SECOND EDITION

Arcana Mundi

MAGIC AND THE OCCULT IN THE GREEK AND ROMAN WORLDS

A Collection of Ancient Texts

Translated, Annotated, and Introduced by

Georg Luck

THE JOHNS HOPKINS UNIVERSITY PRESS
BALTIMORE

The first edition of this book was brought to publication with
the generous assistance of the David M. Robinson Fund and
the Andrew W. Mellon Foundation.

The Johns Hopkins University Press
2715 North Charles Street
Baltimore, Maryland 21218-4363
www.press.jhu.edu

Library of Congress Cataloging-in-Publication Data

Arcana mundi : magic and the occult in the Greek and Roman worlds : a collection
of ancient texts / translated, annotated, and introduced by Georg Luck. — 2nd ed.
p. cm.
Includes bibliographical references (p.   ) and indexes.
ISBN 0-8018-8345-8 (hardcover : alk. paper)
ISBN 0-8018-8346-6 (pbk. : alk. paper)
1. Occultism—Greece—History—Sources. 2. Occultism—Rome—History—
Sources. 3. Civilization, Classical—Sources. I. Luck, Georg, 1926–
BF1421.A73 2006
130.938—dc22
2005028354

A catalog record for this book is available from the British Library.

For Harriet

Contents

Contents

List of Texts

Preface

Since the first edition of this book appeared twenty years ago, a great deal of work has been done in the field of magic in antiquity. New documentary evidence, including amulets and curse tablets, has been found, published, and interpreted, and new ideas have emerged from the evidence—or, perhaps we should say, new aspects have been emphasized.

Greek magical amulets, for example, as edited by Roy Kotansky and others, have become an especially rich source of magical concepts and practices that were generally unknown before. Many amulets have been found in tombs or gravesites (sometimes still around the neck of a corpse). This makes it very clear that the wearer needed protection in the next life as well as on earth—not surprising, considering the daemons lurking in the twilight zone between two worlds. In exceptional cases, the written instructions for making an amulet have survived along with the product. Needless to say, the making of such an object was a magical operation in itself, following a strict ritual, to make sure that the transfer of power was successful.

In a field like this, it seems impossible to come up with explanations that cover all the facts. We are dealing with people living in a distant age, people whose day-to-day lives are quite foreign and sometimes almost incomprehensible to us. Even though we think we know so much about the ancient Egyptians, Greeks, and Romans through literary texts, they are strangers in so many ways. The nonliterary texts speak a more direct language. The magical papyri are different again: they are often semi-literary, often poetic, obviously composed by well-educated people, even though they are designed for practical use, like medical or legal texts or cookbooks, for example. There are cookbooks with literary qualities, after all.

Peter Lamont, a student of parapsychology and a performing magician, has said, in books and interviews, that magic is "an effect which is inexplicable." One might add, "inexplicable at the moment you experience it." For as soon as you know—maybe much later—how it was done, it is no longer magic. But when it happened, and you were there, it most certainly was!

The potential of the human imagination is unlimited. We always hope for the impossible to happen here and now. This is the true reason (not some form of "primordial stupidity") why magic has been around forever and will survive in one form or another as long as there are people on earth. We need it as a complement to our ever-changing construction of reality.

Looking at a number of books recently published by the Johns Hopkins University Press, I came across—almost by coincidence—a clever and amusing book, a real eye-opener, by two French scientists, Georges Charpak and Henri Broch, entitled *Debunked!* in the English translation by Bart K. Holland (2002). The original French title is *Devenez sorciers, devenez savants!* The book shows how easy it is to deceive people today, because, essentially, they want to be deceived. If this is true in our day and age, it certainly was true in ancient times. There is a saying "The world wants to be deceived," *mundus vult decipi,* which appears, in this form, in the *Paradoxa* (1533) edited by Sebastian Franckh.

All the points made in *Debunked!* can be applied to the study of ancient magic, which is, after all, a study of human psychology. For example: Don't tell people what you think you know about them; tell them what they wish were true. Generally speaking, we tend to accept as a fact what we wish to be a fact (principle of selection bias).

One very simple, very powerful factor is the ability of the human brain to recognize patterns in everything and ascribe meaning to them. It is a useful, creative ability, but because it is beyond our control, it jumps to conclusions and sometimes identifies as "extraordinary coincidences" events that may be considered perfectly normal, according to the laws of probability.

Magic as a world view that governs one's entire life in all its compartments and dimensions—not just an occasional experiment but a system of beliefs and a consistent application of "magical thinking" to everything—is hard to imagine today, in an age of science and technology (our own peculiar form of magic), but in antiquity it was common.

One of the aspects of ancient magic that have been emphasized in recent years is the self-identification of the practitioner with a deity: "I am Isis" or "I am Anubis." How can we decide, in any given case, whether this is a mere masquerade designed to impress lesser daemons or a deeply felt certainty, a quasi-religious experience (*homoiosis* 'assimilation'), perhaps induced by trance?

Another aspect that has received special attention is the power of words or inarticulate sounds, including the many names of deities and daemons and the unintelligible *voces magicae*. Magic has always relied to a certain extent on material things, on techniques, but the truly accomplished *magus* was thought to achieve results by the mere use of sounds, whether articulate and meaningful or not. A sequence of vowels, A E I O U Y in various combinations (also as diphthongs), spoken or chanted or hissed in certain ways that had to be learned from a master, could force the agents of the spirit world to obey. To know their names and to pronounce them correctly was in itself a source of power. The Egyptian language was considered to be more effective than Greek, and something was likely to get "lost in translation."

The first edition of *Arcana Mundi* has been translated into other languages. A Spanish version (Madrid: Gredos, 1995) was translated by Elena Gallego Moya and Miguel E. Pérez Molina. Besides a note by the translators, that version includes a new introduction that I prepared, which later appeared in English as "Recent Work in Ancient Magic" (*Ancient Pathways and Hidden Pursuits* [Ann Arbor: University of Michigan Press, 2000], pp. 203-22). For this new edition of the book, that material has been rewritten and expanded and appears now as a prologue under the title "Exploring Ancient Magic." For the German adaptation (Stuttgart: Kröner, 1990), I made a number of changes, partly in response to the reviews that had since appeared. The first Italian translation (Milan: Mursia, 1994) was made by Agata Rapisardi and Cinzia Mascheroni. The second Italian edition, in two volumes (Rome: Fondazione Lorenzo Valla, Mondadori, 1997 and 1999), contains the original Greek and Latin texts as well as additional explanatory notes, and it owes much to Claudio Tartaglini, who, with other scholars, revised the text as he translated it. To him and to Pietro Citati, editor of the series Scrittori greci e latini, I am very grateful.

I have revised the whole book thoroughly myself and made many changes. New texts have been included, for example *no. 2, On the Sacred Disease*. The General Introduction (1–29), published in Spanish in 1995 and in English in 2000, has been brought up to date. The short chapter "Plutarch and the Miraculous" (181–184) is new, as is the section "Ancient Amulets" (218–222). I have slightly expanded the comments on consolations (262) and on the Oracle of Trophonius (303–305). The Epilogue, "The Survival of Pagan Magic" (457–478) has been added as well. The list of *vocabula magica*, an introduction into the terminology of Greco-Roman magic (493–518), is a new feature. Finally, when I became aware of the extensive research done on "entheogens" in recent years, I felt obliged to add an appendix on the possible role of psychoactive substances in ancient rituals (479–488). This led to an afterthought, "The Magical Effects of Panaceas" (488–490). The Bibliography (519–527) has been expanded and updated.

I am very grateful to Michael Lonegro, Humanities Editor of the Johns Hopkins University Press, for support, encouragement, and excellent advice. Thanks to our discussions, the project has gone through several stages before taking this shape. Working with him has helped me improve the book in many ways.

I have been equally fortunate in having the expert assistance of Wei Zhang, a doctoral candidate in the Department of Classics at the Johns Hopkins University, who has been a valuable and reliable help to me in preparing an electronic file of the new manuscript, though it took time from his own research.

Thanks also to Daniel Ogden for his generous and useful comments in his new book.

By his thoughtful and meticulous copy-editing, Brian MacDonald has done me a great favor. I appreciate the care and expertise of Anne Whitmore, who guided the manuscript through production.

As always, I am happy to acknowledge a very special debt to my wife, Harriet.

Abbreviations

ANRW	*Aufstieg und Niedergang der Römischen Welt*
EECC	*Encyclopaedia of the Early Christian Church* (Oxford, 1992)
ERE	*Encyclopaedia of Religion and Ethics,* ed. J. Hastings, 12 vols. (New York, 1908–21)
PGM	K. Preisendanz, and A. Henrichs, *Papyri Graecae Magicae,* 2nd ed. 2 vols. (Stuttgart, 1973–74)
RAC	*Reallexikon für Antike und Christentum*
Suppl. Mag.	R. W. Daniel, and F. Maltomini, *Supplementum Magicum,* Papyrologica Coloniensia 16.1 and 16.2 (Opladen, 1990–92)

Arcana Mundi

GENERAL INTRODUCTION
Exploring Ancient Magic

To say that humankind has lived through three stages—magic, religion, and science—is an oversimplification. At every stage in the history of civilization, the three coexisted, as far as we can tell. There always was religion along with magic and science, and one did not exclude the other or take its place completely. Early advances like the discovery of fire or the invention of the wheel were, in a sense, scientific achievements.

What we can say is that magic anticipated modern science and technology. It was dreaming of something that could not be realized for millennia. The dream of flying through the air by magic has now become reality through machines. The dream of healing disease and prolonging life through magical rituals has become true thanks to modern chemistry and pharmacology.

Ancient magic and modern science have some of the same goals. They also formulate laws—laws that happen to be true in the case of science but largely false (from our point of view) in the case of magic.[1] The expectations are the same as well: both magic and scientific technology promise to give us powers that we, as individuals, do not possess.[2]

Today, we use the increasingly complex technology that is at our disposal without really knowing how and why it works. When it breaks down, we call in an expert to repair it, or we throw it away. In our trust that, ultimately, technology will always work for us, we are like the people of ancient times who relied on magic that seemed to work for them and had worked for their ancestors for a very long time.[3]

In his article "In Search of the Occult," C. R. Phillips III offered a number of valuable remarks on the first English edition of this book.[4] As a starting point, he used the view of magic held by British anthropologists of the nineteenth century. For Edward Tylor, for instance, magic was either bad religion or bad science—bad religion because it had not evolved to Christianity, bad science because it had not evolved to modern technology. And evolved it should have, because Darwin's theories, transferred from zoology to the history of civilization, demanded it.

Phillips quotes E. Leach: "First *science* was distinguished as knowledge and action which depends upon the 'correct' evaluation of cause and effect, the specification of what is correct being determined by the syllogisms of Aristotelian logic and the mechanical determinism of Newtonian physics. The residue was *superstition*. From superstition was then discriminated *religion*. The minimal definition of religion varied from author to author . . . : the residue was then *magic*. Magic was then refined by some into white magic (good) and black magic (bad). Black magic, renamed *sorcery*, was then discriminated from *witchcraft*, and so on."[5]

This is clever, but it seems to be another oversimplification. Things did not happen in this straight, linear way. Moreover, *magic* cannot be neatly separated from *superstition*, while *sorcery* and *witchcraft* are pretty much the same thing today. Sweeping statements concerning *religion* and *magic* can only be made from a secure vantage point, which is, nowadays, that of either modern science or an established religion. If we know what true science is, we are also able, we think, to define pseudoscience. Similarly, if we feel comfortable with our religious faith, we are confident to say what constitutes magic.

Subjective certainty of this kind comes from our awareness that we belong to a solid majority and that we can express our convictions without much risk of being attacked. In antiquity, of course, most people believed in magic, ghosts, and supernatural messages. It is a question of the social consensus. If the community, as a whole, believes in the power of magical operations within a spiritual universe, it will insist on the observation of certain rites and the importance of taboos in everyday life. The occasional failure of magic or the prediction that did not come true cannot shake the near-universal faith in the system.

It is difficult to say what distinguishes religion from magic.[6] For one thing, ancient magic seems to have borrowed extensively from religion, possibly from cults and rituals that are no longer attested and therefore only survive as a form of magic. It could be said that magic tends to grow on a substratum of religion, like a fungus, and that it is able to adopt religious ceremonies and divine names. Magic is the great master of disguises. It operates in a twilight zone and deliberately exploits traditions outside its area while claiming that it achieves better results.[7]

Later on, I try to show that both magic and religion can be derived from shamanism. By introducing this term, we do not really solve any problems: we are just placing them on a different level. Still, this shift may bring us a little closer to a new understanding of the problems. To complicate things further, a case can be made for the survival of ancient magic in the early Church as well as in medieval Byzantium.

Some criteria that have been designed to separate religion from magic should be considered as guidelines, not as the ultimate truth.[8] For example, magic is said to be manipulative, whereas religion relies on prayer and sacrifice; magic applies means to specific ends, whereas religion stresses the ends in themselves (spiritual rebirth, salvation, life eternal); magic concentrates on individual (often selfish or immoral) needs, whereas religion is concerned with the well-being of the community (the family, the tribe, the state); magical operations tend to be private, secretive (they often take place at night, in secluded places), whereas religious rites take place in the open, during the day, visible for all; magic is characterized by a kind of business relationship between a practitioner (who expects to be paid) and his client, whereas the relationship typical for religion is that between a founder, leader, prophet, or "holy man" and a group of followers. Prayers to the gods are normally offered aloud, whereas magical incantations addressed to a daemon are usually formulated silently or pronounced with a special hissing sound, the *susurrus magicus*.

Along the same lines, R. Arbesmann makes a well-balanced but not entirely satisfactory statement: "While in prayer man tries by persuasion to move a higher being to gratify his wishes, the reciter of a magic formula attempts to constrain that being or to force the effect of his own ends by the very words of his formula to which he ascribes an unfailing, immanent power. In the first instance, the answer to man's invocation lies within the will of the higher being; in the second, the binding of the higher being effected by the formula is considered to be absolute, automatically producing the result desired."[9]

But Arbesmann adds a word of caution: "In many ritual acts, it is true, the two attitudes exist side by side and often blend one into the other so completely that it is difficult, if not impossible, to decide which of the two attitudes is present or dominant. It is also true that of the two attitudes the one taken by the reciter of the magic formula is cruder. But this does not warrant the conclusion that the magic formula is older than the prayer and that the latter grew out of the former."

This skepticism is confirmed by our ancient sources. According to Philostratus, in his biography of Apollonius of Tyana, the miracle-worker and "holy man" (*Vita Apollonii* 5.12), some magicians believed that they could change fate by torturing the statues of gods. Because the statues are, to some extent, identical with the deities themselves, they would feel the pain inflicted on their effigies on earth and therefore do almost anything the magician demanded.

But the same sort of thing also occurred in the religious sphere. We hear that, in times of crisis, when the people felt that the gods had failed them, they would punish their statues by taking them out of the temples, whipping them, and dragging them through the streets. When the gods seemed to respond to this kind of treatment and the crisis came to an end, the people would return the statues to their temple, anoint and adorn them, and offer them lavish sacrifices and fervent prayers of thanksgiving. Customs like that survived here and there in Christianity.

Some scholars emphasize that magic, as a way of understanding reality and dealing with it, is radically different from our logical approach, magic representing a prelogical or paralogical mentality. This is obviously true, in a sense, though it also shifts the problem to a different level instead of offering a solution. And one should not forget that there is a kind of logic in magic. No matter how "crude" or "primitive" some of its assumptions and techniques may appear to us, ancient magic did pass through a "scientific" phase during the Hellenistic period and, once more, in Neoplatonist circles. Magicians did not think only in terms of cosmic sympathy or mystic participation; they were aware of space and time and causality.[10]

This is one of the reasons why it can be such a frustrating experience to read a work like Iamblichus' *On the Mysteries*. Essentially, this is a defense of theurgy, but on the surface it is a philosophical treatise, using the methodology developed by generations of Platonists. Iamblichus and other Neoplatonists had inherited the magical lore of the past along with the doctrine of their school. They were convinced that the two could be reconciled and used to explain or justify each other.[11]

Of a *theologos,* a philosopher or priestlike figure who mainly talked about the gods, no miracles or magical feats could be expected, but a *theourgos* who claimed to have a certain power over the gods had to prove his supernatural abilities now and then. This is certainly an area where we cannot exclude the possibility of special effects bordering on fraud. When an exalted mortal such as the emperor Julian was about to be initiated into the higher mysteries, nothing was left to chance, one would assume. We are told that Maximus, the Neoplatonist philosopher and theurgist, impressed Julian by his personality and by the seemingly supernatural phenomena he created (smiling statues of the gods) and thus succeeded in drawing him away from the Church.[12]

Magic generally operates with symbols rather than with concepts. Thanks to the work done by modern anthropologists and psychologists,[13] the world of symbols is better understood today than at the time of Tylor. Symbols help people to associate, to remember, to think. They often serve as a kind of shorthand for concepts that are too complicated to be put into words, and by their very nature they seem to offer a key to reality. No matter how abstruse the drawings in the magical papyri may seem to us, they are symbols for some type of reality and preserve, as "psychograms," certain kinds of experience.

An important concept, the idea of *cosmic sympathy,* was formulated by the Stoic philosopher Posidonius of Apamea (ca. 135–ca. 50 B.C.), called "the Rhodian" after the island where he taught. His concept implies that anything that happens in any part of the universe can affect something else in the universe, no matter how distant or unrelated it may seem. The idea itself must be very old and predates the concept of causality. It is fundamental for magic, astrology, and alchemy.[14]

What is called "sympathetic" magic is based on three principles: similarity (like acts on like); contact (things that touch each other influence each other and may exchange their properties); and contrariety (antipathy works like sympathy). Together, these principles, though they seem partly contradictory, offer explanations to the *magus,* the astrologer, and the alchemist.

Other ways to describe the workings of cosmic sympathy are "Inside is like outside" or "What is above is like what is below." The whole idea involves a constant exchange of energies between the outside world (the macrocosm, the universe) and the inside world (the microcosm, the psyche). Everything around us can be used to our advantage, if we just know how to "plug" into the potential that is there. Of course, there are evil powers around us, too, threatening to harm us, until we protect ourselves by amulets and other forms of countermagic. In addition, there are countless messages—dreams, signs, oracles—that need to be observed and deciphered. There is a saying in the Talmud that reflects a widespread belief: "A dream not interpreted is like a letter not read."

It would be worthwhile to compare *cosmic sympathy* with C. G. Jung's concept of *synchronicity.* Jung introduced this term to designate a coincidence that may not be a coincidence at all. And, perhaps, for someone who believes in magic, there can be no coincidence. Everything that happens has a meaning because a supernatural force is at work, and if one does not understand its significance right away, there are numerous experts and specialists one can consult.

There is also the distinction between *sympathetic* and *contagious* magic, which overlaps, in a sense, with the principles just mentioned. Sympathetic magic seems to work because similar causes produce similar effects. If a man loves a woman who does not desire him, he may fashion an image of her in wax or clay and melt it in fire, hoping that the person represented will feel the heat. This is what happens in Theocritus' *Idylls* 2 [*no. 6*].[15]

If you wish to harm a person, you also fashion an image representing your enemy and pierce it with nails or bind it or break it into pieces. Such figurines, nowadays called *voodoo dolls* (in German: *Zauberpuppen* or *Rachepuppen*), have been found in Athens and elsewhere. Ways of fabricating them are described in the magical papyri. By burning the image of your enemy or throwing something that belongs to him or was in close contact with his body—his hair, clippings of his finger nails, or a piece of clothing—into the flames, you hurt him indirectly. This, too, is a form of contagious magic.

The cosmic force that can either help or hurt has many names. A typical term is the Greek *dynamis.* It is comparable with the *mana* of so-called primitive civilizations, a term preferred by anthropologists. Because it is not always possible to identify the supernatural power that is at work, generic terms like *mana* or *dynamis* are convenient. They often designate the spectacular event that is produced by the power,[16] which acts through certain exceptional people: the shamans, the miracle-workers, the saints.

Dynamis resides in certain things (stones or plants) that are thought to be animated, in utterances (words or names), and in techniques or types of knowledge. The *voces magicae* or *nomina barbara,* the strange, exotic words and names pronounced in rituals had *dynamis,* presumably, because they were unintelligible, but also because some were borrowed from Egyptian and Hebrew. This is true for the Semitic names for the supreme deity, *Adonai* and *Iao.* The former means "Lord," the latter is a contraction of the sacred tetragrammaton JHWH, which also appears as *Jeu.*[17] Near Eastern (Egyptian and Jewish) sorcerers enjoyed a formidable reputation in the Greco-Roman world.

The power of formulas like "God is One"[18] or "Alpha and Omega"[19] can be explained by their obvious importance in a religion foreign to the magical practitioner. If it seemed to work for "them," it was certainly worth a try.

Sometimes, the practitioner assumes the identity of a deity in order to acquire *dynamis* and command respect in the spirit world. He proclaims "I am Osiris" or "I am Anubis" or "I am Jesus Christ."[20] This tells us something about an essential difference between religion and magic. A worshiper of Isis, like the hero of Apuleius' novel, can achieve a union with the deity as the culminating point of a long, demanding initiation. But the magus (someone like Apuleius' hero in a former life) often uses the name of a deity to impress lesser daemons. He may pretend to be Anubis today and Jesus Christ tomorrow, ad hoc, just as it suits him. Pretending that one is not a mere human being but a daemon or a deity is a common type of masquerading in the magical papyri and the Hermetic writings. The *magus* who adopts another identity becomes the person with two images.

There is, however, another aspect to the concept of the double image. The *magus* may not assume the identity of a god or daemon in a calculating, manipulative manner: he may, in trance, become that higher power. There is an element of madness in magic as well as in certain religions.[21] It is the "divine madness" of the shaman. Looking at the evidence, it is hard to avoid the conclusion that trance, ecstasy, enthusiasm, possession—whatever we wish to call an altered state of consciousness—are part of the sorcerer's world, and if it was not always the real thing, it may have been a good facsimile. The evidence also suggests that, in antiquity, it was much more of a "normal" thing to fall into trance and out of it than today. These views will, perhaps, be treated with skepticism by many researchers, but to me there is no way around them, and here the shamanistic background is particularly important. Once we admit the central role of trance, many things fall into place almost at once, and the nature of the tools and the training of the *magus* become more transparent.

The possible role of certain substances will be discussed later (in the appendix). Here, I want to point out four little-known testimonies, two by Greek authors who lived around the time of Jesus, and one by a Jewish writer who lived a generation or two after them.

In his essay on Demosthenes (par. 22), Dionysius of Halicarnassus, the literary critic who was also a historian, says that whenever he is reading one of the speeches of the great orator, he feels "like those who take part in the Mysteries of the Mother Goddess or the Corybantic rites or similar ceremonies, whether they are inspired by scents [*eite osmais*] or sights [*eit' opsesin*, supplied by Radermacher] or by the spirit of the deities themselves to experience so many different visions [*phantasias*]."

Strabo, in his *Geographika* (10.3.7), describes the overwhelming psychological effect of "war dances, accompanied by noise and roaring and cymbals and drums and [the clashing of] arms, also by flutes and shouting" on those who participate in the rites of the Curetes, the Corybants, the Cabiri, the Mother Goddess, and other mystery cults.

Both authors may have witnessed the orgiastic rites for which the cults they name are famous. Dionysius attributes the visions experienced by the worshipers either to odors (from fumigations, incense offerings) or to sights (if the reading is correct) or to the direct intervention of the deities. Strabo, on the other hand, emphasizes the various sounds (music, shouting, probably singing) and the effect of dancing, which, by itself, can lead to trance. But the goal of all these rites is the same: to "become one" with the deity (*henosis, unio mystica*). Once you have entered trance, you are no longer the worshiper, you become the deity you worship.

On a different level, this is also the goal of the *magus* and the *theourgos.* The psychological or neurological process is the same, and the terms used by the Neoplatonists to describe the experience can be applied: *synaphe* 'contact', *synapheia* 'conjunction', *koinonia* 'communion', *henosis* 'union', *homoiosis* 'assimilation' (to the deity), *theiosis* 'deification'. Expressive images are offered to illustrate the experience: spiritual rebirth in the deity, swap of identities, and so on. We find exclamations like: "Hermes, I am you, you are me, your name is my name, and my name is your name."[22] In trance, the *magus,* just like the shaman, may have all kinds of visions—for instance, a trip to heaven or to another world, an experience also attested in the Nag-Hammadi texts and for Apollonius of Tyana.[23]

To Josephus, the Jewish historian (c. A.D. 37–c. 111), we owe two more testimonies whose significance has recently been pointed out.[24] The first is found in *Contra Apionem* 1.232 where the author reports from Manetho, an Egyptian historian, that the Pharaoh Amenophis (perhaps Amenophis IV, 1364–1347 B.C.) wished to become an "observer of the gods" and consulted a seer (or "wise man"), also called Amenophis, who was reputed to "share the nature of the divine because of his ability to predict the future." Here we have an Egyptian "holy man" who has the gift of prophecy and can teach his king the art of "seeing the gods."

Josephus says something very similar about Moses (*Antiquitates Iudaicae* 1.19): in order to lead an exemplary life and be a lawgiver, "one must in the mind observe the works of God." This privilege is equivalent to "seeing God" himself and also to seeing, like God, the whole world from above in a single instant.[25] Josephus speaks of a mystic experience that can be achieved through the knowledge of certain techniques.

Support for this hypothesis may be found at the beginning of the *Alexander Romance,*[26] where Nectanebo(s), another semilegendary Pharaoh who also happens to be a skilled *magus,* is able to "observe the gods" and to associate with them thanks to *lekanomanteia,* a technique of divination, actually an aid of achieving trance through looking into a bowl filled with a liquid. In trance, he sees his deities and, becoming like them, the whole world. Incidentally, according to Genesis 44:5, Joseph, while living in Egypt, practiced a form of *lekanomanteia.*

Dynamis, as we have seen, can be transferred in many ways. In addition to merely pronouncing a name or a formula, the practitioner may absorb it physically by licking or eating it. Thus, at the end of the "Mithras Liturgy" (*PGM* IV.785–89), the devotee is told to write the "eight-letter name" on a leaf and lick the leaf while showing it to the god.[27]

The story of Simon Magus, as told in Acts (8:9–21) is a good illustration of the meaning of *dynamis.* This man who apparently had considerable influence in Samaria in the first century A.D. can be considered to be a *magus*, a type of Near Eastern miracle-worker, and the founder of a new religion, but for the Christians he was a pseudoprophet. His supporters, according to the commonly accepted textual form, called him "the power of God which is called great," *he dynamis tou theou he kaloumene megale,* but the words *tou theou* and *kaloumene* may be a gloss that found its way into the text.[28] What his followers called him (and what he must have called himself) is probably "the great power," *he dynamis he megale.* Simon was impressed by the *dynamis* of the Apostles, which was clearly superior to his own. He wanted to join them and asked them to sell their special kind of magic, whereupon he was sternly rebuked.[29]

In recent scholarship, a further distinction—*direct* versus *indirect* magic—has been advocated. Examples for direct magic would be amulets or written charms (like those offered in Marcellus' *De Medicamentis*) and various drugs and concoctions, but also incantations and invocations of the "great name" of a deity or daemon. Indirect magic, on the other hand, might be illustrated by the summoning of the dead in Book 11 of the *Odyssey,* because Homer describes a kind of magic that leads to another kind. The hero performs a certain ritual, as he has been instructed by Circe, to conjure up the ghosts in Hades, but he needs one particular ghost, that of the seer Tiresias, who, even in Hades, has kept his prophetic powers.

The distinction between *private* and *official* magic has the disadvantage that most magic, as we understand it, was privately practiced and usually just involved the practitioner and the client. Official magic seems very close to religion: it may include rainmaking or fertility rites (the Sacred Marriage), purifications of a community, and the formal cursing of a foreign nation.

The old distinction between *natural* and *ritual* magic has been revived recently, but it is helpful only to a certain point. In a sense, all magic is ritual.[30] Specific rites that may vary from society to society are essential in all kinds of magic.[31] A simple classification would be: (1) rites that reinforce the *mana* (or the *dynamis*) of an individual or a community,[32] promising success in hunting, fishing, and war; (2) rites that reduce the *mana* of an enemy (black magic); (3) apotropaic measures (protection from the evil eye, from daemons, e.g., by means of amulets); (4) purification rites; and (5) healing rites.

Natural magic, on the other hand, is a kind of applied science, often involving trickery or relatively simple experiments that are miraculous only for the naïve and ignorant. The subject was treated abundantly in the Renaissance, for instance by Giambattista della Porta, in his *Magia Naturalis,* first published in 1558 and reprinted many times. The influence of this work can be seen in the *Disquisitiones Magicae* of Martin Del Rio, first published in 1599 and also reprinted several times. There, natural magic is defined (1.2) as "the art or ability created by an effort [*vi creata*], not supernatural, to produce strange and unusual effects whose idea is beyond the common sense and the understanding of people . . . I am speaking of an 'ability created by an effort' in order to exclude true miracles." Here he is speaking as a son of the Church for whom true miracles (such as those attributed to saints) exist.

Another definition of natural (or physical) magic, also found in Del Rio, claims that it is nothing else but a "more accurate knowledge of the secrets of nature" (*exactior . . . arcanorum naturae cognitio*). This goes back to Apuleius who, in his *Apologia sive De Magia,* declared himself to be a harmless scientist and philosopher, definitely not a magician or a miracle-worker, and insisted that the seemingly strange experiments he carried out were done in the interest of research. But he was motivated by *curiositas*—another word for magic—and that made him no less suspicious.

Magika Hiera is the title of a volume published in 1991 that illustrates some trends in contemporary research.[33] It assembles essays on various aspects of ancient magic. C. A. Faraone deals with early Greek "binding spells" (*katadesmoi*); J. H. M. Stubbe ("Cursed Be He That Moves My Bones") discusses funerary imprecations; H. S. Versnel ("Beyond Cursing") looks at prayers for justice and confessions of guilt. J. Scarborough investigates the pharmacology of plants, herbs, and roots (they could serve as remedies and as poisons). From an unfinished word by Sam Eitrem (1872-1966) there is a chapter on dreams and divination, translated by D. Obink and prefaced by F. Graf, who also contributes an essay on prayer in magic and religious ritual. J. Winkler's "The Constraints of Eros" is followed by H. D. Betz on "Magic and Mystery in the Greek Magical Papyri," and C. R. Phillips III concludes the volume with a treatment of socioreligious sanctions on magic entitled "*Nullum crimen sine lege.*"

Versnel's essay is valuable, it seems to me, because he sheds light on an area that has remained largely in the dark so far. It becomes clear now that there was an alternative to taking an enemy to court or putting a curse on him: it was always possible to appeal to a deity. This probably means that someone who was really anxious to win left nothing to chance and did all three things: he talked to his lawyer, consulted a trusted magical practitioner, and also enlisted the help of the gods.

Scarborough shows in detail that real "scientific" knowledge of the properties of plants was available in antiquity. This kind of knowledge—especially if kept secret—represented a powerful kind of magic.

Graf argues that one commonly used criterion to distinguish religion from magic—the religious person approaches the gods respectfully and humbly, whereas the *magus* attempts to force them—is not valid.

Phillips must be right when he says that neither the lawgiver nor the priest nor the philosopher had an interest in clearly defining "unsanctioned religious activities." It seems, however, that attempts were made from time to time. Even so, not surprisingly, a twilight zone remained, and this places us at a disadvantage. If the average Athenian or Roman could not be sure where the boundaries between normal, acceptable practices and strange, possibly illegal, immoral or irreligious activities should be traced, how can we be certain today?

It would be so convenient if we could label all these different areas properly as *religion* and *magic* and *medicine* and so on, but in reality they overlap. In our world—and already in ancient Rome, to a certain extent—things tend to be compartmentalized. For one type of problem, we consult a physician; for another type, a lawyer; for yet another concern, we go to a priest. But we no longer seek the advice of a witch or a sorcerer, because magic is no longer that kind of reality to us, at least not for the academics who write books about it.

In ancient times, magic was essentially a way of dealing with all sorts of problems in life. Still, we have to go back very far in time before we find the *magus,* the one great figure of authority in a society where people talked freely about supernatural experiences and took them for granted—needed them, in fact. Perhaps that figure, a kind of supershaman, is a projection, but it lived on in Greece in the traditions about Orpheus, Empedocles, and Pythagoras and the many miracle-workers (*theioi andres* 'divine men') who came after them.

The divine men have some common characteristics: they practice an ascetic life-style, travel widely (necessary to learn and to reach people), are able to heal (through exorcisms), perform miracles, and spread a message. Some are poets, musicians, creators of myths, philosophers. But their god-given ability to transcend the laws of nature is, so to speak, their passport.

It is more than likely that the archaic shaman was also able to communicate with the dead. The myth of Orpheus certainly points in this direction, and the various techniques of approaching the dead have a long history in Greece, as in Egypt. It makes sense that you consult a specialist if you want to get in touch with your ancestors or a hero or any famous figure of the past.

There were many forms of *psychagogia* 'conjuring up of souls' or necromancy in antiquity.[34] Famous "oracles of the dead" (*nekyomanteia*) are attested already for the fifth century B.C., for example, at Heracleia

Pontica, at Tainaron, at the Acheron in Thesprotia, and at Avernus in southern Italy. They are sometimes, but not always, situated in caves which were believed to be an access to the underworld.

Necromancy may not be such a good term, because predictions of the future were only a relatively small part of the whole business of dealing with the dead. *Psychagogia,* though it has other meanings as well, is perhaps a better word. The *psychagogoi,* especially those from Italy, were much in demand in the classical period and after, though they are hard to distinguish, as a class, from the ordinary *goetes.*

The ritual must have varied from place to place, but incubation—a link to healing rituals—clearly played a role. The oldest form of incubation seems to have been the sleeping (or the resting in a state of trance) on the tomb of an ancestor. Here, it was essential to be stretched out completely, to be in touch with the earth as much as possible. Sleeping—or going into trance—in caves, near springs, and under trees or near points where three ways come together (*triodoi*) was also a form of incubation.

While evocated ghosts are usually experienced in sleep or trance, they are sometimes portrayed as rising before the *waking* eyes of the consulter. Perhaps we should assume a twilight zone between waking and sleeping; this is often, as the annals of psychiatry show, the time when hallucinations occur. There may also have been programming through the priests, who probably used hypnosis and psychoactive substances.

Ventriloquists were more likely to practice a deliberate kind of fraud. The mysterious voice coming out of nowhere could bring a message from a dear departed or from a legendary figure of the past or even from a deity. One thing that the *goes,* who was also a ventriloquist, may have claimed to do for the family dead was granting them absolution (retroactively) for sins committed in this life through a purification ritual for which the descendants had to pay. This may be the meaning of the "initiation of the dead," which is mentioned more than once.

The professionals apparently addressed the dead in a sort of ghost-language, a "mixture of high-pitch squeaking and low droning." Whether this was done in trance or not, it reminds one of shamans in action. It is also reminiscent of the special effects (strange words, gibberish, hissing, and whistling) that the *magus* uttered during his rituals. Perhaps there is also a connection with the peculiar language that the Homeric gods spoke among each other.

But why consult the dead in the first place? What exactly did they know, and how did they acquire their knowledge? One has the impression (in Egypt it may have been different) that the knowledge of the Greek and Roman dead was limited or selective. Some of it they could

derive from other ghosts. There is the idea of a marketplace in the underworld (Ovid, *Metamorphoses* 4. 444; *Tristia* 4. 10. 87–88), analogous to the
Athenian Agora and the Roman Forum, where the latest news, along
with gossip and rumors, was exchanged.

The image of the mythical supershaman seems to live on in the Persian
magos who, as a spiritual heir of Zoroaster, serves within the hierarchy of
the state religion, but also in the Egyptian priest who is attached to the
sanctuary of a syncretistic deity and may, at the same time, be an expert in
various other areas, such as magic or medicine. This is only a hypothesis,
but it finds support in the fragmentary evidence we have about the
apprenticeship of the *magus* and the initiation rites he had to undergo.[35]

To understand Greco-Roman magic, we must look at other cultures,
too. Just as Greek religion and mythology cannot be studied in isolation,
without considering the Near Eastern influences, magic and folklore
should be seen in a larger context.

For the Hittites, magic was a technique that had been invented by their
gods.[36] A Hittite practitioner of magic seems to have belonged to a
privileged group, a caste (like the Persian *magoi,* the Egyptian priests, or
the Celtic Druids), entrusted with secrets that were faithfully transmitted
from generation to generation, ever since they were first revealed by a
deity. This secret knowledge conferred power and status.

Sumero-Accadian magic, as far as it is known, exhibits familiar features.[37] An elaborate daemonology furnishes details that are not always
spelled out in our Greek sources. Daemons are invisible; they are also
innumerable (remember the daemon in Mark 5:9, 15 who says that his
name is "Legion"); they are mostly evil, yet share somehow in the nature
of the divine, and their names are preceded by the divine ideogram; they
move very fast; they can penetrate walls; they control the elements. Obviously, a very fertile imagination was at work. It seems that the witches
and sorcerers in this society were mostly women and foreigners. There
are parallels to this in Greco-Roman culture where the figure of the
witch is well established and foreigners like the "Egyptian prophet" or the
"Etruscan diviner" or the "Marsian enchanter" are fairly common. These
practitioners are sometimes seen as tools of the daemons, but one needs
them for protection. They produce amulets made from gems and shiny
stones, dyed in certain colors, and worn around the neck, waist, wrists,
and ankles.[38]

Thanks to an abundance of written texts and surviving monuments,
Egyptian magic, or *heka,* is quite well known.[39] It was considered an attribute of Re, sometimes represented as an anthropomorphic deity grasping a serpent in each hand. Professional magicians were called "prophets

of *heka*" or "those who know," a kind of euphemism that occurs in other cultures; thus the voodoo term for the *bokor,* the enchanter, is *un qui a connaissance.*

Magic per se was apparently not illegal in ancient Egypt. Only one criminal case, the "Harem Conspiracy" under Ramses III, is documented (from the Papyrus Lee): in this particular case, wax images of gods and men served as voodoo dolls. The sorcerer behind it was put to death for conspiring against the life of the Pharaoh.

The Egyptian deities themselves, like those of the Hittites, practiced magic, and the idea is not totally foreign to Greek myth, if one thinks of minor figures like Circe, who may belong to a pre-Greek pantheon. It was by magical means that Thoth and Isis were able to heal young Horus. On the other hand, even the gods were sometimes powerless against the magic aimed at them by the living and the dead.

For the Egyptians believed that the dead had special powers. They could predict the future, like the ghosts conjured up by the necromancers of the Greeks. They were also held responsible—as the "Letters to the Dead," a special literary genre, testify—for some of the evils that befall the living. The dead were even able to put pressure on the gods by chanting spells and reciting secret names.

That can only mean that Egyptian sorcerers had a "working relationship" with the dead, much like Lucan's witch Erictho. The Greek concept of the *nekydaimon,* the powerful spirit of a deceased person, may have its roots in Egypt. Such spirits were willing or could be forced to perform services for the enchanter. Essentially, this is the concept of the "zombie" in voodoo witchcraft, although it now appears that these creatures are not really dead.

The Egyptian ritual of the "Opening of the Mouth" seems to survive in Greek theurgy. Their priests were able, it is said, to animate by certain formulas (and fumigations?) the statues of the gods and make them smile and speak. Obviously, such a phenomenon—or the illusion—had an overwhelming effect on believers and skeptics, because it showed that the gods were alive and well and caring.

Egyptian sorcerers used particular spells to protect their powers in this world and make sure that they would serve them in the next life as well. Some of them were apparently buried with their books and other tools so that they could continue to practice their craft after death. To this belief in the permanence of secret knowledge we probably owe the preservation of the magical papyri.

On the whole, the spells of ancient Egypt were similar to those found in the Greek papyri. There seems to be a kind of *koine* of magic that reflects a similar way of thinking in different cultures. We are inclined to look for influences, but, as in the world of mythology and folklore, certain ideas, tales, and customs may originate independently. Curse tablets and voodoo dolls have been found in large numbers in Egypt, as in the rest of the Mediterranean world. In the Egyptian texts, the ritual gestures to be executed are often described, but the study of the written documents was probably not sufficient, and one would assume that years of apprenticeship under an established master, followed by initiation rites, were required.

Magic and medicine were like twin sisters in Egypt. Trying to cure an illness is sometimes seen as a struggle between the magician-physician and the daemon of the illness, or, more accurately, the assistant daemon of the practitioner and the evil daemon plaguing the patient. This kind of magical medicine was practiced in Greece long before Hippocrates or one of his disciples wrote the treatise on the "sacred disease."

Particular to Egypt, not yet found in Greco-Roman culture (yet conceivable), are the "healing statues," of which the best-known example is the Statue of Djedher in the Cairo Museum. It represents a kneeling person, arms crossed on the knees, the body covered with pictures and written texts. In front of the statue there is a stele of Horus on crocodiles. A basin around the statue communicates, through a channel, with another, deeper one. Liquids poured over the statue absorbed the *dynamis* of texts and images and could be consumed by the patient, who then bathed in the larger basin or drank from the smaller one. It is the same idea of the physical absorption of magical power we have seen above.

Occult arts are often mentioned in the Bible.[40] Most forms of sorcery documented in other Near Eastern countries were known, at one time or another, to the Hebrews, but they were often practiced by women or foreigners (as among the Hittites), and foreign religions (as among the Greeks) were considered a kind of magic. This seems to be a recurrent pattern.

A very old testimony for the practice of *lekanomanteia* is found in Genesis 44:5, where we hear of the silver cup from which Joseph, while living in Egypt, drinks and which he uses for divination. This could mean that he saw God, under certain circumstances, when he gazed into the liquid in the cup. The "witch of Endor," actually a medium specializing in necromancy, was consulted in secret by Saul, the king of Israel (1 Samuel 28:7), after he had officially banished the "wizards" from his kingdom. The Book of Daniel, probably composed in the second century B.C., tells the story of a young Jewish hostage at the court of the king of Babylon who is more powerful than all the renowned Babylonian magicians and diviners. The author of Wisdom, probably a Hellenized Jew who lived around the middle of the first century B.C., condemns "sorcery and unholy rites" (12:4).

We see clear sanctions against magic in the Mosaic code (Exodus 22:18; Deuteronomy 18:9–13), and these were upheld by the prophets who also attack the magic of foreign nations (Isaiah 44:25). In the Old Testament, magic is often associated with idolatry and the worship of daemons, because it depends, by definition, on a multitude of powers.

A theme of confrontation, of a power contest, runs through the Bible. One could describe it as "our kind of magic versus their kind of magic" or "our religion versus their magic." It is always the true religion that triumphs over a form of magic. Joseph humiliates the Egyptian diviners (Genesis, ch. 41); Moses is more successful than the magicians of Pharaoh (Exodus 7:10–13, 19–23; 8:1–3).

In the New Testament, we witness the confrontation between the Apostles and Simon Magus; the conflict with Elymas, the Jewish consultant (a psychic in residence or a black magician?) to the Roman proconsul (Acts 13: 6–12); and the Jewish exorcists of Ephesus (Acts 19:13–20). In a pointed, dramatic form, the new challenges the old, and the true religion unmasks the false one that is branded as a kind of magic, and not a very good one at that.

On later Jewish magic we are now well informed thanks to the reconstruction of the *Sepher Ha-Razim* by M. Margalioth. This is a magical handbook from the early Talmudic period,[41] and its prescriptions are similar to the ones offered by the Greek magical papyri.

When we talk about Greco-Roman magic, we usually mean Hellenistic magic, as documented by the papyri. This syncretistic, multicultural conglomerate took shape in Egypt when it was ruled by Macedonian kings, before it became a province of the Roman Empire. *Syncretism* does not only apply to the history of religion: it also characterizes the blend of Egyptian, Babylonian, Jewish, and Greek elements that came together and interacted in Alexandria, the great melting pot of the postclassical period.[42] Even though the magical papyri date from a later period, the system they reflect is Hellenistic. They are a very important source for our knowledge of ancient magic, along with the curse tablets, voodoo dolls, and amulets.

The Greek texts, published by K. Preisendanz and A. Henrichs, are now available in English translations, with introductions, notes, and a glossary, thanks to H. D. Betz and a team of scholars. No fewer than fifty recently discovered or newly published texts are included in the first volume, and the Demotic portions of the bilingual Greek-Demotic papyri are also translated. The second volume will include an index of

Greek words, a subject index based on the translations, a collection of parallels between the magical papyri and early Christian literature, and a comprehensive bibliography.[43]

The series *New Documents Illustrating Early Christianity,* edited by G. H. R. Horsley and others, includes a number of magical texts and is useful because of the detailed comments it offers.

What remains to be done is, among other things, an overview of the theology, the religious mood that reveals itself in the magical papyri. There is still considerable disagreement among the specialists. E. R. Dodds, for instance, says that these texts "constantly operate with the debris of other people's religions,"[44] while A.-J. Festugière feels that some documents could be called religious.[45] This is also the view of M. P. Nilsson who wrote, "Several invocations are quite beautiful and marked by a genuine religious spirit."[46]

The prescriptions given in these "working copies of practical magicians" (A. D. Nock) could easily be copied onto other materials. A recently found love charm on a lead tablet shows this process. It was probably written by a professional magician in the third or fourth century A.D. on the basis of *PGM* IV.296–434 or a closely related text.[47] The rolled-up lead tablet, roughly eleven square centimeters in size, was found inside a clay vase, together with a clay statuette of a kneeling woman, with her hands bound behind her back and her body pierced with needles. Such a set of objects looks like a combination of the curse tablet and the voodoo doll. Sometimes, the curse is inscribed on the doll, and occasionally the doll is broken into pieces.[48]

New studies of amulets and magical gems have been published in recent years.[49] It may also be worthwhile pointing out the Byzantine tradition about Apollonius of Tyana and the unusual talismans he set up in many cities:[50] they were large monuments, sacred objects, designed to protect the people from plagues and diseases. A large sculpture of a scorpion, for example, would protect the whole population from scorpion bites. Obviously, one single monumental amulet was sufficient to protect thousands of people, making it unnecessary for them to carry individual amulets at all times.

It is very easy to imagine all the fears, all the obsessions that tortured the superstitious (see Theophrastus' *Portrait* for the type). If one constantly worried about lurking dangers—snakes, scorpions, the evil eye—one would have to wear not just one amulet but many, one for each specific danger, not to mention the endless rituals of purification. The truly superstitious must have been loaded down by the sheer weight of the amulets they carried around the neck, on the wrists, the ankles, the fingers, on every part of the body. Jewelry (precious and semiprecious stones and gems) may originally have served as a protective device, not as an ornament. The same may be true of tattoos and perfumes. The alchemists attached to the temples and the royal palaces of Egypt who manufactured perfumes and incense were bound by secrecy and worked for the priests and the kings. All these substances and devices were meant to concentrate the forces of the earth, the sun, the moon, and the stars and make them useful.

The Hellenistic conglomerate traveled from Egypt to Italy and mixed with native beliefs and rituals, but it is difficult to separate the *koine* from the local traditions.[51] We know very little about Etruscan magic[52] and even less about the sorcerers and witches of the various Italic tribes (the Marsi, the Osci, the Sabelli, for instance), though some of them enjoyed a certain reputation. It is possible that some distinctive features of Roman magic and folklore are really Etruscan. The Etruscan influence is more evident in other areas, but it cannot be excluded in the area that concerns us here.

Divination was one of the specialties of the Etruscans, and the "Etruscan seer" was a familiar figure. Etruscan techniques of predicting the future were integrated into the Roman state religion, even though they could be called "magical" and "foreign" since they must have had their origin in Asia Minor. According to Seneca (*Naturales Quaestiones* 2.32.2) the Etruscans "believe that things do not reveal the future because they occur, but they occur because they are meant to reveal the future."

Cicero's friend Nigidius Figulus no doubt played an important role in the way Hellenistic magic became accepted in Italy: he was a scholar, an astrologer, a clairvoyant—a very unusual type of Roman.[53] If we knew more about him, we would gain a better understanding of the occult arts as they were practiced in Rome.

Through the Law of the Twelve Tables (fifth century B.C.) we catch a glimpse of some ancient types of magic practiced in Italy (and probably elsewhere). One of them is the technique of *fruges excantare* by which a sorcerer could ruin a farmer's harvest or transfer it to another property.[54]

It must have happened, time and again, that in the same year, one farmer did better than the others, although everybody had offered the same prayers and sacrifices to the gods. Hence the one farmer who was more successful than the others must have, in the popular opinion, done something special in secret, and this additional something could only be magic. You could even say that magic is the "extra something" that one does in addition to one's normal religious duties. This strategy is not unusual. The fact that there was an ancient law against this proves that the suspicion was always alive, and envy may have been a powerful motivation. There is also the tendency to blame certain individuals for collective misfortunes, such as famines and epidemics.

The Law of the Twelve Tables (known to us only in fragments) also makes it a criminal offense to recite a *malum carmen,* a spell designed to hurt a person. The law uses the verb *incantare* (as opposed to *excantare*). There is a legal distinction between *malum carmen* and *famosum carmen,* which means "libel" or "defamation." The latter hurts the person's reputation; the former hurts the person physically.[55]

New curse tablets in Latin or Greek come to light from time to time. A fairly recent example is a bilingual inscription on a gold tablet from Dacia, from the late imperial period. In the Greek part, *Adonai* 'Lord' and *theoi hypsistoi* 'highest gods' are invoked, while the Latin part reads as follows: *Demon immunditiae te agitet, Aeli Firme. Stet supra caput Iuliae Surillae* (May the daemon of impurity pursue you, Aelius Firmus. May it stand over the head of Julia Surilla). The letter *F* in the first name is pierced with a needle, and a small cross stands beside the letter *S* of the second name. Incidentally, the oldest specimen of this kind of *defixio* found in Greece dates from the fifth century B.C., and the oldest one found in Italy dates from the fourth century B.C.[56]

In Italy, the belief in the evil eye must be old. *Fascinum* designates a spell caused by envy. The word is probably related to Greek *baskania* 'envy, jealousy', which would mean that there is a common Indo-European root, and that takes us back even further. For the ancients, being jealous of another person's good fortune was at the root of black magic. Even the gods could feel so jealous of a mortal's happiness and success that they would decide to destroy him.

How could you protect yourself against the envy of the gods, the daemons, your fellow mortals? First of all, you must not show any *hybris* 'pride' or 'arrogance'. Second, to feel safe, you must not display your belongings and achievements and everything that is dear to yourself. If someone praises the beauty of your baby, you must spit on it to pretend that it is worthless to you—a precaution that can still be observed in remote parts of Greece. If anyone admires something that you possess, give it to that person at once. It is better to part with a prized possession right away than to live in constant fear of *baskania*. Third, wear an amulet as a protection and make sure that your children also wear one. Amulets, talismans, and *phylakteria* have been found in large numbers in the Mediterranean world.[57] Sometimes, they have abstract shapes; sometimes they represent a part of the human body: an eye (the evil eye) pierced with an arrow, an open hand (the defensive gesture against the evil eye), a phallus (also called *fascinum*).

It is impossible to say which features of Italic magic are unique,[58] but the following practices seem to be characteristic: the "breaking of snakes" (*angues ruptae*), perhaps a kind of fakir trick (a specialty of the Oriental snake charmer); the werewolf phenomenon (*versipellis* 'one who can change the skin'); and the existence of *striges* or *strigae,* that is, women who could transform themselves into birds and were feared as vampires.[59]

Some curious customs cannot easily be labeled as "magical" or "religious." A good example is the rite of Tacita, "The Silent One," an obscure deity, the mother of the Lares, who was worshiped during a period of nine days in February that was sacred to the memory of the family dead. The young girls of a family gathered together around an old woman who did not belong to the clan and who, with three fingers, placed three grains of incense on the threshold of the house, as an offering to the Manes. She then tied a lead doll with threads, recited some formulas, and chewed seven black beans. After that, she cooked the head of a sardine that had been pierced by a bronze needle. After having poured out a few drops of wine, she drank a large share, divided the rest among the girls, and said: "We have tied the hostile tongues, the mouths of our enemies." And as she spoke these words, the old woman left the house, probably not entirely sober.

This is the ritual as described by Ovid, *Fasti* 2.569–82, and much has been written about it.[60] It may be understood as an apotropaic rite, more magical than religious in nature. The old woman who was not part of the family but summoned from outside for this specific purpose looks very much like your friendly neighborhood witch. It was her job to protect the family against the "evil tongue," which could do just as much damage as the evil eye. But what is the connection with the cult of the Manes and the Lares? Is it an attempt to integrate a magical ritual into mainstream religion?

Recently, M. W. Dickie has shed new light on ancient witches.[61] He argues convincingly that the worlds of female magic and prostitution intersected in some ways. The bawd who is also a witch and happens to be addicted to wine is a recurrent theme in Greek comedy and Roman love poetry. This cannot be just a literary cliché, because the tipsy old woman who is summoned to cure the sick by incantations and amulets is also found, at a later date, in the Church fathers. But what does this mean? Were witches always old and habitually drunk? Or were elderly female alcoholics invariably witches and bawds? Something seems to escape us here.

Temple areas apparently were the places in major cities where one could pick up prostitutes, listen to sophists, and consult sorcerers and interpreters of dreams. The same would be true of marketplaces. Again, we see how easily different spheres intersected in the ancient world. Wrestlers, acrobats, charioteers, theatrical entertainers, and other people who were notoriously superstitious always needed professional help. There must have been a regular mafia of athletes and black magicians (the hit men of witchcraft), an underworld of ambition, greed, hatred, and jealousy—not a pretty picture, but all too human.

The crowds, so often present when certain types of miracles happened (as opposed to rituals performed at night, in secrecy) apparently developed a momentum of their own, a *dynamis* that the skillful *goēs* exploited, creating an aura in which the impossible became real. Some itinerant magicians may have performed "gypsy" tricks based on hypnosis and mass suggestion.

A good deal of work has been done in recent years on the miracle-workers, the "holy men," and the "pseudoprophets" of the first and second centuries A.D.[62] Something has been said already about them in connection with such half-legendary figures as Orpheus and Pythagoras. By writing "holy men" in quotation marks, I do not want to suggest that such later figures were always charlatans and impostors. The fact that there were "pseudoprophets" does not disprove the reality of the genuine phenomenon.

Apollonius of Tyana, often represented as a pagan imitator of Jesus, still fascinates historians.[63] He was definitely a cult figure, and new evidence has been found for his cult;[64] there is also a fairly recent edition of his letters.[65] It has been said that the miraculous feats he performed are not essentially different from those reported in the Gospels.[66] On the other hand, it could be argued that Apollonius, unlike Jesus, was inclined to suggest to people that they were possessed and needed to be exorcised by him. There is a curious inconsistency in Philostratus' *Vita:* on the one hand, he presents his hero as a "wise man" along the lines of Pythagoras;[67] on the other, he enriches this tradition with a substantial amount of colorful folklore,[68] perhaps to satisfy the taste of his time.

Simon Magus has already been mentioned. It would be useful to compare him with Alexander of Abonuteichos, the "pseudoprophet,"[69] or the kind of *magus* that Apuleius, at one point, apparently wanted to become.

All these figures are quite different, and yet they have something in common: they aspire to revive the ancient image of the great shaman. What makes it difficult to compare them and describe their common features is the nature of the evidence. In the case of Apollonius, we have mainly the testimony of Philostratus, an uncritical admirer. In the case of Simon Magus and Alexander of Abonuteichos, we have mainly a hostile tradition. As far as Apuleius is concerned, we have his own testimony, but it must be used with caution, because one part of it (the *Apologia*) is, by necessity, self-serving, and the other (the *Metamorphoses*) is partly fiction.

Still, it is not difficult to understand why a brilliant young man, like Apuleius, a Platonist, wished to become a *magus*. He was, as he indicates himself, motivated by *curiositas*, which is, like its Greek equivalent, *peri-ergia*, practically a synonym of magic. Apuleius learned the hard way (*pathei mathos!*) that religion is a far better thing than magic, and he found peace of mind in the mysteries of Isis. His novel is the story of a spiritual pilgrimage that leads the hero from Platonism via the magical arts to salvation.[70]

In conclusion, it may be worthwhile to review briefly the opposition to magic and the occult arts in antiquity. More will be said about this in the epilogue on the survival of magic within the Church.

We have seen so far that magic is often represented as a caricature or parody of religion, something strange and foreign and difficult to control. In Greece as well as in ancient Italy, there was a powerful religious establishment. Any esoteric, nonconformist groups were *eo ipso* suspicious and could be denounced as subversive. In some cultures, as in Egypt, magic was easily tolerated as part of the fabric of daily life, but that was the exception rather than the rule.

In Book 11 of the *Odyssey,* the hero conjures up the souls of the dead. This is essentially a magical ritual, and his instructions come from Circe, who is described as a sorceress. There is no indication that Odysseus is breaking a law or defying a taboo. The fact that he, the great Odysseus, performs such a ritual seems to make it all right.

In the "Homeric" *Hymn to Demeter* (vv. 228–30), on the other hand, witchcraft, here called *epelysie* (perhaps "something that comes upon somebody"), is rejected, but the text is not sound, and the very word has been restored on the basis of another uncertain passage in the *Hymn to Hermes* (v. 37). It is difficult to date the *Hymns,* but, on the whole, they seem to be younger than the Homeric epics.

The evidence is slim, but it appears that, from the point of view of the earliest Greek poets, the Heroic Age accepted magical practices, side by side with religious rituals, without any discrimination. This is documented for Egypt, and it may well be true for the Minoan Age. If this is correct, the criminalization of magic in Greece must have come later, perhaps during the formation of the first city-states.

Plato condemns the abuses of *pharmakeia* but seems to consider them a fact of life. Later philosophers, the Neoplatonists especially, were attracted by magic, daemonology, and theurgy. The Stoics, with few exceptions, believed in divination because they believed in fate.

The oldest Roman legislation known to us, the Law of the Twelve

Tables, condemns various forms of witchcraft. Later, in the late republic and under the emperors, there were drastic measures against the magicians and the astrologers, sometimes also against the philosophers, but the laws were not always strictly enforced.[71]

An edict on an Egyptian papyrus dated 189/90 is particularly intriguing. It was sent out during the reign of Septimius Severus, notorious before his accession to the throne for his habit of consulting astrologers, and notorious afterward for his determination of making this an illegal practice. Just to ask an astrologer the questions, "When will our emperor die? Who will be the next emperor?" was a serious offense, as we know from Ammianus Marcellinus (29.1.25ff.), because it could indicate a conspiracy.[72]

What was the attitude of the Church? For the early Church, the existence of daemons and prophetic utterances in a state of trance were facts of life. It was clearly impossible for the new faith to sweep away many deeply ingrained beliefs and habits overnight. The converts were still somewhat in awe of the power of the ancient idols around them, and they obviously worried about evil spirits in this world. Thus, they wore amulets and practiced protective magic to be on the safe side.[73]

The fourth century witnessed a stiffening of the resistance of the Church against all forms of magic and "pagan superstitions." We see this, for instance, from the writings of Saint John Chrysostom and Saint Augustine and from canon 36 of the Council of Laodicea, held between 341 and 381. This canon specifies that "priests and clergy may not be sorcerers [magoi], enchanters [epaoidoi] or astrologers [mathematikoi] and must not make amulets [phylakteria], which are poison for the soul." Those who still wore such amulets were to be cast out of the Church.[74] If these practices were condemned so strongly, they must have been fairly common, and the archaeological evidence suggests that they did not cease for a long time.

NOTES

An earlier version of this introduction was published in Spanish in *Arcana Mundi*, translated by Elena Gallego Moya and Miguel E. Pérez Molina (Madrid: Gredos 1995), pp. 9–28. An English translation entitled "Recent Work on Ancient Magic" appeared in *Ancient Pathways and Hidden Pursuits* (Ann Arbor: University of Michigan Press, 2000), pp. 203–22. I am grateful to Gredos and the University of Michigan Press for their permission to use some of the same material. I have borrowed a few comments from my reviews of M. D. Dickie, *Magic and Magicians in the Greco-Roman World* (London and New York, 2001), originally published in *New England Classical Journal* (February 2004) and D. Ogden, *Greek and Roman Necromancy* (Princeton and Oxford, 2001), originally published in *International Journal for the Classical Tradition* 10.2 (Fall 2003). The permission of editors and publishers is acknowledged with thanks. Axel Michaels' bibliography "Magie, Stand Oktober 2000" on the Internet (www.sai.uni-heidelberg.de) has been useful to me.

1. See O. Costa de Beauregard, *La Physique moderne et les pouvoirs de l'esprit* (Paris, 1981).

2. Gwyn Griffiths, in Armstrong, *Classical Mediterranean Spirituality*, p. 15.

3. See A. Gell, "Technology and Magic," in *Anthropology Today*, vol. 4 (London, 1988), pp. 81–90.

4. C. R. Phillips III, "In Search of the Occult," *Helios* 15 (1988): 151–70.

5. In *Nineteenth-Century Religious Thought in the West*, ed. N. Smart et al. (Cambridge, 1985), p. 243.

6. See, e.g., C. H. Ratschow, *Magie und Religion* (Gütersloh, 1955); J. Z. Smith, in *ANRW* 2.16.1 (1978), pp. 430–31.

7. There is a new edition of R. H. Lowie, *Primitive Religion* (London, 1997). D. E. Aune, "Jesus II (im Zauber)," *RAC* 17 (1996), cols. 822–37, offers valuable comments on the relationship between religion and magic and the nature of syncretism. A magical text that has been called the "liturgy" of a mystery religion is now available in a new edition, with a translation and a commentary in H.-D. Betz, *The Mithras Liturgy* (Tübingen, 2003).

8. These guidelines were suggested by W. J. Goode, in *Ethnos* 14 (1949): 172–82. I have developed a few details.

9. In *New Catholic Encyclopedia* 11 (1967), p. 667.

10. On the question whether magic may be considered a universal idea, see E. Evans Pritchard, *Theories of Primitive Religion* (Oxford, 1965), p. 111. See also C. H. Ratschow (after A. E. Jensen), "Magie I," in *Theologische Realenzyklopaedie* 21 (1991), p. 689.

11. See G. Luck, in *Religion, Science and Magic*, ed. J. Neusner et al. (New York and Oxford, 1989), pp. 185–225, reprinted in Luck, *Ancient Pathways and Hidden Pursuits*, pp. 110–52.

12. On Maximus, the theurgist who was instrumental in drawing the emperor Julian away from Christianity, see A. Lippold, "Iulianus I (Kaiser)," *RAC* 19 (2001), cols. 448, 467.

13. See C. Lévi-Strauss, *Anthropologie structurale* (Paris, 1958), chs. 9 and 10; F. Isambert, *Rite et efficacité symbolique*, ch. 2.

14. Frazer, *The Golden Bough*, 1:52–219, is still valid in some ways, but see also M. Mauss, *A General Theory of Magic* (London, 1972). Swedenborg, in a way, seems to have rediscovered this ancient concept and based his own occult philosophy on it; see his *Clavis Hieroglyphica Arcanorum per Viam Repraesentationum et Correspondentiarum* (1784). For him, the universe consists of a number of analogous realms whose elements interact, serve as each others' symbols, and are permeated by Divine Light in different degrees of intensity, thereby revealing their properties. Among scientists who explored analogy as a cosmic principle, one should mention E. Geoffroy Saint-Hilaire, *Principes de philosophie zoologique* (Paris, 1830), esp. p. 97.

15. See C. A. Faraone, "Molten Wax, Spilt Wine and Mutilated Animals: Sympathetic Magic in Near Eastern and Early Greek Oath Ceremonies," *Journal of Hellenic Studies* 113 (1993): 60–80.

16. Cf. Bauer, Arndt, and Gingrich, *A Greek-English Lexicon of the New Testa-*

ment, 5th ed. (Chicago, 1979), s.v.; J. Roehr, *Der okkulte Kraftbegriff im Altertum* (Leipzig, 1923).

17. See Horsley, *New Documents,* 1:35. On the *nomina barbara* used in magical and theurgical rituals, see W. Speyer and I. Opelt, "Barbar I," *RAC Suppl.* 1 (2001), cols. 841–44. On the names "Iao" and "Jeu," see D. E. Aune, *RAC* 17 (1996), cols. 1–12, 906–12.

18. Horsley, *New Documents,* 1: no. 69.

19. Ibid., no. 22.

20. See H. Thyen, "Ich-Bin-Worte," *RAC* 17 (1996), cols. 205–9. This way of creating a magical or religious identity is also characteristic of Simon Magus who said of himself "I am the great Power of God" (Thyen, pp. 190–91). Some spells present the *magus* as a successor of an Egyptian priest.

21. J. Boucharlat, *Magie, religion et folie: La Puissance sans la gloire* (Paris, 1991).

22. M. Dupuy, "Union à Dieu," in *Dictionnaire de spiritualité* 16 (1994), pp. 44–45.

23. C. Colpe, "Jenseitsfahrt I," *RAC* 17 (1996), cols. 421, 434–35; Colpe, "Jenseitsreise," ibid., cols. 490–543, and on the shamanistic aspects especially cols. 494–95.

24. J. Dillery, "Josephus, *Contra Apionem* 1, 232," *Classical Journal* 99 (2004): 239–52.

25. *Corpus Hermeticum* 4.2 and 5.5, cited by Dillery, in ibid.

26. *Alexanderroman b,* Bergson 1.3, cited by Dillery, in ibid., p. 241.

27. See F. Eckstein, *Handwörterbuch des deutschen Aberglaubens,* ed. H. Bächtold-Stäubli, vol. 8 (Berlin, 1936–37), pp. 1156–57.

28. See Horsley, *New Documents,* 1:107.

29. Hippolytus, *Refutatio* 6.2.14d; Ps.-Clement., *Refutat.* 1.71; J. M. de Salles-Dabadie, *Recherches sur Simon le Mage,* vol. 1 (Paris, 1969).

30. See L. de Heusch, in *L'Unité de l'homme* (Paris, 1974); Isambert, *Rite et efficacité symbolique;* N. Habel, *Powers, Plumes and Piglets* (London, 1980).

31. For instance by Habel, *Powers, Plumes and Piglets.*

32. See D. O'Keefe, *Stolen Lightning: The Social Theory of Magic* (New York, 1983); Tambiah, *Magic, Science, Religion and the Scope of Rationality;* St. Clark, *Thinking with Demons: The Idea of Witchcraft in Early Europe* (Oxford, 1997).

33. *Magika Hiera,* ed. C. A. Faraone and D. Obink (New York and Oxford, 1991). I am quoting, with permission, from my review in *Classical Outlook* 69 (1992): 140–41.

34. See Ogden, *Greek and Roman Necromancy.*

35. For Aristotle, the *magoi* were Persian priests as well as philosophers who had inherited the teachings of Zoroaster. See A. de Jong, *Zoroastrianism in Greek and Roman Literature* (Leiden, 1997); J. B. Rives, "Aristotle, Antisthenes of Rhodes, and the *Magikos,*" *Rheinisches Museum für Philologie* 147 (2004): 35–54. Their priestly status probably required initiation rites, perhaps conducted by an *archimagos,* but what these rites were like is a matter of speculation. Perhaps they involved a "baptism" with blood, in analogy to the *taurobolium* attested for the cults of Cybele and Mithras. The apprenticeship of the Hellenistic magus may also have ended with an initiation; see R. Turcan, "Initiation," *RAC* 19 (2001), cols. 121–22.

36. See, for instance, M. Vieyra, *Les Religions de Proche-Orient* (Paris, 1977), pp. 533ff.; T. Abusch, *Mesopotamian Witchcraft* (Leiden, 2002).

37. See R. Largement, in *Dictionnaire de la Bible,* suppl. 5 (1953), pp. 706–21.

38. On amulets in general, see note 49.

39. See Lexa, *La Magie dans l'Egypte antique* and the review by G. Roeder, in *Gnomon* 4 (1928): 196–201; W. R. Dawson, "The Magicians of Pharaoh" [Frazer Lecture, 1936], *Folklore* 47 (1936): 234–63; Y. Koenig, *Magie et magiciens dans l'Egypte ancienne* (Paris, 1994); D. Frankfurter, "The Magic of Writing and the Writing of Magic," *Helios* 21 (1994): 189–221; P. Eschweiler, *Das ägyptische Totenbuch. Vom Ritual zum Bild* (Frankfurt am Main, 1999); W. Westendorf, *Handbuch der altägyptischen Medizin,* 2 vols. (Leiden, Boston, Cologne, 1999). On Demotic magic, see R. K. Ritner, in *ANRW* 2.18.5 (1995), pp. 3333–79. On Coptic magic, which has its roots in ancient and Hellenistic Egypt, see Kropp, *Ausgewählte koptische Zaubertexte.* See also W. Vycichl, "Magie," *The Coptic Encyclopedia* 5 (1991), pp. 1499–1509; P. Du Bourguet, "Magical Objects," ibid., pp. 1509–10. Thanks to the Copts, the ancient method of *lekanomanteia* has survived until now. A cup without handles is filled with oil. The magus who reads the spell burns a mixture of incense and places a boy who has not yet arrived at puberty in a circle drawn on the earth. The boy (presumably in trance) sees future events or hidden things (stolen objects). The circle protects him from evil spirits, an ancient precaution. See P. G. Viaux, *Magie et coutumes populaires chez les Coptes* (Sisteron, 1978), p. 55. The knowledge of special fumigations and their effects (aloe, cloves, cardamom, coriander, mastic, olibanum, pepper, sandarac, storax, etc.) stayed alive in the Coptic Church for a long time. Islamic sorcery has its roots in native Arab traditions and in Greek magic; see, e.g., T. Fahd, "Le Monde du sorcier en Islam," in *Le Monde du sorcier,* Sources Orientales 7 (Paris, 1966), pp. 155–204. It survives mainly in the *Picatrix* and an enormous compilation by al-Buni (1225); see I. Toral-Niehoff, *Der Neue Pauly* 7 (1999), cols. 672–73.

40. See A. Lefèvre, in *Dictionnaire de la Bible,* suppl. 5 (1953), pp. 732–39, and especially J. G. Gager, "Moses the Magician," *Helios* 21 (1994): 179–88.

41. Ed. M. Margalioth (Jerusalem, 1966). There is an English translation by M. A. Morgan (Atlanta, 1983). See also J. Neusner, in *Studies in Judaism* (Lanham, Md., 1987), pp. 46–70; Schiffman and Swartz, *Hebrew and Aramaic Incantation Texts from the Cairo Genizah;* J. Naveh and Sh. Shaked, eds. *Magic Spells and Formulae* (Jerusalem, 1993); P. Schäfer and Sh. Shaked, eds., *Magische Texte aus der Kairoer Geniza,* vol. 1, Texte und Studien zum antiken Judentum 46 (Tübingen, 1994).

42. On the term, see, e.g., A. F. Segal, in *Studies in Gnosticism and Hellenistic Religions,* ed. R. van den Broek and M. J. Vermaseren (Leiden, 1981), pp. 340–75.

43. Betz, *The Greek Magical Papyri in Translation, Including the Demotic Papyri,* vol. 1. See also D. Wortmann, in *Bonner Jahrbücher* 168 (1968): 56–111; R. Daniel, in *ZPE* 19 (1975): 249–64; Chr. Harrauer, *Meliouchos: Studien zur Entwicklung religiöser Vorstellungen in griechischen synkretistischen Zaubertexten* (Vienna, 1987); M. Fantuzzi, in *RFIC* 119 (1991): 79–86. Fantuzzi reviews, among other works, R. Merkelbach and M. Totti, *Abrasax: Ausgewählte Papyri religiösen und magischen Inhalts,* vol. 1, *Gebete,* and Daniel and Maltomini, *Supplementum Magicum.* These volumes also include texts inscribed on earthenware vessels, lead and silverware tablets, linen cloth, etc. Thanks to J. L. Calvo Martinez and Dolores Sanchez

Romero (Madrid, 1987), there is now a Spanish translation of selected texts. The material presented in *Supplementum Magicum* is conveniently divided into six categories: (a) *phylakteria* 'amulets'; (b) *agogai* 'love spells'; (c) *arai* 'curses'; (d) *thymokatocha* 'restrainers of wrath'; (e) *charitesia* 'spells to win someone's favor'; (f) *manteia* 'predictions'. This complements the classification found in the *PGM*: (g) how to conjure up an "assistant daemon"; (h) how to conjure up the dead; (i) how to perform black magic; (j) how to heal an illness; (k) how to produce minor miracles (to win in a game or to make yourself invisible). See also Meyer and Mirecki, *Ancient Magic and Ritual Power.* Love magic (next to hate magic) occupied people's minds at all times. The essential procedure is explained very well by A. Touwaide, in *Der Neue Pauly* 9 (2000), p. 900: You needed *philtra,* made from minerals, plants, or animals. The *materia magica* of choice was burned in a ritual performed by a professional magus who could also use other objects, for example, lead tablets with magical inscriptions or a doll representing the target of the operation. Smoke was produced in order to conjure up a deity. Sometimes, the substance was dissolved in a drink (*poculum desiderii*) or brought into contact with the body of the person you desired.

44. Dodds, *Pagan and Christian in an Age of Anxiety,* 73.

45. Festugière, *L'Idéal religieux des Grecs et de l'Evangile,* 282.

46. Nilsson, *Die Religion in den griechischen Zauberpapyri,* 155. See also H. G. Gundel, in *Proceedings of the 12th International Congress of Papyrologists at Michigan* (Toronto, 1970), p. 185.

47. Horsley, *New Documents,* 1: no. 8.

48. On curse tablets, see S. Eitrem and H. Herter, *RAC* 2 (1954), cols. 380–85; K. Preisendanz, *RAC* 8 (1972), cols. 1–19; D. R. Jordan, *Zeitschrift für Papyrologie und Epigraphik* 19 (1975): 254–58; D. R. Jordan, "Contributions to the Study of Greek Defixiones" (Ph.D. diss., University of Chicago, 1985).

49. See F. Eckstein and J. H. Waszink, *RAC* 1 (1950), cols. 397–411; A. Delatte and Ph. Derchain, *Les Entailles magiques Gréco-Egyptiennes* (Paris, 1964); D. Wortmann, *Bonner Jahrbücher* 175 (1975): 63–82; M. Smith, "Salvation in the Gospels, Paul and the Magical Papyri," *Helios* 13 (1986): 63–74; Th. Gelzer et al., *Lamella Bernensis: Ein spätantikes Goldamulett und verwandte Texte* (Bern, 1999). Amulets made for children have been studied by V. Dasen, "Les Amulettes d'enfants dans le monde gréco-romain," *Latomus* 62 (2003): 275–89. It appears that the tombs of women and children are often furnished with all kinds of magical protections. Children's amulets sometimes have the form of a little bell, which the child could ring to chase evil spirits away. The *bulla,* which the Romans inherited from the Etruscans, served the same purpose when filled with pebbles. Snakes shown on Greek amulets are a very old theme that may go back via Crete (Early Minoan Period) to Egypt; see A. Trckova-Flamee, "Motif of the Snake and Its Meaning in the Minoan Iconography," *Eirene* 39 (2003): 119–49. The animals that the *magus* needed for protection (the cat, the hedgehog, the ibis, and others) are typical of shamanism and comparable with the assistant (*paredros*) daemon invoked in ritual magic; see M. Weber, *RAC* 17 (1996), cols. 129–31; M. Weber, *RAC* Lieferung 158 (2003), col. 693; F. Witek, *RAC* Lieferung 17 (1996), cols. 917–18. The "ghost traps," terracotta bowls inscribed with magical texts, may also be considered as amulets. They have been found, e.g., in Babylon, in certain quarters where He-

brews lived, and their Jewish origin seems certain. There is a large collection in the British Museum. See W. Vycichl, *Coptic Encyclopedia* 5 (1991), p. 1508.

50. Petzke, *Die Traditionen über Apollonios von Tyana und das Neue Testament*, pp. 24ff.

51. For new perspectives see J. De Romilly, *Magic and Rhetoric in the Ancient World* (Cambridge, Mass., 1975). On magic and art, see, e.g., J. Vidal, in *Dictionnaire des religions* (Paris, 1984), pp. 993–94.

52. See A. Quattrocchi, *Miti, riti, magie e misteri degli Etruschi* (Milan, 1992).

53. See the excellent treatment of D. P. Harmon, *ANRW* 2.16.3 (1986), pp. 1909–73.

54. See Anne-Marie Tupet, "Rites magiques," *ANRW* 2.16.3 (1986), pp. 2619–27.

55. Ibid., col. 2595.

56. On the gold tablet from Dacia, see Horsley, *New Documents*, 2: no. 12. A well-known example, *CIL* 1.2.2520 (cf. W. S. Fox, *American Journal of Philology* 33, supp. 1 [1912]), has been discussed by Tupet, "Rites magiques," pp. 2602–3.

57. Tupet, "Rites magiques," pp. 2606–10.

58. On magic and medicine in Rome, see A. Oennerfors, *ANRW* 2.37.1 (1993), pp. 157–224.

59. Tupet, "Rites magiques," pp. 2617–26, 2647–53, 2657–68.

60. S. Eitrem, *Hermes und die Toten* (Christiania, 1909); H. J. Rose, *Journal of Roman Studies* 23 (1933): 60; L. Deubner, in *Archiv für Religionswissenschaft* 33 (1936): 103–4.

61. Dickie, *Magic and Magicians in the Greco-Roman World*. On divination as a métier for women, see A. Traill, "A Haruspicy Joke in Plautus," *Classical Quarterly* 54 (2004): esp. 117, n. 3, with a useful bibliography. The author says: "It would not be surprising to find women employed in areas where magic and religion overlap."

62. See, e.g., G. Anderson, *Sage, Saint and Sophist: Holy Men and Their Associates in the Early Roman Empire* (New York, 1994); B. Kollmann, *Jesus und die Christen als Wundertäter. Studien zu Magie, Medizin und Schamanismus in Antike und Christentum*, Forschungen zur Religion und Literatur des Alten und Neuen Testaments 170 (Göttingen, 1996); see the review by P. Dondelinger, *Revue de l'Histoire des Religions* (1999): 483–87; W. Cotter, *Miracles in Graeco-Roman Antiquity: A Sourcebook* (New York, 1999); Ebner et al., *Lukians Die Lügenfreunde oder: Der Ungläubige*; M. Van Uytfanghe, "Biographie II," *RAC Suppl.* 1 (2001), cols. 1124–30 (there is a section on collections of miracles, cols. 1127–30; the author deals briefly, cols. 1128–29, with Aelius Aristides and his *Sacred Orations*). On the gift of spontaneous insight into the human heart that the *magus* shares with the "holy man," see E. Gruenbeck, "Kardiognosie," *RAC* Lieferung 154–55 (2001), col. 129.

63. Among more recent studies, one should mention K. Gross, *RAC* 1 (1950), cols. 529–32; Petzke, *Die Traditionen über Apollonios von Tyana und das Neue Testament*; J. L. Bernard, *Apollonius de Tyane et Jésus* (Paris, 1977). There is a fine translation by C. P. Jones with an excellent introduction by G. Bowersock (Baltimore, 1970).

64. Horsley, *New Documents*, 3:49–50; C. P. Jones, in *Journal of Hellenic Studies* 100 (1980): 190ff.

65. R. J. Penella, in *Mnemosyne* suppl. 56 (Leiden, 1979). Of the 115 letters

preserved as a corpus, together with 16 preserved in Philostratus' *Vita,* Penella rejects or suspects roughly one-third. On no. 53, see C. P. Jones, in *Chiron* 12 (1983): 137–44.

66. See Petzke, *Die Traditionen über Apollonios von Tyana und das Neue Testament.*

67. See Chr. Riedweg, *Pythagoras. Leben-Lehre-Nachwirkung* (Munich, 2002).

68. F. E. Brenk, *ANRW* 2.16.3 (1986), p. 2136; E. L. Bowie, *ANRW* 2.16.2 (1978), pp. 1652–99.

69. One still needs to consult O. Weinreich, in *Neue Jahrbücher* 24 (1921): 192–251, but see now Phillips, in *Helios* 15 (1988): 158, nn. 52–53. See also Luck, in Ankarloo and St. Clark, *Witchcraft and Magic in Europe,* 2:142–48.

70. See A. J. Festugière, *Personal Religion among the Greeks* (Berkeley, 1954), ch. 5; Gwyn Griffiths, in Armstrong, *Classical Mediterranean Spirituality,* 52–64; Luck, *Ancient Pathways and Hidden Pursuits,* 223–38. On the two *lamiae,* see Brenk, *ANRW* 2.16.3 (1986), pp. 2132–33, and on the relationship between Lucius and the charming but treacherous Photis, see R. de Smet, in *Latomus* 46 (1987): 612–23. See also Harrison, *Apuleius: A Latin Sophist,* and P. Habermehl et al., in Apuleius, *De Magia* (Darmstadt, 2002).

71. See Cramer, *Astrology in Roman Law and Politics;* R. MacMullen, *Enemies of the Roman Order* (Cambridge, Mass., 1960), 95ff., 125ff.; Phillips, "In Search," 260ff.

72. On the Egyptian papyrus, see Horsley, *New Documents,* 1: no. 49. On Ammianus Marcellinus as a source for religious beliefs and magical practices, see Phillips, "In Search," 260, 263–64. On the burning of magical books and related texts, see W. Speyer, "Büchervernichtung," in *RAC Suppl.,* Lieferung 10 (2003), cols. 188–89. This was done by the emperors (under Augustus more than 2,000 prophecies in Greek and Latin were destroyed) and by the Church (Speyer, cols. 209–11). Nevertheless, such books have survived. The magical papyri were probably buried in Egypt with their owners. We can only guess under what conditions other books were preserved. On Iulius Africanus and his *Kestoi* (incomplete), see F. Winkelmann, "Iulius Africanus," *RAC* 19 (2001), cols. 508–18; on the *Cyranides,* a Greek treatise on the healing powers of stones, plants, and animals in four books, see J. Scarborough, "Hermetic and Related Texts," in *Hermeticism and the Renaissance,* ed. I. Merkel and A. G. Debus (Berlin, 1988), pp. 19–44. The two authors, "Cyranus" and "Harpocration," clearly believed in the powers of the pagan deities to whom certain stones or birds were sacred. They also give instructions on how to make amulets. A similar text, only preserved in Latin, is the *Compendium Aureum.* It deals with the role of plants and animals in magic. See A. Delatte, in *Bibliothèque de la Faculté de Philosophie et Lettres de l'Université de Liège* 93 (1942).

73. See J. Engemann, *Jahrbuch für Antike und Christentum* 18 (1975): 22–48; D. E. Aune, *ANRW* 2.33.2 (1980), pp. 1507–57.

74. See B. M. Metzger, in *Historical Studies, Pagan, Jewish and Christian,* New Testament Tools and Studies 8 (Grand Rapids, Mich., 1968), pp. 106–7; Horsley, *New Documents,* 3:116.

MAGIC

Introduction

Settling on a precise definition of magic is not easy, so let me begin with a practical interpretation. According to Lynn Thorndike, magic includes "all occult arts and sciences, superstitions and folklore."[1] In truth, however, this is not a satisfactory definition, for magic is but one of the occult sciences. Moreover, Thorndike uses the vague term *superstition,* which characterizes the attitudes of a supposedly more enlightened age and civilization. Finally, he includes *folklore,* which in itself is not an occult art, although folktales are often *about* witches, sorcerers, and the like. In the present context, I would define magic as a technique grounded in a belief in powers located in the human soul and in the universe outside ourselves, a technique that aims at imposing the human will on nature or on human beings by using supersensual powers. Ultimately, it may be a belief in the unlimited powers of the soul.

The multitude of powers can, perhaps, be reduced to the notion of power, or *mana.* The Greek equivalents, found in Hellenistic texts, are *dynamis* 'power', *charis* 'grace', and *arete* 'effectiveness'. This magical *mana* is freely available; all it needs is a vessel or a channel, and the true *magus* is such a medium—even his garments or something he touches can receive and store the *mana.*

In a polytheistic society such as Greece or Rome, it was only natural that the one Power took on the forms and names of many powers—gods, daemons, heroes, disembodied souls—who were willing, or even eager, to work for the *magus.* When the *magus* summoned these powers by means of his magical knowledge and technique, he could either help and heal or destroy and kill.

One important concept in all magic is the principle of cosmic sympathy, which has nothing to do with compassion but means something like "action and reaction in the universe."[2] All creatures, all created things, are united by a common bond. If one is affected, another one, no matter how distant or seemingly unconnected, feels the impact. This is a great and noble idea, but in magic it was mainly applied in order to gain control. Scientists think in terms of cause and effect, while *magi* think in terms of "sympathies" or "correspondences" in the sense defined above. The positions of the planets in the signs of the zodiac, as well as their aspects in relation to one another, govern the characters and destinies of human beings, not by some sort of direct mechanical influence but rather by a hidden "vibration." The microcosm reflects and reacts to the macrocosm because both share certain deep affinities. This doctrine was held, with variations, by Pythagoreans, Platonists, and Stoicists. Among the Stoicists, Posidonius of Apamea (c. 135–50 B.C.) should be mentioned, and among the Neoplatonists, Iamblichus (c. A.D. 250–325), whose treatise *On the Mysteries of Egypt* deals with *theurgy* 'higher magic', which he defines as an activity surpassing the understanding of man, an activity based on the use of silent symbols that are fully known only to the gods. In fact the higher *magus,* or theurgist, does not quite understand what he is doing; the "sympathy" somehow works through him. The secret is "power through sympathy" and "sympathy through power."

Can a clear distinction be drawn between religion and magic? Many approaches to the problem have been tried, but none seems to work well. Four fundamentally different positions on the relationship between magic and religion have been argued: (1) that magic becomes religion (K. T. Preuss); (2) that religion attempts to reconcile personal powers that magic has failed (Sir James Frazer); (3) that religion and magic have common roots (R. R. Marrett); and (4) that magic is a degenerate form of religion (P. Wilhelm Schmidt). It has been said that the religious person prays to a deity in a humble, submissive manner, whereas the *magus* compels his gods by means of threats; that the religious person relies more or less on the goodwill or mercy of a god, whereas the magician uses some special knowledge that gives him power (sometimes he knows the secret name to which a daemon will respond). This may be generally true. And yet we find a religious mood in magical texts [*no. 25*], and the *magi* use rituals and liturgies not unlike those performed in the great religions of the present and the past. Their concerns are the same: health, wealth, good looks, children, protection from dangers or disasters, and so on. For the *magi,* however, there is such a thing as black magic, whereas almost by definition religion itself can do no harm. Still, the threatening of deities is not unknown in religious contexts. When Germanicus, the adopted son of Emperor Tiberius (and much more popular than his adoptive father) died a mysterious death, Tacitus [*no. 15*] did not exclude magical operations, and when the people of Rome heard the news, they stormed into the temples and kicked the statues of the gods into the streets.[3] It is said that even in more recent times Italian fishermen treated the statues of their saints in the same way. Whenever they made a good catch, they offered the saints the usual incense, flowers, and candles; but when the catch was not good, they cursed the statues and kicked them. The law of "sympathy" is in effect: if you kick the statue of your saint or god, he will feel the pain somehow and react.[4]

Hence some scholars believe that there is no fundamental difference between religion and magic. There may be one: praying for something, giving thanks for something, is conceivable in magic, but not the consciousness of sin and the prayer for forgiveness.[5] The *magus* does not recognize sin; he is, in a way, above morality and the law, a law unto himself. In a society in which practically everyone believed in magic and practiced it in one form or another, this contempt for conventional morality and the laws of the state could have encouraged criminal behavior, but the reasons why magicians and astrologers—along with philosophers—were periodically discriminated against in the time of the empire were mainly political.

The roots of magic are no doubt prehistoric. There is reason to believe that some fundamental magical beliefs and rituals go back to the cult of the great earth goddess.[6] In historical times, she was worshiped in Greece and other Mediterranean countries under a variety of names: Ge or Gaia, Demeter, Ceres, Terra Mater, Bona Dea, Cybele, Ishtar, Atargatis. There must have been an important cult of an earth mother in prehistoric Greece long before the Indo-European invaders known as the Hellenes arrived. No doubt the ancient Greeks' own Demeter owes something to that pre-Greek deity, and it is conceivable that the parts of the ritual (human sacrifices, for instance) that were rejected later on survived in secret. The fact that iron knives are generally taboo in magical sacrifices suggests that they may have originated in the Bronze or Stone Age. In other cases the Greeks gave a new interpretation to existing sanctuaries of Mother Earth, for instance in Delphi, where they attached to the old earth oracle, with its prophetess, their god Apollo. The inevitable conflict between an old and a new religion may help to explain why magic, as a profession, remained suspect and feared among the Greeks and why the great witches of Greek mythology, Medea and Circe, are portrayed as evil or dangerous. In fact, they may have been goddesses of a former religion or priestesses of the Mother Earth cult. Their knowledge of roots, herbs, and mushrooms—gifts of the earth—may have been part of their priestly training. Here again, we have the interpretation of a new civilization that conquered an old one.

The early Greeks may well have misunderstood the nature of some foreign religions and cults—they seem to have made very little effort to understand them. Hence, a good deal of magical lore may simply reflect the beliefs and rituals of ancient religions in countries of which the Greeks had only some vague knowledge. One such "creative" misunderstanding has apparently given us the very word *magic,* which is derived from *magoi,* a Median tribe or caste recognized in ancient Iran as specialists in ritual and religious knowledge. Sometimes they are associated with the cult of fire. As we know from Apuleius' *Apology,* the Greeks and Romans saw in the *magoi* the priests of Zoroaster (Zarathustra) and Ormazd (Ahura Mazda), but these two divine or semidivine beings were also considered the inventors of magic [*no. 30*]. This may simply reflect a Greek prejudice dating from the fifth century B.C. The doctrines and rites of a foreign religion were probably reported in a misleading way and understood not as religion but as a sort of perversion of religion. At the same time, because this religion (or whatever it might be) was so exotic, so different, so ancient, the Greeks must have speculated that the *magoi* had access to secret knowledge.[7]

Incidentally, the borrowing of names, concepts, and rituals from foreign religions is one of the characteristics of ancient witchcraft, as the magical papyri attest. Even though cities like Alexandria and Rome were already full of sanctuaries of exotic deities, apparently there was still room for more speculation and more experiment. No doubt the religions of ancient Egypt were similarly misinterpreted or at least simplified by the Greeks of the Hellenistic period who lived in Egypt, and these religious practices survived, through a series of transformations, in the mainstream of magical doctrine.[8]

Ancient history shows us a succession of great empires—Egyptian, Persian, Athenian, Macedonian, Roman—and each of these had its Pantheon of divine powers. As one culture conquered another, it took over some of its gods, usually the ones that could be identified with a native deity, or the ones suitable to become at least the attendants, the courtiers as it were, of native deities. The truly outlandish elements in a foreign religion seem to have been rejected and despised by the conquerors and classified as witchcraft, but the witchcraft continued to have a life of its own. The Greek witches came from Thessaly or the Black Sea, that is, from countries at the end of the world. The Marsi, a tribe or nation of central Italy, maintained their identity until the late second century B.C., it seems. Their civilization apparently was just different enough from the Roman one to make it look somewhat bizarre. Hence, Marsian magicians (perhaps priests of some of their local deities) enjoyed a great reputation in Rome and were especially famous for curing snakebites.

Finally, when the victorious Christian Church began to hunt witches and wizards, its actions were often directed against surviving pagan cults. In continental Europe, as well as in Britain, some worshipers of the ancient Celtic and Greco-Roman gods had refused to convert to Christianity, and the rites they performed (by necessity in secret) were interpreted as magical rites. The Celts worshiped a horned male god that may have reminded the Romans of the god Pan, a minor god to be sure, but one who could drive you into a "panic" terror when you encountered him at noontime. This combination of horned gods, one Celtic, one classical, produced a very powerful deity around which the *pagani* rallied. Indeed, so powerful was this god that the Christian priests cast him as the prototype of the Devil, with horns, hoofs, claws, a tail, and a generally shaggy appearance. These groups also preserved knowledge of the powers of herbs, roots, and mushrooms, and although this knowledge was not included in the fashionable medical science of the day, patients given up by their doctors probably consulted the local witch, and if she cured them, her practice most likely grew.

If this Celto-Roman deity was cast as the Devil, his female worshipers or priestesses naturally were labeled witches, and this may have been the origin of the witch craze in medieval Europe and in early Colonial America. To us, the medieval Church looks monolithic, universal, unshakable, but there must have been just enough evidence of dissension, schism, and this kind of underground paganism for the Church to take the measures it did. There could be no tolerance of anything outside the Church—*extra Ecclesiam nulla salus*—and if these unfortunates resisted conversion, they offered proof of the power the Devil had over them, a power that had to be broken, if not in this world, at least in the next.

Magic as a Social Phenomenon and a Science

There is, in fact, a form of cooperation, or symbiosis, between established religion and magic. The ability to predict the future is certainly an occult power, a form of magic. We hear of many ancient soothsayers and prophets, some of them highly respected, some of them considered mere fortune-tellers; but without question the most important places of divination were the great sanctuaries.

In Delphi, the method of divination practiced by the Pythia, the priestess-prophetess who sat on top of a deep crack in the ground, receiving her trance and her visions from inside the earth, had nothing to do with the cult of the god Apollo. She was a medium who received impulses and messages from the Great Mother, who of course knew the future of the earth and of all mankind. The trance, the ecstasy of the priestess, and her unintelligible language (probably not unlike the *glossolalia* of the early Christians) were alien to the whole Apollonian myth and form of worship as we understand it. But the oracle was so old that the priests of Apollo kept it going, under their control, and over the centuries turned it into one of the most powerful religious, political, and economic centers of the ancient world. Perhaps the priests of Apollo were suspicious of the ancient method, but for many reasons they recognized its value and sanctioned it. Generally speaking, such occult phenomena as trance, visions, and ecstasy were tolerated only within the context of a sanctuary and had to be supervised by the priests of a recognized religion.

It has recently been argued that a drug was used to induce programmed hallucinations during the initiation rites at the temple of Demeter in Eleusis.[9] But use of that same drug at private parties by privileged Athenian playboys like Alcibiades and his set was considered a profanation and desecration.[10] In a religious context the magical drug was tolerated—in fact, was indispensable—but outside of that context it was condemned.

There has been enormous interest in the exorcism of daemons in recent years. Exorcism is the ancient magical technique of driving out daemons from patients who are thought to be possessed. It was practiced in antiquity by "medicine men" and miracle-workers long after Hippocrates had established the foundations of scientific medicine. Christ exorcised, and in the early Church the ability to drive out daemons was considered a spiritual gift, like speaking in tongues. Today, exorcism is still a prerogative of the Roman Catholic Church, and only ordained priests may practice it. This reveals the same tendency to concentrate and institutionalize magical powers within a larger religious context that we observed above.

Thus magic may be called a religion that has been distorted and misinterpreted beyond recognition by a hostile environment almost from the beginnings of history. The environment changed, but the tradition of magic continued through many metamorphoses. By the time of Christ it had become a science, without completely losing its religious character. This process probably took place in Egypt, a country that acted as a melting pot of different civilizations and traditions, combined influences from East and West, and gave birth to an abundance of mystical systems. We discuss the role of Egypt later. At this point, it may be useful to consider the scientific elements that magic had from the earliest times.

Magic, as a science, has always tried to locate the secret forces in nature (*physis*), their sympathies and antipathies. In a sense, the *magi* were scientists (*physikoi*), whose work was not recognized by the "modern" scientists of the day, though they probably borrowed from them. The *magi* were less interested in pure science than in manipulating the powers (*dynameis*) of nature. At the same time, they explored the human soul, its conscious and unconscious states and expressions. They clearly knew about the psychedelic effects of certain plants, but they probably also practiced hypnosis; they used the techniques of fasting, deprivation of sleep, and prolonged prayers. Certain religions used the same techniques. What is today considered to be science or philosophy was at times part of religion or magic in antiquity and was often presented as a vision or a revelation sent by a god: "Religion [in late antiquity] made science its underling. The so-called science of late Antiquity is speculative and mystical and appeals to revelations and dealings with the supernatural world. But, like magic, it always has a practical aim and does not research for the sake of researching. The fundamental idea was the concept of sympathy. . . . The analogies with which Greek rationalism worked shot up like weeds in the hothouse of mysticism."[11]

Ancient magic could arrive at the same results as science, but it did not attribute them to human reasoning or experimentation; rather, it credited them to direct or indirect contact with a supernatural power. Ancient magic usually dealt with the material world, but that world was thought to be governed and controlled by invisible presences. These presences had to be controlled by the *magus,* who wanted to gain knowledge and power through them to change the present and to predict or influence the future. Hence magic in ancient times was an esoteric technique as well as a science, something that was not accessible to everyone but had to be revealed by a god or learned through a process of initiation. There could not be many true *magi* within one environment, and these *physikoi* accepted few disciples.

Ancient magic may have been based on "primitive" ideas, but the form in which it was handed down to us was by no means primitive. On the contrary: magic in this sense existed only within highly developed cultures and formed an important part of them. Not only the lower classes, the ignorant and uneducated, believed in it, but the "intellectuals" down to the end of antiquity were convinced that dangerous supernatural powers operated around them and that these powers could be controlled by certain means.

Magic as a Literary Theme

The best way to look at ancient magic is, perhaps, to survey various literary texts. The Greek and Roman poets were interested in magic and they provide some good descriptions of magical operations. The first magical operation that was recorded in Greek is found in Book 10 of the *Odyssey* [no.1]. It is one of many adventures that the hero of the epic had to endure on his way back from Troy. The epic itself was probably composed in the eighth century B.C., but it reflects the heroic age of Greece, which coincided roughly with the second part of the second millennium B.C. Homer, in other words, is writing about things that were supposed to have happened about five hundred years before he was born. He works from oral tradition—from folktales, myths and legends, and perhaps folk ballads in verse form. The witchlike character, Circe, seems to be characteristic of folktales in many cultures.

One should note that Circe's witchcraft consists in the use of a wand and that Odysseus' defense against her involves an herb called *moly,* which is revealed to him by the god Hermes. Several requisites of magic are here combined: a mysterious tool that looks like a stick but that is obviously endowed with special powers; an herb that was not easy to find; and a god who reveals to one of his favorites a secret that will save him. Thus, at the beginning of recorded Greek literature we find the three elements that will characterize magic as a system in the Hellenistic age: a magical tool, a magical herb (starting a long tradition of herbaria), and a god who reveals an important secret.

Circe is a beautiful woman—a seductress or temptress like Calypso— whom Odysseus visits on her island and who changes his companions into swine. It is not clear why she does this: perhaps because she hates men; perhaps because she represents a more ancient matriarchal society; perhaps because she is just a semidivine power left over from an older culture, a relatively harmless power if one keeps one's distance, but very dangerous if one comes within her reach. This last explanation may have some support in the story of Lucius, as told by Apuleius in the *Metamorphoses* [*no. 31*]: the hero of that novel gets into trouble only when he actually visits the country of witches, Thessaly. Presumably, if Odysseus had stayed away, he would have been safe. But if you believe or half-believe in witchcraft, to enter the territory of a witch is to invite trouble. Although Circe changes Odysseus' companions into swine, she has no power over Odysseus himself, because Hermes has given him a magical herb, the *moly,* whatever it means. But even Hermes cannot protect Odysseus from Circe's physical charms; when Circe realizes that she has no power over Odysseus, she offers him her bed, they become lovers, and he stays for a while.[12]

Circe is a daughter of the Sun, one of the Titans, just as Medea is the granddaughter of the Sun. The Titans represent an earlier generation, or dynasty, of the gods. Not only can Circe transform men into beasts but she can predict the future. This is another magical power. Through her predictions and instructions, Homer links Circe with the other magical motif of the epic, the necromantic scene in Book 11 of the *Odyssey* [*no. 52*]. Following Circe's instructions, Odysseus digs a trench, pours out as an offering to the dead a drink consisting of honey, milk, wine, and water, and slaughters two black sheep in such a way that their blood runs into the ditch. This attracts the shades of the dead in flocks, and by drinking the blood they regain, for a short time, the ability to communicate with the living.

In the centuries after Homer a number of men with supernatural powers emerged who cannot be labeled or classified precisely. They belong partly to the history of Greek philosophy and science, partly to the realm of Greek religion, but they are also *magoi*, or miracle-workers. In his important book *The Greeks and the Irrational*, E. R. Dodds has suggested for them the term *shaman*, and it is certainly possible to see in them highly sophisticated medicine men.[13] The word shaman is derived from Tungusian *saman* 'priest, medicine man'. Shamanism,[14] which is based on animism and ancestor worship, was practiced as a religion by the Indians of North America. To become a shaman required strict training and harsh asceticism, which led up to a kind of delirium, or trance, during which a vision came. Isolation from the community, fasting and praying, and monotonous exercises such as whirling could help produce this experience, but certain drugs were probably also used. In his well-known books *The Teachings of Don Juan* (1968) and *Tales of Power* (1974), to name only two of a series, Carlos Castañeda describes the world of Don Juan, a Yaqui shaman of the twentieth century.

Perhaps the three most famous Greek *magoi*, or shamans, between Homer and the Hellenistic period, when magic became an applied science, were Orpheus, Pythagoras, and Empedocles. All three are strikingly similar, but each clearly has an identity of his own. Pythagoras and Empedocles lived in the fifth century B.C. Orpheus was a more mythical figure, but Orphism, the religious movement named after him, was a reality, and such movements usually have a founder and leader.

Orpheus and Pythagoras are associated with important philosophical and religious groups or schools in the history of Greek culture; Empedocles remains more of a solitary phenomenon, though he did have disciples. The Sicilian medical school that Empedocles is thought to have founded flourished for a long time. All three men are known to have expressed their ideas in poetry and prose, and at some point many of these compositions must have been written down by their followers, but few of these writings are extant. What we have are fragments or substitutions by later authors. The similarities among these three spectacular figures suggest the existence, in Greek civilization, of a type of miracle-worker who was also an original thinker and a great teacher, someone who offered a philosophical theory to explain the universe and the human soul—macrocosm and microcosm—and who may also have been a poet. In all three instances we seem to face the image of the shaman, known from more primitive cultures but superimposed on a great philosopher, teacher, or poet.

Shamanism is a useful term because it is more neutral than *magus* or *thaumaturge* (miracle-worker). Anthropologists, folklorists, and scholars in the field of comparative religion have been working with it for a long time, but it was E. R. Dodds who introduced it into the history of Greek culture. As Dodds writes, a shaman is a "psychically unstable person" who has received a call to the religious (or philosophic) life, who undergoes ascetic discipline (fasting, long periods of praying in solitude), and who acquires supernatural powers and sometimes also the ability to write poetry, which is really such a power (at least it was to the ancients).[15] He can also heal the sick, understand the language of animals, and be at different places at the same time.

This definition fits Orpheus, Pythagoras, Empedocles, and a number of others—including Apollonius of Tyana, who appears much later—quite well. Dodds has been able to show, in particular, that tradition has given Orpheus the main characteristics of a shaman: he was a poet, *magus,* religious teacher, and oracle-giver or prophet.[16] With his music (a kind of magical charm in itself) he could summon birds, soothe wild beasts, and even make trees follow him as he sang and played on his instrument. Like shamans in other cultures, he was able to descend alive into the underworld and return. His magical self lived on as a singing head that continued to give oracles for many years after his death.

The attribution of magical powers to Pythagoras, as recorded in the days of Aristotle,[17] has been discarded by many historians of Greek philosophy of science, but scholars such as W. Burkert tend to accept it as part of the genuine tradition. Pythagoras had a golden thigh; he was greeted by rivers with a resounding "Hail, Pythagoras!"; he had the gift of prophecy; and he could be at different places at the same time. Like Orpheus, he had power over animals, and he, in turn, respected them to the degree that he preached a strict vegetarianism. All these characteristics indicate that Pythagoras was no ordinary human being; he was a "divine man," *theios aner*—or shaman, to use the more objective term.[18]

Empedocles ascribed to himself the powers to heal the sick and rejuvenate the old; he also claimed he could influence the weather (produce rain in the drought or calm a storm) and summon the dead. It is evident that he—or his disciples—thought of him as a miracle-worker. How could he also be a great scientist? Did he start as a magician who lost his nerve and took to natural science, or was he a scientist who later in life converted to a form of Orphism or Pythagoreanism? This is the way Dodds amusingly states the problem, but he adds, in a more serious vein, that we should not ask these questions, for Empedocles was a shaman—a combination of poet, *magus,* teacher, and scientist. To him, there was clearly no contradiction between these various skills or vocations; they formed a unity.[19]

After Empedocles, the scale of these unusual gifts in exceptional individuals seems to shrink; shamanism becomes one-dimensional, so to speak, or specialized. One either has the gift of healing or the gift of prophecy, but no longer the universal range of supernatural powers with which the early shamans were blessed. This specialization, or limitation of spiritual gifts, was observed in antiquity by Paul in his First Letter to the Corinthians and by Plutarch in his essay *On the Ceasing of Oracles.* Compared with the great thaumaturges of archaic Greece, most of the later practitioners of one occult science or another (dream interpreters or soothsayers) seem like shamans who have lost the full range of their powers. It was therefore a great step forward when Dodds taught us to see Orpheus, Pythagoras, and Empedocles as shamans, each sharing with the other two (and with some minor figures, such as Abaris) the distinctiveness of such a personality, but each with his own specific role and message and his personal way of expressing it.

Pythagoras, through both his legend and his doctrine, had great influence on Platonism, but Plato himself says little about magical practices. That he believed in astrology (and other forms of divination) is strongly suggested by the *Timaeus,* and that he believed in daemons is reasonably clear from the Platonic school tradition. In his *Laws* (933A–E) he takes healers, prophets, and sorcerers for granted. These practitioners existed in Athens and no doubt in other Greek cities, and they had to be reckoned with and controlled by laws. But Plato adds that one should not be afraid of them. Their powers are real, but they themselves represent a rather low form of life.

Aristotle is convinced that the planets and the fixed stars influence life on earth, and, in principle at least, he too believed in the existence of daemons. In his *History of Animals* (a better title would be *Biological Researches,* because *historia* originally meant "research," not "history" in the modern sense), he already suggests the magical theory of sympathies and antipathies in the animal world, under the influence of the stars, a theory that reflects a good deal of ancient Greek folklore. Some of these pseudoscientific theories are found in Books 7–10 of the *History,* but because they do not fit our image of Aristotle, there are serious doubts concerning their authenticity. Book 10, for instance, is missing in the oldest extant manuscript; but even though Aristotle himself may not have written it in this form, it seems to reflect the teaching of his school. Books 7 and 9 have also been rejected by modern editors, but it seems that Book 7 uses material from respectable Hippocratic writings and that Book 9 relies on Theophrastus; hence these portions cannot lightly be discarded as later fabrications.[20]

In his collection *Characters,* Aristotle's pupil Theophrastus (c. 370–285 B.C.) has given us the wonderful "Portrait of the Superstitious Person" [*no. 3*]. In Greek, *superstition* is *deisidaimonia,* literally "fear of supernatural powers." Some of the powers mentioned by Theophrastus are bona fide deities that had cults in Athens, and the priests of these deities probably encouraged some of the sentiments the subject of the sketch displays. In addition to the priests, however, the superstitious person consults the "advisers." These are doubtless the more obscure practitioners of the occult arts, but even they appear to be more rational than he. Surely not all Athenians of Theophrastus' time were so haunted by fears, but his portrait is based on personal observation and represents a sort of scientific study.

The Hellenistic period (roughly the last three centuries before Christ) is characterized by a new interest in magic. From this period we have an abundance of texts in Greek and Latin, some literary and some for practical use. Although the magical papyri that are extant were written in the first centuries of the Christian era, their concepts, formulas, and rituals reflect this earlier period, the time when all the occult sciences were developed into one great system. This systematization probably took place in Egypt. The Greeks who lived in Egypt had an opportunity to observe native religions and forms of worship, folklore, and superstition; and, being Greek, they must have tried to make sense of what they saw. Since we owe remarkable descriptions of magical operations to two Hellenistic poets who lived in Egypt in the early third century B.C., it seems appropriate to discuss them first and the magical papyri later, before we try to say something about Hellenistic magic in general.[21]

Apollonius of Rhodes (so called because he spent the last years of his life on the island of Rhodes, though he was born in Egypt) is famous for the epic *Argonautica,* one of the main characters of which is Medea. Our text [*no. 5*] is taken from the account of the return of the Argonauts from the Black Sea. They landed on the island of Crete, but its shores were guarded by a monster called Talos, "a bronze giant who broke off lumps of rock to hurl at them." Talos is introduced by the poet as a leftover from the Bronze Age, as if people then had really been made of bronze; he had survived into the heroic age (the age of myth, in which all this happened), and Zeus had given him to Europa as a guard. It is easy to see why Talos was associated with Crete: on this island Daedalus, the great craftsman, created statues that were so lifelike that they might have walked away had they not been chained to the floor. (This, by the way, is a humorous exaggeration of the realism of Minoan art as seen by the Greeks of a later period. To create such statues seemed a kind of magic in itself. No wonder, Daedalus was also the first human being to fly.) Talos naturally terrified the Argonauts (great heroes that they were). They would have rowed away had Medea not come to their rescue. It was obviously time for her magic, and this quasi-magical monster was a real challenge to her. She knew she could destroy Talos unless there was immortal life in him, that is, unless he was a god. A product of magic could be destroyed by countermagic.

Our text describes the struggle between Medea and the monster. She won because the powers of evil in and around her, which she could control and channel into a single force, were so strong that the monster was literally knocked over. Medea worked herself into a state of trance during which her hatred became material and the "images of death" that she had conceived assumed a reality all their own. This is perhaps the first explicit description of the power of the evil eye and of black magic. We owe it to a very sophisticated Greek poet who professed to be shocked by the mere thought that someone could be hurt by magical operations. Whether or not Apollonius himself believed it, we can be almost certain that most of his contemporaries did.[22]

Theocritus (c. 310–250 B.C.) is mainly known as a pastoral poet, but he also wrote several pieces describing everyday life in the great modern capital Alexandria.[23] One of these (no. 2 in modern editions) has the title *Pharmakeutria,* which is the feminine equivalent of *pharmakeutes* and means "witch" or "sorceress"; it is derived from *pharmakon* 'drug', 'poison', 'potion', or 'spell'. Any herb, chemical, or requisite used in medicine or magic could be called *pharmakon.* We do not know whether Theocritus himself or an ancient editor gave the poem this title, but it is appropriate, even though the woman is certainly not a professional. Our text [*no. 6*] is a long monologue. Simaetha, a young Greek woman who lives in a city, presumably Alexandria, is in love with a young athlete. It was love at first sight, and for some time they were happy together. But now he has not shown himself at her house for eleven days, and she decides to draw him back by magical means, threatening more powerful measures if this love magic does not work. She has already consulted the professionals, of which there may have been quite a few: "Did I skip the house of any old woman who knows magic songs? But this was a serious matter." Then, according to the do-it-yourself principle, she sets up, with a few fairly simple prerequisites, a magical operation at her house. The ingredients she uses are barley groats, bay leaves, bran, wax, liquids (wine, milk, or water) for libations, coltsfoot (an herb), and pulverized lizard (used by alchemists throughout antiquity and the Middle Ages). Her tools are a magic wheel, a bull-roarer, and a bronze gong. She also keeps a fringe from her lover's cloak—in magical thought, any object belonging to a person represents that person—and she shreds it and throws it into the flames. She then addresses various spells and incantations to the full moon in the sky and to Hecate in the underworld, though in some mysterious way the two are identical.

Theocritus' account of this magical ceremony is poetic, not factual, yet there is an amazing degree of truth in it, for extant magical papyri, amulets, and curse tablets, although from a later period, illustrate almost every phase of the operation as he records it, which he does without getting tedious or obscure, as such documents often do.[24]

Literature and Reality

The poets observed magical operations from the outside; but we also have the testimony of the insiders, the professionals. By the end of the last century B.C., Hellenistic magic was fully formed as a system, and all the occult practices that we know of—astrology, alchemy, daemonology—had become applied sciences that could be taught and learned to a certain extent. Much of the instruction was probably carried out in secret, with small groups of disciples studying with a master. The Egyptian priests were supposed to be the keepers of ancient mysteries that they never shared with outsiders, and thus we have practically no information on this kind of apprenticeship. We do have, however, many handbooks and treatises on the more technical sciences, such as astrology and alchemy, and we have a substantial body of recipes and formulas for practical use—that is, the magical papyri. The trend toward specialization continued. The professional astrologer was now usually not a practicing *magus;* as these sciences became more complex, it became more difficult to master them in a lifetime. No doubt some "sorcerers" dabbled in more than one of these arts, and, as an ideal at least, the Faustian type of magician, who is also a great astrologer, alchemist, daemonologist, and physician, was recognized. He was not unlike the "pure" scientist who trained in the school of Aristotle, and he was interested in the whole physical world, in living creatures, plants, stones, and metals; but his experience and methods were different.[25]

Even when the various subjects are kept separate, they explain and interpret one another from our point of view. The astrological texts from Egypt, which F. Cumont discusses, reveal the superstitions that people in late antiquity shared—the hopes and fears, the desires and ambitions, of ordinary men.[26] The magical papyri show us the sort of power that men and women wished to have over others, and the amulets that people wore, also preserved, indicated how the would-be victims defended themselves.

Then, as now, people wished for themselves and for their loved ones health and good looks, wealth, and success in business, politics, sports, and love, and, if they had been hurt or humiliated, revenge. It is curious that in Hellenistic Egypt the ancient native gods (Isis, Osiris, Horus, Anubis, Typhon) became the sources of magical powers. Their names and attributes were borrowed by practitioners of magic who probably took no part in regular Egyptian cults. Similarly, the formula "Jesus, god of the Hebrews" appears in a spell that obviously was not used by a Jew or a Christian. The Lord's Prayer also appears as a magical formula. It is the same phenomenon that we noted earlier: the gods of a foreign culture are not addressed as proper gods, but because they seem to work for that other culture, they are suspected of having powers that could be useful in magical operations.[27]

Later we shall discuss some literary texts (the works of Horace, Virgil, Apuleius, Lucian, and others) that inform us of magical doctrine and rituals. At this point it seems most convenient to look at the magical papyri, those scrolls and leaves from Egypt that, taken together, formed a practicing magician's collection of spells. Although their date is relatively late (third or fourth century A.D.), they reflect much older ideas, and the doctrines and techniques they embody were probably developed in the late Hellenistic period. Many are considered to be copies of copies; in fact, some of them (e.g., the London Papyrus 46) seem to derive from at least two earlier texts, and one (the Oslo Papyrus) appears to be an approximation of a barely legible earlier specimen.[28]

The first magical papyri discovered in Egypt were brought to Europe by Johann d'Anastasy, the Swedish vice-consul in Cairo from 1828 to 1859, an Armenian by birth. He bought a whole collection that had been discovered, he was told, in a grave near Thebes, but no one seemed to know exactly where or when. This amazing collection contained recipes and formulas for all types of magic: love magic, exorcism, curses. At the time it must have created no less of a sensation than the discovery of the Dead Sea Scrolls or of Menander's *Dyskolos,* and its importance should not be underestimated today. One may think of it as the working library of a magician, a library that was buried with him (some time in the fourth century A.D.) to provide him with magical knowledge in the other world.[29] Some of these papyri were acquired by the Leiden Museum of Antiquities in the early nineteenth century, others by museums in London, Paris, and Berlin. The Great Magical Papyrus, for instance, is in Paris; it consists of thirty-six sheets covered with writing on both sides, or a total of 3,274 lines.[30]

What we have is no doubt only a fraction of the magical literature available at one time or another in antiquity. From Acts 19:18–20 we know that Paul made many Ephesians bring out their magical books (which were worth a great deal of money) and burn them; Ephesus was apparently one of the centers of magic, and *Ephesia grammata* are "magical words." The language of the magical papyri would require a separate study. They reflect various levels of literary skill, but generally they are standard Greek; they are not incorrect, but presumably they are closer to the spoken language than to poetry or artistic prose. Many terms are borrowed, it seems, from the mystery cults; thus magical formulas are sometimes called *teletai* (literally, "celebrations of mysteries"), or the magician himself is called *mystagogos* (the priest who leads the candidates for initiation).

Often the texts are written in the form of a recipe: "Take the eyes of a bat . . ." [*no. 26*]. These recipes, along with the appropriate spells and gestures, are supposed to produce a variety of effects: they guarantee revealing dreams and the talent of interpreting them correctly; they send out daemons to plague one's enemies; they break up someone's marriage or kill people by insomnia. There is a definite streak of cruelty in some of these ceremonies, and Theocritus, in the text discussed above [*no. 6*] shows how love magic, which seems harmless enough, can turn into hate magic if the victim does not respond. The same is true for Dido's magical ceremony at the end of *Aeneid* 4 [*no. 11*]. The magician seems to think: "If you won't love me, I'll kill you," a feeling that has caused countless tragedies in literature and in real life.

The magical ostraca are a variety or subspecies of the magical papyri, but the material used (broken pots) was cheaper (some papyri actually recommend the use of ostraca), and the texts had to be shorter. They range chronologically from the fourth century B.C. to Byzantine times, and they operate along the same lines as the spells on the magical papyri. A love spell from Oxyrhynchus, for instance, is designed to break up a woman's marriage and attract her to the sorcerer instead.

The "curse tablets," *tabellae defixionum,* are another important primary source of our knowledge of magic. The term *defixio* is derived from the Latin verb *defigere,* which means literally "to pin down," "to fix," but which also had the more sinister meaning of delivering someone to the powers of the underworld. Of course, it was possible to curse an enemy through the spoken word, either in his presence or behind his back, and this was thought to be effective. But for some reason it was considered more effective to write the name of the victim on a thin piece of lead (other materials were used as well) with magical formulas or symbols and to bury this tablet in or near a fresh tomb, a place of execution, or a battlefield, in order to give the spirits of the dead—which were presumed to hover around such sites on their way to the underworld—power over the victim. Sometimes the curse tablets were transfixed by a nail (the *defixio* dramatized), or they were thrown into wells, springs, or rivers.[31]

The curse tablets cover a much wider range of time than the magical papyri: the first examples are from the sixth or fifth century B.C.; the last, from the seventh century A.D.; they are particularly frequent in the Hellenistic period and toward the end of antiquity. The oldest examples are very simple: "X, bind Y, whose mother is Z," where X is either a (Hellenic) god or a daemon and Y is the victim. It is curious that the victim is identified by his or her mother rather than by the father, as might be expected, since this was the common form of introducing someone. Moreover, it is remarkable that familiar Greek gods can be substituted for magical daemons. Later, as the texts become more elaborate, they contain magical diagrams, series of vowels, and names of foreign gods who are probably considered more powerful than the native ones. Often the curse tablets were aimed at an athlete—a charioteer, for instance—to prevent him from winning. The populace was usually divided in its loyalty to an athlete or a team, and since, no doubt, large bets were placed on the victory or defeat of one or the other, emotions ran high.

Amulets were worn as protection against curses, the evil eye, and evil powers in general.[32] These tokens were often made of cheap material, but precious stones were thought to have special powers; they were also more durable, and so thousands of carved gems that had a magical rather than an ornamental function have survived.[33] One might wear them around the neck or on a ring. On an Egyptian jasper, for instance, there might be carved a snake biting its own tail, two stars, the sun, and the words *Abrasax, Iao,* and *Sabaoth* (*Abrasax* being a magical word, and *Iao* as well as *Sabaoth* being different names for the supreme Jewish-Christian deity).

The word *amulet* is probably derived from *amolitum* (see Pliny *Nat. Hist.*, 28.38, 29.66, 30.138), whereas *talisman* could be an Arabic transformation of Greek *telesma* 'initiation'. Any devotee of magic, whether Gentile, Jew, or Christian, could wear amulets, with their mixture of Babylonian, Egyptian, Greek, and cabalistic elements, regardless of his faith or affiliation.[34] The amulets carry the same formulas as the papyri, though these inscriptions were probably copied from the papyri in a more abbreviated and concentrated form. Again, it seems that the papyri were the working texts of the professional sorcerer and could be put to various uses.[35]

The world of the ancients was full of magical powers, acting in all directions, and many people must have felt constantly threatened. To protect oneself by wearing an amulet was probably not safe enough, and since attack is the best defense, a good deal of black magic was probably performed as a simple measure of precaution: if you suspected someone of putting a curse on you, you put a curse on him and let it be known. Hence a sort of equilibrium was established in which one could exist and pursue one's everyday business.

Something should be said about magical ingredients, tools, and devices. Magical tools were used again and again, just as the spells and incantations were repeated on each occasion. Herbs and other ingredients, however, were in limited supply and had to be replenished. Plant magic and the use of a wand are as old as Homer. Theocritus' amateur witch also used herbs, in addition to a magical wheel, a bull-roarer, and a gong. Moreover, special plates and rings were to be worn during the ceremony. Such a magician's kit, probably dating from the third century A.D., was discovered in Pergamon. It consisted of a bronze table and base covered with symbols, a dish (also decorated with symbols), a large bronze nail with letters inscribed on its flat sides, two bronze rings, and three black polished stones inscribed with the names of supernatural powers. This kit seems to have worked on the principle of a roulette table.[36]

The Roman historian Ammianus Marcellinus (29.1.25–32) describes a kind of ancient Ouija board that was used in a séance in A.D. 371 with very unfortunate results for all the participants.[37] It consisted of a metal disk on whose rim the twenty-four letters of the Greek alphabet were engraved, supported by a tripod made of olive wood. To consult this portable oracle, one had to hold a ring suspended on a light linen thread. After lengthy prayers and incantations addressed to an anonymous "deity of divination" (perhaps Apollo), the ring began to swing from one letter to another, forming words and names, sometimes even sentences in verse form. Two questions that were no doubt frequently asked during such séances were clearly asked during this one—and this made the whole experiment definitely illegal and subversive: "When will our emperor die?" and "Who will be our next emperor?" The first question was answered by the oracle poetically (but accurately it appears); as for the second question, the ring spelled *theta,* then *epsilon,* then *omikron* (giving 'Theo-'). At this point an impatient participant jumped to the conclusion that the oracle was about to spell out *Theodorus,* and the group stopped the whole procedure right there. Somehow the authorities learned of the secret gathering, and all those involved—including Theodorus, who denied all knowledge of it—were arrested, tried, and executed. Seven years later it became evident that the oracle had tried to get the truth across. The emperor Valens was killed, and the name of his successor was Theodosius!

The use of symbols, numbers, and strange words in magic must be very old, though the abracadabra formula is not attested before Serenus Sammonicus, the author of a work *Res Reconditae* (*Secret Matters*), who was murdered in A.D. 212.[38] Symbols are signs that preserve human experience and can create powerful reactions, sometimes more powerful than the reality they represent.[39] Numbers are symbols too, and number mysticism is well attested in Hellenistic magic.[40]

What emerges from the evidence is the permanence and universality of magic in the ancient world. Although some testimonies may be relatively late, the doctrines and practices they reveal are often much older. Certain formulas and recipes were handed down for generations, perhaps with minor changes, and though they are found on tablets and papyri dating from the early Christian era, they probably had been practiced for centuries. Moreover, it is clear that the same type of magic was practiced throughout the Roman Empire.[41]

Types of Magical Operations

Our material permits a division of magical operations into two main kinds, theurgical and goetic. The word *theurgia* calls for a brief explanation. In some contexts it appears to be simply a glorified kind of magic practiced by a highly respected priestlike figure, not some obscure magician. Dodds says: "Proclus grandly defines theurgy as a 'power higher than all human wisdom, embracing the blessings of divination, the purifying powers of initiation, and in a word all the operations of divine possession' (Procl., *Theol. Plat.* [63 Dodds]). It may be described more simply as magic applied to a religious purpose and resting on a supposed revelation of a religious character. . . . So far as we can judge, the procedures of theurgy were broadly similar to those of vulgar magic."[42] Here again we see how difficult it is to separate magic from religion: if Dodds' definition is valid, any theurgical operation must have both a religious and a magical aspect. In a typical theurgical rite the divinity appears in one of two ways: (1) it is seen in trance, in which case the soul of the theurgist or medium leaves the body, ascends to heaven, sees the divinity there, and returns to describe the experience; (2) it descends to earth and is seen by the theurgist either in a dream or when he is fully awake. In the latter case, no medium is needed; only certain "symbols" and magical formulas are required. The "symbols" could be an herb, a stone, a root, a seal, or an engraved gem, and the formulas might include the seven vowels of the Greek alphabet, representing the seven planetary gods.[43] Sometimes the divine presence manifests itself more indirectly, through a medium or a requisite such as the flame of a lamp or the water in a basin.

The term *goeteia* is a synonym for *mageia,* but has even more negative undertones, it seems, just as *theurgia* is definitely more exalted than either. Perhaps these three terms reflect a long battle between believers and nonbelievers, and the attempt by the various groups of practicing believers to distinguish their "magic" from the lower types or techniques that existed at all times. Hence, it could be argued that the term *theurgia* was introduced to make magic a respectable practice for the philosophers of late antiquity, who would have been horrified to be called *magoi* or *goetes,* especially the latter, since that term could also designate a juggler or charlatan—the gypsylike type of fraud who was out to make a quick profit at fairs and festivals all over the Greek world.

The philosophers who were interested in magic described themselves as theurgists, and the lower-class practitioners as *magoi* or *goetes.* According to Plotinus (*Enn.* 4.4.26), theurgy aims at establishing sympathy in the universe and uses the forces that flow through all things in order to be in touch with them. He admits that it works, but he rejects some of its claims and practices (*Enn.* 4.3.13, 4.26.43−44). Thus, the theurgist achieves in reality what the philosopher can only think (Iambl., *Myst.* 3.27).

The term *theurgist* seems to have been introduced by Julianus, a Hellenized Chaldean who lived under Marcus Aurelius. Theurgists formed a late pagan religious sect. They not only talked about the gods as the theologians did; they performed certain actions by which, they claimed, the gods were affected. "Theurgy, like spiritualism, may be described as magic applied to a religious purpose and resting on supposed revelations of a religious character."[44] Their sacred book, *The Chaldean Oracles,* is lost, but parts of it can be reconstructed. They used mediums. Thus, there was an important difference between the theurgists and the theologians: the latter mainly thought and talked about the gods; the former tried to influence them, forced them to appear, even created them.[45]

These theurgical operations appealed to the Neoplatonists, who believed that by ascetic exercises and proper initiation they could either bring divine powers down to earth or make their own souls ascend to heaven. Thessalus of Tralles (first century B.C.) was granted a personal vision of the god Asclepius by an Egyptian priest in Thebes.[46] In other words: theological or philosophical thought is not enough; certain actions, procedures, or rites have to be followed.

But is theurgy really different from magic? In a sense, it is. Franz Cumont called it "a respectable form of magic, an enlightened type of sorcery,"[47] and we may add that the great theurgists of antiquity were highly educated men and women of impeccable reputation, totally different from the sellers of curses and spells.[48]

We know very little about the ritual itself, no doubt because it was kept secret, but it was apparently based on the doctrine of sympathy between things visible and things invisible, beings of this world and beings of another world. The initiation of the emperor Julian gives us an impression of the ritual,[49] but the report we have is sketchy, almost incoherent, full of symbolism and allusions that would make sense only to fellow initiates: "Voices and noises, calls, stirring music, heady perfumes, doors that opened all by themselves, luminous fountains, moving shadows, mist, sooty smells and vapors, statues that seemed to come to life, looking at the prince now in an affectionate, now in a threatening manner, but finally they smiled at him and became flamboyant, surrounded by rays; thunder, lightning, earthquakes announcing the arrival of the supreme god, the inexpressible Fire."

How all these effects were produced is unknown, but they are reminiscent of initiation rites that were required in the mystery religions.[50] There is no evidence that everything was fraud, and it is hard to believe that mechanical tricks, elaborate staging, and so on could fool a man like Julian. It makes much more sense to assume that Julian submitted to some kind of "programming" (months of indoctrination, ascetic exercises, etc.), which, through the use of drugs, either ingested or inhaled, produced an altered state of consciousness at the crucial moment.

In addition to the spoken word (*to legomenon*), certain requisites and rites (*to dromenon*) were necessary. Porphyry gives us a portrait of a theurgist (actually a statue, but the implications are unmistakable, I think), his head wreathed with bandages and flowery branches, his face anointed or actually made up, a laurel twig in one hand, magical symbols on his shoes.[51] And Iamblichus writes: "The theurgist, by virtue of mysterious signs, controls the powers of nature. Not as a mere human being, or as [one who] possesses a human soul, but as one of a higher rank of gods, he gives orders that are not appropriate to the condition of man. He does not really expect to perform all these amazing things, but by using such words he shows what kind of power he has and how great he is, and that because of his knowledge of these mysterious symbols he is obviously in touch with the gods."[52] It seems that even Iamblichus, a believer in theurgy, makes certain distinctions: not everything the great theurgist says and does will have an immediate magical effect; much of it serves to create a mood, an atmosphere that prepares the faithful for greater things to come, such as *autopsia,* the appearance of the divine light without any shape or form.

Theurgy could therefore be defined as an attempt to reestablish, through indoctrination, training, ritual—in short, through "programming"—and possibly through the use of certain drugs, the status of the great shamans of archaic Greece such as Pythagoras (whose biography Iamblichus wrote).

To read about magical operations can be a tantalizing experience. The reader is often led up to a certain point, but the real secret—the words or rites that make the magic work—seems to lie beyond that point. Obviously, there are things that our texts do not reveal, and it makes sense that the magician would not entrust everything to papyrus but would reserve what he considered an essential element to private instruction.[53] Astrology is perhaps the only "occult" science that could be learned from a good handbook. Nevertheless, none of the texts that have survived from antiquity gives us a complete introduction; there are always gaps, perhaps left on purpose, so readers would have to study with a professional astrologer. The same is true for alchemy: the texts are either too general or too technical, and if one wanted to pursue the subject, one would have to be close to an experienced practitioner, watch him, consult him, and use his equipment and his books. There are, at every step, allusions, symbols, a kind of mystic shorthand that would be intelligible and useful only to the initiated and that would have to be explained by a master. It seems safe to venture the statement that magic "worked" only within a group—often a very small group—of devotees and practitioners who gave one another mutual support even when, from an outsider's point of view, their magic failed.

Even the relatively simple, early forms of magic such as those attested in Homer and in Apollonius of Rhodes [*nos. 1* and *5*] involve a kind of ritual. By the end of the Hellenistic period this ritual had become very complex. It generally included *klesis* 'invocation' and *praxis* 'ritual', properly speaking.[54] The invocation summoned a divine power by name, though sometimes, in our documents, the name was not written in: it was either kept secret or left open, a blank for the *magus* to fill in. The name of the god or goddess was not enough; it had to be accompanied by a string of epithets describing the powers of the divinity (*aretalogia*). The *magi* wanted such lists to be as complete as possible, for it might be dangerous to omit one epithet that the god was particularly fond of; hence the lists tended to grow and grow. The invocation was also a means of reminding the divine power of past occasions when he or she had helped the operator in a striking way or performed some sort of miracle. It might also include a specific request for a specific occasion—for example, what the divinity was expected to do for the operator now.

The *praxis* tended to be just as complex as the *klesis*. Long litanies were recited mainly in Greek, but sometimes in a kind of nonlanguage consisting of strings of magical words. Presumably they were recited in a way that could be learned only from an acknowledged teacher. The gestures had to be performed correctly; the right kind of equipment had to be used. Some of these ceremonies must have lasted for several days and nights. Substances (e.g., sulfur) were sniffed, libations were poured, visual and acoustic effects were produced, and, no doubt, drugs were used to help induce a state of trance. We read about weird sounds made by the *magus:* clucking, sighing, groaning, smacking of lips, taking a deep breath and letting it out with a hissing sound.[55] In some cases it was even necessary to eat the magical text, as *PGM* I.14 prescribes: "Write these names with Hermes ink. After having written them as told, rinse them off in spring water from seven springs, drink it on an empty stomach during seven days, when the moon is ascending. But drink a sufficient amount!" Magicians also wrote certain words or names in their own blood.[56]

It seems paradoxical that for certain periods we are better informed on magical rituals than on religious ones. Moreover, although the magical rituals often betray what appears to be a genuine religious feeling, the elements of pressure, blackmail, and sinister threats often build up in and are reinforced by the rituals.

Hellenistic magic represents a conglomerate of many different influences. It borrowed freely from the religions and occult sciences of different cultures (Greek, Jewish, Egyptian, Persian, etc.), but even the religious elements were selected for a practical purpose: the gods of witchcraft were worshiped not for the sake of their glory but for the help they could offer in specific situations. Often these gods were asked to fulfill wishes that the operator would not acknowledge openly; hence, magical prayers and spells were usually "whispered" or "hissed," whereas in the temples of a god or goddess legitimate prayers were uttered aloud. But the syncretism of Hellenistic magic had a parallel in the syncretism of Hellenistic religions in Egypt, a country where many different cultures coexisted, a country that had been open to Eastern influences for centuries and that now, under Greek rulers, had been given a capital, Alexandria, that would become one of the intellectual centers of the world.

Let us turn, then, to the Persian origins of magic. Persian priests, the *magoi,* were supposed to have inherited the lore of the Chaldeans. Chaldea, or "the land of the Chaldeans," was the name of a country (according to Genesis it was the home of Abraham), but a Chaldean could also be an astrologer or an interpreter of dreams, originally perhaps a member of a priestly caste that studied occult rituals and handed them down. Zoroaster (sixth century B.C.) was the greatest teacher, priest, and magician (a figure comparable to Orpheus in some ways) in the early Persian Empire. He lived during the reign of the Achaemenids and wrote many works on magic, astrology, divination, and religion. He is considered the creator of a system of daemonology that was adopted at various stages and in various forms by Jews, Greeks, and Christians. Another great Persian *magus*, Ostanes, accompanied Xerxes on his campaign against Greece (480 B.C.), no doubt as an adviser to the king. After his defeat at Salamis, the king left Ostanes behind, and Ostanes became the teacher of Democritus (born c. 470 B.C.), apparently encouraging his pupil to travel to Egypt and Persia. Democritus is chiefly known as a great scientist (his atomistic theory of the universe anticipates modern physics and chemistry); he may have transmitted Persian magic in one of his many works.

The *magoi* who came to Palestine from a distant oriental country to offer their adoration to the newborn child in Bethlehem are represented as kings and as wise men. Clearly they are skilled in astrology, for a star or an unusual constellation has told them of the birth of a king.

Zoroaster, Ostanes, and the three Magi mark half a millennium. During that time and for centuries to come, the Western world associated Persia with magic and secret lore.

In Egypt, according to our theory, a kind of curriculum of occult sciences was created during the Hellenistic period. To the Greeks living there, many religious ceremonies must have appeared to be magical operations. Then, too, the Greeks probably considered to be magic certain manufacturing processes that the Egyptians kept secret. From the beginning, alchemy seems to have been a mixture of magic and real technology, but the secrecy that enveloped both probably exaggerated the role of the former. Some typically Egyptian features of Hellenistic magic are: (1) Magic is not practiced primarily as a necessary protection from the evil powers that surround the individual; rather, it is a means of harnessing good or evil powers in order to achieve one's goals and desires. (2) The operator of the magical papyri pretends to be a god in order to frighten the gods. This attitude of pretending, of temporarily assuming a supernatural identity, is highly characteristic of magic in general. (3) Magical power is linked to certain words that are clearly differentiated from normal language; they are pronounced in a certain way or written on gems, papyri, and the like, along with certain signs and diagrams. (4) Power is also linked to certain gestures and rites; these rites are similar to the ones used in religious cults but, one would assume, are sufficiently different and distinctive to avoid misunderstandings. It was common, for instance, to sacrifice black animals to the powers of the underworld to make sure that none of the heavenly gods would claim it for himself.

The Greek influence on Hellenistic magic can only be sketched at this point. In a sense, Hellenistic magic was a Greek creation on Egyptian soil: Greek philosophers had given it a basis and built it into a system. In terms of specifics, however, while the magical operations are familiar, the roles of the gods are not. Hermes becomes identified with the Egyptian Thoth, not only as the patron of science and of learning in general, but also as the god who leads souls into Hades. Hecate, the most ancient goddess of the underworld, becomes, along with Persephone, the divinity par excellence of the witches, as does the moon goddess, Selene, who presides over their nocturnal rites. Apollo, the official god of the Delphic oracle, becomes tied to divination in many forms. Pan, as god of the witches, furnishes the traditional image of the Devil; hence he must have played an important role in magical ceremonies in later antiquity, although the texts do not give a coherent picture of this development.

We should also consider the influence of Judaism, and especially Jewish magic, on Hellenistic magic.[57] Alexandria had a large Jewish population in the later Hellenistic period, and it seems to have contributed a good deal to Hellenistic culture in general. On one level we have the daemonology of Philo, a Jewish Platonist, and on another level, all sorts of popular superstitions.[58]

The Old Testament gives us a certain amount of information on magical practices and beliefs, and the very fact that they were outlawed indicates that they existed.[59] In turn, toward the end of the Hellenistic period, Jewish magic was strongly influenced by Greek and Egyptian ideas.[60] By that time many Jews—like the Greeks and Romans—believed in the evil eye, the power of certain words and phrases and of spittle, the omina given by birds, the protection afforded by amulets, and so on.[61] The difference between black magic and white magic was understood. Necromancy was practiced (necromancers were called "bone-conjurers"), as was exorcism (since diseases in general and madness in particular were explained by possession), usually as a last resort when medical science failed.[62]

Because he practiced exorcism and because of some popularized versions of the Gospels, Jesus was considered a magician by some Talmudic teachers and no doubt appeared as such to many Greeks and Romans who did not think of him as a religious leader.[63] It is easy to see how even Moses, in later antiquity, could appear to be a powerful magician in addition to being a great teacher and leader, the inventor of philosophy, learning, writing, and so on, like the Egyptian Thoth. Moses and Aaron perform magic in the Egyptian style before Pharaoh (Exodus 7:8–14, 8:1–15) to compete with the Egyptian sorcerers, and though the sorcerers can duplicate the Jewish magic up to a certain point, Moses and Aaron win the contest because they receive their guidance from the Lord. Magical books were ascribed to Moses in antiquity (PGM XIII).

Solomon's great wisdom was supposed to include magic, and a magical

text, the Testament of Solomon, circulated under his name; it was probably composed in the early third century A.D., but the manuscripts attest-
ing it were not written before the fifteenth and sixteenth centuries.[64] The
much better known Wisdom of Solomon, a biblical book considered
apocryphal by Jews and Protestants, was probably composed in the first
century B.C. In it Solomon says: "God . . . gave me true knowledge of
things, as they are: an understanding of the structure of the world and the
way in which elements work, the beginning and the end of eras and what
lies in-between . . . the cycles of the years and the constellations . . . the
thoughts of men . . . the power of spirits . . . the virtues of roots . . . I
learned it all, secret or manifest." Clearly, Solomon is pictured as the
greatest scientist, but also the greatest occultist, of his time: he has studied astrology, plant magic, daemonology, divination, but also *ta physika*
'science'. Some translators obscure this fact; they write, for instance,
"the power of winds" when the context shows that daemons are meant.
Josephus certainly understood the passage in this way. He writes (*Antiq.
Jud.* 8.45): "God gave him [Solomon] knowledge of the art that is used
against daemons, in order to heal and benefit men." He even adds that
Solomon was a great exorcist and left instructions on how to perform this
kind of healing. This could mean that in Josephus' time, a magical text
that taught how to exorcise daemons in the name of Solomon existed.[65]
In Justin's *Dialogue with Trypho* (85.3) a Jewish magician is addressed as
follows: "If you exorcise a daemon in the name of any of those who once
lived among you—kings, righteous men, prophets, patriarchs—it will not
obey you. But if you exorcise the daemon in [the name] . . . of the God of
Isaac and the God of Jacob, it may obey you. No doubt your exorcists
apply magical techniques when they exorcise, just like the Gentiles, and
they use fumigations and incantations."

In later antiquity, the Jews had the reputation of being formidable magicians, and the various names of their deity—Jao for Yahweh, Sabaoth,
Adonai—appear frequently in the magical papyri. Many outsiders must
have thought of Yahweh as a secret deity, for no image could be seen and
his real name was not pronounced. Here again we see a misunderstood
theology or religious ritual at the basis of speculations on magic.[66] The
roots of *cabala* 'received tradition' are believed to reach back into the first
century A.D., when the first tracts appeared in Palestine.[67] The cabala is
best explained as a system or method of Jewish mystical devotion having
certain magical elements. It flourished in Spain in the twelfth and thir-
teenth centuries but is much older. The cabalists believed in the possibility of direct communion with God, the descent and incarnation of
the soul, and the transmigration of souls. They extracted hidden meanings from the Bible by interpreting it allegorically or by using numerol-

ogy, giving each Hebrew letter in a word or sentence a numerical value. The world, according to them, is inhabited by daemons, and men need amulets to protect themselves. In brief, the cabalistic tradition has preserved, in a systematic and coherent form, blended with Platonist and Neoplatonist doctrine, a good deal of occult science from late Hellenistic times.

Having surveyed the "real" magic, the practical, everyday witchcraft of the period, we can now return to the literary texts.

Other Literary Texts

In his eighth eclogue, Virgil (70–19 B.C.) gives us a free translation or adaptation of Theocritus' second poem [*no. 10*; cf. *no. 6*]. He leaves out a number of details and adds a happy ending—the magic works, and the lover returns—but otherwise, he is quite faithful to the original. Poems such as these describe the life of the so-called lower classes (shepherds and peasants) with a kind of poetic realism, but they are addressed to a highly sophisticated audience. Virgil's amateur witch cannot be assigned to any social class; one would assume that she is a farm girl, but her passion is noble, romantic like that of any Greek heroine, and she speaks in accomplished Latin verse. Undoubtedly, this kind of magic was practiced in Italy as well as in Greece and Egypt. Virgil may have left out something here and there or added some color, but the magical operation as a whole sounds authentic.

A more serious magical ceremony is described by Virgil at the end of Book 4 of the *Aeneid* [*no. 11*]. The hero of the epic, Aeneas, has landed on the coast of North Africa, where he meets Queen Dido, who has just begun to build a new city, Carthage. She is not at all like a witch, but rather resembles an oriental fairy tale queen with a tragic past. She falls in love with Aeneas and wants him to stay with her as her prince consort. One is reminded of the Circe episode in the *Odyssey* [*no. 1*] and of the encounter of Jason and Medea in Apollonius' *Argonautica*. In all these epics, a traveling hero with a mission meets a beautiful, exotic woman who is potentially dangerous, although kind and hospitable as long as her love for the hero lasts. When Aeneas leaves Dido because Fate demands that he found an empire of his own, Dido's love turns to hate. Determined to destroy her faithless lover, she stages a complex magical rite. She builds a gigantic pyre in the main courtyard of her palace and prepares, with the assistance of a famous priestess-witch, an elaborate sacrifice to the powers of the underworld. She realizes that no love magic can bring Aeneas back to her and, despairing, kills herself, giving an ultimate emphasis of doom to her curse. It was commonly believed that suicides, murder victims, men killed in battle—in short, all those who died before their time—could unleash enormous powers of destruction at the moment of their death and for some time afterward. Dido had thus both sealed and extended her curse through her death. She could not destroy Aeneas, who, like Odysseus, was protected by his own gods and reached the coast of Italy safely after many other adventures, but her curse lingered on. Generations later, Rome was almost conquered by Hannibal and his Carthaginian army, but once more the gods of Rome prevented the worst from happening.

In her last wish to hurt Aeneas—and Rome—Dido is more like Medea than Circe [see *no. 13*]. But she also resembles Cleopatra, the queen of Egypt, who in Virgil's lifetime had love affairs with two great Romans: Julius Caesar and Mark Antony. Cleopatra's image was so distorted by contemporary Roman propaganda that her power over these two men may be explained as witchcraft, an art she could easily have learned in the country of her birth. Virgil thus borrowed something from two mythical heroines, Circe and Medea, and something from a historical person, Cleopatra.[68]

Horace (65–8 B.C.) was Virgil's contemporary and friend. Some of his poems (e.g., *Epodes* 5 and *Satires* 1.8) deal with witchcraft. The fifth epode [*no. 8*] is remarkable because here a child is murdered by witches for magical purposes. A clique of witches led by Canidia has kidnapped a Roman boy of noble birth and buried him up to his chin in the ground. Close to his head they place a dish of food which he cannot reach. They intend to starve him to death and then to remove his liver, which, they believe, will grow because of his growing hunger. In vain does the child plead with the degenerate hags; they want his liver in order to brew a particularly powerful love potion. The intended victim of this potion is a man called Varus, who has not yet responded to Canidia's usual spells and brews, and she assumes that he has rubbed himself with a magical unguent given to him by a redoubtable rival of hers. Realizing that he will not be spared, the boy directs a terrible curse against the witches. This curse is a form of magic, too, for the spirits of those who die young or who die a violent death can turn into daemons of vengeance.

Satires 1.8 [*no. 9*] deals with witchcraft in a more humorous vein. Here, the wooden statue of the god Priapus is speaking. The statue has been placed in a beautiful modern park on the Esquiline in Rome as a threat to thieves and birds. But this park was once a cemetery for the poor, and at night, in the light of the moon, the witches, again led by Canidia, still haunt the place, digging for human bones or calling up the shades for necromantic purposes. They also perform other kinds of magic, and these rituals are so revolting that even Priapus, who is not a very refined god, loses his nerve and lets out a resounding fart. This works like a charm: the witches run away screaming; one of them loses her wig, the other her false teeth.

After a careful reading of these two pieces, it is difficult to say whether an educated man and famous author like Horace actually believed in witchcraft. In one poem he seems to take it quite seriously; in the other he makes fun of it. Naturally, the fact that he writes about Canidia with such intense feeling gives her a special kind of reality and makes her, along with Medea and Lucan's Erichto, one of the great witches of ancient literature. That witchcraft was practiced in ancient Rome by women who resembled Horace's Canidia cannot be doubted; that many people were afraid of these women is equally certain. On the whole, however, they seem to have lived underground, so to speak, in the slums of Rome, threatened by laws that, though not always enforced, provided for drastic punishment.

Instead of following a strict, chronological order, it might be better to discuss briefly Seneca, the philosopher and playwright (c. 5 B.C.–A.D. 65), and his nephew, Lucan (A.D. 39–65), the epic poet, because they continue the literary tradition of the superwitch. Seneca's tragedies reflect the taste for the horrible, cruel, and grotesque that seems so characteristic of the early Roman Empire. He selects some of the most gruesome Greek myths for dramatic treatment (*Thyestes*), and he spins out the theme of magic, necromancy, and the like where it is given by the mythical tradition (*Medea* [see *no. 13*]) and even where it is barely indicated (*Heracles on Mount Oeta* [see *no. 12*]). From the dialogue between Deianira and her nurse [*no. 12*] we learn that it was quite common for jealous wives to consult a witch (Seneca projects this into the age of myth); as it turns out, the nurse, very conveniently, is a witch herself. Deianira offers to help by plucking rare herbs in remote places, but she is not sure that magic will work in the case of her unfaithful husband, Heracles; there is at least an implication here that a great hero such as he cannot be influenced by magical means. In the end he is overcome by a deadly poison that Deianira gives him, believing it to be a love charm.

In the two selections from Seneca's *Medea* [*no. 13*] it is remarkable how the image of Medea has changed in the three centuries since Apollonius wrote his epic [*no. 5*]. Her invocations and incantations are no longer left to the reader's imagination: they are spelled out. Her power of hating, which she can switch on, so to speak, and intensify at will, is still the dominant theme, but Medea now has her cabinet of horrors from which to select the most efficient engines of destruction. Her magic involves the whole universe; she claims that she can force down the constellation of the Snake.

The magical papyri illustrate the sense of power that filled the operator during the course of the ritual. Seneca must have known such texts, but he gives them a rhetorical build-up, a literary polish of which the professional magicians were hardly capable. Like Horace, he endows the magical arts with a poetical and terrifying reality. Whether these plays were performed on the stage or were simply recited, they must have shocked a contemporary audience, and shock, *ekplexis,* was supposed to have a therapeutic value. It is probably fair to say that Seneca created horror not for horror's sake but because, as a Stoic philosopher, he believed that the shock produced by horror cleansed the soul of all the emotions that interfere with peace of mind. As a Stoic, Seneca also believed in cosmic sympathy, and thus some of the tenets of magic would have made sense to him, even though he may not have accepted their exaggerated claims.

The ultimate horrors of witchcraft are portrayed by Lucan in Book 6 of the *Pharsalia* [*no. 61*], no doubt in an effort to surpass his uncle, Seneca. Before the decisive battle of Pharsalus (48 B.C.), in which the forces of Julius Caesar defeated those of Pompey, the two armies had been moving through Thessaly, the classical country of witchcraft. There, one of Pompey's sons consults the famous witch Erictho about the outcome of the impending confrontation. In Lucan's epic, Erictho is the most powerful witch, but she is also the most loathsome and disgusting. More powerful and horrible than Medea, she can compel some of the lesser gods to serve her and cause them to shudder at her spells. Through his encounter with Erictho, a frightening apparition, the reader is again supposed to experience shock. In the end he will wonder whether such a monster should be hated or respected: to love her would be impossible, and in this respect she is totally different from Circe, Medea, and Dido, who were all loved, although briefly, by traveling heroes. Shelley admired Lucan greatly, and it is possible that this passage from a poet whom her husband placed above Virgil gave Mary Shelley the idea for her novel *Frankenstein.* The idea of an artificially created human being or a revived corpse may be older, but Lucan was much more accessible to the age of romanticism than any tract of the ancient alchemists who were experimenting with this.

At this point we should probably discuss three historical persons of the first century A.D. who seem to have had at least some of the powers of the shaman documented in earlier times by Orpheus, Pythagoras, and Empedocles. It is almost as if this old tradition of shamanism had been briefly revived. The three men I propose to compare with each other, from a purely historical point of view, on the basis of controversial evidence and with all due caution are Jesus of Nazareth, Simon Magus, and Apollonius of Tyana.[69]

It is difficult to describe Jesus in terms of this particular tradition, but since he was called a "magician" by Jews and Gentiles alike, it seems legitimate to examine some of these charges. From any outsider's point of view, Jesus may have looked like the typical miracle-worker. He exorcised daemons, he healed the sick, he raised the dead, he made predictions, but outside of walking on the waves, he never performed the kind of ostentatious magic that Moses and Aaron performed when they defied the Egyptian magicians. He did not, however, practice necromancy. Nevertheless, within three hundred years of his birth, he was accused of stealing the "names of the angels of might" from Egyptian temples (Arn., *Adv. Gent.* 1.43). The "angels of might" could be translated as "powerful daemons," and the Egyptian concept of "words of power" could be connected with Jesus' belief in angels close to the throne of the Father.[70] Jesus has power over the minds of men, and he represents a limit beyond which the human imagination cannot go. According to the Gospels, he does not practice necromancy, but his life story is colored by features that can be paralleled elsewhere: he is marked by his divine origin, his miraculous birth, the annunciation, and a nativity surrounded by unusual events; he is menaced in infancy; he is initiated into his own ministry by John the Baptist, an earlier evangelist who yields before him; he has to face Satan, a powerful daemon representing the evil forces in the world, and refuses to make a deal with him, winning in a trial of spiritual strength. These encounters and confrontations can be paralleled: Abaris yielded to Pythagoras, just as John the Baptist yielded to Jesus, and Zoroaster had to resist evil daemons.

The important point seems to be this, however: when Jesus was challenged to prove his divinity by performing the kind of magic that many people might expect from him, he refused to do so. He did perform "magic" of a kind spontaneously, but he did so out of compassion, not merely to impress the skeptics or score a point; in fact, he is sometimes slightly impatient with those who need "signs and wonders" to believe in him. It almost seems that magic "flows" out of him, not as a conscious effort, as the result of complicated rituals, but simply because of a power (*dynamis*) that he transmits. Jesus' healing power works when the patient and the bystanders have faith in him (Luke 8), but it also works even when the patient is unaware of being healed (Matthew 8). On the whole, faith does not seem to matter—the power still works, and then faith is created; it is not always a condition. Faith can generate the miracle, but the miracle also generates faith.

It should be noted that Jesus never claimed to perform miracles all by himself; rather, he taught that his power came from the Father and was readily available, without complex sacrifices and incantations. There was no mumbo-jumbo, no hocus-pocus. Moreover, Jesus did not accept any fees for what he did: he considered it part of his ministry to heal the sick, and he passed the gift on to his disciples. Clement of Alexandria (*Strom.* 6.3) says that the pagans were wrong to deny the miracles recounted in the Gospels, for God is infinitely great and can easily perform miracles at any time, without any help from magical arts.

Matthew's report that Jesus was taken to Egypt as an infant was used by hostile sources to explain his knowledge of magic; according to a rabbinical story, he came back tattooed with spells.[71] It is also pointed out in the rabbinical tradition that Jesus was "mad," which probably means "emotionally unstable," one of the characteristics of the shaman, or occasionally "in a state of trance" (e.g., when receiving a vision). The Gospels speak of the "descent of the spirit," the outsiders of "possession by a daemon," and both are possibly describing the same mystic phenomenon, the former as Jesus would explain it, the latter in a negative way. It has even been suggested that Jesus' claim to be "the Son of God" is a formula used in magical rites by the operator who identifies himself closely with the supernatural power that he invokes.[72]

A word of caution should be added here concerning these and similar theories, for that is what they are, theories, not facts. Some of the material comes from sources hostile to Jesus and the early Church; words and facts were either invented or distorted in order to discredit him. The parallels from the magical papyri, even if they were conclusive, are of doubtful value, for they may have been influenced by stories circulating about Jesus. We have seen how eager the magicians were to add to their repertory of formulas, rites, and names, especially if they seemed to work within the context of a new religious movement. At least some contemporary magicians clearly were not just traditionalists; they observed what was going on in the world and added new material to their stock-in-trade. To them Jesus must have appeared to be a very powerful fellow magician from whom they could learn a lot. This certainly does not mean that he was a magician. The outsiders were incapable of realizing what was new and different in Jesus' life and teaching, and they reduced it to their own level. Certain aspects of Jesus' ministry can perhaps be illustrated by certain things contemporary magicians did or said, but the whole of his ministry has no parallel. It is precisely the nonmagical dimension in Jesus that made the early Church grow strong in such a short time; if it had been magic, history might have taken a different course.

Simon is the name of a *magus* mentioned in Acts 8:9ff. and elsewhere.[73] He was active in Samaria about the time of the Crucifixion, and his disciples called him "the power of God which is called the Great Power."[74] Simon was deeply impressed by the apostle Philip's cures and exorcisms and by the gift of the Spirit that came from the apostles' laying on of hands; therefore, he not only "believed and was baptized" but he asked the apostles to sell him their special gift so that he could practice it too. This is the typical attitude of the professional magician, and it illustrates what has been said above. To Simon, the charisma of this new religion is a kind of magic that can be purchased, for a price, and he is prepared to pay for it as he probably had before for the kind of magic he had learned. The sharp rebuke that he draws from Peter—and that he is flexible enough to take in good grace—shows how the early Church drew a line between itself and practitioners of magic such as Simon.[75]

We hear about a Simon again from Justin Martyr (e.g., *Dialogue with Trypho,* ch. 120), who says that he was a *magus* born in Samaria, that his followers worshiped him as the supreme God, and that a Phoenician woman, a former prostitute called Helen, lived with him; she was considered the "primary notion" emanating from him, though in a different context. She was a fallen power for whose salvation he had appeared. Justin also reports that in Rome a statue was erected in his honor on Tiber Island, with the inscription SIMONI DEO SANCTO, "To Simon, the Sacred God." By an amazing coincidence a monument bearing an inscription that begins with the words SEMONI SANCO DEO was found in Rome, but this was clearly a statue of a very old Italic deity known as Semo Sancus, who had a cult on Tiber Island, perhaps nearly extinct by this time, and it is possible that the followers of Simon used the old statue for their own worship. Or perhaps Justin simply misunderstood the inscription SEMONI SANCO DEO for SIMONI DEO SANCTO.

According to other early Christian writers (e.g., Epiph., *Adv. Haeres.* 6.21.2ff.), Simon established his own Trinity, in which he was the Father, Jesus was the Son, and Helen was something like the Holy Spirit; but in another sense, Simon really was all three. This remarkable bit of theology would seem to show how skillfully Simon adapted the Gospel to his own needs. Indeed, it looks as if he started out as a *magus* and then, inspired by the example of Jesus, developed into a cult figure by borrowing from Christianity whatever suited him. He and Helen were worshiped before statues of Zeus and Athena; this, no doubt, was designed to make the ritual more palatable to the Gentiles. The priests of Simon's religion were said by some early Christian writers to practice both magic and free love—a combination of charges that appears throughout history.

From the testimonies that we have, Simon Magus emerges as a kind of shaman, a practitioner of occult science (which he was supposed to have learned in Egypt) with Christlike aspirations. Unlike Jesus, he used daemons for his own purposes, practiced necromancy, and even claimed, according to the *Pseudo-Clementine Recognitions,*[76] to have created a human being. The text may be corrupt, but on the whole the meaning seems clear: Simon claimed to have invoked the soul of an innocent boy who had been murdered and commanded it to enter a new body that he had made from air, thus forming a new human being. He boasts that this was a far nobler achievement than the creation of Adam by God the Father, "for he created a man from earth, but I from air—a much more difficult thing." When people demanded to see this *homunculus*, Simon answered that he had already made him disappear into air again.

The moment of truth came when, according to Acts, Simon and Peter challenged each other before the emperor Nero in Rome. Like earlier confrontations between a mere magician and a true religious leader,[77] it was a contest of spiritual powers. Simon actually managed to fly through the air for a short time, impressing Nero, but Peter broke the spell and made the magician crash to earth so badly that he never recovered. His resurrection within three days, which he himself had predicted (provided he was buried alive), never took place, "because he was not the Christ," Hippolytus notes sarcastically (*Haer.* 6.20.3). The Simon of Acts is sometimes confused with the other Simon, also from Samaria, of the *Pseudo-Clementine Recognitions.* It should be said that Acts is our only source for our knowledge of the elder Simon.

The third *magus* of this period was Apollonius of Tyana, who was born in Cappadocia a few years after Jesus, it seems, and survived into the reign of Nerva (c. A.D. 97). About a century later, Flavius Philostratus wrote a comprehensive *Life of Apollonius of Tyana* [see *no. 28*], which, though not exactly trustworthy, is still our most important source.[78] Philostratus, a professional writer, was a protégé of the empress Julia Domna, mother of the emperor Caracalla. This beautiful and cultured lady was interested in philosophy, religion, and science; Galen, the great physician and medical author, was another of her protégés. She owned a document that claimed to be the memoirs of a certain Damis of Niniveh, a disciple of Apollonius; this she gave to Philostratus as raw material for a polished literary treatment. Philostratus complied, and from his biography, which is eminently readable, the strange, ascetic, traveling teacher and wonder-worker called Apollonius emerges. He is usually labeled a Neo-Pythagorean; actually he is more like a new Pythagoras. He certainly represents, in a different age, the same combination of scientist, philosopher, and *magus,* even though he explains his kind of "magic" as a science. A revival of Pythagoreanism took place in the first century A.D.; its centers were Alexandria and Rome. If we can trust his biographer, Apollonius traveled as far as India, where he exchanged ideas with the Brahmins, who were considered to be true Pythagorean philosophers.

What we know of Apollonius' teaching is fairly consistent with traditional Pythagorean doctrine. Animals have a divine soul, just like human beings; hence it is a sin to kill an animal, either to eat it or to use its fur or skin for clothing or to offer it to the gods as a sacrifice. Vegetarianism and a pure, ascetic life in general are necessary. Apollonius also believed in the transmigration of the soul and claimed to remember his own previous existences, but he explicitly denied certain astonishing feats that were ascribed to him by Philostratus (*Life of Apollonius of Tyana* 8.7)—for example, that he had descended into the underworld and that he could raise the dead. Since he was arrested on charges of magic twice, once under Nero and again under Domitian, he must have had every reason to reduce the miracles he was credited with to reasonable dimensions. His disciples probably made him into more of a thaumaturge than he himself wanted to be. In some ways Apollonius resembles Socrates: he enjoyed lively philosophical debates and was very good at using an opponent's premises against him, leading him on *ad absurdum*. Like Socrates, he had a *daimonion* [see *no. 55*]. Unlike Socrates and Jesus, he published; we know of one treatise, *On Sacrifices*.

In the early fourth century A.D. a new effort was made to discredit the Christians, perhaps in order to justify the persecutions ordered by Diocletian. A high official in his administration, Hierocles of Nicomedia, wrote an anti-Christian pamphlet entitled *The Lover of Truth*, in which he tried to show that Apollonius ranked above Jesus both as a teacher and as a miracle-worker. His thesis was rejected, probably soon after A.D. 310, by the Church historian Eusebius, himself a survivor of the persecutions.[79]

Apollonius was worshiped by his followers as a holy man or a divine being, and he had a shrine in his birthplace, Tyana. At one time, a statue of him stood in the private chapel of a Roman emperor, along with statues of Abraham, Orpheus, Jesus, and others.[80] But even the enthusiasm of the empress Julia Domna and her son Caracalla and the fine literary style of Philostratus could not spread his cult throughout the empire. Julian, an earnest believer in theurgy and a defender of paganism, never mentions Apollonius.

Something should be said about the spiritual movements of later antiquity, which, although often not clearly distinguishable from one another, were, at the time, different. Although they were more like exclusive theologies, and their followers did not necessarily practice magic, they can be labeled "occult sciences."

First we shall discuss Gnosticism.[81] The term is derived from *gnosis* 'knowledge'—not just any knowledge, but knowledge par excellence, "knowing God." To the followers of this ideal, the highest goal in life was to escape from the evil environment surrounding them, to ascend to the realm of the good, which is, at the same time, the ultimate reality. To escape from the visible world by "knowing God" is to be saved. To be a

Gnostic meant to rise above all earthly things and thereby to lose interest in the body, its needs, functions, and emotions. Everything else followed from this; hence it was not necessary to design a system of ethics for the problems of everyday life, as imperial Stoicism and the early Church did.

It has been suggested that Gnosticism derived from Orphism but was also influenced by Babylonian astral religion and by Hermeticism. This is hard to prove, however, because by that time Orphism, like Pythagoreanism, had lost much of its original character.

Some Gnostic leaders—for instance, Carpocrates of Alexandria (c. A.D. 120)—apparently used incantations, drugs, and messages from spirits or daemons, but since much of this information has come down to us through Christian authors who were hostile to the Gnostics, it is not considered reliable. There seems to have been a genuine interest within Gnosticism to reconcile Christianity with contemporary philosophy and occult science, but on the whole the Gnostics were more concerned about understanding how the cosmic mechanisms worked than about switching them on and off.[82]

Hermeticism is a related movement. We have a considerable body of Hermetic writings that promise mankind deeper knowledge of and control over nature.[83] Magic, astrology, and alchemy were all part of Hermeticism. The name itself is derived from Thoth, the Egyptian manifestation of the Greek god Hermes, who is for some the most important god of Greece, Rome, and Egypt around the time of the birth of Christ and is therefore honored by the title Trismegistus, "the thrice greatest." In an attempt to draw in Jewish proselytes, he was even associated with Moses (Euseb., *Praep. Evang.* 9.27.3).[84] Here we observe the tendency to elevate a relatively minor Greek god to the highest possible rank and enrich his image, so to speak, with features borrowed from other religions, especially the most ancient and venerable ones. Such a composite god would be a powerful rival to the popular goddess Isis.[85]

There must have been a good deal of rivalry and competition among these groups. They clearly had much in common, but each one had to have a distinctive feature that demanded total commitment on the part of the neophyte. At this distance it is difficult to see the distinctive features except through the polemic of Christian authors, which helped define the essence of Christianity.

The *Natural History* of Pliny the Elder (A.D. 23/24–79) is a voluminous survey of science, pseudoscience, art, and technology. Reflecting the state of knowledge of the late Hellenistic era, it is based on a hundred or so earlier authorities. This huge compilation deals with cosmology, geography, anthropology, zoology, botany, pharmacology, mineralogy, and metallurgy and their uses in ancient art. It is a mine of information and misinformation, but because almost all the sources that Pliny used are lost, it is of considerable value to us, and it had great influence on later scientific thought. Pliny himself was neither a philosopher nor a trained scientist in the modern sense of the word, but he had read a great deal, always taking notes, and had developed a philosophy, partly derived from Middle Stoics such as Posidonius, in which there was room for the forces of religion as well as those of popular and advanced magic. His attitude, his general curiosity, may be compared with that of Apuleius. He believed in ancient traditions and was convinced that the power of certain herbs or roots was revealed to mankind by the gods, although he also recognized the role of chance. Men stumbled upon the truth by accident; then they tested it by experiment. The divine powers, in their concern for the welfare of mankind, have ways of making us discover the secrets of nature, and this is really what is called progress today. In their wisdom and love, the gods bring us gradually closer to their own status; this is the Faustian aspiration of "being like the gods." There will always be progress of this kind, according to Pliny.[86] How it works in the short term is not so important; in the long term it emanates from benevolent powers. This concept is firmly rooted in Middle Stoicism: here we have a "cosmic sympathy" that, if properly understood and used, operates for the good of mankind.

With all his learning, Pliny preserved many religious and magical beliefs and practices, and much of this tradition was folklore with a scientific pretense. He did not believe in the effectiveness of all magical arts; in fact, he felt that most claims of the professional sorcerers were exaggerated or simply false (25.59, 29.20, 37.75). The sorcerers would not have written down their spells and recipes unless they despised and hated mankind (37.40). If their promises were worth anything, the emperor Nero, who studied magic with the best teachers and had access to the best books, would have been a formidable magician, but in fact he did nothing extraordinary (30.5–6). Pliny's conclusion, however, is cautious: though magic is ineffective and infamous (*intestabilis*), it nevertheless contains at least "shadows of truth" (*veritatis umbras*) that are due to the "arts of making poisons" (*veneficae artes*). Hence, it is the drugs that really work, not so much the hocus-pocus of spells and ritual. Yet, Pliny states, "there is no one who is not afraid of spells" (28.4), and he seems not to exclude himself. The amulets and charms that people wore as a kind of preventive medicine he neither commends nor condemns. It is better to err on the side of caution, for, who knows, a new kind of magic, a magic that really works, may be developed somewhere this very minute. This is why the professional magicians, as we have seen, were always on the lookout for new ideas.

A large part of Pliny's enormous work deals with remedies and drugs to cure diseases. Most of them are herbal preparations. Pliny's medicine is primarily folk medicine, which does not mean that it is totally unsophisticated, for it has a long history that is enriched by valid scientific discoveries.[87] By the time of Pliny, many physicians were using drugs in addition to diet, exercise, baths in mineral springs, and reliance on *vis naturae medicatrix* 'the healing power of nature'. There is one ingredient that Pliny mentions time and again, for both internal and external application, an ingredient whose value is recognized today: honey.

Altogether Pliny gives several thousand recipes for drugs and remedies (especially in Books 20–32). Personally, he prefers herbal simples, but he also notes mixtures, animal remedies, and even drugs concocted by the *magi,* although he dislikes and despises them heartily. Pliny devotes the beginning of Book 30 to the *magi* and refers to them here and there especially in Books 28 and 29.[88] To him they are basically sorcerers, but they might also be priests of a foreign religion, such as the Druids of the Celts in Britain and Gaul. He even includes Moses in a list of famous *magi,* as if he had heard the Old Testament story of Moses' performance before Pharaoh. According to Pliny, the art of the *magi* touches three areas: *medicina, religio,* and *artes mathematicae* (30.1): "healing power," "ritual," and "astrology." This is a curious definition, but perhaps essentially correct, for many professional magicians of that time were probably also healers, performing certain rites and addressing prayers to supernatural powers (*religio*), and many of them no doubt knew something of astrology, even though they did not practice other techniques of divination. Pliny's *religio* is not the same as our *religion,* however; sometimes he uses it in the sense of "superstition," sometimes in the sense of "expression of religious belief or custom" (11.250–51).

In the end, even a well-read, well-educated, enlightened man like Pliny is not sure of what to believe and what to reject. To be on the safe side and to make his work as useful as possible, he hands down, along with many drugs in which he has confidence, a number of superstitions and magical rituals about which he has serious doubts. He dislikes and distrusts professional magicians as a class and calls them "frauds" and "charlatans," and yet he seems to admit, almost grudgingly, that there are certain things they know and can do. His dilemma can best be illustrated by this sentence: "People agree that by simply smearing menstrual blood on the doorposts, the tricks of the *magi,* those worthless quacks, can be rendered ineffective. I would certainly like to believe this!" (28.85).

To the Platonist philosopher Plutarch of Chaeronea (c. A.D. 45–125) we owe the treatise *On Superstition,* which reminds one here and there of Theophrastus' sketch [*no. 3*].[89] Plutarch defines *deisidaimonia* 'superstition' as "fear of the divinity or of the gods," although the examples he uses show that, like Theophrastus, he has in mind a kind of fear that becomes an obsession. Specifically, he mentions magical rites and taboos, the consultation of professional sorcerers and witches, charms and spells, and unintelligible language in prayers addressed to the gods.[90] Although Plutarch himself takes dreams (especially those of the dying) and portents seriously, he reserves the term *superstitious* for those who have excessive or exclusive faith in such phenomena. Clearly, it is a matter of discrimination. He also seems to take for granted other magical practices, such as hurting someone by the evil eye, and offers an explanation of that phenomenon (*Table Talk* 5.7). He also believes in daemons that serve as agents or links between gods and men and are responsible for many supernatural events in human life that are commonly attributed to divine intervention. Thus, a daemon, not Apollo himself, is the real power behind the Delphic oracle. Some daemons are good, some are evil, but even the good ones, in a fit of anger, can do bad things.[91]

In general, Plutarch, though he ridicules the excessive, morbid fear of supernatural powers, accepts a certain amount of what we would call "popular superstition," but he is anxious to select only what is compatible with his own philosophical doctrine, and what he selects he purifies and gives, as far as possible, a rational explanation. He does not discuss ritual magic in any detail, and he seems to reject astrology; in his biography of Romulus (ch. 12) he ridicules a friend of Varro's who tried to determine the date and time of Romulus' birth by working backward from his character and from certain known facts of his life. This operation also led indirectly to a secure date, the astrologer believed, for the foundation of Rome.

A later Platonist, Apuleius of Madaura (born c. A.D. 125), gives us a substantial amount of information on contemporary beliefs in occult science. We have the speech he delivered in his own defense against the charge of magic, circa A.D. 160, and from this *Apologia* (another title is *De Magia* [*On Magic*]) we learn how easy it was, at that time, for a scientist and philosopher to be accused of magical practices. We also learn that the accusation could be used as a pretext to destroy an enemy. Yet Apuleius may not have been completely above suspicion. In his novel, *Metamorphoses* (also known as *The Golden Ass*), a piece of fiction that seems to have autobiographical elements, the hero, Lucius, dabbles in magic as a young man, gets into trouble, is rescued by the goddess Isis, and then finds true knowledge and happiness in her mysteries.[92] It is the story of a conversion. As an extension of his normal philosophical curriculum, a talented, intellectually curious young man attempts to study magic, but he falls in with a group of professional witches who play nasty tricks on him. Delivered from distress and disgrace by the goddess Isis and cured of his un-healthy curiosity, he becomes a deeply religious person, though still a philosopher. To him, religion and philosophy (or science), cleansed of their magical elements, offer, as J. Tatum writes, "a means of making sense of an unpredictable and cruel world."[93] This was exactly the role that magic claimed, but in addition to "making sense" it attempted to "control" the negative powers in the world and promised all kinds of thrills and excitement to the neophyte, and in all this it obviously failed. What can be said of Apuleius can probably be said of many "intellectuals" (as we would call them today) of his period. Magic held tremendous attractions for them, but the more deeply they studied it, the more aware they became of its dangers.

The transformation of Lucius, the hero of the novel, into an ass is described in Book 3 [see *no. 31*]. The main characters are Lucius, the eager young student of magic who is determined to learn the secret of transformation, though he had been warned of the risks; and Photis, the attractive young witch whose mistress, Pamphila, a more advanced sor-ceress, has a kind of magical workshop on the roof of her house—a wooden shelter hidden from view but open to the winds and crowded with her requisites: herbs, metal plates inscribed with magical charac-ters, various ointments in little boxes, and, most gruesome of all, parts of dead bodies stolen from cemeteries or places of execution (*Met.* 1.10, 2.20–21).

Around A.D. 160 Apuleius came to Oea, a city in North Africa, where an illness forced him to stay longer than he had planned. A friend with whom he had studied in Athens introduced him to his mother, a rich widow by the name of Pudentilla, who was about ten years older than Apuleius. When the two got married, the relatives of her first husband feared for the inheritance they expected, and when Apuleius' friend suddenly died in mysterious circumstances, they accused him of murder, later changing this charge to witchcraft. The speech that he delivered in court not only tells us a great deal about magical beliefs and practices, folklore, and superstitions, but it reflects what people thought witches and magicians did in secret. If Apuleius had not convinced the court of his innocence, the presiding Roman magistrate could have sentenced him to death.

In his speech, Apuleius totally rejects the kind of black magic that had been proscribed by Roman law ever since the Twelve Tables, but he also maintains that some of the greatest philosophers have been unjustly ac-cused of magical practices. He mentions, among others, Orpheus, Py-thagoras, Empedocles, and the Persian Ostanes (*Apol.* 27.31). We have seen that these men represented shamanism in early Greece, and that it is difficult to separate philosophy (or religion) from magic in their case. Unlike the ordinary sorcerers, however, they never practiced black magic; this is probably what Apuleius wants to say, for he also includes in his list Socrates (whose *daimonion* was considered a strange sort of god by his accusers) and Plato. It seems clear that the ignorant masses and the educated elite could never agree about the differences between witchcraft and some of the more esoteric philosophic or scientific doctrines.

Like Plutarch, his fellow Platonist, Apuleius firmly believed in the existence of daemons, the intermediaries between men and the gods. They populated the air and were, in fact, formed of air. They experienced emotions just like human beings, and their mind was rational. In a sense, then, the human soul was also a daemon, but there were daemons who never entered bodies.[94] In his treatise *On Socrates' God* Apuleius presented a complete, systematic version of daemonology that was acceptable to later Platonists. The discussion is not always easy to follow, and one can see the dangers of distortions and misunderstandings for outsiders. Philosophers speculated about daemons—magicians invoked them—so what was the difference?

Lucian of Samosata was born about the same time as Apuleius (c. A.D. 125) and died after A.D. 180. Like Apuleius, he traveled from city to city, giving lectures. He also studied philosophy, though he did not belong to any particular school. His philosophical dialogues show the influence of the Platonic dialogues, but he is not a Platonist, and his writings are never as technical as those we have under Apuleius' name. He admires the Epicureans because they fight superstitions in every form.

One of the themes of Lucian's writings is the folly of superstition. It appears, for instance, in a satirical account of the founder of a new cult, Alexander of Abonuteichus, a contemporary of his. Lucian's essay *Alexander,* or *The Pseudoprophet,* obviously hostile, is our main source of information.[95] Alexander claimed to control a new manifestation of the god Asclepius in the form of a snake called Glycon. Thanks to this divine agent, he dispensed oracles and conducted mysteries to which outsiders, especially Christians and Epicureans (a strange combination), were not admitted. He did have a fairly large number of followers, many women and at least one prominent Roman among them. In his essay Lucian takes great pleasure in revealing the "magic" tricks that Alexander performed in order to impress the ignorant and credulous. For example, the questions submitted to the oracle were sealed and came back with an answer, the seal apparently unbroken; Alexander had several methods of opening them, adding a response, and replacing the seal.

Alexander of Abonuteichus was probably just one of many accomplished impostors of later antiquity. If Lucian is right, Alexander knew how to manipulate crowds by his appearance, his delivery of some kind of message, and his skillful use of mechanical devices to produce sham miracles.

Another fraud is ridiculed in Lucian's dialogue *The Lovers of Lies*. Several philosophers, including a Stoic, a Peripatetic, and a Platonist, along with a physician, talk about miracle cures. Some amazing examples are quoted [*no. 47*]. This leads to a discussion of love magic [*no. 29*] and other astonishing feats. Here we find the original version of the story of the sorcerer's apprentice as told by the apprentice himself. His name is Eucrates, and he had studied with a great magician called Pancrates, who had spent twenty-three years underground learning magic from Isis. Pancrates needed no servants: he took a piece of wood—for instance, a broomstick—dressed it in some clothes, and made it into a sort of robot that looked like a human being to all outsiders (Lucian, *The Lovers of Lies*, pars. 34ff.). One day the apprentice overhears the master whispering a magic formula of three syllables, and when the master is away, he tries it on the broomstick. The results are well known from Goethe's poem *The Magician's Apprentice*. At the end of this conversation, even the skeptic (Lucian himself, presumably) is confused and has lost faith in the venerable philosophers who teach the young and perpetuate ancient superstitions. Still, he is not quite sure what to believe and what not to believe.

As far as the story of the great Hyperborean magician is concerned [*no. 29*], Lucian seems to put his finger on the main problem. The magician charges an enormous fee for performing a feat that would have taken place anyway, due to purely natural causes. But the prestige he has, the build-up in front of the audience, the whole hocus-pocus—the public-relations job, as one would say today—are all so impressive that people willingly pay and gladly give him credit, though needless to say he is a fraud.

In another dialogue, *The Ship*, one of the participants tells the others about his fantasies. What he really wants is magical rings from Hermes, rings that will give him eternal youth and the power of inspiring love in those who attract him.[96] This case of wishful thinking is part of the folklore of many countries and finds expression in fairy tales and legends. Such a ring might be compared to the cap that makes one invisible or the wings that enabled Hermes or Daedalus to fly through the air. In response to such fantasies, magic offered an inadequate substitute that seemed to work somehow, with a great deal of faith. It is only fair to say, however, that some very bold shortcut solutions offered by magic have been realized more slowly, but more reliably, by science and technology.

In his dialogue *Menippus*, or *The Necromancy*, Lucian uses motifs from Homer's *Odyssey* [*no. 52*], but he produces a more complex picture of a necromantic ceremony. The satirist Menippus, one of Lucian's heroes, wishes to visit the underworld, and he travels all the way to Babylon to consult one of the *magi*. The preparations he has to make are formidable: purification by ablutions and fumigations, strict diet, sleeping out of doors, taking special precautions. Some of the details seem rather fantastic, while others might be part of the long, slow formation of the shaman; it is Lucian's technique to mix fantasy with "reality," but by the admixture he shows how little "reality" he thought there was to begin with.

The *magi* of later antiquity could be called "Men with the Double Image."[97] Lucian tapped the potentialities of the occult, and he recognized that there are two different ways of making one's way in the world. He engaged in what a psychoanalyst might today call "objective identification" (i.e., he became the god he invoked: "For you are I, and I am you").[98] The people who pointed their finger at him were "Men with the Single Image." They may have envied the *magus'* way of life, his apparent success; they may have been afraid of his power; but they resented his existence, declared his activities illegal, and tried to entrap him.

It is still difficult to draw the line between philosophers (or scientists) who were just that and philosophers who were also "into magic," to use the contemporary idiom. The archaic combination of both survives on a lower level, as it were. A Neo-Pythagorean like Apollonius of Tyana or a Platonist like Apuleius of Madaura[99] could be accused of magical practices and in his defense simply say: "As a philosopher [or scientist] I am interested in everything and ready to investigate every phenomenon under the sun. If there is such a thing as magic—and almost everyone seems to believe there is—I want to find out whether it works or not. But let me assure you that I am not a magician, and any miracles that I seem to perform can be explained in scientific terms."

The professional sorcerers of later antiquity were consulted by women and men of all classes, but among their best clients was the *demi-monde* of popular performers, such as athletes and actors who had to give their best in a limited period of time and were naturally afraid that their rivals or the supporters of their rivals might put a spell on them just then.

Apuleius, accused of witchcraft, was a highly educated man, but most real magicians apparently were not. Augustine (*c. Acad.* 1.7.19ff.) was impressed by Albicerius, a sorcerer who had helped him find a lost silver spoon; this man could also "thought-read" lines from Virgil in the mind of a proconsul. But according to Augustine, he lacked education; hence, he could not be "good." This may seem a curious verdict to us, but ever since Cicero the word *humanitas* had had two meanings: "higher education" and "human feeling"; to lack the first would exclude one to a certain degree from the second. But even among the educated, magic was popular because it helped explain misfortune.[100] For Christians and pagans alike, any sort of misfortune—an accident, an illness, even a nightmare—could be the work of superhuman agents, daemons who either acted on their own or were manipulated by an enemy. The Christian Church, in fact, found it convenient to attribute misfortune to the power of witchcraft. Some theologians believed that God had given the daemons authority to act as his "public executioners" (Origen, *c. Cels.* 8.31), to punish the human race for Adam's sin. Thus the world had become a playground for daemons, an area where they could release their destructive urges: "He has sent upon them the anger of His indignation and rage and tribulation and possession by evil spirits" (Psalms 78:49).

Libanius, a contemporary of Augustine's, reacted to bad dreams as if they were symptoms of magical spells and curses.[101] Whenever a person felt inadequate in relation to his or her image (a lecturer forgot the speech he had memorized; a highly respectable lady fell in love with a man socially far beneath her), black magic was thought to be at work. Thus it is not always just misfortune, but misfortune accompanied by a sense of shame or guilt, that leads one to suspect magical interference.

Gregory the Great (end of the sixth century A.D.) warned that any woman who slept with her husband on the eve of a religious procession was practically inviting a daemon to possess her, and that a nun who ate lettuce without first making the sign of the cross on it might swallow a daemon perched on its leaves. Daemons were everywhere, and only the Church could give protection.[102]

Theodoret (*Hist. Rel.* 13) tells the story of a girl who had become the victim of a love spell, and of Saint Macedonius, who was brought in to exorcise her. The daemon who had taken possession of her excused himself and, naming the sorcerer who had summoned him, declared that he could not leave her easily because he had entered her under great stress. The girl's father then lodged a complaint against that sorcerer before the governor, but Saint Macedonius managed to chase the daemon away before it could be used as a witness in court.[103] The story shows that the Church was able to deal with daemons, but is also shows that the Church accepted the fact of possession by the agency of witchcraft. These daemons had been sent by someone outside the Church, and it was the Church's duty to counteract their evil power.

The belief in daemons is much older than Plato, but it found a home in Platonism and Neoplatonism, and if philosophers, on the authority of Plato, spoke of daemons as real, it is clear that the common people, Christians and pagans alike, also were looking for ways in which to deal with them. The Bible did not offer much technical knowledge—Jesus' exorcisms are always unique and could not be duplicated from any information given in the Gospels—so even the Christians sought guidance elsewhere, in the ancient magical traditions.

The Neoplatonists—at least some of them—became the most ardent defenders of ritual magic and theurgy, perhaps as part of a last effort to suppress Christianity. Plotinus (c. A.D. 205–270), the founder of the school, seems to have had psychic powers [*no. 33*] and certainly took magic seriously [*no. 32*], though it is doubtful he should be called a magician.[104] He believed that the soul was clothed in an ethereal covering, the *ochema*, which was illuminated by divine light so that spirits and souls (or daemons) could be seen. The soul itself could ascend toward the Absolute through ecstasy. Perhaps one could say that certain inexplicable things went on around him, and no doubt after his death his students speculated a great deal about what had really happened.

Porphyry (c. A.D. 232–304), in his *Letter to Anebo,* criticizes the exaggerated claims of certain Egyptian theurgists: they threatened to frighten not only the daemons, or the spirits of the dead, but the Sun and the Moon and other divine beings of higher order; they pretended to be able to shake the heavens, to reveal the mysteries of Isis or interfere at a distance with her sacred rites. How can blatant lies force the gods to tell the truth? And why do the Egyptian theurgists insist that Egyptian is the only language these gods understand? What Porphyry attacks is not the theory that magic works, but the techniques employed by its Egyptian practitioners and their blatant self-advertisement.

Iamblichus (c. A.D. 240–330), another Neoplatonist, replies to Porphyry's letter in a work entitled *On the Mysteries of Egypt* [*no. 34*], which is basically a defense of ritual magic and theurgy and which deals, from a philosophical point of view, with the techniques of inducing the presence of daemons or gods.[105] Iamblichus firmly believes that the world is managed by a host of daemons and that the magician-priest, if he has been duly initiated and trained, can get in touch with these subordinate deities and control them to a certain degree. In this work, which is an important source for understanding religious feeling in antiquity, Iamblichus describes in detail the visions he has had of spirits, probably hallucinations in a half-waking state.

The full-scale persecution of magic by the state begins in the fourth century A.D.[106] The emperors clearly felt uncomfortable at the thought that astrologers might be able to predict their death accurately and that magicians might put a curse on them. At times even the wearing of an amulet was considered a crime. In a parallel movement, the Church now also condemned witchcraft, but for different reasons. The fears of the Church were not unfounded, for the emperor Julian, "the Apostate" (A.D. 361–363), rejected the Christian faith and tried to restore the old religion. From that point on, the two ruling forces of the empire, Roman law and the Church, combined to fight witchcraft, and this alliance continued into the Middle Ages.

Ancient Magic and Psychic Research Today

Many phenomena described in ancient texts as magical feasts might now be called paranormal, supernormal, or parapsychical.[107] Today, parapsychology has become an academic subject, and experiences similar to those reported by ancient authors have been observed and studied over a long period of time. Experiments have been conducted in order to understand the nature of extrasensory perception (ESP), telepathy, psychokinesis, and the like, and the literature available is enormous. In some ways we have come a little closer to understanding the stories and speculations that have reached us from antiquity. If telepathy is real, we can no longer dismiss as fraud stories like the vision of Sosipatra [*no. 51*]. Of course, there were cases of fraud: supernatural lights and voices could be created by simple devices. From Hippolytus (*Haer.* 4.35) we hear of a glass-bottomed cauldron of water that was placed over a small skylight, and of a seer who, gazing into the cauldron, saw in its depths various daemons, who were actually the magician's accomplices in the room below.[108] People wanted to see daemons, so a clever operator gave them daemons. Whenever a magician makes grandiose claims, charges a fee, and then produces certain special effects, we ought to be suspicious. But there also seem to be cases that are above suspicion.

Labeling phenomena reported by Greek and Roman writers with modern terms does not really explain them, and it can confuse the issue. *Telepathy,* for instance, is derived from two Greek words (*tele* 'at a distance' and *pathos* 'experience'), but, coined in the nineteenth century A.D., it was never used by the ancient Greeks. Similarly, *medium* looks like a Latin word and is a Latin word, but it was never used by Latin authors in antiquity to describe a person who helped the living communicate with the spirits of the dead; in this sense, this term too was coined only in the nineteenth century. These terms are useful, but they do not explain what really happens. *Mediumship* may be a real supernormal phenomenon and yet have nothing to do with messages or manifestations from the spirit world. In short, such things may happen, but the traditional explanation is false.

The main difficulty consists in applying modern terms to events and experiences described by ancient sources, for even if the modern term seems to fit, we should not assume that simply because it has a label the phenomenon is now explained once and for all. Where an ancient author speaks of his *visions,* we might use the term *state of consciousness;* where an ancient author uses the term *ecstasy,* we might prefer *trance.* Ever since William James breathed in nitrous oxide for the first time, we have known that our normal waking consciousness is but one particular state of consciousness, and that there are others, potential or real, that are separated from it only by a screen, as it were.

Thus the psychical research[109] done over the past century or so is valuable for our understanding of occult science in the ancient world as long as we keep these difficulties in mind. Moreover, as Dodds has pointed out, there is a difference between the occultist and the psychical researcher: "The occultist, as his name betokens, values the occult *qua* occult: that is for him its virtue, and the last thing he will thank you for is an explanation. . . . The genuine psychical researcher . . . is attracted to [occult phenomena] because he believes that they can and should be explained, being as much a part of nature as any other facts. . . . Far from wishing to pull down the lofty edifice of science, his highest ambition is to construct a modern annex which will serve, at least provisionally, to house his new facts."[110] Much of this cannot yet be explained. Dodds quotes from Augustine (*De Gen. ad Litt.* 12.18) as follows: "If any one can trace the causes and modes of operation of these visions and divinations and really understand them, I had rather hear his views than be expected to discuss the subject myself."[111] But Augustine does not doubt the reality of the visions themselves.[112]

Telepathy, mediumship, and *automatism* are among the most useful terms in our attempt to understand "occult" phenomena in the ancient world, but they do not all belong in the sphere of "magic." Telepathy could be discussed in the chapter on divination. For a Greek or a Roman, mediumship would have been a case of possession and hence might seem to belong in the chapter on daemonology. The question is, Should we put ourselves in the position of the ancients and use their concepts and terms? Up to a point this might be useful, but there is also some value in testing the modern terms by applying them to experiences that were felt to be "magical" or "miraculous" by the ancient narrators.

The vision of Sosipatra, as reported by Eunapius (*Lives of the Philosophers and Sophists* [*no. 51*]), is a good example of supernatural knowledge of an event that happened (at that very moment, it would appear) at a distance from the seer and was verified soon afterward. Livy relates how his friend, the augur Caius Cornelius, actually saw Caesar's victory over Pompey at Pharsalus, thousands of miles away (Plut., *Caes.* 47; Gell., *Noct. Att.* 15.18), and there are other stories of this kind, usually involving important battles. Should this be called "telepathy" or "clairvoyance"? Or is it that "sixth sense" which, according to Democritus,[113] "animals, wise men, and gods" have in common? Or should we simply call it the *psi* faculty, the term parapsychologists use today?

Like Freud, Dodds believed that before the development of language there was an archaic method by which individuals understood one another, a kind of shared consciousness, going back, perhaps to a time when human beings were not yet aware of themselves as individuals.[114] Once this awareness developed and language came into use, that other faculty functioned at an unconscious level and was used only under special circumstances, in an emergency. Normally this faculty manifested itself in dreams or in states of mental dissociation; in fact, the normal consciousness rejects any "occult" communication from outside.

The standard definition of *telepathy* as "the communication of impressions of any kind from one mind to another, independently of the recognized channels of sense" (F. W. H. Myers) would fit a number of cases reported from classical antiquity, and it seems that Democritus (c. 400 B.C.) based his account of divination on that concept. He believed that images are constantly flowing through space, some of them sent out by living persons. These images penetrate the body of the recipient and appear to him, for instance, in a dream. The more excited or emotional the sender, the more vivid the images.[115] In our age of television the idea of images traveling through space at tremendous speed is not unfamiliar. Democritus' sender of telepathic images could be compared to a television station, the recipient to a television set. The comparison does not explain anything, of course, but it seems clear that Democritus, who also anticipated the modern atomic theory, observed genuine cases of telepathy and tried to explain them scientifically.

King Croesus of Lydia's testing of the famous oracles of the Greek world by making them guess a bizarre event that took place under his control, at a certain moment, was an experiment in telepathy (Herodotus 1.47).[116] The king assumed that the oracle who guessed right would also advise him best about the future. Croesus' envoys to the seven greatest oracles were to ask, on a prearranged day, "What is the King of Lydia doing on this very day?" Only the Delphic oracle came up with the correct answer: the King of Lydia was cooking a most unusual dish consisting of lamb and tortoise, in a copper pot. The story has a sad ending, however. After this rather frivolous or, as some Greeks thought, blasphemous experiment, Croesus put his trust in the Delphic oracle, asked a crucial question, received an ambiguous answer, attacked Persia, and was defeated. This story may be a Greek invention, but the idea of such an experiment may well have occurred to a Middle Eastern ruler of that time.

The "Tale of the Wicked Innkeeper" is quoted by several Stoic philosophers as an example of the truth that is revealed to us, under certain circumstances, in dreams.[117] Two travelers arrive at Megara together. One has to stay at an inn, the other spends the night at the house of a guest-friend. The second man has a vivid dream: he sees his fellow traveler being killed by the innkeeper, jumps out of bed to run to his aid, but then says to himself that it was only a dream and goes back to bed. But now he has a second dream, in which the other man informs him that he has, indeed, been murdered and tells him to go to one of the city gates early in the morning: there he must stop a dung cart because his body is hidden in it. This the man does, the corpse is found, and the innkeeper is arrested as a murderer. Whether the story is genuine or not we cannot tell, although it does sound authentic. How to explain it, as Dodds says,[118] is even more difficult: is it telepathy from a man being murdered (in the case of the first dream) and clairvoyance on the part of the dreamer (in the case of the second dream), or are there other explanations?

Psychokinesis has received a good deal of attention in recent years. It can be defined as the moving or alteration of objects without direct physical contact. This ability is attributed to daemons in some legends of early saints,[119] and in Philostratus' *Life of Apollonius of Tyana* (4.20), the daemon, after having been forced to leave a possessed youth, overthrows a statue nearby. There is a story of a walking statue in Lucian's *Lovers of Lies* (ch. 21), but this seems to be a joke aimed at the belief in animated statues.[120] Some cases that have been reported could be considered instances of the "poltergeist" phenomenon. The house in which the future emperor Augustus was nursed as a baby—some said he was born there— was supposed to be inhabited by such a force, and when a new owner, either in ignorance or because he was too curious, tried to sleep in a certain room, he found himself ejected, mattress and all, by a "sudden, mysterious force" (Suet., *Aug.* 6).

There are various states of "mental dissociation," as they are called today: dreams, slight distractions, hallucinations of the dying and the mentally disturbed, and "mediumistic" states voluntarily induced.[121] For a Greek or Roman, any form of dissociation may have been considered a case of possession. As Dodds, from his personal experiences as well as from his knowledge of the ancient sources, points out, the "more extreme symptoms" are interpreted as signs of possession, and the experience of symbolic physical phenomena confirms the religious authority of the possessed and his or her utterances. Lights are seen, not always by all witnesses, at the moment when the medium is falling into trance or emerging from it; this means, no doubt, that these sittings were usually held in dark or semidark rooms.[122] Levitation of the medium when in trance is also reported,[123] but this seems to have a religious rather than a magical significance, because in different cultures it is consistently the mark of a good and holy person: Indian sages (i.e., fakirs or yogis), Jewish rabbis, Christian saints—even Jesus, according to the apocryphal Acts of Peter (32)—had the gift.[124]

Phenomena of materialization are also described as "spirit forms," which can be shapeless or take on a recognizable shape;[125] they have been compared to the "ectoplasm" that some modern spiritualists claim to have seen emerge from and return to the body of a medium.[126]

Automatism is another modern term applied to certain occult phenomena. It means, essentially, that someone else or something else is taking over and that one loses, for a while, control over a sense or a muscle. Dodds distinguishes four main types of automatism: (1) visual, (2) auditory, (3) motor or muscular, and (4) vocal, actually a subspecies of (3) because, in speaking, muscles are used.[127]

Visual automatism[128] is the modern term for scrying or crystal-gazing— that is, the technique of seeing images in crystal balls, mirrors, or water that reveal the future or, less frequently, secrets of the past and present. *Catoptromancy*, the use of a mirror for this purpose, was already practiced in Athens in the fifth century B.C.[129] When water is used, the terms are *hydromancy* (divination by water) or *lecanomancy* (divination by means of a bowl). The latter method seems to have originated in Babylonia, where oil was poured on water, and the shapes it formed were observed and interpreted. A similar custom has survived in Europe into the twentieth century: the pouring of melted lead into a pan of water on Halloween or New Year's Eve to see what the New Year will bring (Halloween is the Celtic New Year's Eve). The oil or lead is not necessary, for the scryer ought to be able to see figures in the water. Nor is this technique always used for divination: the theurgist may use catoptromancy or hydromancy to see God. In ancient times this technique was used for the most mundane of purposes, such as recovering money or valuable objects that had been stolen or lost, but it was also practiced by magician-priests, within an established sanctuary, as part of a mystic ritual to produce visions of gods.

Auditory automatism is the hearing of supernormal voices.[130] Technically speaking, an Old Testament prophet hearing the voice of Yahweh is a case of this kind of automatism. The phenomenon was more frequent among the Jews (who had no image of the Lord) than among the Greeks and the Romans, it seems, but Socrates' *daimonion* is a notable exception; although it did not deliver long messages to his inner ear that he could share with others, it always stopped him from doing one thing or another.

Whether he actually heard anything at all or just felt a kind of restraint, we cannot know. Later texts such as the pseudoplatonic *Theages* make him deliver oracles, but they seem to be the work of authors who did not know Socrates himself.

It would be wrong to say that an individual who experiences visual or auditory automatism is entirely passive, just the recipient of visions and voices. There is also a more active, "muscular" or "motor" automatism, which, according to Dodds, accounts for automatic writing and drawing, table-tilting, and the so-called Ouija board.[131] Actually, vocal automatism or mediumship could also be treated as a form of "muscular automatism," though, as Dodds says, it involves "a much more profound degree of dissociation than the types so far considered, and has correspondingly made a much deeper impression on the popular imagination of all periods."[132] The type of Ouija board described earlier is a good example; it is an experiment that can easily be reproduced today.

Eighty Egyptian priests moving the statue of a god at the oracle of Zeus Ammon "wherever the will of the god directed them" (Diod. Sic. 17.50.6) must have been an even more impressive sight, but it involved the same unconscious muscular movement or pressure that activates the Ouija board. Although the technique had its origin in Egypt, it was practiced in Antium (not far from Rome), in the sanctuary of Fortuna, as late as the fifth century A.D. Macrobius (*Sat.* 1.23.13) describes the "moving statues of the Fortunes which give oracles" at Antium.[133] The details are not known, but we may imagine several statues, each one representing Fortuna, the goddess of Chance, each one carried by a group of priests in a certain direction, "as the deity moved them." One direction perhaps meant yes, another one no, but the spectacle must have been striking, and because there were several statues, more applicants could be dealt with. It is possible to think of the whole operation as a kind of gigantic Ouija board.

Automatic speech or *mediumship* are modern terms that have been used to explain cases of possession reported from ancient times,[134] and in a sense the Pythia at Delphi, a woman in trance who spoke with a voice not her own, was a case of possession; the only question was, who possessed her—Apollo himself or some minor daemon? All we can say is that her state of consciousness was autosuggestively induced and that she had very little control over it. Not everyone was suitable to serve as a medium, but "young and unsophisticated persons" were the best candidates.[135] How they were put into trance we do not know, but a simple ritual such as the putting on of special vestments, sitting in a holy place, touching holy water, reciting prayers, or chanting hymns may have operated as an autosuggestion. At this distance in time it is difficult to determine whether this phenomenon was spontaneous or induced. "Speaking with tongues" (*glossolalia*) was, in a sense, an early Christian equivalent of the unintelligible utterances of pagan prophets and prophetesses; an interpreter who was also psychic, but in a different way than the medium, was needed (see 1 Corinthians 12:10).

Hypnotism was probably practiced in antiquity, though no detailed account of its use has survived.[136] The technique of inducing (in the absence of drugs) a trancelike state in a person and thus rendering that person more susceptible to external suggestions and directions is probably very old and may have been handed down as a secret in certain sanctuaries in Egypt and Greece. In more recent times, the Austrian physician Franz Anton Mesmer (1734–1815) discovered in himself a quality he called "animal magnetism," and he used it to cure or relieve certain disorders. After Mesmer that trancelike state was called "mesmerism." Then, in 1842, the Scottish surgeon James Braid coined the term *neurohypnotism*, which is still used in shortened form. Although it is derived from the Greek word *hypnos* 'sleep', *hypnosis* was never used in the modern sense by any ancient writer. Instead, the Greek word *ekstasis* 'stepping outside oneself' was used to describe this trancelike state, whether spontaneous or induced, hypnotic or mediumistic.

It would be tempting to investigate the relationship between the ancient *magi* of the Western world and the yogis and fakirs of India, who seem to be able to control the automatic processes of the body, can live without food and drink for days, have visionary and telepathic experiences, and are said to perform miraculous feats. Such paranormal happenings are documented but remain largely unexplained. There are peculiar parallels between the Greek and Latin texts and modern eyewitness reports from India. Is it possible that some of the early Greek shamans learned their techniques in India, where these traditions are still alive? A discussion of the whole problem would require a book in itself.

We have seen the many different forms magic took in classical antiquity. It is a great distance from Homer's Circe to Lucan's Erictho, and there are many differences between the *magi* of early Greece and the sorcerers of later centuries, but they all have one thing in common: they all personify the desire of man to impose his will on nature and to become, like Prometheus, like Dr. Faustus, "equal to the gods." Much of ancient magic in a sense anticipates (as a dream, at least) modern science and technology; but much of it also reveals man's continuous yearning for *gnosis,* the knowledge or understanding of hidden things.

NOTES

1. Thorndike, *A History of Magic and Experimental Science,* 1:2.

2. Festugière, *La Révélation d'Hermès Trismégiste,* 1:76, 89.

3. Suet., *Calig.,* ch. 5.

4. R. Ehnmark, in *Ethnos* 21 (1956): 1; E. R. Goodenough, *Jewish Symbols in the Graeco-Roman Period,* 13 vols. (New York, 1963–68), 2:155; M. Smith, *Jesus the Magician,* ch. 1.

5. M. Smith, *Jesus the Magician,* ch. 1.

6. A. Dieterich, *Mutter Erde,* 3rd ed. (Leipzig, 1925); I. F. Burns, in *ERE,* 4:145; E. O. James, *The Cult of the Mother Goddess* (London, 1959).

7. Bidez and Cumont, *Les Mages hellénisés;* R. N. Frye, *The Heritage of Persia* (London, 1962), p. 75.

8. P. Ghalioungui, *Magic and Medical Science in Ancient Egypt* (London, 1963), p. 18.

9. R. Wasson, C. A. P. Ruck, and A. Hofmann, *The Road to Eleusis* (New York, 1978); 2nd ed., with a preface by Huston Smith (Los Angeles, 1998). See G. Luck, in *American Journal of Philology* 122 (2001): 135–38.

10. D. MacDowell, in his commentary on Andocides, *On the Mysteries* (Oxford, 1962), app. N.

11. M. P. Nilsson, *Greek Piety,* trans. H. J. Rose (New York, 1969), pp. 14–15.

12. C. M. Bowra, *Homer* (New York, 1972), pp. 125–28.

13. Dodds, *The Greeks and the Irrational;* W. K. C. Guthrie, *A History of Greek Philosophy,* 6 vols. (Cambridge, 1962–81), 1:146ff., 2:12ff.

14. On shamanism, see, among others, J. A. MacCulloch, in *ERE,* 11:441ff.; M. Eliade, *Le Chamanisme et les techniques archaïques de l'extase* (Paris, 1951); H. Findeisen, *Schamanentum* (Stuttgart, 1957).

15. Dodds, *The Greeks and the Irrational,* p. 140.

16. Ibid., p. 147.

17. Arist. frag. 191 Rose (3rd ed.) (= pp. 130ff. Ross).

18. Burkert, *Lore and Science in Ancient Pythagoreanism,* pp. 162ff.

19. Dodds, *The Greeks and the Irrational,* pp. 145–46.

20. Thorndike, *A History of Magic and Experimental Science,* 1:26ff.

21. Apollonius of Rhodes and Theocritus, both of whom represent the Alexandrian style in Greek poetry.

22. On the evil eye, see F. T. Elworthy, in *ERE,* 5:608ff.; E. A. W. Budge, *The Mummy: Chapters in Egyptian Funereal Archaeology,* 2nd ed. (repr., New York, 1964), pp. 316ff.

23. H. Schweizer, *Aberglaube und Zauberei bei Theokrit* (Basel, 1937).

24. Similar rituals have been observed in other cultures. In his *Popular Antiquities of Great Britain,* 2 vols. (London, 1870), 1:379ff., John Brand quotes and illustrates a poem by Thomas Gray:

> Two hazel nuts I threw into a flame,
> And to each nut I gave a sweetheart's name:
> This with the loudest bounce me sore amaz'd,

That in a flame of brightest colour blaz'd.
As blaz'd the nut, so may thy passion grow,
For 'twas thy nut that did so brightly glow.

This appears to be a magical guessing game. A girl throws nuts into a fire, giving to each the name of a young man, in order to find out which one truly loves her. Maybe this is not real love magic, as in Theocritus, but is closely related to it.

25. Festugière, *La Révélation d'Hermès Trismégiste*, 1:189.

26. Cumont, *L'Egypte des astrologues*.

27. Bell, *Cults and Creeds in Graeco-Roman Egypt*, pp. 71ff.; A. D. Nock, in *Journal of Theological Studies* 15 (1954): 248ff.

28. Hull, *Hellenistic Magic and the Synoptic Tradition*, pp. 23ff.

29. K. Preisendanz, in *Zentralblatt für Bibliothekswesen* 75 (1950): 223ff.

30. The Greek magical papyri were published by K. Preisendanz, E. Diehl, S. Eitrem, and others (Leipzig) in 3 vols.: 1 (1928), 2 (1931), 3 (1941). Only a few copies of volume 3 survived the Second World War. A new edition of the whole was prepared by A. Henrichs of Harvard University, 2 vols. (Stuttgart, 1973–74). Counting the more recent discoveries, almost two hundred magical papyri have been published to date. The London and Leiden papyri (= *PGM* LXI and LXII) were published by Bell, Nock, and Thompson, in *Proceedings of the British Academy* 17 (1931): 235ff. They are available in English thanks to H. D. Betz (Chicago, 1986; 2nd ed., 1992) and a team of other scholars.

31. On curses, see A. E. Crawley, in *ERE*, 4:367ff.; G. van der Leeuw, *La Religion dans son essence* (Paris, 1948), pp. 395ff.

32. See Bonner, *Studies in Magical Amulets*.

33. On these gems, see S. Eitrem, in *Symbolae Osloenses* 19 (1939): 57ff. Their use must be old; see Saggs, *The Greatness That Was Babylon*, pp. 303ff.

34. F. C. Burkitt, *Church and Gnosis* (Cambridge, 1932), pp. 35ff., deals with Gnostic amulets.

35. These texts gave the magician elaborate instructions for his own operations, but brief excerpts could be used for the amulets the magician then sold to his customers.

36. R. Wünsch, *Antikes Zaubergerät aus Pergamon*. In a little-known article, "Die pergamenische Zauberscheibe und das Tarockspiel," *Bulletin de la Société Royale de Lund* 4 (1935–36), S. Agrell tries to establish a connection between the symbols found in the three concentric circles round the edge of the dish and the twenty-two cards of tarot.

37. E. R. Dodds, "Supernatural Phenomena in Classical Antiquity," first published in *Proceedings of the Society for Psychical Research* 55 (1971) and reprinted, with additions, in his book *The Ancient Concept of Progress*, pp. 156ff.

38. *Abraxas*, another magical word, is often found on gems. *Hocus-pocus* appears much later, and its etymology is controversial; some derive it from the pseudo-Latin formula *Hax Pax Max Deus Adimax*, which was first used in the Middle Ages by vagrant scholars who performed magical tricks; others see in it a parody of *hoc est corpus*, "this is the body," which is spoken by the priest during Holy Communion.

39. C. Wilson, *The Occult* (New York, 1971), p. 106. The pentagram as protection against evil spirits seems to be very old, and it survives far into the Middle

Ages; see M.-T. d'Alverny, in *Antike und Orient im Mittelalter*, ed. P. Hilpert (Berlin, 1962), pp. 158–59.

40. Reitzenstein, *Poimandres*, pp. 256ff.

41. J. M. R. Cormack, "A Tabella Defixionis in the Museum of . . . Reading," *Harvard Theological Review* 44 (1951): 25ff.

42. Dodds, *The Greeks and the Irrational*, p. 291.

43. These symbols were secretly placed by the operator in the hollow inside the statue of a god; see ibid., p. 292. Sometimes, aromatic essences were added for theurgical operations.

44. Dodds, *The Ancient Concept of Progress*, pp. 200–201; see also Dodds, *The Greeks and the Irrational*, appendix.

45. See E. des Places, in *Entretiens de la Fondation Hardt* 21 (1975): 78–79.

46. See Festugière, *La Révélation d'Hermès Trismégiste*, 1:56ff.

47. F. Cumont, *Lux Perpetua* (Paris, 1949), p. 362.

48. See Thorndike, *A History of Magic and Experimental Science*, 1:319ff.

49. J. Bidez, *La Vie de l'empereur Julien* (Paris, 1930), p. 79.

50. See J. E. Harrison, in *ERE*, 7:322; G. Luck, in *American Journal of Philology* 94 (1973): 147ff.

51. See Porphyrius, *De Philosophia ex Oraculis Haurienda*, ed. G. Wolff (Leipzig, 1856), pp. 164–65; and Euseb., *Praep. Evang.* 4.50ff., in the edition of E. des Places (*Sources Chrétiennes* 262 [1979]), where O. Zink discusses the fine robes, the liquids and flowers, and the gestures used in magical operations of this kind.

52. Iambl., *Myst.* 6.6.

53. The correct manner of uttering certain sounds and words was an orally transmitted secret; see Dodds, *The Greeks and the Irrational*, p. 292. Oral tradition obviously played an important role in the teaching of magic and other occult techniques, and our knowledge must remain incomplete or uncertain because that tradition has been lost. We hear of all sorts of eerie sounds (hissing, howling, clucking, whistling) that were produced by the professionals during a session.

54. Hull, *Hellenistic Magic and the Synoptic Tradition*, pp. 42–43.

55. *PGM* 7:786ff., 13:946.

56. D'Alverny, in *Antike und Orient im Mittelalter*, p. 164.

57. Blau's *Das altjüdische Zauberwesen* is still useful.

58. Barb, in Momigliano, *The Conflict between Paganism and Christianity*, pp. 118–19.

59. J. Dan, in *Encyclopaedia Judaica* 10 (1971), s.v. "Magic."

60. Blau, *Das altjüdische Zauberwesen*, pp. 27, 43.

61. Ibid., pp. 96ff.

62. Ibid., p. 53.

63. Hull, *Hellenistic Magic and the Synoptic Tradition*, p. 129; M. Smith, *Jesus the Magician*, pp. 45ff. The thesis of S. Eitrem in *Die Versuchung Christi* (Oslo, 1924) that the purpose of the Temptation, according to the synoptic Gospels, is to *induce* Christ to *become* a magician should have received much more attention than it did; but see H. J. Rose's comments in *Classical Review* 38 (1924): 213.

64. Cf. C. C. McCown, ed., *The Testament of Solomon* (Leipzig, 1922); K. Preisendanz, in *PW*, suppl. vol. 8 (1952), cols. 684ff.

65. See D. Winston, trans., *The Wisdom of Solomon*, Anchor Bible Series, vol. 43

(Garden City, N.Y., 1979), pp. 172ff. The author of this apocryphal book was clearly familiar with Middle Platonism and may have belonged to the circle of Philo of Alexandria.

66. Hull, *Hellenistic Magic and the Synoptic Tradition*, p. 31.

67. See G. Scholem, in *Encyclopaedia Judaica* (1971), 10:489ff.; B. Pick, *The Cabala* (La Salle, Ill., 1974).

68. It seems worthwhile to note that Aphrodite, Circe, Medea, and Dido live on in Germanic mythology in at least two versions, the tale of Tannhäuser and the tale of the Lorelei. Tannhäuser was a knight-errant and minstrel who spent—not altogether against his will—many years with Frau Holde (or Hulda, or Holle) in the mountain of Venus. Frau Holde ("the lovely woman") appears to be a pagan goddess (related to Aphrodite) who, with her whole court, survived the victory of Christianity over paganism. Living deep inside a mountain, she could be found by privileged heroes such as Tannhäuser. (Incidentally, the dwarfs and elves of European fairy tales also live in mountains; they are usually interpreted as ancient nature daemons who were driven from society but not completely eliminated by the Church.) Tannhäuser is spellbound by this ancient yet eternally beautiful and seductive goddess, but finally he manages to tear himself away and goes on a pilgrimage to Rome, where he confesses his sins to Pope Urban. According to the Old German ballad, Tannhäuser says to the pope: "Lady Venus is a beautiful woman, lovely and graceful, and her voice is like sunshine and the scent of flowers. . . . If I owned all of heaven, I would gladly give it to Lady Venus; I would give her the sun, I would give her the moon, and I would give her all the stars." The pope replies: "The devil whom they call Venus is the worst of all. I could never save you from her beautiful claws."

In the end, Tannhäuser is saved by a miracle that even the pope has to acknowledge. He has been forgiven. But according to the ancient folktale, the pagan goddess of love has been degraded to the role of an evil witch, though the Church still recognizes her great power over men. Tannhäuser, the poet, returns to the pagan cult of beauty but must humble himself before the head of the Church. In his study *The Science of Folklore* (pp. 106ff.), Krappe maintains that the whole story is un-German, that it never was popular in the Middle Ages, and that it is Celtic in origin, even though Tannhäuser is a German name. It may be Celtic, but the main point seems to be that it replaces the Greek island on which an ancient goddess survived as a witch, with a mountain in the North, which serves as the underground domicile of a formerly powerful Roman goddess.

Similarly, the Lorelei is a seductive woman who sits on a rock in the Rhine, combing her golden hair, luring to their death the boatmen who cannot take their eyes off her. She is arrested and tried as a witch, but the bishop who presides over the ecclesiastical court is so moved by her loveliness that he lets mercy prevail. Again, Krappe (p. 92) feels that this is not a genuine German folktale. It is apparently not attested in any medieval source, and it might indeed be, as Krappe thinks, a creation of the romantic era, at least in the form in which we know it. Heine's haunting song

> Ich weiss nicht, was soll es bedeuten,
> dass ich so traurig bin;

ein Märchen aus uralten Zeiten,
das kommt mir nicht aus dem Sinn

has made it popular since then, but the romantic poet is right: It is a story from times immemorial; Homer's Circe is still alive.

69. A. D. Nock, in *Beginnings of Christianity*, vol. 5, ed. F. J. F. Jackson and K. Lake (London, 1933), pp. 164ff.; P. de Labriolle, *La Réaction païenne*, 6th ed. (Paris, 1948), pp. 175ff.; E. M. Butler, *The Myth of the Magus* (Cambridge, 1948), pp. 66ff. See also note 78 below.

70. See Hull, *Hellenistic Magic and the Synoptic Tradition*, p. 38.

71. See M. Smith, *Jesus the Magician*, pp. 150ff.

72. Ibid., p. 151.

73. See R. S. Casey, in Jackson and Lake, *Beginnings of Christianity*, 5:151ff. See also G. N. L. Hall, in *ERE*, 11:541ff.; and P. Carrington, *The Early Christian Church*, 2 vols. (Cambridge, 1957).

74. The formula, curious as it seems, has an authentic ring; perhaps it is an adaptation of some of Jesus' sayings.

75. There is a parallel story in Acts 13:6–12. While they were at Paphus, on Cyprus, Paul, John, and Barnabas met a Jewish *magus* and pseudoprophet called Elymas. He was part of the household of the proconsul, Sergius Paulus, a Roman who was anxious to "hear the word of God." When the Jewish *magus* tried to influence the Roman proconsul against the Christian missionaries, Paul, "filled with Holy Spirit," looked at him, cursed him, and struck him with blindness, whereupon the proconsul became a believer. This event can be dated within a year or two of A.D. 45; see Nock, in Jackson and Lake, *Beginnings of Christianity*, 5:182ff. Nock's discussion of Jewish *magi* of the period—the role that someone like Elymas might have played in the household of a Roman official (a kind of spiritual adviser), the scene of confrontation before someone in authority, and the fate of the *magus* beaten at his own game—is still important.

76. *Recogn. Clement.* 2.15; *Homil. Clement.* 2.26. These passages are quoted in P. M. Palmer and R. P. More, *Sources of the Faust Tradition* (New York, 1978), p. 16. The implications are that Simon killed the boy; see the witches in Horace's fifth epode [*no. 8*].

77. Moses and the Egyptian magicians before Pharaoh (Exodus 7); Paul and Elymas before the proconsul (Acts 13:6–12).

78. See note 69 above; cf. Thorndike, *A History of Magic and Experimental Science*, 1:242ff.; T. Whittaker, *Apollonius of Tyana and Other Essays* (London, 1906); and W. R. Halliday, *Folklore Studies* (London, 1924), ch. 6.

79. Gabriel Naudé, a French scholar of the seventeenth century, wrote an *Apology for All Great Men Who Were Wrongly Accused of Magic* (first published in French, Paris, 1625; repr., 1985). Among those defended are Pythagoras and Socrates; Apollonius is characterized as a religious leader who patterned himself after Christ; and Philostratus' *Life of Apollonius of Tyana* is presented as an imitation of the Gospels.

80. S.H.A., *Sev.* 29.2; see M. Smith, *Jesus the Magician*, pp. 88–89.

81. See C. H. Dodd, *The Bible and the Greeks* (London, 1935); R. Bultmann, *Das Urchristentum im Rahmen der antiken Religionen* (Zurich, 1949), pp. 181ff.; W. C.

van Unnik, *Evangelien aus dem Nilsand* (Frankfurt, 1960); R. M. Grant, *Gnosticism: A Source Book* (New York, 1961).

82. New Gnostic texts have been found in the Coptic Library of Nag Hammadi. See G. MacRae, in *Interpreter's Dictionary of the Bible,* suppl. vol. (Nashville, Tenn., 1976), pp. 613–19.

83. Festugière and Nock, *Corpus Hermeticum,* 4 vols.

84. Witt, *Isis in the Graeco-Roman World,* p. 207.

85. On the survival of Hermeticism, see W. Shumaker, *The Occult Sciences of the Renaissance* (Berkeley and Los Angeles, 1972), pp. 201ff.; F. A. Yates, *Giordano Bruno and the Hermetic Tradition* (Chicago, 1978).

86. Pliny, *Nat. Hist.* 2.62; Manil., *Astron.* 1.95ff.; Sen., *QNat.* 6.5.3, 7.25; Dodds, *The Ancient Concept of Progress,* p. 23.

87. Aspirin, the most widely used drug in the world and one of the least expensive, has been called a "magical" drug because medical science does not know exactly how it works. Its active ingredient, salicylic acid, has been used in the form of willow bark in scientific medicine since Hippocrates (c. 400 B.C.) and in folk medicine—for instance, by the American Indians—for many centuries. See *The World Almanac Book of the Strange* (New York, 1977), pp. 13–14.

88. See W. H. S. Jones, in *Proceedings of the Cambridge Philological Society* 181 (1950–51): 7–8.

89. J. E. Harrison, *Prolegomena to the Study of Greek Religion,* 3rd ed. (Cambridge, 1922), pp. 4ff.

90. F. E. Brenk, *In Mist Apparelled: Religious Themes in Plutarch's "Moralia" and "Lives"* (Leiden, 1977), p. 59.

91. J. Dillon, *The Middle Platonists* (Ithaca, N.Y., 1977), pp. 216ff.

92. Tatum, *Apuleius and the Golden Ass,* pp. 28–29; he refers to A. D. Nock, *Conversion* (Oxford, 1933), pp. 138ff., a detailed treatment of Book 11 of Apuleius' *Metamorphoses.*

93. See Tatum, *Apuleius and the Golden Ass,* pp. 62ff., for a discussion of "spiritual serenity and the surrounding world." Philosophy and science are both ingredients of a higher kind of magic.

94. Dillon, *The Middle Platonists,* pp. 317ff.

95. Elymas (see note 75 above) is called *pseudoprophetes,* which corresponds to Lucian's term *pseudomantis.* But Elymas is also called, in Acts, *magos,* while Alexander is labeled *goes.* At this period, the terms must have been almost synonymous, though *goes* tends to be more negative. The essential information on Alexander is found in H. J. Rose's excellent article in the *Oxford Classical Dictionary,* 2nd ed. (1970), p. 42.

96. See Caster, *Lucien et la pensée religieuse de son temps,* pp. 307ff.

97. This is the term used by Brown in *Religion and Society in the Age of St. Augustine,* p. 124.

98. Dodds, *Pagan and Christian in an Age of Anxiety,* pp. 72ff.

99. Abt, *Die Apologie des Apuleius von Madaura und die antike Zauberei,* pp. 108ff.

100. This concept was introduced in a classic work by Evans-Pritchard, *Witchcraft, Oracles, and Magic among the Azande;* it has been applied to later antiquity by Brown, *Religion and Society in the Age of St. Augustine,* p. 131.

101. Libanius' *Autobiography,* ed. J. Martin (Paris, 1979), is remarkable; see

esp. pars. 245ff. His speech "On Witchcraft" also is very revealing; cf. C. Bonner, "Witchcraft in the Lecture Room of Libanius," *Transactions and Proceedings of the American Philological Association* 63 (1932): 34ff.

102. Gregory the Great, *Dial.* 1.4, 30. The best edition is that by A. de Vogüé (*Sources Chrétiennes* 251 [1978]). There are many curious tales of the supernatural in the *Dialogues.*

103. Brown, *Religion and Society in the Age of St. Augustine,* p. 37.

104. Merlan, in *Isis* 44 (1953): 341ff.; Armstrong, in *Phronesis* 1 (1955): 73ff.

105. Iamblichus, *Les Mystères d'Egypte,* ed. and trans. E. des Places (Paris, 1966); cf. Dodds, *The Greeks and the Irrational,* pp. 278ff.

106. Barb, in Momigliano, *The Conflict between Paganism and Christianity,* pp. 102ff.

107. See Dodds, *The Ancient Concept of Progress,* pp. 156ff. In a letter to Dodds, M. P. Nilsson had written in 1945: "I am persuaded that the so-called parapsychical phenomena played a very great part in late Greek paganism and are essential for understanding it rightly."

108. Dodds, *The Ancient Concept of Progress,* pp. 191–92.

109. See Wilson, *The Occult;* A. Koestler, *The Roots of Coincidence* (London, 1972).

110. E. R. Dodds, *Missing Persons: An Autobiography* (Oxford, 1977), pp. 97ff. This is a charming and enlightening book.

111. Ibid., p. 111.

112. In fact, Augustine was a careful observer of occult phenomena, as P. Brown, *Augustine of Hippo* (London, 1967), pp. 413ff., has shown; cf. Dodds, *The Ancient Concept of Progress,* p. 174, n. 1.

113. H. Diels and W. Kranz, *Die Fragmente der Vorsokratiker,* 12th ed. (Berlin, 1966), 68A. 116; cf. Dodds, *The Ancient Concept of Progress,* p. 162.

114. Dodds, *Missing Persons,* pp. 109ff.

115. Diels and Kranz, *Die Fragmente der Vorsokratiker,* 68A.77; Dodds, *The Ancient Concept of Progress,* pp. 161–62.

116. Dodds, *The Ancient Concept of Progress,* pp. 166–67.

117. For testimonies from Chrysippus, Cicero, and other authors, see ibid., pp. 172–73.

118. Ibid., p. 172.

119. Ibid., p. 158, n.1; p. 206, n. 2.

120. P. Boyancé, in *Revue de l'Histoire des Religions* 147 (1955): 189ff.

121. Dodds (*The Ancient Concept of Progress,* p. 204) points out that dissociation is a psychological state that occurs in all cultures.

122. Iambl. *Myst.* 3.5; Dodds, *The Ancient Concept of Progress,* pp. 203ff.

123. Iamblichus was apparently capable of this; cf. Eunap., *Lives of the Philosophers and Sophists,* p. 458 Boissonade.

124. Dodds, *The Ancient Concept of Progress,* p. 205.

125. For instance, Proclus, the Neoplatonist, in his commentary on Plato's *Republic* 1.110.28 (Kroll).

126. Dodds, *The Ancient Concept of Progress,* p. 204.

127. Ibid., pp. 186ff.

128. Ibid.

129. Aristoph., *Ach.* 1128ff.; A. Delatte, *La Catoptromancie grecque et ses dérivés* (Paris, 1932), pp. 133ff.; Dodds, *The Ancient Concept of Progress,* pp. 186ff.

130. Dodds, *The Ancient Concept of Progress,* pp. 191ff.

131. Ibid., pp. 193ff.

132. Dodds discusses "motor automatism" and "vocal automatism" or "mediumship" (ibid., p. 193).

133. Ibid.

134. Ibid.

135. Iambl., *Myst.* 3.19, quoted by Dodds in *The Ancient Concept of Progress,* pp. 193ff.

136. Dodds, who was an experienced hypnotist, was inclined to dismiss the experiment described by the philosopher Clearchus (frag. 7 Wehrli), whereby a "soul-dragging" wand rendered a sleeping boy insensitive to pain (*The Ancient Concept of Progress,* pp. 193ff.). Apuleius' description of boys "lulled to sleep either by spells or soothing odors" (*Apol.* 43) is, to Dodds, more suggestive of hypnosis.

Texts

I

The oldest Greek text in which a magical operation is mentioned forms part of Homer's *Odyssey*. In this episode the hero confronts a sorceress, Circe, on her own territory. Her power is established when she transforms some of Odysseus' companions into swine. She accomplishes this by mixing a magical drug into the special cheese mixture that she serves them and by touching them with her magic wand. Here we see the typical modus operandi of the witch (no chant or formula is mentioned, just a direct order), but unlike later witches, Circe is beautiful. This leads one to suspect that in mythological terms she is not really a witch, but a minor goddess, a survivor from an earlier generation of gods, removed—like Kronos—to a distant island and of no great concern to anyone, except, of course, if one enters her territory. Her power, whatever it may be, is inferior to that of the ruling dynasty of gods, the Olympians, and one of them, Hermes, equips Odysseus with a magical antidote, the mysterious herb *moly*, and provides the necessary instructions.

It is clear that witchcraft was part of Greek folklore from the earliest times. Some of Homer's material may go back to the Bronze Age, and an epic like the *Odyssey*, with its rich heritage of folktales and sailors' yarns, would have been incomplete without a tale of magic and, no less important, countermagic, for wherever people believe in witchcraft, they believe in ways of protecting themselves. They wear an amulet because they are convinced that they need it, to be on the safe side.

Homer, *Odyssey* 10.203–347

[*Odysseus is speaking.*]
    I counted up my strong-greaved companions, divided them into two groups, and appointed a leader for each group. One of them I led myself, the other was led by godlike Eurylochus. Quickly we shook lots in a

bronze helmet. The lot of the great-hearted Eurylochus jumped out. So he left, along with his twenty-two men, all weeping. We who were left behind wept too.

In a clearing in the woodland glen they discovered the house of Circe; it was well protected, put together with well-polished stones. All around it were mountain wolves and lions. She had bewitched them by giving them evil drugs. They did not attack my men, but stood up on their hind legs, wagging their long tails, as dogs go fawning about their master when he comes from a dinner, for he always brings them some treats. With such affection did the wolves with their strong claws and the lions fawn about my men. But they were scared when they saw the terrifying beasts. They stood before the gate of the goddess with the neatly braided hair and heard Circe singing melodiously inside as she walked up and down at her great, immortal loom, weaving a delicate, lovely, shining fabric, as goddesses do.

Polites, a natural leader, my best, my dearest companion, said to the others:

"Friends, inside a woman is singing beautifully, walking up and down at her great loom—the whole building echoes—either a goddess or a woman. Come on, let us call her."

They shouted and called her. At once she opened the shining doors, came out, and invited them in. They were naïve enough to follow her, all of them except Eurylochus, who waited outside, suspecting some treachery. She led them inside, asked them to sit on high chairs and benches, and mixed for them a dish of cheese and barley, clear honey, and Pramnian wine. But into the mixture she also put some dangerous drugs that would make them forget completely their native land. After she had given this to them and they had drunk it, she quickly struck them with her wand and locked them into her pig pens. They had the head, the voice, and bristles, and the shape of a pig, but their minds were the same as before. So they went in, crying. Circe cast before them acorns, chestnuts, and cornelian fruit, the kind of food that pigs, who sleep on the ground, usually eat.

Eurylochus returned at once to the fast black ship to tell the story of his companions and their tragic fate. He was unable to bring out a single word, though he tried; his heart was struck with great anguish, his eyes were filled with tears, and he only wanted to lament. We were all shocked and asked him questions. Finally he told us of the disaster that had befallen his companions:

"Glorious Odysseus, we went, as you had ordered, through the woods and discovered, in a clearing in the woodland glen a beautiful well-protected house constructed of polished stones. Inside, somebody—a goddess or a woman—sang sweetly as she walked up and down at her great loom. We shouted and called her. Quickly she opened the shining doors and came out, inviting us in, and all the others, naïve as they were, followed her. But I stayed outside, suspecting some treachery. They all vanished completely, and none of them reappeared, though I sat there waiting for a long time."

I slung my great bronze sword with the silver studs and my bow across my shoulders. I told him to lead me along the same path he had taken before. But he clasped my knees in both hands and implored me in a plaintive voice, saying:

"Son of Zeus, I do not want to go; please do not force me, but let me stay here. I know that you will not come back yourself and that you will not bring back any of your companions. Let us rather flee, those of us that are left; it is still possible to escape our doom."

I answered:

"Eurylochus, you may stay right here and eat and drink near the hollow black ship. But I am going. It is absolutely necessary."

I left the ship and the shore. As I went through the awesome woods and was approaching the great house of the sorceress Circe, Hermes with the golden rod met me as I came close to the house, looking like an adolescent in the flower of manhood, with a new-grown beard. He took my hand, spoke my name, and said to me:

"Where are you going, my poor friend, through the wild woods, all by yourself, not knowing the place? Your companions move around in Circe's house, looking like swine, crowded into her pig pens. Are you going there to set them free? I tell you, you will not come back; you will stay there with the others. But look, I will help you and rescue you from your troubles. Here, take this fine medicine—it will save your life and protect you from evil—and enter Circe's house. I will tell you all about Circe's deadly tricks. She will prepare a potion for you and mix drugs into the food, but in spite of it she will not be able to bewitch you, for the fine medicine that I will give to you will prevent her. Let me explain the details. As soon as Circe strikes you with her long wand, you must draw from beside your thigh your sharp sword and pounce on her as if you wanted to kill her. She will be frightened and ask you to sleep with her. Never reject the bed of a goddess, but let this set your companions free and be pleasant for you. You must make her swear a great oath by the gods not to plan any more evil against you, lest she weaken and unman you once you are naked."

The Argus-killer gave me an herb that he had plucked out of the ground and explained its nature to me. It was black at the root, and its flower was like milk. The gods call it *moly*. It is difficult for mortal men to dig it up. But to the gods everything is possible.

Then Hermes went away, over the wooded island, to great Olympus, and I went to Circe's house; my heart was agitated as I went. I stood at the gate of the goddess with the lovely locks and shouted; the goddess heard my call. Quickly she opened the shining doors and came out, inviting me in; I followed her nervously. She led me in and asked me to sit down on a beautiful, well-made chair with silver nails; there was a stool under my feet. In a golden dish she prepared a potion for me to drink; but with evil thoughts in her mind she had slipped a drug into it. After she had given it to me and I had drunk it, unbewitched, she struck me with her wand and called out, saying:

"Go now to the pig pen and lie down there with your friends."

I drew my sharp sword from beside my thigh and pounced on Circe as if I were about to kill her. She let out a loud scream, ran under my stroke, clasped my knees, and wailed:

"Who are you? Where are you from? What is your city? Who are your parents? I am amazed: you drank the poison, yet you are not bewitched. No other man could ever resist my poison once he had drunk it and it had passed the fence of his teeth. There is a mind in your breast that cannot be bewitched. You must be the resourceful Odysseus! The Argus-killer with the golden staff has always told me that you would come here from Troy in a fast black ship. But please, sheathe your sword, and then let us go to bed to make love and learn, in love, to trust each other."

I answered:

"Circe, how can you expect me to be kind to you? You have turned my companions into swine in your house, and now that you have me here you ask me deceitfully to come into your bedroom and go to bed with you, in order to weaken and unman me once I am naked. No, I do not want to go to bed with you, goddess, unless you agree to swear a great oath to plan no further mischief against me."

She swore immediately what I had asked her to swear. When she had sworn the oath and completed it, I climbed into the beautiful bed of Circe.

2

This attack on shamans who treat epilepsy seems to be one of the earlier works in the collection of medical writings known as the *Corpus Hippocraticum,* and it is dated in the late fifth or early fourth century B.C. Because the nature and origin of epilepsy were not understood, dealing with it was left to priests and practitioners of magic. The author of the treatise speaks as a scientist, but he also professes his belief in the Greek gods; for him, the practitioners he attacks are really false prophets and sacrilegious impostors. The skill with which the author turns their arguments against them seems to show the influence of the Sophists. He dismisses the dietary rules imposed by the "charlatans," although the ones that he suggests himself (in another context of the treatise) are not much different. There is a note of sarcastic humor when he tells them to take the "stuff" that they cleansed out of the patient to the temples of the gods where it allegedly came from. Another touch of sarcasm may be found in the idea that all the Libyans ought to suffer from epilepsy because of their contacts with goat meat and goat skins. But he delivers a devastating attack on the "healers" when he says that, if their healing powers are real, they might be capable of practicing black magic as well.

The author must have observed the dubious practitioners he denounces at work. They are neither real physicians nor real priests, but they fill a kind of void between the two professions and make a living this way. The author scornfully dismisses their claims and does not credit them with any success in the treatment of epilepsy. In fact, they cannot possibly be successful, because they treat a disease that has natural causes by an appeal to supernatural forces. Basically, we have here the scientist confronting the shaman or pseudoshaman who survives from a former age.

Hippocrates, *On the Sacred Disease* 1–4 Jones

The truth about the so-called sacred disease is this: in my opinion it is not any more divine or sacred than the others, but it has a natural cause and a . . . [text uncertain]. Because of their ignorance and its strange character—it is unlike any other disease—people thought that it was of divine origin. They are unable to understand it and continue to believe in its divine nature; at the same time, their simple-minded therapies—purifications and incantations—prove the opposite. Or should we consider it divine because of its strange nature? But in that case there would be many sacred diseases, not just one, for I will show that other diseases are no less bizarre or amazing, and yet no one calls them sacred. For example, quotidian, tertian, and quartan fevers seem to me no less divine and caused by a god than this disease, but no one wonders at them. Then again, I see men who are mad, insane, and do strange things for no apparent cause. I know that many people groan and yell in their sleep, others choke, jump up, and run outdoors and are out of their minds, until they wake up, and then they are healthy and normal as before, even though they are pale and weak, and this happens not once but many times. There are other examples of all kinds, but it would take too much time to discuss each one separately.

I think that the first people who have characterized epilepsy as "sacred" are those who are in our own day sorcerers [*magoi*], purifiers [*ka-*

thartai], mendicant priests [*agyrtai*] and charlatans [*alazones*]. These people pretend to be very reverent of the gods and to have superior knowledge. They hide behind the idea of the divine and disguise the fact that they have nothing with which to fight the disease and bring relief. To make sure that their ignorance does not become evident, they spread the belief that this disease is "sacred." They added a plausible story to make their method of healing safe, as far as they are concerned. They used purifications [*katharmoi*] and incantations [*epaoidai*] and told people to refrain from bathing and from eating many foods inappropriate for the sick. Among fish they banned red mullet, black-tail, gray mullet, and eel (for those are the most dangerous). Among meats (they banned) goat, deer, pork, and dog (for those upset the stomach most). Among poultry (they banned) cock, pigeon, the otis bird, and all the birds considered to be most substantial. Among vegetable (they banned) mint, leek, and onions (their pungency is bad for a sick person). They also prohibited the wearing of a black cloak (for black is the color of death), and the lying on goatskin or the wearing of it. One should not place one foot on another or one hand on another (for this means binding). These rules they impose because of the "sacred" nature of the disease, as if they had superior knowledge. They talk of other causes, too, so that they may become famous for their skill, if the patient recovers, and if he dies, they always have a good excuse, because they are not at all to blame, but the gods. Since they have not given the patient a drug to eat or to drink and since they have not ordered baths, they cannot be held responsible. (If that is true), then none of the inland Libyans could be in good health, for they lie on goatskins and eat goat meat, since their blankets, their cloaks, and their shoes are all made from goatskins. They only have goats. But if one gets sick from eating this sort of thing or having it close to one's body, and if one gets well from abstaining from all this, then the deity can no longer be held responsible, and purifications will be useless. On the contrary, it is the food that heals and harms, and the divine has no influence at all.

This is why, in my opinion, those who deal with these diseases in this particular way, do not really consider them to be "sacred" or "divine." Can the diseases be dislodged by purifications and therapies of this kind? Then how can we prevent them from attacking people, making them sick, by similar techniques? Thus, the cause is no longer "divine" but human. The person who is capable of relieving you from such an illness by thorough purifications and through magic, is also capable of making you sick through similar techniques! This is another argument against divine influence. With such claims and schemes they pretend to have some higher knowledge, and they deceive people by giving them "sacred" cleansings and purifications. They mostly talk about the "divine" and "supernatural powers." In my opinion, their talk does not prove that they are (really) pious, as they believe; in fact, it proves that they are impious, because, in a way, they deny the existence of the gods. In fact, their supposed piety, their devotion to the gods is downright impious and unholy, and I will show you why.

They pretend to know how to draw down [katagein] the moon, to eclipse the sun, to make storm and sunshine, to bring rain and droughts, to make the sea impassable and the earth sterile, and other things like this. The ones who "know" about such things will tell you that such effects can be achieved through certain rites or some other skill or operation. But to me, they are impious, because they believe that the gods do not exist and have no power. They are capable of anything and everything, and that makes them surely terrible in the eyes of the gods! If a person can draw down the moon by magic, by sacrifice, if he [she] can make the sun disappear and bring bad weather or good, I personally cannot see anything divine in this: if the power of the divine is defeated and enslaved by human cleverness—this is done by humans! Perhaps it is not so; perhaps it is just fine [text uncertain] that human beings trying to make a living invent all sorts of things and make elaborate claims, especially as far as this particular illness is concerned. They stick the blame for each form of the disease on a [different] god—for they do not blame one single deity but several gods for these problems. If the patient sounds like a goat and bellows, or if he has convulsions on the right side, they say that the "Mother of the gods" is responsible. If he shrieks loudly, they compare him to a horse and declare that Poseidon is responsible. If a patient passes stool, as is often the case under the compulsion of the disease, the deity named is Enodia. If the stools come frequently and are rather thin, like those of birds, Apollo Nomios must be responsible. If foam comes out of his mouth and he kicks with his feet, Ares gets to be blamed. If the patient is tortured by fears, terrors, manias in the night, jumps out of his bed and runs outside, they talk about "attacks of Hecate" or "interference of ghosts" (heroes). They use purifications and incantations—things that are totally unholy and irreligious, in my opinion. For they purify with blood and such things those who are in the grip of a disease, as if they were the victims of pollution or avenging ghosts, or as if they were bewitched by human beings or as if they had committed sacrilege. These patients have done none of these things, and they ought to treat them in the opposite way: sacrifice, pray, bring them to the sanctuaries, supplicate the gods. As it is, they do nothing of the sort; they just purify them. Some of the "refuse" [reading katharmata with Jones] they bury in the earth, some of it they throw in to the sea, and some of it they carry off to the mountains where no one will touch it or step on it. But they ought to take it into the temples and return it to the god, if the god indeed is responsible! But I don't believe that the human body is polluted by a god, the utterly corrupt by the perfectly holy! If the body happens to be polluted or made to suffer by some outside influence, then—in my opinion—it could only be purified and made whole [holy] by the god—not polluted by him! It is the divine that purifies and makes holy [whole] the greatest and most unholy of our errors and the dirt that attaches to us as a consequence [text uncertain]. We mark our boundaries for the temples, the sanctuaries of the gods, so that no one who is not pure should cross them. When we enter, we are sprinkled thoroughly—not as if we were considered polluted but to be cleansed of any former pollution we might have. This is my opinion concerning purifications.

3

Theophrastus (c. 370–285 B.C.) studied with Aristotle, whom he succeeded as head of the school in Athens. In addition to a large number of specialized philosophic, scientific, and critical works, most of which are lost, he wrote for a larger public a collection of thirty character sketches, portraits of the miser, the garrulous type, the superstitious person, and so on. These sketches were doubtless based on his own amused observations of real people, but they also show the influence of contemporary Greek comedy with its repertory of psychological "types," the braggart and the grouch, among others. Many of Menander's plays are titled after the particular type whose habits and principles are presented on the stage. Theophrastus must have been an avid theater-goer, and since he was a contemporary of Menander's (though some thirty years older, he survived him), he had an opportunity to see all of Menander's plays performed, and probably many of those produced by Menander's colleagues and rivals. Comparatively few of these comedies have survived, either in the original or in Latin adaptations. If we had more of them, we would get an invaluable picture of Athenian society in the postclassical period. Because literally hundreds of plays are lost, however, an "extract," like that by Theophrastus, must fill a few gaps.

In his "Portrait of the Superstitious Person" Theophrastus begins, as he learned from his teacher Aristotle, with a definition of superstition; only then does he list the characteristic features of the psychological type he is describing. Reading his account, his contemporaries would recognize with pleasure certain of their friends or acquaintances. In a sense, these sketches may have been born out of gossipy, malicious conversations about local characters, but then much good literature is gossipy and can be malicious!

Today we would probably say that the superstitious type, as described by Theophrastus, is a neurotic person weighed down and hemmed in by an unusual number of taboos—not only the normal, contemporary, local taboos, but some ancient and rather exotic taboos as well. There are taboos that one has to respect in any society, but there is no limit to the number of taboos one may impose upon oneself. Theophrastus is saying that some people need more taboos than others in order to function.

Theophrastus, *Characters*, "Portrait of the Superstitious Person"
(ch. 28 Jebb)

Superstition would seem to be simply exaggerated fear of supernatural powers.

The superstitious type is the sort of person who will wash his hands at a fountain and sprinkle himself from a temple font, to cleanse himself from a pollution. He will take a laurel leaf into his mouth and walk around like this all day. If a weasel [or: a cat] crosses his path, he will not walk any farther until someone else has passed him or until he has thrown three stones across the road. When he sees a snake in his house, he will invoke the god Sabazius if it is the "red snake"—but if it is the "sacred snake," he will at once establish a shrine on the spot. Whenever he passes a "pile of shiny stones" at the crossroads, he will pour oil from his flask on them, and he will fall on his knees and worship them before he continues on his way. If a mouse gnaws a hole in a barley sack [in his house], he goes to the "adviser" and asks him what to do. If the "adviser" tells him to take the sack to a cobbler and have it stitched up, he will not pay attention to his advice but will go his own way and offer a special sacrifice. He is capable of purifying his house quite often, saying that it has come under a spell of Hecate. If he startles an owl as he walks along, he may be frightened and shout "Glory be to Athena!" before he continues. He will never walk on a [flat] tombstone or come near a corpse or a woman who has just given birth, saying that it is better for him not to be polluted. On the fourth and seventh days of the [last ten days of the] month he will order his servants to mull wine, while he goes out to buy myrtle wreaths, frankincense, and smilax; when he comes back to his house he will put wreaths on the busts of Hermaphroditus all day long. Whenever he has had a dream, he will consult the interpreters of dreams, the seers, the augurs, to find out to which god, to which goddess, he ought to pray. He will also go to the "Orphic priests," in order to be initiated. This is the kind of person who will sprinkle himself thoroughly with seawater every month, along with his wife—or, if the wife is busy, with the nursemaid—and his children. Whenever he sees someone at the crossroads who is crowned with garlic [reading *estemmenon tina,* with Kayser], he will go away, pour water over his head, call the priestesses [of Hecate], and make them carry a squill or a puppy round him for purification. If he sees a madman or an epileptic, he shudders and spits into his bosom.

4

"Aesop" is the semilegendary author of a fairly large number of prose tales. This tale about a sorceress is preserved in a Byzantine collection, but it must be older (probably fifth–fourth century B.C.) and may be based on a real event.

One of the specialties of this witch was *katathesis,* the laying to rest of divine wrath. This was, of course, the domain of the priests of the official cults within the city-state. No wonder that the woman was charged with *asebeia* and condemned to death. The fact that she "did well for herself" would indicate a substantial clientele who preferred her services to those of the established priests, perhaps because she promised a more direct access and quicker results or because her ritual was more impressive. Perhaps she was cheaper. We can only guess.

Her claims must have been similar to those of the *agyrtai* and *manteis* that Plato (*Republic* 364b6–c2, *Laws* 909b2–4) attacks.

Paradoxically, Plato's teacher, Socrates, was also condemned to death for introducing "religious innovations," but he was hardly the type of *agyrtes* or *magos,* and in his case the charge was a pretext.

Aesop, Fable 56 Perry

A sorceress was claiming that she could placate the anger of the gods with her incantations. She performed a large number of them and did well for herself. Because of this some men charged her with making innovations in religion and took her to court. As a result of these accusations she was condemned to death. Someone saw her as she was led away from the court and said: "Poor woman! You claimed to be able to avert the anger of higher powers. How was it that you could not even persuade mere mortals?" This story could be used against a fantasizing woman who promises great results but is incapable, as it turns out, to achieve even modest ones.

5

This episode about Medea from a Hellenistic epic, the *Argonautica,* by Apollonius of Rhodes (early third century B.C.), is based on old folktales and myths. Medea is in the same class as Circe, and later ages have labeled her a witch, but she may be a minor goddess from a distant age, a remote civilization. She has fallen in love with Jason, the leader of the Argonauts, helps him win the Golden Fleece, and protects him and the other heroes on the way back to Greece. At one point they are threatened by a bronze monster called Talos, who patrols the shores of Crete, where they would like to land. Talos is a sort of robot, himself a magical creature, unless he is a survival of an earlier, more powerful race of men. The men of the heroic age are helpless against him, but Medea destroys him with her evil eye and by her knowledge of ritual magic.

This is the oldest extant Greek text that describes the effect of the evil eye and gives a tentative explanation of the powers involved. We see that magic was, by Apollonius' day, understood as a science. Apollonius had lived in Egypt, where he no doubt had had an opportunity to study occult arts.

Apollonius of Rhodes, *Argonautica* 4.1635–90

Rocky Carpathus greeted them from afar. They were planning to cross over from there to Crete, which is the biggest island in the sea.

But Talos, the bronze man who broke off lumps from a massive rock, prevented them from tying the rope to the land, as they entered the shelter of Dicte's harbor. He had been left over from the Bronze race of men who had sprung from ash trees, and he survived into the heroic age. Zeus had given him to Europa to be a guard of the island by running three times around Crete on his bronze feet. Well, the rest of his body and his limbs were made of bronze and invulnerable, but way down under a tendon near his ankle he had a blood vessel; it was covered by a thin membrane, and to him it meant the difference between life and death.

The Argonauts, totally overcome by fatigue, were terrified and quickly put the ship astern, rowing away from the shore. They would have rowed away from Crete in a gloomy mood, thirsty and exhausted as they were, had not Medea spoken to them as they pulled back: "Listen, I think that I and I alone can kill for you that man, whoever he is, even if his body is completely of bronze, provided that there is no immortal life in him. But keep the ship where it is, outside the range of his rocks, till I have finished with him." Rowing hard, they wrenched the ship out of range of his missiles, waiting to see what novel scheme Medea would carry out.

She held a fold of her purple cloak close to both cheeks and went up on deck. Grasping her hand in his, Jason accompanied her as she passed between the benches.

Then she sang songs of incantation, invoked the daemons of death, the swift hounds of hell that whirl around the air everywhere and fall on living creatures. On her knees she called them three times in song, three times in prayer. She put herself into a sinister mood, and with her own evil eye she put a curse on the eye of Talos. She gnashed at him her devastating fury and hurled forth images of death in an ecstasy of rage.

Father Zeus! It comes as a great shock to my mind that fearful death does not face us by illness and wounds alone but that someone can hurt from a distance! Yes, Talos was brought down helplessly, though made of bronze, by the force of Medea, the cunning sorceress. As he was lifting up some heavy lumps to prevent them from entering the anchorage, he nicked his ankle on a sharp rock. His divine blood ran out of him like molten lead. For a short time he remained there, on the jutting cliff on which he stood. But like a tall pine tree high up in the mountains which the woodmen left half-felled from their sharp axes before they came down from the wooded hills—first it is shaken by the winds in the night, but then it breaks at the bottom and crashes down—thus he stood for a little while, swaying sideways on his sturdy legs, but then he fell down helplessly with a mighty crash.

That night the heroes camped on Crete.

6

Theocritus lived in Alexandria at some time during the first quarter of the third century B.C. and had a good opportunity to observe the Greeks who had settled in the new capital of Ptolemaic Egypt. This stay inspired a few realistic poems about daily life in the great city. They are numbered among Theocritus' *Idylls,* though they are not "idyllic" at all; the Greek word *eidyllion* originally meant "short text," but because Theocritus was chiefly known as a pastoral poet, the name attached itself to the genre and, by extension, to most of Theocritus' poems that have come down to us. This particular poem is more like a mime, and its dramatic form (one long monologue) made it ideal for recitation. The monologue of Simaetha is dramatic in character (though it was probably not delivered on a stage), with another character, her maid, Thestylis, present and the ingredients she mentions ready at hand. The imagination of the audience had to supply all this. It was a special art (like that of the mime today, but using the words of a poet) to make the audience actually see everything as the story was told.

Theocritus may not have been a believer in magic himself, but he must have been familiar with magical practices, for almost every detail he mentions can be documented from the magical papyri and other sources. The ceremony he describes dramatizes Simaetha's passion for the handsome young athlete, Delphis, who treats her rather coolly. Simaetha's love is so overpowering that she would literally do anything to get Delphis back; and if she cannot have him, she threatens to harm him—like Dido in the *Aeneid* [*no. 11*].

Theocritus, *Idylls* 2

[*Simaetha is speaking.*]

Where are the bay leaves? Bring them, Thestylis! Where is the love magic? Tie a thread of fine purple wool around the bowl that I may bind with a spell my lover who is so cruel to me. For eleven days he has not visited me, alas, and does not even know whether I am alive or dead; nor did he—heartless as he is—knock at my door. Of course, Eros and Aphrodite have carried his fickle heart elsewhere. Tomorrow I will go to Timagetus' wrestling school and reproach him for the way he treats me. But now I will bind him with fire magic. Shine brightly, Moon; I will softly chant to you, Goddess, and to Hecate in the underworld—the dogs shiver before her when she comes over the graves of the dead and the dark blood. Hail, grim Hecate, and stay with me to the end; make these drugs as powerful as those of Circe and Medea and golden-haired Perimede.

Draw to my house my lover, magic wheel.

First, barley groats must cook on the fire. Throw them on, Thestylis! Idiot, where are you with your thoughts? Has it come to the point that even you make fun of me, scamp? Throw them on and say at the same time: "I throw on Delphis' bones."

Draw to my house my lover, magic wheel.

Delphis brought me trouble, and for Delphis I burn this bay leaf. As it crackles in the flames with a sharp noise and suddenly catches fire and we don't even see its ash, so may Delphis' flesh melt in the flame.

Draw to my house my lover, magic wheel.

Now I shall burn the husks of corn. Artemis, you have the power to move even the steel in Hades or anything else that is hard to move. . . . Thestylis, the dogs are howling around the town: the Goddess is at the crossroads. Quick, bang the gong!

Draw to my house my lover, magic wheel.

Look, the sea is still and the winds are still, but never stilled is the pain deep in my heart; I am all on fire for the man who made me a wretched, useless thing, who took my maidenhood but did not marry me.

Draw to my house my lover, magic wheel.

As I melt, with the goddess's help, this wax, so may Delphis of Myndus waste at once from love. And as this bronze rhombus whirls by the power of Aphrodite, so may he whirl about my door.

Draw to my house my lover, magic wheel.

Three times I pour a libation, mighty Goddess, and three times do I cry: "Whether it is a woman who lies with him now or a man, may he forget them as clean as Theseus once in Dia, they say, forgot Ariadne with the lovely locks."

Draw to my house my lover, magic wheel.

Coltsfoot is an Arcadian herb, and because of it, all the fillies and the swift mares run madly over the hills. May I see Delphis in such a state, coming to this house like a madman from the bright wrestling school.

Draw to my house my lover, magic wheel.

Delphis lost this fringe from his coat: I now shred it and cast it into the wild flames. Ah, cruel Love, why do you cling to me like a leech from the swamps and drain all the dark blood from my body?

Draw to my house my lover, magic wheel.

I shall crush a lizard and bring him an evil drink tomorrow. But now, Thestylis, please take these magic herbs and smear them on his threshold while it is still night, and whispering say: "I smear the bones of Delphis."

Draw to my house my lover, magic wheel.

Now that I am alone, how can I lament my love? Where shall I begin? Who brought this curse upon me? Eubulus' daughter, my friend Anaxo, went as a basket-bearer to the grove of Artemis, in whose honor on that day many wild animals, among others a lioness, were led around in the procession.

Tell me, Moon Goddess, how my love began.

Theumaridas' Thracian nurse—kind soul—who used to live next door, begged me and urged me to see the procession, and I, poor wretch, went with her in a nice long linen dress and Clearista's wrap over it.

Tell me, Moon Goddess, how my love began.

I was halfway down the road, near Lycon's place, when I saw them walking together, Delphis and Eudamippus. Their beards were more golden than helichryse and their breasts much shinier than you, Selene; for they came directly from their athletic workout at the gymnasium.

Tell me, Moon Goddess, how my love began.

One look, and I lost my mind, and my poor heart was aflame. My beauty faded. I was no longer interested in the procession, and I have no idea how I got home, but a dry fever shook me, and I was in bed ten days and ten nights.

Tell me, Moon Goddess, how my love began.

Sometimes my complexion would be like fustic, and all the hair on my head fell out, and all that was left of me were skin and bones. Whose place did I not visit? Did I skip the house of any old woman who knows magic songs? But it was a serious case, and time went by so fast.

Tell me, Moon Goddess, how my love began.

So I told my maid the true story: "Please, Thestylis, find me some remedy for this bad disease. The man from Myndus possesses me completely; it is terrible. Go to Timagetus' wrestling school and keep watch, for there he goes and there he likes to sit."

Tell me, Moon Goddess, how my love began.

"And when you are sure that he is alone, give him a quiet nod and tell him: 'Simaetha invites you' and lead him here." This is what I said. She went and brought smooth-skinned Delphis to my house. When I saw him stepping lightly across the threshold of my door—

Tell me, Moon Goddess, how my love began—

I felt chillier than snow all over, and from my forehead the sweat ran damp like dew, and I was unable to make a sound, not even as much as a baby whimpers in his sleep to his dear mother. My beautiful body went stiff all over like a doll's.

Tell me, Moon Goddess, how my love began.

My faithless lover looked at me and then fixed his eyes on the ground, sat down on a couch and said: "Really, Simaetha, your invitation beat my coming to you by no more than I recently beat charming Philinus in a race."

Tell me, Moon Goddess, how my love began.

"I would have come, I swear it by sweet Eros, with two or three friends, in the evening, carrying in my pocket apples of Dionysus and on my head white poplar leaves, the holy plant of Heracles, twined all around with crimson bands."

Tell me, Moon Goddess, how my love began.

"If you had let me in, that would have been very nice, for I am considered agile and handsome among young men, and if you had only let me kiss your lovely lips, I could have slept. But if you had pushed me out and barred the door, then, believe me, axes and torches would have marched up against you."

Tell me, Moon Goddess, how my love began.

"But now I must first say thanks to Cypris and after Cypris to you, lady, because you have rescued me from the fire, already half-burned, by inviting me to this house. You know, Eros sometimes kindles a hotter blaze than Hephaestus on Lipara."

Tell me, Moon Goddess, how my love began.

"With dangerous madness Eros scares a maiden from her bedroom and makes a young bride leave her husband's bed when it is still warm."

This he said, and I—so easily persuaded—took him by the hand and drew him down on the soft couch. Body quickly warmed to body, and cheeks burned hotter than before, and we whispered sweetly to each

other. To make a long story short, dear Moon Goddess, our main purpose was achieved, and both of us came to our desire. He found no fault
with me till yesterday, nor I with him. But today, when the horses of rosy
Dawn ran up the sky, bringing her out of the Ocean, the mother of
Philista, our flute player, and of Melixo came to see me. She said among
many other things that Delphis was in love, and she did not know for sure
whether it was love for a woman or a man, only this: he constantly called
for unmixed wine, and his toast was "To Love!" and finally he left in a
hurry, saying that he must decorate that house with garlands. This is the
story my visitor told me, and she is no liar. For I swear he used to come
three or four times a day, and often he would leave his Dorian oil flask
with me. But now it has been eleven days that I have not seen him. Does
this not mean that he has found other delights and has forgotten me?

Now I will bind him with my love magic, but if he still causes me pain,
he shall beat on the gate of Hades, such evil drugs, I swear, I keep for him
in my box; it is something, Goddess, that I have learned from an Assyrian
stranger.

But farewell, Queen! Be happy and turn your horses toward the Ocean.
I shall bear my desire as I have endured it till now. Farewell, Selene, on
your shining throne! Farewell, all you other stars that follow the chariot of
silent Night.

7

The following Roman spells can be roughly ascribed to three different
periods: the first is from the second century B.C., the second is from the
first century B.C., and the third is somewhat later (the time of Marcellus
Empiricus?). Nevertheless, they are very similar, and they show that this
kind of folk medicine was old and did not change much over the centuries. Cato the Elder (who distrusted doctors) takes us back to a time
when the owner of an estate was an authority on everything and, if an
accident happened, had to administer some kind of first aid. The symbolism of the split reed and the iron is fairly obvious, and the impressive
mumbo-jumbo of pseudo-Latin also fulfilled its purpose. The daily recitation of the second formula made it necessary for the owner to visit the
patient every day. Clearly this magic had some kind of rational basis.

Varro's formula is more "magical" because it involves a superior power
—the "you" that is mentioned. It also uses the concepts of analogy and
transmission: the feet that touch the earth communicate their pain to the
earth. Spittle is often used in healing, and to be sober during a religious or
magical ritual is a form of ascetic discipline.

This last point is also stressed by Marcellus in the third spell (if he actually wrote it). The real Marcellus, as the title of the text shows, was a professional physician. The spell is like a form: one has to fill in the appropriate words ("swelling in tonsils"). Here the magical gesture is as important as the words spoken. The language is obscure toward the end, but this is no doubt intentional. *Religio* evidently means "spell" in this context.

A: Cato, *On Agriculture,* par. 160

If something is out of joint, it can be set by the following spell: Take a green reed, four or five feet long, split it in the middle, and let two men hold it to their hips. Begin to recite the following formula: *moetas vaeta daries dardaries astataries dissunapiter,* until the parts come together. Put a knife on top of it. When the two parts have come together and touch each other, grip them with your hand, make a cut left and right [on the reed?], tie it onto the dislocation or the fracture, and it will heal. But you must recite every day for the dislocation [the formula] *haut haut haut istasis tarsis tardannabou dannaustra.*

B: Varro, *On Agriculture* 1.2.27

Stolo smiled and said: "I will use the same words that he wrote down—or rather, the ones I heard from Tarquenna: whenever someone begins to feel pain in his feet, you can heal him when you think of him. [Say:] 'I think of you; heal my feet; let the earth retain the illness; let health remain here, in my feet.' He prescribes to recite this twenty-seven times, to touch the earth, and spit. Must be recited sober."

C: [Marcellus Empiricus?] *De Medicamentis* 15.11 (= 113.25 Niedermann)

To be recited when sober, touching the relevant part of the body with three fingers: thumb, middle finger, and ring finger; the other two are stretched out. Say: "Go away, no matter whether you were born today or earlier, created today or earlier: this disease, this illness, this pain, this swelling, this redness, this goiter, these tonsils, this abscess, this tumor, these glands and the little glands, you call forth, I lead forth, I speak forth, through this spell, from these limbs and bones."

8

In his *Epodes* (the title can be translated as "incantations") Horace describes a fantastic human sacrifice performed by witches. The victim is a boy whom the witches have kidnapped. In an ordinary sacrifice, the liver was considered an important organ because it gave clues to the future; in this case the witches want to use the boy's liver in a love potion they are planning to prepare. The boy, realizing the fate that awaits him, first pleads with the witches and, when this has no effect, curses them. His curse is an act of black magic in itself. In it, the boy distinguishes between right and wrong on the one hand and human fate on the other. The witches then commit the criminal act of killing an innocent child, and they seem to get away with it—that is, they escape the arm of worldly justice—but sooner or later they will be punished for their vicious deed.

Scholars have wondered why Horace in this piece and in the next [*no. 9*] makes such an effort to paint witchcraft as loathsome and despicable. He seems to hate Canidia (who appears here and there in his poems) with a passion, almost as if he had loved her once. The answer may be that Augustus (whose ideas Virgil and Horace often translated into poetry) was planning drastic legislation to stamp out witchcraft in the Roman Empire and that, through Maecenas, he enlisted the aid of two great poets of his age, Virgil and Horace. Little is known about the legislation itself, but it seems to have been in effect over the following centuries and to have served as the government's main tool in prosecuting the occult sciences.

Horace, *Epodes* 5

[*The kidnapped boy speaks.*]

"By all the gods in heaven who rule over the earth and mankind, what does this tumult mean? What is the meaning of the fierce looks of all these women, fixed on me? I implore you by your children—if you really ever gave birth to any, assisted by Lucina, whom you called—I beg you by this useless purple ornament of mine and by Jupiter, who must disapprove of all this, why do you stare at me like a stepmother or a wild beast wounded by a spear?"

The boy made these complaints with a trembling voice. He stood there, his badge having been taken away from him. His childish body would have softened the cruel heart of a Thracian. But Canidia, small vipers braided in her hair on her unkempt head, ordered wild fig trees torn from graves, funeral cypresses and eggs smeared with the blood of a loathsome toad and the feathers of a screech owl that flies by night, the herbs which Iolcus and Hiberia, rich in poisons, send, and bones snatched from the mouth of a hungry bitch, all to be burned in Colchian flames.

Sagana, her robes tucked up, sprinkled water from Avernus throughout the house. Her rough hair bristled like a sea urchin or a running boar. Veia, totally unscrupulous, was digging up the floor with a solid spade, groaning as she labored. They wanted to bury the boy in such a way that only his face would stick out, like that of a swimmer who seems suspended on the water by his chin. Then they would slowly torment him to death by making him look at food that was changed twice or three times a day. Finally, when his eyes, fixed on the food denied to him, dimmed, they intended to cut out his marrow and his parched liver to make a love potion.

In Naples, where people have time to gossip, and in all the neighboring towns, it was believed that Folia from Rimini, known for her masculine lust, was there too. She can force down the stars and the moon from heaven by singing magic songs from Thessaly.

At this point savage Canidia began to gnaw her uncut thumb nail with her yellow teeth. What did she say? What did she not say?

"Night! Diana, who rules over silence when secret rites are performed! You are the faithful witnesses of my doings. Now is the time to help me. Now you must turn your wrath and your divine power against the house of my enemy. Now that the wild beasts, relaxed in sweet slumber, hide in the fearful forests, let the dogs of the Subura bark at the aging playboy, drenched with a perfume more perfect than my hands ever made! Let everybody laugh at this. But what happened? Why are the horrible drugs of barbarian Medea not as powerful as they once were? She used them to take revenge on her husband's arrogant mistress, the daughter of great Creon—and got away! A robe she sent as a gift, saturated with poison, took off the young bride in a blaze of fire. And yet I have not missed any herb or root growing in a rough spot. Does he sleep [reading *an dormit* with D. R. Shackleton Bailey for *indormit*] in the perfumed bedroom of every harlot, without a thought of me? Ah! Ah! he moves around, protected from me by the song of a witch who knows more than I do.

"Varus! You are about to shed many tears, and you will hurry back to me, drawn by extraordinary drugs, and even the recitation of Marsian spells will not help you recover your sanity. You scorn me, but I will prepare a more potent drug; I will pour you a more potent drink. As surely as the sky will never drop below the sea and the earth never float above, as surely must you burn with passionate love for me like pitch in sooty flames!"

When he heard this, the boy no longer tried, as he had before, to appease the ruthless hags with gentle words. Though he did not know what to say, he broke the silence and poured out a malediction worthy of Thyestes:

"Magic drugs cannot [reading *maga non* with M. Haupt] upset right and wrong; they cannot upset human destiny. I shall pursue you with curses: a deadly curse cannot be undone by any sacrificial victim. So I am doomed to die. But when I have breathed my last I shall haunt you as a terrifying appearance in the night; I shall, as a ghost, attack your faces with hooked talons, for such is the power of the divine Manes. Crouched on your anguished hearts I shall terrorize you and rob you of your sleep. In every quarter of the city a crowd will gather, throw stones at you, and crush you, you filthy old hags. Your unburied limbs will then be scattered by the wolves and the vultures that live on the Esquiline. I hope that my parents, who must, alas! survive me, will not miss that show."

9

Horace's other witchcraft piece is funnier, less frightening. Here the god Priapus delivers a monologue, telling us what happened one night as he was guarding the new park established on the Esquiline. Because the park had once been a cemetery for the poorest of the poor, witches still frequented it to dig for bones and herbs and to conjure up the souls of the dead. They also performed some black magic on the spot. Priapus is so anguished and disgusted that he has to interrupt the goings-on.

In this text the witches are made to look ridiculous and pathetic. Because a minor god like Priapus can chase them away, the power they claim for themselves cannot be real.

Horace, *Satires* 1.8

[*The statue of Priapus is speaking.*]

Once I was the trunk of a fig tree, a useless piece of wood. A craftsman, not sure whether he would make a bench or a Priapus, decided that it was to be the god. So I am a god, a holy terror to thieves and birds: my hand and the red shaft that sticks out indecently from my crotch threaten the thieves; the bundle of reeds planted on my head frightens the birds—they are a nuisance!—and forbids them to settle in what is now a park. Once the bodies of slaves, thrown out of their narrow cells, were carried here in cheap coffins by their fellow slaves to be buried. This place served as a common grave for the poorest of the poor. Here a tombstone gave to that clown Pantolabus and to Nomentanus, the big spender, "A thousand feet in front, three hundred deep" and announced, "This plot does not go to the heirs." Now the air is clean on the Esquiline, and people can live here and go for walks on the sunny embankment where not so long ago they found it depressing to look at a field disgraced by white bones. But I have to worry and watch out not so much for the thieves and the wild animals that are accustomed to haunting this place as for women who work on the minds of men with magic songs and potions. There is no way in which I can wipe them out or, once the wandering moon has shown her graceful face, keep them from gathering bones and poisonous herbs.

With my own eyes I have seen Canidia walk barefoot, her black dress tucked up over her knees, hair undone. She and her older companion, Sagana, were howling. Their pale faces made them horrible to look at. They began to dig up the earth with their fingernails and to tear a black lamb to pieces. The blood ran into a ditch, to summon up the souls of the dead and make them answer questions. They had two dolls—one of wax, the other, larger one of wool; [the wool one] was meant to punish the smaller, waxen one, which stood submissive like a slave about to be put to death. One of the witches called "Hecate!" the other "Dreadful Tisiphone!" You could see serpents sliding, hell hounds running. The Moon blushed because she refused to be witness to all this and hid behind some large monuments. If I tell not the whole truth, let white turds of crows disgrace my head, and let Ulius and frail Pediatia and that thief Voranus come to piss and shit on me!

Must I go on and on and tell how the ghosts—they sounded shrill, desolate—carried on a conversation with Sagana, how the witches furtively buried a wolf's beard together with teeth from a spotted snake, how the wax doll blazed with larger flames, how horrible it was for me to witness the things that those two Furies said and did? But revenge was near: I made a fart that split my figwood buttocks; it sounded like a pig's bladder exploding. They ran back to town: Canidia lost her teeth, Sagana her pompous wig, and they dropped their herbs and magic bracelets. What a joke! You would have laughed, had you seen it.

10

Virgil's eighth eclogue ("pastoral poem") is an adaptation of Theocritus' second idyll [*no. 6*]. Written more than two hundred years after Theocritus' poem, it stays very close to the original story line in many details. Most of the magical ingredients are the same, though the bull-roarer and the magical wheel are replaced by two dolls, one made of clay, the other of wax. Virgil also introduces the werewolf theme: Moeris, a local warlock who has sold Simaetha some powerful herbs, is a werewolf. Virgil leaves out the whole love story that Simaetha tells in Theocritus' idyll, but he adds a happy ending: the magic works, and Daphnis comes back. The skillful use of the refrain (suggesting magical chants that are repeated over and over again) is another technique Virgil has learned from Theocritus. Poems like these are realistic and accurate in the details they represent, but they are not meant to be factual reports of a real ceremony. Rather, they create an atmosphere that makes the reader feel the meaning of the goings-on. In this sense, poetry is a kind of magic in itself: the Latin word *carmen* means "poem" as well as "magical chant."

Virgil, *Eclogues* 8.64–109

Bring water, tie a soft fillet around this altar, and burn on it fresh twigs and male frankincense that I may succeed in turning my lover from sanity to madness by magic rites: all we need now is songs.

Draw home from the city, my songs, draw Daphnis home.

Songs can even draw the Moon from heaven; by songs Circe transformed Odysseus' men; by singing the cold snake in the meadow bursts.

Draw home from the city, my songs, draw Daphnis home.

To begin with, I shall twine around you three strands composed of three threads, each of a different color, and three times I shall carry your image around the altar; the divinity likes the odd number.

Draw home from the city, my songs, draw Daphnis home.

Tie the three colors with three knots, Amaryllis; please, tie them and say: "I tie the bonds of Venus."

Draw home from the city, my songs, draw Daphnis home.

As this clay gets hard and as this wax gets soft in one and the same fire, so may Daphnis from love of me. Sprinkle salted barley meal and kindle the fragile laurel twigs with pitch. Cruel Daphnis makes me burn: I burn this laurel for Daphnis.

Draw home from the city, my songs, draw Daphnis home.

With love possessed is the heifer that has been searching for the young steer through the woods and the tall groves and sinks, weary and lost, in the green rushes near a water bank and never thinks of going away when the night falls: may such love possess Daphnis, and may I not care to heal him.

Draw home from the city, my songs, draw Daphnis home.

My faithless lover once left behind these clothes, dear pledges of himself. Earth, I now commit them to you, right under the threshold: these pledges must bring Daphnis back to me.

Draw home from the city, my songs, draw Daphnis home.

Moeris himself gave me these herbs and poisons gathered near the Black Sea (they grow in abundance near the Black Sea). I have often seen Moeris turn into a wolf by their power and hide in the forest, and often seen him conjure up souls from the depth of their tombs and move to other fields the crops that had been sown.

Draw home from the city, my songs, draw Daphnis home.

Bring ashes, Amaryllis, and throw them over your head into the running brook, and don't look back! With these will I attack Daphnis; he cares nothing for gods, nothing for songs.

Draw home from the city, my songs, draw Daphnis home.

"Look: the embers on the altar have caught, all by themselves, with a flickering flame while I was slow to fetch them. Let this be a good sign!"

It must mean something . . . and Hylax is barking in the doorway! May we believe it? Or do lovers make up dreams for themselves?

Spare him, my songs! Daphnis is coming from the city! Spare him, my songs!

I I

In his *Aeneid,* Virgil returns once more to the theme of love magic and its potential transformation into black magic. Simaetha in Theocritus' second idyll threatens to hurt her unfaithful lover; the woman in Virgil's eighth eclogue hints at this possibility. Dido in Book 4 of the *Aeneid* actually curses Aeneas, because she realizes that love magic will not work, and then she kills herself.

Dido, once she is deserted by Aeneas, is the victim of different emotions: hate and love, frustration, shame, and anger. The conflict between these feelings is so strong that Dido goes into a deep depression, as we would say, and resolves to take her own life. To mask the preparations for her suicide she stages an elaborate magical ceremony under the supervision of a famous priestess who is also a powerful witch. As a great and noble queen she is opposed to magic, but in this situation she is willing to give it a try.

Although the magic is intended at least partly for show, most ancient readers of this passage would have felt that it worked. Dido's curse does not harm Aeneas himself, for like Odysseus, he has powerful divine protectors, and he has not left her frivolously, but because he had a mission. The curse comes true many generations later, when the descendants of Aeneas, the Romans, become involved in three murderous wars against the Carthaginians, and Dido's "avenger"—none other than Hannibal—comes very close to total victory.

Dido's self-sacrifice has a magical meaning. By killing herself, she releases her own spirit and turns it into a daemon of revenge, thus lending additional emphasis to her curse. In ancient times, everyone was thought to have special powers at the moment of death, and the souls of those who died before their time or died a violent death (Dido fits into both categories) were especially suitable for black magic.

Virgil has created a magnificent scene in which magic is only one element. The psychological portrait of Dido in her despair is drawn with great understanding, and the reader, though he may be shocked by her thirst for revenge, nevertheless feels compassion for the unfortunate queen.

Virgil, *Aeneid* 4.450–705

At this point poor Dido, frightened by her fate, prayed for death. She could no longer stand the sight of the arch of heaven, and she saw something that made her even more anxious to carry out her plan and leave the light: when she placed offerings on the altars on which incense was burning, she saw—horrible to say—that the sacred milk turned black and that the wine she had poured turned into ghastly blood. She told no one what she had seen, not even her sister.

There was also in the palace a marble shrine of her former husband which she tended with very special reverence; it was decorated with snow-white fur and festive leaves. Now she thought she heard a voice coming from its inside—the words of her husband, who was calling her. It was the time when dark night covered the earth, and only the screech owls on the rooftops delivered their funeral laments, again and again, drawing out the mournful notes.

Moreover, many predictions of ancient prophets terrified her with their sinister meaning.

In her dreams she was pursued by cruel Aeneas himself, rushing madly after her. Constantly she dreamed of being left by herself, of going without companions on a long trip, seeking the people of Tyrus in a desert land, just as Pentheus, driven out of his mind, sees the swarm of the Eumenides and a double sun and a double vision of Thebes, or as Orestes, the true son of his father, Agamemnon, is driven across the stage, fleeing before his mother, who is armed with torches and black snakes; and the Avenging Furies crouch on the doorstep.

Thus, overwhelmed by grief, she conceived a mad scheme and decided to die. She worked out by herself the time and the method. She approached her sister, who was sad, and talked to her; her face did not betray her plan, and the way she looked even left room for hope:

"Dear sister, I have found a way—wish me luck—that will either bring Aeneas back to me or help me get rid of my love for him. Near the far end of the Ocean, where the sun sets, at the limits of Ethiopia, is a place where Atlas, the giant, turns on his shoulders the axle that is fitted to the sphere of the burning stars. A priestess of the Massylians who lives there has been recommended to me: she is the custodian of the temple of the Hesperides, and she used to bring the dragon his food and guard the sacred boughs on the tree, sprinkling liquid honey and sleep-inducing poppy seed. She guarantees that she can relax with her incantations all those she wishes to, but she also threatens to inflict harsh pains on others. She says that she can stop the flowing of a river and turn the course of the stars around. She conjures up ghosts by night. You might hear the earth roar under her feet and see ash trees marching down from the mountains. I swear by the gods, my dear, and I take you as a witness, darling, that I hate to get involved in magic arts. Please raise secretly a pyre in the inner courtyard, under the open sky, and place upon it the weapons of my lover which he left hanging in my bedroom—how faithless he is! Put all his clothes on top and our conjugal bed, which has been death for me. It is very important to wipe out all traces of that horrible man, says the priestess."

She fell silent. Her face turned pale. And yet Anna could not believe that her sister would conceal her death under strange rites, nor could she understand such a fantastic scheme, nor did she fear anything more serious than what had happened at the time of Sychaeus' death. So she arranged everything as she was told.

When the huge pyre was constructed of piled faggots and cleft ilex in the innermost part of the palace, under the open sky, the queen hung the place with garlands and funeral wreaths. On top she placed Aeneas' clothes, the sword he had left behind, and, on a bed, his image. She knew very well what would happen. Altars were all around. The priestess, her hair undone, called three times with a thundering voice the gods, the Erebus, the Chaos, Hecate with her three heads, and the three faces of the virgin goddess Diana. She sprinkled water that was supposed to have come from the springs of Avernus. Potent herbs with the milk of black poison that had been cut with bronze sickles by moonlight were obtained. They also obtained the love magic torn from the forehead of a filly at birth before the mother could snatch it.

Dido herself, the holy cake in her pure hands, stood near the altars, one of her feet bare, her robes flowing loose. In the hour of her death she called on the gods and the stars that knew her fate. She also prayed to any just and mindful divinity that might care for abandoned lovers.

Night fell. Weary creatures enjoyed restful sleep all over the earth. The woods and the cruel sea were at rest. It was the time when the stars are halfway in their gliding course, when all the fields are silent and the beasts and colorful birds that live on smooth lakes or in thorny thickets all rest peacefully under the silent night, forgetting their burdens. But not so the Phoenician lady in her distress: she never relaxed in sleep or drew the night into her eyes or her heart. Her pain grew twice as intense, her frantic love swelled once again, and she was tossed up by a high wave of anger.

She began to express the various feelings that stirred in her heart:

"What shall I do? Shall I try my luck with my former suitors and risk being laughed at? Shall I humbly beg to become the wife of one of the Nomad chiefs whom I have rejected so many times as husbands? Well, perhaps I ought to follow the fleet of the Trojans and obey their most outrageous orders? They, of course, are happy that I, at one time, gave them help and assistance, and the memory of the favor I once did them is no doubt still fresh in their minds. But even if I wanted to do this, who would want me? Would they let a hateful woman—arrogant as they are— travel on their ships? Ah, you fool, you still don't know, you still don't understand the treachery of the descendants of Laomedon! And then? Shall I alone, an exile, follow the cheering sailors? Or shall I join them, surrounded by the men of Tyrus and my whole army, and order my people to set the sails to the winds, forcing them to cross the sea once more? It was hard enough for me to uproot them from their former city, Sidon. No. Die as you deserve, and let the sword end your pain. Sister, you started it all. I was mad, but you gave in to my tears, burdened me with all this misery, and cast me before an enemy. Why was it not possible to live, the way animals do, a blameless life, without getting married again and without getting involved in such distress? I have not kept the faith that I promised to the ashes of Sychaeus."

These were the heavy laments that burst out from her heart.

[*In the meantime the god Mercury appears to Aeneas in a dream, warns him of Dido's wrath and her thoughts of revenge, and urges him to sail at once. Aeneas obeys the divine order.*]

Dawn left the saffron-colored bed of Tithonus and spread her early morning radiance over the earth. From her watchtower the queen saw the early light turn white and Aeneas' ships depart with their sails squared to the wind. She noticed that the harbor was empty, not an oarsman left. Three, four times she struck her lovely breasts and tore her golden hair and cried:

"God! He is leaving! A foreigner may mock my kingdom? Will no-body fetch arms? Won't my men from all over the city pursue him? Won't they drag their ships out of the dockyards? Let's go! Hurry! Carry torches, hand out missiles, pull on the oars! But what am I talking about? Where am I? What madness transforms my mind? Poor Dido, have you finally realized what crime has been committed? You should have realized it earlier, when you offered him your kingdom! There is faith and loyalty for you! And they say he took his household gods with him and carried his old weary father on his shoulders! Why could I not tear his limbs apart and throw them into the sea? Why not kill his companions, why not kill his son Ascanius and serve him as food for his father's meal? The outcome of the fight would have been doubtful. All right, but whom was I to fear, since die I must? I should have thrown firebrands into his camp, heaped flames on his decks, destroyed father and son and the whole race, and flung myself on top of everything! Sun god, you let your flames shine

over all the works of the world! Juno, you know my sorrows and understand them! Hecate, they howl at you in the night at the crossroads in the
cities! Avenging Furies! Gods of dying Elissa! Listen to me! Turn your
power to my misfortune: it deserves your attention! Listen to my prayers!
If it is preordained that this hateful man must reach a harbor and may land
somewhere, if Jupiter's fates demand this, then let it happen. But let him
be harassed in a war against a fierce, aggressive nation! Let him be driven
homeless from his country! Let him be torn from the embrace of Iulus!
Let him beg for help! Let him see the tragic deaths of his people! And
once he has yielded to the harsh terms of a peace treaty, may he not enjoy
his kingdom and a pleasant life! May he die before his time and lie
unburied somewhere in the sand! This I pray. These are my last words,
poured out with my blood. But then, men of Tyrus, you must pursue his
race and all his descendants with your hatred. This sacrifice you must
offer to my ashes. Let there be no friendship, no treaties between our
peoples! Avenger, whoever you are, arise from my bones! Attack the
Trojan settlers with the torch and the sword! Do it whenever an opportunity makes you strong! I pray: let shores fight against shores, sea against
sea, arms against arms! Let this and future generations carry on the war!"

These were her words. Her thoughts moved in various directions. She
wanted to end as soon as possible the life she hated. Briefly she spoke to
Barce, Sychaeus' old nurse, for her own nurse was buried, a heap of black
ashes, in the old country: "Dear nurse, please go and bring me my sister
Anna. Tell her to quickly sprinkle river water over herself and bring along
the animals, the sacrificial offerings I mentioned. Yes, let her come. And
you must cover your head with a pure fillet. I am determined to go
through with the sacrifice to the god of the underworld that I prepared
and began in the ritual manner. I want to end my sorrows and hand over
to the flames the pyre of the Trojan leader."

This she said. The old woman ran eagerly as fast as she could. Dido,
trembling and almost overcome by her enormous endeavor, staring out
of bloodshot eyes, with spots here and there on her quivering cheeks that
were marked already with the pallor of impending death, burst into the
innermost courtyard of the palace and in a state of madness climbed up
the pyre, pulling out the Trojan sword, a gift not meant for such use. At
this moment she saw the clothes of the Trojan and the familiar bed. She
paused for a while to think and weep, then sank on the bed and spoke her
very last words:

"Clothes, you were dear to me while fate and the gods allowed it.
Now take my soul and deliver me from my distress. I have lived long
enough to finish the course that Fortune gave me. I will go now, a
majestic shade, underground. I have built a splendid city, seen my ram-

parts rise; I have punished my wicked brother to avenge my husband; and I would have been happy, oh, too happy! if only the Trojan ships had never come near our shore."

She buried her face in the pillows and cried: "I shall die unavenged, but die I must. Yes! Yes! I want to go into the darkness. May the cruel man from Troy enjoy the sight of this fire, and may he carry away my death as an evil foreboding!"

Still speaking, she collapsed; she had stabbed herself. The attendants saw it, saw the sword foaming with blood, her hands splattered. Their cries went up to the palace roof. The news spread wildly through the city. The whole palace trembled with the laments, the sobbing and howling of the women, and the echo of the loud wailing resounded from heaven. It seemed as if Carthage or ancient Tyrus had fallen from an enemy attack, wild flames rushing across the tops of houses and temples.

Dido's sister heard it. She almost fainted from the shock but ran hysterically through the crowd, goring her face with her nails and beating her breasts and calling her dying sister:

"Dido! What is this, dearest? Did you want to trick me when you called me? Is this—oh, no!—what your pyre, your fire, your altars meant? You have left me. How can I say what I feel? You died and would not let your sister join you? But you should have called me to share your death! The same pain inflicted by the sword, the same hour would have carried both of us away. Did I build the pyre with my own hands and call on the gods of our fathers—to be left out when you lay down, cruel sister? You have destroyed yourself and me, the people of Sidon, its leaders, and your city! Bring water: I want to wash her wounds and catch with my lips her last breath if it still lingers."

She climbed up the high steps, embraced and caressed her dying sister, and, sobbing, dried the dark blood with her robes. Dido tried to open her heavy eyes, but her strength failed her; a hissing came from the deep wound in her breast. Three times she tried to raise herself on her elbow; three times she fell back on the bed. With wandering eyes she searched for the light in the sky, and when she found it, she moaned.

Great Juno felt sorry for her drawn-out suffering and painful death and sent Iris down from Olympus to free her struggling soul from the body to which it clung. Since she was dying neither by fate nor by a death she deserved, but before her day, poor woman, and fired by sudden madness, Proserpina had not yet taken from her head the blond lock nor handed her over to Orcus below. So Iris, covered with dew, flew down through the sky on crocus-colored wings, displaying in the sunlight a thousand different colors. She stood near Dido's head and spoke: "I take this lock, as I was told to do, as an offering to Dis, and I release you from this body."

She cut off the lock. All at once the warmth drained from Dido's body, and her life vanished into the air.

12

The story of Heracles' death through a kind of love magic has been dramatized by Sophocles in *The Women of Trachis* and by Seneca (if he was the author) in *Heracles on Mount Oeta*. The myth itself embodies the ancient belief that certain drugs can kill even if they are absorbed by the skin rather than ingested. Heracles' wife, Deianira, was carried across a river by the Centaur Nessus. When he tried to make love to her in midstream, Heracles shot him from the other side with his poisoned arrows. The dying Centaur persuaded Deianira to preserve some of his blood, telling her it was a potent love charm, to be used whenever she felt that Heracles was unfaithful to her. This happens; she impregnates a new garment with the Centaur's poisonous blood and sends it to her husband, who then dies a slow and painful death. According to one version, he cannot die and has to burn himself alive on a gigantic pyre constructed on Mount Oeta. Perhaps Virgil had this scene in mind when he described Dido's suicide; both Dido and Heracles were victims of love.

Although the myth reflects magical concepts, Seneca (unlike Sophocles) has stressed this by making Deianira's nurse—that is, her confidante —a witch. But even her powers are not sufficient to restore Heracles' love, and in the end Deianira has to resort to the dead Centaur's deadly magic.

Seneca (?), Heracles on Mount Oeta, vv. 449–72

[*Deianira wants to regain Heracles' love.*]

DEIANIRA'S OLD NURSE: Has your love for illustrious Heracles vanished?

DEIANIRA: No, it has not vanished, nurse: it remains with me and sits deeply, firmly in my heart, believe me. But angry love hurts very much.

NURSE: It often happens that wives pull their marriage together by magic arts and prayers. I once ordered a landscape to bloom in the middle of winter; I have stopped a thunderbolt in its flight; I have shaken the sea, though there was no wind, and smoothed the stormy ocean. The dry earth opened up in fresh springs; rocks began to move; doors were forced open by me. Shades stood still; the Manes spoke; the hound of hell fell silent; for my prayers are an order. The sea, the earth, the sky, and Tartarus obey me. Midnight saw the sun, and the day saw night. When I begin my chants the laws of nature lose their power. Let me change his mood: my songs will find a way.

DEIANIRA: Do you want me to gather the poisonous herbs that grow beside the Black Sea or on high Pindus in Thessaly to break his will? Sooner will the moon desert the stars and come down to earth, forced by a magic song; sooner will the winter solstice see a harvest; sooner will a fast thunderbolt be stopped by an incantation; sooner will everything be turned upside down; sooner will noon be bright with all the gathered stars: but he alone will never change.

13

In his tragedy *Medea*, Seneca presents the heroine as a witch whose power has no limits. These two scenes are typical. In the first one she invokes various deities in order to curse her enemies. Like Deianira, like Dido, she feels abandoned and betrayed by the man she loved, and she is determined to hurt him as deeply as she can. What distinguishes her from Deianira and Dido is the fact that she is a professional witch, not just an amateur, and she knows exactly what she is doing.

The second passage probably inspired Lucan's necromantic scene. In it Medea invokes the powers of the underworld while she cooks in her cauldron all kinds of magical herbs.

Much of both scenes is sheer rhetoric, designed to create a mood. To us it is just one tedious detail after another, but contemporary audiences probably experienced the kind of frisson that one gets nowadays from horror movies. It is not great literature, perhaps, but it catered to a need. It dramatized aspects of the old myths that had not been shown before.

A: Seneca, *Medea*, vv. 6–26

[Medea invokes various gods to curse her enemies.]

MEDEA: . . . and Hecate with the three bodies! You offer your light, which knows the secret rites. Gods by whom Jason made his vows to me! Gods to whom Medea must pray in particular: Chaos of eternal night! Realms remote from the heavenly gods! Shades of the sinners! Ruler of the gloomy kingdom! Queen whom he abducted but kept more faithfully than Jason kept me! I pray to you with a voice that threatens doom. Now, now is the time to help me, avenging goddesses, your hair bristling freely with snakes, black torches in your bloody hands! Appear in the same horrible shape you had when you once stood in my bridal chamber! Bring death to my husband's new wife, death to her father and to the whole royal house! And let me wish an even more terrible curse on the bridegroom: to live, wandering from city to city in foreign lands, poor, exiled, anguished, hated, homeless! May he wish to have me back as his wife! Let him go to the house of strangers where they already know him. And, finally, the worst I can wish on him: children who are like their father, like their mother. There, there I have my revenge: I have given birth!

B: Seneca, *Medea,* vv. 670–843

[*Medea prepares a deadly poison.*]

MEDEA'S OLD NURSE [*observing Medea*]: I am frightened, horrified. Something terrible is going to happen. It is amazing how her anger grows, inflames itself, and renews its former strength. Often have I seen her mad, assailing the gods, pulling down the sky, but now Medea plans something more monstrous, yes, more monstrous than ever before. As soon as she hurried away, out of her mind, and entered her cabinet of horrors, she spread all her materials, even those she had long been afraid to use, and unfolded a host of terrors, secret, occult. She touched with her left hand a magic utensil and invoked all the plagues which the hot sands of Libya produce and which the Taurus, covered with arctic snow, imprisons; she invoked every monstrosity on earth. Drawn by her magic incantations, a whole army of reptiles appears from their hiding places. A fierce dragon hauls its enormous body, darts its triple tongue, and looks around for victims to kill. It hears the magic song and stops and wraps its bloated, knotty rump in spirals around itself.

Medea cries: "Small are the evils, weak the weapons that hell can produce: I shall claim my poison from heaven. It is time, high time, to carry out a most unusual scheme. I want the Snake that lies up there to come down here like a gigantic torrent. I want the two Bears—the big one, useful to Greek ships, and the small one, useful to Phoenician sailors—to feel the Snake's enormous coils. Let the Snake-Keeper at long last relax the tight grips of his hands, and let the poison pour out. I want Python, who dared to challenge the divine Twins, to obey my song and appear! I want Hydra and all the snakes that Hercules killed to come back, renewed from their death. Leave Colchis and come here, watchful snake, put to sleep for the first time by my songs!"

After she had summoned up all kinds of snakes, she stirred together poisonous herbs: whatever impassable Eryx produces on its rocks; what the Caucasus, sprinkled with Prometheus' blood, grows on peaks covered with eternal snow; the poisons that the warlike Medes and the fast Parthians carry in their quivers; the poisons that the rich Arabs smear on their arrows; the juices that Suebian noblewomen gather in the Hyrcanian forest under a cold sky; whatever the earth sprouts in spring, when birds build their nests or, later, when the numbing winter solstice has destroyed the beauty of the landscape and shackled everything with icy frost; every kind of plant that blooms with deadly flowers; every virulent juice in twisted roots that causes harm. All this she takes. Mount Athos in Thessaly has contributed some poisonous herbs, huge Pindus others; some tender leaves were cut on the peaks of Pangaeum with a bloody sickle; some grew near the Tigris, which hides deep currents; some near the Danube; some near the Hydaspes, which runs lukewarm water and carries many gems; some near the Baetis, which gives its name to a country and sluggishly joins the Hesperian Sea. This plant was cut as Phoebus started the day; that stalk was lopped off deep in the night; this crop was mown with a magic fingernail.

She plucks the deadly herbs and squeezes out the poison of the snakes and mixes them with hideous birds: the heart of the night owl, which brings sorrow, and the vitals of hoarse screech owls, cut out alive. The mistress of crime sorts out other ingredients and arranges them: this one has the ravening power of fire, that one the paralyzing cold of icy frost. The words she speaks over her poisons are not less frightening. Listen: her frenzied step has sounded. She sings. The whole world trembles at her first words.

MEDEA: I pray to the silent crowd, to the gods of doom, the dark Chaos, the shadowy house of gloomy Dis, the caves of horrible Death circled by the bank of Tartarus. Shades, your torments have ceased: hurry to this new kind of wedding! The wheel that tortures Ixion's limbs must stop and let him touch the ground; Tantalus must drink undisturbed the water of Pirene. A heavier punishment must weigh on my husband's father-in-law alone. Let the slippery stone make Sisyphus roll backward over the rocks. You, too, Danaids, whose wasted efforts are mocked by your pitchers full of holes, assemble! You are needed today.

Come now, Star of nights! My offerings call you. Come, wearing your most sinister expression, threatening with all three faces.

For you have I loosened my hair from its band, according to the custom of my people. On bare feet have I wandered through remote groves and conjured water from dry clouds. I have pushed the seas down to the bottom. I have conquered the tides, and the Ocean has sent its heavy waves farther into the land. I have upset the cosmic laws, and the world has seen at the same time the sun and the stars. The Bears have touched the sea, which was forbidden to them. I have changed the order of the seasons: my magic chant made the summer earth bloom, and, compelled by me, Ceres saw a winter harvest. Phasis has turned its rushing streams back to its source, and the Danube, split into so many mouths, has checked its currents and become a sluggish river in all its beds. The waves have roared, the sea swelled madly, but there has been no wind. The dwelling of an ancient grove lost its shadows at the command of my voice. The day was over, yet Phoebus still stood in the middle of the sky.

Moved by my magic songs, the Hyades are falling. Phoebe, it is time to be present at your sacred rites.

For you my bloody hands are wreathing these garlands, each entwined with nine serpents; to you I present these limbs which rebellious Tiphys had when he shook the throne of Jupiter. This contains the blood of Nessus, the treacherous ferryman: he offered it as he died. These are the ashes left from the pyre on Mount Oeta: it drank the poisoned blood of Hercules. Here you see the torch of Althaea, the avengeress: she was a good sister, but a bad mother. These are the feathers that the Harpy left in her unapproachable lair after she had fled from Zetes. And finally you have the quill of the Stymphalian bird after it had been wounded by the arrows of Lerna.

Altars, you made a sound. The goddess is favorable. I can see how her approach moves my tripods.

I see the fast chariot of Trivia. It is not the chariot that she drives in the night when her face is full and shining. It is the one that she drives when she stays closer to the earth, troubled by the threats of Thessalian witches, her face sad and pale. Yes! Pour out from your torch a gloomy, pallid light through the air! Frighten the peoples with a new kind of horror! Let precious Corinthian bronze gongs sound to help you, Dictynna! On the bloody turf I bring you a solemn offering. A torch snatched from the middle of a funeral pyre illuminates the night for you. For you I toss my head, bend my neck, speak my words. For you I have tied loosely, as is the custom at funerals, a fillet round my flowing locks. For you I wave the branch of sorrow from the Stygian stream. For you I will bare my breasts and, like a Maenad, slash my arms with the sacrificial knife. Let my blood flow to the altar. My hand must learn to draw the sword, and I must learn to endure the sight of my own blood. There! I have cut myself and given my sacred blood.

If you resent the fact that I call on you too often in my prayers, please forgive me, daughter of Perses: the reason why I call on your bow again and again is always the same: Jason.

Poison now the robes of Creusa! As soon as she puts them on, let a hidden flame burn her marrow deep inside. Within this dark-golden box lurks an invisible fire. Prometheus gave it to me: he stole the fire from heaven and pays for this with his ever-growing liver. He taught me by his art to store magic powers. Hephaestus gave me fires covered by a thin layer of sulfur, and from my cousin Phaethon I received powerful shafts of lightning. I hold contributions from the middle part of Chimaera; I have flames that were snatched from the parched throat of the bull; those I mixed thoroughly with Medusa's gall, and I told them to preserve secretly their deadly effect.

Add your sting to these poisons, Hecate, and preserve in my gift the seeds of fire that are hidden in it! Let them deceive the sight and endure the touch; let the heat penetrate Creusa's heart and veins; let her limbs melt and her bones go up in smoke, and let the bride, her hair on fire, shine brighter than the wedding torches!

My prayers have been heard: three times has fearless Hecate barked, and she has sent out the fire of damnation from her torch that brings sorrow.

14

Encolpius ("Bosom Pal"), the narrator and antihero of Petronius' novel *Satyricon*, describes an embarrassing episode. A beautiful woman by the name of Chrysis ("Goldie") had offered herself to him, but he had completely failed in her arms. Now he is most anxious to restore his sexual powers. First he tries the conventional remedies of the day: a spicy meal of onions and snails (considered an aphrodisiac) and some wine—not too much. He goes for a leisurely stroll and abstains from sex with his boyfriend, Giton. The next day, at the rendezvous with Chrysis, he discovers that she, too, has given the problem some thought and has brought her own personal witch with her. The witch ties a kind of amulet around his neck, for his temporary impotence might have been caused by black magic. The threads of different colors (probably black, white, and red) remind us of the threads in Virgil's eighth eclogue [*no. 10*]. Spittle is often used in healing rites, and the spell, of course, is necessary to ask for supernatural help. The pebbles might have been just ordinary stones, but certain minerals were thought to have magical properties, just like herbs. The purple cloak wrapped around them is supposed to enhance their power to form another amulet. The magic works instantly.

Petronius, *Satyricon,* ch. 131

Having parted from Chrysis with such a promise, I now devoted myself to that body of mine that had been of so little use to me. Instead of taking a bath, I applied a light massage, and then I ate a fortifying meal: onions, snails' necks without sauce, and just a little wine. Before going to sleep I went for a very leisurely stroll and then to bed without Giton; I was so anxious to soothe the lady that I was afraid to let the dear boy give me a workout.

The next day I got up, physically and emotionally in one piece, and went down to the grove of plane trees where we had met before, although that ill-omened place made me nervous. Under the trees I then began to wait for Chrysis, to be my guide. I had only walked a few steps and sat down at the place where I had been yesterday when Chrysis appeared, dragging a little old woman behind her. She greeted me and said: "How about it, my delicate lover: have you made up your mind to be normal today?" The old woman pulled a string made from threads of different colors from her dress and tied it around my neck. Then she took some dirt, mixed it with her spittle, and with her third finger made a mark on my forehead in spite of my resistance. [What may be the spell is lost in a lacuna in the text.] After having recited the spell, she told me to spit three times and to drop inside my garment three times in a row some pebbles over which she had said a spell and which she had wrapped in purple cloth. Then she tested the power of my loins by touching me there.

15

After the mysterious death of Julius Caesar Germanicus, the adopted son of the emperor Tiberius, at Antioch in A.D. 19, a gruesome discovery was made. According to Tacitus, workmen who searched Germanicus' residence found under the floor and between the walls a collection of objects obviously put there by someone who wanted the commander out of the way. Even though Germanicus was almost universally popular, he had at least two enemies: Gnaeus Calpurnius Piso, governor of Syria; and Piso's wife, Plancina. As Germanicus lay dying, he expressed the belief that these two had poisoned him, but his friends suspected black magic, which, of course, could include poison. Piso was later prosecuted by the Senate and took his own life; his wife escaped condemnation in A.D. 20 but was accused again years later and also committed suicide. Tacitus does not commit himself, although the list of objects allows no other interpretation: someone who believed in the powers of black magic planted them in order to destroy the prince. Whether poison was used for good measure we do not know.

This is a fairly well-documented example of the interaction between the worlds of politics and magic. No doubt this sort of thing happened many times; we just do not hear about it very often from reliable sources.

Tacitus, Annals 2.69

The terrible impact of his illness was intensified by his conviction of having been poisoned by Piso. Under the floors and between the walls of his house the remains of human bodies were found and dug up. There were also spells and curses and lead tablets with the name "Germanicus" engraved and, furthermore, half-burned ashes, smeared with blood, and other tools of evil magic by which, it is believed, souls [i.e., the life force of human beings] can be handed over to the divinities of the underworld.

16

The language of this inscription from the late first century A.D. is very formal, but the story is clear. The city of Tuder (Todi) had been in grave danger because a curse had been placed on several members of the city council. The inscription does not explain how this became public knowledge, but someone may have started a rumor. By suggesting that some of the councillors were in danger, it was possible to frighten all of them. In magical operations the victims were often allowed to know that something was going on. This gave them a last chance to pray to the gods for protection, unless they wished to launch a magical counterattack. In this instance the man who set up the inscription, L. Cancrius Primigenius, made a vow to Jupiter Optimus Maximus. He vowed to set up the inscription in the temple (and probably to offer a sacrifice) if more details about the curse, especially the names of the intended victims, came to light. Thanks to Jupiter this happened—we are not told how—and the details were duly recorded. The names of victims had been written on tablets, and the tablets had been buried near some tombs. The communal slave, who may have had a grievance against the city council, is not identified, but no doubt he was convicted of sorcery and executed.

CIL 11.2.4639

For having saved the city, the city council, and the people of Tuder, L. Cancrius Primigenius, freedman of Clemens, member of the committee of six men in charge of the worship of the Augustans and the Flavians, the first to be honored in this way by the order, has fulfilled his vow to Jupiter Optimus Maximus, because through his divine power he has brought to light and protected the names of the members of the city council, which, by the unspeakable crime of a worthless communal slave, had been attached to tombs so that a curse could be put upon them. Thus Jupiter has freed the city and the citizens from the fear of danger.

17

This curse, inscribed on a lead tablet from Africa (third century A.D.), was found in a tomb. Its victims are two teams of charioteers. The chariot races in the circus—and most major cities throughout the Roman Empire had one—were among the most popular of spectator sports, and emotions ran high during these events. Our inscription identifies four teams. Distinguishable by the color of their uniforms, they were known as the Reds, Whites, Greens, and Blues. This tablet was obviously inscribed by a fan of the Blues and the Reds, for he delivers the opposite teams—riders and horses—to an anonymous daemon. He strengthens the spell by invoking the name of the Jewish deity: *Iao* and *Iasdao* seem to be variants of *Yahweh* (Jehovah). *Iasdao* was perhaps pronounced with a hiss, *susurrus magicus;* the series of vowels *a e i a* often appears in magical texts.

Lead tablet from Africa, late Empire (no. 286B Audollent)

I conjure you, daemon, whoever you may be, and order you, to torture and kill, from this hour, this day, this moment, the horses of the Green and the White teams; kill and smash the charioteers Clarus, Felix, Primulus, Romanus; do not leave a breath in them. I conjure you by him who has delivered you, at the time, the god of the sea and the air: Iao, Iasdao, Oorio, Aeia.

18

A section of the Great Magical Papyrus in Paris is entitled "Astonishing Love Magic." The papyrus was written in the early fourth century A.D., but it contains ideas and materials that are older. Like most magical "recipes," it follows the format "take this," "do this," "say this," and so on. It is a rather elaborate love charm, and some parts of it remind one of Theocritus [*no. 6*], while others are reminiscent of Horace [*no. 9*]. The magician has to fashion two dolls, one representing himself, the other the woman he desires. The doll representing the woman then has to be pricked with thirteen iron needles at certain spots, and the appropriate formulas have to be recited. The symbolism is fairly obvious, and there is a certain weird logic behind the whole thing. Such were the working papers of the professional sorcerer.

This so-called love charm has nothing to do with love, however. It is a tool that was used to possess and subjugate a woman who, presumably for good reasons, had rejected the suitor who ordered this performance. There is certainly a cruel, vindictive, and aggressive tone throughout the charm. It continues with more prayers, formulas, and rites, and one has the feeling that after a certain amount of all this either the magician or his customer (who may have been present) or both must have been totally exhausted.

Great Magical Papyrus in Paris (PGM IV.297–408)

Amazing love charm:

Take wax [or clay] from a potter's wheel and form two figures, one male and one female. Make the male one look like Ares in arms, holding a sword in his left hand and pointing it at her right collarbone. Her arms must be (tied) behind her back, and she must kneel. Fasten the magical substance on her head or neck. On the figure of the woman you want to attract write as follows. On the head: ISEE IAO ITHI OUNE BRIDO LOTHION NEBOUTOSOUALETH. On the right ear: OUER MECHAN. On the left: LIBABA OIMATHOTHO. On the face: AMOUNABREO. On the right eye: ORORMOTHIO AETH. On the other: CHOBOUE. On the right shoulder: ADETA MEROU. On the right arm: ENE PSA ENESGAPH. On the other: MELCHIOU MELCHIEDA. On the hands: MELCHAMELCHOU AEL. On the breast write the name, on her mother's side, of the woman you want to attract. On the heart: BALAMIN THOOUTH. Under the abdomen: AOBES AOBAR. On her sexual organs: BLICHIANEOI OUOIA. On her buttocks: PISSADARA. On the sole of the right foot: ELO. On the other: ELOAIOE. Take thirteen bronze needles and stick one in the brain and say: "I am piercing your brain, NN." Stick two in the ears, two in the eyes, one in the mouth, two in the midriff, one in the hands, two in the genital organs, two in the soles, saying each time: "I am piercing such and such a member of NN, so that she may remember me, NN alone." Take a lead tablet and write on it the same formula and recite it. Tie the lead leaf [i.e., the lead tablet] to the two creatures with thread from the loom after making three hundred sixty-five knots, saying, as you have learned: "Abrasax, hold her fast." As the sun is setting, you must place it near the tomb of a person who has died an untimely or a violent death, along with flowers of the season.

The formula to be written and recited: "I am handing over this binding spell to you, gods of the underworld, HYESEMIGADON and KORE PERSEPHONE ERESCHIGAL and ADONIS, the BARBARITHA, chthonic HERMES THOOUTH PHOKENTAZEPSEU AERCHTHATOUMI SONKTAI KALBANACHAMRE and to mighty ANUBIS PSIRINTH who has the keys to the realm of Hades, to gods and daemons of the underworld, to men and women who have died before their time, to young men and women, from year to year, from month to month, from day to day, from hour to hour. I adjure all the daemons in this place to assist this daemon. Arouse yourself for me, whoever you are, male or female, and enter every place, every neighborhood, every house, and attract and bind, attract NN, daughter of NN, whose magical substance you have. Make NN, daughter of NN be in love with me. Let her not have sexual intercourse with another man, neither from front nor from behind, let her not have pleasure with another man, only with me, NN, so that she, NN, is unable to drink or eat, to love, to be strong, to be healthy, to enjoy sleep, NN without me, NN, because I adjure you by the fearful, the awesome name, the name at whose sound the earth will open, the name at whose terrifying sound the daemon will panic, the name at whose sound rivers and rocks will explode. I adjure you, daemon-dead [i.e., the spirit of a dead person], male or female, in

the name of BARBARITHA CHENMBRA and in the name of ABRAT ABRA-
SAX SESENGEN BARPHARANGES and in the name of MARMAREOTH MARMA-
RAUOTH MARMARAOTH MARECHTHANA AMARZA MARIBEOTH. Listen to my
commands and to the names. Just arouse yourself from the repose that
holds you, whoever you are, male or female, and enter every place, every
neighborhood, every house, and bring her, NN, to me, and keep her
from eating and drinking, and let her, NN, not enjoy the attempt of any
other man, not even that of her own man, only my own, NN. Yes, drag
her, NN, by her hair, by her heart, by her soul to me, NN, every hour of
life [or: eternity], night and day, until she comes to me, NN, and let her,
NN, remain inseparable from me. Do this, bind her for all the time of my
life and force her, NN, to be my, NN, servant, and let her not flutter away
from me for even one hour of life [or: eternity]. If you accomplish this for
me, I will let you rest at once. For I am BARBAR ADONAI who hides the
stars, who governs with his bright splendor the heaven; [I am] the lord
of the world, ATHTHOUIN IATHOUIN SELBIOUOTH AOTH SARBA THIOUTH
IATHRIERATH ADONAI IA ROURA BIA BI BIOTHE ATHOTH SABAOTH EA
NIAPHA AMARACHTHI SATAMA ZAUATHTHERE SERPHO IALADA IALE SBESI
IATHTHA MARADTHA ACHIL THTHEE CHOOO OE EACHO KANSAOSA ALK-
MOURI THYR OSO MAI. Attract her, bind her, NN, make her love me,
desire me, yearn for me, NN, (add the usual), because I adjure you,
daemon-dead, in the name of the terrible, the great IAEO BAPH RENE-
MOUN OTHI LARIKRIPHIA EYEAI PHIRKIRALITHON YOMEN ER PHABOEA, to
bring her, NN, to me, to join head to head, glue lips to lips, join belly to
belly, approach thigh to thigh, fit the black together with the black, and
let her perform, her, NN, sexual acts with me, NN, for the time of my life
[or: for all eternity].

19

King Psammetichus, to whom this text is dedicated, may be as fictitious as
Nephotes, the magician who addresses him, but the magic itself is probably much older than the papyrus. The kings of Egypt were thought to live
forever (hence the spectacular tombs built for them), and during their life
on this earth they must have had the best magicians money could buy—
witness their confrontation with Moses, in Exodus 7. The Pharaoh learns
from them how to have visions in a bowl of water, how to hear voices, and
how to receive revelations from "the ruler of the universe." But even the
Pharaoh needs a "mystagogue"—that is, a guide to initiate him into the
higher mysteries, and he apparently has to pretend to be a mummy and to
create or reproduce a whole mythology in his prayer. Obviously, to arrest
the great Osiris and bring him before an even greater god is no mean feat.

The first part of the ritual is supposed to produce a specific vision (that of the seahawk), which, in itself, is only a signal to proceed with another ritual. The real vision appears in a bowl of water on whose surface there is a film of olive oil. This is the technique of lecanomancy, here incorporated into an elaborate ritual. Watching the shapes forming on the surface of the water, the magician falls into a state of trance, during which he hears voices. The gods who send these voices then must be properly released.

Great Magical Papyrus in Paris (*PGM* IV.154–242)

Nephotes to Psammetichus, immortal King of Egypt, greetings. Since the great god has appointed you immortal King and nature has made you an outstanding sage [or: an excellent magician], I too, wishing to show you my willingness to work, have sent this magical procedure, which, with the greatest ease, accomplishes a holy power. After you have tried it out yourself, you too will be amazed at the extraordinary nature of this operation. By looking into a visionary bowl, on whatever day you wish, in whatever place you wish, you will see god in the water and receive a voice from god, speaking in verse in response to your requests. You will also know [taking *oiseis* as a future of *oida*] the ruler of the universe and whatever you propose; he will also speak to you on other things you may ask about. You will achieve results by following these instructions.

First, connect with Helios in this manner: At any sunrise you choose, provided it is the third day of the moon [i.e., of the month, or (perhaps) after the new moon], go up to the roof of a very tall house and spread a pure linen garment on the floor. Do this with a mystagogue [i.e., an experienced magician]. As for you, crown your head with black ivy. When the sun is in mid-heaven, at the fifth hour, lie down naked on the linen, looking upward. Order your eyes to be completely covered with a black band. Wrap yourself [in linen], as if you were a corpse, close your eyes, keep your direction toward the sun and begin [the ritual] with the following words.

Prayer: "Mighty Typhon, master and ruler of the kingdom above, lord ABERAMENTHOOU [formula], prince of darkness, bringer of thunder, whirlwind, nightflasher, breather-forth of hot and cold, shaker of rocks, bulldozer of walls, whisperer in the waves [or: boiler of waves] who stirs up the depths of the sea, IO ERBET AU TAUI MENI: I am he who has searched with you the whole world and found great Osiris whom I brought to you in chains. I am he who fought at your side with the gods [others: against gods]. I am he who closed the double doors of heaven and who put to sleep the dragon whose sight no one can stand [or: who must not be looked at], who stopped the sea, the streams, the flowing of rivers, until you have become the [absolute] ruler of this kingdom [or: as far as your kingdom extends]. As your soldier, I have been defeated by the gods, and I have been thrown face down on the ground because of [their] empty wrath. Raise up, I beg you, I implore you, I, your friend, and do not throw me on the ground, ruler of the gods, AEMINAEBARTHER-RETHORABEANIMEA. Give me strength, I beg you, and grant me this favor that, whenever I call on any of the gods by my spells to come, he will be seen coming to me at once. NAINE BASANAPTATOU EAPTOU MENOPHAESME PAPTOU MENOPH AESIME TRAUAPTI PEUCHRE TRAUARA PTOUMEPH MOURAI ANCHOUCHAPHAPTA MOURSA ARAMEI IAO ATHTHARAUI MENOKER BORO PTOUMETH AT TAUI MENI CHARCHARA PTOUMAU LALAPSA TRAUI TRAUEPSE MAMO PHORTOUCHA AEEIO IOY OEOA EAI AEEI OI IAO AEI AI IAO."

When you have said this three times, there will be a sign of a [mystic] union, but you, being armed with a magical soul, must not be alarmed: a sea falcon flies down and hits your body with its wings. This means in no uncertain terms that you must get up. Get up, put on white garments, sacrifice uncut incense in grains on an earthen altar and say: "I have become attached to your holy frame, I have been given power by your holy name, I have shared your outflow of good things, lord, god of gods, ruler-daemon. ATHTHOUIN THOUTHOUI TAUANTI LAO APTATO. When you have done this, descend as one who is lord of a godlike nature thanks to the mystic union, which has been accomplished. [text missing] of a vision through bowl-divination combined with the evocation of a dead person [text and punctuation uncertain, but this seems to be a new section, and something may be missing at the beginning]. Investigation. Whenever you want to investigate things, take a bronze vessel, either a bowl or a saucer, whichever you prefer. Pour water into it—rainwater, if you call on the heavenly gods, seawater, if [you call] on the gods of the earth, river water, if you call on Osiris or Sarapis, springwater, if you call on the dead. Holding the vessel on your knees, pour green olive oil into it. Bend over the vessel and recite the prescribed spell. Address any god you desire and ask him any questions you wish. He will reply and tell you everything. After he has spoken to you, dismiss him with the dismissal formula. Having used this spell, you will be amazed.

Spell to be recited over the water: AMOUN AUANTAU RIPTOU MANTAUI IMANTOU LANTOU LAPTOUMI ANCHOMACH ARAPTOUMI. Come to me, god NN, let me see you, and do not frighten my eyes. Come to me, god NN, listen to me, for this is the will and the command of ACHCHOR ACHCHOR ACHACHACH PTOUMI CHACHCHO CHARACHOCH CHAPTOUME CHORCHARACHOCH APTOUMI MECHOCHAPTOU CHARACHPTOU CHACH-CHO PTENEACHOCHEU [a hundred letters].

20

This prayer of thanksgiving comes as a surprise in a body of magical recipes and spells. It seems to contradict the theory that the magician uses gods as his tools, compelling them to perform, whereas the religious person approaches them humbly, asking for help. The god addressed in this prayer is very much like the Judeo-Christian God, and because this text was written down as late as the fourth century A.D., it is quite possible that its author was influenced by Christian theology, though not a Christian himself. The success of Christianity may have persuaded him that here was a powerful magic that might be used to good advantage, especially if the ancient magic did not work anymore. If so, this text is another example of the flexibility of the magicians: they were always on the lookout for new methods, even if they involved a kind and benevolent god rather than the threatening daemon of earlier days. For a similar text, see Festugière and Nock, *Corpus Hermeticum* 2:353ff.

Magical Papyrus in the Louvre (*PGM* III.1–25)

We are grateful to you from all our soul, with the heart stretched out to [you], unutterable name, honored with the appellation "god" and blessed with the holiness of god, by which you have shown to everyone and everything your fatherly kindness, love, friendship and sweetest power, having granted us intellect, [speech] and knowledge: intellect to understand you, speech to call upon you, knowledge to know you. We rejoice, because you have shown yourself to us; we rejoice, because—although we are [mortal] creatures—you have made us divine through knowledge of you. As human beings, we have only one way of showing our gratitude to you: by coming to know your greatness. We have come to know it, o [life] of human life, we have come to know it, o womb of all knowledge, we have come to know it, o womb pregnant through the Father's begetting; we have come to know it, o eternal presence of the Father's impregnation. After having worshiped your abundant goodness, we have asked you no [other favor except this]: let us continue in knowledge of you and grant us [as a] protection that we may never fall away from [a life] such as this.

21

Here is another example of love magic from the Great Papyrus in Paris. Similar to an earlier text [*no. 18*], it illustrates the total power over a woman that the magician (or his client) desires. The spell is written in the form of an impassioned monologue directed at a vessel of myrrh, which is burning during the whole operation. There is a kind of poetry in the intensity of the appeal to the magical substance and the detailed anticipation of its effect, and there is the same lack of compassion for the victim, who is treated as a mere sex object, not as a human being.

Great Magical Papyrus in Paris (PGM IV.1495–1546)

Spell of attraction over myrrh that is burning. While the myrrh is burning over coals, recite the formula. Formula: You are Myrrha, the bitter, the difficult. You reconcile those who fight each other; you burn and force those who do not acknowledge Eros to fall in love. Everyone calls you Zmyrna, but I call you flesh-eater and heart-burner. I am not sending you to distant Arabia; I am not sending you to Babylon, but I am sending you to NN, whose mother is NN, to help me with her, to bring her to me. If she is sitting, let her not sit; if she is talking to someone, let her not talk; if she is looking at someone, let her not look; if she is going to someone, let her not go; if she is walking about, let her not walk about; if she is drinking, let her not drink; if she is eating, let her not eat; if she is kissing someone, let her not kiss; if she is enjoying something pleasant, let her not enjoy it; if she is sleeping, let her not sleep. Let her think of me, NN, alone; let her desire me alone; let her love me alone, and let her do all my wishes.

Do not enter her through her eyes, not through her sides, not through her nails, not through her navel, not through her members, but through her soul and settle down in her heart and burn her guts, her breast, her liver, her breath, her bones, her marrow, until she comes to me, NN, loving me and doing all my wishes. Because I adjure you, Zmyrna, by the three names ANOCHO ABRASAX TRO and by the even more compelling and potent ones KORMEIOTH IAO SABAOTH ADONAI to carry out my commands, Zmyrna. As I burn you and [as] you are powerful, so you must burn the brain of the woman I love, NN. Inflame her guts and rip them out, shed her blood, drop by drop, until she comes to me, NN, whose mother is NN.

22

For this magical operation, a cat must be "made into an Osiris," that is, killed. The euphemism originates from the belief that Osiris represents the dead Pharaoh and therefore, by extension, any dead creature. To be "osirified," therefore, means to be given a new life in another world, for, as the spell shows, the dead cat is capable of attracting a daemon. The magician blames the death of the cat on his enemies—the names are to be filled in—because they forced him to engage in magical rites in the first place. This is very ingenious. The last few lines show that this magic can be used to influence the outcome of the races in the circus. A simple drawing of the circus, the chariots, and the charioteers is sufficient.

Magical Papyrus in the Louvre (*PGM* III.591–609)

[Take a] cat and [make] it into an Esies [Osiris] [by submerging] its body in water. As you are drowning it, recite [the spell] over its back.

Spell during the drowning: "Come hither to me, you who are in charge of the form of the Sun, cat-faced deity, and look at your [own] form which has been brutalized by your opponents, NN, so that you may pay them back and accomplish the NN feat, because I am calling you, sacred spirit. Be strong and vigorous against your enemies, NN, because I adjure you by your names BARBATHIAO, BAIN CHOOOCH NIABOAITHABRAB SESENGENBARPHARARGES . . . PHREIMI: raise yourself up for me, cat-faced deity, and accomplish the NN feat. [The usual].

Take the cat and make three lamellae: one [to be placed] in its anus, one [to be placed] in its [mouth], one [to be placed] in its throat, and write the appropriate formula with cinnabar [ink] on a pure sheet [of papyrus] [and then] [the names of] the chariots, the charioteers, the chariot boards and the racehorses. Wrap this around the cat's body and bury it. Light seven lamps on seven (7) unbaked bricks and make an offering to him by fumigating storax gum. And be of good cheer!

23

This papyrus, entitled "Sacred Book, Called the 'Monad,' or 'Eighth Book of Moses,' about the Holy Name," was written down in the fourth century A.D., but the material seems to be several centuries older.

The first rite described is to be used for an exorcism. Sulfur and bitumen ("Jew's pitch," found in antiquity in Palestine and Babylon) are strong-smelling substances that are believed to have the power to drive daemons away. The "Name" is probably the holy name of the Old Testament, Yahweh.

The second ritual invokes the snake Aphyphis, in Egyptian myth the enemy of the sun god. By calling a snake by this name, the magician will enlist the sun god's help. To bring a corpse back to life requires an appeal to a daemon, a reference to the Egyptian god Thayth, and a recitation of the Name, presumably Yahweh.

The last spell includes an invocation of Christ as well as the "Name" of another deity (perhaps Yahweh) and the Greek sun god. But it is possible that "Christ"—and perhaps the whole passage from "Hear me, o Christ" to "thrice eight times"—is a Christian interpolation. The very nature of this type of magic demanded that it be updated and rewritten from time to time.

Magical Papyrus in Leiden (PGM XIII.242–44, 261–65, 277–82, 290–96)

If you say the Name to someone who is possessed by a daemon while holding sulfur and bitumen to his nose, the daemon will speak at once and depart.

If you want to kill a snake, say: "Stop! For you are Aphyphis. "Take a green palm branch, hold its heart, split it in two and say the Name over it 7 times, and it [the snake] at once will split or burst.

Resurrection of a dead body. "I adjure you, life spirit walking in the air: enter this body, inspire it, empower it, resurrect it by the power of the eternal god, and make it walk about in this place: for I am he who acts through the power of [Th]ayth, the holy god." Say the Name.

For release from bonds. Say: "Hear me, o Christ, in [my] torments, help me in [my] constraints; you who are merciful in the hour of violence; you who are so powerful in the universe; you who have created Constraint, Punishment and Torture." [Say it] twelve times a day [or: during twelve days?], hissing [or: whistling] thrice eight times. Say the whole name of the Sun, beginning from [A]CHEBYKROM.

"Let every bond, every force be loosed, let every iron be broken, let every rope, every strap, every knot, every shackle be opened, and let no one use force against me, for I am" (say the Name).

24

To send dreams to someone, the magician has to draw a rather complicated figure on a linen sheet and recite a formula. This forces a minor daemon to go to the bedroom of X and give him a dream—the dream to be specified by the operator. The minor daemon is threatened by the authority of a major one in drastic terms. The "sending of dreams" is not a common magical operation, but it may have been practiced whenever a dream was required to reveal the future.

Magical Papyrus in Leiden (PGM XII.121–43)

Spell for sending dreams by Zminis of Tentyra:

Take a pure linen cloth and—according to Ostanes—draw on it with myrrh ink a figure that looks like a human being but has four wings, with the left arm outstretched along with the two left wings and the other arm bent with the fist clenched. On the head [draw] a royal crown and over its elbow a cloak, with two spirals on the cloak. Above the head [draw] bull horns and on the buttocks a bird's rear end, with feathers. Have his right fist held close to the stomach, and on either ankle there should be a sword extended [outward].

On the rag write the following names of the god and whatever you want him [,NN,] to see and in what way: "CHALAMANDRIOPH IDEARZO THREDAPHNIO ERTHEBELNIN RYHAONIKO PSAMOMERICH. To you I speak and also to you, most powerful daemon: go to the house of that person and tell him this."

Afterward take a lamp which is neither red nor inscribed, put a wick in it, fill it with cedar oil and light it. Recite the following 3 names of the god [or: recite 3 times the names of the god]: "CHALAMANDRIOPH IDEAR-YOTH THREDAPHNIO ERTHABEANIC RHYTHANIKO PSAMMORICH. Hear me, sacred names of the god, and you, too, Good Daemon, whose power is very great among the gods, hear me. Go to NN, into his house, where he sleeps, into his bedroom, and stand beside him, terrifying, frightening with [through] the great and mighty names [of the god] and tell him this: 'I adjure you by your power, by the great god Seith, by the hour in which you were born [appointed] a great god, by the god who will reveal it [?] now, by the 365 names of the great god—to NN this very hour, this very night, and, in a dream, tell him this.'

If you do not listen to me and refuse to go to NN, I will tell the great god, and he will spear you through and chop you up, member by member and feed your flesh to the mangy dog that lives among the dung heaps. For this reason listen to me now, now, quickly, quickly, so I won't have to tell you a second time."

25

The following three texts are invocations of a supreme cosmic deity, but the context shows that this particular deity is needed for magical pur-poses, even though the language is religious. A and B are from the famous "Eighth Book of Moses," a formidable collection of magical spells and incantations, interspersed with myths, hymns, and prayers. Moses was reputed in antiquity to be a great magician as well as a lawgiver and priest. The god invoked here is similar to Moses' deity (he is a creator-god, is invisible, but sees everything), but he combines the attributes of some pagan deities in the form of an *aretalogia* or doxology. Moreover, he is identified as the "Aion of Aions." Originally, *aion* meant "a very long time, an eternity," but in biblical Greek it also designates a limited historic period (e.g., "the present age"), and in late Hellenistic Greek in general its meaning was "the world," a time concept having become a space concept. Time and space were given their own deity, and so Aion became an all-embracing god. In B, the god has a secret, unspeakable name (in addition to Aion?)—and yet the daemons can hear it and are terrified. Perhaps this means that the name (the factor that would make the spell potent) cannot be revealed here but will be given at some other point, or it is hidden in the *voces magicae*. The "heptagram" is a sequence of the seven vowels of the Greek alphabet. The "four winds" are the four cardinal points, East, South, West, and North. C consists of tolerably good dactylic hexameters. The "living beings" may be the signs of the zodiac; in that case, "ways" would refer to their courses (see A). At the end we seem to have a whole family of Aions.

A: Magical Papyrus in Leiden (*PGM* XIII.64–71)

The [text of the] sacred stele to be written in the natron:

I call on you who are greater than all, the self-created who sees all and is not seen. For you gave to the sun its glory and all the power, to the moon [the ability] to wax and wane and to have fixed courses, yet you have not taken anything away from the primordial darkness, but you have established equal proportions. For when you appeared, the universe [or: the cosmic order] came into being, and light appeared. All things are in subjection to you whose true form none of the gods can see. You can change into all forms; you are invisible, Aion of Aions.

B: Magical Papyrus in Leiden (*PGM* XIII.760–65)

Here is the instruction [for reciting] the heptagram and the spell to which the god pays attention. [The spell]:

Come to me, you from the [four] winds, divine ruler of all, who breathed spirit into men to [give them] life, lord of all beauty in the universe. Listen to me, lord, whose name is secret, unspeakable—the daemons are terrified when they hear it . . .

C: Magical Papyrus in Leiden (*PGM* XII.245–53)

Who has shaped the forms of living beings? Who has found [their] ways? Who was the begetter of fruits? Who raises up mountains? Who told the winds to accomplish their yearly tasks? What Aion nourishing Aion rules Aions?

26

As one reads this text, one discovers another type of love charm. Although intended to induce insomnia, the sending of sleepless nights to a woman is not the ultimate purpose of this spell; rather, she is supposed to lie awake, thinking of the sorcerer or the client who ordered this. The symbolism of the puppy dog and the bat's eye is fairly obvious: bats are awake at night and see in the darkness, and barking dogs keep people awake. The three-forked roads outside ancient cities were useful for magical purposes because there were tombs nearby, and Hecate as well as Kore (i.e., Persephone), deities of the underworld, were thought to appear at these places at night. Both Hecate and Kore are invoked in this spell, along with some more obscure deities and daemons (although Brimo is often identified with either Persephone or Hecate).

The text is uncertain at the very end of the passage, but because provisions are made to remove the magical device from its spot near the crossroads, one may assume that the sleepless nights are not intended to last forever but can be ended as soon as the woman discovers her love for the magician.

Great Magical Papyrus in Paris (PGM IV.2943–66)

Attraction spell through insomnia:

Take the eyes of a bat and release it alive. Take a piece of unbaked dough or unmelted wax and shape a puppy dog. Put the right eye of the bat into the right eye of the puppy dog. Similarly the left into the left. Take a needle, thread it with the magical substance [*ousia*] and stick it through the eyes of the puppy dog, so that the magical substance is visible. Put the puppy dog into a new drinking vessel, attach a label [i.e., a tablet, or: a papyrus strip] to it and seal it with your own ring, which has crocodiles head to head [or: tail to tail; or: head to tail] to each other. Deposit it at a crossroad after having marked the spot, so that you can find it, should you wish to recover it.

Formula to be written on the label: "I adjure you three times in the name of Hecate PHORPHORBA BAIBO PHORBORBA that NN lose the fire in her eye or even lie awake with nothing on her mind except me, NN, alone. I adjure you in the name of Kore who has become the goddess of the crossroad, who is the true mother of . . . (write any name you wish) PHORBEA BRIMO NEREATO DAMON BRIMON SEDNA DARDAR. All-seeing one IOPE make her, NN, lie awake for me for all [eternity]."

27

Kronos, younger son of Heaven and Earth, father of Zeus, was the leading deity of an earlier generation of gods, the Titans, his brothers. He probably belongs to a pre-Greek civilization. After Zeus and the other Olympian gods took over, the Titans were driven from heaven. What happened to their leader, Kronos, is told in different versions. According to one story (reflected here) he was chained and imprisoned; according to another one he was exiled on a distant island, where he fell into an everlasting sleep, dreaming the destinies of the world.

In our spell, Kronos is presented as a god in chains who is therefore full of resentment and needs to be soothed and flattered. Naturally, he can be dangerous to the magician too, but the magician can protect himself by wearing the white linen robe of a priest of Isis and fashioning an amulet of the shoulder blade of a boar (very durable material) by scratching a picture of Zeus on it—Zeus with the sickle, the emblem of power that he took away from his father. This will humiliate Kronos and render him harmless to the wearer of the amulet.

Note that the formula of dismissal at the end of the document is very similar to the earlier formula of invocation, but the "magical words" appear in the reverse order which makes sense. There are, however, several inconsistencies, perhaps due to scribal error. Ideally, all the words should be identical. At the beginning and at the end of the first formula one should, perhaps, read IAEIOI. But it is difficult to decide which series should be corrected after which; and it is just a conjecture that the first one may be more "correct" than the second one.

Great Magical Papyrus in Paris (PGM IV.3086–3124)

A sought-for divination ritual addressed to Kronos, called "Little Mill":

Take two measures of sea salt and grind them with a handmill while reciting the formula several times, until the god appears to you. Do this at night, in a place where grass grows. If, while reciting it, you hear the heavy step [of someone] and the clanking of iron, the god is coming, bound with shackles and holding a sickle. You must not be afraid since you are protected by the talisman which will be explained to you. Be clothed in pure linen, the garb of [a statue or a priest] of Isis. Sacrifice to the god a burnt offering of sage, with the heart of a cat and horse manure.

The formula to be recited while you are grinding is this. Formula "I call you, the great, the holy one, the one who created the whole inhabited world, who suffered a great injury from your own child, whom Helios bound with steel fetters, to save the universe from complete collapse, you [who are] male-female, father of thunder and lightning, you who hold down [or: rule] those under the earth: AIE OI PAIDALIS PHRENOTEICHEIDO STYGARDES SANKLEON GENECHRONA KOIRAPSAI KERIDEU THALAMNIA OCHOTA ANEDEI. Come, master, god, and tell me about the NN matter; you must [obey]. For I am the one who rebelled against you PAIDOLIS MAINOLIS MAINOLIEUS. This you must recite while the salt is being ground.

But the formula that compels him is: KYDOBRIS KODERIEUS ANKYRIEUS XANTOMOULIS. You must recite this when he approaches you in a threatening manner, in order to soothe him and make him answer your questions.

This is the sought-after talisman: on the shoulder blade [or: the rib] of a young pig, carve Zeus holding a sickle and this name: CHTHOUMILON. It could also be the shoulder blade [or: the rib] of a black, scaly, castrated boar.

Dismissal: "ANAEA [or: ANEDEI] OCHETA [or: OCHOTA] THALAMNIA KERIDEU KOIRAPSIA [or: KOIRAPSAI] GENECHRONA SANELON [or: SANKLEON] STYGARDES [or: PHRENOTO?] CHLEIDO PHRAINOLE PAIDOLIS IAEI [or: AIE] [OI]. Go away, ruler of the world and retreat to your own domain, in order to keep the universe intact. Be gracious to us, lord."

28

Apollonius of Tyana, philosopher and miracle-worker of the first century A.D., was reported to Tigellinus, Nero's "chief of police," we would say today, and was promptly arrested. But the charges against him, written on a scroll, disappeared magically. Tigellinus then interrogated him in secret and was so impressed that he released him.

It is clear from the story told in document A that Apollonius could have been executed at the order of Tigellinus, as so many others were, even without a trial. Apollonius consistently denies having any supernatural abilities—for instance, the gift of divination. Like Apuleius, about a century later, he claims that he is merely a philosopher, a scientist who observes certain natural phenomena and interprets them correctly. But according to his biographer, Philostratus, he sees things that no one else sees, and he certainly believes in daemons, for he deals with them: but then, many serious philosophers of the time believed in daemons, and Pythagoras, whose doctrine Apollonius professed to teach, was that strange combination of philosopher and miracle-worker that we call "shaman."

In document B, Apollonius is in a similar situation, but here his biographer gives us his formal *Apologia* before the emperor Domitian. In many respects it corresponds to Apuleius' *Apologia,* delivered in court about a century later, but unlike Apuleius' speech it can hardly be considered authentic; Philostratus no doubt composed the sort of speech that Apollonius *might* have delivered under the circumstances, though it is possible that he found some of the material in his source.

Apollonius was accused of witchcraft because he predicted a plague at Ephesus. The argument of the prosecutor was that only a wizard could have made such a prediction. The fact that Apollonius also saved the people of Ephesus from the plague did not interest the court. In maintaining that this kind of foreknowledge is not supernatural, Apollonius compares himself with two "pre-Socratics," Thales and Anaxagoras (since he calls them both Ionians, he may be thinking of Anaximander or perhaps the name is corrupted, in the textual tradition), and with Socrates himself.

How does Apollonius explain his "psychic" abilities? First, by his diet. Although he does not explain it here in detail, it is clear that he was a vegetarian and probably avoided wine. This life-style is in accordance with Pythagoras' teaching, but it is also something that Apollonius might have learned in India, where he lived for a while. In modern terms, he might be called a strict practitioner of yoga.

Another argument Apollonius presents in his defense is the fact that he gave full credit to Heracles for ending the plague; he dedicated a temple to the god. A real magician would have claimed all the credit for himself. This distinction is important. By paying tribute to a god, Apollonius removes the miracle from the sphere of magic and places it in the religious sphere. The fact that he actually *saw* the plague in human shape is puzzling, but for Apollonius evil daemons were responsible for diseases whether they affected a person or a whole community.

Finally, Apollonius rejects the charge or insinuation that he offered human sacrifices to perform black magic. He is against *all* bloody sacrifices (i.e., he would never ritually kill an animal, much less a human being). He describes the magician as "the sort of person who prays with his eye on a knife" (an interesting and rather unusual detail), meaning that the magician promises in his prayer to the god the gift of sacrifice he is about to offer with his knife. This may also be an allusion to human sacrifices, a crime practitioners of magic were accused of. Apollonius argues that if he himself had done any such thing, his *daimonion* would have left him long ago; the fact that it still advises him proves that he is pure.

A: Philostratus, *Life of Apollonius of Tyana* 4.44

An epidemic broke out in Rome, called a "flu" by the doctors; its symptoms: coughing, and when the patient tried to speak, his voice was affected. The temples were full of people supplicating the gods because Nero had a swollen throat and his voice was hoarse. Apollonius thundered against the ignorance of the crowd, though he did not chastise anyone in particular; in fact, he talked sense to Menippus, who was furious at this sort of thing, and restrained him, telling him to forgive the gods if they enjoyed the farces of clowns. This remark was reported to Tigellinus, who sent the police to take him to prison and summoned him to defend himself from the charge of impiety against Nero. A prosecutor was appointed in his case who had already ruined many people and had quite a record of such Olympic victories. He held in his hands a scroll in which the charge was written out, and he brandished it against Apollonius like a sword, saying that it had been sharpened and would destroy him. But when Tigellinus unrolled the scroll and did not find in it a single trace of writing, but looked at a perfectly blank book, he began to suspect that he was dealing with a daemon. Apparently Domitian later felt this way about Apollonius, too.

Tigellinus now led Apollonius into the secret tribunal where magistrates of his rank try in private the most important cases. He told everyone else to withdraw and kept asking Apollonius questions. "Who are you?" Apollonius gave his father's name and that of his country and explained why he practiced philosophy: he said that he practiced it in order to know the gods and to understand human beings, because it was more difficult to know someone else than to know oneself. Tigellinus asked: "How do you drive out daemons and ghostly phantoms, Apollonius?" He answered: "In the same way as I would drive out the murderous and the impious." This was a sarcastic remark aimed at Tigellinus, for he had taught Nero every kind of cruelty and perversion. Tigellinus asked him: "Could you prophesy, if I asked you to?" Apollonius answered: "How could I, seeing that I am no prophet?" "And yet," Tigellinus remarked, "they say you predicted that some great event would happen and yet not happen." "What you heard is true," Apollonius answered, "but you must not ascribe this to any gift of divination, only to the wisdom which god reveals to the wise." Tigellinus asked: "Why are you not afraid of Nero?" Apollonius answered: "Because the same god who made him seem so terrifying also gave me the gift of being without fear." Tigellinus asked: "What do you think of Nero?" Apollonius said: "I have a better opinion of him than the rest of you; for you consider him worthy to sing, but I consider him worthy to be silent." Tigellinus was astonished and said: "You may go, but you must post a bond for your person." Apollonius asked: "And who might post a bond for a person that no one can bind?" These answers struck Tigellinus as being divinely inspired and above the nature of man, and since he was afraid of fighting with a god he said: "You may go wherever you wish, for you are too powerful to be controlled by me."

B: Philostratus, *Life of Apollonius of Tyana* 8.7.9–10

My prosecutor interrupts me—you have heard it yourself, your Majesty—and says that I am not accused of having saved the city of Ephesus from the plague, but for having predicted that it would be visited by an epidemic. This, he says, is beyond science and represents a miracle, and that I could never have reached such a degree of truth if I were not a magician, an unspeakable creature. Well, what would Socrates say, at this point, of the knowledge that he received from his *daimonion?* What would Thales and Anaxagoras say, both Ionians, one of whom predicted an abundant olive crop, the other a series of dramatic changes in the weather? That they predicted these things because they were magicians? And yet they were brought before courts of law on different charges, and we never hear of anyone accusing them of witchcraft simply because they had the gift of foreknowledge. That would have seemed ridiculous, an improbable charge against scientists, even in Thessaly, where women had a bad reputation for pulling the moon down to earth.

How, then, did I sense the disaster threatening Ephesus? You have heard the statement made by the prosecution that my life-style is different from that of others, that I follow a diet of my own which is light and more pleasant than the luxurious meals of the others. I have said that myself at the beginning of my speech. This diet, Your Majesty, keeps my senses in a kind of mystic atmosphere and prevents them from coming in contact with any interference, but allows me to see, as if in the shining surface of a looking glass, everything that is happening or will happen. For the true scientist will not wait for the earth to send up its exhalations nor for the air to be polluted, if the evil influences should come from above, but he will sense these things when they are imminent—not as soon as the gods, of course, but sooner than the ordinary person. For the gods perceive the more distant future, men what is happening, scientists what is about to happen. Please ask me privately about the causes of epidemics, Your Majesty; they are too scientific to be discussed in public. Is it then my life-style alone which makes my sense perceptions so subtle, so keen, that they take in the most spectacular, the most miraculous, phenomena? You can look at the facts from different points of view, but especially from what happened in Ephesus in connection with that epidemic. I actually saw the physical appearance of the epidemic—it looked like an old beggar—and once I saw it, I subdued it and did not so much bring the disease to an end as eradicate it. And who was the god to whom I had prayed? The sanctuary that I founded in Ephesus to commemorate the event shows it, for it is dedicated to Heracles, the "Averter of Evil." I chose him for my helper because he is the god whose knowledge and courage once purged Elis of a plague, when he washed away the miasma that used to rise from the ground when Augias was king.

Your Majesty! Would you think that someone whose ambition it is to be considered a sorcerer would ever attribute his own achievement to a god? Who would admire his magic if he gave credit for the miracle to a god? And what magician would pray to Heracles? For these accursed men attribute such miracles to the trenches they dig and to the gods of the underworld, from which Heracles must be separated, for he is a pure god and kind to men. Another time I prayed to him in the Peloponnesus, too, for there was an apparition of a Lamia; it haunted the surroundings of Corinth and devoured handsome adolescents. Heracles helped me in my struggle and did not ask for extraordinary gifts—just a honey cake and some frankincense and the opportunity of working for the good of mankind. For in the days of Erechtheus, too, this had been the only reward for his labors. Your Majesty need not resent my mentioning Heracles; Athena had him under her special care because he was good and a savior of mankind.

But since you command me to justify myself in the matter of the sacrifice—I know that this is what your gesture means—please listen to my defense: it is the truth. In everything I do I have the salvation of mankind at heart; yet I have never offered any sacrifice on their behalf nor will I ever offer one nor will I ever touch one that has blood in it; I am not the sort of person who prays with his eye on a knife or offers the kind of sacrifices that the prosecution alleges. The prisoner who stands before you is not a Scythian, Your Majesty, nor a native of some savage country. I have never mixed with Massagetes and Taurians, and if I had, I would have converted them from their traditional sacrifices. But what degree of madness would I have reached if—after talking so much about divination and the conditions under which it works or does not work, and understanding better than anyone else that the gods reveal their plans to holy and wise men, even if they have no prophetic gifts—I would become guilty of murder and operate with entrails that are an abomination to me and wholly unacceptable to the gods? If I had done such a thing, the divine voice of the *daimonion* would have left me as being impure.

29

Lucian of Samosata, a satirist of the second century A.D., has left some eighty pieces, most of them short dialogues. Because of his wit and his irreverent criticism of contemporary customs and institutions, he has been called "the Greek Voltaire." He makes fun of popular religious ideas (e.g., in the *Icaromenippus* and in the *Assembly of the Gods*) and of certain superstitions (as in *The Lovers of Lies*). It is clear from the present passage that Lucian himself did not believe in magic, though many of his contemporaries, even educated men, still did.

The person who tells the story is, as a matter of fact, a teacher of philosophy who tutors a young man in the doctrine of the Aristotelian school. (Incidentally, we are informed that the works of the master were studied in this order: *Analytics,* i.e., Logic, then *Physics*—to be followed no doubt by *Metaphysics*, i.e., "that which comes after *Physics.*") This philosophy teacher finds himself in the curious role of having to procure a magician for his pupil. The magician is found and produces first, for a fee, the ghost of the young man's father, and then the living body of the lady he loves. The description of the ritual is full of ironic distortions and exaggerations of details, which, in themselves, are not implausible. Clay figures were used in magic, but this one can actually fly, and so on.

The fact that the whole ceremony—though it literally worked like a charm—was unnecessary is another of Lucian's jokes. A famous exorcist is then mentioned, the "Syrian from Palestine," who had healed many people for a fee.

Finally, one of those present affirms his belief in spirits. The narrator (Lucian himself, one assumes) each time intersperses his doubt in the politest possible Attic manner.

Lucian, *The Lovers of Lies*, pars. 14–17

"Very soon after Glaucias' father had died and he had taken over the property, he fell in love with Chrysis, the wife of Demeas. He had hired me as his philosophy tutor, and if that love affair had not kept him so busy, he would have mastered already the whole Peripatetic doctrine, for even at the age of eighteen he did Analytics, and he had studied Physics from beginning to end. Well, he was at his wit's end with this love affair and told me everything. It was only natural—after all, I was his teacher—for me to bring to him that Hyperborean magician at a fee of four minas down (an advance toward the cost of the sacrifices was required) and sixteen more if he should find Chrysis' favor. The magician waited for the moon to wax, for this is the time when such rites are usually performed. Then he dug a pit in an open court of the house.

"Around midnight he first conjured up for us Alexicles, the father of Glaucias, who had died seven months before. The old gentleman was against this love affair and grew quite angry, but finally he told his son to go ahead and love her. Then the magician produced Hecate, who brought Cerberus along with her. He also drew down Selene [the moon], who presented a variety of apparitions: first she looked like this and then like that. First she appeared in the shape of a woman, then she was a very handsome bull, and then she looked like a puppy dog. Finally the Hyperborean formed a kind of miniature Cupid out of clay and said to him: 'Go and fetch Chrysis.' The clay [figure] flew away, and shortly afterward the lady stood at the threshold, knocked at the door, came in, embraced Glaucias as if she were madly in love with him, and stayed with him until we heard the cocks crowing. Then, as dawn was approaching, Selene flew back to the sky, Hecate plunged into the earth, all the other phantoms disappeared, and we sent Chrysis off. If you had seen this, Tychiades, you would no longer have doubted that there is much power in magic."

"You are right," I said. "I would have believed this, if I had seen it, but as things are, you will perhaps forgive me if I am not quite as clear-sighted as you. I do, however, know the Chrysis of whom you speak; she is an amorous lady and quite willing, and I don't see why you needed the clay ambassador and the magician from the land of the Hyperboreans and Selene in person in order to get her, when for twenty drachmas you could have brought her to the Hyperboreans! For the lady is very responsive to that kind of spell [i.e., money], and her reaction is totally different from that of phantoms: if they hear the clinking of bronze or iron, they take off—so you say yourselves—but when she hears the clinking silver [coins] anywhere, she moves in the direction of the sound. Moreover, I am amazed at the magician; he was able to make the richest ladies love him and take whole talents [large sums] from them, and yet he was so penny-wise that for only four minas he made Glaucias irresistible?"

"You are ridiculous," Ion said, "to doubt everything. You know, I should really like to ask you what you have to say about all those who deliver men possessed by daemons from their terrible predicament by—there is no doubt about it—exorcising them! No need for me to dwell on this. Everybody knows about the Syrian from Palestine, the expert in these matters, and how many people he took care of—those who collapsed before the full moon, those who rolled their eyes, those whose mouths filled with foam—and yet he made them well and sent them home in a normal frame of mind, having healed them from whatever plagued them, for a substantial fee. They lie there and he stands beside them and asks, 'Where do you come from? Whence did you enter this body?' The patient himself says nothing, but the daemon answers, either in Greek or in a foreign language, depending on the country he comes from, and tells him how and from where he entered this person. Then he swears an oath, and if the daemon does not obey, he threatens him and drives him out. As a matter of fact, I saw one coming out, all black and smoky."

I said: "So what? You see that sort of thing, but you also perceive the ideas that Plato, your founding father, defines, and yet they are a hazy vision to those of us whose eyes are weak."

"Do you mean," said Eucrates, "that Ion is the only one who has seen that sort of thing? Are there not many others who have met spirits, some at night and some by day? I have seen things like that not only once but practically thousands of times. At first I was upset by them, but now, having gotten accustomed to them, I no longer think that I am seeing anything abnormal, especially since the Arab gave me the ring made of iron from crosses and taught me the spells with many names. But perhaps you won't believe me either, Tychiades?"

I said: "How could I not believe Eucrates, the son of Deinon, a learned and distinguished [text and meaning uncertain] gentleman, when he freely expresses his own opinions in his own home?"

30

Apuleius, a Platonist and traveling lecturer of the second century A.D. who had a certain interest in occult science, found himself accused of witchcraft. In the North African town of Oea (Tripoli today) he was visited during an illness by a friend, Sicinius Pontianus, and met through him his mother, Pudentilla, a wealthy and not unattractive widow a few years older than Apuleius. When Apuleius married Pudentilla, he was accused of witchcraft by his wife's relatives, who apparently were unwilling to let her fortune go to a foreigner.

In the trial held at Sabrata, before the Roman proconsul, Claudius Maximus, Apuleius defended himself, and the speech he delivered in court (or, more likely, a revised version) is preserved. It contains a great deal of information on magic. Had Apuleius been convicted, the penalty would have been death.

Apuleius' speech first deals with the vague rumors that had been spread in the community to discredit him. Those rumors had led to the formal charge that Apuleius was a *magus*. To reject this, Apuleius first discusses the original meaning of *magus*. He even quotes from Plato's *Alcibiades* and *Charmides* to show how highly the Persians regarded "magic" and the *magi*: magic formed part of the education that the royal princes received; hence it must have been a religion, a philosophy, rather than some kind of witchcraft. The second testimony, taken from Plato's *Charmides,* is doubtful; Zalmoxis seems to have been a god of the dead worshiped by the Getae, a semicivilized Thracian tribe, and what Plato says about the "healers of Zalmoxis" cannot be substantiated.

Apuleius then shows that even his accusers do not believe in the reality of witchcraft and use it only as a pretext to destroy him; for if he were the formidable magician they make him out to be, they would be worried about their lives. There is no question that throughout the centuries the charge of witchcraft has been used again and again as a way of disposing of someone who has become unpopular.

In refuting the other arguments of the prosecution, Apuleius shows himself to be a skillful trial lawyer. The only serious charge is the experiment with the boy, the altar, and the lantern. Boys were considered natural mediums in antiquity; Apuleius gives an explanation for it and refers to Varro's story concerning Nigidius Figulus, a contemporary of Cicero's who was interested in the occult. The boy with whom Apuleius experimented apparently went into a trance, which must have frightened the eyewitness but could hardly have surprised Apuleius. To that extent the experiment was successful, but Apuleius—for obvious reasons—says nothing about any revelations.

Apuleius, *Apology,* or *On Magic,* chs. 25–27, 42–43

I will now deal with the actual charge of magic. He [the accuser] has spared no effort to light the flame of hatred against me, but he has falsely raised everyone's expectations by some old wives' tales he told. I ask you, Maximus [the judge], have you ever seen a fire started from stubble, crackling sharply, shining far and wide, getting bigger fast, but without real fuel, with only a feeble blaze, leaving nothing behind? This is their accusation, kindled with abuse, built up with mere words, lacking proof, and, once you have given your verdict, leaving no trace of slander behind.

Aemilianus' slander was focused on one point: that I am a *magus.* So let me ask his most learned advocates: what is a *magus?* I have read in many books that *magus* is the same thing in Persian as *priest* in our language. What crime is there in being a priest and in having acquired an accurate knowledge, a science, a technique of traditional ritual, sacred rites and theology, if magic consists of what Plato interprets as the "cult of the gods" when he talks of the disciplines taught to the crown prince in Persia? I remember the very words of that divine man [Plato]. Let me recall them to you, Maximus: "When the young prince has reached the age of fourteen, he is handed over to the royal tutors. There are four of them, chosen as the most outstanding among the Persian elders. One is the wisest, one the most just, one the most restrained, one the bravest. One of them teaches [the crown prince] the 'magic' of Zoroaster, the son of Ormazd, which is the worship of the gods. He also teaches [him] the art of being king." Listen to this, you who rashly slander magic! It is an art acceptable to the immortal gods, an art that includes the knowledge of how to worship them and pay them homage. It is a respectful theology dealing with things divine, and it has been the priestess of the gods ever since it was founded by Zoroaster and Ormazd. In fact, it is considered one of the chief elements of royal instruction, and in Persia no one is allowed lightly to be a *magus* any more than they would let him be king.

Plato also writes, in a different context, about a certain Zalmoxis, a Thracian, but an expert in the same art, that "incantations consist of beautiful words." If this is so, why should I not be permitted to learn the "beautiful words" of Zalmoxis or the priestly traditions of Zoroaster? But if my accusers, after the common fashion, think of a "magus" primarily as a person who by verbal communications with the immortal gods and through the incredible power of his incantations can perform any miracles he wants, I am astonished that they are not afraid to accuse a man who, as they admit themselves, has such powers! For there is no protection against such a mysterious, such a divine, power as there is against other dangers. If you summon a murderer before the judge, you come with a bodyguard; if you charge a poisoner, you take special precautions with your food; if you accuse a thief, you watch your possessions. But if you demand the death penalty of a *magus,* as they define him, what escort, what special precautions, what guards, can protect you against an invisible, inevitable catastrophe? None, of course, and so this is not the kind of charge a man who believes in the truth of such things would make.

But because of a fairly common misunderstanding the uneducated often accuse philosophers. Some of them think that those who investigate the simple causes and elements of matter are antireligious, and that they deny the very existence of gods, as for instance, Anaxagoras, Leucippus, Democritus, Epicurus, and other leading scientists. Others, commonly called "magi," spend great care in the exploration of the workings of providence in the world and worship the gods with great devotion, as if they actually knew how to make the things happen that they know to happen. This was the case with Epimenides, Orpheus, Pythagoras, and Ostanes. Similarly, later on, the "Purifications" of Empedocles, the "Daemon" of Socrates, the "Good" of Plato, came under suspicion. I congratulate myself to be associated with so many great men.

I am afraid, nevertheless, that the court may take seriously the silly, childish, and naïve arguments brought forward by my accusers in order to substantiate their charges—for the simple reason that they have been made. My accuser asks: "Why have you tried to get specific kinds of fish?" Why should a scientist not be allowed to do for the sake of knowledge what a gourmand is allowed to do for the sake of his gluttony? He asks: "What made a free woman marry you after having been a widow for fourteen years?" Well, is it not more remarkable that she remained a widow for such a long time? "Why did she, before she married you, express certain opinions in a letter?" Well, is it reasonable to demand of someone the reasons for someone else's opinions? "She is older than you, but did not reject a younger man." But this alone is proof enough that no magic was needed: a woman wished to marry a man, a widow a bachelor, a mature lady a man her junior. And there are more charges just like that: "Apuleius has in his house an object that he devoutly worships." Well, would it not be a worse offense to have nothing to worship? "A boy fell to the ground in Apuleius' presence." What if a young man, what if an old man, had fallen when I was there, perhaps stricken by illness, perhaps simply because the ground was slippery? Do you think you can prove your accusation of magic by such arguments, the fall of a little boy, my getting married to my wife, a serving of fish?

[*Apuleius deals with the subject of fish and argues that he was motivated only by scientific interest; then he turns to the incident of the boy who suddenly fell down in his presence.*]

My accusers, in accordance with common beliefs, claim that I bewitched a boy by an incantation with no witness present and then took him to a secret place with a small altar and a lantern and only a few accomplices present, and there he was put under a spell and collapsed; he lost consciousness and was revived. They did not dare go any further with their lie. To complete their fairy tale, they should have added that the boy uttered a lot of prophecies. For this, of course, is the benefit of incantations: prophecy and divination. This miracle involving boys is not only a popular superstition but is confirmed by the authority of learned men. I remember reading in the philosopher Varro, a thoroughly learned and erudite man, stories of this kind, and especially this one. There was at Tralles an inquiry by means of magic about the outcome of the Mithridatic War: a boy was gazing at a reflection of Mercury in water and then foretold the future in one hundred sixty lines of verse. Varro also tells that Fabius, having lost five hundred denarii, came to consult Nigidius, who inspired some boys by a spell to reveal where exactly a pot with part of the sum was buried and how the rest had been dispersed; one denarius actually found its way to the philosopher Marcus Cato, who acknowledged having received it from a servant as a contribution to the treasury of Apollo.

I have read these and many similar stories about boys in magical rituals, but I cannot make up my mind whether to believe them or not. But I do believe Plato when he says that there are divine powers that rank both by their nature and location between gods and men and that all kinds of divination and magic miracles are controlled by them. It also occurs to me that the human soul, especially a boyish, unsophisticated soul, can be lulled to sleep by soft music and sweet smells and hypnotized into oblivion of reality, so that gradually all consciousness of the body fades from memory and the soul returns and retreats into its own true nature, which, of course, is immortal and divine, and thus, as if it were in a kind of slumber, can predict the future. Well, no matter whether this is true or not, if one were to believe this sort of thing, the boy with the gift of prophecy, whoever he is, from what I hear, must be handsome and healthy, also intellectually alert and articulate, to make sure that the divine power takes up lodgings in him, as if he were a respectable abode—if it is really appropriate for such a power to squeeze itself into the body of a boy! It could also be that the boy's mind, when awakened, quickly applies itself to the business of divination, which may be his natural, spontaneous gift, which can easily be picked up without being dulled or damaged by any loss of memory, since it is well implanted in him. For, as Pythagoras used to say, you must not carve a statue of Hermes from just any piece of wood. If this is true, please tell me who that healthy, sound, gifted, handsome boy was whom I chose to initiate by my incantation. As a matter of act, Thallus—you mentioned his name—needs a physician, not a magician.

31

Lucius, the hero of Apuleius' novel, *Metamorphoses,* traveled to Thessaly in order to study the practice of magic, because Thessaly was traditionally considered the country of witches. Because we know that Apuleius was attracted to magic and got into trouble because of that, we might reasonably assume that the novel is partly autobiographical. Lucius, eager to learn important secrets, befriends Photis, the maid of a famous witch, and asks her to help him get transformed into a bird. Unfortunately Photis—it is not quite clear whether by accident or on purpose—picks the wrong ointment, and Lucius finds himself transformed into a donkey.

The antidote at first seems very simple: all Lucius has to do is eat roses in order to regain his human shape. As the story goes on, however, obstacle after obstacle is placed between Lucius and roses. In the end he is saved by the intervention of the goddess Isis and decides to become one of her devotees. Thus, a rather frivolous and ribald novel ends with a conversion and an initiation scene. Cured of the curiosity that caused him so much hardship, Lucius literally finds salvation and is reborn into one of the great mystery religions of the ancient world.

Apuleius, *Metamorphoses,* or *The Golden Ass* 3.21–28

In this delightful way Photis and I spent quite a few nights. One day she came to me trembling with excitement and told me that her mistress was still making no headway by other techniques in her love affair and was therefore going to transform herself into a bird the following night to fly to her darling. So Photis urged me to prepare myself carefully to watch secretly this important event. Early in the night she led me on tiptoe, without making the slightest noise, to the upstairs bedroom and told me to peep through a chink in the door and see what was going on. First I saw Pamphile strip completely. Then she opened a small chest, took out several boxes, opened one of them, and took some ointment out of it.

This she rubbed for a long time between her hands and then applied it to her whole body, from the tips of her toes to the top of her head. At the same time she had a long, secret conversation with her lamp and shook all her limbs vigorously. Her outlines began to fluctuate gently, and soft feathers began to sprout, strong wings grew, her nose became crooked, horny, her nails took on the shape of talons. No doubt about it: Pamphile had turned into an owl. She gave a plaintive hoot, hopped about a few times to test her flying ability, and then took off and flew away with powerful wing strokes.

Well, she had transformed herself by magic technique as she had wished; but I just stood there, glued to the spot, not bewitched by any spell, but hypnotized by what I had seen, and I was not at all sure that I was really Lucius. My mind was wandering, my stupor bordered on madness, I dreamed and was awake at the same time. I kept rubbing my eyes to find out whether I was awake. At long last I regained my aware-ness of reality; I took Photis' hand, held it close to my eyes, and said: "Please, do me a great favor; this is a very special moment; show me that you love me by doing something very unusual but very important for me and let me have a tiny little bit of that ointment; I beg you by these lovely breasts of yours, my honey child. I am your slave! Do me a favor that I can never repay (I shall always be indebted to you) and help me! You are my Venus: I want to be your winged Cupid!"

"Oh, really?" she said, "My little fox, my darling, you want me to chop off my own legs? You are helpless as you are, and I can hardly protect you from those Thessalian she-wolves; where shall I find you, when will I see you again, after you have become a bird?" I protested: "The gods in heaven forbid that I commit such a crime! Even though I were to fly on the proud wings of an eagle across the whole sky, as the trustworthy messenger or the cheerful armor-bearer of great Zeus, I would always get rid of my feathery glory and fly back to my little love nest. By that sweet knot in your hair in which my soul is tied up, I swear that I shall never love any other woman as much as my Photis. There is something else that occurs to me: once I have used the ointment and become a bird, I will have to stay far away from all houses, for what lady would like to have an owl—such a fine, cheerful bird!—as a lover? Don't we know that those birds of night, when they have flown into someone's house, cause great anxiety and are caught and nailed to the main door to pay by their own torments for the bad luck their ill-omened presence threatens to the household? But I almost forgot to ask: what do I have to say or do to get rid of the feathers and become good old Lucius again?" She replied: "Don't worry about this problem. My mistress showed me every single step by which such creatures can regain their human shape. And you mustn't assume that she did this out of kindness; she simply wanted me to be able to help her with an appropriate antidote after her return. Watch and you'll see what a tremendous effect is produced by quite ordinary little herbs: a small amount of anise, along with some laurel leaves, is put into spring water to make a bath and a potion."

She impressed this on me repeatedly and, trembling with fear, sneaked into the room to take one of the boxes out of the chest. I embraced and kissed her first; then I begged her to wish me a good flight; then I quickly took off all my clothes, greedily plunged my fingers into the box, dug out quite a lump and rubbed my whole body with it. After this I just stood there, flapping my arms, first one, then the other, trying to act like a bird, but no feathers and no wings, appeared anywhere. Instead my hair turned into bristles and my tender skin into hide; my fingers and toes seemed to shrink and contract into hooves, and from the end of my spine a long tail began to sprout. My face became enormous, my mouth enlarged, my nostrils dilated, my lips were pendulous, my ears oversized and hairy. The only good thing about this wretched transformation was that my genitals had increased in size, although it had become difficult for me to embrace Photis.

In despair I considered all the parts of my new body and I realized that I was not a bird but a donkey. I wanted to complain about what Photis had done to me, but I was deprived of human gestures and a human voice; and all I could do was to let my lower lip hang down and look at her sideways with moist eyes and reproach her silently. When she saw what shape I was in, she beat her face violently with her own hands and cried: "What an idiot I am! Oh, I could die! I was nervous and in a hurry and took the wrong box; the two looked exactly alike, and that fooled me. But fortunately there is a quite simple antidote to reverse this kind of transformation. You need only nibble some roses and you will at once get rid of your donkey's shape and become my dear Lucius again. If only I had made some garlands last evening, as I always do, so you wouldn't have to wait even one night. Anyway, first thing in the morning the remedy will be brought to you in a hurry!"

She was very upset, and I, though by now a complete ass and a beast of burden instead of Lucius, still retained my human ability to reason. For a long time I intensely debated within myself whether or not to kick and bite that wicked, scheming bitch to death. But my better sense checked this reckless impulse; I was afraid to cut off all hope for a remedy by inflicting the death penalty on her. I let my head hang and shook it sadly, but decided to swallow my humiliation for the time being and accept my cruel fate. I walked into the stable to join my trusty saddle horse. There I found another ass, one of Milo's (who had once been my guest-friend) that shared the stable. I thought that if dumb animals had any sense, any instinct of loyalty, my horse would recognize me and, feeling sorry for me, would offer me hospitality and a cozy place. But let Jupiter, the god of hospitality, let the mystic divinities of faith, hear this! That fine horse of mine and that ass put their heads together and formed at once a conspiracy against me; they were worried about their food, of course. As soon as they saw me approaching the manger, they laid their ears back and attacked me furiously with their hooves. They chased me away, as far as they could, from the barley which I myself had offered the evening before to my grateful servant!

This is the way they treated me! I was relegated to a remote corner of the stable. There I meditated on the rudeness of my colleagues, and since I was sure to be, with the help of the roses, Lucius again the next day, I planned my revenge on that disloyal horse. Suddenly I noticed at the very center of the middle column that supported the beams of the stable a statue of the horse goddess, Epona, sitting in a small shrine; the statue had been carefully adorned with rose garlands that were still fresh. I realized at once that here was the remedy, the help that I needed, and I abandoned myself to hope. I stood up on my hind legs and stretched my forelegs out as far as I could, and I made a tremendous effort to extend my neck and my lips in order to reach the garlands. But as I tried, my bad luck wanted it that my slave, who had been ordered to take care of the horse, suddenly saw me, jumped up, and shouted angrily: "I have had all I can take from this creature! Just a moment ago he was after the food of the other animals, and now he is after the statues of the gods! I'll be damned if I don't beat the disrespectful brute until he is too weak and too lame to move!" He looked around for some weapon and happened to find a bundle of faggots which was lying there; from that he picked a thick, knobby stick bigger than all the others and started whacking me with it (oh, it hurt!), and whacking me until someone made a tremendous noise and banged deafeningly against the door; at the same time people in the neighborhood, in a state of panic, shouted "Robbers!" This frightened him, and he ran away.

Almost at once the main gate was forced open and a gang of robbers rushed in. Armed men searched all parts of the house; neighbors arrived in a hurry from here and there to help, but they were powerless against the fast action of the enemies. They all had swords and carried torches that illuminated the night; reflected on the steel, the flames were brighter than the rising sun. There was a storage room in the center of the house, well locked and well secured by solid bolts; it was full of Milo's treasures. This room they attacked with heavy axes and broke it open. Once they had opened it they carried out the treasures, tied them quickly into bundles, and divided them among themselves. But there were more packages than men to carry them. Their overabundance of wealth totally defeated them, so they led us two donkeys and my horse out of the stable, loaded us with the heavier bundles, and, threatening us with sticks, drove us out of the house, which was empty by now. They left one member of the gang as a spy so that he could report on the investigation of the crime and drove us with relentless beatings at great speed over trackless mountain passes.

32

In his philosophical treatises, Plotinus, who was himself credited with supernatural gifts, discusses magic. As is often the case, it is difficult to follow his train of thought, possibly because he developed his thoughts as he lectured to his disciples and did not care to revise his notes or those taken by others.

It is clear from the first sentence of this text, however, that Plotinus believes in magic, although he is not certain how and why it works. He first deals with the concepts of sympathy and antipathy. These forces, he argues, exist in the universe by themselves and are contained by it, and magic simply reinforces them.

Ritual magic, as Plotinus no doubt saw it performed, required a special costume and the recitation of special formulas. He compares magic to music, for both affect the irrational part of the human soul.

Plotinus makes it clear that magic is something that happens between people, although he does not exclude the influence of cosmic forces; again, the analogy of music helps us understand what is happening: the vibrating strings of one lyre set off vibrations in another instrument.

To pray to the stars (i.e., the planets named after gods) is meaningless, according to Plotinus, and yet the stars do have a certain influence on all life on our planet. This leads back to the concept of cosmic sympathy: "He who demands something from the universe is no stranger to it"—that is, magic works because we belong to the universe.

Some magicians are bad, but their magic works too, because the force is available; because they use magic for an evil purpose, however, they will be punished sooner or later. Whatever harm the magician may be able to do to human beings, he cannot affect the universe, and even his power on this earth is limited, because the "wise man" (a concept Plotinus has borrowed from the Stoics) certainly can defend himself against black arts. The life of contemplation—that is, "the philosopher's life"—is free from any magical influence.

Plotinus, *Enneads* 4.4.40–44

How should one explain magical operations? Perhaps by sympathy, by the fact that there is a natural harmony between similar things and disharmony between dissimilar things, or else by the fact that there are a great many different powers that together affect a single living creature [or: that collaborate toward the unity of the cosmic organism]. For there are many attractions and magical operations without anyone to set them in motion. The true magic in the universe is "love and its opposite, hatred" [Empedocles]. The first sorcerer, the first witch doctor, is the one whom people know well and whose potions and spells they use against each other. For since it is natural for them to love, and since [everything] that makes them love attracts them to each other, a technique of love attraction [reading *holkes*, with Kirchhoff, for *alke* or *alkes* of most manuscripts] through witchcraft has originated, and the practitioners of this craft [simply] unite by physical contacts natures that are already drawn to each other and have an inborn love for each other. They [the practitioners] join one soul to another, just as if one were to join together [i.e., graft] plants that have grown at a distance from each other. They also use the figures that have power, by dressing up in certain ways [or: assuming certain attitudes?], and in certain ways they silently draw to themselves powers and are in one toward one [or: are in and toward universal unity?]. For if one were to assume [the existence of] such a person [the magician] outside the universe, he would not attract nor draw down any [special powers] by his spells or incantations. But now, since he does not work in another place, as it were, he is able to lead them, knowing the ways by which in the living universe one creature is led to another.

It is only natural for the soul to be directed by the tune and the specific sound of incantations and the attire [or: attitude?] of the operator, for that sort of thing has its own attraction, just like gestures [or: attitudes?] and words that inspire pity. For it is not our willpower or our reason that is charmed by music, but the irrational part of our soul. That sort of magic is not extraordinary; yet an audience that is bewitched [by music] feels love, even if it does not demand this [effect] from the performing musicians.

One should not believe that prayers [are fulfilled] because the will [of the gods] is listening. This is not what happens to those who are bewitched by incantations, nor does a man who has been bewitched when a snake puts a spell on people understand [what is happening to him], nor does he feel [it], but he knows, when it has already happened; the ruling part [of his soul, i.e., his intellect] remains unaffected.

From [the one] to whom a prayer has been addressed, something has gone out to the person [who prayed] or to another. But the sun or any other heavenly body [to whom a prayer was addressed] does not listen [or, understand?].

The effects of a prayer are real because one part [of the universe] is in sympathy with a[nother] part, as [one may observe] in a properly tuned string [on a lyre]. When it has been struck in its lower part, the upper part vibrates as well. And it often happens that when one string has been struck, another one, if I may say so, feels this, because they are in unison and have been tuned to one and the same pitch. If the vibration travels from one lyre to another, [one can see] how far the sympathetic element extends. In the universe, too, there is one universal harmony [or, tuning?], even though it is made up of discordant notes. It is also made up of similar notes, and all are related, even the discordant ones. Even things that are harmful to men—passionate impulses, for instance, that are drawn, along with anger, into the nature of the liver [i.e., the liver as their physical organ and center]—did not come [into the world] to be harmful [to men]. If, for example, one were to take fire from fire and hurt someone, yet without approaching him with any evil intention [reading *allon, hoi me mechanesamenos elthen,* modifying Seidel's suggestion, after Ficino's translation], he who took the fire [would be] responsible, because, you know, he delivered, as it were, something from one place to another, and it [i.e., the accident] happened because the person to whom the thing was transferred was unfit to receive it.

For this very reason the stars will need no memory—our whole discussion leads up to this point—or any sense perceptions transmitted to them. Hence they have no power of conscious assent to [our] prayers, but one must admit that with or without prayer their influence is real, since they [like us] are part of the One. Since there are many powers that are not guided by a conscious will, some spontaneously, some through a technique, and since this is happening in one living organism [the universe], some elements are helpful, some harmful, to one another, according to their nature. Medical art and magic art compel one element to surrender part of its own specific power to another element. In the same way, the universe also distributes something of itself to its parts, both spontaneously and because it feels the attraction of something else to part of itself which is essential to its own parts, because they share the same nature. After all, he who demands [something from the universe] is no stranger [to it].

He who demands it may be bad. This should not surprise you. Bad men draw water from a river too. The giver does not know the one to whom he gives; he simply gives. And yet the gift [reading *ha dedotai*] agrees with the nature of the universe. Therefore, if someone takes from that which is available to everyone, although he had no right to it, punishment will catch up with him according to the law of necessity.

One must admit, then, that the universe may be afflicted, although its ruling part must be admitted to be completely free of any affliction. Since affliction can come to its parts, we must admit that they can be afflicted. But since nothing that happens in the universe is against its nature, it must be free of affliction, because it is in contact with itself. The stars, too, can be affected, inasmuch as they are parts [of the universe], and yet they remain unafflicted because their will is not affected, because their bodies, their natures, remain unharmed and because, even if they communicate something through their soul, their soul is not diminished, and their bodies remain the same; if something is leaking from them, it escapes unnoticed, and whatever augments them, if anything augments them, is not noticed either.

What influence do witchcraft and magic drugs have on the wise man? As far as his soul is concerned, he is not affected by witchcraft, and his rational part could hardly be affected, nor would it change its conviction; but to the extent that he has in himself the irrational element of the universe, he might suffer to that extent, or rather this [element] might suffer [in him]. But [no one could provoke in him] love by magic drugs, for to be in love requires the assent of the one [i.e., the rational] soul to the affect of the other [i.e., the irrational] soul. Just as the irrational part is affected by incantations, thus he [the wise man] will cancel out those outside powers by counterincantations. He might suffer death from such [evil] influences or diseases or every kind of bodily affliction, for the part of the universe [which is in him] may be affected by another part of the universe itself—but his [real] self remains unharmed.—It is perfectly consistent with nature that one is not affected [by magic] right away, but at some later time.—Even daemons are not exempt from being affected in their irrational part—it is [, after all,] not unreasonable to attribute memory and sense perceptions to them and [to assume] that they are being charmed and led by science [i.e., magic] and that those among them who are closer to our region listen to those who call them, [the more readily,] the closer their contact with our region. For everything that is in close contact with another is bewitched by the other; the thing with which it is in contact bewitches and leads it; only that which is in contact with itself cannot be bewitched. Therefore all action and the whole life of the man of action is influenced by witchcraft; in fact, he is attracted by the things that charm him. Hence the phrase "for fair of face is the people of magnanimous Erechtheus." What knowledge establishes a contact [?], or is one attracted not by the arts of magic but by those of nature, as illusion works and connects one to another, not by proximity but by charms?

This leaves only the life of contemplation to be uninfluenced by witchcraft: for no one practices witchcraft on himself.

33

Plotinus had an enemy, Olympius of Alexandria, who tried to hurt him through magic. This passage from Porphyry's biography of Plotinus offers a good illustration of Plotinus' own teaching concerning magic [*no. 32*]. First, we are told that the sorcerer in vain appealed to the stars; second, that Plotinus, being a "wise man," was able to resist the evil forces directed at him and, in fact, to redirect them against the very operator who had unleashed them. Thus, the real anguish that Plotinus had felt at one point rebounded on the magician himself. Such personal experiences apparently helped shape Plotinus' ideas on magic in general.

Porphyry, *Life of Plotinus*, ch. 10

Among those who pretended to be philosophers there was a certain Olympius of Alexandria who, for a short time, was a student of Ammonius. Because of his ambitions he treated Plotinus with disrespect. Olympius' scheming went so far that he even attempted to direct, through magical operations, the evil influences of stars at Plotinus. But he realized that his attempts fell back on himself, and he said to his friends that the psychic powers of Plotinus were so strong that the attacks of those who wished to hurt him rebounded on themselves. Plotinus did sense the attempts of Olympius and said that his body had felt, at the time, like a purse whose strings had been pulled together; his limbs had been squeezed just like that. Olympius, however, since he ran the risk of hurting himself rather than Plotinus, gave up.

34

Iamblichus, a later Neoplatonist, discusses magic as a science. He actually uses the term *theurgy*, which has become a more exalted word for "ritual magic," implying, as it does, that higher gods, not mere daemons, are involved. His main problem is this: How can we use, for magical purposes, beings that are obviously superior to us? Why should they obey us? The answer is ingenious: we, as human beings, trained by great teachers, are complete entities in a sense that mere daemons are not, and we will always find even higher entities that will support us against the lesser ones, because we are more "in tune" with them.

Iamblichus, *On the Mysteries of Egypt* 4.2

What we will now discuss is something that we occasionally experience. It happens now and then that commands are addressed to spirits which do not use their own powers of reasoning and have no basis for judgment. There is a reason for this. For since our mind has the ability to reason and to judge reality, and since it concentrates in itself many different vital powers, it is used to giving orders to creatures that have no reason and are complete with the possession of only one faculty. So it calls on them as on superior beings, because it tries to draw away from the whole universe that surrounds us the elements that contribute to the full order of things, toward those which are contained within individual creatures. But it commands them as subordinate beings because certain parts of the world are often purer and more perfect by nature than those which spread all over the world. For example, if one being is intellectual and another entirely without soul or purely physical, the more limited one has greater authority than the one that stretches over a larger space, even if it is greatly surpassed by the other in size and power of control.

There is yet another principle behind this. All of theurgy has a double aspect: on the one hand, it is practiced by men and keeps our natural place in the universe; on the other hand, it is supported by divine signs and rises upward through them because it is connected with the higher powers; it moves harmoniously according to their direction and may indeed even put on the appearance of the gods. In accordance with this distinction the magician naturally calls upon the powers of the universe as superior ones, since he who calls upon them is a human being, but he also commands them, since he has assumed by his secret formulas the holy appearance of the gods.

35

The Christian writer Eusebius of Caesarea (c. A.D. 260–340) deals with magic in his *Preparation of the Gospel,* a work that is designed to show that even before the ministry of Jesus pagans had at least a glimpse of the word of God. He rejects what are, to him, the errors of paganism, but he does not dismiss all the claims made for magic.

For the pagans, the statues of the gods in their temples actually were the gods and could be used for magical operations. Eusebius does not reject this outright, even though his questions show that he has some doubts.

He then submits that many "supernatural" events are not the work of gods or daemons but the result of human fraud.

Finally he suggests natural causes for seemingly supernatural effects, and this takes us very close to the modern point of view. We can only observe, not always explain, what happens in nature. After a sufficient body of data has been collected, the true explanation may be found, and then what seemed like witchcraft becomes science. From our modern point of view, this seems a very sensible statement.

Eusebius also explains the psychological factors that enter into this process: a mood of expectation can be created in a certain way, an audience can be hypnotized, so to speak, but to Eusebius, who is deeply suspicious of paganism, all this may be part of a fraudulent scheme.

Eusebius, *The Preparation of the Gospel* 4.1.6–9

It is easy for anyone who is willing to show that all the claims made for the oracles are misleading and the fabrication of charlatans. Even for the pagans it is obvious that lifeless statues are not gods, and in the first book it has been shown that not even the stories of their mythical theology have any concepts that are serious and worthy of a deity; in the second and third books we have shown that neither their philosophical interpretations as allegories of natural forces have provided a straightforward explanation. But let us [now] consider the third question: How should one look at the powers lurking in statues? Can one have a pleasant relationship with them? Are they good and truly divine or the very opposite of all this?

If someone were to study this subject thoroughly, he might possibly come to the conclusion that everything is a mystification produced by charlatans and consists of fraud. Thus he would demolish their [the sorcerers'] prestige by showing that the stories told about them [the gods] are certainly not the work of a god, and not even the work of an evil daemon. For the oracles in verse, skillfully arranged, are the work of clever men; they are fictitious and designed to deceive; they are expressed in such a vague, ambiguous manner as to fit both of two possible outcomes of a prediction quite well.

One might also say that portents that seem miraculous and deceive the masses can be explained by natural causes. For in all of nature there are many kinds of roots, herbs, plants, fruits, and stones, as well as the various forces inherent in matter, whether they are dry or humid. Some of them have the power of repelling and driving away; others are magnetic and attract; some can separate and split up; others can assemble and concentrate; others can relax, make wet, rarefy; some save and others destroy; some transform and bring about a change in the present condition, one way or another, for a short while or a long time; their effect may be felt by many people or only a few; some of them lead the way, and others follow; some agree with others and increase and decrease along with them; some, indeed, are conducive to health and belong in the realm of medical science, while others produce illness and are harmful. Thus certain phenomena are due to the necessary effect of natural causes, and they wax and wane with the moon.

There are thousands of antipathies between living beings, roots, and plants: certain perfumes go to the head and make you sleepy, whereas others produce hallucinations. Moreover, the places, the locations where something is going on, also contribute a great deal, not to mention the instruments and the apparatus that sorcerers have held ready long beforehand to help them in their art. They [the charlatans] also benefit from all sorts of outside assistance to bring off their deceit: helpers who receive the visitors with a great show of interest and find out what their business is and what they wish to know. The inner sanctum and the recesses inside the temple, which are not accessible to the public, also hide many secrets. The darkness certainly helps them in their fraudulent scheme, and the mood of expectation, the fear the visitors experience when they think they are approaching the gods, and all the religious prejudices they have inherited from their ancestors [all contribute to the effect].

36

The following text deals mainly with theurgy, a form of ritual magic that was apparently practiced in late antiquity by certain religious and philosophical groups. As we have seen [*no. 32*], Plotinus believes in magic in general, but he does not accept the claims of the Gnostics that they can control cosmic powers by magical rites and use them for specific purposes, such as curing a disease by exorcising a daemon. For Plotinus, this is an insult to the gods. Whatever actually happens, whatever makes magic work, the gods are not involved. Plotinus leans toward "natural" or "scientific" causes, and since magic, according to him, uses natural forces, it is a kind of science. He attacks the practice of exorcism and ridicules the concepts on which it is based. No doubt, at the time when this was written, exorcists were still in demand, but Hippocratic medicine, of which Plotinus must have been aware, had been in existence for six or seven centuries.

Plotinus, *Enneads* 2.9.14

There is another way in which they [the Gnostics] grossly insult the purity of the higher powers. When they write out incantations, as if they were addressing those powers—not only the soul, but the powers above as well—what else are they doing but, if I may say so [reading, with Müller, *hos logo* for *kai logo*], forcing [the gods] to obey magic, to be led and influenced by witchcraft, charms, and formulas spoken by them? [Does this mean that] any of us who is highly accomplished in the art of reciting such formulas in the right way—songs and sounds, breathing and hissing—and everything else which works, according to their writings, has control over the higher powers?

If they are reluctant to put it this way, [let me ask,] how can incorporeal things be affected by sound? By the kind of phrases they use to make their theories look more sublime, they take away, without realizing it, the sublimity of those powers. They claim that they can cure themselves [reading *hautous* with Heigl] of diseases; if they mean that they can do this by self-discipline and a rational way of life, "fine," as the philosophers would put it. But in fact they assume that diseases are caused by daemons, and they claim that they can exorcise the daemons by their words. When they claim this, they may look quite sublime in the eyes of the average person who is in awe of the powers ascribed to magicians, but they would scarcely convince any sensible person [when they assert] that diseases do not have their origin in fatigue, or overeating, or lack of food, or a process of putrefaction, or, generally speaking, in changes that have their origin inside or outside.

Their treatments of illness make this clear. If the patient has diarrhea, or if a laxative has been administered, the illness passes through the downward passage and leaves the body. It is the same with bloodletting. Fasting also heals.

Does this happen because the daemon has been starving and the drug has made him waste away? Does he sometimes leave at once and sometimes remain inside? If he remains inside, how is it [possible] that the patient is feeling better, even though the daemon is still inside? Why did he leave—if he actually left? What happened to him? Did he perhaps thrive on the illness? In that case, the illness is different from the daemon. Moreover, if the daemon enters the body without any cause [i.e., in the absence of illness], why are we not always sick? And if there was a cause, why do we need the daemon to get sick? The cause is sufficient to produce a fever. It would be ridiculous to suppose that as soon as the cause operates, the daemon, standing by, moves in at once, as if to reinforce the cause. No, it is quite clear what they mean, what they intend, when they say all this, and for this reason above all—but for other reasons as well—did I mention their doctrine concerning daemons.

37

Porphyry seems to describe here a kind of séance during which some people he knew asked the "higher powers" all sorts of trivial questions. Such questions were also presented sometimes to the great oracles. For

Porphyry, as for his teacher, Plotinus, this procedure is absurd unless it is conducted as an experiment, "for the sake of research." How dare you bother the gods with such trivialities? he asks. They should be consulted only about serious questions—for instance, the nature of the Good, the nature of Happiness—but somehow they seldom are, and if they are, no profound answers ever come across. Porphyry admits that such séances could be fraudulent.

Porphyry, *Letter to Anebo*, chs. 46–49

I ask whether there might not be another way to Happiness, one that has escaped notice so far. I also wonder whether one should consider [mere] human opinions in matters of divine prophecy and theurgy, or whether the soul makes great things out of irrelevant premises. But there are other methods of foretelling the future, and, perhaps, those who have [the gift of] divine prophecy, can actually foresee [the future] but are not fortunate. For they do foresee the future but are unable to make good use [of their gift]. Therefore I want you to show me the way to Happiness and [tell me] what it essentially is.

There is an intense verbal debate going on among us, as we [reading *eikazomenon* for *eikazomenou*] try to form an idea of the Good based on human reasoning. There are those who have established communion with the Higher Power: but, if they have conducted their investigation in a negligent way, they have exercised their skill in vain, [asking] about where to find a runaway slave or the purchase of a piece of land, or the success of a marriage or a business venture, troubling the divine mind [with trivialities].

If they have been careful, those "in touch" may very well give absolutely true answers to many questions, but they have nothing trustworthy, nothing reliable to offer on Happiness, even though they can give thorough assessments of difficult things that are unprofitable to mankind. Thus, they were not really in touch with gods or good spirits, but with that well-known "spirit of deception," or the thing was human invention, a fiction of mortal nature from beginning to end.

38

In this text Iamblichus tells us clearly that the theurgists of his day invoked the powers that dwell in heaven, on earth, and in the underworld. This apparently puzzled some philosophers and theologians, because they thought that the gods dwell only in heaven.

In a rather poetic way Iamblichus tries to explain that the power of the gods is like the power of light: it gives illumination as well as warmth, and it fills the whole universe, yet it is one. He calls the stars "the brilliant image of the gods." The divine element, so to speak, is everywhere, and it cannot be understood in terms of time or space.

Iamblichus, *On the Mysteries of Egypt* 1.9

I assume you are not asking the difficult question "If the gods dwell only in heaven, why do those who practice theurgy invoke the powers that dwell on earth and below the earth?" As to the first principle, that the gods dwell only in heaven, it is not true. Everything is full of them. You are asking instead, I think, "How can some be said to be in the water or in the air? And how is it that some were assigned different places than others? Were they somehow given, as if by fate, the dimensions of bodies, even though their powers are infinite, indivisible, incomprehensible? How will there be a union among themselves, seeing that they are isolated by their own distinct dimensions and separated from each other according to the different nature of the places and the bodies they inhabit?"

There is one excellent solution to all these problems and many, many more like them: to consider the ways of divine allotment. No matter whether it distributes parts of the whole, such as the sky or sacred cities and areas or sacred precincts or holy statues, it illuminates everything from outside with its rays just like the sun illuminates everything with its rays from outside. Just as light embraces everything that it makes brighter, thus the power of the gods embraces everything that partakes of it. And just as light is present in the air without mixing with it [proof: no light remains in the air once the light-giving element has gone away, but it still keeps warmth once the warmth-giving element has withdrawn], thus the light of the gods shines separately and proceeds, stabilized in itself, throughout the whole universe. The visible light, in fact, is a continuum, the same everywhere. Thus it is impossible to cut off part of it or to confine it in a circle or to isolate it from its source.

According to the same principle, the whole universe, since it is divisible, can be separated in relation to the one and indivisible light of the gods. That light, too, is entirely and absolutely one. It is present as an indivisible entity for all those who are able to partake of it. By its perfect power it has filled everything; by its infinite superabundance of creativity it transcends everything in itself; in all respects it is united to itself and connects the end with the beginning. Imitating this process, the whole sky, the whole universe, goes through its circular motion. It is united with itself. It leads the elements in their circular whirl; it includes all beings that are within one another and move toward one another; it defines by equal measures even the parts that are located at the farthest ends. It produces one continuity, one harmony of the whole with the whole.

If you look at the clear images of the gods [i.e., the stars], united in this way, would you not hesitate to form a different opinion of the gods, their originators, and assume that they have sections and divisions and body-like outlines? As far as I am concerned, I think that just about everyone feels that way. For if there is no principle, no symmetrical relationship, no shared substance, no connection, either potential or actual, between the organized and the organizing element, they have no reality, if I may say so, since no lateral tension, or any internal tension or circumference in space, or division into parts, or any other equation of this type, is being generated in the presence of the gods.

39

It is clear from this text that Iamblichus considers himself a theurgist and that, to him, theurgy is a very special experience that cannot be analyzed logically. He establishes a boundary line between a purely theoretical approach to theurgy and a deeper understanding of it. We hear the voice of a philosopher who sincerely believes in the power of the ancient gods and seeks for means and techniques to demonstrate this power to un-believers or skeptics, the voice of a man who assumes that the gods re-spond to goodness and perfection in man. All this is expressed in the terminology of the Neoplatonist school, with its curious transitions from things as they are to things as they should be, and vice versa.

Iamblichus, *On the Mysteries of Egypt* 2.11

The following problems, which you raise when you denounce the igno-rance and fraud concerning these matters as a kind of wickedness and depravity, encourage me to expose the true doctrine about them. These problems are not controversial; everyone is in full agreement. For who would not admit that a science which concerns the being is most appro-priate to the gods [leaving out "of the divine cause" in the Greek text, probably a gloss], whereas the ignorance which tends toward the non-being falls quite short of the divine cause of the true ideas? But since I have not discussed this adequately, I will add [now] what I left out, and since my opponent defends himself more like a philosopher and a ra-tionalist, not according to the efficient technique of the priests, I feel I ought to speak about these matters more like a theurgist.

Let us admit that ignorance and deceit are wrong and irreligious. At the same time, they do not necessarily give the lie to what one offers properly to the gods and to divine acts, for it is not thought, either, that connects the theurgists with the gods. For what could prevent those who reason only theoretically from experiencing actually a theurgic union with the gods? In fact, things are quite different. It is the mystic realization of the unutterable things, the things that are achieved beyond all concept according to the divine will and the power of the silent symbols [that are] understood only by the gods, that bring about the theurgic union. Therefore, we do not achieve these effects by our thought, for in this way their effectiveness would be intellectual [only] and would depend on us. Neither of these is true. For even if we do not think [about it,] the signs themselves, by themselves, perform their proper operation, and the inexpressible power of the gods to whom they [the signs] belong recognizes itself, by itself, and its own images, without having to be awakened by our mental processes. It is not natural for the one containing to be shaken up by the one contained, the perfect by the imperfect, the whole by the parts. Therefore, the divine causes are not primarily called into action by our thoughts, but they [our thoughts], along with all the best dispositions of our soul and our [ritual] purity, must be there first, as auxiliary causes of a sort. What properly awakens the divine will are the divine symbols themselves. Thus the actions of the gods are stirred up by themselves and do not receive from any of the subordinate beings any kind of initiative for their proper energy.

I have discussed these things at length to make sure that you do not believe that the whole power of theurgic action depends on us.

40

According to this anecdote, Iamblichus' disciples asked him to perform some special feat for them. He does not oblige them right away but puts them off until a proper occasion arises. His first comment stems from his own doctrine: to demand a miracle from the gods is an act of arrogance and therefore dangerous. But he also believed—at least at one point—that miracles, as we call them, are not caused by the intervention of gods at all. In the end he succeeds in materializing two divine presences, Eros and Anteros. Eros is the god of love, but Anteros, in this context, cannot be the opposite of love, that is, hate. The prefix *anti* also suggests a substitute or surrogate for love, something like love, but not quite the real thing. The disciples are convinced by what they see, and from then on they accept everything their teacher tells them.

Eunapius, *Lives of the Philosophers and Sophists* 5.2.7

The disciples wanted to test Iamblichus in something more important, but he said: "No, it does not depend on me; we must wait for the right moment." Some time later they decided to go to Gadara. This is a place in Syria where there are hot springs, inferior only to those at Baiae in Italy, with which no other baths can be compared. So they traveled in the summer season to Gadara. Iamblichus happened to be bathing, his disciples were bathing with him, and they insisted on the same request as before. Iamblichus smiled and said: "It is irreverent to the gods to give this kind of demonstration, but for your sake it shall be done." There were two hot springs, smaller, but more pleasant than the others. He told his disciples to find out from the natives their ancient names. They did what he had told them and said to him: "This is not something we made up, but this spring is called Eros and the one next to it has the name Anteros." Right away he touched the water—he happened to be sitting on the ledge of the spring where the overflow runs off—recited a brief summons, and conjured up from the depth of the spring a boy. The boy had fair skin and was not too tall but well-built, his golden locks were shining on his shoulders and his breast, and he looked exactly like someone who was taking a bath or had just come out of a bath. The disciples were awestruck, but Iamblichus said: "Let's go to the next spring," and led the way, lost in deep thoughts. Then he went through the same sort of ritual at this other place and conjured up another Eros, similar to the former one in all respects except that his hair was darker and flowed in the sunlight. Both boys hugged Iamblichus and clung to him as if he were their real father. He sent them off to their proper places and went away, after completing his bath, while his disciples showed their reverence. After this the crowd of his pupils demanded nothing more, but considering the proofs that had been given to them, clung to him as if by an unbreakable chain and believed everything.

41

Maximus of Ephesus, the most famous theurgist of the fourth century A.D., had great influence on the emperor Julian but was executed under Valens. Eunapius, the author of this biographical sketch, gives us his own impression of the great teacher and then refers to Eusebius (not the Christian writer of Caesarea) and to Julian himself to show how Maximus' charisma worked. Apparently we face once more the type of philosopher-teacher-theurgist that seems to go back to Pythagoras. Without a miracle the message was not complete: the teaching was about miracles, and the miracles, when they happened, reinforced the teaching. Young Julian is looking for a teacher who combines these abilities, and through Eusebius he finds Maximus, but after Maximus he goes on to an even greater hierophant with prophetic powers.

Eunapius, *Lives of the Philosophers and Sophists*
7.11.6—10; 7.1.1—3; 7.2.1; 7.3.6—6.3 (G. Giangrande)

Then they brought so-called monks into the sacred places. These looked like human beings, but their life-style was swinish, and they openly suffered and committed all sort of unspeakable atrocities. Yet this sort of thing, the contempt of the divine, was considered a form of religion. In those days, any person who wore a black robe and was willing to behave indecently in public acquired absolute power: such progress in morals has been made by mankind! But these events have been recorded in works of general history. They installed these monks even in the temple of Canopus, condemning people to worship slaves, worthless ones at that, instead of the intelligible gods. For they collected the skulls and bones of people who had been imprisoned and condemned to death by courts of law, pretending that they were gods. They fell on their knees before them and believed that they could derive power by wallowing on their tombs. Slaves who had served [their masters] badly, who had been wasted by flagellations, who carried scars [as signs] of their wickedness on their bodies were actually called "witnesses" and "deacons" and "ambassadors" of the requests coming from the gods. And yet the earth supports these gods! All of this naturally contributed to the great reputation of Antoninus as a prophet and seer, because he used to say to everyone that the sanctuaries would be transformed into tombs.

He who writes this has seen the man [i.e., Maximus] in person. I was still young, and he was old when we met. I listened to his voice, which sounded like that of Athena or Apollo in Homer. The pupils of his eyes were sort of winged, his beard was white, and his eyes revealed the impulses of his soul. There was a harmony all over him when you listened to him and looked at him, and when you were close to him, you felt overwhelmed through both sense organs, because the rapid movement of his eyes and the flow of his speech was too much for you. When there was a discussion, no one, not even the most experienced, the most eloquent, dared to contradict him. They all surrendered to him in silence and accepted everything he said, as if it had come from tripods [i.e., from an oracle]. Such was the charm that sat on his lips.

When Julian [the Apostate] heard this, he did not leave the philosopher but spent most of his time with Eusebius [Neoplatonist, student of Aedesius] and Chrysanthius [also a student of Aedesius]. Chrysanthius had the same kind of soul as Maximus [a fellow student], and he, too, was able to get into trance and share his inspiration with others [meaning uncertain, but probably an allusion to theurgy]. He devoted himself to [occult] knowledge, and his whole character was similar.

Eusebius said: "Maximus is one of our older and most advanced students. He is so enormously gifted and has such an extraordinary command of words that he does not care about the [normal] kind of proofs [that the gods exist] but gives in to some mad impulses and urges. Not so long ago he summoned us to the temple of Hecate, and there he showed us many witnesses [or: testimonies] on his behalf. We met him there and reverenced the goddess. He said to us: 'Be seated, dear friends, and watch what is about to happen, and [decide] if I am in any way different from most.' This is what he said. We were all sitting there. He now burned gum of frankincense and sang to himself some kind of a hymn from beginning to end. His demonstration reached such a level that the statue [of Hecate] began to smile, at first, and then clearly laughed. We were stirred up by this phenomenon, but he said: 'None of you should be frightened by this; in a moment, even the torches in the hands of the goddess will light up.' Before he finished speaking, light burst forth from the torches in all directions. Well, for the time being, we were overwhelmed and left that spectacular miracle-worker.

"But you should not be amazed; neither am I. Instead, you should understand that purification through reason [or: speech] is very important." When the divine Julian heard this, he said: "Well, good-bye and stick to your books! You have shown me the man I was looking for." He said this, kissed Chrysanthius on the head and left at once for Ephesus. There he met Maximus, attached himself to him and devoted himself to wisdom in all its dimensions. Maximus suggested to him also to invite the divine Chrysanthius to join them, and when he came, the two of them were barely capable to satisfy the boy's large appetite for [occult] knowledge. Julian made good progress, but then he heard that there was even more to learn in Greece, from a hierophant of the Two Goddesses [Demeter and Persephone], so he rushed there eagerly. I am not allowed to reveal the name of the hierophant in charge at the time. It was he who initiated the writer [into the Mysteries], and he descended by birth from the Eumolpidae. He also predicted, in the presence of the writer, the destruction of the sanctuaries and the ruin of all of Greece. Furthermore, he testified clearly as to who would succeed him as a hierophant, though the man was not worthy to touch the hierophantic thrones, because he had been consecrated to [serve] other gods. And yet he had sworn a most solemn oath that he had never presided over other cults. Nevertheless, this man had presided [over another cult], and he was not even an Athenian!

He [the authentic hierophant] reached such a level of prophetic power that he predicted that in his lifetime the sanctuaries would be totally devastated and razed to the ground. The other one, he said, would see this happening in his own lifetime, dishonored by his excessive ambition. The cult of the Two Goddesses would end before his death, and he, stripped of his honor [i.e., the priestly office], would neither be a hierophant any more nor reach an old age. And so it happened.

MIRACLES

Introduction

Miracles can be defined as extraordinary events that are witnessed by people but cannot be explained in terms of human power or by the laws of nature. They are therefore frequently attributed to the intervention of a supernatural being. In this sense, an act of healing can be considered a miracle, for it involves a healer who is divine or who is especially favored by a higher being acting through him.[1]

The definition, tentative as it may be, shows us how difficult it is to separate miracles from the power of performing magic (the Greek word *dynamis* covers both), because magic does produce miraculous effects, and miracles can be attributed to magic.

The problem is partly semantic, partly cultural, partly theological. We have seen that the word *magic* was borrowed by the Greeks from the Persians to describe religious rites totally foreign to them, totally different from their own, and therefore suspect. The word *miraculum* (from *mirari* 'to marvel'), on the other hand, is a Latin word with a long history; in the modern sense, it is attested only in later Latin.[2] The Latin Bible also uses the term *signum* 'sign' to translate the Greek *semeion;* it uses *prodigium* 'marvel' to translate *teras,* and *virtus* 'power' to translate *dynamis,* as both the power to perform miracles and the resulting miracle itself.

The cultural problem has already been formulated. To rephrase it, one person's religion may be another person's magic.

The theological problem is related to the other two. A believer would readily accept the term *miracles* for what the New Testament calls "signs" and "wonders" (how to explain them is a different matter), but he would not use the term *magic;* from a different point of view, Jesus has been called a "magician" and put into the category of "wonder-workers" (*thaumatourgoi*) such as Apollonius of Tyana. Clearly, this is more than a semantic difficulty: it is ultimately a matter of faith.

One difference seems to be implied in many of the texts: magic can be performed privately, secretly; miracles, especially in the sense of "signs," have to be seen and experienced in the open by many people.

Another difference should not be overlooked: magic is often hard work; it may require hours, even days, of concentrated effort and sometimes an elaborate apparatus. Miracles tend to happen spontaneously and require only the miracle-worker and some very simple materials—a garment, for instance—that are thought to be charged with his *dynamis*. A miracle might be described as instant magic, but magic is not a continuing miracle; it is rather the exercise of a profession.[3]

Some characteristics of the miracle are *to paradoxon* 'the extraordinary' (in the sense of "the totally unexpected"),[4] *to teratodes* 'the strange', and *to phoberon* 'the fearsome'. These words describe the emotions and comments of the people witnessing the miraculous event. Miracles, of course, are always welcome (while magic may be evil), but even so they inspire fear, because one is in the presence of a strange power.

One should keep in mind what Pierre Janet has said about miracles:

> From time to time it has been the fashion to laugh at miracles and to deny that they occur. This is absurd, for we are surrounded by miracles; our very existence is a perpetual miracle, and every science has begun by the study of miracles. What may be called miraculous is part of a very large category of phenomena which conflict with scientific determinism. . . . When such phenomena are rather indifferent to us, we describe them as "fate"; but when we welcome these undetermined phenomena, we speak of them as miracles. If I am told that some unknown person has won the first prize in a lottery, I say that he has done so by chance; but if I am myself the winner, I talk of a miracle.[5]

The Bible offers stories of miraculous cures. The miracles performed by Moses in his contest with the Egyptian wizards (Exodus 7) are magical in nature,[6] but for Josephus (*Ancient History* 2.284ff.) they are proof of divine authenticity; thus he makes Moses say that the deeds performed by him are superior to the magical art of the Egyptians because things divine are superior to things human. What Moses actually does is almost exactly what the Egyptian magicians were trying to do, except that he does it much better, and it is not magic for effect or profit, but a kind of miracle to demonstrate that his god is superior to their gods. Magic in itself would be suspect, but if it serves to confirm the supreme authority of a god, it is legitimate. This may explain why so many rites that we would call magical today were practiced in a sanctuary and thus removed from the sphere of everyday life.

The Old Testament prophets were able to effect miraculous cures and even raise the dead, and Jesus, who was considered a new prophet by some of his contemporaries, did the same. But this is only part of his ministry, for he is not a professional faith healer, and—unlike Apollonius of Tyana—he never gives any medical advice concerning diet, bathing, or exercise.

What we call "miracles" are very often extraordinary cures of diseases and physical conditions. The term *faith healing* is commonly used, but this is open to the objection that faith in the healer is not always necessary.[7] Hence the terms *divine healing* or *spiritual healing* have been suggested, and perhaps they are more useful. If diseases were caused by divine powers or by evil spirits, they could also be healed by a divine power acting through someone, or by a holy spirit driving out an evil one. Sometimes, as in the case of incubation discussed earlier (see chapter 1), a ritual had to be followed, but very often the touch of the healer is sufficient. The healer is not always a religious figure; one of the prerogatives of royalty in antiquity as well as in the Middle Ages was the ability to effect miracles.[8]

Many patients whose miraculous cures are recorded had probably sought help from conventional medicine at one point, going to the healer as a last resort. Many, of course, would go to the healer in the first place rather than to a physician. Although what we would call scientific medicine had been practiced since Hippocrates (a contemporary of Socrates' [fifth century B.C.]), folk medicine continued to exist side by side with it.

A pilgrimage to Epidaurus is difficult to interpret in these terms. If you were deeply religious you might prefer this from the beginning. It should also be said that the priests were not merely faith healers: they seem to have had some medical knowledge. Still, the miraculous cures recorded in the famous sanctuaries were ascribed to divine intervention: the priests' knowledge and the ritual they prescribed were only supposed to open the way, as it were, for the god to act upon the patient, and the miracle had to be recorded to the glory of the god. In this sense, the whole procedure, from the preparatory rites to the final recording of the cure on the walls of the temple, was very much a part of worship. The Egyptians apparently believed that anything left behind by a grateful patient had prophylactic powers. In this, as in other aspects, the cult of Asclepius seems to continue Near Eastern traditions.[9]

The ancient concept of "miracle" can best be explained in the following way.[10] Nature is permeated by a divine power. We see the processes in the universe, the macrocosm, as analogies (on a much larger scale) of processes in the laboratory, the microcosm. The ancient alchemists wanted to achieve the ultimate miracle—the transformation of lead into gold, for instance—but they communicated with the gods in order to achieve this. Similarly, ancient physicians, although they prescribed diet, drugs, exercise, and other "natural" or "scientific" therapies, did not always exclude divine intervention. Either they identified God with Nature or they distinguished certain events which they thought they could explain in "natural" terms from those which seemed "spontaneous" because they could not be explained rationally. The latter might be called "miraculous." Thus, many ancient physicians from Hippocrates to Galen were probably opposed to the rites of exorcism and purification that were practiced by the shamans, but this does not mean that they were pure scientists in the modern sense of the word. The miraculous was part of their world, and it is unlikely that they discouraged their patients from making a pilgrimage to Epidaurus. Advice that would be considered "unprofessional" today was very much a part of Greek and Roman culture.

A miracle often implies an instant cure witnessed by astonished spectators; on the other hand, we have records of cures that required a certain amount of time, like those told by Aelius Aristides [*nos. 45, 46*], but that were still considered somewhat extraordinary. Of the fifty or so miracles ascribed to Jesus in the four Gospels, roughly three dozen can be called healings (excluding resurrections from the dead), and many of those refer to psychological states and psychiatric disorders.[11] Several cures of organic diseases are also recorded in the synoptic Gospels (Matthew, Mark, and Luke). Matthew (8:5–13; see also Luke 7:1–10 and John 4:46b–54), along with Mark (7:24–30), deals with patients who did not know that they were being treated: one is the "boy" (son or slave) of the centurion (or royal official) of Capernaum; the other is the young daughter of the Syrophoenician (or, according to Matthew 15:21–28, Canaanite) woman.[12] These stories have one thing in common: the patient is closely associated with or related to a non-Jew, and Jewish readers might have been offended at the thought that Jesus had entered the house of one who was unclean. Yet he was so moved by their faith that he consented to cure the patient, even though it had to be done at a distance.

When Jesus commissions the Twelve (Matthew 10:1–15), he gives them authority over unclean spirits (daemons), the power to drive them out, and he charges his disciples to heal every disease and infirmity. Physical illness or emotional disturbances still had not been clearly separated from sin and could be considered a form of divine punishment. Therefore, salvation, the ministry of the Apostles, had to include physical, mental, and spiritual health. It has been suggested that one of the reasons for the growth of the early Church was its care for the sick (in other words, the sinful) who were neglected by the medical establishment of the period.[13]

In Book 22 of the *City of God* Augustine describes a long series of miracles, including some that he had witnessed or helped to bring about (ch. 8). One involved a high-level civil servant in Carthage who had suffered for a long time from a large number of fistulae in his rectum. He had been operated on already, but the surgeons said that one more operation was necessary. The patient, who feared the agonizing pain that he knew the surgeons' knives would inflict, begged Augustine and one of his associates—both not yet priests, but already, as Augustine writes, "servants of God"—as well as two bishops, one priest, and several deacons to be present during the operation. They comforted him and prayed with him for a long time. What Augustine actually writes is this: "Whether the others prayed . . . I do not know; as far as I was concerned, I could not pray at all." He could only think: If God does not hear these prayers, what prayers does he hear? The next day the servants of God were there when the surgeons arrived, but the surgeons, after removing the bandages, could not find anything on which to operate. A miracle had happened literally overnight.

In the texts translated here, it is mostly the so-called neurotic illnesses that are cured in such a way as to suggest divine intervention. Ancient Greek drama relates the tensions that existed within families or communities, and even though modern medical terms did not exist then, the problems were the same as those encountered today. Yet medical science, then as now, was more interested in particular physical symptoms that could be dealt with than in a patient's stress and anxiety.[14] The almost instant relief that successful operations afforded made surgeons rich and famous. Simple drugs, diet, exercise, and bathing in certain springs had curative powers, too, but their effects were less spectacular. Beyond such treatments, however, there was always the need for a sympathetic person to whom one could confess one's problems or who might even grasp them intuitively.

Plutarch on the Miraculous

Plutarch was a deeply religious person, rooted in tradition, and living at a time when many Greeks had lost their faith in the ancient gods. He was also a philosopher, a historian, and an accomplished and very prolific writer. All this makes him a unique source of information for us. His so-called theological essays (those dealing with gods or religious institutions and related topics) are particularly important. They reflect the thoughts of a very perceptive, very cultured observer of supernatural phenomena. As such, a brief discussion of Plutarch's views on extraordinary phenomena may clarify a few points.[15]

When Plutarch speaks of events that ultimately defy explanation, the terms he uses most frequently are *tekmerion, semeion, thauma* and *anomalia*.

He uses the first term, *tekmerion,* when he deals, for instance, with the indications or instructions given by the gods to the pioneers who founded the earliest Greek colonies (*On the Oracles of the Pythia,* 408a). He describes in similar terms the miraculous lamp in the sanctuary of Zeus Ammon in Libya (*On the Failure of the Oracles,* 410b): this lamp was always kept burning, but, according to the priests, it used up ever diminishing amounts of oil. From this *tekmerion* the priests concluded that the years were becoming shorter. The term has a similar meaning in Acts 1:3 (the only example in the New Testament): "After his suffering, he showed himself to these men [i.e., the apostles he had chosen] and gave many convincing proofs that he was alive." The exhalations that filled a certain area within the temple at Delphi with a sweet odor are also a *tekmerion* for Plutarch (*On the Failure of the Oracles,* 437c). Such phenomena reveal some kind of anomaly, a gap or a break, so to speak, in the natural order of things. Usually they indicate a divine presence. They are "signs" or "clues" that make a person think, reflect, speculate.

Closely related is the term *semeion,* which can also be translated as "sign." It is very frequent in the New Testament where it often has the same meanings as in Plutarch. The letter E, for instance, is a *semeion,* a "symbol" of the Pentad, the Pythagorean group of five; this is the numeric value of the letter in Greek arithmetics (*On the Epsilon in Delphi,* 387e). The history of the Delphic oracle, which rose from modest beginnings to become an internationally recognized religious center, is a sign of the actual presence of the god Apollo (*On the Oracles of the Pythia,* 409c). Elsewhere (*On the Failure of the Oracles,* 410d), small things in nature are, for Plutarch, models or suggestions of a higher reality or, once again, signs of a divine presence. Here and there, *semeion* designates an event foreshadowing the future (often in an ambiguous way), or providing a clue that helps the observer judge the nature of an apparition (*On Socrates' Daimonion* 577d; cf. 588a, 593d, 585e).

In *God's Slowness to Punish* (550d–e) Plutarch offers a summary of Platonic theology. Here, he ponders on the attitude of human beings when they look at celestial phenomena: they "marvel" at them, and this feeling of "marvel" (*thauma*) is at the beginning of all philosophy and science. The term *thaumasion* 'marvelous' appears, for instance, in *God's Slowness to Punish* (565f). "Amazement" is the natural reaction of a person to a supernatural occurrence. In his essay *On Socrates' Daimonion* (589f–592f), Plutarch tells the story (*mythos*) of a certain Timarchus who consulted the oracle of Trophonius and traveled to another world. During his trip many strange things happened to him. (The account has remarkable similarities with early Christian apocalyptic writings.) In the end, a voice from heaven predicts Timarchus' death, and he dies, as predicted.

Plutarch's beautiful essay *On the Soul* survives only in fragments. There he tells (frag. 176 Sandbach) the story of a man named Antyllus who—like Timarchus—traveled to another world, saw many strange things, and returned. We would call this, perhaps, a shamanistic experience.

The term *anomalia,* as used by Plutarch, designates something that seems to defy the laws of nature, something supernatural and strange (*On the Failure of the Oracles,* 410b, 413e). The word does not occur in the New Testament.

Plutarch uses other terms to indicate something extraordinary, super-human, or truly amazing. In the essay *On Isis and Osiris* (330b), he speaks of the "great deeds" (*megalai praxeis*) of "divine men and women," such as Semiramis, Sesostris, Manes, Cyrus, and Alexander the Great—deeds that border on the fabulous.

In the *Oracles of the Pythia* (379e) he preserves some stories told by the tourist guides at Delphi: a colossal bronze column dedicated by Hieron collapsed on the very day the tyrant died far away, in Syracuse. A statue lost its eyes (made of precious stones) when the man who had dedicated it fell in the battle of Leuctra. Evidently, a certain mysterious *dynamis* is alive in the gifts offered to the god of Delphi, and it manifests itself now and then in a certain synchronicity with distant events, to testify to the god's telepathic powers.

Alas, most people, says Plutarch, are only superficially impressed by the marvelous or miraculous. They are like children: when their curiosity is satisfied, they walk away, ignoring the divine message that is there for them to receive (*Oracles of the Pythia* 409d). But miracles are all around us, and they never cease.

NOTES

1. See J. A. MacCulloch, in *ERE,* 8:676ff.

2. Isaiah 29:14 is difficult to interpret. The Vulgate has: "Ideo ecce ego addam ut admirationem faciam populo huic miraculo grandi et stupendo." The New English Bible (1970) translates "therefore I will yet again shock this people, adding shock to shock."

3. The crowds, so often present when certain types of miracles happened, seem to have developed a kind of momentum of their own, a *dynamis* that the miracle-worker exploited; one could say that miracles have performance character. In Homer, miracles are sometimes performed by the will of a god, but the devices used may be magical; see E. J. Ehnmark, *Anthropomorphism and Miracle* (Upsala, 1039), p. 6.

4. See Weinreich, *Antike Heilungswunder,* pp. 198ff.

5. Pierre Janet, *Psychological Healing,* trans. E. Paul and C. Paul, 2 vols. (New York, 1925), 1:21.

6. Hull, *Hellenistic Magic,* p. 46.

7. L. Rose, *Faith Healing* (Harmondsworth, 1971), pp. 11ff., admits the success of "unorthodox" medicine but claims that it has nothing to do with religious beliefs and practices; he prefers to consider it a form of psychotherapy. See also E. Thrämer, in *ERE,* 6:540ff.; and J. C. Lawson, *Modern Greek Folklore and Ancient Greek Religion* (1910; repr., Cambridge, 1964), pp. 60ff.

8. See M. L. P. Bloch, *The Royal Touch,* trans. J. E. Anderson (London, 1973). Pyrrhus of Epirus, Vespasian, and other ancient rulers were thought to have the "king's touch."

9. Rose, *Faith Healing,* p. 24.

10. C. J. Singer, *Greek Biology and Greek Medicine* (Oxford, 1922); L. Edelstein, *Ancient Medicine,* ed. O. and C. L. Temkin (Baltimore, 1967), pp. 205ff.

11. Rose, *Faith Healing,* p. 27.

12. Rose (ibid.) does not refer to the story in Matthew.

13. Ibid., pp. 28–29.

14. See U. Maclean, *Magical Medicine* (Harmondsworth, 1974), p. 177.

15. See H. D. Betz, *Plutarch's Theological Writings and Early Christian Literature* (Leiden, 1975).

Texts

42

The sanctuary of Asclepius at Epidaurus (a small city-state on a peninsula of the Saronic Gulf) was famous for its cures. Although the temple was built no earlier than the fourth century B.C., the cult seems to have been older. Around the temple there was a whole complex of other buildings, some of them designed for the convenience and entertainment of the patients, who often spent weeks or months there seeking relief. There were porticoes, baths, a gymnasium, at least one inn, and a theater, which has been preserved. Attached to the temple was a special dormitory, necessary for the procedure of "incubation" for which Epidaurus was famous, though it was also practiced elsewhere—for instance, at the oracle of Trophonius at Lebadea. The patients who spent the night in the dormitory received—perhaps not right away, but sooner or later—a vision of the god of healing, Asclepius, in their dreams. He inquired about their symptoms and indicated the therapy they needed. In principle, every god that a Greek or Roman believed in might appear to him, no matter where he slept, but only a few gods at a few places were thought to be able to give sound medical advice. On the other hand, incubation could be used for other purposes; the god then acted like an oracle, answering specific questions—for instance, telling the visitor where to find a lost article.

Incubation might be called "dreaming under controlled conditions," and it is still a mystery how the priests could practically guarantee dreams of this kind. Incubation must involve, somehow, a magic procedure, for a god is conjured or summoned ritually, but it is performed within a religious context, under the supervision of priests who may have had some medical knowledge. Perhaps a drug was administered, and hypnosis may have been used. The details of the ritual itself are not known. There may have been ablutions, prayers, processions, and fasting, and it is said that the patient sometimes had to sacrifice an animal and sleep on its hide. The moods of hope and expectation were heightened by hundreds of inscriptions on the walls of various buildings recording previous cures and by the hymns of praise sung by aretalogists.

Trained physicians were probably available, for Asclepius was, after all, the patron god of Greek medicine, and it is said that the temple of Asclepius on the island of Cos—a rival institution—was founded by disciples of the great Hippocrates. But it also seems that many went to Epidaurus as a last resort, after the conventional medicine of their time had been unable to give them the help they wanted.

The god often prescribed specific diets, exercise, baths—just what a resident physician at one of the well-known spas in Europe might do today. Some sanctuaries were actually located near mineral or radioactive springs, and even though their healing powers are not quite established today, the Greeks and Romans believed in them. Sometimes the god would also prescribe a fairly simple drug.

Since the advice he gave usually made sense and since some cures took a long time, one should perhaps not speak of these cures as miracles, for miracles tend to happen suddenly, mysteriously. But the priests ascribed them to divine intervention, many patients seem to have accepted this, and some of the stories—such as those of very long pregnancies—border on the miraculous.

The whole operation therefore has a magical, a medical, and a religious aspect, it seems. One wonders whether people with minor ailments went to Epidaurus for a vacation, just as the rich and the fashionable went to Baden-Baden in the nineteenth century.

The inscriptions mostly speak for themselves. Not all of the patients were firm believers (see the doubters of nos. 3 and 4), but faith apparently was not absolutely necessary: the god did what he did and thus implanted a new faith in the person he had healed, but he also punished a man who defrauded him (no.7). As number 8 shows, the god also had a sense of humor.

IG 4.951–52 (=Dittenberger, *Sylloge*⁴ 1168–69)

God   Good Fortune   Cures of Apollo and Asclepius

1. *Cleo had been pregnant for five years.* When she had been pregnant for five years she turned to the god for help and slept in the inner sanctum. As soon as she came out of there and the sanctuary, she gave birth to a boy who, as soon as he was born, washed himself in the spring and walked around with his mother. Because this happened to her, she had an inscription set up:

It is not the size of the tablet that should be admired,
but the divine intervention.
Cleo bore her burden in her womb for five years
Until she slept here [in the temple] and he [the god]
made her well.

2. *A young woman three years [pregnant]*. Ithmonika of Pella [?] came to the sanctuary and slept in the inner sanctum to find out about her child. She fell asleep in the temple and had a vision: in her dream she asked the god to give her a baby girl. The god told her that she would become pregnant and that he would grant her any other wish she might have, but she said that she had no further demands. She became pregnant and remained pregnant for three years, until she approached the god, asking for help in giving birth. As she slept in the inner sanctum, she had a dream. She dreamed that the god asked her whether she had not gotten everything she had wanted and whether she was not pregnant, but about the baby he said nothing. But when he asked her whether she needed anything else, and he found out what it was, he said he would do this, too. Since she had come to him for help in this situation, he said he would grant her that, too. After this she quickly left the inner sanctum, and as she came out of the sanctuary, she gave birth to a baby girl.

3. *A man whose fingers, all but one, were paralyzed*. He came to the god asking for help. When he looked at the tablets in the sanctuary, he did not believe in the [miraculous] cures and made fun of the inscriptions. As he slept in the sanctuary, he had a vision. He dreamed that he was playing dice in the temple, and as he was about to make a throw, the god appeared to him and leapt onto his hand and stretched out his fingers. As the god left, still in his dream, the patient clenched his fist and extended the fingers one by one. After he had managed to stretch them all, the god asked him whether he still refused to have faith in the inscriptions on the tablets around the sanctuary. He said "No." "All right," the god answered, "but since you did refuse to believe what is not unbelievable, from now on your name will be 'the Doubter.' " When it was day, the man left and was cured.

4. *Ambrosia from Athens, who was blind in one eye*. She came to the god seeking help, but as she walked around the sanctuary, she laughed at some of the cures, because it seemed implausible and impossible to her that the lame and the blind could be healed simply by having a dream. She slept in the sanctuary and had a dream. She dreamed that the god stood close to her and said that he would make her well; in return he asked her to dedicate in the sanctuary a silver pig as a memorial to her stupidity. As he

said this, he cut open her weak eye and poured in some medicine. When it was day, Ambrosia left and was cured.

5. *A dumb boy.* This boy came to the sanctuary to get his voice. As he was presenting his preliminary sacrifice and performed the customary ritual, the acolyte who carried the fire for the god looked at the father of the boy and asked him: "Will you promise that if he gets the wish that brought him here, he will bring within a year the sacrifice that he owes for his cure?" The boy at once cried out: "I promise." The father was amazed and told him to say it again. He said it again and was well from that moment.

6. *Pandarus, a Thessalian, who had marks on his forehead.* He slept in the sanctuary and had a vision. He dreamed that the god put a bandage over the marks and told him to take the bandage off after he left the inner sanctum and dedicate it in the temple. When day came, the man got up and took off the bandage, and his face was clear of marks. He dedicated the bandage in the temple, and it had on it the marks from his forehead.

7. *Echedorus received the marks of Pandarus in addition to the ones he already had.* This man (Echedorus) had received from Pandarus a sum of money to offer to the god in Epidaurus on his behalf, but did not deliver it. As he slept in the sanctuary he had a vision. He dreamed that the god stood over him and asked him whether he had received any money from Pandarus of Euthenai to dedicate in the temple. He said that he had received nothing of the kind from Pandarus, but that he would paint a picture and set it up if the god would heal him. After this the god tied the bandage of Pandarus around his marks and told him to take off the bandage when he came out of the inner sanctum, wash his face in the spring, and look at himself in the water. When it was day he came out of the inner sanctum and took off the bandage, but it did not have the marks. As he looked into the water he saw that his face now had the marks of Pandarus in addition to the markings he already had.

8. *Euplanes, a boy from Epidaurus.* He suffered from stones and slept in the temple. He dreamed that the god was standing over him and asked him: "What will you give me if I make you well?" He replied: "Ten dice." The god laughed and said that he would relieve his condition. When day came, he left and was cured.

9. A man was blind in one eye to such an extent that he had only the eyelids left, nothing in between; the area was completely empty. Some of those who were in the temple blamed his naïveté in thinking that he would be able to see, even though nothing was left of his eye except the empty socket. As he slept in the inner sanctum he had a vision. He dreamed that the god was cooking some medicine and then opened his

eyelids and poured it in. When day came, he left and was able to see with both eyes.

10. *The drinking vessel.* A porter who approached the sanctuary, walking with difficulty, fell down near the Decastadion [a race course]. He got up and opened his pouch and looked at the broken objects in it. When he saw that the drinking vessel from which his master used to drink was shattered, he was upset and sat down, trying to put the pieces together. A traveler passing by saw him and said to him: "Poor fellow, why are you wasting your time piecing that drinking vessel together? Even Asclepius of Epidaurus could not make it whole again." When the slave heard this he put the pieces into the pouch and went into the sanctuary. After he got there, he opened his pouch and took out the drinking vessel, and it was whole again! He told his master what had happened and what had been said. When the master heard this, he dedicated the vessel to the god. [Eighteen letters are missing.]

43

Asclepiades of Prusa practiced medicine in Rome for many years and died there an old man circa 40 B.C. He had studied Epicurean philosophy as well as the medical science of the day, and he defined health as "a smooth flow of atoms through the body." Illness meant to him that somehow that flow had been blocked. He prescribed diets rather than drugs, and he taught that every kind of therapy should be safe, work fast, and be pleasant to take. Pliny, in his *Natural History* (Books 7 and 26), mentions him with approval.

This highly regarded practitioner who was trained as a physician and had studied Epicurean physics was also able to perform miracles, according to Apuleius. But was this really a full-fledged miracle? Asclepiades may have observed something, or his instincts may have told him that his body was still alive, though the man had been pronounced dead by other doctors. Such cases are known in medical history.

What makes this particular event a "miracle" is perhaps the drama staged by the great doctor: he obviously had not been consulted by the family, but now he stops the funeral, creates an uproar, forces the mourners to take sides, infuriates the heirs, and finally triumphs. All this happens in public, is witnessed by a large crowd, and the story naturally spreads and is magnified.

Asclepiades has this in common with the early Greek shamans: he is a miracle-worker as well as a scientist, which shows that there was still a demand for such figures.

Apuleius, *Florida,* ch. 19

The famous Asclepiades, one of the leading physicians—in fact, the great-est of all, with the exception of Hippocrates—was the first to discover, among other things, how to cure patients with wine, at the right time, of course, and he knew exactly when the time was right, because he carefully observed the irregularity or abnormal rapidity [reading *praeceleres,* with Stewech, for *praeclaros* of the manuscript tradition] of the pulse beat in the veins.

One day, when Asclepiades returned from his country house to the city, he noticed, in a suburb, the preparations for an enormous funeral, with a great many people, a huge crowd, standing around to pay their respects, all looking very gloomy and wearing their oldest clothes.

He came closer, either curious to find out—he was human, after all—who it was, since nobody had answered his question, or, perhaps, to find out whether his medical experience would allow him to discover anything [text and meaning uncertain]. In any case, it was destiny that brought him to the person who lay there, stretched out and practically buried already. The poor creature's whole body had already been sprin-kled with aromatic essences, his face already covered with a fragrant cream, and he had already been arrayed [in the customary way] for his funeral and prepared for the pyre.

Asclepiades examined him very carefully, noted certain symptoms, palpated the body again and again, and discovered in him a hidden spark of life. At once he cried: "This man is alive! Throw away your torches! Take that fire somewhere else! Tear down the pyre! Move your funeral dinner from the tomb to the dining room!"

The crowd began to mutter. Some said that one should take the doctor seriously, but others, in fact, made fun of medical science. Against the protest of all the relatives [reading *omnibus,* with Stewech, for *hominibus* of the manuscript tradition]—they either could hardly wait for their inheri-tance [reading *avebant,* with Colvinus, for manuscript's *habebant*] or they still did not believe him—Asclepiades with a certain difficulty and with great effort obtained a brief respite for the dead man, rescued him from the hands of the undertakers, and brought him back to his house, re-claimed from the threshold of the underworld, if I may say so. There he quickly revived his breath, and immediately stimulated by certain drugs, the life force that had been languishing in the recesses of the body.

44

The Apellas Inscription (c. second century A.D.) is remarkable because it shows that this particular patient was almost constantly in touch with the god Asclepius. The god tells him to come to his sanctuary (to make a pilgrimage, as it were), gives him good advice as he sets out, and provides a weather forecast as Apellas enters the sanctuary. The god also prescribes a diet and a form of exercise right away. It all sounds very sensible, and divine care is evident, but one wonders whether part of the secret of these cures was not the total change of daily habits that was imposed on the patients. Someone who may have been accustomed to eating heavily spiced meat is told to eat only bread and cheese, with celery and lettuce, for a while; someone who may have been fond of Grecian wine is told to drink only milk with honey. If the patient adheres to this diet for a while, he may feel better physically; this, after all, is the idea behind the diets that are fashionable today. Then he may go home and sin again, but the god at least gave him a chance.

We can only guess at the identity of the "Place Where Supernatural Voices Are Heard." It could have been a hall where the patients meditated, concentrating on their problems, waiting for voices to speak to them. Or the patients may have heard the voices in a dream.

Before he leaves, Apellas is told by the god to write all this down, and that is what he did.

IG 4.955 (= Dittenberger, Sylloge⁴ 1170)

When P. Aelius Antiochus was priest, I, Marcus Iulius Apellas, from Idrias (a suburb of Mylasa), was summoned by the god, for I was often falling into illnesses and suffering from indigestion. During my journey by boat he told me, in Aegina, not to be so irritable all the time. When I entered the sanctuary, he told me to keep my head covered for two days (it was raining during this time), to eat bread and cheese and celery with lettuce, to bathe without any assistance, to run for exercise, to take lemon rind and soak it in water, to rub myself against the wall in the bath near the "Ears" [i.e., a place where "voices" were heard?], to go for a walk on the "Upper Portico," to swing on a swing [or: to engage in passive exercise?], to smear myself with mud, to walk barefoot, to pour wine all over myself before climbing into the hot pool in the bathing establishment, to bathe all alone, to give an Attic drachma to the attendant, to offer a joint sacrifice to Asclepius, Epione, and the goddesses of Eleusis, and to drink milk with honey. One day when I drank only milk, the god said: "Put honey in your milk, so it can strike through [or: have the right effect, i.e., act as a laxative]." When I urged the god to heal me more quickly, I had a vision: I was walking out of the sanctuary toward the "Ears," rubbed with salt and mustard all over, and a little boy holding a smoking censer was leading me, and the priest said to me: "You are cured; now pay the fee." I did what I had seen [i.e., acted out my vision]. When they rubbed me with salt and liquid mustard, it hurt, but after I had taken a bath, it hurt no longer. All this happened within nine days after my arrival. The god touched my left hand and my breast. On the following day, as I was offering a sacrifice, the flame leapt up and burned my hand so that blisters appeared. Soon afterward my hand healed. I stayed on, and the god told me to use anise with olive oil for my headache. Actually, I had no headache. But after I had done some studying it happened that I suffered from congestion of the brain. Taking olive oil, I got rid of my headache. [I was also told] to gargle with cold water for my swollen uvula—for I had asked the god for help with this problem, too—and the same treatment for the tonsils. The god also told me to write all this down. I left, feeling grateful and restored to health.

45

Aelius Aristides was a prominent sophist (i.e., a professional lecturer and teacher) of the second century A.D. He was educated at Pergamon and Athens and later performed in Italy and Asia Minor. While staying in Smyrna, he fell seriously ill, suffered for a long time, and finally went to the sanctuary of Asclepius at Pergamon, where he experienced a cure. His *Sacred Orations* (a series of six in a collection of fifty-five formal speeches that have survived) describes how a god appeared to him in dreams and gave him medical advice, which he always (or almost always) strictly followed, no matter how strange it appeared at first.

Two passages from the second of these orations are fairly typical. In the first passage, Aristides describes a dream that turned out to be very similar to a dream that one of the temple wardens had during the same night. The technique of incubation was practiced in Pergamon as it was in Epidaurus, and the patients and the temple wardens apparently got together to discuss their dreams; the fact that the two dreams were so similar obviously meant something.

To what should one attribute the coincidence? Partly, perhaps, to the long conversations the patients and wardens had during weeks and months of close proximity, but also to the fact that Aristides was a deeply religious person. His faith was strong, and mystic experiences, as we would call them today, were familiar to him. Among the priests and temple wardens serving the god, there must have been at least a few who were, like Aristides, firm believers; some of them may even have been "psychics," as we would say today, and could "tune in" to some congenial patients and "pick up" now and then one of their dreams. This probably did not happen regularly, but it happened.

This is only a tentative explanation in modern terms—the terms themselves actually explain very little—but it is one that Aristides would have accepted, though he might have maintained that both dreams were sent by the god. At the same time it seems clear that long conversations between Aristides and the temple warden created a certain rapport. They obviously discussed his illness, and Aristides must have talked about his career, for he was a renowned figure, and public recognition meant a great deal to him. The situation in which he found himself in the dream—standing on a stage, addressing a festive crowd in white (corresponding to an audience in formal wear today), delivering a grand ceremonial speech for a special occasion—must have been familiar to him.

We also learn from Aristides that physicians were available for consultations at Pergamon, that they made house calls at dawn if necessary, and that they sometimes doubted the dream messages that came from the god. This doctor, for instance, worries about Aristides' weakened constitution. What the bad weather has to do with the drinking of wormwood in vinegar is not quite clear, unless the god also prescribed that it be taken out of doors. The solution for many patients may have been to compromise between the god's orders and the doctor's advice. It is typical of Aristides' attitude that he does not listen to the doctor in this instance.

Aelius Aristides, *Sacred Orations* 2 (= 48, 30–35 Keil)

One of the two temple wardens was called Philadelphus. One night he had the same dream vision that I had, though it was a little different. Philadelphus dreamed—this much I still remember—that there was, in the sacred theater, a crowd of people, all dressed in white and gathered together to honor the god. I was standing in their midst, delivering a speech and singing a hymn in praise of the god and saying, among many other things, how the god had saved my life on many occasions, for instance, just recently, when he told me to drink wormwood diluted in vinegar, to make it less distasteful to me. He also talked about a sacred stairway, I think, and about an epiphany of the god and some miracles that he performed. This was Philadelphus' dream.

And this was my own experience: I dreamed that I was standing in the propylaeum of the sanctuary and that many other people were gathered there, too, as if they had come for the ceremony of purification, and that they were dressed in white and generally looked very festive. There I spoke about the god and addressed him as, among other things, the "Distributor of Destinies," because he does assign destinies to men. The expression came to me from my own experience. I also mentioned the drink of wormwood, which had been some sort of revelation. It was, in fact, an unmistakable revelation, just as one feels unmistakably in thousands of cases the presence of the god. You can, for instance, feel his touch, you can realize his coming with a kind of consciousness halfway between sleeping and waking. You want to look up to him and are deeply afraid that he might vanish too soon; you sharpen your ears and listen, half-dreaming, half-awake; your hair stands on end, you shed tears of joy, and humble pride fills your heart. Who could express this experience in words? Anyone who belongs to the initiated will know and recognize it.

After having had this vision, I called Theognotus, the physician, and when he came I told him my dream. Its divine character astonished him, but he did not know what to make of it, since it was winter and he was worried about my weakened condition; I had been confined to bed for months. It seemed to us a good idea to call in Asclepiacus, the temple warden in whose house I stayed and to whom I used to tell my dreams. The temple warden came, but before we could say a word to him he began to tell us this: "I have just come from my colleague"—he meant Philadelphus—"for he called me about an extraordinary dream he had last night concerning you."

And so Asclepiacus told us the vision of Philadelphus, and Philadelphus himself, after we called him, confirmed it. Since our dreams agreed, we applied the remedy, and I drank more of it than anyone had ever drunk before, and the following day, at the god's direction, I drank an equal amount. It is impossible to describe the relief the potion brought me and how good it made me feel.

46

In this passage from the second of his *Sacred Orations* Aristides is still unwell, partly because he has followed bad advice instead of doing what the god told him to do. But he is now ready to obey the god unconditionally. In the midst of winter Asclepius orders him to smear his body with mud and then to wash himself in the sacred spring. Such springs, incidentally, could have been radioactive, and the mud nearby may have had certain properties recognized by modern medicine.

Running three times around the temple in the midst of winter, smeared with mud, even wrapped in layers of clothing, seems rather outlandish, but this time Aristides did as the god ordered, without consulting the doctor, who would no doubt have advised against it. These were truly heroic measures, but apparently they worked.

Aelius Aristides, *Sacred Orations* 2 (= 48, 74–78 Keil)

It was during the spring equinox, when people smear mud on their bodies in honor of the god, but I was unable to move, unless he were to give me a sign to make a special effort. So I hesitated, although as far as I remember it was a very warm day. A few days later a storm came up, the north wind swept across the whole sky, and black clouds gathered. It was winter once more. This was the kind of weather we had had when the god ordered me to smear myself with mud near the sacred spring and to wash myself right there. People stared at me this time, too, and the mud and the air were so cold that I considered it a special treat to run to the spring; the water, more than anything else, was enough to warm me.

But this was only the beginning of the miracle. The following night, the god told me again to smear myself with mud, in the same way as before, and to run three times around the temple. The impact of the north wind was beyond words, and the frost was getting even more severe; there was no piece of clothing thick enough to protect yourself; the coldness went right through it and hit you in the side like a missile. Some of my companions, even though they did not have to do it, decided to join me and do what I did, because they wanted to give me moral support. I smeared myself and ran, giving the north wind ample opportunity to mangle me. Finally, I arrived at the spring and washed myself. One of my companions had turned around immediately; another fell into convulsions and had to be carried hurriedly into a bath building, where they warmed him up with great difficulty.

But then we had a real spring day. After that the winter temperatures returned, and we had very cold weather and icy winds again. The god told me to take mud, apply it to my whole body, sit down in the courtyard of the gymnasium of the sanctuary, and invoke Zeus, the "greatest and best of the gods." This, too, happened in the presence of many witnesses. But what was even more miraculous than anything I have ever told before is this: after it had been snowing for forty days or more, and some of the ports as well as the sea along the whole shore near Elaia where one descends from Pergamon were covered with ice, the god ordered me to put on a short linen tunic and nothing else, and to suffer through the whole ordeal in this garment, then leave my bed, and wash myself in the spring outside.

47

The following conversation concerns various kinds of folk medicine and the scientific medicine of the day. Someone states that the god Asclepius is actually on the side of scientific medicine, and then another person tells the story of a Babylonian miracle-worker who instantly healed a man who had been bitten by a snake. The Babylonian healer could also destroy all the snakes that infested the farm on which the accident happened. Moreover, he was able to fly through the air and walk on water.

All this sounds impressive, but the way in which it is told suggests that the narrator doubts all the tales he relates. The old dragon who failed to obey the wizard's command is a built-in clue, and so are the heavy brogues that the wizard wore as he flew through the air. Lucian has a way of weaving together popular beliefs and giving them a twist that makes them look ridiculous.

Lucian, *The Lovers of Lies*, pars. 10–13

"It seems to me," Dinomachus said, "that when you talk like this you do not believe in the gods, at least not if you refuse to admit that such cures by invocation of holy names are possible."

"Don't say that, my dear friend," I replied. "Even if the gods exist, there is nothing to prevent that sort of thing from being untrue all the same. As far as I am concerned I worship the gods, and I notice the cures they effect and all the good that they do when they heal the sick by drugs and medical science. In fact, Asclepius himself and his sons cured their patients by applying beneficial drugs, not by wrapping them in lions' skins or weasels' skins."

"Never mind him," said Ion. "I will tell you a fantastic story. I was still a boy, about fourteen years old, when someone came and told my father that Midas the vine-dresser, normally a strong and hard-working farm-hand, had been bitten by a snake around noon and was lying there, his leg already gangrenous. As he was tying up the twigs and twining them about the poles, the creature had crept close to him and bitten his big toe; then it had quickly slipped back into its hole as he was groaning in agony. While the story was still being told, we saw Midas being carried on a stretcher by his fellow slaves, all swollen and livid, his skin clammy, his breath very faint. Of course, my father was distressed, but one of his friends who was there said to him: 'Don't worry; I will go at once and fetch the Babylonian, one of the Chaldeans, they say, and he will cure the fellow.' To make a long story short, the Babylonian came and brought Midas back to life: he drove the poison from his body by means of a spell and by tying to his foot a piece of stone that he had broken off the tombstone of a dead virgin. Well, perhaps there is nothing extraordinary about that, even though Midas himself picked up the stretcher on which he had been carried and marched off to the fields, so powerful was the spell and the piece from the tombstone!

"But the Babylonian did other things which were truly prodigious. Early one morning he came to the farm, recited seven sacred names from an ancient book, purified the place by sulfur and torch, walked around it three times, and thus conjured forth all the reptiles that lived inside the boundaries. As if drawn toward the spell, large numbers of snakes, asps, vipers, horned snakes, darters, common toads, and puff toads arrived on the scene. Only an old dragon was left behind, perhaps because he was too old to drag himself out or because he had misunderstood the command. The magician noted that not all were present and so elected one of the youngest snakes to be sent as a messenger to the dragon, who presently appeared, too. When they were all assembled, the magician breathed on them, and they were immediately burned up by his breath. We were amazed."

"Tell me, Ion," I said, "did the messenger snake, I mean the young one, lead the dragon, who, as you say, was rather ancient, by the hand, or did the dragon have a stick and lean on it?"

"All right," said Cleodemus, "you make fun of this. But let me tell you that at one time I was even more of an unbeliever than you as far as these things are concerned, for I was convinced that they could not possibly happen. All the same, when I saw for the first time the stranger, the foreigner, you know—he said he came from the land of the Hyperboreans—fly through the air, I believed at once and surrendered, though I had resisted for a long time. What was there to do when I saw him flying through the air in broad daylight and walking on water and going through fire leisurely and on foot?"

"You actually saw this?" I asked. "The Hyperborean flying through the air and walking on water?"

"Yes, certainly," he answered, "and he wore heavy brogues on his feet, the kind that those people usually wear."

48

After having escaped Nero's secret police, Apollonius and his disciple, Damis, are in danger once more under the emperor Domitian, who twice (A.D. 89 and 95) banished "philosophers" from Italy, "philosophers" being a label that covered also practitioners of what we call the occult sciences.

Although the master and his disciple are imprisoned, in chains, Apollonius is calm, for he knows already that they will be freed by court order very soon, and even if that order of release should not come through, they would, in fact, be free—in the sense of the Stoic paradox that the wise man is always free. To emphasize this truth, Apollonius performs an instant miracle: he slips out of his shackles and then into them again.

Philostratus uses the story to discuss magic and miracles in general, and in doing so he applies Apollonius' own ideas. We are given a short account of how magic was thought to work in people's lives—in sport, in business, in love—wherever instant success depended on circumstances beyond the individual's control. Whenever people felt that they had failed, they suspected a spell directed at them, or they blamed themselves for not having used more potent magic.

But Apollonius, in spite of his performance of miraculous feats, in spite of the accusation that he was a dangerous magician, declared that there was no such thing as magic. How, then, did he explain his own success? By the power of the mind? It is true that he usually did not perform an elaborate ritual, did not offer any sacrifice, and yet it would seem that he spoke with tongue-in-cheek, as if he wanted to say: "What seems like magic to you is some higher form of science to me, but you'll never understand the difference, so why bother to explain it?"

Philostratus, *Life of Apollonius of Tyana* 7.38–39

Damis said to Apollonius a little before noon: "Man from Tyana"—for Apollonius enjoyed being addressed in this way—"what is going to happen to us?" Apollonius replied: "What has happened to us already, of course, nothing more. No one is going to kill us." Damis asked: "But who could be as invulnerable as that? Will you ever be free again?" Apollonius answered: "As far as the judge is concerned, today; as far as I am concerned, right now," and as he said this, he extricated his leg from the fetters and said to Damis: "Here, I have given you proof that I am free; now cheer up!"

It was then for the first time, Damis says, that he truly understood Apollonius' nature and realized that it was divine, superhuman. Without offering any sacrifice—and how could he have done this in prison?—and without saying a prayer, without even saying a word, he made fun of his fetters and then inserted his leg again, behaving like a prisoner in chains.

Naïve people attribute things like that to witchcraft, and they make the same mistake in judging many human actions. Athletes use magic, and so do all those who eagerly compete for victory, although it contributes nothing at all to their success, and if they happen to win, the wretched creatures rob themselves of all credit and attribute it to witchcraft. Even if they lose, they still believe in it, saying: "If only I had offered that other sacrifice! If only I had used that other incense! I would have won!" That's what they say, and that's what they believe.

Magic also comes to the doors of merchants, just like that, because it is easy to see how even they attribute their success in business to a wizard, but their failure to their own reluctance to spend more money and to their not having offered all the necessary sacrifices. Lovers especially are addicted to magic; they are sick anyway, and their disease makes them gullible, so they consult old hags about it and, not surprisingly, visit practitioners of this kind and listen to their nonsense. Some will give them a magic girdle to wear, some will give them stones from the unspeakable depths of the earth or from the moon and the stars, and they are given all the spices that grow in the gardens of India, and for this the impostors get splendid sums of money but don't give their customers any help at all. If men are successful in love, either because their darlings feel something for them or because their gifts make an impression on them, they sing hymns of praise to magic, as if it had produced this effect, but if the experiment does not work out, they blame it on some omission, saying they should have burned such and such an herb or offered such and such a sacrifice or melted such and such a substance, and that this was absolutely essential but hard to get.

The various techniques by which they work signs from heaven and all sorts of other miracles have been recorded by certain authors, who enjoyed a hearty laugh at the expense of this kind of art. Let me say only this: young people should not be allowed to associate with such practitioners, lest they become accustomed to these things, even as a joke. But this digression has led me far enough from my topic; why should I attack any further a thing which is condemned by nature as well as by law?

49

In Philostratus' *Life of Apollonius* we find a parallel to the story of Asclepiades as Apuleius told it in his *Florida* [*no. 43*]. A grand funeral procession arouses Apollonius' curiosity. He asks permission to look at the body of a young woman who, he is told, died in the middle of her wedding, and he brings her back to life. The biographer asks the same question that has been asked before: was the person actually alive, but in a state of coma? If so, the restoration of her life could not be called a miracle, properly speaking, even though the effect on the crowd was the same, because no one could possibly know the true reason, and the healer himself would not reveal what happened.

Philostratus, *Life of Apollonius of Tyana* 4.45

Here is another miracle that Apollonius performed. A young woman had died, it seemed, in the very hour of her wedding, and the bridegroom was following her bier, howling. This was only natural, since his marriage had been left unfulfilled, and all of Rome mourned with him, for the young woman belonged to a family of consular rank. Apollonius happened to witness this sad event and said: "Put down the bier; I shall stay the tears that you are shedding for this young woman." At the same time he wanted to know her name. The crowd thought that he was going to deliver the kind of oration that is appropriate in such a situation, the kind that stirs up lamentations, but he did nothing of the kind; he simply touched the young woman and said something inaudible over her and woke her up from what had seemed death. The young woman spoke out loud and returned to her father's house, like Alcestis, after she had been brought back to life by Heracles. The relatives of the young woman offered Apollonius 15,000 sesterces, but he said that he would be glad to give the money to the young woman as dowry. Now, did he detect in her body a spark of life that had not been noticed by those who had taken care of her? Apparently it had rained at the time, and yet a kind of vapor went up from her face. Or had life been totally extinguished, and he brought her back to life with the warmth of his touch? This is an insoluble mystery, not only for me but for those who were present at the time.

50

Apollonius has a discussion with other philosophers when he is suddenly called upon to perform an exorcism, and he does it, at a distance, because the victim cannot be brought to him.

This story is different from most other accounts of exorcisms because it has some bizarre, almost humorous, features. The way in which the mother describes the predicament of her son characterizes her as a naïve, uneducated woman. She believes that the daemon that possesses her son is in love with him; this is unusual. Finally, the daemon has a story of his own to tell: he hates women because his wife, a long time ago, disappointed him.

One might almost think that Philostratus—or his source—told this story with tongue in cheek.

Philostratus, *Life of Apollonius of Tyana* 3.38–39

The discussion was interrupted when among the wise men a messenger appeared. He brought with him some Indians who needed to be rescued [or: saved]. Thus he presented a poor woman who implored them to do something for her son.

She said that he was sixteen years old and had been possessed by a daemon for two years, and that the daemon had a sarcastic and deceitful nature.

When one of the wise men asked her on what basis she made this claim, she answered: "My son is rather good-looking, and the daemon is in love with him and won't allow him to think normally, or go to school or to archery practice, or to stay at home, but drives him out to desert places. The boy does not even have his own voice, but speaks in a deep, hollow tone, the way grown-up men do, and when he looks at me, his eyes don't seem to be his own. All this makes me cry and scratch my cheeks. I try to talk sense into him, to a certain degree, but he doesn't even know me. As I was planning to come to you—in fact I have been planning it since last year—the daemon made himself known to me, using my son as a mouthpiece, and told me that he was the ghost of a man who had been killed in a war a long time ago, and that he had been very much in love with his wife at the time he was killed. But he had been dead for only three days when his wife married another man, thus mocking her previous marriage. Since then (the daemon said) he had begun to loathe the love of women and had transferred himself into this boy. He promised to give the boy many precious and useful gifts if I would not denounce him to you. This made an impression on me, but he has put me off again and again; he has complete control over my house, and his intentions are neither reasonable nor honorable."

Apollonius asked if the boy was nearby. She said no, although she had tried very hard to make him come here, "but the daemon," she said, "threatens to throw me into a crevice or a precipice and to kill my son if I bring him here for trial." "Be of good cheer," the wise man said, "for he will not kill him when he reads this," and he snatched a letter from his pocket and gave it to her. The letter, of course, was addressed to the daemon and contained the most alarming threats.

51

The story of Sosipatra's early youth sounds like a fairy tale. Two old men arrive one day on her father's estate, are treated hospitably, and offer in exchange to educate the little girl, under certain conditions. The father agrees—he does not have much choice—and his daughter is then initiated by the two into the ancient mysteries. We are not told who they are, but they are described as minor gods or benevolent daemons. In later years Sosipatra became a famous philosopher and "psychic," as we would say today.

One might speculate that such stories were told in order to defend paganism against the increasing power of Christianity. Eunapius, like Julian the Apostate, is trying to say that the ancient gods are not dead, that they still walk the earth and take care of human beings, at least of some chosen ones, as they had done in the days of the Golden Age. In this way they establish, as it were, a hidden elite, a secret aristocracy that will take over

in the days to come, after Christianity has been defeated. Sosipatra represents the qualities that Julian wished to achieve, but according to this story
she achieves them through divine grace as well as through years of training of some sort.

Eunapius, *Lives of the Philosophers and Sophists* 6.6.5–8.3

Eustathius, a man of great qualities, married Sosipatra, who actually
made him look average and insignificant because of the abundance of
her wisdom. Her reputation traveled so far that I must speak of her in
this catalogue of wise men at some length. She was born in Asia Minor,
near Ephesus, where the river Caystrus flows through a plain, crosses it,
and gives it its name. Her ancestors, her whole family, were wealthy
and prosperous. When she was still a little child, she seemed to bring a
blessing to everything: such beauty and good manners brightened her
early years.

She was five years old when two old men—both of them past their
prime, but one even older than the other—carrying voluminous purses
and dressed in leather garments, came to a country estate belonging to
Sosipatra's parents. They persuaded the manager—this they were easily
able to do—to entrust to them the care of the vineyards. When a harvest
beyond expectation was the result—the owner was present, and little
Sosipatra was with him—there was boundless amazement and a feeling
that some divine influence was involved. The owner of the estate invited
the two men to his table and treated them with great respect; at the same
time, he took the other workers on the estate to task because they had not
achieved the same results.

The two old men enjoyed the [typical] Greek hospitality and food but
were also impressed and beguiled by the unusual beauty and charm of
little Sosipatra and said [to her father]: "We usually keep our powers
secret and unrevealed. This great vintage [?] that you praise so much is
only a joke, mere child's play, nothing compared to our unusual abilities.
But if you want from us a worthy compensation for this food and hospitality, not financially or in the form of perishable gifts, but something
far above yourself and your way of life, a gift as high as heaven, reaching as
far as the stars, then you should hand over your Sosipatra to us, because
we are in a deeper sense [than you] her parents and her guardians. For the
next five years you need fear neither illness nor death for your little girl,
but remain calm and confident. You must not set foot on this estate until,
in the course of the annual revolutions of the sun, the fifth year has come.
Riches will spring up and well up of their own accord from your estate,
and your daughter will think unlike a woman or any average human

being; in fact, you yourself will see something greater in your child. If you are a sensible man, you ought to accept our proposition with open arms, but if you are bothered by suspicions, let us assume that we have said nothing."

At this the father, although biting his tongue and cringing [with fear], put the child into their hands and gave her over to them. Then he called his manager and said to him: "Supply the old gentlemen with everything they want and ask no unnecessary questions." He said this, and even before the light of dawn began to appear, he left, as if he were running away from his daughter and his estate.

The old men—whether they were heroes or daemons or belonged to some race even more divine—took the girl. No one found out into what mysteries they initiated her, and even to those who were most eager to learn, it was not revealed into what rites they consecrated her.

Soon the time came, and the accounts of the estate's revenues were due. The girl's father came to the farm and found her so tall that he hardly recognized her; her beauty seemed to be of a different kind than before. It took her a while to recognize her father. He greeted her with great reverence, almost as if he were seeing another woman.

When her teachers came and the meal was served, they told him: "Ask the girl whatever you wish." Before he could say anything the girl told him: "Please ask me, father, what happened to you on your journey." He said: "All right, tell me." [The reader ought to know that] because he could well afford it, he traveled in a four-wheeled carriage, and a lot of accidents happen to that type of carriage, but she described every detail— what was said, the dangers, the fears he experienced—as if she had traveled along with him. The father was absolutely astonished; in fact, this was more than astonishment, it was a state of shock, and he was convinced that his daughter was a goddess. He fell on his knees before the men and implored them to tell him who they were. Slowly and reluctantly—but perhaps obeying the will of a god—they revealed to him that they had been initiated into the so-called Chaldean wisdom, and even that much they told in an enigmatic way, looking down to the ground. When Sosipatra's father clung to their knees in supplication, begging them to take over the estate, keep his daughter under their instruction, and initiate her into even higher mysteries, they nodded their assent but did not say anything more. To him this seemed like a promise or an oracle, and he felt greatly encouraged, even though he could not understand the meaning of all this. In his heart he praised Homer profusely for having sung of a supernatural, of a divine, experience such as that:

Yes, and gods, looking like strangers from abroad,
assuming all kinds of shapes, wander through the cities.
(*Od.* 17.485–86)

For he certainly believed that he had met gods disguised as strangers.

While his mind was full of all this, he was overcome by sleep, but the two men left the table, taking the girl along, and handed her very affectionately and carefully the whole set of robes in which she had been initiated, and added certain mystic symbols; they also put certain booklets into Sosipatra's chest, ordering her to seal it up. She was overjoyed by the men, no less than her father had been. When dawn began to break and the doors were opened and people went to their work, the [two] men left along with the others, as was their custom. The girl ran to her father with the good news, and one of the servants brought the chest. The father asked for all the cash of his own that was available and from the estate agents all that they had for their necessary expenses and sent for the men. But they were nowhere to be seen. He said to Sosipatra: "What is this, my child?" After a moment's thought she replied: "Now at last I understand what they said to me. For when they handed me these things—and they wept as they did it—they said to me: 'Child, take care [of them], for we shall travel to the Western Ocean, but soon we shall return.'" This was absolutely positive evidence that those who had appeared [to them] were daemons [blessed spirits]. So they had departed and went to whatever place they went. The father took back the girl, who now was fully initiated and filled with the divine spirit, though modest [about it], and allowed her to live as she wished, never interfering with her affairs, though he was sometimes a little annoyed at her silence.

As she reached full maturity, never having any other teachers, the works of the poets, philosophers, and orators were [constantly] on her lips and texts that others who had spent a great deal of painstaking trouble over [and] understood only dimly and with difficulty she could interpret casually, effortlessly, and with ease, making their meaning clear with her light, swift touch.

Well, she decided to get married, and beyond dispute Eustathius of all men was the only one worthy to be her husband.

III

DAEMONOLOGY

Introduction

Attested since Homer and used frequently in the *Corpus Hermeticum,* in the writings of Philo Judaeus, and many other ancient sources, the Greek word *daimon* originally meant "divine being." In fact, in the early texts the distinction between *daimon* 'divine being' and *theos* 'god' is not always clear. By the later Hellenistic period, however, the distinction between *theos* 'god' and *daimon* 'evil spirit' had become fairly common. "Evil spirit" is the meaning that *daimon* has in Matthew 8:31, the only passage in the New Testament where it is clearly attested. Sometimes the noun *daimon* is qualified by the adjective *kakos* or *poneros,* both of which mean "bad," "evil" (e.g., Iambl., *Myst.* 3.31.15), but on the whole there seems to be a kind of dissociation between the terms *theos* and *daimon,* the former being applied to the highest divine beings, the latter to various lower species. Given the nature of Greek mythology or theology, these higher gods could not always be considered uniformly "good" or "kind," but they also could not be classified as persistently "evil."

A related word, *daimonion* (which is neuter; *daimon* is masculine or feminine), had a similar history. In classical Greek usage (e.g., Eur., *Bacch.* v. 894) it could simply designate "a divine being," but the tendency to differentiate it from *theos* is apparent in the charge made against Socrates that he introduced "strange [new] *daimonia*" in Athens (Xen., *Mem.* 1.1.1). Because Socrates himself explained his *daimonion* as an inner voice that warned him whenever he was about to do something wrong, it could not be considered simply an evil power, at least not within the Platonist tradition, for Plato states that "every *daimonion* is something in between a god and a mortal" (*Symp.* 202E). In fact, later Platonists such as Plutarch (*Dio* 2.3), and early Stoics as well (Chrysipp., *SVF* 2.338), felt it necessary to add the adjective *phaulos* 'bad' if they wanted to make it clear that they were speaking of an evil influence.

In popular usage such qualifications were apparently not necessary, for in the New Testament, as well as in the pagan texts, we hear of *daimonia*

207

that entered into persons and caused illness, especially mental illness. If an exorcist was able to drive out the *daimonion,* he was thought to have cured that person. *Daimonia* were supposed to live in deserted places (a ruined city is called a "habitation of daemons" in Revelation 18:2). The following concept seems to be behind this phrase. After a city has been destroyed by an enemy, its inhabitants killed or dragged away as slaves, only the former gods of the community—degraded to the rank of daemons—remain in the ruins. They are organized under the leadership of Beelzebub, or Beelzebul (Luke 11:15, 18–19), whose name is probably derived from Baal, the main god of the Philistines. The name itself could mean either "lord of the flies" or "lord of filth," but the fact that Beelzebul (or Beelzebub) is the prince of daemons, from the Hebrew point of view, shows clearly that the supreme god of one culture has become the Satan of a hostile culture and that his subordinate gods have been degraded.

Such beings were worshiped by other nations as well (e.g., by the Persians and Babylonians) and were thought to be capable of performing miracles like the pagan deities that were demoted by the Christians. But an ordinary ghost, an apparition without tangible body, also could be called a *daimonion* (Ignatius, *To the Smyrn.* 3.2).

Another term, originally neutral, but later charged with emotion, is *angelos* 'messenger'. In Homer, as well as in Luke 7:24, *angelos* is a human messenger sent out by a real person. But on Attic curse tablets,[1] "messengers" could be supernatural agents connected with the underworld, and the Neoplatonists associated them with gods and daemons: Porphyry, for example (*Marc.* 21), speaks of "divine angels and good daemons" when he means benign supernatural powers. At the same time, the term *messenger* was colorless enough in itself to allow all sorts of different interpretations. Depending on who it was who sent him, a spirit might be an "angel" or a "daemon." The complexity was such that Iamblichus had to ask the question how one could distinguish among gods, archangels, angels, daemons, planetary rulers, and mere "souls,"[2] especially since the lower order of spirits occasionally posed as the higher ones. Iamblichus himself was reputed to have unmasked a bogus Apollo, conjured up as such by an Egyptian magician, but it turned out to be only the ghost of a gladiator.[3] Thus, cases of mistaken identity in the world of supernatural beings were possible, and only very advanced theurgists were credited with the ability to distinguish clearly between a true theophany and the appearance of an ordinary ghost boosted temporarily to an exalted status by a fraudulent practitioner or simply as a result of mistaken identity.

The Nature of Daemons and the Early History of the Belief in Spirits

The belief in daemons seems to have originated in Mesopotamia. We are fairly well informed on the daemonology of the Babylonians.[4] Apparently they organized daemons into armies, or hierarchies, and distinguished between categories—for example, field daemons, graveyard daemons, and so on. Illness was caused by daemonic possession and could be healed by exorcism. There were ways of protecting one's house against evil spirits. Similar theories and practices are attested in Egypt.[5]

Evil spirits, called *daimones, alastores,* and *Erinyes,* are well documented in Aeschylus' *Oresteia.*[6] It seems pointless to ask whether the dramatist himself believed in their existence: the story, as he told it, required them. They can be generated by murder itself or by the curse of its victim, as in Horace's fifth epode [see *no.8*]. But, as in *Macbeth,* a murder that has not yet been committed sends *daimones* backward in time, as it were, to enter the heart of the murderer.

There is a close connection between the belief in fate and the belief in daemons: the daemons know future events long before they happen, because they are fated to happen long before human beings plan them or execute them. Hence, Plutarch associated daemons with oracles [see *nos. 92, 93, 94*]. We are dealing here with very ancient beliefs that the philosophers—Platonists and Stoics alike—tried to interpret "scientifically."

A wide range of unexplained pathological conditions—epilepsy, insanity, even sleepwalking or the delirium of high fever—were interpreted as the work of evil spirits.[7] Automatic speech, although perhaps not a "pathological" condition, made a much deeper impression on the observer than did most other paranormal phenomena: "A female automatist will suddenly begin to speak in a deep male voice; her bearing, her gestures, her facial expression are abruptly transformed; she speaks of matters quite outside her normal range of interests, and sometimes in a strange language or in a manner quite foreign to her normal character; and when her normal speech is restored, she frequently has no memory of what she said."[8] It is as if a power from above had taken over her body. Indeed, this is how ecstasy is described by Lucan [*no. 90*] and Seneca [*no. 88*].

The world of the ancients was populated by all sorts of spirits. Even if they did not take over a human body in order to express themselves or to work some mischief, contacts and communications could be established with them.[9] But on the whole, the ancients believed that only the "unquiet dead"—that is, those who had died before their time, met with a violent death (being murdered or killed in battle), or been deprived of proper burial—were earthbound and readily available.[10] Those were the spirits the magicians used, because they were thought to be angry about their fate and therefore ruthless and violent.

Daemons and the Spirits of the Dead

The ancients' belief in daemons was closely connected with their attitude toward the dead, and something ought to be said about that here.[11] The dead were divided into several classes. There were, for instance, the dead of the family. They had a kind of shadowy existence, as the custom of feeding them at certain times shows. A mixture of oil, honey, and water was poured onto the grave, or even through a tube that led into the grave, while the living were having a picnic nearby.

How could the dead be in Hades and in their graves at the same time? The ancients apparently believed that only their shades (two-dimensional images of their former selves) went down to Hades, while their bones or their ashes retained, magically, a particle of the extinguished life force, at least for a time. Hence the theme of the "grateful dead," as expressed, for instance, by the Hellenistic poet Leonidas of Tarentum, in a bucolic epitaph (*Anth. Pal.* 7.657.11–12): "There are ways, yes, there are ways, in which the dead, even though they are gone, can return your favors." And in an anonymous epigram (*Anth. Pal.* 7.330) that cannot be dated, we hear of a man who built a tomb for himself and for his wife, so that "even among the dead he might have her love."

Perhaps the Greeks of the classical age had inherited two different concepts of survival and tried to reconcile them as best they could. In the fifth century B.C. a third concept appeared, that of the soul, the *psyche,* which ascends to heaven, as witnessed in the epitaph for the Athenians who fell in the battle of Potidaea (431 B.C.): "Heaven has received their souls, earth their bodies."[12] But *heaven* in Greek is *aither* 'the upper air', as distinguished from *aer* 'the air we breathe'; it is also the divine element in the human soul. Incidentally, the soldiers who had died for their country were treated like the family dead, because the *polis* was an extended family and owed a collective duty to those who had sacrificed their lives for the community. Their names were registered, their deeds honored.

In general, the ancients also believed in a nameless, unidentified multitude of ghosts who had to be taken care of at least once a year, in Athens during the Anthesteria, the festival of flowers in spring, when pots of cooked fruits were offered to them.

Necromancy is defined as the art of predicting the future by means of communicating with the dead.[13] The forms of communication vary, as the texts from Homer to Heliodorus show. As a technique, necromancy falls within the domain of magic (it is practiced by witches such as

Erictho), but because it deals with the dead, it can also be discussed as part of daemonology, and because its aim is very often the revelation of future events, it is definitely a form of divination. This difficulty in classification shows once more how closely related the occult sciences were in antiquity. It is more or less an arbitrary decision to treat necromancy in this chapter.

The practice itself seems to be very old. We read in 1 Samuel 28:6ff. how King Saul in disguise consulted the "woman of En-dor," although he himself had "made away with those who call up ghosts and spirits"—in other words, he had outlawed necromancy in his kingdom. At her visitor's request the woman conjured up the ghost of Samuel, and as soon as she saw him, she knew the identity of her visitor, who apparently could only hear the ghost's voice but did not actually see it. The ghost's gloomy prediction was fulfilled the next day, and that is the dramatic finale of the First Book of Samuel. Manasseh, one of the last kings of Judah, practiced soothsaying and divination and dealt with ghosts and spirits (2 Kings 21:6); this must be an allusion to necromancy, and it is made clear that the Lord, because of these "abominable things," brought disaster on Jerusalem and Judah. The Second Book of Kings ends soon afterward. From the references to necromancy in the Old Testament, one gains the impression that it was practiced commonly in other Near Eastern cultures, while it was anathema in Israel.

In Book 11 of the *Odyssey* [*no. 52*] Odysseus himself, instructed by Circe, plays the role of the necromancer, and the ceremony is performed with great dignity and compassion; there seems to be no stigma attached to it. It is perhaps significant, however, that Virgil felt it necessary to transform the theme in the *Aeneid*. Instead of conjuring up the dead, Aeneas descends into the underworld to visit them. His consultation with the Sibyl of Cumae and the rites he must perform contain magical elements,[14] but the Sibyl herself is an ecstatic prophetess, comparable with the Pythia in Delphi; at the same time she acts as Aeneas' guide through the horrors of the underworld. More than a consultation, Aeneas' visit is the revelation of a whole philosophy of life; as such, it is comparable with an initiation into the Eleusinian mysteries.[15]

In historical times, necromancy was condemned. Plato, both in his *Republic* (364B–E) and in his *Laws* (905D–907D), rejected the idea that gods or daemons could be influenced by spells and rituals, and he prescribed severe penalties for anyone who practiced necromancy; he himself considered it fraudulent, and he was concerned with its harmful results (*Laws* 909B; 933A–E).[16] During the years of Roman imperialism, there were heavy sanctions.[17] In Cicero's time a few Neo-Pythagoreans seem to have been attracted by necromancy, but in general it was considered a particularly loathsome form of magic. The dead themselves resented being disturbed, as we see from Lucan [*no. 61*] and Heliodorus [*no. 74*], and since necromancers were, almost by necessity, body snatchers, they came in conflict with the laws against desecrating tombs.[18]

The great necromantic scene in Aeschylus' *Persians* [*no. 54*] is quite different from the ritual in the *Odyssey*. Perhaps it reflects Greek notions of a Persian ritual. Here, after the defeat of Salamis, the widow of King Darius, assisted by the Chorus (representing the Persian nobility), conjures up the ghost of her husband to find out what caused the catastrophe and what course of action the Persians ought to take. Thus, necromancy, retrospective as well as divinatory, was practiced at the Persian court, presumably as a religious ritual, but Persia was a foreign country, and we have seen that, for the Greeks, the Persian *magi* were not only priests but also sorcerers.

Both Seneca and his nephew, Lucan, wrote under Nero, who was interested in magic, especially in necromancy.[19] It is difficult to reconstruct from their poetic accounts any historical reality, and it seems doubtful that either Seneca or Lucan ever saw a real necromancer in action. Both poets stress the sinister, shocking, revolting aspects of such ceremonies, Lucan even more than his uncle. In addition to the general atmosphere of horror, Lucan introduces some pseudoscientific speculation on how to revive a corpse. His superwitch, Erictho, pours boiling blood into the body of a soldier who had recently been killed, but she also injects many other substances. Here we may well have the prototype of Frankenstein, for Mary Shelley probably knew of this passage through her husband, a great admirer of the Roman poet.

Plutarch [*no. 66*] refers to a regular oracle of the dead (*psychomanteion*), probably near Cumae in southern Italy, but there is no elaborate ceremony: the procedure reminds one of the incubation rites in the temple of Asclepius at Epidaurus. The person who wished to get in touch with the dead fell asleep in the sanctuary and had a dream or vision. The element of shock and horror is absent, and yet, in a remote sense, this, too, is necromancy.[20]

In a necromantic scene from the *Aethiopica*, Heliodorus [*no. 74*] uses familiar elements but adds several new twists: the Egyptian witch performs the ceremony on the body of her own son, who reproaches her for it; one of the involuntary eyewitnesses is a priest, who should never be exposed to such rites; the witch turns nasty and tries to kill the intruders, but ends up killing herself instead.

In necromantic ceremonies the dead are compelled by the magician to appear, but cases of spontaneous possession of a living person by a dead one are discussed by pagan theurgists and by Jewish and Christian writers.[21] The main controversy seems to be whether the "daemonic agents" are really the evil spirits of the dead or are actually independent daemons. Obviously, the distinction is difficult to draw, especially since the "agents" tended to veil their identity or even to lie about it until forced by the exorcist to confess their true name and origin.[22]

Heroes and Hero Worship

Heroes form a special class among the dead. Some heroes were the ghosts of kings of old,[23] who were considered powerful even after death, at least for a time, because they had been powerful in life. Others, like Achilles or Odysseus, who had ruled over small kingdoms, were worshiped as heroes because of their glorious deeds. The distinction could easily become blurred. The fact is that there were many heroes' tombs, *heroa,* all over Greece and parts of Asia Minor. Some of them became objects of a cult that seems to have continued from the end of the heroic age down to classical times, but after a while the worship ceased, and finally even the location of the tombs was forgotten, until they were rediscovered almost in their ancient splendor, like the royal graves of Mycenae.

Historical persons could be heroized; Alexander the Great is an example,[24] and worship of the Roman emperors was a form of hero worship. But even philosophers after their death sometimes became cult figures for the members of their schools: Plato and Epicurus might be mentioned.

The hero belongs to the local community that he protects, but his power does not really extend beyond those boundaries. Though usually benevolent to the people of the community, he could turn into a ghost or, like a daemon, cause epilepsy or mental illness.[25]

Ghosts and Related Phenomena

Tales about haunted houses seem to have been as popular in antiquity as they are today,[26] and the belief that spirits dwell at their place of death or burial is no doubt much older than Plato (*Phd.* 81C–D):[27]

> You know the stories about souls that, in their fear of the invisible, which is called "Hades," roam about tombs and burial grounds in the neighborhood of which, as they say, ghostly phantoms of souls have actually been seen; just the sort of apparition that souls like that might produce, souls that are not pure when they are released [from the body] but still keep some of that visible substance, which explains why they can be seen . . . it is clearly not the souls of the good but those of the wicked that are compelled to wander about such

places, as the penalty for a bad way of life in the past. They must continue to wander until they are once more chained up in a body.

This belief survived throughout antiquity and was accepted by early Christians.

It is not easy to differentiate between ghosts, heroes, and daemons, for they all have something in common. Ghosts, though mostly evil, are associated with their tomb (or the place where they died), just as heroes are. Various Greek ghosts have names (Empusa, Gorgo, Lamia, Mormo) that seem to underline their daemonic character; Ephialtes, for example, is a ghostlike nightmare daemon.

Vampires, a special kind of ghost, are not clearly attested in ancient literature. But it seems that Lamia, who will sooner or later eat her human lover, has vampirelike features, and the theme is common in Greek folklore. Herodotus says that Periander had sexual relations with his wife after he had killed her (accidentally, it seems), and the story is repeated by Nicolaus of Damascus (*FgrH* 90F58 Jacoby), probably following another early source, because Nicolaus adds "from love." But this may be a case of necrophilia. Phlegon of Tralles (under Hadrian) tells the story of a vampire in a collection entitled *Strange Stories,* which was used by Goethe in his wonderful ballad *The Bride of Corinth* [*no. 56*].

There is no pre-Christian evidence for the "poltergeist" phenomenon,[28] nor do we ever hear of the *âme en peine* 'the soul in pain' who is being punished for a crime committed in life and who sometimes can be redeemed by a prayer. The idea is certainly not alien to the Platonic concept of ghosts; in fact, it may be a Christian variation of it.

The greatest collection of ghost stories that has come down to us from antiquity is the *Dialogues* of Gregory the Great (pope from 590 to 604).[29] The persons involved are all contemporaries, known to Gregory or his friends, and the ghosts often announce that they suffer in purgatory or that they have been relieved by prayers or masses.

The Greek word *phasma* is usually translated as "apparition" or "phantom" (see Hdt. 4.15: *phasma anthropou* 'spectral appearance of a man', etc.). Such apparitions have been reported over the centuries and they have taken on various forms: in Lucian's *Ship* one of the characters has seen Hecate at noon; in Philostratus' *Heroicus* someone has seen Protesilaus and his companions, and someone else has witnessed the Giants on the Phlegrean fields.

The actual substance of such apparitions or phantoms was discussed by the Neoplatonists. To them, as Dodds points out, the "materialization" of immaterial beings presented a difficult problem.[30] Among the solutions offered, we may mention that of Proclus (Commentary on Plato's *Rep.* 1.39.1ff.): what we see is not the god himself but an emanation from him, partly mortal, partly divine, and even this we do not see with our physical eyes but with the eyes of our astral body, according to the principle "like is perceived by like."

Some daemons are close to the gods themselves. They might be called "angels" in the Jewish or Christian sense. They can be associated with planets and fixed stars and, like those heavenly bodies, with plants and minerals on earth. Thus, the "sympathy" between stars and earthly organisms or objects that is part of the astrological doctrine could be combined with daemonology. The lower a daemon is placed in the hierarchy, the more malevolent he may be presumed to be, mischievous by nature and at times inclined to play nasty tricks. Some of these daemons like warm places but hate the light; hence, they look for human bodies to enter.

Black magic is essentially the technique of conjuring or summoning up one of these lower, nonincarnated daemons, arousing his or her anger, and channeling that anger in the direction of a victim. In ancient times this could be a risky business for the magician himself, and he usually had to take all sorts of precautions. Unlike the theurgist, the common magician did not attempt to influence the higher gods; he was satisfied with daemons of a lower rank; these may have been fallen deities who once had enjoyed great prestige, but who now were considered barely good enough for the everyday practical requirements of a sorcerer.[31] We do hear, however, of the invocation of heroes such as Orpheus (*PGM* VII.451) or Homer (Apion of Alexandria, under Tiberius, claimed he had done this in order to ask the great poet about his real parents and birthplace).

Philosophers on Daemons

Daemonology became part of philosophy in the school of Plato, especially with Xenocrates, who succeeded Plato's direct successor, Speusippus, as head of the school (339–314 B.C.). There can be little doubt that the traditions concerning Socrates' *daimonion* had something to do with this great, absorbing interest, whether or not Socrates himself actually thought of that "inner voice" as a kind of being. "I seemed to hear a voice," Socrates is made to say in the *Phaedrus* (242B), but this voice never offered positive advice; it always stopped him from doing something wrong, as if it were an "inward sense of inhibition" (F. W. H. Myers). Nor was it a great flash, a spectacular vision of the kind that great religious leaders (Moses, Jesus) experienced; it was more like a small light that would manifest itself and then go away.

In later Platonism, Socrates' *daimonion* was interpreted as a guardian angel or spiritual guide; according to the modern view, as expressed by Dodds but foreshadowed in Hermias,[32] the *daimonion* could be called the suprarational personality that controls the whole of our lives, including involuntary functions such as dreaming. Socrates' accusers certainly chose to interpret the *daimonion* as a strange god—hence the charge of "impiety" made against Socrates. What Plato thought about it is not quite clear. In the myths of the *Phaedo* (107D–E) and the *Republic* (617D, 620D–E) he speaks of guardian daemons who accompany a man through life, know his innermost thoughts, his most secret actions, and, after death, act as his advocates or accusers before the throne of judgment.[33] These guardian daemons are linked by Apuleius (*De Genio Socr.* 154) with Socrates' *daimonion,* but the connection may have been made before Apuleius, and it is not inconceivable that Plato, in his "unwritten doctrine" (i.e., his oral teaching, which was reserved for his most trusted disciples), gave an interpretation along these lines.

Aristotle (who remained a Platonist in some respects) has been called "the father of scientific daemonology." His theory of the subordinate gods of the planetary spheres seems to anticipate the daemonology of Plutarch and Apuleius and even Iamblichus, but some of it may be part of the doctrine of the Academy to which Aristotle belonged for twenty years. Here, as in other areas, Aristotle may simply have formulated some ideas that had been discussed earlier by Plato and his most intimate disciples.

Guardian Spirits

In the Hellenistic period, the belief in a kind of guardian angel, a "good daemon" (*agathodaimon*), was fairly common. Some also believed in an "evil spirit" (*kakodaimon*), but Menander, in one of his plays (frag. 714 Sandbach [= 550–51 Kock]), rejects this as a poor excuse for one's own shortcomings. "To each human being is assigned at the moment of his birth a good spirit, his guide through the mysteries of life. We should not believe that the spirit is evil and can harm our lives; he is good, and there is no evil in him. Every god must be good. But those who are bad themselves, who have bad characters and make a muddle out of their lives, managing everything badly through their own foolishness [text uncertain] . . . they make a divine being responsible and call it 'bad,' while they are actually bad themselves."

Pagans, Christians, and Skeptics on Daemons

Under the influence of Xenocrates, Plutarch developed a complex dae-monology that, in many points, is close to that of Apuleius[34] and can be said to represent a kind of Platonic *koine*. According to Plutarch (*De Genio Socr.* 589B), daemons are spiritual beings who think so intensely that they produce vibrations in the air that enable other spiritual beings (i.e., other daemons), as well as highly sensitive men and women, to "receive" their thoughts, as through antennae or vibrations like those coming from a lyre. Thus the phenomena of clairvoyance, prophecy, and the like can be explained.

Plutarch's tendency, especially in the treatise *On the Ceasing of Oracles*, is to assign to daemons some of the functions traditionally assigned to the gods. Unlike the gods, daemons grow old and, after many centuries, die. Thus he explains the fact that the great oracles of the ancient world have declined: daemons, not gods, were in charge of them, and these daemons are now old and dying. In his essay *On the Ceasing of Oracles* (419B) Plutarch tells the famous story of the death of the great Pan: Thamus, the Egyptian pilot of a ship, had been told by a mysterious voice to make the announcement, when passing a certain spot, that "the great Pan is dead." He did this, and the most pitiful sounds of mourning were heard at once. The meaning of the story is fairly obvious: now that the great daemon Pan was dead, the lesser daemons realized that their lives would soon come to an end.[35]

The "pagan theologians" (probably some Neoplatonist theurgists) quoted by Eusebius in *Preparation of the Gospel* 4.5 divide the world into four classes of higher beings: gods, daemons, heroes, and souls. The sublunar sphere is the region of the daemons. The gods generally control them, but there are spells by which an unnamed daemon can be used to threaten the gods themselves. Thus daemons can take the place of gods, and it is essentially up to the magician to decide who is more powerful than whom. In the end, as Eusebius points out, the fourfold division breaks down, and there is evidence of other classifications.

Daemons could become visible, but often they manifested their pres-ence by a sign. Philostratus, in *Life of Apollonius of Tyana* 6.27, tells the story of the ghost of an Ethiopian satyr who was very amorous and pursued the women of a village. Apollonius set up a trap—a trough full of wine—and though the ghost remained invisible, the wine was seen to disappear from the trough.

For centuries, Christians continued to believe to a certain degree in the reality, the power, of the pagan gods. They were not as powerful as

God the Father and the Son, but they had to be reckoned with as the evil spirits they were now thought to be. Ideally, if you were a good Christian, Christ would protect you, just as pious Jews might feel safe from magicians and the influence of the stars. Still, those powers were there, and under certain circumstances one might be at their mercy.

Wherever we discover the belief in daemons and daemonic possession, we also find the belief in the technique of exorcism. In antiquity, exorcism was practiced by Egyptians,[36] Jews,[37] and Greeks,[38] and the Christians found it useful.[39]

Not everyone, however, accepted these beliefs. Again, Lucian represents the voice of skepticism. In his *Lovers of Lies* (pars. 29ff.), a Pythagorean philosopher by the name of Arignotus is introduced. He had read a large number of Egyptian books on magic (corresponding to our magical papyri, no doubt), and he apparently was able to liberate a house from a daemon by talking to the daemon in Egyptian; elsewhere in *The Lovers of Lies* (par. 17) a Syrian exorcist drives daemons out of the bodies of "lunatics," and someone actually witnesses one coming out, all black and sooty. Needless to say, these stories are reported tongue-in-cheek. But the fact that the Church accepted the reality of daemons, of daemonic possession and the efficacy of exorcism, shows how people's minds were literally in the clutches of fear, and how, in the absence of medical knowledge, a kind of psychotherapy, administered by the Church, had to be developed. Benedict (c. A.D. 480–543) was reputed to be the most successful *effugator daemonum,* and his medal is worn to this day as an amulet against evil spirits.

Ancient Amulets

Amulets were worn not only to protect the person from the powers of evil but also to assure good health, success, and prosperity. Most ancient amulets or talismans are made of stone or metal, but specific charms and spells could also be written on scraps of papyrus, which were rolled or folded to be worn.

In their earliest and simplest form, amulets were probably strings or narrow bands tied around the neck, an arm, an ankle, or across the body. Various additions then were improvised or elaborated by specialists. The wearing of jewelry almost certainly originated in this custom. A precious gem or a beautiful necklace may be viewed as a highly developed, artistic form of a primitive amulet, even though its function is mainly aesthetic, no longer protective or magical. Similarly, scents were worn originally as a protection. Daemons could be extremely sensitive to smells.

Certain precious or semiprecious stones had special powers, and a whole body of precepts developed from this belief. Part of it is preserved in texts entitled *Lithika* (*About Stones*). The amethyst (literally "remedy against drunkenness") was supposed to protect the wearer against the unpleasant consequences of heavy drinking—perhaps because of its color. Other gems had a more active function: not only did they protect, they could also establish contacts with superior powers. How this was done is not completely clear—perhaps by warming them in the hand, holding them in the mouth, or sniffing them.

The magical papyri offer a great deal of information on the design of amulets and the style of their inscriptions. This seems to have changed very little over the centuries. One section of the Paris papyrus (PGM IV.256ff.) gives precise directions for making an amulet (*phylakterion*): on a thin silver plate (*leptis*) a sacred name containing a hundred letters is to be inscribed with a bronze stylus. The finished amulet is to be worn around the neck on a thong made of donkey leather. It is interesting that the use of a bronze tool is prescribed, at a time when everybody used tools made of iron. This rule, which we see observed in magic and religion throughout antiquity, probably means that we are dealing with rituals that go back to an age when bronze was the most "advanced" metal (as opposed to stone and wood).

By their very nature as a protective device, all amulets would seem to represent "white magic," and it is hard to imagine a person who would wear a curse tablet around the neck. And yet some Greco-Egyptian amulets clearly express the wish to hurt another person. Were they intended to be used in a ritual, or was the desire to destroy an enemy "so passionately felt that the person [wished] . . . to be constantly reminded of it"?[40]

Once the amulet was crafted, a ritual of consecration (*apotelesma, kathierosis, telete*) had to be performed over it, in analogy to the consecration of cult objects and holy substances in religion. Apparently, this was not always necessary. The mere carving of a suitable design and the addition of letters or words could be considered an act of "consecration" (magical enhancement through ritual), or the crafting was a ritual in itself, because certain words were spoken during the process. Of course, the very act of writing or carving was, to the ignorant and illiterate, a kind of magic.

Many people probably wore their amulet every day, others perhaps only when they felt the need for extra protection, going to war or embarking on a voyage or feeling sick. A story about Pericles, the Athenian statesman, provides an example of the latter. During his last illness, a friend visited him and asked him how he was. Pericles pointed to the amulets that had been hung about him, implying that there was not much hope; otherwise he would not have let the women try this ultimate remedy in which he hardly believed himself.

The chariot races in the circus and other public events provide good examples for the use of amulets. Before and during the races, emotions ran high, and both the charioteers and their horses were the target of curse tablets. The teams had their fans and support groups, and large bets were involved. That the charioteers wore amulets can be taken for granted, but their horses, too, were hung with protective devices, such as little bells; they are clearly visible on frescoes and sculptures depicting scenes in the circus.

The original function of the bell was to protect the wearer from evil spirits. This explains not only the cowbells still in use today in the Swiss Alps but also the function of the church bells that summon the faithful: originally, their metallic sound was meant to protect the faithful from the daemons, the demoted deities of paganism. All daemons fear the sound of metal.

A woman who puts on her jewelry and perfume on a Sunday morning to go to church to the sound of the bells does not realize that, in terms of ancient magic, she is protected by three powerful amulets.

Daemonology existed as a "pure" science, without any application to magic, but on the whole, it seems to have been destined for practical use, not for speculation alone. And yet, just like alchemy, daemonology also had its mystic, contemplative side. There must have been a certain fascination in considering the ranks and hierarchies of daemons, in pronouncing their fantastic names. Platonists, such as Plutarch, who spent a great deal of their creative energies in thinking and writing about daemons, were certainly not magicians or exorcists; on the other hand, this part of their metaphysical doctrine was more than just an intellectual exercise; in a sense it helped them understand the forces that were purported to control life.

NOTES

1. E. Ziebarth, in *Nachr. Gesellsch. Wiss. Gött.*, 1899, pp. 105ff.
2. Iambl., *Myst.* 2.3; Dodds, *The Ancient Concept of Progress*, pp. 209-10.
3. Dodds, *The Ancient Concept of Progress*, p. 210.
4. Saggs, *The Greatness That Was Babylon*, pp. 302ff.
5. G. van der Leeuw, *La Religion dans son essence* (Paris, 1948), pp. 129ff., 236-37.
6. Dodds, *The Ancient Concept of Progress*, pp. 55-56.

7. Ibid.

8. Ibid., p. 195. Dodds refers to T. G. Oesterreich's important work *Possession, Demoniacal and Other,* trans. D. Ibbetson (New York, 1930).

9. Only the Epicureans and the Skeptics seem to have denied *ex cathedra* the possibility of communicating with the ghosts of the dead.

10. Dodds, *The Ancient Concept of Progress,* p. 206.

11. Dodds discusses the ancient belief that some human souls might after death be promoted to the rank of daemons (ibid., p. 209, n. 1).

12. The epitaph was published by W. Peek in *Griechische Versinschriften* (Berlin, 1955), 1:8–9.

13. Cf. the account given by F. Cumont, *Lux Perpetua* (Paris, 1949), pp. 97ff.; and Dodds, *The Ancient Concept of Progress,* p. 207.

14. See F. L. Griffith, *Stories of the High Priests of Memphis* (Oxford, 1900), pp. 44–45. Virgil was considered a sorcerer in the Middle Ages; see D. Comparetti, *Virgilio nel medio evo* (Florence, 1872).

15. G. Luck, in *American Journal of Philology* 94 (1973): 147ff. This was Bishop Warburton's theory, rejected by Gibbon but not at all improbable.

16. Dodds, *The Ancient Concept of Progress,* p. 117.

17. T. Mommsen, *Römisches Strafrecht* (Leipzig, 1899), p. 642; Barb, in *The Conflict between Paganism and Christianity in the Fourth Century,* ed. Momigliano, pp. 102ff.; Dodds, *The Ancient Concept of Progress,* p. 207.

18. Brown, in Douglas, *Witchcraft: Confessions and Accusations;* Dodds, *The Ancient Concept of Progress,* p. 207.

19. Suet., *Nero* 34.4.

20. Dodds, *The Greeks and the Irrational,* p. 111; Dodds, *The Ancient Concept of Progress,* p. 207, n. 3.

21. Dodds, *The Ancient Concept of Progress,* p. 157, n. 2, quotes Lactantius, *Div. Inst.* 2.2.6, and other testimonies.

22. Dodds, *The Ancient Concept of Progress,* pp. 208–9; Ogden, *Greek and Roman Necromancy,* is a very good treatment.

23. Not all became heroes, as Dodds, *The Ancient Concept of Progress,* p. 153, suggests; there seems to be a difference between Atreus, who, though not a very admirable character, was once a powerful king, and Heracles, who earned the right to be worshiped.

24. See Luc., *Phars.* 10.20ff.

25. Some heroes may be "faded gods"—that is, powers who were originally divine but who, unlike the immortal gods, had died and were worshiped at their tombs rather than in temples, as the gods were. But the ritual surrounding the worship of these heroes seems to have been different from the normal worship of the dead.

26. Pliny, *Ep.* 7.27; Lucian, *The Lovers of Lies,* pars. 30–31.

27. On the Babylonian belief in ghosts, see Saggs, *The Greatness That Was Babylon,* pp. 309ff.

28. Dodds, *The Ancient Concept of Progress,* p. 158.

29. E. Bevan, *Sibyls and Seers* (London, 1929), p. 95.

30. Dodds, *The Ancient Concept of Progress,* p. 205.

31. J. Leipoldt and S. Morenz, *Heilige Schriften* (Leipzig, 1953), p. 187.

32. Dodds, *The Ancient Concept of Progress,* p. 192, n. 5, offers testimonies from the later Platonist tradition.

33. J. Dillon, The *Middle Platonists* (Ithaca, N.Y., 1977), p. 320.

34. Ibid., pp. 216ff., 17ff.

35. See G. A. Gerhard, in *Sitzb. Heidelb. Akad.,* 1915; Gerhard, in *Wiener Studien* 37 (1915): 323ff. and 38 (1916): 343ff.

36. On exorcism in Hellenized Egypt, see Cumont, *L' Egypte des astrologues,* pp. 167ff.

37. See Joseph., *Jewish Antiquities* 8.5.2, on a case of exorcism performed in the presence of the emperor Vespasian.

38. Philostr., *Life of Apollonius of Tyana* 3.38, 4.30.

39. See K. Thraede, in RAC 7 (1969), cols. 44ff. The *Rituale Romanum* is still the official handbook of the Roman Catholic Church for states of possession and the ritual of exorcism.

40. Bonner, *Studies in Magical Amulets,* p. 17.

Texts

52

The earliest extant description of a necromantic ceremony is found in Book 11 of Homer's *Odyssey*. It is the model for Aeneas' descent to the underworld in Book 6 of Virgil's *Aeneid* and the magical operation of the witch Erictho in Book 6 of Lucan's *Pharsalia*. Unlike Erictho, Odysseus is not a professional, but he follows the instructions of a "witch" (actually a minor goddess), Circe, as Homer makes clear (*Od.* 10.487ff.).

The ditch that Odysseus must dig is apparently not very deep, but it seems to serve as an access to and, afterward, an exit from Hades. Around it the hero pours libations—milk, honey, wine, and later (not specifically mentioned) the blood of a ram. The sacrificial animal must be black in order to alert the heavenly gods that this offering is not intended for them, but rather for the deities of the underworld.

As might be expected, the ghost of the last person to die is the first to appear, presumably because it has not yet found its permanent place in Hades or may not yet have been admitted to Hades, since the body has not been properly buried.

The ghosts are eager to drink from the blood of the ram in the ditch, to regain, at least for a short time, some semblance of life, but Odysseus guards with his sword the precious substance and saves it for the ghost of the great seer Tiresias. As soon as Tiresias appears, Odysseus puts away his sword, and after the seer has delivered his prophecy, the other shades are allowed to drink just a little of the blood, Odysseus' mother, Anticleia, first. What she says helps us understand how Homer and his contemporaries viewed death: as the separation of body and soul.

Both Anticleia and Tiresias speak as if Odysseus has actually descended into Hades. This is strange, for he has been standing all the time right there, near the pit, but perhaps, by magical substitution, the pit symbolizes the underworld. Homer is showing us two "truths" that seem to contradict each other: How can Odysseus at the same time go to the underworld and remain above ground? Because, through magic, he descends symbolically, or because a part of him actually descends while his body remains above?

In the end, Homer's Odysseus, like Dr. Faustus in Goethe's drama, is granted visions of the beautiful heroines of Greek myth whom he could not have known before because they had died long ago. Here we detect Homer's sense of humor: his hero, who was so strongly attracted to living women, is allowed to enjoy, as a special privilege, at least a glimpse of some famous beauties of the past.

Homer, *Odyssey* 11.12–224

The sun went down, and all the paths across the sea were in darkness. Our ship had reached the limits of the deep Ocean; the nation of the Cimmerians lives there, and they have a city, all wrapped in mist and clouds. Never does the Sun shine upon them and look at them with his beams, not [in the morning,] when he climbs up the starry sky, nor [in the evening,] when he turns back from heaven toward the earth. Gloomy night is spread over these poor people.

After we had landed there, we beached the ship and took out our sheep. We walked along the Ocean shore until we came to the spot that Circe had described.

There Perimedes and Eurylochus held the victims while I drew my sharp sword from my hip to dig a ditch about a cubit long and a cubit deep. Around it I poured libations for all the dead, first of milk and honey, then of sweet wine, and finally of water; on top I sprinkled shiny barley. On my knees I then prayed to the dead, those insubstantial beings, and promised them after my return to Ithaca the sacrifice of a heifer, the best to be found on my estate, and a funeral pyre full of precious things. Especially for Tiresias I promised to sacrifice a ram, all black, a choice male from my flocks.

After praying to the nation of the dead and making my vows to them, I took the sheep and cut off their heads over the ditch in such a way that the dark blood dripped into it. From the depths of Erebus flocked the souls of the dead, the deceased: young women and adolescents, old men who had suffered a great deal, delicate maidens who never got over their first sad experience, soldiers who had been wounded by bronze spears and still held their bloodstained weapons. They all crowded around the trench, coming from different directions, and their wailing was weird. The fear that makes one pale overwhelmed me. I ordered my companions to hurry up and skin the sheep that lay there, slaughtered by my merciless sword, and burn them, praying to the gods [of the underworld], great

Hades and terrible Persephone. I myself sat there, holding my sharp sword that I had drawn from the hip, to prevent the dead, those insubstantial beings, from coming any closer to the blood until I had my answer from Tiresias.

The first that came was the soul of my companion Elpenor, for he had not yet been buried deep in the wide earth. We had to leave his body, unlamented and unburied, in the house of Circe, because there was urgent work to be done. When I saw him I felt sorry for him and began to cry and said to him quickly:

"Elpenor, how did you get down into the gloomy darkness? You were faster on foot than I on my dark ship."

I said this, and he answered in a wailing voice:

"Divine son of Laertes, resourceful Odysseus: the harsh verdict of a god and far too much wine were my downfall. I had stretched out on Circe's roof, and it did not occur to me to step on the long ladder to climb down again. Instead, I fell headlong from the housetop and broke one of the vertebrae in my neck. My soul went down to Hades. But now, on my knees before you, I beg you—in the name of those who are not here, your wife, your father who cared for you when you were a baby, and in the name of Telemachus, whom you had to leave behind in your house all by himself—I beg you, my lord, to remember me. I know that once you leave from here, from the house of Hades, you will steer your well-built ship to the island Aeaea. Please do not leave me behind, unlamented and unburied, forsaking me, lest I become for you a tool of divine retribution, but cremate me with all the weapons that I still have, and heap over me, at the edge of the foaming sea, a mound, so that future generations may remember an unhappy man. Please do this for me, and fix on my tomb the oar that in life I pulled among my companions."

Thus he spoke, and I said to him in reply:

"Yes, my poor friend, I shall take care of everything and see that it is done."

So the two of us sat there, carrying on a sad conversation, I with my sword held away from me, over the blood, while the phantom of my friend, on the other side [of the ditch], had a great deal to say.

Then came the soul of my dead mother, Anticleia, daughter of noble Autolycus; when I had left for sacred Ilion she had been alive. I felt sorry when I saw her and began to cry. Nevertheless, even though it hurt very much, I would not let her come closer to the blood; first I had to consult Tiresias.

And the soul of Tiresias of Thebes came, holding a scepter of gold. He recognized me and said:

"Divine son of Laertes, resourceful Odysseus, what made you leave the sunlight, my poor friend, and come here to visit the dead in their joyless place? Please get up from that pit and turn away your sharp sword so that I may drink the blood and tell the truth."

So he spoke. I drew back and pushed my sword with the silver hilt into its scabbard.

The great seer drank the dark blood and then said to me:

"You have come, glorious Odysseus, in order to be told about a pleasant way home, but a god will make it hard for you. I do not think that you will escape the attention of the Earth-Shaker, who still holds a grudge against you and hates you because you blinded his son. Yet in spite of this, though suffering great hardship, you may get there, if you and your companions choose to control yourselves when your well-made ship first comes to the island Thrinacria, finding a refuge from the dark-blue sea. You will find there at pasture the oxen and the fat sheep of Helios, who sees everything and hears everything. Now, if you think of your safe return and leave those alone, you may very well get back to Ithaca, though under great hardships, but if you harm them, I would predict ruin to your ship and your companions. And even if you escape, you will come home after a delay and in sad shape, in someone else's ship, having lost all your companions. You will find trouble in your house, arrogant men who eat up your livelihood, suitors of your godlike wife who try to win her with gifts. You will surely punish them for their violence when you come home, but once you have killed these pretenders in your house, either by deceit or openly with your sharp sword of bronze, you must take up your well-made oar and go away until you come to men who know nothing of the sea, who eat food that is not spiced with salt, who know nothing of ships whose cheeks are painted red and nothing of well-made oars that act as wings for ships. I shall give you an obvious clue that you cannot possibly miss: when you meet another traveler who says that you carry a winnow fan on your handsome shoulder, then you must stick your well-made oar into the ground and offer a splendid sacrifice to the lord Poseidon: a ram, a bull, and a boar who covers sows. And then you can go home again and offer splendid hecatombs to the immortal gods who rule over the wide heaven, to all of them in order. Death will come to you from the sea, and it will not be violent at all, but it will end your life when comfortable old age has worn you out. You will be surrounded by your prosperous people. I am telling you the truth."

This he said, and I spoke to him in reply:

"Tiresias, clearly the gods themselves have spun this [destiny of mine]. But come now, tell me something, and give me a true answer: I see here the soul of my dead mother, but she sits in silence near the blood, and she has not yet deigned to look at her son or to speak to him. Tell me, sir, what will make her recognize my presence?"

This I said, and he quickly gave me this reply:

"It is easy for me to tell you this and make you understand: If you allow any of the dead, the deceased, to come near the blood, he will give you a true answer; but if you begrudge it to him, he will go back to the place where he came from."

Having said this and delivered his prophecy, the soul of the lord Tiresias went back into the palace of Hades. I waited patiently right there until my mother had come and drunk the dark-colored blood. At once she recognized me, and lamenting she quickly said to me:

"My child, how did you get here, under the fog and the darkness, still alive? This is a hard experience for the living. Large rivers and frightful waters lie in between: first of all the Ocean, which cannot be crossed on foot; one needs a well-made ship. Have you come here from Troy, with your companions and your ship, after wandering for a long time? Have you not yet been in Ithaca and seen your wife in your palace?"

[*Odysseus then asks his mother how she died; she answers that it was her longing for him that shortened her life.*]

So she spoke, but I debated within myself and wanted to take the soul of my dead mother in my arms. Three times I started out because I had this urge to take her in my arms, and three times she slipped out of my hands like a shadow or a dream, and the pain in my heart grew even sharper. I said to her quickly:

"Mother, why do you not wait for me when I want to embrace you, so that even in Hades we can hold each other and share the sad pleasure of mourning? Or has noble Persephone sent me a shadow to make me grieve and lament even more?"

So I spoke. My queenly mother answered at once:

"No, no, my child, unfortunate beyond all other mortals! Persephone, the daughter of Zeus, is not deceiving you; this is the law for all mortals when they die: the sinews no longer hold the flesh and the bones together, but the force, the violence, of the fire consumes all that as soon as the spirit has left the white bones, and like a dream the soul flutters and flies away. You must work your way back to the light as soon as possible and find out all of this, so that you can tell it afterward to your wife."

[*Before he leaves, Odysseus is allowed to see the ghosts of many beautiful heroines of Greek myth.*]

53

In his survey of myths explaining the early history of the world, Hesiod (c. 800 B.C.) describes five successive generations or races: the golden, the silver, the bronze, the heroic, and the iron. He knows that he lives in the last of these, and that the one before, the heroic age, is but a distant memory. The golden race did not completely disappear but lived on in the form of "kind spirits" or "benevolent daemons," a privilege granted to it by Zeus, who also assigned to them certain functions and areas; thus they act as his invisible agents or ambassadors.

Zeus in his wrath wiped out the silver race because it refused to worship the Olympian gods. If we may judge from Near Eastern parallels, it would appear that these people, like the people of Israel at times, worshiped foreign gods, perhaps those of the Egyptians, and neglected their own. Yet, for some obscure reason, the "spirits" of the people of the silver age were worshiped by subsequent generations of Greeks, although they occupied a lower level than did the "kind spirits" mentioned above.

Thus Hesiod seems to establish a hierarchy: (1) the Olympian gods; (2) the spirits of the upper order, who are good; and (3) the spirits of a lower order, who are basically bad. The fact that the Greeks worshiped the spirits of the lower order, too, should not surprise us. They could blame these spirits for all the bad things that happened in the world and so exonerate the gods and the daemons of the upper order. Thus, even at this early stage of Greek religion and folklore, a simple system of theodicy was in place. It is also clear that the phrase "blessed spirits of the second rank" is something of a euphemism. People were afraid of calling them by their real name, that is, "evil spirits," just as they were afraid of calling the Furies by their real name, substituting the term *Eumenides* ("the kind ones") instead and paying them due tribute in order to appease them.

At any rate, these are the two classes of daemons that Hesiod reckons with in the following text, and his authority was such that the distinction was accepted by subsequent generations and even became the basis of philosophical systems. Hesiod is quite firm when he declares that the heroes of the age of myth did not survive into his own time as "spirits." Some of them, he claims, did not survive at all; others were removed to the isles of the blessed, somewhere at the end of the world. These isles (or one of them, at least) are ruled by Kronos, who once headed a pre-Olympian dynasty of gods.

This passage is an important example of early Greek theology. Whatever daemons you honor, good ones or bad, Hesiod seems to say, do not believe that they are the spirits of the heroes of old (i.e., the men and women of the heroic age). Yet we know that in classical and postclassical times hero worship was very common in Greece. Since hero worship is not attested in Homer, and Hesiod is close in time, we may speculate that the practice began to become popular in this period. Hesiod's version influenced later philosophical thought, but hero worship flourished as well.

Hesiod, Works and Days, vv. 109–93

First the immortal gods who live on Olympus created a golden race of mortal men. This was in the time of Kronos, when he was king in heaven. They lived like gods, without any sorrow in their hearts, free of cares and pain, and they were not subject to wretched old age, but, always youthful of limbs, they enjoyed festive days, far from all evil. When they died it was as if they were overcome by sleep. All good things were theirs. The bountiful earth produced willingly all kinds of food, and plenty of it. In peace and quiet they gladly lived on their land, blessed with all the goods. After the earth hid this race of men in darkness, they became venerable daemons on earth, guardians of mortal men [watching over retribution and crimes, clothed in mist, walking over the whole earth,] giving wealth. This was one of their royal privileges.

Next, the Olympian gods created a far inferior race, the silver race, quite unlike the golden one in body and mind. For a hundred years a child grew up by his loving mother's side and played in a completely childlike state in his home. But when these people were fully grown and had reached maturity, they lived only for a very short while, and they were unhappy because of their foolishness. They could not refrain from hurting each other badly, nor did they want to honor the immortal gods and offer sacrifice at the holy altars of the blessed ones, as it was right for men, according to their own rites. Zeus, the son of Kronos, in anger put them away because they would not offer honor to the blessed gods who live on Olympus. After this race of men, too, was hidden in the earth, they were called "blessed mortals of the second rank," but they certainly had their honor, too.

Then Zeus the father made a third race of mortal men, the bronze race, totally unlike the silver race. They came from ash trees and were terrible and violent and constantly engaged in the deplorable works of Ares and crimes. They never ate bread, and their stubborn souls were as hard as steel [; they were unapproachable. Terrible arms of great strength grew out of the shoulders on their solid frames]. Their armor was of bronze, of bronze were their houses, and they worked with bronze tools. Black iron did not yet exist. They killed each other with their own hands and went down, nameless, into the moldy house of cold Hades. Formidable as they were, black death took them away, and they left the sun's shiny light.

When this race also was hidden in the earth, Zeus, the son of Kronos, made another one, the fourth, on the bountiful earth. It was more just and better, a godlike race of heroes who are called demigods, the one just before us in the wide world. Terrible wars and savage battles destroyed them, some before Thebes, the city of Cadmus with the seven gates, fighting over the flocks of the descendants of Oedipus; others before Troy, where ships had taken them across the great gulf of the sea, for the sake of Helen with the lovely hair. [For some of them this was the end of their lives, and death covered them.] Others were given by Zeus, the son of Kronos, an existence, a way of life far from men, at the end of the world, far from the immortal gods; and Kronos is their king. There they live, their hearts free of sorrow, on the Islands of the Blessed, near the Ocean with the deep whirlpools, happy heroes for whom the bountiful earth bears ripe honey-sweet fruit three times a year.

I wish I did not have to live among the men of the fifth race; if only I had died before or could have been born later! For this now is truly a race of iron. Neither by day nor by night will toil and misery ever cease for them. The gods will always send them painful sorrows. Zeus will destroy this race of mortal men, too, when their babies are born with gray hair. The father will not resemble his own children, nor the children their father; the guest will not be welcomed by his host, the friend by his friend, the brother by his brother, the way it used to be. Soon they will not honor their aging parents but will blame them and hurt them with poisonous words, sinful men who have no respect for the gods! They might even refuse to give their old parents the payment for their nurture, putting might before right.

54

In his tragedy *The Persians,* Aeschylus presents a necromantic ceremony in the Persian capital, after the news of the defeat at Salamis (480 B.C.) has arrived. The Queen Mother, Atossa, comes out of the royal palace in black robes, carrying the gifts of milk, honey, holy water, wine, and olive oil, along with a wreath. At the tomb of her husband, Darius I, she deposits the wreath and pours out libations.

While she performs this ritual, the chorus sings hymns of praise to the dead, and some of these may have been sung in Persian or what sounded like Persian to a Greek audience, for the chorus says in Greek, at one point: "Does our blessed, godlike king hear me, as I utter, in my unintelligible foreign language mournful laments of all sorts?" Since Persian was not a foreign language for a Persian audience, it would appear that the poet, at least for the first performance of his play, added laments in Persian or what could have passed for Persian. If these songs ever existed in the written text of the play, they must have been deleted soon thereafter, for the Greek scribes were reluctant to copy what seemed to them to be sheer nonsense. But on stage the effect may have been tremendous, and the use of foreign words or phrases in magical ceremonies is well attested in the magical papyri.

Darius is deified in death, like the Egyptian Pharaohs, the rulers of Mycenae, Alexander the Great, and later the Roman emperors. Even in Hades he has certain powers and privileges (unlike, e.g., Homer's Achilles). He is willing to appear and is granted a brief leave of absence from Hades in order to give advice to his people in an emergency. Darius wears the crown, the robes, and the saffron-colored sandals in which he was buried.

The scene has certain comical undertones—the reference to Persian as an unintelligible language (in Persia!), and the royal ghost's complaint that it is much easier to go down to Hades than to come back.

The ceremony itself is best described as a poetic and dramatic rendering of an authentic ceremony, although it was probably more Greek than Persian.

Aeschylus, *Persians* vv. 607–99

ATOSSA (*Queen Mother of Persia*): So I have come out of the palace once more, without my chariot, without my splendid robes, bringing to the father of my son propitiatory libations, gifts that soothe the dead: white milk, sweet to drink, from an unblemished cow; honey, the essence of light, the distillation of the bees that work on blossoms; holy water from a pure spring; this refreshing, unmixed drink from an ancient vine, its mother in the fields; and here is the fragrant fruit of the pale green olive that lives its abundant life among the leaves; there are flowers woven into a garland, the children of the generous earth.

But come, my friends; sing hymns of praise to the dead, while I offer them these libations, and conjure up the spirit of Darius; I shall pour these offerings, for the earth to drink, to the gods of the underworld.

CHORUS: Royal lady, venerable to the Persians! Let the libations flow down into the chambers of the earth, and we, in our hymns, will pray to the guides of the dead beneath the earth to be gracious to us.

Yes, holy gods of the underworld, Earth and Hermes and you, king of the dead, send up to the light a soul from below, for if he knows any new remedy for our distress, he alone among mortals might tell us what to do.

Does our blessed, godlike king hear me, as I utter, in my unintelligible foreign language, doleful laments of all sorts? Or must I shout my wretched misery? Does he hear me down below?

Earth and all you other rulers of the shades, allow the glorious spirit, the god of the Persians who was born in Susa, to leave your palace. No one like him was ever buried in Persian earth; please let him come.

Dear is that man, dear is his tomb; dear are the qualities that are buried there. Aidoneus, you guide the shades to the upper world, let him come, Aidoneus, the divine lord Darius! Ah!

He has never sent his people into death by waging ruinous, senseless wars; so the Persians called him "divine counselor," and he was a divine counselor indeed, for he led his armies well.

Our king, our ancient king, come here, come back! Rise to the top of your tomb! Lift the saffron-colored sandals on your feet! Show us the crest of your royal crown! Approach, merciful father Darian! Oh!

Lord of our lord, appear and listen to our pitiful, unheard-of sorrows! The darkness of Styx is hovering in the air; the whole youth of your nation has perished. Approach, merciful father Darius! Oh!

Alas! Alas! Your friends wept many tears when you died . . . [The text of the following two verses is uncertain.] Our country has lost all its triremes; we have no more ships, no more ships!

GHOST OF DARIUS (*rising from the tomb*): Faithful of the faithful, companions of my youth, old men of Persia! What is this pain that afflicts our nation? The earth groans: it is beaten and torn. As I look at my wife standing near my tomb, I am alarmed, though I have accepted her libations gladly. But you, standing close to my tomb, are chanting laments, and in shrill songs that bring back souls you call on me most pitifully. There is no easy exit from the underworld, you know—mainly because the gods down there are better at seizing than at letting go! But since I have certain powers even among them, here I am. Go ahead; I must account for my time. What is this sudden tragedy that has hit the Persians so hard?

CHORUS: I am afraid to look at you; I am afraid to speak to you; I still feel that ancient awe of you.

DARIUS: I know, but since I have listened to your laments and have come back from the world below, put aside your awe of me, make a long story short, and tell me everything in brief from the beginning to the end.

[*The Chorus is still afraid to speak; so the ghost now addresses Atossa, who tells him the news of the Persian defeat. Darius puts the blame on his son Xerxes alone, while Atossa also holds his counselors responsible. The Chorus then asks the ghost for a word of advice, and he gives it to them: never attack Greece again. After having urged Atossa to be kind and compassionate to her defeated son, he "departs to the darkness beneath the earth" (v. 839).*]

55

What Socrates himself said about his *daimonion*, the "inner voice" that gave him advice, we do not know; but in the *Apology*, which his disciple Plato wrote, there is a memorable passage. Socrates was sentenced to death by his fellow citizens because two accusations made against him were considered proven: (1) that he had corrupted the youth; (2) that he had introduced new gods.

History shows that unpopular figures have often been attacked on moral and religious grounds. In a sense, the campaign against Socrates may be called a witch-hunt. In the speech that Plato makes him deliver in court, he explains how his *daimonion* worked, but he does not actually say what he thought it was. The experience, to him, was very real; he is not using poetic language to describe something fairly trivial that might happen to any of us. According to Xenophon, another disciple who also wrote an *Apology* for his master, Socrates used to call his *daimonion* "the voice of god" (Xen., *Apol.* 12). Because the great oracles of the ancient world were considered the mouthpieces of gods, Socrates' *daimonion* might be called his "private oracle."

The true nature of Socrates' experience has often been discussed by Platonists—for example, by Apuleius in *On Socrates' Genius* and by Plutarch in *On Socrates' Sign*. Modern psychologists have written about it. Obviously, even his contemporaries did not understand the phenomenon, and some chose to misunderstand it. To call it *daimonion* would, indeed, arouse the suspicion that Socrates was worshiping a secret, nameless deity. If this deity (or daemon or spirit) worked for him, it gave him special powers that were inaccessible to others—hence the accusation of atheism and the implication of witchcraft. Only sorcerers paid tribute to nameless deities in private. But Socrates was no sorcerer. Neither was he a pure rationalist, although Plato stresses this aspect of his personality. One could call him a mystic, a Greek kind of yogi, who is at the same time a brilliant thinker.

Plato, *Apology of Socrates* 33B8–E8, 39C1–40C3

Now why is it that some people enjoy spending a good deal of time in my company? Citizens of Athens, you have heard the reason; I have told you the whole truth. The reason is this: people enjoy hearing me cross-examine those who think they are wise but are not. This, of course, is not unpleasant. I maintain that I have been told by the god to do this—in oracles, in dreams, and in any other way in which any divine power has ever told a human being to do anything. This is true, citizens of Athens, and it can easily be proved. For if I really have corrupted some of the young and am now corrupting some, surely when they were grown up and realized that I gave them some bad advice when they were young they would come forward by themselves and accuse me and wish to see me punished. Or else, if they were unwilling to do anything about it themselves, some of their relatives—their fathers, their brothers, or anyone else close to them—would now remember and demand punishment. At any rate, I see many of them right here in court—first of all Crito, who is about my age and belongs to the same tribe, father of Critobulus over there; then Lysanias of Sphettus, father of Aeschines over there; also Antiphon of Cephisus, father of Epigenes. And there are others whose brothers have been my companions in that pursuit: Nicostratus, son of Theozotides, brother of Theodotus—Theodotus, by the way, is dead, so he could not be invited—and Paralius there, son of Demodocus, whose brother was Theages.

[*Socrates maintains his innocence, and he knows that his defense is strong, but he is willing to accept the death sentence, though the charges against him are malicious and unfair.*]

Now I wish to make a prophecy to you, my fellow citizens who have sentenced me to death, for I have now reached the point where human beings are particularly apt to deliver prophecies—shortly before they die. I tell you, my friends, my murderers, that very soon after my execution a punishment much worse than the sentence of death that you passed on me will catch up with you, God knows! Now you think you have accomplished something by removing the danger of having to give an account of your lives, but I tell you, the very opposite will happen to you. For you will run into many more critics than before; I have tried to restrain them until now—you did not notice it—and they will be even more obnoxious, because they are so much younger, and you will be even more annoyed. If you think that by executing people you can prevent others from criticizing your unnatural way of life, you are mistaken, for this kind of deliverance cannot possibly come true and is not attractive; but the other one, which consists in becoming a better person instead of interfering with others, is very easy and most attractive. You have condemned me, and this is my parting prediction.

To me, my judges—for I am sure it is right for me to call you "judges"—a wonderful thing has happened. The familiar prophetic voice of my "spiritual guide" has manifested itself very frequently all my life and has opposed me, even in trivial matters, whenever I was about to do something wrong. What has happened to me now, as you can see for yourselves, might well be thought and is generally held to be the ultimate evil. And yet, when I left my house early this morning, the sign of the god did not oppose me, nor [did it manifest itself] on my way here to the court, nor at any moment during my speech when I was about to say something. On many other occasions it made me stop short in the middle of a speech, but in this matter it opposed nothing I did or said. What should I assume to be the reason for this? I will tell you: what is happening to me must be good, and those of us who consider death an evil must be wrong.

56

Phlegon of Tralles (Asia Minor) was a freedman of the emperor Hadrian, served on his staff, and wrote several books, among them *Mirabilia* (*Marvelous Facts*) from which this amazing tale is taken. It seems to have been fairly well known in antiquity, for Proclus, the Neoplatonist (fifth century A.D.) refers to it in his Commentary on Plato's *Republic* (pp. 115–16 Kroll). He gives an outline that supplies the missing beginning, and he tells us that this happened in Amphipolis, during the reign of Philip. This must be Philip II of Macedonia, the father of Alexander the Great, who ruled from 356 to 336 B.C. Phlegon's tale is cast in the form of a report from the governor of Amphipolis to a friend close to the king, who may eventually have been informed of all this.

From Proclus we learn that Philinnion died shortly after her wedding. This does not place her among the *agamoi*—the restless ghosts of those who had died unmarried—but it suggests that she clung to life on this earth and was ready to return, because her desire for love had just been aroused and was, in a way, stronger than death.

There is a similar story in Philostratus' *Life of Apollonius of Tyana* (4.25). A handsome young athlete, and aspiring philosopher, falls in love with what he thinks is a beautiful and affectionate woman who also seems to be wealthy. Apollonius, however, unmasks her at once as a dangerous kind of ghost, an *empousa* who would eventually devour her lover. At a reception just before the planned wedding, Apollonius denounces her and makes all her fine possessions disappear, whereupon she admits her true identity as a vampire and then, one assumes, disappears before she has a chance to feed on the young philosopher-athlete. This possibility is not implied in Phlegon's tale, although the man dies tragically and, perhaps, is united in another world with Philinnion.

In his ballad "The Bride of Corinth," Goethe added a brilliant new twist to the tale he found in Phlegon. It is a haunting poem in the deepest sense of the word, and it stirs up all sorts of emotions. According to Goethe, the young man who comes to spend the night in Corinth (not in Amphipolis) is the fiancé of the dead girl. The wedding was postponed, because her parents (not herself) have converted to Christianity, and he has remained faithful to the ancient gods. The girl's death was hastened, or so it seems, by her fear that marriage was no longer possible, and her frustration brings her back from the grave. That first night she spends with the guest-friend—her fiancé—is to be their wedding night. Her desire for love and sex—denied by her parents, denied by the Church—is stronger than death. Her lover never quite understands what is happening. He enjoys the bliss that is offered to him, but he is doomed to die, and his bride fears that she is doomed to go, as a vampire, after other young men. Still, as the last stanza tells us, the lovers will be cremated together, joined in death and joined to the ancient gods and ultimately happier than if they had been married in the Church by "priests with their humming songs."

Phlegon of Tralles, *Mirabilia* 1

[*The beginning of the story is missing, but we can guess the following: Philinnion, the daughter of Demostratus and Charito, has died. Her ghost comes back and visits young Machatas, a guest-friend, in his room. The old nurse discovers this by coincidence.*]

She [the nurse] came to the door of the guest room and by the light of the lamp saw the girl close to Machates. The sight was so astonishing that she could not stay there any longer but ran to the girl's mother and shouted at the top of her voice: "Charito! Demostratus!" telling them to get up and come to see their daughter by themselves. For—so she said— the girl had appeared alive and was there, by some divine will, with the guest, in the guest room. As she heard this strange tale, Charito's soul was filled with panic. She felt faint because the news was so amazing and the excitement of the nurse so obvious. Thinking of her daughter, she began to cry. Finally, she accused the old woman of being out of her mind and told her to go away at once. But now the old woman reproached her and, speaking openly, said that she was perfectly sane and normal, and that it was not she who was afraid to see her own daughter. At long last Charito, partly because the nurse told her so, partly because she wanted to know what was going on, came to the door of the guest room. But by now, some time had elapsed, since the nurse had brought the news two hours ago, and they came too late; the couple was already asleep. The mother, peering into the room, thought she recognized her daughter's clothes and general appearance, but she was unable to find out the truth that night and thought that she should keep quiet. She hoped to catch the girl by getting up early or, if she was too late, ask Machates about everything; for she knew that he would never lie about such a serious matter. So she said nothing and left. At dawn they realized that the girl had slipped away unnoticed, either by the will of the gods or by chance. When Charito came to the room, she was angry with Machates because the girl had disappeared, but she told him the whole story from the beginning, as it had happened, hiding nothing, embracing his knees and asking him to tell her the whole truth. He felt very uncomfortable at first and was upset, but finally he told her the girl's name: Philinnion. He also told her how she had first visited him and how great her desire for him was. She had said that she was coming to him without her parents' knowledge. To convince the mother, he opened his trunk and took out the things the girl had left behind: the golden ring she had given to him and the girdle she had left the night before. When Charito saw this clear evidence, she cried aloud and tore her clothes and her cloak, threw the hairnet from her head, fell to the ground, clutched the tokens to her breast, and started to grieve all over again.

When the guest saw what was happening—everyone lamenting, over-come by emotion, as if they were just now preparing the girl's burial—he became troubled and begged them to stop. He promised Charito to show the girl to her if she came to him again. She accepted this, urged him to keep his word and left. Night came, and it was that hour when Philinnion was accustomed to visit him. Everybody was awake, anxious to see her arrive and kept a lookout. She came, entered the room at her usual time and sat down on the bed. Machates pretended that nothing had changed, but he wanted to find out what was going on, even though he could hardly believe what he had been told. He wanted to find out whether the woman he was making love with—the woman who so faithfully visited him at the same time every night and who ate and drank with him—was actually dead. He was very doubtful of what they had told him and preferred to believe that some grave-robbers had opened her tomb and sold her clothes and her gold jewelry to her father. At any rate, he had to know the truth; so he sent the slaves in secret to call the parents.

Demostratus and Charito arrived at once. When they saw her, they were at first speechless and terrified by the unexpected sight, but then they cried out and hugged their daughter. But Philinnion said: "Mother! Father! It is not fair of you to begrudge me those three days with the guest in my father's house. I was not causing any trouble for anyone. Now, because of your meddling, you will have to grieve all over again, and I have to return to my appointed place. I came here not without the will of the gods." She said this and was dead. Her body was stretched out on the bed, for all to see. Her mother and her father threw themselves upon it, and the house was filled with shouting and laments because of this calam-ity. What had happened was unbearable, incredible.

The rumor of these events quickly spread through the city, and I was notified. During the following night I kept back the crowds that were flocking to the house, taking precautions that there should be no distur-bance, because a story of this kind was going from mouth to mouth. By early dawn the theater was already full. The whole affair was presented. A decision was made that we should first go the tomb, open it up and find out whether the body was on its bier or whether her place was empty. It was not yet six months since the girl had died. When we had opened the vault, which was the resting place for all her deceased family members, we saw bodies or bones—in the case of those who had died a long time ago—lying on the other biers, but on the bier on which Philinnion had been laid and put to rest, we found only the iron ring that had belonged to the guest and the gold-plated cup that Machates had given to her on the first of their days together.

We were amazed and terrified and went at once to the guest room in Demostratus' house to find out whether the dead girl was really there. We saw her lying on the ground and gathered at the place of the assembly. What had happened was shocking and hard to believe. There was excitement in the assembly, and practically no one knew what to think about all this.

Hyllus was the first to stand up. He is not only considered the best prophet in the city, but he also has the reputation of being a very good augur, and he has practiced his craft with exceptional skill. He told us to cremate the girl outside the city limits—no good could come out of her being buried within the city limits once more—and to propitiate chthonic Hermes and the Eumenides. Everybody should then be purified. We should cleanse the temples and perform the customary rites for the chthonic deities. To me he spoke privately about the king and what had happened. He told me to offer sacrifices to Hermes, to Zeus as patron of guests, and to Ares, and to be scrupulous with my offerings. He gave these instructions, and we carried them out.

Machates, the guest whom the ghost had visited, fell into a depression and committed suicide.

If you decide to write to the king about this, let me know, so that I can send you one of my men who knows all the details.

Farewell.

57

Ancient ghost stories attest the popular belief in some form of survival of the person after death. Ghosts are, in fact, visible daemons, as Pausanias' description of "Cemetery Hill," near Marathon, shows. Just as invisible daemons were worshiped throughout Greece, visible ones also might have their cult, although they were usually considered a nuisance and people shunned haunted places then as now because they often indicated the presence of evil—murder, for instance, or violent death in general.

It is obvious that an ancient battlefield on which thousands of men had been killed in the prime of their lives would yield a certain number of permanent ghosts (even ghost horses!), apparitions that were still reported in the time of Pausanias, who wrote a travel guide to Greece circa A.D. 150.

The English word *ghost* itself shows how ancient beliefs sometimes survive. It can mean "soul" or "spirit," as opposed to the body, but it can also mean "a spectral apparition," and the third person of the Trinity is called either "the Holy Spirit" or "the Holy Ghost." Similarly, the German word *Geist* has a fairly wide range of meaning, with "spirit" in one sense or another fitting most of them.

Pausanias traveled all over Greece in the second century A.D. and visited the famous sites. He listened to the stories of the tourist guides as he looked at the monuments, but he also did some research on his own.

In the battle of Marathon (490 B.C.) many men lost their lives, and their bodies were buried there. Such an ancient battlefield—ancient even in the days of Pausanias—is no ordinary place. Every now and then the battle is reenacted at night, but it is dangerous to go there and wait for it to happen. The ghosts do not like idle curiosity.

All of the fallen soldiers are considered "heroes," but three divine or semidivine beings are singled out for special worship: Marathon, the eponymous hero of the site; Heracles, who was believed to have helped the Greeks; and a mysterious apparition called Echetlaeus, who used his plowshare as a weapon.

Pausanias, *Description of Greece* 1.32.3–5

Before turning to the description of the islands, I will deal once more with the counties. There is a county called Marathon, halfway between Athens and Carystus in Euboea. It was in this part of Attica that the foreign army [i.e., the Persians] landed, was defeated in battle, and lost some of its ships as it took off again. In the plain there is a grave for the Athenians, and on it there are slabs with the names of the fallen, arranged according to their tribes. There is another grave for the Boeotians of Plataea, and one for the slaves, because slaves had fought there for the first time [along with the free].

There is also a separate monument for one man, Miltiades, the son of Cimon, though his end came later, after he had failed to take Parus and had been brought to trial by the Athenians because of this.

At Marathon you can hear all night horses whinnying and men fighting. No one who stays there just to have this experience gets any good out of it, but the daemons do not get angry with anyone who happens to be there against his will.

The people of Marathon worship both those who died in the fighting, calling them "heroes" and [a semidivine being called] "Marathon," from whom the county derives its name, but also Heracles, saying that they were the first among the Greeks to acknowledge him as a god.

They say also that a man took part in the battle who looked and was dressed like a farmer. He slaughtered many of the Persians with his plowshare, and when everything was over he disappeared. But when the Athenians consulted the oracle, the god would not tell them anything except to honor "Echetlaeus" [i.e., the man with the plowshare] as a hero.

58

Pausanias' description of a famous painting that could be seen in Delphi in ancient times gives us the common Greek view of Hades. Part of it served as an illustration of Odysseus' consultation of the seer Tiresias [*no. 52*]. It was clearly represented as a real *katabasis* 'descent', either because the painter, Polygnotus, understood the text in this way, or perhaps because he could not represent the seeming contradiction between descent and nondescent that we have noticed above.

The way in which he made visible the topography of the underworld, with all its inhabitants known from myth, literature, and earlier works of art, was much admired in antiquity. In a sense, the painting was monumental and encyclopedic, and the wealth of detail must have been astonishing. In another sense it worked on the emotions of those who still believed that this was life after death, at least for those who had sinned or committed a crime on earth. The mystery religions and the characteristic ethical doctrine preached at Delphi, where the painting stood, held out hope for those who put themselves under the gods and began a new life.

The artist included some characters that seem to belong to the realm of folklore rather than literature—for example, the daemon Eurynomus, who eats the flesh of corpses (i.e., causes their decaying). Pausanias tried to look him up in the *Odyssey* as well as in other early epics that are no longer extant, but he could not find this particular daemon. Guides were no doubt available to explain the details, and thus, perhaps, they created a new mythology for the benefit of the tourists.

Pausanias, *Description of Greece* 10.28.1–29.1

[*One part of the large painting of Polygnotus in the Lounge at Delphi shows the fall of Troy and the departure of the Greeks.*]

The other part of the painting, the one on the left, shows Odysseus, who has descended into the so-called Hades to consult the soul of Tiresias about his safe return home. The details of the painting are as follows: There is water that looks like a river, obviously the Acheron, with reeds growing in it and fish swimming in it whose forms appear so dim that one would take them to be shadows rather than fish. There is a boat on the river, with the ferryman [Charon] at the oars. Polygnotus has followed, it seems to me, the poem *Minyad,* for there is a passage in the *Minyad* that refers to Theseus and Pirithoous: "But then they could not find within its anchoring-place the boat upon which the dead embark, the one that Charon, the old ferryman, steered."

In addition, Polygnotus painted Charon as a man well advanced in years. The passengers in the boat are not altogether clearly visible [or: are not very well known]. Tellis seems to be a young adolescent, Cleobaea still a young woman; she holds on her knees a chest of the kind they usually make for Demeter. As far as Tellis is concerned, I have only heard that the poet Archilochus was his grandson, and of Cleobaea it is said that she brought the mysteries of Demeter from Parus to Thasus.

On the bank of the Acheron, just under Charon's boat, there is a remarkable group. There is a man who treated his father unjustly, and he is now being strangled by his father. In those days people honored their parents above anything else. [A digression follows.] Next to the man who abused his father, and who for this suffers his full share of punishment in Hades, there is a man who pays the penalty for sacrilege. The woman punishing him is skilled in drugs, especially harmful ones. Clearly in those days people were very religious. [A digression follows.]

Higher up than the figures just mentioned is Eurynomus. The guides at Delphi say that he is one of the daemons in Hades and that he eats the flesh off the corpses, leaving them only their bones. Homer's *Odyssey* and the epic entitled *Minyad* and the *Nostoi*—they do refer to Hades and its horrors—know nothing of a daemon called Eurynomus. But let me describe at least what he is like and how he is represented in the painting. His color is black-blue, like flies that buzz around meat, and he is showing his teeth, and he sits on the skin of a vulture. Immediately after Eurynomus there are Auge of Arcadia and Iphimedea. Auge went to the court of Teuthras in Mysia, and of all the women who had shared Heracles' bed, according to myth, Auge was the one who gave birth to a son just like his father. Iphimedea was greatly honored by the Carians of Mylasa.

Even higher up than the figures just mentioned are two companions of Odysseus, Perimedes and Eurylochus, carrying victims for sacrifice; the victims are black rams.

59

This exorcist's ritual from the Great Magical Papyrus in Paris is far more complicated than any of the exorcisms described in the Bible. Certain substances have to be cooked in olive oil, certain words written on a tin tablet, certain formulas recited. In the main formula the daemon possessing the patient is threatened by divine names from different cultures: Egypt, Israel, Greco-Roman paganism, Christianity, and some others that cannot be clearly identified. The whole adds up to a massive attack on the daemon. If the god of one culture is powerless, the combination of many gods will certainly help. In some cases the powers of the gods to whom the daemon must eventually yield are emphasized by striking examples (sometimes called *historiolae*).

The food taboo prescribed at the end is interesting. It does not necessarily mean that the magician who designed this ritual was Jewish. He may simply have used Hebrew words (or what he thought were Hebrew words) and assumed that ritual purity, according to the Jewish custom, made the words more effective. An exorcist of this type probably did not belong to any of the great religions of the time, one would assume; but this did not prevent him from borrowing from them in order to reinforce his magic.

Great Magical Papyrus in Paris (*PGM* IV.3007–86)

A well-tested formula by Pibeches for those possessed by daemons. Take oil from unripened olives together with the "mastigia" plant and lotus pith, and cook it with colorless marjoram, saying: "IOEL. OS SARTHIOMI. EMORI. THEOCHIPSOITH. SITHEMOCH. SOTHE. IOE. MIMIPSOTHIOOPH. PHERSOTHI AEEIOUO IOE. EO CHARIPHTHA." Go out of NN! Common formula. Write the protective charm on a tin tablet: "IAEO. ABRAOTHIOCH. PHTHA MESENPSINIAO. PHEOCH. IAEO. CHARSOK" and attach it to the patient. This is an object of horror for every daemon, and it frightens him. Stand facing [the patient] and begin the exorcism.

The formula of the exorcism is the following: I adjure you in the name of the god of the Hebrews, Jesus. "IABA. IAE. ABRAOTH. AIA. THOTTH. ELE. ELO. AEO. EOU. I I IBAECH. ABARMAS. IABARAOU. ABELBEL. LONA. ABRA. MAROIA. BRAKION." You who appear in fire, you who are in the midst of land, of snow and of fog: Tannetis, let your pitiless angel descend, and let him arrest the daemon that flies around this creature shaped by God in his holy paradise. For I pray to the holy god through Ammon: "IPSENTANCHO" [formula]. I adjure you "LABRIA IACOUTH. ABLANATHANALBA. AKRAMM. [formula]. AOTH. IATHRBATHRA. CHACHTHABRATHA. CHAMYN CHEL. ABROOTH. OUABRASILOTH." Otherwise "IELOSAI IAEL."

I adjure you by him who appeared to Israel in a pillar of light and a cloud by day, who has saved his people from Pharaoh and has brought upon Pharaoh the ten plagues, because he would not listen. And I adjure you, every daemonic spirit, to speak, no matter who you are, in the name of the seal that Solomon placed on the tongue of Jeremiah, and he spoke. So you must speak, too, whoever you are, whether daemon of heaven or air, or earth or under the earth or of the underworld, Ebusaean or Chersaean or Pharisaean. Speak, whoever you are, for I adjure you in the name of the light-bearing, invincible god, the one who knows what is in the heart of every living being, who has created the human race from dust, who has brought [it] out of uncertainty, who gathers the clouds, sends rain upon the earth, who blessed its fruits, whom every heavenly power of angels and archangels blesses.

I adjure you in the name of the great god Sabaoth who made the river Jordan flow backward and made impassable the Red Sea through which Israel had passed.

I adjure you in the name of him who revealed the hundred forty languages and distributed them according to his own command. I adjure you in the name of him who, with his beams of fire, has burned down the stiff-necked giants, to whom the wings of the Cherubim sing praises. I adjure you in the name of him who has built the mountains around the sea [or] a wall of sand, and who ordered it not to overflow. And the deep obeyed. You must obey, too, every daemonic spirit, for I adjure you in the name of him who shakes up the four winds from the holy eternities, who looks like the sky, like the sea, like the clouds, who carries the light, the invincible one.

I adjure you in the name of him who dwells in Jerusalem, the pure [city], for whom and near whom the inextinguishable fire burns for all eternity, through his holy name "IAEOBAPHRENEMOUN" [formula], before whom the hellfire trembles and flames leap all around, and iron explodes, and every mountain is seized by fear from the depth of its foundations. I adjure you, daemonic spirit, whoever you are, in the name of him who looks down on the earth and makes its foundations tremble, who has brought the universe from nonbeing into being.

But I urge you who make use of this exorcism not to eat any pork, and every spirit, every daemon, no matter of what kind, will be subject to you. As you perform the exorcism, blow once [at the patient], beginning at the toes, blowing all the way up to the face, and the daemon will be arrested. Stay pure! For the formula is in Hebrew and is kept [pure] among pure men.

60

Whether Seneca's tragedies were actually performed on stage or were merely recited is still the subject of controversy. This necromantic scene from one of his dramas (written during the first half of the first century A.D.) was narrated, perhaps because it would have been difficult to show the action on stage. As a Stoic philosopher, Seneca was interested in contemporary science (he wrote a scientific work, *Quaestiones Naturales* [*Scientific Problems*] in prose); he also condemned superstitions and wrote a work (now lost) on that subject. In one of his *Moral Essays* (*De Beneficiis* [*On Good Deeds*]) he writes: "No normal human being is afraid of a god. It is insane to fear what is good for you, and no one can love what he fears" (4.19.1).

Since fear—mostly fear of unknown powers—is such an important element in magic, it is puzzling that Seneca paid any attention to magic at all, and yet he did, not only here, but also in his *Medea*. Perhaps, like authors before him, he looked upon magic as a literary theme that offered great possibilities. Descriptions of magical ceremonies were apt to shock the reader and the audience, and ever since Aristotle, the "shock effect" had been considered one of the functions of drama. As a philosopher, Seneca wanted to help his readers overcome fear; as a playwright, he thought it necessary to terrify them, in order to achieve a *katharsis,* a kind of purification of the nervous system. The magical scene is not necessary for the plot of the play; Sophocles and other dramatists did not use it. One suspects, then, that Seneca threw it in for the sake of its "shock effect."

Did Seneca or his nephew, Lucan [see *no. 61*], ever witness a necromantic ceremony? We do not know, but since Nero himself was interested in this sort of thing, it is quite possible. We know from the magical papyri that such rituals were performed, but to reconstruct them from this dramatic text would be a mistake. On the other hand, the theme already had a long history, and Seneca may have borrowed from literature rather than from life—for example, from the "daemonic personifications" in Book 6 of Virgil's *Aeneid*—adding some touches of his own.

Seneca, *Oedipus,* vv. 530–626

CREON: Far from the city, near the valley through which the Dirce flows, there is a grove, dark with oak trees. Cypresses, lifting up their heads from the deep woods, dominate the forest with their evergreen masses. Ancient oak trees stretch out their twisted branches, rotting from decay. The ravages of age have broken the side of this tree; that one, about to fall because its roots have grown weak, leans precariously against another trunk. There are laurel trees with bitter berries, basswood trees with light leaves, myrtle from Paphus, elms that will someday move oars through the wide sea, the fir tree that grows toward the sun and exposes its knotless sides to the Zephyrs. In the middle of the woods there is an enormous tree whose heavy shade weighs on the smaller plants and which guards the grove all by itself, spreading out its branches in a wide perimeter. At its foot there is a sinister pool which never sees the sunlight, still and stagnant in eternal frost. A brackish swamp surrounds the sluggish spring.

When the old priest had entered this place he acted quickly. The place itself offered night. The earth was dug up, and a fire, snatched from a pyre, was thrown on top. The seer drapes himself in a funereal robe and waves a branch. The black garment reaches down to his feet. The old man in his sinister apparel draws nearer, gloomily. Yew, the plant of death, crowns his head. Black sheep and black oxen are dragged to the ditch. The flame consumes the sacrificial meal, and the cattle, still alive, struggle in the deadly fire. The priest now calls the shades and him who rules over the shades and him who guards the entrance to the pool of death. He lets the magic spells roll and sings in ecstasy threatening words that either appease or force the frail shades. He pours an offering of blood on the altar and lets the animals burn whole. He floods the ditch with blood and pours the white milky liquid on top; with his left hand he sprinkles wine. Once more he sings, looks down on the ground, and calls the shades with an even louder, more ecstatic voice.

The pack of Hecate barks. Three times the hollow valley echoes with a mournful sound. The ground trembles, the earth quakes.

"They have heard me!" cries the seer. "The spells that I have poured out are working! The dark chaos is breaking open, and the peoples of Dis are allowed to come to the world above!"

The whole forest sinks into the ground, its leaves bristling. The oaks split open. The whole grove quivers in horror. The Earth gives way and groans deep inside. (Is it because she resents the fact that Acheron's hidden depths are opened up? Or is it because the Earth herself has thunderously ripped her structure to let the dead pass through? Or is it because three-headed Cerberus, mad with rage, has pulled on his heavy chain?) Suddenly the Earth yawns and opens up an enormous chasm.

I saw with my own eyes the stagnant pools among the shades; with my own eyes I saw the bloodless gods and the night that is truly night. My blood turned cold, stopped, and froze in my veins.

A wild cohort jumped forth. The whole offspring of the dragon stood there in arms, the armies of the two brothers born from the teeth sown near Dirce, the merciless destruction of the people of Thebes! There was a yell coming from the black Furies, blind Madness and Horror, and all the other creatures that eternal Darkness produces and hides. There was

Bereavement tearing at her hair, Disease barely holding up her weary head, Old Age, a burden to herself, and halting Fear. My courage fell. Even the old priest's daughter, who was familiar with his sacred rites and magic arts, was shocked. But he, fearless and bold, conjured up the bloodless folk of savage Dis.

At once they appeared, flying through the air like delicate mist, breathing the air under the open sky. The crowds attracted by the seer's voice were more numerous than the leaves that grow on Mount Eryx, more numerous than the flowers that come out on Mount Hybla in the middle of spring when swarming bees form a tight ball in the air, more numerous than the waves that break on the Ionian Sea, more numerous than the birds that escape from the winter and from the threats of icy Strymon and cut through the sky to exchange arctic snow for the mild climate of the Nile. Nervously the trembling souls seek hiding places in the shady grove.

First, Zethus emerged from the ground, his right hand holding on to a bull with fierce horns. Then, with a lyre in his left hand, came Amphion who moved rocks with his sweet sounds. Finally, Niobe, the daughter of Tantalus, came, among her children, lifting her proud head safely, count-ing the shades. Delirious Agave, worse as a mother [than Niobe] ap-peared, followed by the whole crowd that tore the king in pieces, and be-hind the Bacchants, Pentheus, mutilated, but still savage and threatening.

Often was Laius conjured up, and finally he lifted his disgraceful head, but he sat down at a distance from the crowd, hiding his face. The priest insisted and doubled his incantations until Laius showed the features he had concealed so far. I shudder as I describe him: there he stood, his body horribly covered with gore, his hair dirty, disgusting, and covered with filth. In ecstasy he yelled.

[*Laius' ghost now reveals that his son Oedipus, king of Thebes, is responsible for the plague that has befallen the city; Oedipus has killed him and married his own mother; Oedipus must be punished.*]

61

From this text it would appear that Lucan tried to surpass his uncle Seneca in the description of horror. He created in this unfinished epic on the civil war between Caesar and Pompey a kind of superwitch, Erictho, who is consulted by the "worthless" son of Pompey on the eve of the decisive battle of Pharsalus (48 B.C.). Since Lucan wished to compete with Virgil as an epic poet, it is safe to say that this necromantic scene in Book 6 of his work was designed to invite comparison with Book 6 of the *Aeneid,* the hero's visit to the underworld.

Lucan first enumerates various methods of divination, but adds that for Pompey's son necromancy is the only reliable way of exploring the future. The rites involved are presented as monstrous and disgusting, but the poet goes on and on, as if he enjoyed all the gruesome details. It is a neat literary trick: Lucan professes to be shocked by the magical practices he describes, and yet they seem to give him a certain thrill.

Erictho has enormous power and no scruples whatsoever about using it. The central idea of the whole passage—the revival of a corpse—may have been discussed as a scientific problem at the time. Shelley, who admired Lucan and placed him above Virgil as a poet, must have read this passage with his wife, Mary, for it is almost certainly the nucleus of Frankenstein's experiment.

Lucan, *Pharsalia* 6.413–830

When the leaders had pitched their camps in the doomed part of the world, everyone was disturbed by a feeling that the battle was near. Obviously the grim hour of decision was approaching, and destiny was moving in. Worthless characters trembled and feared the worst, but a few, anticipating an uncertain outcome, built up morale and coped with hope and fear alike.

Among the idle crowd was Sextus, the unworthy son of the great Pompey. Later, in exile, he was to become a pirate, haunting the sea around Sicily, disgracing the glory that his father had won in naval battles. Goaded by fear, he wanted to know ahead of time the course of fate. He could stand no delay and was tormented by all the events that the future held; so he did not consult the tripods of Delus or the Pythian caverns, and he cared not to find out what the sound made by the bronze cauldron of Jupiter at Dodona means—Dodona, which produced the first human food—nor did he ask for someone to read the future in the entrails, to interpret the signs of birds, watch the lightnings of heaven, investigate the stars by means of the Assyrian science, or practice any other science that is secret but not unlawful.

He was familiar with the occult knowledge of the cruel sorcerers that are an abomination to the gods, the gloomy altars where funeral rites are performed; he knew that Pluto and the shades below can be relied upon, and he was perverse enough to believe that the gods above have little knowledge. The very region [of Thessaly] supported his vicious, insane delusions: the camp was close to the habitation of Thessalian witches, whose bold criminal acts surpass our imagination and whose specialty is the impossible.

Moreover, the earth of Thessaly produces poisonous herbs in the mountains, and the rocks feel it when magicians sing their deadly spells.

Many plants grow there that may compel the gods, and the woman who came from Colchis [Medea] picked in Thessalian country many herbs that she did not bring along. The impious incantations of a horrible race attract the attention of the gods, who turn a deaf ear to so many nations, so many peoples. The witch's voice alone reaches through the remote regions of heaven and conveys compelling words even to a reluctant deity, a deity not distracted by care for the sky and the revolving firmament. When her unspeakable mumbo-jumbo has reached the stars, a Thessalian witch can call away the gods from every altar except her own, even though Persian Babylon and Memphis, full of mysteries, may open every shrine of their ancient magicians.

Through the song of a Thessalian witch, a love that is not willed by destiny enters an insensible heart, and respectable old men burn with forbidden passions. Not only are their poisonous potions or the tumor full of juice that they snatch from the forehead of a foal—the indication that its mother will love it—so powerful: no, men's minds are destroyed by magic spells, even if they have not been poisoned by any dangerous drug. Men and women who are not joined in marriage and not attracted to each other by charm or beauty can be drawn together by the magic power of a thread that is being twirled.

The decrees of nature cease to operate; nights grow longer and delay the days; the heavenly sphere does not obey the law; the swift firmament slows down, as soon as it has heard a magic spell; and Jupiter is amazed that heaven does not rotate on its swift axis, although he keeps pushing it hard. At one time [the witches] fill everything with rain and hide the warm sun behind a veil of clouds; there is thunder in the sky, and Jupiter knows nothing about it; by the same kind of spell they disperse the large expanses of wet mist and the disheveled locks of the clouds. There are no winds, but the sea swells, and then again it is forbidden to feel the power of a storm and lies silent, even though the south wind tries to stir it up and the sails that carry a ship against the wind belly out. The waterfall on the face of a steep cliff hangs suspended in midair, and rivers do not run in their natural directions.

The Nile does not rise in the summer; the Maeander straightens out its course, and the Arar rushes the sluggish Rhone. The mountains lower their peaks and flatten out their ridges; Olympus looks up at the clouds, and the snows of Scythia thaw without any sun, even in the midst of a harsh winter. When the tide is moved by the moon, Thessalian charms defend the shore and drive back the tide. The earth, too, shakes off the axis of her solid mass, and her gravity stumbles and tends toward the center of the universe. Struck by the voice [of a witch] the mass of this enormous structure splits and offers a view of the sky that rotates around it. Every animal that has the ability to kill and is equipped by nature to do harm fears the Thessalian witches and provides them with murderous techniques. The greedy tiger and the lion, noble in his wrath, show their best manners and lick their hands; the snake unfolds his frosty coils just to please them and stretches at full length on ground that is covered with dew; the bodies of knotted vipers break apart and get joined together again, and serpents collapse, because human poison is blown at them.

Why do the gods trouble to obey these spells? Why are they afraid of ignoring them? What mutual agreement puts pressure on the gods? Must they obey, or does it give them pleasure to do so? Is this allegiance caused by some obscure religion, or do the witches enforce it with silent threats? Do witches have power over all the gods, or are their incantations effective against only one particular god, who can inflict the compulsion inflicted upon him on the whole world?

These witches first brought down the stars from the fast-moving sky, and by their techniques the clear Moon, attacked by dreadful, poisonous incantations, grew dim and burned with a dark and earthly light, just as if the Earth had cut off the Moon from the reflections of her brother, the Sun, and projected its own shadows into the light from heaven. The Moon is so strongly affected by magic spells and pulled down so hard that she finally drops her foam from a close distance on the plants below.

These criminal rites, these wicked practices of a horrible race, were scorned by savage Erictho as being too pious, and she degraded a science that was already tainted with rites unknown. To her, it was a sacrilege to seek shelter for her abominable person in a city or in a normal house; she lived in deserted tombs and inhabited graves from which the ghosts had been driven, and the deities of hell loved her. Neither the heavenly gods nor the fact that she was still living prevented her from visiting [reading *ambire* for *audire*] the assemblies of the dead or from knowing the dwellings beyond the Styx and the mysteries of Dis in hell. The face of the loathsome witch is haggard, hideous, and decomposed; her features inspire fear because of their hellish pallor; they are covered with disheveled hair and are never seen when the sky is bright: only if rain and black clouds conceal the stars does the witch emerge from the tombs she has stripped and try to catch the lightning of the night. As she stomps over a fertile cornfield, she burns the seeds, and her breath poisons air that was wholesome before.

She never prays to the heavenly gods, never invokes divine aid by a suppliant hymn, knows nothing about the entrails of a sacrificial victim. She only enjoys placing upon an altar the burning logs and the incense that she has stolen from a kindled pyre.

As soon as they hear her voice uttering a magic prayer, the gods grant her every kind of horror; they are afraid to hear the second spell. She buries alive those whose souls are still in control of their bodies, and Death catches up with them against his own will, because years of life were still due them. Or else she brings back dead bodies from the grave, by turning around the funeral procession; corpses actually escape death. This witch snatches the smoking ashes, the burning bones of the young, from the midst of the pyre and grabs the very torch the parents were holding, and collects the pieces of the bier that are fluttering in black smoke, the burial garments that crumble into ashes and the cinders that smell of the corpse. But when the bodies have been put into stone sarcophagi, which drain off the body fluids and absorb the liquid marrow, drying out the corpse, she feasts greedily, savagely, on all the limbs, thrusts her fingers into the eye sockets, scoops out gleefully the frozen eyeballs, and gnaws the yellow nails on the withered hand. With her teeth she bites through the fatal noose on the rope and plucks the corpse dangling from the gallows; she scrapes criminals off the cross, tearing away the rain-beaten flesh and the bones baked in the glaring sun. She takes off the nails that pierce the hands, the black juices of corruption that drip all over the corpse, and the clotted fluids, and when a tendon resists her bite, she pulls it down with her weight. Wherever any corpse lies unburied on the ground, she sits near it, before any birds or beasts arrive, but she has no intention of dissecting the body with a knife or with her nails; she waits for the wolves to tear it apart and then snatches the prey from their hungry throats.

She is ready to commit a murder whenever she needs the fresh blood that gushes forth when a throat is slit and whenever her ghoulish repasts require flesh that still throbs. She also slits open women's wombs and delivers babies by an unnatural method, in order to offer them on a burning altar. And whenever she needs evil spirits as her henchmen, she creates them herself [by killing someone]. Every human casualty serves her in some way. She rips off the bloom on the face of a child's body, and when an adolescent dies, her left hand cuts off a lock of his hair. Quite often, when a dear relative dies, the horrible witch bends over his body, and as she kisses him, she mutilates his face and opens his closed mouth with her teeth; then she bites the tip of the tongue that lies in the dry throat, pours whispered sounds between the cold lips, and sends a secret message of horror down to the shades of Styx.

Her reputation in the country made her known to Pompey [the son], and he picked his way across deserted fields, when night occupied the high heaven, and the sun beneath our earth marked the hour of noon. Faithful, trusted creatures who assisted her in her crimes went to and fro among the ruined tombs and burial places till they saw her far away, sitting on a steep rock where the Balkan mountains slope down and extend their ridges toward Pharsalia.

She was experimenting with a spell unknown to other sorcerers and to the gods of witchcraft, and she composed an incantation for an unheard-of purpose. She was worried that the civil war might wander off to some other part of the world and that Thessaly might miss this tremendous slaughter, and so the witch poisoned the countryside near Philippi [i.e., Pharsalus] with her spells and sprinkled it with her horrible drugs, to stop it from letting the war move elsewhere, because she wanted to have all those dead to herself and make use of the blood of the whole world. She was hoping to mutilate the bodies of slaughtered kings, to sweep off [reading *auerrere* for *auertere*] the ashes of the whole Roman people, and to get hold of the bones of the aristocracy, in order to control its shades. She had only one passionate concern: what part of Pompey's stretched-out corpse she might snatch, or on what limb of Caesar's she might pounce.

The worthless son of Pompey spoke first and said to her: "You are the pride of Thessalian witches. You have the power to reveal to mankind its future, the power to change the course of events. Please tell me exactly what turn the hazard of war is going to take. I am not just a Roman plebeian—I am the son of Pompey, and everyone knows me—and I shall either rule the world or inherit disaster. I am worried because my heart is struck with doubts; on the other hand, I can deal with dangers that are spelled out to me. Chance hits us unexpectedly and unforeseen—take this power away from it! Torture the gods—or leave them alone and extort the truth from the dead! Open up the seat of Elysium, summon Death himself, and force him to tell us which one of us will be his prey. It is a difficult task, I know, but it might be of interest, even to you, to find out which way the hazard of this enormous issue is going to go."

The ruthless witch is glad that her reputation is so widespread and answers: "Young man, if you wanted to change a minor decree of fate, it would be easy to steer the gods into any course of action, even against their will. When the planets with their beams commit one single soul to death, witchcraft has the power to delay the event. Even if all the stars promise to people a ripe old age, we can cut short their lives by our magic herbs. But if the chain of causes goes back to the origin of the world and universal fate suffers if you want to make a minor change, then the whole of mankind must expect one single blow, and Fortuna has more power than the Thessalian witches—we admit it ourselves. If you just want to know what will happen to you, there are many easy ways that lead to the truth: earth and sky, the seas, the plains, and the rocks of Rhodope will speak to us. But the obvious method—since there is such an abundance of men who were recently killed—would be to pick one body from the Thessalian fields; then the mouth of a corpse that is still warm because death occurred only a short time ago will speak clearly [to us], and it will not be a dismal shade, with limbs dried in the sun, hissing sounds that our ears cannot make out."

Thus the witch spoke, and by her magic she made the night twice as dark as before. She wrapped her sinister head in a veil of smog and moved among the bodies of the slain that had been cast out and denied burial. At once the wolves fled and the vultures pulled out their talons and flew away, still hungry; meanwhile, the witch picked out her "prophet"; she inspected the innermost organs, cold in death, and found that the tissue of the hardened lung was undamaged, and she looked for the power of speech in the dead body. Now the destiny of many men killed in battle is hanging in the balance: who is the one she might want to call back to the upper world? Had she attempted to raise a whole army of dead from the plain and make them fight again, the laws of the underworld would have yielded to her, and an entire host, brought up from Stygian Avernus by the power of a monstrous witch, would have joined the ranks.

At last she chose a corpse, inserted a hook into its throat, and attached the hook to a rope taken from the gallows [text and translation uncertain]; with this contraption she dragged the wretched corpse over rocks and stones, to bring it back to life, and placed it beneath a high rock of a hollow mountain that savage Erictho had condemned to witness her rites.

The ground there descended abruptly and led down almost as far as the dark caverns of the underworld. A gloomy wood with drooping leaves borders it, and it is shaded by yew trees that the sun cannot penetrate and that never turn their tops toward the sky. Inside the caves there is darkness and gray mold caused by eternal night; only magic can produce light. Even in the gorge of Taenarus the air is less sluggish and stagnant—it is the gloomy zone between the hidden world and our own, and the rulers of Tartarus are not afraid of letting the shades go that far. Although the Thessalian witch imposes her will on destiny, it is doubtful whether she actually sees the shades of the underworld because she has dragged them there [i.e., to her cave] or because she has descended [into the underworld] herself.

She wrapped herself in a dark, hellish robe of various shades, threw back her hair, revealed her face, and tied her shaggy locks with vipers serving as ribbons.

When she saw that young Pompey's companions grew pale and he himself trembled and stared at the ground, she turned her lifeless face toward him and said:

"Drop your fears! Let not your hearts flutter any more! Right now a new life, a true life, from its looks, will be given to him, so that you can hear him speak, no matter how much you are afraid. And even if I were to show you the pools of Styx, the shore that consists of hissing flames, and you could see, by my magic, the Furies, Cerberus shaking his mane of snakes, and the chained bodies of the Giants, you would have no reason to fear the shades that are afraid of me, cowards!"

Now first of all she pierced the breast of the corpse, opening new wounds in it, which she filled with boiling blood. The inner organs she washed clean of gore and poured in a generous portion of moonjuice. With this she mixed everything that nature conceives and brings forth under evil stars: foam from the mouth of dogs that have rabies; the inner organs of a lynx; the vertebra of a frightful hyena; the marrow of a stag that had lived on a diet of snakes; the Echeneis, which holds a ship motionless in the middle of the ocean, even though the south wind stretches her ropes; eyes of dragons; stones that produce a sound when warmed under a breeding eagle; the flying serpent of Arabia; the viper born from the Red Sea, which guards the precious shell; the skin that the Libyan horn snake peels off when it is still alive; the ashes of the Phoenix, which places its body on an altar in the East. All this was there in abundance.

After she had thrown in ordinary poisons that are known by their names, she added leaves soaked in unutterable spells and herbs on which her own disgusting mouth had spat when they first appeared and all the poisons that she herself had given to the world.

Finally her voice, more capable than any herb of invoking the powers of hell, first uttered inarticulate sounds that seemed completely different from human speech. You could hear the barking of dogs in that voice, the howling of wolves, the moaning of the restless owl and of the screech owl that flies by night, the shrieking and roaring of a wild beast, the hiss of a serpent, the sound of waves beating against rocks and of forests in the wind, the thunder that detonates from a cloud—all these noises were in her voice. Then she utters the rest in a Thessalian spell, and her voice reached as far as the Tartarus:

"Furies! Horrors of hell! Tortured sinners! Chaos, eager to destroy countless worlds! Ruler of the underworld, who suffers for endless centuries because the death of the [heavenly] gods does not come soon enough for him! Styx! Elysium, where no Thessalian witch is allowed to enter! Persephone, who hates her mother in heaven! Hecate, third personification of my own goddess, Hecate, who enables me to communicate with the dead in a secret language! Custodian of the vast domain, who feeds the savage Dog with bits of human flesh! Sisters who must now spin a second thread of life! Ancient Ferryman of the burning waves, who is exhausted from rowing back the shades to me! Listen to my prayer!

"If these lips of mine that call you have been tainted sufficiently with crime, if I have always eaten human flesh before chanting such spells, if I have often cut open human breasts still full of life divine and washed them out with warm brains, if any baby could have lived once his head and inner organs were placed on your dishes—grant me my prayer!

"I am not asking for a shade lurking in the depths of Tartarus, a shade that has become accustomed to darkness long ago; no, I am asking for one that has just left the light and was on his way down; he still lingers at the very entrance of the chasm that leads down to gloomy Orcus, and even though he obeys my spell, he will join the Manes just once. Let a shade who was just recently one of Pompey's soldiers tell his son the whole future; and remember that you ought to be grateful for the civil war!"

When she had spoken these words, she raised her head, her mouth foaming, and saw standing beside her the ghost of the unburied corpse. It was afraid of the lifeless body, the hated confinement of its former prison, and it shrank from entering the wound in the breast, the inner organs, and the tissue split open by the fatal wound. Poor wretch! You are cruelly deprived of death's last gift: the inability to die [a second time].

Erictho is surprised that the Fates have the power to cause this delay. Angry at Death, she whips the motionless corpse with a live snake, and through the chinks in the ground which she had opened up with her spells, she barks at the shades and breaks the silence of their realm:

"Tisiphone and Megara! Are you listening to me? Will you not use your savage whips to drive his wretched soul through the wasteland of Erebus? Just wait, I shall conjure you up by your real names and abandon you, hounds of hell, in the light of the upper world. Over graves and burial grounds I shall follow you and watch you and drive you away from every tomb and every urn! And you, Hecate, with your pale and morbid aspect, whose face is usually different, made-up, when you visit the gods [above], I shall show you to them as you really are and forbid you to change your hellish face! Shall I tell what kind of food it is that keeps you there, Persephone, under the huge mass of earth, what bond of love unites you with the gloomy king of night, what defilement you suffered to make your mother not want to call you back? On you, lowest of the rulers of the world, I shall focus the sun breaking open your caves, and suddenly daylight will hit you. Will you obey? Or must I recruit him who always makes the earth tremble when his name is invoked, who can look at the Gorgon's head unveiled, who lashes a frightened Fury with her own whip, who dwells in the part of Tartarus that is hidden from your view, for whom you are the 'gods above,' who commits perjury in the name of Styx?"

At once the clotted blood began to boil, heated the blackish wounds, circulated in the body, and reached the extremities of the limbs. Struck by it, the vital tissues in the cold breast began to vibrate, new life stole into organs unaccustomed to it and struggled with death. Every limb began to shake, the sinews stretched, and the corpse, far from rising slowly, limb by limb, from the ground, jumped up as if rebounding from the earth and stood at once erect. His eyelids were wide open, his eyeballs bare. His face was not yet that of a living person; it looked as if he were already dead. He remained pale and stiff and in a daze, thrust upon the world as he was. His lips were locked and produced no sound; voice and utterance were only given to him in order that he might deliver an oracle.

The witch said: "Tell me what I command and your reward will be great, for if you speak the truth, I shall make you safe from witchcraft as long as the world lasts. On such a pyre, with such fuel, shall I cremate your corpse, chanting at the same time a Stygian spell, so that your shade will never have to respond to the incantations of any witch. This privilege should make it worth your while to have lived twice: neither spells nor herbs will venture to interrupt your long sleep of oblivion, once I have given you death. From the tripod [of Delphi] and the prophets of the gods one expects an ambiguous answer, but whoever seeks the truth from the shades and has the nerve to approach the oracles of grim death must leave with clear information. Please do not hold back anything: tell me what will happen and where; provide the voice through which Fate may speak to me."

She added a spell that furnished to the ghost the knowledge of all she was asking.

The corpse, looking sad and shedding many tears, spoke: "You have called me back from the high shore of the silent river. There I did not see the Fates spinning their gloomy threads, but I learned from all the dead that a terrible strife divides the Roman shades and that the civil war has shattered the peace of the underworld. Some great Romans have left the Elysian fields; others have come from gloomy Tartarus [reading *Elysias alii sedes, at Tartara maesta / diuersi liquere duces*]. They revealed [to me] what the Fates have in store. The blessed shades looked sad; I saw the Decii, father and son, who had devoted their lives to the gods in battle; Camillus and the Curii were crying; and Sulla complained about Rome's fortune. Scipio was mourning because an unlucky descendant of his was destined to perish on Libyan soil; and Cato, an even fiercer enemy of Carthage [than Scipio], lamented the death that his descendant prefers to slavery. Only one of the blessed shades did I see rejoicing: the first consul after the expulsion of the kings, Brutus.

"But dangerous Catiline has torn and broken his fetters and is exulting, and so are fierce Marius and Cethegus with the naked arm. I saw the delight of the Drusi, those infamous demagogues who had proposed unreasonable laws; I saw the delight of the Gracchi, who had tried the impossible. Their hands were chained by everlasting links of steel, and they themselves were locked in the prison of Hades, but they applauded, and the whole bunch of criminals demanded the fields of the blessed. The king of the stagnant realm opened wide his gloomy residence; he sharpened steep rocks and hard steel for fetters and prepared tortures for the victor.

"But take this consolation with you, son of Pompey: the dead are looking forward to welcoming your father and his family in a quiet retreat, and they are reserving a place for the house of Pompey in the brighter region of their kingdom. Let not the glory of a short life trouble you; the hour will come that wipes out the distinction between the leaders. Hurry up and die, be proud of your great soul when you descend from graves, however small, and trample on the shades of the gods of Rome. Whose grave will be near the Nile, and whose near the Tiber? That is the question, and [in the end] the [whole] battle between the two rivals is merely about their place of burial. Do not ask about your own destiny: the Fates will reveal it to you, and I shall be silent; your father himself, a more reliable prophet, will tell you everything [when he appears to you] on Sicilian soil, and even he will not know where to summon you and whence to keep you away. . . . [A spurious line follows in the text.] Beware of Europe, Africa, and Asia Minor, poor wretches; Fortune will divide [reading *distribuet*] your tombs among the lands over which you once triumphed, and in all the world you will find no safer place than Pharsalus."

Having delivered his prophecy he stood there in silence and sorrow and pleaded to die once more. Magic spells and herbs were needed before the corpse could die, and death, having used up its powers already, could not claim his life again. The witch now built an enormous pyre of wood. The dead man walked to the fire, and Erictho left him there, stretched out on the lighted pile, and allowed him finally to die. She then walked back with Sextus to his father's camp. The sky was now taking on the color of dawn, but she ordered night to hold back the day and give them thick darkness, until they set foot safely within the encampment.

62

When the great oracles of the ancient world—Delphi, for example—began to lose their prestige, a good deal of concern arose among pagan theologians and philosophers. Plutarch, the Platonist, who had held a priesthood for life at Delphi since A.D. 95, devoted one of his treatises to the problem. The theory he seemed to favor is this: not the gods themselves—the Apollo of Delphi, for instance—but some minor deities are responsible for the maintenance, the continuity, of the oracular spirits at the famous shrines. Unlike the Olympian gods, these daemons grow old and finally, after many centuries, die. It is an interesting theory, for it implies the belief in a cosmic force that is more concentrated or more intense at certain points on the globe than at others. When this force is detected at a certain place, that place becomes "holy." But if the force gradually vanishes, the holy place will be deserted.

To illustrate his point, Plutarch tells the famous story of the death of "the Great Pan," who was clearly a powerful daemon; the lesser daemons knew at once their time had come when they heard of his death.

Substituting mere daemons for the Olympians helped uphold the prestige of the ancient gods against the skepticism of some philosophical schools and the attacks of the Christians. In the end, the Christians claimed that no valid distinction could be drawn between such gods and daemons.

Plutarch, *On the Ceasing of Oracles* 14–15, pp. 418E–419E

[*Cleombrotus, one of the participants in the dialogue, has just proposed a theory that daemons or minor gods, not any of the major divinities, are responsible for the oracles. This theory does not appeal to Heracleon, another participant in the dialogue.*]

"To say that it is not the gods," said Heracleon, "who are in charge of the oracles, since the gods ought to be free of earthly concerns, but that daemons, the servants of the gods, are in charge does not seem such a bad idea to me, but to take, by the handful, so to speak, lines from Empedocles and impose on these daemons sins and delusions and errors sent by the gods, and to assume that they finally die, as if they were human beings—this seems to me a little too rash and rather uncouth."

At this point Cleombrotus asked Philip who this young man [i.e., Heracleon] was and whence he came, and after learning his name and his city, he said: "Heracleon, we have become involved in strange discussions, but we know what we are doing. When you discuss basic ideas, you need basic principles if you want to come anywhere near the truth. But you are inconsistent, because you take back something that you just granted: you agree that daemons exist, but by denying that they can be bad and mortal, you no longer admit that they are daemons. For in what respect are they different from the gods if, as regards their substance, they possess immortality and, as regards their qualities, freedom from emotion and sin?"

As Heracleon was silently thinking about this, Philip said: "No, Heracleon, we have inherited evil daemons not only from Empedocles but also from Plato, Xenocrates, and Chrysippus, and Democritus, too, who by his prayer to meet 'propitious daemons' clearly acknowledged the existence of another class—tricky and full of evil intentions and urges.

"As to the question whether daemons can die, I have heard a story from a man who was neither a fool nor an impostor. The father of Aemilianus, the professor of rhetoric whose students some of you have been, was called Epiterses; he was a schoolteacher and lived in the same town I did. He told me that he once made a trip to Italy and embarked on a ship that carried commercial goods and a large number of passengers. It was already evening; they were near the Echinades Islands. The wind dropped, and the ship drifted near Paxi.

"Most of the passengers were awake, and some were still drinking after having finished their dinner. Suddenly a voice was heard from Paxi loudly calling 'Thamus! Thamus!' Everybody was astonished. Thamus happened to be our pilot, an Egyptian, but he was not known by name even to many of us on board. The voice called twice, and he remained silent, but the third time, he answered. The caller, raising his voice, now said: 'When you get across to Palodes, announce that the Great Pan is dead.'

"On hearing this, Epitherses said, everybody was amazed, and they argued among themselves whether it might be better to do what they were told or not to get involved in something and let the matter go. So Thamus decided that if there should be a breeze he would sail past and say nothing, but with no wind and a smooth sea all around he would announce what he had been told. When he came near Palodes, and there was no wind, no wave, Thamus looked from the stern toward the land and said the words as he had heard them: 'The Great Pan is dead.' He had not yet finished when there was much wailing, not just from one person, but from many, mingled with shouts of amazement.

"Since there were so many persons on board, the story soon spread in all of Rome, and Thamus was sent for by the emperor Tiberius. Tiberius became so convinced that the story was true that he ordered a thorough investigation concerning Pan; the scholars at his court—and there were many of them—guessed that he was the son of Hermes and Penelope."

But Philip also had several witnesses among those present; they had heard the story from Aemilianus when he was an old man.

Demetrius said that among the islands near the coast of Britain many were isolated and deserted, and some had the names of daemons and heroes. He himself, by order of the emperor, had made a voyage of exploration and observation to the nearest of these islands. It had only a few inhabitants: holy men who are all considered inviolate by the Britons. Soon after his arrival there was great tumult in the air and many portents were observed: thunder exploded and lightning hit the earth. When things had quieted down, the people on the island said that one of the more powerful spirits had passed away.

63

In the dialogue *On the Ceasing of Oracles* Plutarch also discusses daemons in general. He tends to dissociate the gods from any direct contact with human beings and to introduce daemons as intermediaries. In referring to Hesiod [*no. 53*], he interprets—correctly, it would seem—Hesiod's distinction between good and bad daemons. His attempt to compute the average life expectancy of a daemon seems a little farfetched, but his description of the transformation of bodies and souls is beautiful, for it asserts eloquently the reality of a higher, spiritual order of existence.

Plutarch, *On the Ceasing of Oracles* 9–11, pp. 414E–415D

[*Lamprias says:*] It is really naïve and childish to believe that the god himself enters the body of the prophet and speaks forth, using his lips and his voice as an instrument as in the case of the ventriloquists who were once called "Eurycleis" but now are known as "Pythones." For if you mix a god with human functions, you violate his majesty and you disregard his dignity and the excellence of his nature.

[*Cleombrotus answers:*] You are right, but since it is difficult to grasp and define how Providence acts and to what point one should let it enter, some maintain that the god has absolutely nothing to do with it, while others see in him the cause of everything. Both positions are equally far from a balanced and responsible view. I agree with those who say that Plato, when he discovered the element that underlies all created qualities—the element that is now called "matter" and "nature"—relieved philosophers of many serious problems. But there are those who have discovered that the race of daemons, halfway between gods and men, communicates between the gods and mankind and establishes a relationship between them and us, and they have created, in my opinion, more problems of an even more serious nature. It is irrelevant whether this theory goes back to the *magi* who followed Zoroaster or is Thracian and belongs to Orpheus, or is Egyptian or Phrygian, as we may guess from seeing how the ritual of both [of the latter] countries includes many themes relating to death and mourning, and that these form part of their ceremonies and liturgies.

Among the Greeks, Homer seems to use both terms indifferently. He sometimes calls the gods "daemons." Hesiod was the first to distinguish clearly and explicitly between four different classes of rational beings: the gods, the daemons, the heroes, and mankind. This means that he believed in a transformation by which the men of the Golden Age became good daemons in great numbers, and by which some of the demigods were admitted to the ranks of the heroes.

Others assume a transformation of bodies as well as souls. Just as one sees water generated from earth, air from water, fire from air, as matter moves upward, thus the superior souls undergo a transformation from men to heroes and from heroes to daemons, but from the rank of daemons only a few are purified over a long period of time because of their excellence and come to partake altogether in divine nature. But it also happens that some of them cannot gain control over themselves and are degraded and clothed once more in mortal bodies and have a dark, dim life, like mist.

Hesiod thinks that at the end of certain periods of time death comes to daemons, too. For in the speech of the Naiad he says, alluding to their life-span:

> The raucous crow lives as long as nine generations of men in their
>   prime;
> the deer lives four times as long as the crow,
> the raven three times as long as the deer,
> the Phoenix nine times as long as the raven,
> but we Nymphs with our beautiful locks, the daughters of Zeus,
>   who holds the Aegis,
> live ten times as long as the Phoenix.

Those who misinterpret the term *generation* come up with a very high number. In fact, it means only "one year." Thus, daemons reach an age of nine thousand seven hundred twenty years, which is less than most mathematicians calculate but more than Pindar gives to the Nymphs when he says that "their life-span is equal to that of a tree" and that is why they are called "Hamadryads."

64

In this passage from his dialogue *On the Ceasing of Oracles*, Plutarch makes the point that the gods do not operate directly; rather, they communicate

through daemons, their servants, messengers, assistants, or secretaries. Daemons, for example, supervise sacrifices and mystery rites; they punish the guilty and sustain the oracles.

Plutarch, *On the Ceasing of Oracles* 15, p. 418C–D

Allow me to bring this preliminary discussion to a suitable conclusion, for we now have reached that point. Let us venture to say, too, after so many others have said it, that when daemons in charge of divination vanish, the oracles vanish along with them and are gone. When daemons go into exile or emigrate, the oracles lose their power, but when the daemons come back, even after a long time, the oracles speak again, like musical instruments when there are players who know how to use them.

65

In his treatise *On Isis and Osiris,* Plutarch offers further speculations on the nature of daemons. He quotes from Hesiod, Empedocles, Plato, and Plato's disciple Xenocrates, who has been called "the father of scientific daemonology." The emphasis here is on evil daemons. Some of them are what we would call the "fallen angels" of pagan antiquity. Others seem to be evil by nature—for example, Typhon, who, in the myth and ritual of Isis and Osiris, represents the eternal villain, the permanent antagonist in a kind of cosmic drama between benevolent and malevolent deities.

To Plutarch, who witnessed the rapid growth of the Isis cult during his lifetime, these Egyptian deities, even the good ones, looked like daemons that had been promoted to higher ranks in return for exceptionally good behavior. In other words, Plutarch was pragmatic enough to recognize a measure of success even in the religious sphere. Isis and Osiris were definitely not part of the Greek Pantheon, but the appeal of their cult in the late Hellenistic and early imperial periods is a fact. According to Plutarch, their success as deities was based on a kind of advancement within a divine hierarchy, which, of course, required the approval of all the highest authorities and was, therefore, acceptable. This spiritual advancement reflects an upward mobility within the hierarchies that we already know on earth, and thus our search for the supreme power must go on.

Plutarch, *On Isis and Osiris* 26–27, p. 361A–E

It would seem that daemons have a complex and abnormal nature and purpose; hence Plato assigns to the Olympian gods that which is on the right side and the odd numbers, and to the daemons the opposite of these. Xenocrates believes that unlucky days and all holidays that are characterized by beatings or lamentations or fasting or bad language or obscene jokes are not proper occasions for honoring gods and good daemons. He believes that there are in the atmosphere great, powerful presences that are also ill-tempered and unpleasant and enjoy the sort of thing just mentioned and, if they get it, cause no further trouble.

Hesiod calls the good, kindly daemons "holy daemons" and "guardian of mankind," and he says that "they give wealth, which is their royal privilege."

Plato calls this category "interpreting" and "ministering," halfway between gods and men, carrying upward the prayers and wishes of men and bringing to us from the realm of the gods oracles and welcome gifts.

Empedocles says that daemons get punished for the bad things they do and the duties they neglect:

> The power of the aether drives them into the sea;
> the sea spits them out onto the soil of the earth;
> the earth sends them to the rays of the tireless sun;
> and the sun throws them into the whirlpool of aether:
> one region receives them from another, and they all hate them.

The daemons are punished and purified up to the point when they take back the place and rank that are naturally theirs.

Stories like these and similar ones are told, they say, about Typhon. His jealousy and vicious temper made him do terrible things: he stirred up everything and flooded the whole earth and the sea with evils. Later, he had to pay the penalty. The avenger was Isis, the sister-wife of Osiris: she quenched the insane fury of Typhon and put an end to it. But then she did not simply forget the struggles and trials that she had been through, or her wanderings and the many brave and wise things that she had done. She would not accept silence and oblivion, but into the holiest ritual [the initiation rites of the Isis mysteries?] she introduced symbols and representations of her former sufferings. She sanctified these as a lesson in piety and an encouragement for men and women who are the victims of similar predicaments. She and Osiris were promoted to the rank of gods from that of benevolent daemons because of their admirable conduct. This happened later to Heracles and Dionysus. It seems appropriate that they receive joint honors as gods and daemons. Their power is everywhere, but especially in the regions above the earth and beneath the earth.

66

Many ancient philosophers wrote "Consolations" for their friends and patrons and even for themselves to give help and comfort in times of

bereavement. Two essays or addresses of this kind are attributed to Plutarch: one to his wife on the death of their daughter, Timoxena; the other to Apollonius, a friend. The second essay was probably not written by Plutarch, but it represents the genre quite well.

The sophist Antiphon (fifth century B.C.) is said to be the "inventor" of this genre. He had an office in or near the marketplace of Corinth where he comforted people who mourned the death of a family member or a dear friend, combining the roles of priest and psychiatrist, presumably for a fee. Antiphon also conceived a method or technique to achieve *Freedom from Distress*. It is lost, but some of his advice may live on in Platonism (Crantor, *On Mourning,* a famous work, also lost) and Stoicism (Panaetius, *Consolation Addressed to Quintus Tubero*). Cicero wrote a celebrated *Consolatio* for himself, to get over the death of his beloved daughter, Tullia; again, the work is lost, but its main ideas can be reconstructed on the basis of his *Tusculanae Disputationes.*

According to one of the arguments used in this kind of literature, death is not the evil that most people consider it to be; it is, in fact, a blessing. A few stories are then told to illustrate this truth. In the present text the third story is particularly important in our context, for it documents the existence, in antiquity, of "oracles of the dead" (*psychomanteia* 'soul oracles'). In this case the oracle is consulted not about the future but about the past. A father has suddenly lost his only child and suspects foul play. He visits a *psychomanteion,* probably the one at Cumae, near Naples, which is associated with the famous sibyl located in the region (see Virg., *Aen.* 6). There he offers a sacrifice, falls asleep, and has a vision. The procedure is a form of incubation, although in this case the vision is sought not for the sake of finding a cure for a disease but in order to establish a fact in the past. It might be said, however, that the father's anxieties and suspicions about his son's death could easily have become an obsession and manifested itself in a nervous disorder. At the same time, he simply wants to know the truth, and the truth is revealed to him by two *psychai* 'souls', that of his father and that of his son. The message that the "soul," or "daemon," of his son delivers to Elysius (the name sounds as if it had been invented for the occasion) is simply that we do not know what death really is and that people die because their natural time has come, even if we do not understand it.

The story may be unhistorical, but it shows that the Greeks and Romans believed in various means of communicating with the dead. Dreams were one of them. The special function of the *psychomanteion* was to set up the conditions under which such dreams would occur. The technique or techniques used were probably similar to those employed for incubations.

Plutarch, *Consolation Addressed to Apollonius* 14, p. 109A–D

Pindar tells us that Agamedes and Trophonius, after having built the temple of Delphi, demanded their pay from Apollo. The god answered that he would pay them seven days later and urged them, in the meantime, to enjoy themselves. They did as they were told, and on the seventh night they died in their sleep.

The delegates of the Boeotians went to Delphi to consult the god, and Pindar is supposed to have urged them to ask [on his behalf] the question, "What is best for man?" The priestess answered that he ought to know the answer, if he really was the author of the story about Trophonius and Agamedes. On the other hand, if he wanted to find out by himself, it would become clear to him in the very near future. From this response Pindar concluded that he should prepare himself for death, and in fact he died shortly thereafter.

And here is the story about the Italian [i.e., South Italian Greek] Euthynous. He was the son of Elysius of Terina, a prominent man in that community because of his qualities, his wealth, and his reputation. Euthynous died suddenly, and no one knew why. It occurred to Elysius—as it might have occurred to anyone—that perhaps his son had died of poisoning, for he was his only child, destined to inherit a substantial fortune. Because he did not know how to verify this suspicion, he went to an oracle of the dead [*psychomanteion*]. After he had offered the prescribed sacrifices, he fell asleep and had a vision. His father appeared to him, coming toward him. When Elysius saw his father, he told him in detail everything that had happened to his son and urged and implored him to find the cause of death. His father answered: "This is exactly why I came. Take from this person here the object that he brings to you. From this you will find out everything that distresses you." The person he pointed out was a young man who followed him and resembled Euthynous [the son], both in age and in stature. When he asked him who he was, the young man replied: "I am the soul [literally, the daemon] of your son." And as he said this, he gave the father a little scroll. Elysius unrolled it and saw written on it three lines:

> Truly, the minds of men are lost in ignorance.
> Euthynous died in accordance with fate.
> It was not right for him to live, nor for his parents.

This is what you can read in the accounts of ancient writers.

67

Here we have a piece of folklore that was not included in the *Odyssey,* although it may be quite old. One of Odysseus' companions keeps plaguing as a ghost the inhabitants of a Sicilian town who had stoned him to death for raping a local girl. The Delphic oracle is consulted and supports the daemon, because he was a hero, after all, and a cult is established in his honor. Every year the most beautiful girl in the whole community must be given to the daemon-hero as his wife. What is meant by the word *given* is not quite clear, but the context seems to suggest a human sacrifice, not just a *hieros gamos,* a "sacred wedding" or a ritual rape. The girls always either died or disappeared, it would seem. The real hero of the story, a famous boxer, Euthymus, falls in love with the intended victim and wrestles with the daemon, just as Heracles wrestled with Death in Euripides' *Alcestis,* driving him "out of the land." Euthymus then marries the girl, and they live happily ever after: in fact, he never dies, but becomes a daemon (a good one, no doubt) himself. Pausanias saw a painting, a copy of a much older original, that illustrated this quaint story. In it the evil daemon, Lycas by name, appears as an "awfully black" figure, terrifying in appearance, dressed in a wolf's skin (*lykos* means "wolf" in Greek). Perhaps this is the origin of the story of Dracula and the wolf-man. It should be noted that throughout the story the terms *hero* and *daemon* are used interchangeably.

Pausanias, *Description of Greece* 6.6

[*Euthymus was a famous boxer; he was born in southern Italy and returned there after one of his Olympic victories.*]

When Euthymus had returned to Italy, he fought the Hero. This is the story. During Odysseus' wanderings after the fall of Troy, they say that he was carried by winds to various cities of Italy and Sicily. He landed with his ships at Temesa. One of the sailors got drunk and raped a young woman, and for this crime he was stoned to death by the villagers.

Odysseus paid no attention whatsoever to the death of this man and sailed away, but the daemon of the man who had been stoned to death by the people never missed an opportunity to murder someone in Temesa, attacking all age groups. Finally the whole population was ready to leave Temesa and Italy altogether, but the Pythia would not let them. She told them to appease the Hero by measuring out for him a holy precinct, building him a temple, and giving him as his wife every year the most beautiful young woman to be found in Temesa. They did, of course, what the god had ordered, and the daemon did not terrorize them any further.

Euthymus happened to come to Temesa at the time when the customary tribute was paid to the daemon. When he found out about their problem, he expressed the wish to enter the temple and have a look at the girl. When he saw her, his first reaction was to feel sorry for her, but his second was to fall in love. The girl swore to marry him if he saved her. Euthymus prepared himself and waited for the entrance of the daemon. He fought him and won, and the Hero—since he had been driven out of the land—dived into the sea and disappeared. Euthymus had a splendid wedding, and the people there were free forever from the daemon.

I also heard another story about Euthymus: he reached a ripe old age and managed to escape death, leaving human life in some different way. From a merchant who has sailed there I have learned that Temesa is still inhabited.

This is what I have heard, but I also know the following from a painting that I happened to see. It was a copy of an older painting. There is young Sybaris and the river Calabrus and the spring Lyca, and a hero's sanctuary nearby and the city of Temesa. Among these figures there is also the daemon whom Euthymus drove out: his color is terribly dark, and he is really terrifying to look at; a wolf's skin serves as his dress, and according to an inscription on the painting his name was "Wolf-Man."

68

The story of Thelyphron is a tragicomic episode in Apuleius' novel, *Metamorphoses*. Apuleius was interested in witchcraft himself, and the novel undoubtedly has autobiographical elements. This particular episode reflects the popular belief that witches needed corpses or parts of them for their magical operations; therefore, corpses had to be guarded carefully until they were cremated. People who could afford it hired a guard. Here, a young man who desperately needs money takes on a job that turns out not to be as easy as it appeared. In the course of the story the corpse is called back to life twice, once in secret by the witches and once in front of a crowd by a famous Egyptian "prophet"—that is, a necromancer—dressed in linen robes, with palm-leaf sandals on his feet and a shaven head. The circumstances of his death are cleared up by the dead man himself [as in *no. 66*].

Apuleius, *Metamorphoses*, or *The Golden Ass* 2.21–30

When I was still a minor under the care of a ward, I traveled from Miletus to the games in Olympia, and since I also wanted to visit this famous province, I wandered through all of Thessaly and arrived in Larissa under an unlucky star. My travel funds were quite low, and I felt so poor that I walked all over the place looking for means of support. In the middle of the marketplace I saw a tall, elderly man. He was standing on a stone and announced in a loud voice that he was hiring someone to guard a corpse. I said to a passerby: "What is this I hear? Are the corpses in this country in the habit of running away?" He answered: "Hush! You are obviously very young and very much a stranger, and so of course you don't know that you are in Thessaly, where the witches generally gnaw the flesh off dead men's faces and use it as an ingredient in their magic." I said: "Could you please tell me what it involves to stand guard over a corpse?" He replied: "Well, first one has to remain completely awake all night, the eyes wide open, never closed for a second, and always concentrated on the corpse; one must never take them off [it], not even glance sideways, because the evil witches can transform themselves into any animal they like and approach so stealthily that they can even deceive the eyes of the Sun and of Justice with the greatest ease. They take on the shape of birds or dogs or mice or even that of flies. By their horrible spells they manage to put the guards to sleep. No one can say for sure what tricks these vicious women invent to satisfy their lust. And yet for this wretched job the pay is usually not higher than four or six ducats. Oh—I almost forgot to tell you: if the corpse is not delivered intact in the morning, the guard must furnish from his own face that part that has been eaten off the corpse and is missing."

When I heard this I mustered up my courage, approached the crier at once, and said to him: "You need not shout any more. Here is your guard, ready. Let me know the pay." He answered: "A thousand drachmas will be deposited in your name. But listen, young man: you must be very careful if you want to watch this corpse and guard it properly against those awful harpies; he is the son of one of the chief men in the city." I said: "Don't be ridiculous. Save your worry. You see before you a man of iron who never sleeps and has sharper eyesight than Lynceus or Argus—who is, in fact, all eyes." I had hardly finished speaking when he quickly led me to a house whose main entrance was locked. He took me through a small back door and opened a dark room with closed windows. Then he showed me a weeping lady all in black, walked up to her, and said to her: "Here is the man I hired; he has taken the responsibility of guarding your husband." She pushed back the hair that hung into her face on both sides, showed a face that was impressive even in mourning, and said, looking at me: "I beg you, make sure you do a really good job." I said: "Don't worry, just add a good tip."

She agreed, got up, and led me into another room. There she showed me a body covered with a shiny linen shroud which she herself removed in the presence of seven witnesses. She wept over him for a long time and then appealed to the conscience of all those present as she pointed out the parts of the body while someone carefully took an inventory in legal language: "Look," she said, "the nose is there, the eyes are unhurt, the ears in good shape, the lips not damaged, the chin in one piece. You are witnesses to this, fellow citizens." When the inventory was signed and sealed, and she was about to leave, I said to her: "Madam, will you arrange for me to have everything I need?" She asked: "Well, what do you need?" I answered: "A fairly large lamp and enough oil to last till daybreak, warm water with a few flasks of wine, a cup, and a plate full of leftovers." But she shook her head and said: "Leave me alone, you fool. You want to dine and have a good time in a house of mourning in which for days and days not even smoke was seen? Do you think you have come here for a party? Don't you think it would be more appropriate to the occasion to mourn and weep?" As she said this, she looked at a maid and said: "Quick, Myrrhine, give him a lamp and oil, lock him in the room to do his job, and leave at once."

Thus left alone, I rubbed my eyes to comfort the corpse and to keep myself awake during the vigil, and I sang to amuse myself. Twilight fell and turned into night, and night grew deeper, and it was really time to go to sleep, and it was probably past midnight. I was scared to death, especially when all of a sudden a weasel slipped in and stood there looking at me intently. The nerve of the tiny animal annoyed me. I said: "Move on, you filthy creature, and get back to the likes of you in the garden before I let you have it. What are you waiting for?" It turned around and disappeared from the room at once. Almost immediately I fell into a deep sleep—it was like sinking into a bottomless pit—and even the Delphic oracle could not have determined which of the two of us lying there was more dead than the other. I was practically lifeless, nonexistent, and needed a guard myself.

The truce of the night was broken by the crowing of the "crested cohort." I finally woke up in a state of terror and ran over to the corpse. I held the lamp close to see his face clearly and checked all the details. Everything seemed to be in order. At this moment the poor widow, still weeping, burst into the room, accompanied by the witnesses of the evening before. She threw herself on the body, kissed it again and again for a long time, and then, guided by the lamp, registered everything. She turned around and called for her steward Philodespotus and told him: "Give this fine guard his pay at once." It was handed out to me and she said: "I thank you very much, young man. You have done me a tremendous service, and you will be a friend of the family from now on." I was absolutely overjoyed at this unexpected benefit and at the bright gold coins I was tossing up in my hand, and I said to her: "But madam, please consider me one of your servants, and whenever you need my help be sure to call on me." I had hardly said this when all her people jumped on me, called me a scoundrel, cursed me, and attacked me with all kinds of improvised weapons: one of them boxed me in the face, another dug his elbows into my back, a third hit me in the ribs very hard; they kicked me, pulled my hair, ripped my clothes. I was almost torn to pieces, just like Adonis [text uncertain], that arrogant youth, or Musaeus or Orpheus [?], and kicked out of the house in terrible shape.

I stopped in the next street and recovered somewhat, and as I remembered my tactless and ill-omened remark, I had to admit to myself that I deserved even more beatings than I had received. Meanwhile, the dead body had been mourned and saluted for the last time and was now being carried according to ancient tradition (he belonged, after all, to the aristocracy) in a solemn funeral procession across the marketplace.

An older man in black, looking sad and crying as he tore his fine white hair, approached the bier, clutched it with both hands, and cried, his voice tense and choking with sobs: "Fellow citizens! I appeal to your sense of honor and your love for our city! This man has been murdered! Help! A shocking deed has been done, and you must punish this evil, wicked woman drastically. She and no one else has poisoned this poor young man, my nephew, to oblige her lover and to inherit her husband's estate!" Thus the old man continued to appeal to one person after another with pitiful complaints. The crowd went wild, and since such a crime seemed plausible, they were ready to believe it. People shouted for fire, demanded stones, and incited a bunch of young men to kill the woman. She produced well-rehearsed tears and, calling on all the gods, swore in the language of true religion that she could never have committed such a horrible crime.

The old man said: "Let us leave the judgment of truth to divine providence. Here is Zatchlas, an outstanding Egyptian necromancer who has made an agreement with me some time ago to bring back briefly, for a considerable fee, the spirit of the young man from the underworld and to revive his body by restoring it back to life from death." As he said this he brought forward a young man dressed in linen robes, with palm-leaf sandals on his feet, his head completely shaven. The old man kissed his hands repeatedly and touched his knees; then he said: "Reverend sir, have mercy, have mercy! I implore you by the stars of heaven, by the gods of the underworld, by the elements of nature, by the silence of the night and the hidden sanctuary of Coptus and the flooding of the Nile and the mysteries of Memphis and the sacred rattles of Pharus! Grant him the brief enjoyment of sunshine! Pour a little light into eyes that are shut forever! I am not quarreling with fate, nor am I denying the earth what belongs to it: I only ask for a few spare moments of life to have at least the consolation of revenge." The necromancer, favorably impressed by these words, placed a magic herb on the lips of the dead man and another on his breast. Then he turned to the east and prayed in silence to the glorious Sun for success. The whole scenario looked so impressive that all those present could hardly wait to see a tremendous miracle happen.

I managed to push my way into the crowd and to climb on a slightly raised stone directly behind the bier, and I watched everything with great interest. Soon the breast of the corpse began to heave as breath returned to it; the vein of life began to pulsate; the whole body was filled with spirit. The corpse sat up, and it was the young man who spoke: "Why on earth did you have to call me back briefly to the business of life when I had already my drink of Lethe and was floating on the Stygian swamp? Leave me alone, I beg you, leave me alone, and allow me to have my peace." This was the voice we heard coming from the body. The prophet sounded a little more excited as he cried: "Why don't you reveal and relate to the people all the hidden details of your death? Don't you realize that I am able to invoke the Furies with my incantations and have your weary limbs tormented?" The one on the bier understood this and with a deep sigh addressed the people: "I have been finished off by the evil practices of my young bride; she sentenced me to drink poison; the bed that I had to vacate for her adulterous lover was still warm." That fine wife of his showed great presence of mind and without any regard for the gods argued stubbornly with her husband, who argued back. The crowd got all heated up, but people disagreed violently: some wanted to see that wicked woman buried alive at once with the body of her husband; others insisted that the false testimony of a corpse ought not to be accepted.

The whole disagreement was settled by the following words of the young husband. With another deep sigh, he said: "I will give you clear proof of the truth and nothing but the truth, and I will tell you something that absolutely no one else can know." He pointed his finger at me and continued: "This is the man who guarded my corpse throughout the whole night most conscientiously and carefully while the witches were waiting to attack my remains. To this purpose they had taken on various shapes, but in vain, for they were unable to fool his vigilance and dedication. Finally they enveloped him in a cloud of sleep, and when he was buried in deep slumber they kept calling my name again and again, until my lifeless limbs and my cold body clumsily and reluctantly obeyed their magic commands. Now this man was alive, of course, but he slept like a corpse, and since he had no idea that his name was the same as mine, he stood up and walked around without resisting, exactly like a ghost. Even though the doors of the room had been carefully locked, through a tiny hole in the wall they cut off first his nose and then his ears. So he suffered mutilation in my place. To improve on their deceit, they glued on his head a pair of wax ears shaped exactly like the ones they had cut off, and they also gave him a fake nose. And now, there he is, poor fellow. He thinks he was rewarded for his dedication, but he was rewarded for his own mutilation!"

I was horrified as he said this, and tried to touch my face. I grabbed my nose: it came off. I felt my ears: they just dropped. Everyone pointed at me and wagged their heads, and there was thunderous laughter. Bursting into a cold sweat, I tried to escape between the legs of the people standing there. And I was never able to go home again, mutilated and ridiculous as I was, but I let my hair grow on both sides to cover the place where my ears had been, and for cosmetic reasons I glued a compact bandage on my face to make up for the lack of my nose.

69

According to his biographer, Philostratus, Apollonius of Tyana, the philosopher and miracle-worker, was successful as an exorcist. The young man he healed is described as a "playboy" who belonged to a prominent family and whose problem had not been recognized until Apollonius came to town. The reference to "singers on wheels" is curious; apparently these were ambulant satirists who used their carriages as platforms. The practice seems to have survived in the context of the carnival along the Rhine, from Basel to Cologne.

The exorcism worked by Apollonius is different from Jesus' miracles. The way this daemon responds to the philosopher, and the feat he performs for the benefit of the crowd—to prove that he really is a daemon—seem unique. After he is healed, the young man naturally becomes a disciple of Apollonius.

The act of exorcism is quite simple: an angry look and a stern admonition from the master are enough to drive the daemon out.

Philostratus, *Life of Apollonius of Tyana* 4.20

Apollonius was discussing the problem of libations, and a young playboy happened to be present at his lecture. The young man had such a terrible reputation that he had once been the target of songs from "cabarets-on-wheels." He was from Corcyra and traced his pedigree back to Alcinous the Phaeacian, the host of Odysseus. Apollonius went on about libations and urged his audience not to drink from one particular cup but to keep it for the gods without touching it or drinking from it. At one point he urged them to have handles attached to the cup and to pour the libation over the handle, this being the part from which men practically never drink. The young man burst into loud, vulgar laughter. Apollonius looked at him and said: "It is not you who behave in an insulting manner, but the daemon who drives you to do this, and you don't know it." The young man actually had no idea that he was possessed. He used to laugh at things that made no one else laugh, and then fall to weeping without any reason, and he often talked and sang to himself. Now, most people thought it was the exuberance of youth that led him into these moods, but actually he was the mouthpiece of the daemon, and when he seemed to be drunk, he was not [text uncertain]. When Apollonius looked at him, the ghost [in him] began to cry in fear and anger—it sounded like people being burned and racked—and swore to leave the young man alone and never possess any person again. Apollonius spoke angrily to him, the way a master speaks to a shifty, scheming, shameless slave, and ordered him to leave the young man alone and show by a sign that he had done so. The daemon said: "Yes, I will throw down that statue over there," and he pointed at one of the statues in the King's Portico, for this is where all this took place. Now, it would be impossible to describe the commotion of those in the crowd and the way they clapped their hands in wonder when the statue first began to sway gently and then crashed down! The young man rubbed his eyes, as if he had just woken up, and looked toward the radiant sun. He was very embarrassed when he saw everyone staring at him. He no longer seemed dissolute, nor did he have that crazy look: he had returned to his own true self, just as if he had been cured by a drug. He gave up his fancy clothes and elegant apparel and all the other requisites of his Sybaritic way of life and fell in love with [philosophical] austerity, put on the [philosopher's] cloak, and modeled his character after that of Apollonius.

70

Plotinus (c. A.D. 205–270) was the last great creative thinker of pagan antiquity. He thought of himself as a Platonist, but in fact he transformed Platonism into a new synthesis that also contained Pythagorean and Stoic elements. This new philosophical school—Neoplatonism—appealed to the educated classes because it seemed to explain in rational or near-rational terms some of the mysteries of life while at the same time salvaging traditions cherished by pagan culture.

Because Plotinus was born in Egypt, a theurgic ceremony performed by an Egyptian priest in a temple of Isis may have had special meaning for him. The priest offers to grant Plotinus a vision of his own "familiar spirit." This is a Greek interpretation of the Latin word *genius,* for which the Greeks had no exact equivalent. There were many spirits or daemons in the universe, but according to ancient Roman belief, only one "belonged" to an individual.

The priest, who has expected an ordinary "familiar spirit," is amazed that Plotinus' *genius* belongs to a different species of powers altogether. We learn that at these ceremonies an attendant is needed to hold a couple of chickens. The chickens will be strangled at once if the spirit that appears turns out to be threatening. This sacrifice was probably conceived as an instant peace offering, after which the spirit would leave without harming any of the participants. In this case the attendant panics, strangles the chickens, and the daemon leaves, but before he leaves, Plotinus gets a good look at him.

A monograph entitled *On the Spirit That Allotted Us to Himself* is preserved among Plotinus' writings (*Enn.* 3.4 [= tract 15 Harder]), but no mention is made of this incident there; it may be an anecdote that Plotinus told some of his students. In fact, the tract is little more than an interpretation of some Platonic passages (from the *Phaedo,* the *Timaeus,* the *Republic,* etc.) dealing with daemons.

The belief in the existence of daemons seems to have been an essential part of Neoplatonism, but the ability actually to see one's own guardian spirit was a privilege granted to only a few. Those who, like Plotinus, were granted the gift, apparently encouraged their disciples to study hard, to work on themselves, and to achieve the spiritual progress that would lead them to a higher level of awareness.

Porphyry, *Life of Plotinus* 10, pars. 56–60

From the time of his birth Plotinus had some very special gifts. An Egyptian priest came to Rome and became acquainted with him through a friend. This priest wanted to give Plotinus a demonstration of his [occult] science and invited him to be present at an appearance of his familiar spirit. Plotinus accepted willingly. The conjuring took place in the temple of Isis because this was, as the Egyptian said, the only "pure place" that he could find in all of Rome. But when the spirit was conjured and was asked to show himself, a god appeared that did not belong to that category of spirits. At this point the Egyptian cried: "Blessed are you who have a god as a familiar and not a spirit of the lower class!" But there was no opportunity to ask the apparition any questions or even to look at it any longer, because the friend who shared the experience strangled the chickens that he held as a safeguard, either because he was jealous or because he was afraid of something. Because Plotinus had a higher divine being as a familiar, he concentrated his divine eye for a while on that being. This experience prompted him to write an essay, *On the Spirit That Allotted Us to Himself,* wherein he tried to give reasons for the difference between familiars.

71

Iamblichus (c. A.D. 250–325), a student of Plotinus' disciple Porphyry, discusses daemonology from a Neoplatonist point of view, probably using *Enn.* 3.4 (= tract 15 Harder) as a starting point. The text is difficult and no doubt corrupt in several places, but the message seems clear: the true philosopher must be able to distinguish the different classes of daemons from each other as well as from the higher gods.

Iamblichus, *On the Mysteries of Egypt* 1.20.61–63

You formulate the problem of "what distinguishes the daemons from the visible and the invisible gods"—the ones that are invisible but connected with the visible ones. Taking this as a starting point, I will show what the difference is. The visible gods are joined to the intelligible gods and have the same form as far as they are concerned. The daemons on the other hand are quite different as far as their substance is concerned, and they barely look like them. This is how the daemons are different from the visible gods. They differ from the invisible gods in regard to their invisibility, for the daemons are invisible and cannot be perceived in any way by the senses. But the gods even transcend rational knowledge and perception tied to matter [or: reading *anylou* for *enylou* in the Greek, "immaterial perception"]. Because the gods are unknown and invisible they are called "invisible," but they are invisible in a completely different manner than are the daemons. Well now, being invisible, are the daemons superior to the visible gods in respect of their being invisible? Not at all. The divine, no matter where it is and how far it extends, has the same power and domination over everything that is subordinate. Therefore, even if it is visible, it rules over the daemons of the air, even if it dwells in the terrestrial region, for neither the environment nor the part of the universe affects in any way the authority of the gods; their total substance remains the same everywhere, indivisible, unchangeable, and all the lower orders worship it in the same way, according to the law of nature.

72

Iamblichus continues to discuss disembodied spirits here. It may seem strange that a distinguished theologian and philosopher would spend so much time and ingenuity on the subject of daemonology, but once the existence of such beings was admitted—and we have the testimony of

Plotinus as well as the long Platonist tradition to document this belief—
they had to be defined, distinguished, classified. Daemonology had become a science, and it was developed according to scientific principles. It
was important to recognize the true character of a vision [as in *no. 70*]. It
could be dangerous, or at least embarrassing, to mistake a god for a mere
guardian spirit, or vice versa. Hence the subject also had a practical value.

Iamblichus, *On the Mysteries of Egypt* 2.1.67–2.69

I must also explain to you first how a daemon is different from a hero and
from a soul, and whether the difference is in the substance, the potential,
or the activity.

I maintain that daemons are produced according to the generative and
creative powers of the gods in the most remote [or: the lowest] termina-
tion of the progression and its ultimate division. Heroes are produced
according to the vital principles in divine beings. The first and perfect
measures of the souls are their final product, and they begin their division
at this point.

Because their substance is generated in this way from different causes,
the substance itself must be different. That of the daemons is productive:
it fashions the cosmic organisms and completes the perfection of every
single creature. The substance of the heroes is life-giving, rational, and
consists in control over the souls. To the daemons one must attribute the
generative powers that control the organism and the connection of soul
and body. It seems right to assign to the heroes the life-producing powers
that rule over men and are detached from creation.

Following this we must also define their activities. We must assume
that those of the daemons are cosmic in a higher sense and have a wider
extension as far as their effects are concerned, whereas those of the heroes
are not as far-reaching and are oriented toward the disposition of the
souls.

After these classes have been defined we come to the next one [the
soul]. It descends to the end of the divine orders and has been allotted
from these two [upper] orders certain shares of powers. It also grows from
other, special, additions that come from itself. At different times it projects different images and principles and ever-different lives. It uses a
variety of lives and ideas, according to the individual regions of the
universe. It joins whatever organism it wants to join and withdraws from
it whenever it wants to. It presents thoughts that are related to things that
exist and will exist. It attaches itself to the gods in virtue of essential or
potential harmonies other than those which associate daemons and heroes with them [the gods]. It has less of the eternity of the similar life and
energy , but because of the goodwill of the gods and the radiation of light

given out by them, it often rises to the higher order of the angels. This happens when it no longer remains within the boundaries of the soul but perfects itself completely into an angelic soul and an immaculate life. Hence the soul seems to present in itself all sorts of substances and activities and a variety of thoughts and all kinds of ideas. If the truth must be told, the soul is always defined according to one specific criterion, but when it associates itself with leading causes, it joins different causes at different times.

73

In his work *The Preparation of the Gospel,* Eusebius of Caesarea (c. A.D. 260–340) wanted to show that pagan history and pagan civilization played a role in God's plan to save the world. In the course of the work he gives a summary of that part of pagan theology which dealt with daemons and their relationship with gods and heroes. That evil daemons had been worshiped from time immemorial has been noted already [*no. 53*]. The main edge of Eusebius' polemic against the pagan theologians (mostly the Neoplatonists) is what he sees as their exclusive worship of evil powers; he accuses them of offering only a kind of lip service to their benign deities.

The oversimplification may have been made in the interests of Christian propaganda. Moreover, from a strict Christian point of view, all pagan deities were evil, and to worship any of them was a sin. To a pagan believer it may have seemed safe to honor, above all, the evil powers, since the benevolent ones were good anyway, although this reasoning does not seem to be sound theology.

Eusebius points to an important aspect of ancient religion: ever since heroic times, certain powers had been worshiped because they were powerful and fearsome, not because they were considered loving or good. Hence the world was ready to embrace the new religion, with its message of divine love.

Eusebius, *The Preparation of the Gospel* 4.5.1–3

The Various Parts of Pagan Theology

Those who have a thorough knowledge of pagan theology apply a classification that is different from the one proposed above and divide the whole doctrine into four parts: first of all they distinguish the supreme god; they say they know that he rules over everything and that he is the father and the king of all the gods. After him there is a second category of gods; then comes the category of daemons; and as number four they list the heroes. All these, they say, share in the idea of the Good, and thus in a sense lead and in another sense are led, and every substance of this kind, they say, can be called light because it participates in light. But they also say that Evil is in control of what is inferior; this is the category of the evil daemons; there is no friendship between them and the Good; they certainly have an enormous power in the sphere that is totally opposed to the Good; and everything of this kind they call "darkness."

Having distinguished these categories, they say that heaven and the ether as far as the moon are assigned to the gods; to the daemons, the region around the moon and the atmosphere; to the souls [of the dead], the terrestrial regions and the subterranean spaces. Having established these distinctions, they say that one must first of all worship the gods of heaven and of the ether; then the good daemons; in the third place the souls of the heroes; and in the fourth place one must soothe the evil and malevolent daemons. After they have made these distinctions in theory, they confuse everything in practice, and instead of worshiping all the powers mentioned, they worship only the evil powers and serve them exclusively, as I will show in a later part of my discussion.

74

Heliodorus, author of the novel *Ethiopian Tales,* or *The Story of Theagenes and Charicleia,* probably lived in the third or fourth century A.D. Like Apollonius of Tyana, whose biography by Philostratus apparently made some impression on him, he seems to have been, at least for part of his life, a Neo-Pythagorean. Later, according to tradition, he converted to Christianity and became bishop of Tricca in Thessaly.

In this episode of his novel the heroine, Charicleia, accompanied by Calasiris, an elderly Egyptian priest, witnesses—much against her will—a necromantic scene. An old woman, obviously a witch, revives the dead body of her son. The ditch she digs, the libation she pours, and the sword she manipulates remind us of the Homeric *Nekyia* in the *Odyssey* [*no. 52*], but there is also a doll made of dough mixed with fennel and laurel. The whole operation is successful up to a point, but we are told by the dead man himself that it is a sinful endeavor because it violates the will of the Fates, and that death (actually provided by law) would be an appropriate punishment for her. Moreover [see *no. 61*], the dead resent being called back to life.

All this is made even worse by the fact that a priest, a holy man beloved by the gods, is forced to be a witness to the horrible scene "that can be performed only at night," as the witch says. We learn from this that certain pagan priests were not even allowed to watch magical rites, much less perform them. Nevertheless, Calasiris is able to gather some helpful information from the dead man.

Heliodorus, *Aethiopica, or Ethiopian Tales* 6.14–15

[*Calasiris, an elderly priest of Isis, and Charicleia, the beautiful young heroine of the novel, are traveling together through Egypt and come across a large number of dead bodies. It looks as though, not long ago, Persians and Egyptians had fought a fierce battle. The only living being in sight is an old Egyptian woman who is mourning the loss of her son. She tells the two travelers to spend the night there and promises to escort them to the next village in the morning.*]

Calasiris told Charicleia everything the old woman had said to him [in Egyptian] by translating it faithfully. They walked away from the slain bodies for a short distance and came to a little hill. There Calasiris stretched himself out, using his quiver as a pillow, while Charicleia sat down, using her purse as a cushion.

The moon rose and illuminated everything with her bright light; it happened to be the second night after the full moon. Calasiris felt his age and was tired from the journey, so he fell asleep. Charicleia, however, kept awake by her worries, became the eyewitness to a gruesome spectacle, but one that is not unfamiliar to Egyptian women.

The old woman, feeling undisturbed and unobserved, first dug a ditch and then lit a pyre that had been built on either side of it. After placing the body of her son in between, she lifted from a tripod that was standing there an earthenware jug of honey, one of milk, and another one of wine, and poured their contents into the ditch, one after another. Then she took a male figure made of dough, crowned with laurel and fennel, and threw it into the ditch. Finally she grabbed a sword, began to shake, as if in a trance, addressed the moon in many prayers that sounded wild and exotic, cut herself in the arm, wiped off the blood with a laurel branch, and sprinkled it over the pyre.

After performing more bizarre magic of this kind, she bent down to the body of her son, chanted something into his ear, and forced him, by her spells, to stand up straight.

Charicleia had already observed the first part of the ceremony with growing fear, but now she really began to shudder, and because of the horror she felt at this appalling spectacle, she woke up Calasiris and made him, too, watch what was going on.

Thus the two sat in the dark without being seen, but they could easily observe what was happening in the light coming from the pyre. Since they were not too far away, they could also hear what the old woman said, for she now began to ask the dead man questions in a fairly loud voice.

She wanted to know whether his brother, her surviving son, would return home safe and sound.

The dead man did not say anything in reply; he just nodded, without giving a clear indication to the old woman whether she might expect to see her wish fulfilled or not. Suddenly he collapsed and lay with his face on the ground. She turned the body on its back, continued relentlessly with her questions, and whispered, or so it seemed, even stronger incantations into his ears. Holding the sword in her hand, she jumped back and forth between the ditch and the pyre, aroused him once more, and as he stood up, renewed her questions and forced him to make his prediction not just by nodding but in clear language.

While the old woman was occupied with this, Charicleia kept urging Calasiris to move closer to the action and to ask questions about Theagenes. He refused, saying that it was a sin even to watch this spectacle, and they were excused only by the fact that they had no choice. He added that priests were not allowed to take part in such rites or even to be present; their own predictions were the result of the correct kind of sacrifice and a prayer coming from a pure heart, whereas impure outsiders were operating, in fact, with earth and bodies, just like the Egyptian woman whom, by chance, they were able to observe.

Before he could finish his sentence, the dead man began to mumble in a dull, deep voice that sounded as if it came from a closed vault or a cavern:

"Mother, so far I have been very patient with you, and I have tolerated the fact that you are sinning against human nature, that you violate the law of the Fates, and that you try to move by your magic what may never be moved. For even the dead respect their parents, at least up to a certain point. But by your behavior you undermine and destroy this respect, for you have not only applied ruthless methods to begin with, but you have now pushed your ruthlessness to the extreme by forcing a dead body not only to get up but also to nod and talk, without taking care of my burial, but preventing me from joining the other souls, only thinking of your own concerns. Listen to what I wanted to tell you before but did not, out of respect for you: Neither will your [other] son return alive, nor will you yourself escape death by the sword. Since you have always devoted your life to sinful practices such as these, you shall very soon meet the violent end that is destined for all people like you. In addition, not only have you had the nerve to perform such mysteries, mysteries veiled in silence and darkness, all by yourself, but you have just now betrayed the fates of the dead in front of witnesses. One of them happens to be a priest, but that is not the worst, for he is wise enough to keep such things under the seal of secrecy and never to mention them; he is also, by the way, beloved by the gods. This is why he will be able to stop his two sons from fighting each other and reconcile them instead—they are getting ready for a duel to the death with swords—if only he will hurry up. What is more serious is this:

a girl sees and hears everything that is happening to me; a young woman overwhelmed by love, she has wandered through the whole world for the sake of her beloved, but after a thousand troubles, a thousand dangers that will lead her to the limits of the earth, she will live happily and in royal style with him ever after."

Having said this, he collapsed and lay still.

The old woman understood at once that the two strangers were the spectators. She grabbed the sword and, mad with fury—you could tell from her expression—she wanted to attack them and looked for them everywhere, suspecting that they were hiding somewhere among the bodies. She was determined to kill them, if only she could find them, because they had maliciously, or so she thought, disturbed her magic by watching her. As she was searching in blind rage among the corpses, she did not see the end of a spear sticking up. It pierced her body, and she fell to the ground, dead.

Thus, she at once fulfilled her son's prediction, as she deserved.

75

The name Abrasax (or Abraxas) appears frequently in magical texts as a powerful daemon who can protect the wearer of the amulet against other daemons, as the text of this amulet shows. The wearer of the amulet cannot know what dangerous force is attacking her; therefore, different possibilities are considered: a daemon, a ghost, and "something that is shivering," which could mean "something that makes you shiver," perhaps a spirit of sickness. The amulet was probably commissioned by the parents of a little girl; they may have been Christians, as the names suggest, but they are still in awe of the daemons of pagan witchcraft. The Church condemned such amulets, but they were still worn for a long time. Campbell Bonner, *Studies in Ancient Amulets* (Ann Arbor, 1956) is still a very valuable study.

Abrasax Amulet (*Suppl. Mag.* 13 = *PGM* LXXXIX)

SO SO ABRASAX [character] ABRASAX. I am ABRASAX ABRASI CHO OU. Come to the aid of little Sophia also known as Priscilla. Restrain and render harmless the attacker of little Sophia also known as Priscilla. If it is shivering, restrain it; if it is a ghost, restrain it; if it is a daemon, restrain it. SO SO ABRASAX ABRASAX. I am ABRASAX ABRASI CHO OU. Restrain and render harmless the things that attack little Sophia also known as Priscilla, on this very day. If it is shivering, restrain it; if it is a daemon, render it harmless.

76

The text is written on a lamella found in a stone sarcophagus (third century A.D.) discovered in Althenburg, Austria, the Roman Carnuntum. The Greek term for "migraine," *hemikranion*, literally "half of the head," is the root of our modern word. Antaura, the daemon that causes migraine, is represented as a wind that comes from the ocean and is on the way to someone's head. Artemis, the great goddess of Ephesus, stops the daemon and sends it somewhere else, possibly into the head of an animal (a deer or an ox). A little story, a mini-myth, sometimes called *historiola,* is attached to certify the potency of the charm.

Amulet against Migraine (R. Kotansky, 1994, no.13)

For migraine. Antaura came out of the sea. She shouted like a deer. She roared like an ox. Artemis of Ephesus meets her: "Antaura, where are you headed?" "Into the half of the head." "You surely will not go into . . ."

IV

DIVINATION

Introduction

Foretelling the future, interpreting the past, and, in general, discovering hidden truth (by way of clairvoyance, precognition, telepathy, and other such phenomena) was called *divinatio* by the Romans. The noun is derived from the verb *divinare* 'to predict', which is no doubt related to *divinus* 'divine' in the sense of "pertaining to a god or to the gods." The linguistic evidence in antiquity shows that the gift of predicting future events or grasping things by extrasensory perception was something that came from the gods, and this is confirmed by myth. According to Aeschylus (*Ag.* 1203ff.), Cassandra had been given her prophetic powers by Apollo to win her love. Similarly, Tiresias was endowed with the gift of prophecy, either by Zeus or by Athena, to compensate him for the curse that had made him blind.

The Greek word for "prophetic power" or "gift of divination" is *manteia;* the word for "prophet" or "prophetess" is *mantis.* The Greeks were probably right in connecting these two words with *mainomai* 'to be mad' and *mania* 'madness', but of course they were not thinking of permanent insanity; rather, they meant an abnormal state of mind that lasted for a short time. The word *ekstasis* also is used to describe this abnormal state; it means "stepping out of one's self" and is best understood today as "trance," though in antiquity it could mean a form of "possession." The association of prophetic powers with "madness" seems to be a very old idea among the Indo-European tribes, as the etymology shows,[1] and the descriptions of prophetic trance [*nos. 87* and *90*] stress this particular aspect. It should be said, however, that this is only one form of divination; there are forms (e.g., the interpretation of dreams, or astrological forecasts) that do not require—in fact, they preclude—an abnormal state of consciousness.

Something should be said about the original meaning of the words *prophet, prophecy,* and the like. In Greek, *prophetes* literally means "a person who speaks for someone else," and that someone else is usually a god, though in Delphi the priests who interpreted the obscure utterances of the Pythia were also called *prophetai*. The Pythia was the *mantis,* directly inspired by Apollo, but her message from the god had to be put into comprehensible form, into verse, for those who consulted the oracle. These *prophetai* were not directly in touch with the god; they were one step removed. Plato (*Timaeus* 72A) says that the term *prophetes* should be reserved for those priestly interpreters who translated the frenzied utterances of the ecstatic seer (*mantis*) into intelligible Greek. But, in general, *prophetes* is a person who speaks for a god, or through whom a god speaks and reveals his plans. This is true for the prophets of the Old Testament, for John the Baptist, for Jesus—for anyone who proclaims a divine message with a special sense of mission.

Divination had its roots in Mesopotamia. The gift of prophecy and the status it confers were taken for granted in the Old Testament. Prophets were men of God who had the privilege of seeing him in a vision or hearing his voice, but then it became their duty to bring his message to the community. The prophetic books of the Old Testament, with their magnificent poetry, show that this was by no means an easy job; he who had to spread God's message usually encountered indifference or downright hostility, especially if he denounced heresy and vice and prophesied doom. The Greek myths of Cassandra and Tiresias also show that the gift of prophecy was a blessing and a curse in one.[2]

The Babylonians believed that the decisions of their gods, like those of their kings, were arbitrary, but that mankind could at least guess their will. Any event on earth, even a trivial one, could reflect or foreshadow the intentions of the gods because the universe is a living organism, a whole, and what happens in one part of it might be caused by a happening in some distant part. Here we see a germ of the theory of "cosmic sympathy" formulated by Posidonius, the Stoic. Lists of unusual happenings were kept in Babylonia, and later (perhaps through Etruscan influence) in Rome. These observations could then be matched with events that affected the whole country: the death of a ruler, a famine, a war. Among the techniques practiced, we find astrology, liver divination, and the interpretation of dreams; the birth of freaks and the strange behavior of animals also were thought to have special meaning.

Cicero's work *On Divination* (*De Divinatione*) is the most important ancient text we have. It should be read in conjunction with his treatises *On the Gods* (*De Natura Deorum*) and *On Fate* (*De Fato*), because certain forms of divination were part of religion, and the doctrine that all things are determined or decreed by fate naturally favored the belief that divination was possible. Cicero's three treatises give us a fairly full picture of Hellenistic theology as it was taught in the various philosophical schools.

As far as divination is concerned, Cicero himself remains skeptical, but he borrows a good deal from philosophers who firmly believed in the various methods of predicting the future. One of the leading minds of what is now called Middle Stoicism, Posidonius of Apamea (c. 135–50 B.C.), seems to have written a book in which he tried to show, from the many cases he had collected, that divination actually works. In order to find a philosophical reason for the phenomenon, he established the principle of "cosmic sympathy," which is at the basis of all occult sciences. Thus we know from Cicero (*Div.* 1.64) how Posidonius explained dreams that came true: in sleep the human soul communicates either with the gods directly or with an "immortal soul" (i.e., one of the many daemons that throng the air beneath the moon). These divine beings know the future, and they often share their knowledge with human souls when they are not encumbered by the body.

Natural and Artificial Types of Divination Dreams

According to Cicero (*Div.* 1.11; 2.26), who seems to follow Posidonius, there are two main types of divination: natural and artificial.[3] The most obvious form of natural divination is by dreams; we have just seen how Posidonius accounted for dreams that anticipated future events. Dreams are called "the oldest oracle" by Plutarch (*Conv. Sept. Sap.* 159A). Often the dreamer himself understood the meaning of his dream; but sometimes he would consult a professional interpreter. Their lore is preserved in dream books such as Artemidorus' *Oneirocritica* (*The Art of Judging Dreams*).[4]

A special way of inducing meaningful dreams is known as incubation (in Greek, *enkoimesis* 'sleeping in a temple'). In certain sanctuaries—for instance, in the temple of Asclepius at Epidaurus—the visitor had to follow an established ritual (fasting, praying, bathing, sacrificing) and then spend the night in the temple. In his sleep he would see the god and receive from him advice about the problem that had brought him there, usually a serious illness. By following the god's advice, many patients whose doctors had given up on them recovered miraculously, and many of their cures are recorded in inscriptions and in literary works—for example, in the *Speeches* of Aelius Aristides (second century A.D.), who had been healed himself. Hence, this special kind of divination is also called *iatromancy.*

The dream experience seems to have been fairly predictable. The prescribed ritual no doubt conditioned those who sought help; the holy place, the presence of kindly priests, and the records of earlier cures inscribed on the walls to document the reality of divine healing must have heightened their expectations; almost certainly they were also given a drug, along with hypnosis. For many patients these ancient sanctuaries were a kind of last resort, like Lourdes today.

Physical and mental sickness may be considered borderline conditions that allow the body to release certain powers that it does not normally possess. Aristotle (frag. 12a Ross) tells a story about his friend Eudemus, who during a serious illness had instant knowledge of his recovery and was at the same time able to predict the imminent death of Alexander, king of Pherae. Similarly, Augustine (*De Gen. ad Litt.* 12.17) reports the case of a mentally disturbed person who was regularly visited by a priest and "saw" him during all the phases of his journey between his own house, twelve miles away, and that of the patient.[5]

Like other forms of divination, the interpretation of dreams was practiced at an early date in Mesopotamia.[6] In Egypt this art was in the hands of priests and was so highly regarded that King Esarhaddon of Assyria, when he conquered Egypt in 671 B.C., took a number of these priests back to Assyria with him. The Papyrus Chester Beatty 3 (c. 1800 B.C.) contains an elaborate manual that is similar to the dream book of Artemidorus, which was written two thousand years later: eating donkey meat in a dream is good (it means a promotion); making love to one's mother is good ("he will be supported by his fellow citizens"); diving into a river is good ("his sins will be taken away from him"); having intercourse with a pig is bad ("he will lose his possessions"). The Egyptians believed that man, in his sleep, had access to a universe that is different from the one we normally inhabit and that, though the body is asleep, the soul is somehow awakened to a new life.

In the Old Testament, dreams are one way in which man communicates with God, though it is admitted that some night visions are meaningless or even misleading. The dreams experienced by kings, priests, and prophets are naturally more significant than those had by others, and kings sometimes slept in holy places if they need help from God: Solomon's dream at Gibeon (1 Kings 3:4–15; 2 Chronicles 1:3–12) is an incubation dream; Joseph's dream (Genesis 37.5–11) is one of the oldest dreams of prediction on record; and Pharaoh's dream (Genesis 41:1–45), which none of the Egyptian "magicians and sages" could interpret, is explained to him by Joseph, because he "has the spirit of God in him." Because dreams come from God—or from a god—only he who has the divine spirit in him will be able to understand them. Curiously, Pharaoh does not have the authority to interpret his own dream.

The Talmudic tradition also recognizes the value of dreams. According to Rabbi Jochanan, "Three kinds of dreams come true: the dream in the morning, the dream someone [else] has about you, and the dream that is interpreted by another dream." Clearly, if a dream needs interpretation, the best interpretation comes from God, in the form of another dream.

The earliest dream in Greek literature is found in Homer's *Iliad* (2.5ff.). It is a deceitful dream sent by Zeus to Agamemnon, the commander in chief of the Greeks before Troy, "in order to destroy many Achaeans in their camp," as Homer says, and eventually make the Greeks realize how valuable a fighter Achilles, who has just been insulted by Agamemnon, will prove to be. The dream vision urges Agamemnon to attack the Trojans at once, which is bad advice. Clearly the gods can send false dreams, and in the assembly of elders in which the dream is discussed, Nestor, the wisest of the Greeks, says: "If any other man had told us about this dream, we would declare it false and turn away from it; but now it was he who claims to be by far the greatest among the Achaeans who had the vision." The fact that the supreme commander experienced the dream and was ready to take it as a good omen seems to exclude any doubt.

In the *Odyssey* (19.562ff.) Penelope develops a kind of theory of misleading and trustworthy dreams. She uses the image of two gates, one made of ivory, one of horn. The deceptive dreams fly through the gates of ivory, and those which accurately predict the future fly through the gates of horn. But it is difficult to distinguish one from the other, and in this particular instance, Penelope's instinct tells her that her dream is not true, although she would like to believe in it.

According to Hesiod (*Theog.* 211–13), dreams are creatures of the Night, along with Sleep, Doom, Death, and other sinister personifications. It is strange that Hesiod, in the seventh century B.C., seems to ignore pleasant dreams, of which there is no lack in early epic poetry; he thinks only of frightening visions, deceptive dreams, and nightmares.

A powerful religious movement that originated in Greece in the seventh century B.C. is known as Orphism. Some Orphic theories concerning the soul impressed later poets and thinkers such as Pindar, Aeschylus, Sophocles, and Plato. They taught that, during sleep, the soul was freed and could leave the body in order to communicate with higher beings. While the body is awake, the soul (or "the subconscious," as we might say) is asleep, but when the body is asleep, the soul is wide awake and acquires what we today would call extrasensory perception. The soul, as Aeschylus says (*Ag.* 178; cf. 975 and Fraenkel's notes),[7] sits in the heart like a prophetess in her chair and interprets the visions of the blood. This striking image anticipates later philosophical theories.

Similarly, Euripides (*Iphigenia Taurica* 1261ff.) says that dreams are creatures of the Earth. Text and interpretation of this choral passage are controversial, but the playwright seems to compare the dreams with the visions of the Pythia, who was also believed to receive her insights from the Earth. The chorus, consisting of Greek women, takes it for granted that dreams "tell what happened first, what happened later, and what will happen in the future."

In Plato's *Phaedo* (60C–61C) Socrates reminisces in prison about a recurring vision in which the dream figure—always the same—urges him to "make music." The expression is ambiguous in Greek; it could refer to any of the arts and crafts sacred to the Muses, including what we call "music," but it might also refer to poetry or philosophy, for Socrates felt that, for many years, he had been "making music" through philosophical discussions. Perhaps we ought to translate the order of the dream figure as "Be creative!" To Socrates the highest form of creativity was philosophical (or scientific) investigation. But after his trial, awaiting execution, he realizes that some supernatural power wants him to write poetry while there is still time, and he does this by versifying some of Aesop's fables that he knows by heart.

This is obviously the type of dream called *chrematismos* 'oracular response' by Artemidorus and *admonitio* 'command' by Chalcidius (also fifth century). This type, Macrobius writes, "occurs when in sleep the dreamer's parent, or some other respected or impressive person, perhaps a priest, or even a god, reveals without symbolism what will or will not happen, what should be done or avoided."[8]

That Socrates paid attention to the messages delivered by dreams and that he placed them on the same level as the responses given by the established oracles and the "inner voice" that he listened to is clear from a passage in his *Apology* (33C): "God has ordered me to do this, both through oracles and dreams and in all the other ways used by divine providence for giving its commands."

Xenophon, like Plato a disciple of Socrates, believed that divination through dreams was possible and should not be neglected (*Cyr.* 8.7.21): "It is in sleep that the soul really shows its divine nature; it is in sleep that it enjoys a kind of insight into the future; and this apparently happens, because it is completely free in sleep."

Plato went one step further when he claimed that we can control our dreams and that such control is, in fact, essential (*Rep.* 571C). Before going to sleep we must awaken our rational powers and concentrate on noble thoughts. If we do not indulge our baser appetites too much and if we are able to free ourselves from passions, we shall see in our dreams the truth; otherwise we will be the victims of absurd visions.[9]

In one of his early dialogues, when he was still under the influence of Plato, his teacher, Aristotle said: "The mind recovers its true nature during sleep" (*On Philosophy*, frag. 12a Ross). In his later writings (*On*

Sleep, On Dreams, On Divination in Sleep, all parts of the *Parva Naturalia* [*Short Scientific Treatises*]) he is more cautious when dealing with dreams. He denies, for instance, that they are sent by a god, for if the gods wished to communicate with men, they could do so in the daytime, and they would show more discrimination in choosing the dreamers.[10] To him, dreams are affections of the central organ of consciousness. The dreamer is sensitive to the slightest disturbances in his organism, and these will affect his dreams. While asleep, he may hear a faint noise and dream of a thunderstorm.

Dreams certainly have their meaning, according to Aristotle, and physicians should tell their patients to pay attention to dreams. The best dream interpreter, he says, is the man who spots analogies and recognizes the true image behind the dream reflection, for the true image is often broken or distorted or changed through the dream process, just as an image reflected in water is distorted by ripples on the surface.

Aristotle recognizes the common origin of the following three phenomena: dreams, the hallucinations of the sick, and the optic illusions of the sane. Although dreams are not divine, they are daemonic, "for Nature is daemonic"[11] (a profound remark). If a dream comes true, it may just be coincidence, but there are two types of dreams that can be taken as predictions: those that disclose foreknowledge of the dreamer's state of health, and those that initiate their own fulfillment by strongly suggesting to the dreamer a course of action.[12]

We can take it for granted that most of Aristotle's contemporaries believed in dreams, for we hear of various practices of averting an outcome threatened by bad dreams. People either "told it to the sun" or prayed or took ablutions or offered sacrifices.[13] This was a form of psychotherapy, and even for the fatalist the law of predetermination was not broken, because the prevention of catastrophe, once the warning had been issued in a dream, could easily be predetermined.

The Stoic philosophers were busy collecting case histories of predictions (in dreams, oracles, etc.) that came true, mainly in order to provide an empirical base for their theory of predetermination. Cicero, in his treatise *On Divination,* uses these collections, along with some personal reminiscences, mainly to show that they were open to doubt. Posidonius, a Stoic thinker who had considerable influence on later philosophers, was convinced that divine powers communicate with human beings through dreams, and that they do this in three different ways: (1) the soul, being divine, is allowed to see the future as only gods or daemons see it; (2) the air is full of disembodied souls (daemons), which enter the organism of the dreamer; (3) the gods speak directly to the dreamer.

We have already seen how the Stoics dealt with an argument that was designed to weaken their doctrine of fate. If dreams effectively warn human beings of impending dangers, the whole irrevocable chain of events becomes problematic. A man dreams of being shipwrecked and consequently cancels the passage on a ship he has reserved. The ship, indeed, goes down with every soul on board, but the man who stayed at home is safe. How does this agree with the Stoic doctrine that no one can escape his fate? Seneca (*Scientific Problems* 2.37–38), probably following Posidonius, offers an answer: "Certain events have been left suspended, as it were, by the immortal gods, so that they may end happily if one addresses prayers to the gods and makes vows. Therefore this [happy outcome] is not against fate: it is, in itself, part of fate."

Such a reply to the skeptic's objections looks deceptively simple, but it breaks the wholly impersonal chain of events ruled by fate by introducing a personal power that can be influenced—the power of the gods. The Stoics, however, seem to have been satisfied by this reply. Their need to believe was probably greater than their urge to doubt.

A Greek novel written in the second century A.D. by Achilles Tatius, who, according to tradition, became a Christian and rose (just like Heliodorus, another novelist) to become a bishop, gives a different explanation: "The divine power often wishes to whisper about the future to human beings in the night, not in order to protect them from a tragic event (because fate cannot be controlled), but to help them accept such an event when it occurs. For when disasters come all at once, unexpectedly, they produce a sudden shock and overwhelm us totally, but if people are prepared for them and can think about them beforehand, it dulls a little the sharp edge of pain."[14]

Lucretius (*De Rerum Natura* 4.749–822, 961–1036) puts the doctrine of Epicurus into Latin verse, and from his poem, written in the first century B.C., we can see that the Epicurean theory of dreams owes more to Aristotle than to Plato. According to Lucretius (i.e., Epicurus), we see in our dreams the things with which we are concerned during our waking hours: lawyers dream of their cases; generals, of their battles; Lucretius himself, of the book that he is planning to write. In short, we dream of the activity that absorbs our main energies, our hopes, and our ambitions. But we also dream of things that give us pleasure, such as music, dancing, plays, and entertainment in general, for sleep is a period of relaxation.

Since Lucretius, following Epicurus, wants the gods to be entirely carefree and blissful, he cannot admit that they are the least bit concerned about human affairs; therefore, they cannot send dreams warning of impending disaster. A purely rational explanation of dreams appealed to the Epicureans, and Aristotle, perhaps following Democritus, had given one, at least tentatively.

But most people continued to believe in the meaning of dreams, as we can see from the existence of dream books. The oldest preserved dream book dates from the second century A.D. Its author, Artemidorus of Daldi, was a professional interpreter of dreams with scientific and didactic interests. Not only did he collect more than three thousand dreams from those who consulted him, but he also took a good look at the people themselves. Thus, though bizarre in many ways, his book is a document of human psychology.

Artemidorus attempts to establish various levels of classification of his dream book. He distinguishes between dreams proper, visions, oracles, fantasies, and apparitions; then again, he separates dreams that forecast events from dreams that are concerned with the present.

Symbolism is the key to understanding the dream mechanism, according to Artemidorus. Some of the symbols are fairly obvious. An abyss means impending danger; a blossoming tree, happiness and prosperity. Bathing in clear water symbolizes good fortune; in muddy water, the opposite. A candle being lighted announces a birth in the family; one already lit hints at success; one burning dimly indicates distress of some kind.

In a sense, Artemidorus already anticipates the Freudian concepts of wish fulfillment and wish substitution; thus he says that the dreamer, if he is in love with a woman, will not see the object of his passion in his dreams, but he will see, for example, a horse, a mirror, a ship, the sea, or a woman's garment (Artem., *Oneirocr.*, preface to Book 4). It is up to the dream interpreter to find out whether his client is in love, and then he will understand the nature of the symbolism. In general, the client's personality, his habits, his profession, his recurrent dreams, have to be considered, for all of these might affect the symbolism of his dreams. Being struck by lightning, for instance, has at least fifteen different meanings, and only a long interview can bring out the specific nuance.

The most famous passage in Artemidorus' *Oneirocritica* is 1.79, which concerns the "dream of Oedipus" [*no. 97*] and its variations. Calmly and in an almost clinical manner, Artemidorus discusses various types of dreams involving sexual intercourse with one's mother. The theme of incest is compounded by bizarre practices (even necrophilia, it seems), and each variation of the theme has its own meaning.

Sometimes Artemidorus' approach is empirical. Among the thousands of dreams he must have listened to in his professional career, he matches some with the experiences the dreamers had afterward, and he draws certain conclusions. The ancient astrologers worked in the same manner, and they, too, used symbolism. Perhaps it is characteristic of all occult sciences that they have a "scientific" or "empirical" basis, but that they also resort to images, symbols, and analogies that no modern scientist would accept and leave room for instinct, intuition, and "psychic readings."

Marcus Aurelius, a Stoic who became emperor of Rome in A.D. 161, records in his *Meditations* that he received medical advice in dreams (1.17.20). In a remarkable passage (9.27) he urges the reader, in almost biblical terms, to feel kindly toward those who hate him, and reminds him that even his enemies benefit from dreams and oracles, although for their own, presumably crooked, purposes. But though Marcus Aurelius believes in various forms of divination, he rejects magic, exorcism, and "such things" (1.6). This shows how selective a highly educated Greek or Roman could be: he might accept one of the "occult" sciences but be hostile toward others.

In the first century A.D., mainly in Rome and Alexandria, a new version of the Pythagorean school appeared. Its doctrine was a blend of (presumably) genuine Pythagorean tradition, Platonism, Stoicism, and other philosophies that had been formulated since Pythagoras' death. Among other things, these late disciples had inherited from Pythagoras an interest in occult phenomena. Apollonius of Tyana, who is usually labeled a Neo-Pythagorean (he is discussed in chapter 1), was a healer, exorcist, and miracle-worker. A later philosopher, Iamblichus, actually a Neoplatonist, wrote a *Life of Pythagoras* (c. A.D. 300) in which he claimed (65, 114) that Pythagoras, like Plato, was convinced that sleep and dreams could be controlled. To fall asleep while listening to soft, soothing music would create a mood in which light, pleasant, and meaningful dreams might be expected. From this point of view, dreaming was considered to be a creative activity that demanded a certain technique and a specific training that might be compared with biofeedback today. The emphasis was definitely on spiritual discipline; any kind of food, drink, or drug that would stupefy body and soul was strictly forbidden. The Neo-Pythagoreans were especially interested in the "admonition" type of dream, called *admonitio* by Chalcidius and *chrematismos* by Artemidorus (*Oneirocr.* 1.2). (The Greek noun is derived from the verb *chrematizo*, which means "to give a revelation, in a dream or an oracle"; it also occurs in the New Testament.)

This new version of Pythagoreanism had a strong influence on Neoplatonism. Indeed, it was a Neoplatonist, Synesius (c. A.D. 373–410; he became a Christian bishop in 409 or 410), who theorized in his book *On Dreams* that dreams are preludes to real events and put us in the right mood for what is to come. Synesius argued that since no two people are completely alike, there can be no rules for all dreams; we have to find our own interpretation. This theory seems to have been directed against Artemidorus' style of dream books, with their vague symbolism and even vaguer empiricism. Synesius himself found that his dreams helped him in his work: they gave him ideas. Once, when he went hunting, a dream suggested to him a new kind of trap.

To Synesius, dreams could be both revealing and obscure, but even in their obscurity some revelation might abide. He knew people who had no education but who dreamed that they were talking with the Muses and woke up as great poets. "Make your bed on a Delphic tripod," Synesius says, "and you will lead a nobler life. Everyone, woman or man, can do it, because sleep is the most readily available oracle of all. The soul is lucid and mobile only when the body is asleep" (*De Insomniis* 144B).

Christians and pagans alike believed in the meaning of dreams, and dream books continued to be written throughout Byzantine times. Several of them have been preserved, the best known, perhaps, under the name of Achmes.

What has been written on dreams in modern times often seems to echo ancient theories.[15] In his *Interpretation of Dreams*, Freud quotes Aristotle and Artemidorus and follows their clues. According to the school of C. G. Jung, "Many crises in our lives have a long unconscious history. We move toward them step by step, unaware of the dangers that are accumulating."[16] And E. R. Dodds, who has tried to combine psychoanalysis and anthropology with the more traditional methods of classical scholarship, writes that certain dreams (he calls them culture-pattern dreams) are closely related to myth,[17] because, as Jane Harrison once put it, myth is the dream-thinking of the people, just as the dream is the myth of the individual. In other words, we create in dreams our own mythology, but only part of it comes from personal experience, distant or near; some images flow from the "collective unconscious" we have inherited from our ancestors.

It is almost impossible to understand a culture without knowing about its typical dreams and the typical interpretations of them. But the material we have is scanty, and much of it may have been edited or manipulated in some way. Still, since we are all dreamers, we can probably sense the hidden mechanisms that produced certain dreams in ancient times, for more than likely they also give rise to dreams today.

Oracles as Institutions

Dreams were called "the oldest oracle" by Plutarch, and everyone could have prophetic powers in dreams. But there existed, throughout the ancient world, establishments where predictions were regularly delivered by prophets. Not every prophet was associated with such a sanctuary, however; diviners practiced everywhere, and most did not enjoy the status of the Delphic Pythia or the Sibyl of Cumae. In fact, these free-lancing diviners were in a sense "shrunken" shamans who had only one gift left, the gift of prophecy, unlike Orpheus or Pythagoras, who controlled a whole range of occult powers.[18]

As early as Homer, divination came under the control of religion and was concentrated in a few shrines that soon became prominent and wealthy. At a very early date, Apollo seems to have been in charge of trance mediumship, while Asclepius, his son, guaranteed true dreams. Some of the ancient divinities, such as Hecate, were still invoked to grant a glimpse into the future.

What is an oracle? The word has three basic meanings: (1) a response given by a priest or priestess at the shrine of a deity; (2) the shrine itself (thus we speak of the Delphic oracle as a sanctuary where oracles were delivered to those who consulted it); and (3) the "real" oracle, the power that inspired the messages that emanated, as it were, from another world and had to be interpreted.[19]

The techniques used to obtain predictions varied from shrine to shrine, and it is difficult to understand them at this distance in time. To dismiss them altogether as fraud, as the philosophers of the Enlightenment did, hardly seems reasonable, however. Bernard de Fontenelle (1657–1757) compared the ancients' belief in oracles with their belief in the gods, one that he assumed was not very deep: "Act like the others and believe whatever you like." It was essential to conform publicly, to offer the right sacrifice in the right way; if one did this, one could make fun of it in private. Thus, "You might or might not believe in oracles, but they continued to be consulted for centuries, because custom has a hold on people which need not be reinforced by reason."[20] Fraud was certainly involved in some cases.

An Egyptian oracle in the oasis of Siwa in the Libyan Desert, that of Ammon, or Amun ("The Hidden One"), may have had some influence on the organization of the sanctuaries at Delphi and Dodona in Greece.[21] Statesmen from Athens and Sparta went there in the fifth and fourth centuries B.C., and Alexander the Great consulted it too. We know very little about the method of divination that was practiced there.

Since the Delphic oracle is the most famous institution of its kind in Greece, it might be useful to discuss it first. Phenomena such as prophecy, ecstasy, enthusiasm, clairvoyance, trance, and talking in tongues can perhaps be best illustrated by our knowledge—inadequate as it is—of what happened at Delphi, for at least part of the collective experience of thousands of visitors has been recorded.

Before we discuss the oracles as institutions where prophecy was practiced, we should say something about prophecy as a form of divination.[22] The foretelling of events as the result of a vision or hearing the voice of a divine being or entering a state of inspiration is well documented in the ancient Near East. We know of prophets (1 Samuel 10:5ff., 19:24) who came before the "canonical" prophets Isaiah and Jeremiah, for instance.

The nature of Old Testament prophecy has often been studied[23] and is, strictly speaking, outside the limits of this book. In the New Testament John the Baptist and Jesus are called "prophets" in the Gospels; Jesus was even taken to be one of the ancient prophets come to life again (Mark 8:28, etc.). In the early Church, people who had the special gift of uttering words in trance were called "prophets" (the word is sometimes translated as "charismatists"), for example, in Jerusalem (Acts 11:27, 15:32) and in Antioch (Acts 13:1). In a very early Christian text, *The Teaching of the Twelve Apostles* (*Didache*, probably composed c. A.D. 150, but some sections are older), we find references to these "charismatists." They are distinguished from the "apostles" (or "missioners") and from the "teachers" (see 1 Corinthians 12:28). Unlike the teachers, the "charismatists" were inspired, and unlike the "speakers in tongues," their message was intelligible, though they might forget immediately afterward what they had said. The genuine "prophets" were highly regarded by the community, but apparently there were also impostors who faked their gift as an easy way to make a living (*Didache* 11–12).

"Speaking in tongues" (*glossolalia*), a form of inspired ecstatic utterance, is not exclusively a Christian phenomenon; it occurred in various religious contexts of the Hellenistic period,[24] and it is described in an old testimony concerning the Delphic Pythia (Heraclitus, quoted by Plutarch, *De Pyth. Or.*, p. 404D): "She is in trance [*mania* 'madness'], does not smile, speaks in inarticulate, harsh sounds, but she is in touch with the god." A much later witness, Lucian (*Alex.*, par. 23), writes that the sibyl's speech sounds like Hebrew or Phoenician, and that those who do not understand her are amazed. The point, of course, is that it is neither Hebrew nor Phoenician nor any other language known to man (the use of Semitic words in magical Greek formulas is something else), but just a broken, inarticulate, incoherent outpouring of sounds.

In the early Church, being "filled with the spirit" created three spectacular gifts: (1) prophecy; (2) "speaking in tongues"; (3) the power of healing. "Speaking in tongues," as distinguished from "prophesying," referred to the unintelligible sounds of ecstatic speech.[25]

Speaking a "foreign" (i.e., unintelligible) language and predicting future events was also taken to be a symptom of possession.[26] This is not surprising, for the trance of the Pythia has also been described as a form of possession. Apollo takes over, fills her, controls her. The difference lies in the nature of the divine power that "takes over" a human being: a beneficial divine power on the one hand, a malevolent daemon on the other.

Prophetic ecstasy is usually explained as "trance," a state of consciousness induced by a divine power in which the normal mind is suspended and normal language is often replaced by unintelligible utterances. Galen, a medical authority of the second century A.D., describes it as "a madness that lasts only a short time," and, indeed, the Greek language itself reflects the connection of *mania* 'madness' with *mantis* 'seer'. The phenomenon has been studied many times,[27] but like related phenomena such as hypnosis, it is not fully understood today.

Prophetic ecstasy is a characteristic of the shaman.[28] It can be brought about by a kind of self-hypnosis—for example, by the monotonous murmuring of prayers or magical formulas, by taking drugs (herbs, mushrooms, toxic substances such as ergot) and inhaling aromatic vapors (from burning an incenselike resin on a bed of coals), or by dancing or engaging in other forms of exercise (the whirling dervishes). A strict ritual preceding the actual trance (fasting, bathing, lack of sleep), the presence of the priests in their robes, the awesome surroundings—all this could prepare (or "program," as we would say today) the medium. The trance could also be faked, as we know from Lucan (*Phars.* 5.124–61), because the real experience of divine possession was often traumatic and was thought to shorten the medium's life. But judging from Lucan's episode, there were signs that gave a faked ecstasy away.

Prophetic visions or insights are described in Homer more than once. Helenus, the Trojan seer (*Il.* 7.44–45), "understood in his mind the decision that the gods in their deliberations had made." Toward the end of the *Odyssey* (20.345ff.) the suitors who are doomed to die so soon at the hands of Odysseus, the hero who has already returned, eat and drink, laugh and scoff, as usual, but "their laughing jaws are no longer their own, and the meat they eat is defiled with blood, and their minds foretell grief." They continue to laugh and eat, but somehow they sense that disaster is near. The soothsayer Theoclymenus interprets it for them when he shouts: "Poor wretches! Do you realize what terrible fate will befall you? You heads, your faces, your knees are wrapped in darkness; the sound of wailing has broken out like fire; your cheeks are running with tears! The walls and the beautiful pillars are splashed with blood! The entrance to the court and the court itself are full of ghosts headed toward the underworld, the darkness! The sun has completely gone from the sky, and the mist of evil has spread across it!" The suitors respond with more merry laughter.

It is a remarkable scene: a sense of disaster hangs in the air, and even the suitors feel it, benighted as they are, but the seer Theoclymenus actually sees it all in a flash. This kind of sudden vision, which can be excruciating[29] for the seer himself and usually is not fully realized by those who are about to suffer, seems typical, and Homer's audience must have recognized it at once as a case of clairvoyance, an authentic phenomenon, not just a literary device.

The ancients also believed that in a state of trance, the soul leaves the body and is granted visions. Such a state can be induced by a ritual.[30] The highest form of ecstasy is the union of the soul with the divinity or the One (Plot., *Enn.* 6.9.11), not as the gift of the One, but as the result of human effort or discipline. This does not appear to be a purely Neoplatonist concept; it is probably connected with the much older Greek idea that man alone—without the help of the gods, and even, like Prometheus, against the gods—can achieve great things. It also seems related to the idea that magic or theurgy can practically compel divine powers to become accessible to human beings, in other words, to make trance possible in the first place. But trance does not always lead to this ultimate experience, though it may open up another world.

It is difficult to understand trance, because the "psychics" who have it are not always articulate. In his *Autobiography,* John Cowper Powys, an English author with Welsh roots, comes close to a description that seems meaningful even to those who have never had such an experience. One day, in San Francisco, he felt stirring within him "that formidable daimon which. . . can be reached somewhere in my nature, and which when it is reached has the Devil's own force. . . . I became aware, more vividly than I had ever been, that the secret of life consists in sharing the madness of God, I mean the power of rousing a peculiar exultation in yourself as you confront the Inanimate, an exultation which is really a cosmic eroticism."[31]

Ecstasy is sometimes distinguished from *enthusiasm,* which means, literally, "being full of God," but it can also be translated as "possession" or "inspiration." In their own language the ancients tried to describe an experience that was very real to them, but since they could not find a scientific explanation for it, they had to create an image—that of having a god inside (*enthusiasmos*) or being touched (or filled) by the spirit (*inspiratio*).[32]

Naturally, prophetic ecstasy could occur anywhere, at any time, even outside the great sanctuaries such as Delphi, but the ancients tried to control these irrational phenomena, to keep them under the strict supervision of a body of priests. Perhaps we should substitute the term *clairvoyance* for *prophecy,* for, according to F. W. H. Myers, clairvoyance is "the faculty or art of perceiving, as though visually, with some coincidental truth, some distant scene," and such distance could be in time as well as in space. Some ancient seers were no doubt true visionaries.[33] The terms *premonition* and *precognition* also have been used, but they do not explain why and how these experiences occur.[34] The Pythia, the entranced woman at Delphi, can be described as a "medium" or an "automatist," but these are just labels; at most, they allow comparisons to be drawn with experiments conducted in more recent times.

One distinction should perhaps be made. A prophetic vision may occur spontaneously and out of context, so to speak, like the vision of the seer Theoclymenus in the *Odyssey,* or the vision of Cassandra shortly before she and Agamemnon are murdered. In these cases it almost seems that a certain location is already charged or filled by the vibrations of a terrible event that is about to happen, and a "psychic" picks up these vibrations. Similarly, a "psychic" may pick up from a certain location vibrations of dramatic events that happened in the past: Cassandra had this ability, too (Aesch., *Ag.* 1194ff.).[35] Precognition, retrocognition, and telepathy may be different aspects of the same gift.

On the other hand, one wonders whether the Delphic Pythia and her *prophetai,* who dealt with the questions of visitor after visitor, day after day, can be called "psychic" in the same sense. The inarticulate response of the Pythia meant only one thing to the visitor: the oracle was working; the priestess was in touch with the god. But her answer also had to be interpreted, and at this point all kinds of rational considerations may have entered: politics, economics, diplomacy. The oracle, as delivered to the visitor, was a finished product. At best, it contained a genuine vision, but one that had been filtered through some of the shrewdest minds in all of Greece. An oracular response of this kind clearly differs from the apocalyptic visions of John on the island of Patmos.

Revelation means the "disclosure" or "uncovering" (*apocalypsis*) of God's will through visions and dreams, but primarily through the initiative of God, not through a special technique or concerning one particular religion as a whole or, more narrowly, its mystic doctrine of the Last Things. In one sense Judaism and Christianity are revealed religions; in another sense their eschatology concerns an apocalypse, because it predicts the ultimate conflict between the supreme powers of good and those of evil, with the good prevailing. This type of religious thought may have been accepted by some Jews from Zoroastrianism, the ancient Persian state religion (see Porph., *Plot.*, ch.16), and the tradition was continued by the early Christian Church. Hermeticism, on the other hand, is a philosophy that was revealed to mankind by the Egyptian god Thoth, the equivalent of Hermes, and such occult sciences as alchemy and astrology were considered by their practitioners to be the gift of a god. Thus, in later antiquity, the element of revelation distinguished religion from philosophy, occult science from science.[36]

Sanctuaries where divination was exercised regularly, as part of the cult of a god, are known as oracles (in Latin, *oracula;* in Greek, *manteia* or *chresteria*).[37] But as noted earlier, an oracle is also the response of the god to a question asked by a visitor to the shrine.

The method of divination varied from shrine to shrine.[38] Sometimes the will of the god was explored by the casting or drawing of lots (*kleroi, sortes*)—for example, dice or sticks or bones. The word *sortilegus* originally designated a soothsayer who practiced this particular method of divination (*sortes legere* 'to pick up lots'); later, by extension, it referred to any type of prophecy or sorcery. It must be a very old technique, for it was practiced at Clarus, Praeneste, Antium, and elsewhere. A later variant is the consultation of scrolls or books (bibliomancy) by opening them at random or pricking them with a needle: Homer, Virgil, and the Bible (*sortes Homericae, sortes Virgilianae,* and *sortes Biblicae*) were the obvious texts chosen.[39] This do-it-yourself method could easily be carried out at home, but when important decisions were at stake, the great shrines were still visited. One suspects that traveling to a famous oracle—Delphi, for instance, or Antium—was a way of life, like a pilgrimage in the time of Chaucer, and that the actual consultation was only part of a rather complex religious and social experience. Of course, there were certain methods that could not be duplicated anywhere else—the genuine trance of the Pythia at Delphi, for instance, or the rustling of the leaves of the sacred oak at Dodona.

Two collections of oracles might be mentioned here: the *Sibylline Oracles* and the *Chaldean Oracles.* Sibyls were women who, like Cassandra or the Delphic Pythia, prophesied in trance. Ten places in the Mediterranean world are known as residences of Sibyls, although originally there seems to have been only one. The Sibyl of Cumae is known from Book 6 of Virgil's *Aeneid,* and the ecstatic character of her prophecy is made clear by the poet (6.77–102); later she becomes the hero's guide through the underworld. A collection of prophecies written in Greek hexameters and attributed to various Sibyls was kept in Rome, in the temple of Apollo on the Palatine, for consultation by a special committee at the command of the Senate in times of crisis. This original collection was destroyed in a fire in 83 B.C.; a second collection, drawn from different sources, was destroyed in A.D. 405. What still exists today under the title *Sibylline Oracles* is a forgery,[40] although some genuine Greek oracles are interspersed through it. Part of it is Jewish propaganda against pagan culture and the beginnings of Roman imperialism (from the second century B.C. on); these texts were later rewritten, interpolated, and enlarged to suit the Christian polemic against paganism and the empire as well.[41]

The *Chaldean Oracles* appear to have been the work of one Julianus, who lived under Marcus Aurelius and is considered the founder of theurgy. Proclus and Iamblichus, the Neoplatonists, wrote commentaries on them. Where these "oracles" originally came from, no one knows. Dodds does not think that Julianus forged them; they remind him more of the trance utterances of modern "spirit guides."[42] Thus Julianus may have listened to the "revelations" of a visionary or a medium, transcribed them into verse, and supplied explanations. They contain guidelines for a cult of the sun and fire, but they also give instructions on how to conduct theurgical operations—for instance, how to conjure up a god.[43]

The most famous oracle of the ancient world was in Delphi.[44] Its origins probably go back to Minoan times, and for many centuries it must have been a sanctuary of the great earth goddess *Ga*, or *Gaia*. The Greek name *Delphoi* may be connected with *delphys* 'womb', since the Pythia in a sense did receive her inspiration from the womb, the inside of the earth. Another clue is given by the *omphalos*, a very old stone that once stood in the adytum of the temple of Apollo and marked or represented the "navel" of the earth, as the inscription *Gas* 'of the earth' indicates. The fact that at the oracle the most important function is performed by a woman implies that this was originally the sanctuary of a goddess, not a god. The very nature of the Pythia's trance suggests the influence of the earth, and her name recalls the ancient Python snake, which was thought to be female and presumably was the cult image under which the great earth goddess was worshiped.

Moreover, as is often the case, Greek mythology seems to have preserved part of the historical truth by making Apollo kill the Python. The oldest version of the myth appears in the *Homeric Hymn to the Pythian Apollo* (perhaps sixth century B.C.). It suggests that toward the end of the second millennium B.C., when Greek-speaking Dorians invaded the pre-Greek world of what is now called Greece, they took over some of the existing sanctuaries and changed their character, at least to a certain extent. Apollo replaced Gaia, and her cult image, the snake, was smashed, but the prophetic ecstasy of the priestess was, with great foresight, preserved as an institution.

How the Pythia's trance was induced is still a mystery. The most recent archaeological excavations have shown that there was a chasm from which she could have breathed a kind of natural gas.[45] Scholars who chewed large numbers of laurel leaves felt no special effect. Drinking the holy water or bathing in it can no longer be tested; these may have played a certain role, along with fasting, praying, and staying awake in inducing the trance that led up to the ultimate vision.[46] But the possibility of a psychoactive substance (an "entheogen"), perhaps laurel leaves mixed with hemp or poppy seeds smoldering on a bed of coals, remains an attractive hypothesis. For many Greeks and Romans it was a case of possession, of a god or daemon taking over. In modern terms the Pythia can be described as a "medium" or a "vocal automatist."[47] Telepathy and clairvoyance cannot be excluded: Tacitus (*Ann.* 4.52) says that the priest at Clarus, another famous oracle, would merely ask for the names of the clients present, then retire to a sacred grotto, drink the sacred water, and give the appropriate answers to questions he had not even heard. Plutarch (*De Garr.*, ch. 20) reports that the Pythia did this in certain cases; this means, perhaps, that certain Pythias did have the gift of clairvoyance, while others did not.

The sanctuary of Apollo at Clarus, near Colophon, seems to have been very old, but the oracle became especially famous during the imperial period.[48] The "prophet," assisted by a priest and a "thespiode" (i.e., a "singer of prophecies"), followed the procedure described above. Dodds is inclined to attribute this feat to thought-reading, though he also points out that the utterances of the prophet (who was generally uneducated, like the Pythia) were enigmatic and therefore had to be interpreted; this interpretative step appears to have been the function of the "thespiode," whose contribution to the psychic process is difficult to estimate.[49]

Divination was practiced in many different ways at the oracles of the ancient world. We are especially well informed about the procedure at the oracle of Trophonius, mainly thanks to Pausanias (9.39.2–14),who writes from personal experience. Trophonius was a local deity of chthonian character. Over the centuries, his sanctuary seems to have attracted a steady stream of visitors, including a number of prominent Romans. It is quite different from the oracles of Apollo at Delphi or Clarus or the Oracle of Zeus at Dodona, because it seems to have retained some very ancient features, due to the association of its deity with the earth and the underworld. It deserves a digression.

The consultation of the oracle at Lebadeia was surrounded by a number of complicated taboos and rituals—things you were not allowed to do and things you had to do. For one thing, only those who were seriously in search of an answer to their questions could expect to be admitted. Idle curiosity was actively discouraged, and the whole procedure was such that one really had to be determined to go through with it.

There was a fixed period of preparation, which included ablutions (only cold water was permitted), fasting (or at least abstention from certain types of food), induction of trance by dancing and possibly flagellation, and various sacrifices offered to Trophonius and other deities.

When the candidate was deemed to be ready by the priests, he was anointed with a special kind of oil by two boys aged thirteen. Then he had to drink from two springs; first from Lethe, to forget everything he remembered up to that moment; then from Mnemosyne, to remember everything he was about to experience during his (symbolic) visit to the underworld. Then he had to worship a very old wooden idol representing the god. A specific set of garments (white and red) was prescribed; but according to other sources, the postulant had to be naked.

Then he was allowed to begin his ascent to the sanctuary on the top of a hill. It had the shape of an oven. Once he had entered it, he saw a very small opening leading to the *adyton,* the "inner sanctum." When he squeezed through the opening in the prescribed manner, he found himself in a subterranean cave. He felt a strong current that practically sucked him through the opening. The darkness was almost total; there was only a ray of daylight coming through a tiny window. As a protection against the sacred snakes who lived there, he had to carry honey cakes in both hands. He heard indistinct human voices and a kind of distant bellowing; some reported that they had had a vision of the god himself, perhaps in a dream, which would mean that they had fallen asleep. There are varying reports about the length of time the postulant spent underground: it could have been a few hours; it could have been several days.

He returned to the world above in the same way he had left it, but with his feet first. Then the priests made him sit on the "Throne of Memory" and asked about his experiences, taking notes. Relatives or friends had to be waiting for him to guide him away. It took him a long time to recover and—it is said—to "learn to laugh again"; hence the proverbial comment about one who looked gloomy and lost in thoughts: "He has consulted Trophonius!"

There can be no question that the whole ritual was based on a very good knowledge of human psychology. Over the centuries, the priests had accumulated, thanks to the "Throne of Memory" routine, a great deal of information, which they were able to refine. The ascetic practices are not unlike those that were customary at other sanctuaries, but trance induced by dancing and possibly whipping is unusual. The oil used for anointing may have had psychoactive ingredients, but how the water from the springs had the desired effects is difficult to explain; unless the drinking was accompanied by a form of hypnosis. One thing is certain: the whole experience was overwhelming, unforgettable, a life-changing event. Obviously, it was not free of charge, but no matter how high the fee might have been, the postulants got their money's worth.

Were the answers to the questions useful? Probably, because the answer to his question was already in the mind of the postulant, but in a latent state. All the oracle did was activate it, and so it become true *for him*. At many oracles the behavior of animals was observed. At Dodona not only was the rustling of the leaves of the sacred oak of Zeus considered meaningful, but so, too, was the flight and cooing of the sacred doves on and around that tree. At the oracle of Apollo at Sura, in Lycia, omens were read from the movements of sacred fish that were kept in a tank. At Epirus, tame snakes were kept in a grove of Apollo, and when the priestess fed them, and their appetite was good, an abundant harvest could be predicted. The behavior of the underground snake of Lanuvium (an ancient city in the Alban hills where Juno was worshiped as Sospita) was interpreted in a similar way. According to Propertius (*Eleg.* 4.8.5ff.), once a year, when the giant snake was heard whistling for food, girls were sent down the "sacred way" into a dark cave. They could see nothing, but they felt the head of the snake as it snatched the food from a basket. If the snake accepted the food, it was a sign that the girls were chaste (though Propertius does not say this explicitly), and the farmers shouted: "The year will be fruitful!"

All these customs reflect a form of animal worship, which predated by centuries the arrival of the Olympian gods in Greece. It is interesting to note that animals representing three realms—earth, water, and air— played a role in divination. Snakes were associated with chthonian deities and with heroes, as we see in Delphi, where the Python represented the earth goddess herself. Birds were even more important. The interpretation of their flight, their cries, and other behavioral patterns was the subject of a special art, augury, a topic we turn to later in this chapter.

The Rise and Fall of the Oracles

Two questions about the oracles have been asked but have never been answered conclusively: (1) How did oracles, some more than others, gain their enormous prestige and influence in the ancient world? (2) Why did they eventually decline?

To deal with the first question, we ought to consider, as Dodds did, the religion, culture, and social life of Greece in the archaic and classical periods.[50] It is a historical fact that the belief in the authority of the oracle of Delphi was deeply rooted in the minds of the educated and the uneducated, and that this belief could not be shaken by striking proof that the oracle was fallible and downright subversive—for instance, when it discouraged the Greeks from resisting the might of the Persian Empire in the early fifth century B.C. The advice was terrible; the Greeks ignored it and won, but they soon forgot that the oracle had failed them completely. This can only mean that the Greeks believed in oracles because they needed them. They had neither the divine legacy of Scripture nor an established church, and their feelings of guilt and fear could only be controlled, it seems, by faith in a constantly renewable and more or less dependable divine revelation. The Delphic oracle gave them this and more.

The Delphic priests seem to have developed over the centuries a theology and a moral philosophy that stressed purity in ritual as well as in everyday life. Those who entered the temple were greeted by two large inscriptions: "Know thyself" (i.e., realize how unimportant you are, compared to the gods) and "Nothing in excess" (no idle admonition, for the Greeks, far from being the rational beings they are thought to have been, tended to do things in excess).

Socrates believed in the Delphic oracle, as he believed in his own *daimonion,* and so did his disciples Xenophon[51] and Plato[52] (the latter, perhaps, with certain reservations).

The importance of Delphi in world religion, politics, and economics has been compared with that of the Vatican today, and the comparison, taken with a grain of salt, is helpful. News of anything that happened in that *piccolo mondo antico* must have reached Delphi—which no doubt had a large network of agents and consultants—in record time. Delphi was also a financial center where gifts from kings and city-states to the god Apollo were kept and displayed. In addition, Delphi offered banking facilities: currency could be exchanged, and certain gifts were actually treated as investments. In the period of colonization, which expanded Greek influence beyond the Mediterranean, the advice of the oracle determined the choice of new sites for settlements.[53]

Before the Roman period few doubts concerning the good faith of the priests serving at the oracles were expressed, although the possibility of fraud in certain instances was not rejected. In the Enlightenment, oracles were regarded as a triumph of charlatanism and deceit and as evidence of the strange superstitions of the ancient world. The best-known attempt to discredit all oracles, as mentioned above, is Bernard de Fontenelle's *Histoire critique des oracles,* which was first published in 1687. Fontenelle, who was neither a historian nor a classical scholar, made two points: (1) oracles could not possibly have been inspired by divine powers; (2) they did not cease with the birth of Christ. The critique stirred up a lively controversy because it was felt to be an attack on the *fable convenue,* on all superstitions and bigotry that had been tolerated and encouraged by powerful institutions in all ages, not just in antiquity. Among other things, Fontenelle maintained that "custom, which need not be reinforced by reason, has enormous influence on people." It was, according to him, perfectly possible for a Greek or a Roman to ridicule the Delphic oracle in private, but to go through the motions of traveling there, offering the right kind of sacrifice in the customary way, and consulting the god just for show: "Act like the others, believe whatever you like." This was certainly true for many educated Greeks and Romans of the Hellenistic and imperial periods, but probably not for earlier centuries.

The second question—Why did the oracles decline and finally disappear?—is discussed by Plutarch in his essay *On the Ceasing of Oracles*.[54] Some of the reasons he offers are social and economic. Oracles can flourish only if they are visited regularly by large crowds that spend considerable sums of money or leave splendid gifts behind. As a result of wars and, later, as a result of Roman rule, the population and prosperity of central Greece had declined in the Hellenistic period. An impoverished Greece could no longer support the oracles. The fact that the ancient city-states had lost their independence was an additional factor. Their rivalry, both political and economic, had no doubt been manipulated and exploited by the great oracles. Under Roman rule this was no longer possible, and Rome itself had no interest in supporting the oracles, though distinguished Romans, out of curiosity, still visited the shrines.

To these explanations, other scholars have added the following: the expanding belief in astrology and similar types of do-it-yourself oracles; the publication of the *Sibylline Oracles* and similar collections; and, above all, the growth of Christianity.

Plutarch's main argument, however, is theological. Defending the supreme authority of the gods, he claims that they are not responsible for the operation of the oracles dedicated to them. Instead, he says, some very powerful daemons are in charge, but since daemons are mortal, they grow old and eventually die. To illustrate this, he tells the haunting story of the death of Great Pan (which supposedly occurred under Tiberius). As Plutarch interprets it, Great Pan was an important daemon, and the news of his death frightened all the minor daemons because they knew at once that the time of their own deaths had come. There is also a Christian explanation: Christ chased these daemons from the world.[55]

Speculation about the death of Pan continued in the Renaissance and afterward. Rabelais thought that Pan was Christ, for *pan* means "all," and Christ is mankind's All.[56] This idea was taken up by Fontenelle in his *Histoire critique des oracles*. The fact that Christ was crucified at about the same time that Great Pan died suggested to him that it was Jesus' death and resurrection that upset the daemons so much, because they realized that they could no longer control mankind. But Fontenelle also considered the possibility that Jesus and Great Pan might be "daemons" of approximately the same rank and that the death of one would affect the other.

Even if the story of Great Pan has no foundation whatsoever, it seems to sum up the mood of an entire era, and its historical truth is that of a myth, albeit a late myth. The lifetime of Plutarch (c. A.D. 45–125), who took the myth seriously, coincides with the time in which almost all the books of the New Testament were written.

Augury

An important form of divination in Greece and Rome was augury (*augurium*), the interpretation of the flight, sound, and manner of feeding of birds. The technique was practiced so commonly that *augur* became the word for any soothsayer, diviner, or prophet. Cicero, who was an augur himself, though he did not take the office very seriously, states that this craft was practiced in the ancient Near East in different cultures.[57] From Greek mythology we know that in the heroic age there were seers who understood the "language of the birds"—Calchas, Melampus, and Tiresias, among others. Moreover, it should be noted that these seers could interpret other phenomena as well. According to Homer (*Il.* 2.308ff.), Calchas understood at once an event that involved a dragon (a huge snake) and nine sparrows. Melampus understood the speech of all creatures, including birds, because snakes had licked his ears (Schol. Hom., *Od.* 11.290). Tiresias, who once observed two snakes coupling (Hyg., *Fab.*, no. 75), was blind when he received his prophetic gift, and thus would have been unable to observe birds flying; yet he, too, is labeled an augur. Strangely enough, we find the same association with birds and snakes in this list of great seers that we noted earlier. This should not be surprising, however, for snakes represent the divine powers of the earth, while birds might be envisaged as being in closer contact with the Olympian gods. The fact that Calchas, Melampus, and Tiresias were not committed to augury alone indicates that the oracles coming from the ancient earth goddess through her messengers, the snakes, had not been completely superseded by the oracles coming from the heavenly gods through their messengers, the birds. As might be expected, Greek mythology describes an age of transition.

In Greek, a bird of omen or augury is called an *oionos*, and a person who "foretells from the flight and cries of birds" is known as an *oionistes, oinethetes,* or *oionoskopos.* A whole family of words was built up around this ancient custom. For many centuries, no important decision affecting a country or an army was made without first consulting the birds.

According to Cicero (*Div.* 1.92), this divination technique was known in Asia Minor as well as in Greece. In Rome it was entrusted to a college of *augures.* This college, one of the most distinguished in Rome, originally consisted of three members, but was gradually increased to sixteen. The etymology of *augur* is uncertain, but the traditional derivation *avis* 'bird' and *gero* 'to carry' seems impossible; it may be an Etruscan word. Strictly speaking, the augurs were not diviners; it was their function to find out, by observing certain signs, whether the gods approved of a certain plan of action. The signs were divided into *oblativa* 'casual ones'[58] and *impetrativa* 'those one watches for'. In observing wild birds, the augur defined (in words) a specific area of the sky or the land, called *templum,* and only what happened within this area was considered significant.

Alectryomancy was another method by which the Romans explored the will of the gods. It consisted in consulting the sacred chickens that were carried along on military campaigns. If, before a battle, the chickens ate their food so greedily that some of it fell from their beaks, this was considered an excellent omen.

Auguria were taken before any important public event, such as elections or a governor's entrance into a province, and this naturally gave the augurs great power, a power they occasionally misused for political reasons. A synonym or near synonym for *augurium* (the difference in meaning, if any, is not clear) is *auspicium* (probably from *avis* 'bird' and an old verb, *specio* 'to watch'). This term was extended to cover many types of divination, from "the observation of things in heaven" to "frightening portents." Only certain magistrates had the right to take *auspicia,* and only consuls, praetors, and censors were allowed to perform the more elaborate ritual of the "major auspices."

The "Etruscan Art"

The inspection of the entrails of a sacrificial victim, especially of the liver (hepatoscopy) was thought to give a clue to the future. The technique was called *Etrusca disciplina* 'Etruscan art', or *haruspicina* (sc. *ars*), or *haruspicium* (analogous to *auspicium*), and its practitioners were known as *haruspices.*[59] The first part of the word, *haru-,* is compared by linguists with the Greek *chorde* 'guts', and the second part seems to be derived from the Latin verb *specio* 'to watch,' which we have already encountered. The Romans learned this technique from the Etruscans, but the Etruscans apparently brought it with them from the Near East, for we know that it was practiced by the Babylonians and the Hittites.[60]

In Rome, a body of sixty *haruspices,* headed by a chief *haruspex,* became

a threat to the *augures,* a rival group, but the two techniques were practiced side by side for centuries.

The Etruscans apparently created a myth to explain the origin of this
form of divination.[61] Cicero tells the story, but not in a very reverent manner (*Div.* 2.50). An Etruscan farmer was plowing his field near
the town of Tarquinii, about sixty miles from Rome, when a childlike
creature suddenly emerged from one of the deeper furrows. That creature introduced himself as Tages and proceeded to reveal the secrets of
haruspicina to all the Etruscans who had, in the meantime, assembled
around him and were eagerly writing down every word. This marked the
beginning of a doctrine that was later expanded, but as Cicero adds,
rather sarcastically, "This is what we hear from them [the Etruscans]; this
is what *their* writings [the priestly books] preserve; this is the origin of
their science."

Cicero talks about the Etruscan diviners the way a Victorian English-
man might talk about the Welsh Druids: they represent a different culture, and he is puzzled (and amused) that this foreign ritual could still have
such a hold on the Roman imagination. Elsewhere (*Div.* 2.51) he quotes
with approval something that Cato the Elder (c. 200 B.C.) once said:
"How can two *haruspices,* upon meeting, not laugh at one another?"[62]

The *haruspices* observed and interpreted three kinds of phenomena: the
entrails of animals; unnatural things or events in nature; and lightning
(Cic., *Div.* 1.12, 2.26). The Etruscan *haruspex* Arruns, as described by
Lucan (*Phars.* 1.584ff.), is probably not historical, but his qualifications
would fit any practitioner of the craft: "He knows thoroughly the course
of the thunderbolt, the marks on entrails still warm and the messages of
winged creatures that fly through the air. He orders . . . the destruction of
monsters which nature had produced, as abnormal births [reading *dissors,*
with Oudendorp, for the manuscripts' *discors*] from mixed [reading *mixto,*
with Grotius, for *nullo*] seed and gives instructions to burn the abominable offspring of a barren womb with wood from a tree of bad omen."
Just before the outbreak of civil war, he performs a sacrifice (1.609ff.) and
observes one horrifying omen after another; the liver, for instance, has
two lobes, one of which is limp and flabby, while the other throbs with a
hectic rhythm. When he sees this, the *haruspex* knows that a catastrophe is
imminent, but he does not have the courage to tell the truth—that a civil
war between Caesar and Pompey is unavoidable. The passage from Lucan
also shows how we ought to understand "unnatural things or events in
nature" (*monstra*). These include teratological, that is, abnormal or monstrous, formations in animals or plants, misshapen organisms of any kind,
and strange meteorological phenomena. Such events were normally reported from all parts of Italy, to be analyzed by the experts, and if they

occurred more frequently in one particular year, rumors of an impending crisis began to circulate.

The interpretation of lightning was also part of the "Etruscan science." It was important to note from which of sixteen sections of the sky the lightning came and what spot or object on earth it hit.

Other Methods of Divination

There are so many other methods of divination that it is almost impossible to list them, except, perhaps, a few that are labeled with a specific name. Most of them did not require any apparatus or technical expertise and could be practiced almost anywhere. The catalogues compiled by scholars are rather tedious to read, but since this is a chapter of cultural history—and one that provides some curious insights into human psychology—a brief survey seems appropriate. The information we have comes from various sources, many of them late and not very explicit, but it seems that much of the material was originally compiled by Marcus Terentius Varro (116–27 B.C.) in Book 41 of his monumental work, *Antiquitates Rerum Humanarum et Divinarum* (*The History of Rome and Its Religion*). Varro was one of the greatest scholars of his time and an authority on Roman religion, and later writers—the Church fathers, for example—used him extensively, but the work as a whole is lost.

The body movements of human beings, especially their involuntary behavior (twitching, sneezing, etc.), provided omens. A visible part of someone's body might suddenly move spasmodically and give, to the observer, some indication of the future.

The various methods of divining from inanimate objects were divided by Varro into four classes that corresponded to the four elements: geomancy, aeromancy, pyromancy, and hydromancy (*Schol. Dan. Virg. Aen.* 3.359; Isid., *Etym.* 8.9.13). Actually, the phrase *inanimate objects* is misleading, because to the ancient Greeks and Romans, especially to Platonists and Stoics, nothing was wholly inanimate. Divination was possible because there was part of the cosmic soul in everything.

Geomancy was the art of divining by means of lines formed by throwing earth on a surface. *Aeromancy* consisted in casting sand or dirt into the wind and studying the shape of the resulting dust cloud; or in throwing seeds into the wind, allowing them to settle on the ground, and interpreting their pattern (though this is also considered a form of *aleuromancy*).[63] The modern method of teacup reading might be compared, even though the element is water rather than air. *Pyromancy* (or *empyromancy*) is divination by fire or signs derived from fire: if incense is placed on fire, we speak of *libanomancy;* if flour is thrown on the flames, this is a form of *aleuro-*

mancy; if an egg is broken over the fire, the term is *oöscopy.*[64] When the shoulder blade of a sheep is heated over the coals, one uses the term *omoplatoscopy* or *scapulomancy.*

All these methods were practiced at one time in one or more parts of the ancient world. The fire and the preferred materials strongly suggest a sacrifice offered to a god—Apollo, for example—because incense and grain were used as offerings, either along with a slaughtered animal or instead of it, from time immemorial. Since the deity was thought to be present at such a ceremony, it was he or she who conveyed the omen, but it may have been the duty of a priest to interpret it. Any sacrifice of this kind could be performed in private, but the more solemn the occasion, the greater the likelihood that more people were present.

The various subdivisions of *hydromancy,* or divination by water, are not always clearly defined.[65] The term *scrying* is used for "crystal gazing," but, strictly speaking, water or any other translucent or shiny surface could have been substituted for the crystal, which is not attested before Byzantine times.[66] This technique allows the "medium" to see a series of hallucinatory moving pictures "within" the shining object.[67] Not everyone, at least not in modern times, can be a "medium": F. W. H. Myers, who was a classical scholar and a psychic, estimated that perhaps one man or woman in twenty can experience hallucinations of this kind.[68]

At least two methods of scrying were used in antiquity. In one the translucent object was a mirror—not necessarily in the modern sense of the word, but a highly polished metal surface, a soldier's shield for instance. This method is called *catoptromancy.* In the other a glass or bowl of water was used, and for this the terms *lecanomancy* (divination by bowl) and *hydromancy* are attested.

Hydromancy,[69] like many other methods of divination, seems to have originated in Babylonia and reached the Greco-Roman world via Egypt, in the first century B.C. or earlier.[70] It was fairly popular throughout antiquity and in Byzantine times. In Europe, during the Middle Ages and later, it was associated with witchcraft, and in some countries severe penalties prohibited this seemingly harmless practice.

One ancient method is described by M. P. Nilsson: "Scrying was done by gazing at the surface of water, a method . . . which reminds us of modern crystal-gazing. A medium, an innocent boy, was chosen after he had been tested and found suitable. . . . The medium, with his eyes shut or bandaged, lay on his belly, with his face over a vessel containing water. Thereupon certain ceremonies were gone through which led up to the trance into which the medium passed by staring at the surface of the water, wherein he saw the beings summoned up by the magician, and then gave answers to the questions asked."[71]

The methods varied according to the nature of the shiny object used and the medium employed; sometimes a pregnant woman was substituted for the "innocent" boy (*innocent* here meaning "lacking sexual experience"). Sometimes the term *gastromancy* (divination by the belly) was used, because the vessel filled with water was called *gastra* 'belly-shaped vessel'.[72]

Other requisites mentioned are a small altar, a statue of a god, and a lantern (Apul., *Apol.*, ch. 42). A magical papyrus in London (*PGM V*) describes how to obtain an oracle from Serapis. One needs a bowl, a lamp, a bench, and a young boy. The prescribed ritual involves the invocation of Serapis, pouring the water into the bowl, lighting the lamp (at this point the boy probably stretches out on the bench so that he can look down into the bowl), waiting for visions in the water, a prayer to dismiss the god, and a charm to protect the boy.

We would call the boy a medium. When he sees certain things in the water (a throne carried by four men crowned with olive branches, preceded by a censer bearer, is mentioned), the priest knows that the medium is now in trance. These images can vary from cult to cult, from age to age. In this case we are probably getting a glimpse of a ritual procession in honor of the god Serapis in the late Hellenistic period. In theory, other images could be substituted, but this particular vision has survived for centuries, for we have a remarkably similar account of the same kind of ceremony from an English traveler, E. W. Lane, who visited Egypt in the nineteenth century.[73] The images that the boy-medium sees at the beginning of his trance are also certainly scenes of temple life in Egypt two thousand or more years ago. One possible explanation is that this technique was taught by one generation of magicians to the next for centuries, and that along with the technique a certain way of "programming" the medium was inherited. This programming could have been done when the boy was hypnotized. The long survival of these ancient practices, at least under certain circumstances, is truly astonishing.

Crystal gazing, or *crystallomancy*, is not referred to by this name before Byzantine times, but the practice itself seems to be older.[74] The favorite mineral used by the ancient diviners was the beryl, a transparent stone pale green in color and passing into light blue, yellow, and white; the green variety of the transparent beryl is the emerald, while the pale bluish-green variety is the aquamarine. All these stones were used in antiquity, but in modern times "crystal balls" made of clear glass have been substituted.[75]

No doubt many other techniques of divination were known to the ancients but no detailed descriptions have survived. The term *rhabdomancy* appears in a gloss without further explanation. Translated as "divination by means of a rod or wand," it is connected with a passage from Herodotus (4.67) in which we are told that the Medes, the Persians, and the Scythians used a stick or rod for divining. How they used it is not known, but it is reasonable to assume that Herodotus was speaking of the "divining rod" used for dowsing or "water witching" to this day.[76] No clear reference is found in any ancient author, though on the strength of Numbers 20:7–11 Moses is sometimes called the first dowser, that is, if the staff with which he struck the rock twice, after speaking to it, was a divining rod, not a magic wand.

According to the historian Ammianus Marcellinus (29.1.25ff.), participants in magical operations involving a kind of Ouija board were brought to trial for high treason.[77] Their instrument, produced as evidence, was a tripod of olive wood that supported a circular metal dish. On the rim of the dish were engraved the twenty-four letters of the Greek alphabet. A ring hanging from a thin linen thread began to swing from letter to letter, spelling out words and arranging the words into hexameters. Then someone asked the crucial question: "Who will be our next emperor?" Slowly the ring began to spell: first a *theta,* then an *epsilon,* then an *omikron*—it could only mean Theodorus, or so they thought. Unfortunately, they were wrong. One of them informed a so-called friend, and soon afterward they were all arrested, tried, and put to death, and Theodorus, though he insisted to the end that he knew nothing of the whole experiment, was put to death also. Had they only been a little more patient, the divination board would have told them the truth. Seven years later the reigning emperor, Valens, was killed, and his successor was—Theodosius.

A board similar to the one described above was excavated at Pergamon,[78] but it is not really a member of the Ouija board family; it is more like a roulette table, for the answers it provides seem to be determined by chance alone.

Chiromancy, or palmistry, is mentioned in the second century A.D. by Pollux (2.152), but apparently it was practiced in the Far East at least two thousand years before that. Originally it was based on intuition combined with symbolism, and some of the symbolism was derived from astrology. Lines in the hand forming a triangle (trine, 120° in astrology) were considered a good sign, whereas lines resembling a square (90° in astrology) were interpreted as a bad omen.

Tarot cards, as popular today as they were in the Middle Ages, were possibly created in Egypt as part of the Cabalistic tradition. When they were brought to Spain by Jewish scholars, they were adapted to medieval society; for example, the medieval clergy was symbolized by cups or chalices, the nobility by swords, merchants by pentacles, and peasants by wands. In subsequent centuries these class distinctions lost their meaning, and the cards were filled with new magical significance as practitioners interpreted the changing social scene. Basically, tarot is a variation of the sortilege technique, for each card represents the elaboration of one symbol.

The preceding survey of the methods used in ancient divination, incomplete as it is, shows that almost anything could be used to predict the future—the human body, the organs of an animal, minerals, artifacts, the four elements, even the stars. Almost anything that could be experienced or observed, anything that attracted attention, anything that could be manipulated—in a simple way or in an elaborate ritual—had some meaning for the individual or the community. Certain techniques were confined to certain places. Some required highly skilled practitioners, but many were devised for the use of the ordinary person. In a universe where supernatural powers were thought to influence every act and thought, ancient divination was essentially a form of psychotherapy. It helped people cope with their worries about the future, and it forced them to reach decisions after all the rational angles had been explored.

The divination techniques described in the following texts are different, but the principle is the same: the participants in these rituals assumed that the future was somehow present, either visible in trance or written in the sky (astrology is treated in chapter 5) or understandable through dreams. Some of these techniques were more elaborate than others. The professional dream interpreter needed his dream books; the professional astrologer, his astrolabe, his ephemerids, and other tools. The Pythia in Delphi prophesied in trance, a state of consciousness that could be induced naturally, by a form of self-hypnosis, or artificially, by psychoactive substances, most likely a kind of incense. Divination often worked because the person who asked the questions already, in the subconscious, knew the answers. This may sound paradoxical, but the evidence of the texts, if read carefully, confirms it.

Essentially, ancient divination was a form of communication between gods and men. The oracles were sanctuaries where gods were thought to reside and be willing to talk to men and women under certain conditions, sometimes through an intermediary (the prophet), sometimes directly (in a dream).

NOTES

1. See Dodds, *The Greeks and the Irrational,* p. 70.
2. See H. Gunkel, *Die Propheten* (Tübingen, 1917).

3. All the basic information is given in A. St. Pease's article in the *Oxford Classical Dictionary* (2nd ed., 1970), s.v. "Divination."

4. There is a French translation of Artemidorus' *Oneirocritica,* with valuable notes, by A.-J. Festugière (Paris, 1975) and an English one by R. J. White (Park Ridge, N.J., 1975). Dodds, *The Greeks and the Irrational,* ch. 4, is devoted to dreams. See also G. E. V. Grunebaum and R. Caillois, eds., *The Dreams and Human Societies* (Berkeley and Los Angeles, 1966). On incubation, see L. Deubner, *De Incubatione* (Giessen, 1900).

5. Dodds, *The Ancient Concept of Progress,* p. 174.

6. The dream book of Ashurbanipal has been published and translated by A. L. Oppenheim in *Transactions and Proceedings of the American Philosophical Society,* n.s., 46 (1956). The dreams sent by the gods to kings, priests, or wise men were considered self-explanatory, so to speak, because these persons had the authority to interpret them.

7. Aeschylus' *Agamemnon* is a tragedy about a Greek ruler who won a war and returned with a prophetess, Cassandra, as his captive; she foresaw his and her own doom. E. Fraenkel's monumental commentary (1950) offers insights into the phenomena of ecstasy and prophecy.

8. Dodds, *The Greeks and the Irrational,* p. 120.

9. According to Plato, prophetic dreams originate in the rational soul but are seen by the irrational soul as images reflected on the smooth surface of the human liver; see the reference to the *Timaeus* in ibid.

10. Ibid.

11. Ibid.

12. Ibid.

13. Dodds, *The Ancient Concept of Progress,* p. 183.

14. Achilles Tatius, *The Adventures of Leucippe and Clitophon* 1.3.2.

15. See W. O. Stevens, *The Mystery of Dreams* (New York, 1949); and E. Fromm, *The Forgotten Language* (New York, 1959), esp. pp. 47ff., on Freud and Jung. See also A. Faraday, *Dream Power* (New York, 1972).

16. C. G. Jung et al., eds., *Man and His Symbols* (Garden City, N.Y., 1964), p. 51.

17. Dodds, *The Greeks and the Irrational,* p. 104.

18. W. R. Halliday, *Greek Divination* (London, 1913), ch. 3. "Bacis" may have been the name given to a whole group of inspired prophets who were active in the seventh and sixth centuries B.C. Another legendary figure, "Musaeus," seems to be related to "Orpheus"; he is a healer as well as a diviner.

19. R. Flacelière, *Greek Oracles,* trans. D. Garman (New York, 1963). F. W. H. Myers' *Essays Classical* (London, 1904) and M. P. Nilsson's *Cults, Myths, Oracles, and Politics in the Ancient World* (Lund, 1951) also are important.

20. Bernard de Fontenelle, *Histoire critique des oracles,* ed. L. Maigron (Paris, 1908), p. 70.

21. See S. A. B. Mercer, *Religion of Ancient Egypt* (London, 1949), pp. 157ff.

22. See A. Guillaume, *Prophecy and Divination* (London, 1938).

23. See, e.g., H. H. Rowley, *The Servant of the Lord* (Oxford, 1965).

24. See E. Rohde, *Psyche,* 3rd ed. (Tübingen, 1903), 2:18ff.; Reitzenstein, *Hellenistische Mysterienreligionen,* pp. 236ff.

25. See J. Hastings, ed., *Dictionary of the Bible*, 2nd ed. (1918), s.v. "Tongues, gift of"; A. Mackie, *The Gift of Tongues* (New York, 1922).

26. Dodds, *The Ancient Concept of Progress*, p. 174, quotes from a Byzantine author, Psellus, *How Daemons Work*, ch. 14, and points out that the *Rituale Romanum*, still the official Roman Catholic handbook for exorcists, cites as criteria of possession "the ability to speak or understand an unknown language and to reveal things distant or hidden."

27. Rohde, *Psyche*, 2:18ff.; Oesterreich, *Die Besessenheit;* Dodds, *The Greeks and the Irrational*, pp. 77ff.

28. See I. M. Lewis, *Ecstatic Religion: An Anthropological Study of Spirit Possession and Shamanism* (1971; repr., Harmondsworth, 1975).

29. This anguish of prophetic revelation is well attested and may be compared to Jung's "painful process of individuation."

30. See Dieterich, *Eine Mithrasliturgie*, pp. 2ff.

31. John Cowper Powys, *Autobiography* (New York, 1934), p. 531.

32. See R. A. Knox, *Enthusiasm: A Chapter in the History of Religion* (New York, 1950).

33. See E. Bevan, *Sibyls and Seers* (London, 1929).

34. Dodds, *The Ancient Concept of Progress*, pp. 176ff., gives a very instructive survey of possible explanations; he distinguishes clairvoyance from precognition, for apparently only the latter is explained by "divine images" (pp. 162, 202). One cannot help feeling that occult phenomena, like religious experiences, may be labeled and classified, but that the labels in themselves are no explanation.

35. On "retrocognition," see ibid., p. 160, n. 3. Sir Wallis Budge, in *By Nile and Tigris* (London, 1922), p. 122, tells us that he once relived in a room a horrible event that had actually taken place a long time ago. He goes on to explain that places can be like phonograph records, and that the psychic is like the needle that brings out the sound (i.e., the experience that is engraved in the place).

36. See S. Morenz, *Egyptian Religion* (Ithaca, N.Y., 1973), pp. 32ff.

37. See note 19 above.

38. Since the Egyptian oracle Amun, or Ammon was famous in Greece, one may assume that the Greeks inherited this form of divination from an older culture; see Mercer, *Religion of Ancient Egypt*, pp. 157ff.

39. Verses from Homer were written on papyrus, and then one particular verse was selected by throwing dice or pricking the papyrus with a needle; that verse was then interpreted as a response to one's question; see A. Vogliano, in *ACME* 1 (1948): 226ff.

40. An English translation is found in R. H. Charles, *Apocrypha and Pseudepigrapha of the Old Testament* (Oxford, 1913), vol. 2.

41. See P. Fraser, *Ptolemaic Egypt*, 3 vols. (Oxford, 1968), 1:708ff.

42. Fragments of the *Chaldean Oracles* were compiled and edited by W. Kroll (Leipzig, 1894). For Dodds' comments on them, see *The Greeks and the Irrational*, pp. 283ff.

43. See H. Lewy, *Chaldaean Oracles and Theurgy;* and the more recent edition by H. Tardieu (Paris, 1978).

44. See H. W. Parke, *Greek Oracles* (London, 1967).

45. Plutarch himself seems to have believed in "prophetic exhalations from the earth"; see *On the Cessation of Oracles,* ch. 44.

46. Cf. G. Luck, in *Gnomon* 25 (1953): 364.

47. Dodds, *The Greeks and the Irrational,* pp. 70ff., 87ff.

48. K. Buresch, *Klaros* (Leipzig, 1899); C. Picard, *Ephèse et Claros* (Paris, 1922).

49. Dodds, *The Ancient Concept of Progress,* pp. 168, 198–99. On Trophonius, see G. Radke, in *RE* 7A (1932), cols. 673ff.; A. Schachter, *Cults of Boeotia,* vol. 3 (London, 1994), 66ff.

50. Dodds, *The Greeks and the Irrational,* pp. 74–75, 93.

51. M. P. Nilsson, *Greek Popular Religion* (New York, 1940), pp. 123-24.

52. Dodds, *The Greeks and the Irrational,* pp. 217–18, 222–23.

53. Nilsson, *Cults, Myths, Oracles, and Politics in the Ancient World,* pp. 95ff.

54. Plutarch, *De Defectu Oraculorum,* ed. R. Flacelière (Paris, 1947).

55. Euseb., *Praep. Evang.* 5.17; see also D. A. Russell, *Plutarch* (New York, 1973), p. 145.

56. Rabelais, *Pantagruel* 4.28, quoted by Flacelière, in his edition of Plutarch's *De Defectu Oraculorum,* p. 79; see also Russell, *Plutarch,* p. 145.

57. Cic., *Div.* 1.92.

58. *Oblativa* were comparable to *enodia,* chance appearances of animals during a walk or a journey. In German folklore, a black cat that crosses one's path means bad luck.

59. See Sir James Frazer's translation of Pausanias' *Description of Greece* (London, 1898), vol. 4; and G. Dumézil, *Archaic Roman Religion,* trans. P. Krapp (Chicago, 1970), vol. 2.

60. Models of the liver of a sacrificial animal—no doubt used for teaching purposes—have been found in Boghazköi (Hittite territory) and in Piacenza (Etruscan territory). This would support the hypothesis that the Etruscans learned this particular technique of prediction from the Babylonians and taught it to the Romans.

61. See Cic., *Div.* 2.50, and Pease's note in his edition.

62. The answer, Cicero implied, is that they know only too well that the ritual is all a fraud.

63. See *The World Almanac Book of the Strange* (New York, 1977), p. 402.

64. The egg could also be broken over water, and the shape that it formed would then be interpreted.

65. The *Shorter Oxford Dictionary of the English Language* (Oxford, 1975) adds: "or the pretended appearance of spirits therein."

66. To *scry* is apparently a shortened form of to *descry,* i.e., "to discover by observation."

67. Dodds, *The Ancient Concept of Progress,* pp. 186ff.

68. F. W. H. Myers, *Human Personality and Its Survival of Bodily Death* (London, 1906), 1:237, quoted in Dodds, *The Ancient Concept of Progress,* pp. 186ff. In ancient times, young boys and girls were used, and their success rate seems to have been rather high.

69. Bouché-Leclerq, *Histoire de la divination dans l'antiquité,* 1:185ff., 339–40.

70. Dodds, *The Ancient Concept of Progress,* p. 188.

71. M. P. Nilsson, *Greek Piety,* trans. H. J. Rose (New York, 1969), pp. 146ff.

On modern methods, see T. Besterman, *Crystal Gazing* (London, 1924); J. Melville, *Crystal Gazing and Clairvoyance* (Wellingsborough, 1970).

72. The term *gastromancy* is ambiguous, for it may also refer to ventriloquism.

73. See E. W. Lane, *An Account of the Manners and Customs of the Modern Egyptians,* 3 vols. (London, 1846), quoted in Hull, *Hellenistic Magic,* pp. 21–22.

74. Dodds, *The Ancient Concept of Progress,* p. 186, n. 2.

75. For more information on scrying, see ibid., pp. 186ff.; there Dodds tells the story of a conjurer who used a device in order to fake a vision.

76. See W. Barrett and T. Besterman, *The Divining Rod* (New Hyde Park, N.Y., 1968). Minerals, ores, oil, and water have been located by this method. It does not always seem to work, but its success, on the whole, is undisputed; the phenomenon itself remains unexplained.

77. Dodds, *The Ancient Concept of Progress,* pp. 193–94, tells the story as described by Marcellinus and others.

78. See Wünsch, *Antikes Zaubergerät.*

Texts

77

Heraclitus, the "obscure philosopher," lived around 500 B.C., a time when the Delphic oracle already enjoyed its full prestige and prosperity. In this statement he tries to define the "obscurity" of the oracle, which must have perplexed those who wanted clear-cut answers to their questions or explicit guidance in difficult situations. It has often been suspected that the oracles' ambiguity was deliberate: because several possibilities could be read into a prediction, the god would be right, no matter what happened.

Heraclitus prefers a different explanation. He distinguishes between two different ways of communicating (besides not communicating at all), "to speak out" and "to signify." The first way is the one we use in everyday conversation; the second is that of the poets, but also of some philosophers, notably Heraclitus himself. The relatively few fragments that are preserved from Heraclitus' works suggest that he modeled his style on that of the Delphic oracle, always saying too little rather than too much. Perhaps this has been the guiding principle of all great diviners throughout the ages; Nostradamus' predictions, published in the sixteenth century and still not fully understood today, are a good example of this cryptic style.

Heraclitus, quoted by Plutarch in *The Oracles of the Pythia*, 21, p. 404d

I think you know what Heraclitus said: "The Lord to whom the Delphic oracle belongs does not speak nor does he hide: he signifies."

78

The excerpt from Xenophon's *Memorabilia* (*Recollections of Socrates*) could be discussed under "Daemonology" as well as under "Divination." It is an attempt, after Socrates' execution, to absolve him from the charge of having "introduced strange gods." Such a charge was indeed serious, for the gods might punish a whole community for the sacrilege committed by one person. Xenophon testifies that his teacher honored all the gods an Athenian was expected to honor, but that he also believed in a "spiritual force" that was, in a way, his own private oracle. It gave him "clues"; like the Delphic oracle, it did not spell things out. Apparently Socrates always knew what this inner voice meant, but when he was asked to give advice to his friends, he did not always want to take full responsibility for it, and so he would send them to one of the established oracles.

In speaking of his teacher, Xenophon also discusses divination in general. Socrates, like most Greeks of his time, including such eminently sensible men as Xenophon himself, firmly believed in divination, not only as a possibility but as a practical necessity. The methods used (augury, prophetic voices, secret tokens, sacrifices) did not matter so much, although Socrates clearly preferred his own method. Divination worked because the gods (or, ultimately, human nature) made it work.

According to Socrates, in order to be successful in life, man needs all the expertise in his field that he can acquire, but he also needs some kind of knowledge of the future. Without this knowledge, he cannot prosper. It is curious that Socrates, who is so often labeled a rationalist, believed so firmly in the influence of irrational forces in our lives.

Xenophon, *Memorabilia,* or *Recollections of Socrates,* 1.1.1–9

I have often wondered by what arguments Socrates' prosecutors were able to persuade the Athenians that he deserved to die, according to [the laws of] the city. The indictment against him said in effect: "Socrates is guilty of rejecting the gods that the city worships and of introducing new deities of a different kind; he is also guilty of corrupting the youth."

First of all, what proof did they offer for his rejecting the gods that the city worshiped? He could often be seen performing sacrifices both at home and at the public altars of the city; he never practiced divination in secret. It was common knowledge that Socrates claimed to be guided by a "spiritual force" [*daimonion*], and this was probably the main reason for the charge that he was introducing new deities. But what he introduced was in no way more unusual than the beliefs of other people in divination by augury, prophetic voices, secret tokens, and sacrifices. For they do not believe that the birds or the people they meet by coincidence actually know something that might help the person who needs an oracle; [they believe] that the gods give us clues through them, and this is what Socrates believed, too. Only, while most people say that they have been dissuaded or encouraged by the birds or those they met by chance, Socrates said exactly what he meant: he said that the "spiritual force" gave him clues. Many of his companions were advised by him to do this and not to do that, just as the "spiritual force" guided him. Those who followed his advice were successful, those who did not, had cause for regret. And yet who would not admit that he did not want to appear as a simpleton or an impostor to his friends? But that is what they would have thought of him, if he had made predictions as if inspired by the god, and then he would have been unmasked as a liar. Obviously, Socrates would not have given this advice if he had not been confident that what he said would come true. And who else could have given him that confidence but a god? And since he had confidence in the gods, how could he possibly not believe in them?

Another way he had of dealing with close friends was this: the things that had to be done he told them to do as best they could. But if the outcome of something was doubtful, he sent his friends to the oracle to find out whether or not this ought to be done. Those who wanted to take good care of their household or of the state, he said, needed divination in addition [to their expertise]. For the carpenter's craft or that of the smith or the farmer or the ruler of men or the knowledge of dialectics or logic or economics or tactics—all these subjects he thought could be acquired by the human mind, but the most important part of these sciences had been reserved by the gods to themselves, and it was not accessible to men. You may plant a field well, but you do not know who will reap the harvest; you may build a house well, but you do not know who will live in it; you may be a good commander, but you do not know whether you will be successful in your command; you may be a good politician, but you do not know whether your politics will be good for the state; you may marry a beautiful woman, but you do not know whether she will bring you grief; you may gain powerful connections in the state through your marriage, but you do not know whether you will be exiled because of them. If any man thinks that none of these pursuits is controlled by a divine force and that all of them depend on human reason, he must be mad [in the Greek text here there is a play on the words of *daimonion* 'divine force' and *daimonan* 'to be possessed']. But it would also be mad to seek by divination something that men are allowed by the gods to learn by using their reason, to ask, for example: Is it better to hire an experienced coachman to drive my carriage or one who has no experience? Is it better to hire an experienced sailor to steer my ship or one who has no experience? This applies to everything that can be determined by counting, measuring, or weighing. To put such questions to the gods he considered an act of impiety. He said that we must learn what the gods have allowed us to achieve by learning, and that we must try to find out from them through divination what we, as human beings, cannot know for certain; the gods will give a clue to those whom they favor.

79

The questions people asked the oracle at Dodona were written on thin lead tablets and apparently stored in the archives of the sanctuary. Many of them have been excavated and published. The responses of the oracle seem to have perished. As this selection (mostly from the third century B.C.) clearly shows, some questions were rather trivial in nature.

Dodona, an oracle of Zeus, was situated in the mountains of Epirus in northwestern Greece. We know that it had been established in remote antiquity, for Homer writes of it (*Il.* 16.233–35; *Od.* 14.327–28, 19.296–97). A gigantic oak, the tree of Zeus, formed the center of the cult, and the rustling of its leaves was thought to reveal the will of the god. Zeus was worshiped at Dodona as Zeus Naios, and his consort was not Hera but Dione—actually a feminine form of Zeus, although Homer knows her as one of Zeus' many mistresses. The priests were called *Selloi* and are described by Homer as "those who do not wash their feet and sleep on the ground" (*Il.* 16.234–35); the priestesses were called "the Old Ladies" or "the Pigeons." These designations seem to document the long history of the sanctuary, for washing one's feet and sleeping on beds were relatively modern customs, and the name "Pigeons" reminded visitors of the ancient cult legend according to which a pigeon flying from Thebes in Egypt had lighted on the oak tree and, speaking with a human voice, ordered the institution of the oracle.

The questions asked represent various concerns and worries of individuals and communities. It is difficult for the modern-day reader, reading the query in line 793, to understand why a city-state like the Mondaiatai would send a special delegation to Dodona just to find out whether a loan to a certain lady would be a safe investment or not. The city fathers probably let a number of similar requests pile up and sent them to the oracle in a batch, and from such a batch only this tablet has survived.

The man Heracleidas, in line 1160, must have been married before, but in his previous marriage(s) he had remained childless. His new wife is not yet pregnant, and he is getting impatient. The man in 1163 whose wife is pregnant worries whether he is the father or not. It is difficult to see how the oracle would answer such a question. Surely the priests were aware of the tragedy they would cause by confirming the husband's suspicions. An ambiguous answer in the true "oracular" style would not have helped, either.

The query in 1165 concerns another business venture. It seems to involve a switch from one type of farming to another or, possibly, the expansion of a farm operation. On the reverse side of the tablet we read a note that was obviously added by the priest in charge or his clerk; it consists of (1) a brief rubric; (2) the abbreviated name of the petitioner; (3) a number. Since the name is abbreviated almost beyond recognition, we may assume that everyone was given a number and that the combination of rubric and name was meant to exclude any possible error.

Questions Asked at Dodona
(Dittenberger, *Sylloge*[2] 793; *Sylloge*[3] 1160–61, 1163–65)

793. The state of the Mondaiatai consults Zeus Naios and Dione about the money requested by Themisto, whether she can afford it and whether it is all right to lend it.

1160. Heraclides asks Zeus and Dione for good fortune and wants to know from the god about a child, if he will have one from his wife Aegle, the one he has now.

1161. Nicocrateia would like to know to what god she ought to offer sacrifice in order to get well and feel better and make her illness go away.

1163. Lysanius wants to know from Zeus Naios and Dione whether the child Annyla is expecting is his or not.

1164. Is it more profitable for me and of much greater advantage to buy the house in the city and the piece of land?

1165. Cleotas asks Zeus and Dione whether it is profitable and to his advantage to raise cattle. [On the reverse:] About cattle. K<LE><OYTAS>. No. 5.

80

This inscription from the late first century B.C. records a decree of the Senate of the city-state of Anaphe, but it also includes the question that one citizen, Timotheus, submitted to an oracle, as well as the oracle's response.

Timotheus must have been a wealthy man. He was willing to build, for his city, a temple to Aphrodite. Such a gift, seemingly spontaneous, was often a form of taxation, but it also lent a certain amount of prestige to the donor. Officially, this oracle had to be consulted about the whole project and about the specific location of the temple. There is no need for Timotheus to describe the location—the god will know. In the end, the god approves the project and states his preference for one location over the other; he also gives further instructions, which ultimately lead to this record.

On this inscription, see now Eran Lupu, *Greek Sacred Laws: A Collection of New Documents* (Leiden, 2004), 36–37.

Timotheus Wants to Build a Temple
(Dittenberger, *Sylloge³* 977, 25–36 = *IG* XII 3, 248)

Timotheus asked the god whether it would be advantageous and appropriate for him to ask the city to build a temple of Aphrodite in the place he has in mind, in the precinct of Apollo of Asgelata, and let it be public property, or [build] it in the sanctuary of Asclepius, in the place he has in mind.

The god answered that he should ask [the city to have it built] in the precinct of Apollo and, after the completion of the temple, have the decree, the oracle, and the request inscribed on a stone slab. The Senate made a decision on these matters and granted him his request, provided the Assembly would approve of it, too.

81

This fragmentary inscription in three pieces was found on a hill near the Pergamene Gulf on the site of the ancient city of Demetrias. According to epigraphers who have studied it, it dates from the first century B.C.

The text of the inscription shows that even minor cities (not well known in history) could have an oracle of their own. In this instance the oracle of Apollo of Corope is called an ancient institution, which in this context probably means not more than "pre-Hellenistic." In the first century B.C. the great oracles were declining, and an effort was begun in Demetrias to reorganize the whole procedure of oracular consultation and to establish stricter rules. It is clear from the inscription that the secular authorities of the city, including the chief of police, were responsible for parts of the operation. Presumably they had neglected their duties in previous years, and the implication is that complaints had been made against them. But the visitors themselves had not always behaved properly either: they had not always worn their best garments, or they had been drunk and disorderly. Some of them may even have tried to bribe the officials in order to get preferential treatment. The strict rules prescribed represent an effort at reform, an attempt to restore the oracle to its former prestige. About the method of divination employed at the oracle the text says nothing.

On this inscription, see now Eran Lupu, *Greek Sacred Laws*, 10-11.

Procedure at an Oracle
(Dittenberger, *Sylloge*³ 1157, 1–69 = *IG* IX 2, 1109)

During the priesthood of Crino, son of Parmenio, on the tenth of the month of Areius. Proposal of Crino, son of Parmenio of Homole, priest of Zeus Acraeus, of Dionysiodorus, son of Euphraeus of Aeole, prefect of Magnesia, of the commanders Aetolius, son of Demetrius of Pagasae, Cleogenes, son of Amyntas of Halae, Menes, son of Hippias of Eole and of the magistrates Menelaus, son of Philippus of Iolcus, Aenias, son of Nicasibulus, and Alexander, son of Meniscus of Spalautra, and Menander, son of Nicias of Corope:

Whereas our city devoutly worships all gods, especially Apollo of Corope, and honors him with the most signal honors because of the blessings it has received from the god who gives, through his oracle, clear instructions, both in general and individually, concerning health and welfare;

and whereas it is right and appropriate, since the oracle is ancient and has been held in high esteem by our forefathers, and since many foreigners visit the seat of the oracle, that the city should take very careful measures for the proper maintenance of the oracle;

the Council and the People have decreed that whenever an oracular consultation has been completed, the priest of Apollo appointed by the city who happens to be in charge at the time, and one representative of the commanders, the guardians of the law, one delegate from both ruling bodies and one from the prytanies, the treasurer and the secretary of the god, and the speaker [for the god] must attend.

If any one of those mentioned above is sick or out of town, he must send someone else. The commanders and the guardians of the law must enroll staff-bearers from among the citizens, namely, three men under thirty who shall have the authority to punish unruly elements. The staff-bearers shall be paid from the collected contributions an allowance for two days, a drachma a day. If one of the enrolled [staff-bearers] fails to show up, he shall pay a fine of fifty drachmas to the city, after the commanders and the guardians of the law have established his culpability. When those mentioned above are present at the oracle and perform the sacrifice according to tradition, with a favorable result, the secretary of the god shall collect, immediately after the sacrifice, the petitions of those who wish to consult the oracle, write all their names on a white tablet, exhibit the white tablet at once in front of the temple, and lead them in, calling them up according to the order of their names, unless someone may have the privilege of being called ahead of the others. If the person called up is not present, the secretary shall lead in the following one, until the one called up [before] happens to arrive.

In the sanctuary, the persons entered on the lists shall sit properly, in shining [i.e., festive] garments, crowned with laurel wreaths, clean and sober, and they shall receive the tablets from those who deliver the oracle. When the consultation has been completed, they shall deposit the tablets into a vessel and seal it with the seal of the commanders and the guardians of the law and also with that of the priest, and they shall let it remain in the sanctuary. At dawn the secretary of the god shall bring in the vessel, show the seals to those mentioned before, open them, read from the list the names in their order, and give back to each one the tablet . . . [with] the oracles . . .

The staff-bearers shall take precautions about maintaining order. In the Assembly of the people, in the month of Aphrodision, before everything else, the examiners shall, in the presence of the people, administer to all persons mentioned before the following oath: "I swear by Zeus of Acra and by Apollo of Corope and by Artemis of Iolcus and by all the other gods and goddesses that I have performed all my duties as specified in the decree which was authorized concerning the oracle in the year of the priesthood of Crino, son of Parmenio."

After they have sworn this they shall be released from their responsibility. If anyone does not take this oath, the examiners and any one of the citizens who wishes [to shall be] free to bring a complaint against him on the grounds of every single offense [that he may have committed]. If the examiners do not take any of the actions mentioned before, they will be responsible to their successors in office and to anyone else who wishes [to bring a charge against them]. To make sure that this decree is enforced forever, the ten annually chosen commanders and the guardians of the law shall hand over this decree to the officials who will be elected in the future. Furthermore, a copy of the decree shall be inscribed on a stone slab at the expense of the "Wall Builders" [officials responsible for repairs to the city walls] and is to be set up in the sanctuary of Apollo of Corope.

82

Cicero's treatise *On Divination* is essentially an attack on the Stoic doctrine of divination as it was presented by Posidonius. In this passage, Cicero deals with oracles. He argues that oracles flourished only as long as people were naïve and credulous; as soon as the skepticism of the New Academy (i.e., the nondogmatic Platonists with whom Cicero had studied in Athens) had undermined the Stoic position, the oracles began to decline.

Cicero quotes two famous responses of the Delphic oracle. One had been given to Croesus, the last king of Lydia (sixth century B.C.); the other, to Pyrrhus, the last strong king of Epirus (fourth-third century B.C.). In both cases, an ambitious king was planning to attack a foreign power—Croesus, the Persians; Pyrrhus, the Romans. In both cases the god of Delphi was consulted. And in both cases the answer given was ambiguous: Croesus was defeated and thus destroyed his own kingdom; Pyrrhus, although "able" to defeat the Romans, achieved only a "Pyrrhic victory" and had to retire to Greece with about one-third of his army and without the strength needed to strike once more.

Even though the oracle had the last word, Cicero argues that it was misleading in both cases and did not keep its part of the bargain. The truth of the matter is that the oracle was a paid consultant who did not always give the best advice to clients.

Cicero also questions whether the oracular responses are historical. Had not, perhaps, Herodotus made up one, Ennius the other? The second response, not preserved in Greek, sounds especially suspicious: we have only this poetic version in Latin, yet at that time the oracle no longer went to the trouble of putting its responses in verse, and certainly not in Latin verse.

That the prestige of the oracles had declined in Cicero's time is well attested, and the philosophers came up with various explanations. The Stoic theory that Cicero quotes appears in a slightly modified form in Lucan [no. 90] and also in Plutarch [no. 92]. The historical or economic reasons are difficult to assess, but there seem to have been three major ones: (1) in the first centuries of our era there was a tendency to move away from the great religious centers, to find a more personal relationship with the deity, a relationship that needed no elaborate apparatus; (2) Greece, like Judea, was incorporated into the Roman Empire, and the Romans did not do a great deal to support the famous old sanctuaries; (3) the countries occupied by the Roman legions were soon impoverished, for, due to the Roman tax system, any wealth that might have gone to Delphi or Dodona went to Rome instead.

Cicero, On Divination 2.115–16

A famous oracle was given to the wealthiest ruler of Asia Minor:

When Croesus crosses the Halys, he will destroy a mighty empire.

He thought that he was going to destroy his powerful enemy; [in fact] he lost his own. No matter which of the two events happened, the oracle would have been right. But why should I believe that this oracle was ever given to Croesus? Why should I believe that Herodotus is more reliable than Ennius? Was Herodotus less likely to make up something about Croesus than Ennius about Pyrrhus? For who ever believed that the oracle of Apollo made the following response to Pyrrhus?

> I tell you, descendant of Aeacus, that you are able to conquer the Romans.

First of all, Apollo never answered in Latin. Second, the Greeks never heard of this particular oracle. Moreover, in the time of Pyrrhus, Apollo no longer spoke in verse.

But the main point is this. Why are oracles of this kind [text and sense uncertain] no longer issued at Delphi, not only in our own time, but for some time [text uncertain], so that the oracle has fallen into total neglect [sense uncertain]? When the Stoics are pressed by this argument, they answer that over a long period of time the power of the place from which the breath came—the breath that moved the mind of the Pythia to produce oracles—had become weak. It is as if they were speaking of things like wine or sauces that lose their taste due to age. We are dealing with the power of a place that is not only a natural but actually a divine power. But how can it become weak? "Through age," you may say. But what kind of age is this that can weaken a divine power? And what can be so divine as a breath coming from the earth, moving the mind (of the Pythia) to such a degree that she not only knows future events long before they happen but also expresses them in metrical form? When did this power disappear? Perhaps after people became less gullible?

83

In his treatise *On Divination,* Cicero deals with various aspects of Stoic doctrine as presented by Chrysippus (c. 280–207 B.C.), who defended it vigorously against the doubts of the skeptics (2.130). Cicero is also familiar with Posidonius (c. 135–50 B.C.), who, it seems, had collected a substantial body of evidence to support his thesis that divination worked. But the Stoics, as Cicero shows (1.82), also used purely logical arguments. If, as the Stoics maintained, the gods are omniscient, all-powerful, and concerned for the welfare of mankind, it follows that they know what the future will bring and are willing to share their knowledge with us because it may help us.

In another excerpt (1.72) Cicero distinguishes between "natural" and "technical" divination. Interpreting one's own dream is an instance of natural divination, but various other techniques of predicting the future have to be learned.

Divination as a science may be based on statistics (1.109–10). Cicero uses the words "frequency of records," but that is what we mean by "statistics"; such statistics were probably kept over centuries by the Babylonians and Egyptians, but no doubt also by the Greeks and Romans. The augurs, for instance, might note the behavior of birds at a certain moment and tie their observations to striking events that followed soon afterward. Even respectable historians like Livy listed unusual phenomena that were reported during a given year and worried the people, but he leaves it up to the reader to match these "warnings" with actual events. In a sense, this method is scientific, and it does not require the intervention of a god or a daemon, though practitioners may claim that it was a god who originally revealed these secrets to mankind. An ancient legend may serve as an example: Tages, a divine being who looked like a child, was unearthed by a farmer in a field near Tarquinia and there revealed the secrets of the "Etruscan discipline" of divination to a committee of twelve Etruscans.

In the last excerpt (2.33) Cicero reluctantly admits the validity of the Stoic concept that the universe is a living organism and that all its parts are connected by "cosmic sympathy," but he rejects the practical application of these principles. A haruspex looks at the liver of a freshly slaughtered sheep and tells a person where to dig to find a buried treasure. How does the universe enter into all this?

Cicero, On Divination, excerpts from Books 1 and 2

2.130. Chrysippus defines divination as "the power to see, to understand, to interpret the signs that are given to men by the gods."

1.82. That divination really works is shown by the following Stoic argument: "If the gods exist but do not reveal to men the future, either they do not love men, or they do not know what will happen, or they think that men have no interest in knowing the future, or they consider it beneath their majesty to warn men about the future, or even the gods are unable to warn us of what lies ahead. But they certainly love us, for they mean well and are friendly to mankind; they certainly know what they themselves have planned and established; it is definitely in our interest to know what will happen, for knowing it will make us more careful; it is entirely consistent with their majesty, for nothing is more important [to them] than to do good deeds; and of course they are able to predict the future."

1.72. Everything that is interpreted by guesses or observed and recorded in specific events belongs to the kind of divination, as I have said above, that is called "technical," not "natural." The *haruspices* [interpreters of internal organs of sacrificial animals, prodigies, lightning], the *coniectores* [soothsayers], and the *augures* [bird watchers] belong to this [category]. This sort of thing is rejected by the Peripatetics but is defended by the Stoics.

1.109–10. Could there be a relatively easy science of technical predictions, but a more hidden one of divine predictions? For events that are foreshadowed in internal organs, in lightning, and in the stars [are interpreted] by a science based on long observation, and a long tradition adds in every subject, through accumulated observations, an incredible amount of knowledge. This kind of knowledge is possible, even without any influence, any impulse from the gods, because statistics [literally, "the frequency of records"] indicate what happens as a result of something else and what it means.

The other type of divination is "natural" and must be, as I have said before, and, as the greatest philosophers thought, theologically speaking, seen in relation to the gods, for we have breathed in, we have imbibed our souls from the gods. Since the universe is filled to the brim with an everlasting sense, with a mind that is divine, it follows logically that the spirits of men are directed by the contact with divine souls.

1.118. The Stoics do not believe that a god is actually present in the dividing lines of livers or in the sounds that birds make, for this is unsuitable for gods, unworthy of them, and simply cannot be imagined. They believe that from the beginning the world was designed in such a way that certain events would follow certain signs—signs in internal organs, in birds, in lightning, in portents, in stars, in dream visions, in the utterances of madmen. Those who really understand these things do not often go wrong; bad guesses and bad interpretations are wrong not because the facts mislead them but because the interpreters are incompetent.

2.33. What relationship do these things [i.e., the entrails from which the seers predict the future] have to the nature [of the universe]? Let us admit that it is held together by one common feeling and that it forms a unit—I see that this is the opinion of the physicists and especially of those who think that the whole universe is one—but what connection is there between the world and the discovery of a treasure?

84

Cicero's treatise *On Divination* is not systematic; he returns to the same questions in different parts of the work.

The argument he makes in 2.41 is directed against the Stoic doctrine that the gods care for us and therefore want us to know the future [see *no. 83*]. Cicero (or his skeptic source) turns this around and says that there can be no knowledge of the future; hence there are no gods. Whether Cicero himself was an agnostic or a freethinker is a different matter; here he simply wants to show that the Stoic argument does not prove what it is supposed to prove.

Another argument the Stoics were fond of using is the concept of a universal consensus of mankind (2.81)—namely, all nations worship gods; therefore, all nations practice divination. Cicero reduces this argument ad absurdum by saying (1) that the Stoics themselves ignore the universal consensus when it does not serve their cause, and (2) that nothing is as universal as stupidity.

Cicero makes another point by asking these questions: Why should the gods give us any clues concerning the future, and, conceding that they actually give them, why are they usually so vague? The gods are supposed to help us because they love us. Why, then, do they make things needlessly difficult for us? Warning us of a disaster is not an act of kindness unless they also tell us how to avoid it. Cicero also mentions catastrophes that occur without warning, noting that, post factum, a seer could always claim that he had foretold them.

Finally, he reports a few typical *omina* or *portenta* that to the average Roman could be interpreted only as signs of impending disaster. Here Cicero argues from a strictly philosophical point of view, and it is interesting to see that, for him, philosophy (or science) begins with Thales of Miletus (sixth century B.C.). Science (or philosophy), Thales contended, ought to liberate the human mind from irrational fears and superstitions by showing that everything has a natural cause and that there is no need to invoke supernatural powers. To understand the natural causes does not mean to control them, however, and in a sense, mankind is just as helpless as before science enlightened it.

Cicero, *On Divination*, excerpts from Book 2

2.41. The Stoics actually argue when they are particularly eager [to make their point]: "If there are gods, there is divination; the gods exist; therefore, there is divination." It would make much more sense to say: "There is no divination; therefore, there are no gods."

2.81. [The defender of divination objects:] But all kings, peoples, nations, make use of auspices. [Cicero retorts:] As if anything were as universal as the fact that people are stupid! As if you yourself would agree with the majority whenever you form a judgment! How many are there who deny that pleasure is a good? Most people even call it the highest good. Do their numbers shake the Stoics in their conviction? Or do the masses bow before the Stoics' authority in most matters?

2.54–55. What is this premonition sent by the gods, this so-called warning of impending disasters? What do the immortal gods have in mind when they give us clues that we cannot understand without interpreters and—this is my second point—against which we are defenseless anyway? No decent human being would do that: predict to a friend an imminent disaster from which there is no way of escape. Physicians often realized the truth, but they never tell the patient that he will die of a certain illness. For the prediction of misfortune is accepted [only] when advice on how to avoid it is joined to the prediction. In what way did portents or their interpreters help the Spartans in the past or, more recently, the Romans? If they are to be considered signs of the gods, why are they so obscure? If the gods really wanted us to know the future, they should have stated it clearly; if they did not want us to know it, they should not even have hinted at it.

[*Prodigies and portents have no hidden significance; they can always be explained by natural causes.*]

2.58. It was reported to the Senate that bloody rain fell, that the river Atratus was flowing with blood, that the statues of the gods had been sweating. Do you think that Thales or Anaxagoras or any other scientist would have believed these reports? There is no blood, no sweat, except from a living body.

2.60. Or does it frighten you when some monstrous birth from a beast or a human being is described? To make it short: all these phenomena have a natural explanation. Whatever is born, no matter what it may be like, must have its origin from nature; therefore, even if it turns out to be abnormal, it cannot exist outside of nature. So by all means investigate the cause of a strange phenomenon, if you can; if you cannot find any, you may take it for granted that nothing could have happened without a cause, and whatever terror [reading *terrorem* with Lambinus for *errorem*] the strangeness of the phenomenon may have given you, the principles of science will drive it away.

85

Cicero here reports the doctrine of "natural divination" as formulated by Posidonius who believed that the air around us is full of invisible souls or spirits. Some of them are on the way to being incarnated, some have just left a dead body, some are absenting themselves temporarily from a sleeping person. There must be a certain intercourse, an exchange of ideas, between these mobile spirits and the gods.

It seems that Posidonius had recorded a number of case histories that, to him, proved beyond a doubt that divination was possible, and he developed this theory to explain the phenomenon. He was also convinced that the dying develop special powers of precognition or have some sort of remote control, and as an explanation he offered the theory that the soul, the divine part of the human personality, leaves the dying body and thereafter is able to use its full powers.

Many such stories were told and believed. One of the reasons why Stoicism was such a popular philosophy in the late republic and early empire was its appeal to popular beliefs and the use it made of them.

Cicero, On Divination 1.63–64

When, in sleep, the mind is separated from the companionship of the body and is not in touch with it, it remembers the past, sees the present, foresees the future. The body of the sleeper lies as if he were dead, but his mind is alert and alive. This is true to a much higher degree after death, when the mind has left the body altogether; therefore, when death approaches, the mind is much more divine [or: prophetic]. For those who are seriously, critically ill see the very approach of death; therefore, they very often have visions of the dead, and at this point they are especially anxious to be worthy of praise; but those who have not led the kind of life that one should lead regret their sins deeply. To show that the dying foresee the future, Posidonius quotes the following example. A man on Rhodes was dying and named six of his contemporaries in the order in which they were going to die. Posidonius thinks that there are three ways in which the gods cause dreams in men: first, because the mind foresees the future all by itself; second, because the air is full of immortal spirits on which the seal of truth appears as if it had been imprinted on them; third, because the gods themselves talk with those who are asleep.

86

Cicero now criticizes Posidonius' theory of dreams. Experience tells us that not all of our dreams come true; in fact, in a lifetime most dreams offer no clues about the future. To this the Stoic might reply that we seldom remember all the details of a dream, and even if we did remember most of them, we would be unable to interpret all of them properly. It is true that the serious interpreters of dreams—Artemidorus, for instance— insisted on being told all the details of a dream and claimed to know their true meaning.

Cicero dismisses this argument. If this were true, why would the gods, caring and benevolent as they are supposed to be, not spell out the meaning for us? The Stoic might answer: Not everyone has the same kind of dreams: most people have senseless, incomplete, confusing dreams, and only the wise man dreams in a clear, consistent, and meaningful manner.

Cicero's sarcasm aside, the Stoics were not totally wrong. There are dreamers and there are dreamers, and in antiquity there was even a technique that taught people how to prepare themselves for veridic dreams, through diet, exercise, prayers, meditation, and the like.

Cicero, *On Divination* 2.127–28

Well, who would be bold enough to say that all dreams are true? "Some dreams are true," says Ennius, "but not necessarily all." But what kind of distinction is this, anyway? Which does he consider true, which false? And if the true ones are sent by a god, where do the false ones come from? For if they, too, are divine, what could be more inconsistent than the god? And what is sillier than to vex the minds of men with false, deceitful visions? If true visions are divine, and false ones are human, what kind of arbitrary distinction are you proposing? Does this mean that a god makes this, nature that? Should one not rather assume that the god made everything—but this you deny—or nature made everything? But since you deny the former, one must necessarily admit the latter. "Nature" I call the entity that must always fill the mind that is based on activity and movement. When the mind cannot make use of the limbs and the senses because the body is tired, it encounters vague visions of different kinds from residual impressions, as Aristotle says, of things that it did or thought about while awake; when those get out of control, strange kinds of dreams result.

87

This scene from Seneca's *Agamemnon* only remotely resembles any part of Aeschylus' tragedy of the same title, but the story is roughly the same: Agamemnon, king of Mycenae and supreme commander of the Greeks during the Trojan War, returns in triumph to Mycenae after an absence of more than ten years. He brings with him his captive Cassandra, the most beautiful of King Priam's daughters. Apollo, who had fallen in love with her at one time, had bestowed on her the gift of prophecy, but when she disappointed him, he put a curse on her: though her visions of doom would inevitably come true, no one would believe her. This curse plagues her during her whole career as a prophetess. When her brother Paris is born, she predicts that he will some day ruin Troy, but no one wants to hear the truth; she also warns the people against the Wooden Horse, but no one listens.

During the sack of Troy, Ajax, the son of Oileus, had dragged her away from the altar of Athena, where she was seeking refuge. Later, Agamemnon claimed her as his personal property. Now that he has returned, his wife, Clytemnestra, and her lover, Aegisthus, are planning to murder him as well as his mistress, and that is what Cassandra foresees.

The chorus observes Cassandra entering into a state of trance. For the description, Seneca uses a few details from Virgil's *Aeneid* 6.77–82 and 6.98–102 (the trance of the Sibyl of Cumae). A theme that sometimes occurs in such descriptions [see also *no. 90*] is that of a prophetess who is unwilling to abandon herself to the god who is taking over and seeks to control her. This act of taking possession of the prophetess is often described in almost sexual terms, as a kind of rape. In Seneca's text, part of Cassandra's eccentric behavior is explained as her desperate struggle against the overpowering presence of the god. Also, to have vivid premonitions of disaster without being able to do anything about them was surely a painful experience. In addition, the physical shock of trance was considered traumatic and health-damaging.

With bitter irony Cassandra calls herself a "false prophet," because this is what people have always called her. Now nature seems to change around her: the sun disappears from the sky, darkness descends, there are two suns, two royal palaces of Mycenae. This double vision seems to be characteristic of trance. Then Cassandra sees the queen, ax in hand, and her victim, Agamemnon, in the shape of a lion, about to be killed. She also hears the voices of members of her family, the royal family of Troy, all dead—Priam, Hector, Troilus, Deiphobus. She sees the Furies and other monsters of the underworld, and realizes they are ready to receive new shades, including herself. Although she is doomed, the brutal, humiliating end of the Greek conqueror is a sad triumph for the conquered Trojans, and Cassandra does not fail to make this point.

Seneca, *Agamemnon*, vv. 710–78

CHORUS: Suddenly the priestess of Phoebus is silent. Her cheeks are pale, and her whole body shakes. Her fillets stiffen; her soft hair stands on end; her inner being hisses frantically with a choking sound. Her glance wanders unsteadily in different directions; her eyes seem to twist and turn inward and then again just to stare motionless. Now she lifts her head up into the air, higher than usual, and walks erect. Now she is getting ready to unseal her vocal chords against their will; now she tries to close her lips but cannot keep her words inside. Here is a priestess in ecstasy who fights against her god!

CASSANDRA: Sacred heights of Parnassus! Why do you prick me with the goads of a new kind of madness? I have lost my mind; why do you sweep me away? Leave me, Phoebus! I am no longer yours. Extinguish the flame that you have kindled deep in my breast! What good does it do if I rush around like mad? Who needs my bacchantic frenzy? Troy has fallen: What is left for me, "the false prophet," to do? Where am I? The kindly light is gone; deep darkness blinds my sight; heaven, covered with gloom, hides itself from me.

But look! There are two bright suns in the sky; there is a double Argus with two towering palaces!—I can see the groves of Ida where the fateful shepherd sits, appointed to judge between the mighty goddesses.—Kings, beware of incestuous offspring! That country boy shall overturn a royal house!—Who is that madwoman? Why does she carry a naked sword in her hand? She is dressed like a Spartan but carries the ax of the Amazons. Who is the hero she attacks? Now my eyes are focusing on another face— but whose? An African lion, the king of beasts, his neck formerly so proud, lies there, bitten by a vicious tooth, bloodied by the bite of a bold lioness.

Shades of my dear ones, why do you call me? I am the only one still alive. I shall follow you, father, I, the witness of Troy's funeral. Brother, help of the Trojans, terror of the Greeks, I see you. But I do not see you in your former splendor, your hands still hot from the burning ships! Your body is mangled, your arms bruised by heavy bonds. Troilus, you met Achilles too soon; I shall follow you. Your face, Deiphobus, is unrecognizable—a gift from your new wife.

I am glad to wade through the depth of the Stygian pool, to see the savage dog of Tartarus and the realms of gloomy Dis. Today the ferry of black Phlegethon will carry over two royal souls—one of a conqueror and one of the conquered. Shades, hear my prayer. Water by which the gods swear, hear my prayer. For a short while open the cover from the world of darkness, that the ghostly crowd of Trojans may have a look at Mycenae. Look, wretched souls: the Fates have made a full turn!

The squalid sisters are threatening us. They brandish their bloody whips; they hold half-burned torches in their left hands; their pale cheeks are bloated; black funereal robes gird their emaciated loins. The fearful noises of night come alive. The bones of a huge body, rotten and decayed long ago, lie there in a slimy swamp. Look, Old Tantalus forgets his thirst and no longer tries to drink water that eludes his lips; he is sad because someone will die very soon. But our ancestor Dardanus rejoices and walks around in regal manner.

CHORUS: Her ecstatic rambling has stopped abruptly. She has fallen on her knees in front of the altar like a bull that received a badly aimed stroke on his neck. Let us lift her up.

88

In this later scene from Seneca's *Agamemnon,* one of Cassandra's predictions [see *no. 87*] comes true: the assassination of Agamemnon. Since the playwright has already dealt with the phenomenon of trance (or ecstasy), he pays little attention to it here, but the words *madness, ecstasy,* and *vision* indicate to the audience what is going on. The sun's standing still has nothing to do with Cassandra's vision, however; the sun stops in its course because it is shocked and indignant at what it has seen.

This monologue is more rhetorical than the earlier one and less informative, but it serves an important dramatic function: the violent action does not have to be shown on stage; the audience experiences it not through a messenger's report, not "from the top of the walls" (*teichoskopia*), but literally through the walls of the royal palace, thanks to Cassandra's special gift.

Seneca, *Agamemnon,* vv. 867–908

CASSANDRA: Something momentous is happening within, something comparable with the Ten Years [of the Trojan War]. Ah, ah, what is this? Rise, my soul, and take the prize of your madness. We, the conquered Trojans, are now victorious. All is well, Troy has risen again. When you fell, father, you dragged Mycenae with you. Your conqueror turns to flight. Never before has the ecstasy of my prophetic mind given me such a clear vision. I see it, I am in the midst of it, I am enjoying it! No blurred picture deceives my sight. Let us look at it:

A banquet for many guests is being held in the royal palace, just like that last one we had at Troy. The couches are shining with Trojan purple. They drank their wine from the golden cups that once belonged to ancient Assaracus. In his embroidered robes Agamemnon himself lies on a raised couch, his body draped in the magnificent spoils of Priam. His wife is urging him to take off the garments that belonged to the enemy; she wants him to put on the robes that her faithful hands have woven.

I shudder. My soul trembles. Shall an exile kill a king, an adulterer kill the husband? Yes, the fateful day has come. The end of the banquet will see the murder of my lord. Blood will drip into the wine. The deadly robe, thrown treacherously over him, will tie him up and deliver him to his assassins: the large, impenetrable folds envelop his head and leave no way to his arms. With a shaking hand the weakling stabs at Agamemnon's side but does not manage to thrust the sword in all the way; he stops, dumfounded, in the midst of the act of wounding him. Agamemnon is like a bristling boar deep in the woods, entangled in a net and trying to escape from it, but the more he struggles, the tighter he draws his bonds, and his rage is in vain. So the king struggles to throw off the folds that move around him on all sides and rob him of his sight, and though he is enmeshed, he still seeks his assailant. But now Clytemnestra, enraged, snatches a double ax. Like a priest at the altar who marks with his eyes the oxen's neck before he strikes with his ax, the ruthless woman aims now this way, now that. He is hit! The deed is done! His head, not yet wholly severed, hangs by a slender thread; blood streams from his trunk; his lips quiver. And yet they will not leave him alone: Aegisthus still attacks the lifeless victim and keeps hacking at the corpse, and Clytemnestra helps him as he stabs. In committing this enormous crime, the two of them show who they are: after all, he is Thyestes' son, and she is Helen's sister. The sun stands still. . . .

89

From another drama ascribed to Seneca, *Heracles on Mount Oeta,* comes this brief reference to a prediction the oracles of Delphi and Dodona had made to the hero years ago. Now that he lies dying, Heracles realizes that the prediction is about to be fulfilled. He had killed the Centaur, Nessus, when he tried to rape Deianira, as he carried her through a stream. Heracles killed the Centaur with one of his poisoned arrows from the shore, but before he died, Nessus persuaded Deianira to keep some of his blood as a love potion. A few year later, when Heracles fell in love with another woman, his jealous wife smeared the drug on a garment and gave it to him. As soon as the hero put it on, the poison from his own arrow began to destroy him slowly.

The same story was dramatized by Sophocles in the *Women of Trachis,* and it has a parallel in the myth of Medea.

Heracles, as befitted his stature, consulted two of the most famous oracles of Greece about his death, and their predictions agreed. They were also enigmatic: how could Heracles, the great conqueror who had even come back from the underworld, die at the hands of a man he had already killed?

Seneca, *Heracles on Mount Oeta,* vv. 1472–78

HERACLES: Very well; it is fulfilled. My fate becomes clear: this day is my last. The oracular oak and the grove that shook the temples of Cirrha with a rumbling that came from Parnassus once predicted this destiny to me: "Heracles! You, the conqueror, will fall some day by the hand of a man you have killed. This is the end destined to you after you have traveled all over the earth, the seas, and through the realm of the shades."

90

In his *Pharsalia,* an unfinished epic on the civil war between Caesar and Pompey, Lucan describes a consultation of the Delphic oracle by a distinguished Roman, Appius, who wishes to know the outcome of the war. This consultation is supposed to have taken place in 49 or 48 B.C., shortly before Caesar's decisive victory at Pharsalus. The scene has a counterpart in a later book of the epic, in which one of Pompey's sons, immediately before the battle, approaches a famous Thessalian witch, Erictho, and asks her the same question [*no. 61*]. The poet's interest in various methods of divination is evident. He addresses himself to a question that was much debated at the time: why the prestige of the great oracles had declined. At the same time, he reintroduces an old theme: Odysseus had conjured up the dead in Book 11 of the *Odyssey,* and Aeneas had descended into the underworld in Book 6 of the *Aeneid;* the aim of both had been to learn of future events.

First, Lucan attempts to explore the secret behind the Delphic oracle. As a Stoic, he believes in a divine power that manifests itself in different forms in different parts of the universe. An earlier age had called this power "Apollo." Lucan does not reject the ancient myth, but he offers a more "modern" explanation. He assumes that there is a divine power above and a divine power beneath the earth and that they are the same power.

Lucan acknowledges that the Delphic oracle had declined for political reasons. The Roman emperors (and already the Senate during the late republic) had done their best to undermine the authority of the oracle. Any non-Roman methods of predicting the future had, in principle, become suspect because of the power they gave to the practitioner or the institution involved. This is one of the reasons why astrologers (along with philosophers!) were periodically expelled from Italy. But the very fear of this power shows how firmly rooted the belief in divination was. On this question Lucan probably reflected the views of his uncle, Seneca, who had had a good deal of political experience and knew one emperor, Nero, from close association.

According to Lucan, the Delphic priestesses were not unhappy when fewer and fewer visitors came, because they knew that their health was overtaxed by their duties; to produce one genuine trance after another was hard work. In this instance, the Pythia, who had been recruited in a great hurry and almost at random, it seems, because the priests were not prepared for the visit of such an illustrious Roman, tries to fake an ecstasy but does not get away with it. By telling us what she did not do, Lucan lists the characteristics of a real trance: inarticulate cries that fill the temple, quivering sounds, whispers, hair standing on end, and, as a sort of subterranean accompaniment, a small earthquake that is felt in the temple. (How this last effect was produced we do not know.) If any of these signs were not in evidence, the visitor, feeling cheated, would insist on the real thing.

Scared into submission, the young woman in Lucan's story goes into a real trance, her very first. The god takes over, fills her with his presence, and literally drives her mad, for a while at least. Apollo "rapes" her and rides her and remains in total control.

The poet makes an effort to understand the nature of the Pythia's vision, and he approaches the problem in terms of the Stoic concept of time. Somehow, in this one moment, the whole past and the whole future of mankind are concentrated, for they are part of a colossal scheme that transcends the human mind. The Pythia is allowed to pick from her grandiose vision only one detail—one that is important to the visitor. Her ecstasy then reaches a new climax and she collapses.

Following this, Lucan inserts a brief diatribe. Why do the gods not reveal such essential information to mankind more willingly? It is the same argument that Cicero used in his treatise *On Divination*. Have the gods not yet decided who is to win the war?

Or do they have an ulterior plan: let Caesar win now in Thessaly, but have him assassinated dramatically four years later in the Senate?

Then there is another description of the visible aspects of trance: rolling eyes, constantly changing expression, flushed face, sighing and moaning.

When the Pythia returns to her normal state of consciousness, she has forgotten everything she saw.

Lucan, *Pharsalia* 5.86–224

Which one of the gods is hidden here? What divine power, exiled from heaven, agrees to live here, locked up in dark caves? What heavenly god supports the weight of the earth, holding all the secrets of the eternal course of events, sharing with the sky knowledge of the future, willing to manifest himself to the nations, suffering the contact of men? He must be great and powerful, no matter whether he merely predicts fate or if everything he proclaims becomes fate. Perhaps a large portion of the main god is embedded in the earth and rules it, supporting the globe that is suspended in empty space, and it may be this part that comes out of the cave of Delphi and can be breathed in, though it belongs to Jupiter in heaven. When this divine power has been received in the heart of the virgin [the priestess], it strikes the human soul of the prophetess with a sound and opens her lips, as the top of Mount Etna in Sicily boils over from the pressure of the flames and as Typhoeus, trembling under the timeless mass of Inarime where he lies, breathes smoke out of the rocks of Campania.

Such a divine power is, however, accessible to everybody and does not refuse itself to anyone: it only keeps itself from human passions. Here no evil prayers are whispered quietly. The god sings of predetermined events that cannot be changed and leaves no room for human desires. To the just he is kind, and he has often given a new country to the emigrants of entire cities, as to the Tyrians, or he showed people a way to remove the threats of war, as the sea near Salamis remembers; he softened the wrath of the earth by showing how to end its sterility; he also cleaned up pestilential air. The Delphic oracle fell silent when rulers became afraid of the future and stopped the gods from speaking. Our age misses this gift of the gods more than any others. But the priestesses of Delphi are not unhappy that they may no longer speak; in fact they are glad that the oracle has ceased. For if the god enters someone's heart, premature death is the penalty or the reward for having received him; the human organism is battered by the sting and the surge of that ecstasy, and the pounding of the gods shakes up the fragile souls.

Appius comes to find out the final destiny of the Western world and demands an answer from the tripods that have not moved for a long time and the large rock that has remained silent. When the chief priest was ordered to open up the sanctuary and to lead into the presence of the god a frightened prophetess, he seized Phemonoe who was strolling free of cares among the Castalian springs and the distant groves and forced her to rush through the gate of the temple. The priestess of Apollo was afraid to stop at the awesome entrance and tried—in vain—to discourage by deceit the prominent Roman from his ardent desire to know the future.

She said to him: "Roman! What wicked search for truth brings you here? The Parnassus is silent and prevents the god from speaking from the depth. Perhaps the spirit has left those caves and has traveled to the end of the world. Perhaps, when Delphi was burned by the barbarians, ashes flew into the vast underground spaces and barred the passage for Apollo. Perhaps Delphi speaks no longer by the will of the gods, and the predictions of the ancient Sibyl that have been entrusted to the Romans are sufficient to learn the future. But perhaps Apollo who never admitted evildoers to his temples has not, in our time, found anyone who deserves to hear him."

The deceit of the priestess was obvious, and her very fear revealed the fact that she refused herself to the god. A twisted fillet binds her hair in front, and a white headband with a laurel branch from Phocis holds the locks that flow down her back. She still hesitates and pauses, but the priest pushes her by force into the temple.

Afraid of entering the oracle-giving recess of the inner sanctuary, she stops near the entrance of the temple, pretends that she is possessed by the god, and utters words that she makes up, but her heart remains unmoved. No inarticulate cries or whispers indicate that divine ecstasy inspires her mind. She could do more harm this way to the oracle and to Apollo's reputation than to the important person to whom she gave a false prophecy. Her words do not rush forth with a quivering sound; her voice is unable to fill the expanse of the huge temple; her hair does not bristle and shake off the laurel wreath; the temple floor does not tremble, the trees do not move. These are all signs that she is afraid of entrusting herself to Apollo.

Appius notices that the tripods do not move and cries out in fury: "The gods whom you fake and I will punish you as you deserve, wicked woman, unless you descend at once into the cave! I have come to consult you about a world torn by a great war. Stop giving me your own words!"

Scared at last, the young woman takes refuge by the tripod. She is led into the vast chasm, and there she remains, and now her soul, which has never had this experience before, draws in the divine power that the spirit of the rock, still active after so many centuries, conveys to her. At last Apollo takes over the soul of the Delphic priestess. Never before has he forced his way so fully into the body of a prophetess, driving out her normal consciousness and taking the place of everything that is human in her heart.

Frantically, out of her mind, she runs through the sanctuary. Her neck no longer belongs to her; her bristling hair shakes off the fillets and garlands of Apollo as she whirls, tossing her head, through the empty space of the temple, and as she runs she kicks over the tripods that are in her way. She boils over with a tremendous fire, because she is full of your wrath, Apollo! You do not only use your whip on her and inject fire into her vitals as you goad her; she also feels your curb, and as a prophetess she may not reveal as much as she is allowed to know. All time concentrates in one complex; all the centuries descend on her heart—poor woman!—and the great chain of events lies open; the whole future struggles to come into the light; destinies fight destinies to be expressed in her voice. She sees everything; the first day and the last day of the world, the dimensions of the Ocean, the sum of the sands!

As the Sibyl of Cumae in her cave on Euboea resents the fact that her trance should be of service to many nations and out of this great heap of destinies picks haughtily only the ones affecting Rome, thus Phemonoe, possessed by Phoebus, is troubled and has to search for a long time before she finds the fate of Appius—the man who has come to consult the god who is hidden in the land of Castalia—concealed among the fates of more important men. When she finds it, madness and ecstasy begin to flow in earnest from her foaming lips. She moans and utters loud, inarticulate cries. Then her wailing rises in the huge temple. Finally, when she is totally overpowered, she shouts these words: "Roman, you will not take part in this crucial battle. You will escape the horrible dangers of war. You alone will dwell in peace in a broad hollow on the coast of Euboea."

Apollo closes her throat and cuts short any further words.

Oracles! Guardians of destinies! Secrets of the universe! Apollo, master of truth! The [other] gods have not hidden a single day in the future from you. Why are you afraid to reveal the final act in the tragedy of a great nation, the massacre of captains, the death of kings, and the destruction of so many other countries dragged along by the bloodbath, the catastrophe of Rome? Have the gods not yet decided to perpetrate this horrible crime? Are the stars still hesitant to sentence Pompey to death? Are the fates of thousands still held in suspense? Or are you silent so that you can permit Fortune to wield the avenging sword, punish mad ambition, and have a tyrant undergo once more the punishment at the hands of a Brutus?

The priestess throws herself against the temple doors. They open from the impact and she rushes out, driven from the sanctuary. But her frenzy continues, and the god, who has not left her body, is still in control. After all, she has not told the whole truth. Her eyes roll wildly, and her glance roams over the whole sky. The expressions on her face change constantly: now she looks frightened, now fierce and menacing. A fiery flush spreads over her features and colors her pale cheeks, but her pallor does not seem to indicate fear; rather it inspires it. Her heart is overtired but cannot relax; voiceless sighs that sound like the moaning of a turbulent sea after the north wind has ceased to blow still heave her breast.

As she returns to the ordinary light of day from the sacred light that has showed her the future, she is enveloped by darkness. Apollo sends Lethe from Styx into her innermost being to wash away the secrets of the gods. The truth flees from her heart. Knowledge of the future returns to Apollo's tripod. She falls to the ground, barely recovered.

91

In chapter 14 of his First Letter to the Corinthians, Paul of Tarsus writes of spiritual gifts. Speaking in tongues is one gift, delivering prophecies is another. The two are not the same, according to Paul, though they might seem to be closely related.

The Pythia did not always make sense when she uttered prophecies, and what she uttered had to be translated into normal Greek by the priests.

The early Christian communities were composed of Jews and Gentiles, two groups that had different cultural and religious traditions. The Jews had inherited the tradition of the Old Testament prophets, who spoke in a highly poetic but quite understandable idiom. The Greeks were accustomed to ecstatic outpourings that had to be translated into intelligible Greek by trained interpreters.

Paul seems to want to reconcile both traditions. He concedes that they are both legitimate, but he expresses a preference for the prophetic style of the Old Testament. He is rather diplomatic, but he has not much use for the ecstatic type of utterance unless it is kept under control and translated for the congregation.

It required true genius to reconcile such different traditions within a new religious group, and Paul, though he prefers one, recognizes the validity of the other. Apparently the Corinthians still liked to hear someone speak "in tongues" now and then, for the very fact that the language was unintelligible proved that it emanated from another world.

Paul, First Letter to the Corinthians 14:1–33

Seek love, but strive also after other spiritual gifts, especially prophecy. For he who speaks in tongues is talking with God, not with people, for no one understands him: he speaks mysteries in a state of inspiration. But when someone prophesies, he speaks to people and gives them spiritual strength, encouragement, and comfort. The person who speaks in tongues gives spiritual strength to himself, but the prophet gives spiritual strength to the community. I want all of you to speak in tongues, but I am even more anxious for you to prophesy. The prophet is greater than the one who speaks in tongues—unless he can interpret [himself], so that the congregation may receive spiritual strength.

Now, brothers, if I come to you speaking in tongues, what good shall I do you, unless what I say to you is revelation or knowledge or prophecy or instruction? Inanimate things produce voices, too—a flute, for instance, or a kithara—but all the same, if I do not give their sounds intervals, how can we recognize the melody on the flute or the kithara? Or again, if I blow an indistinct signal on the trumpet, who will prepare for battle? In the same way, if you speak in tongues without giving a clear message, how can anyone understand the meaning of your speech? You will be talking to the wind. It happens that there are many kinds of sound in the world—nothing is soundless—but if I do not understand the meaning of something that is said, I will be a foreigner in the eyes of the speaker, and he will be a foreigner as far as I am concerned. Since you are eager for the gifts of the Spirit, you, too, must work toward the spiritual strengthening of the congregation, in order to excel.

Therefore, the person who speaks in tongues must pray for the gift of interpretation. If I pray in ecstatic language, the spirit in me prays, but my mind is unproductive. What does this mean? I shall have to pray as the Spirit moves me, but I shall also have to pray with my mind; I shall sing hymns as the Spirit moves, but I shall also have to pray with my mind. For if you praise God in ecstatic language, how can the person who occupies the place of the "outsider" know when to say "Amen" to your prayer of thanksgiving, if he does not understand what you are saying? Your prayer of thanksgiving is fine, but the "other person" does not feel uplifted spiritually. Thank God, I speak in tongues more often than all of you, but in the congregation I would rather say five words through my mind than thousands of words in ecstatic language.

Brothers, do not become children in your minds; be childlike, as far as evil is concerned, but be mature in your minds. It is written in the Law: "Through men of foreign tongues and on the lips of foreigners will I speak to this nation, and even so they will not listen to me" [Isaiah 28:11–12; Deuteronomy 28:49], says the Lord. Hence the tongues are meant as a sign not for the believers but for the unbelievers. If the whole congregation is assembled and all are speaking in tongues and some "outsider" or unbeliever walks in, will he not say that you are insane? But if the whole congregation utters prophecies and some unbeliever or "outsider" walks in, he will feel convinced by everyone, search his soul because of everyone. The secrets of his heart are laid bare, and so he will fall on his face and worship God and announce: "Truly, God is among you!"

What does all this mean, brothers? When you get together, each of you has a hymn, has a piece of instruction, has a revelation, has a message in ecstatic language, has an interpretation. All of this must be directed toward spiritual strengthening. If it is a matter of speaking in tongues, let two speak, or at most three, and only one at a time, and one person should interpret. If no interpreter happens to be there, the [ecstatic] speaker should not address the congregation at all, but talk to himself and to God. Only two or three prophets should speak, and the rest should examine [what they say]. If someone else, being seated, has a vision, let the first speaker stop. For all of you can utter prophecies, one by one, so that the whole congregation may receive instruction and comfort. The prophetic spirit is controlled by the prophets, for God is the author of peace, not of disorder.

92

Plutarch deals with the Delphic oracle in several of his philosophical treatises and dialogues. His interest may be explained by the fact that he held a priesthood there for life, from A.D. 95. His *Pythian Dialogues* seem to be late works; the group includes *On the Ceasing of Oracles, On the E at Delphi,* and *On the Oracles of the Pythia.* In them he discusses various problems of daemonology and divination. The explanation of clairvoyance he proposes would have been acceptable to Platonists as well as Stoics; this shows what a strong influence Posidonius had on Middle Platonism. Plutarch states that every soul has the gift of clairvoyance, whether it is embodied or not, but as long as it coexists with the body, this faculty is relatively weak, though it is there nonetheless, more evident in sleep or in trance ("inspiration") than in our normal state of consciousness.

Plutarch also believes that certain forces are transmitted through the air, or in water, and that these forces somehow enter a body and produce a change in the soul. Plutarch must have spoken to informants who had actually experienced trance and who tried to describe to him what happened to them, how they felt, and so on. Not surprisingly, he has to resort to images in the end.

Plutarch, *On the Ceasing of Oracles* 39–40, pp. 431–32F

If the souls that have been separated from a body or never shared existence with one at all are daemons according to you [i.e., the Platonists] and the divine Hesiod [*Works and Days,* v. 123], "Holy dwellers on earth, guardians of mortal men," why should we deprive embodied souls of that power, that natural gift, by which daemons foresee and predict the future? It is not likely that any faculty, any dimension, is added to the souls after they leave the body, beyond those that they had before, but they have them always; they are merely weaker as long as the soul is joined to a body. Some are completely imperceptible and hidden, others weak and dim, just as ineffective and slow as people who try to see in a fog or move in water, and they need a great deal of care in restoring their proper function, a period of recovery and a cleansing to remove that which hides it. The sun does not become bright the moment it bursts through the clouds; it is always bright, but to us it appears somber and dim when we see it through mist. In the same way the soul does not acquire the power to prophesy when it has left the body—as if it were emerging from a cloud—but it has that power right now, though it is blinded by its association and cohesion with the mortal element. We should not be in awe or skeptical; all we need to do is look at the faculty of the soul that is the reverse of prophecy, the one called "memory": what an achievement it shows by keeping and preserving the past, or rather the present! Nothing that is past has any kind of existence or reality, but as soon as it happens, it is gone, all of it—actions, words, and experiences—for, like a stream, time bears everything away. But this faculty of the soul [i.e., memory] somehow gets hold of things that are not real and invests them with shape and substance. An oracle given to the Thessalians concerning Arne told them to mind "the hearing of the deaf and the sight of the blind." For us, memory is the hearing of things that cannot speak and the sight of things that are invisible. Therefore, as I have said, it is not astonishing that something that no longer exists can also anticipate many things that have not happened so far. The future fits the soul even more closely and feels the same way: it reaches out toward that which will happen and leaves behind what is in the past, is finished, only remembering it.

It may be that, through heat and expansion [i.e., expansion through heat], certain pores open up and visualize the future, just as the fumes from wine set things in motion and reveal things that are put away and forgotten:

> the ecstasy of Bacchus
> and the state of madness have great prophetic powers,

according to Euripides. Whenever the soul warms up and becomes fiery, it rejects the diligence mandated by mortal reasoning, which often disregards and downgrades enthusiasm. [*Another image follows a little later: ecstasy is like a hot steel knife dipped into water.*]

Therefore, all souls have this power [of prophecy]; it is innate, though dim and hardly real, and yet it often fully blossoms and radiates in dreams and sometimes in the hour of death, when the body becomes purified or acquires a disposition suitable for that purpose, a disposition through which the reasoning faculty, the ability to think, is relaxed and released from the present and can turn [reading *epistrephomenon*] to the irrational imaginary range of the future. It is not true, as Euripides says [frag. 973 Nauck²], "the best seer is he who makes the best guess"; no, it is the intelligent man who follows the rational part of his soul, the part that leads the way by making reasonable guesses. The prophetic gift is like a writing tablet without writing, both irrational and indeterminate in itself, but capable of images, impressions [reading *kai pathesi*], and presentiments, and it paradoxically grasps the future when the future seems as remote as possible from the present. This remoteness is brought about by a condition, a disposition, of the body that is affected by a change known as "divine inspiration."

Often the body all by itself attains this condition, and the earth sends up to human beings the sources of many faculties other than this, some of which produce trance, illness, even death, but others that are helpful, pleasant, and beneficial, as can be seen from the accounts of those who have experienced them. But the flow, the spirit of prophecy is the most divine, the most sacred, whether it spreads all by itself through the air or together with running water, for when it enters the body, it produces in the soul a strange, unusual disposition. It is difficult to describe its character accurately, but a number of analogies offer themselves.

93

Once more, Plutarch asserts the universal value of divination. It is a natural activity of the human soul, and one should not be surprised that it exists. Even the term *foretelling* is misleading; one should simply use the word *telling.*

The distinction he makes between an event that happens after having been foretold, and the foretelling of an event that will happen, is hard to grasp, and it looks like one of the subtleties of Stoic logic that Cicero struggled with in his treatise *On Fate.* It also seems strange that Plutarch calls certain predictions "lies," even though they are confirmed by events. Perhaps what he is saying is this: in the "ocean of time"—that is, during a period of millions of years—all predictions that have ever been made will come true. This may be similar to the modern paradox according to which a million monkeys working at a million typewriters during a million years will eventually produce the works of Shakespeare. But for Plutarch, it seems, the prediction of an event in the very distant future is not a valid prediction. To be useful in human terms, it has to be fulfilled within a reasonably short time.

Plutarch, *On the Oracles of the Pythia* 10, pp. 398–99

Boethus answered: "What kind of event can there be that is not a debt owed by time to nature? Is there anything so strange, so unexpected, on land, on sea, in cities, among men, that it cannot be predicted before it actually happens? And this can hardly even be called 'foretelling,' just 'telling,' or even better: throwing away and scattering words that have no basis into infinite space. Occasionally chance meets them as they wander around and, of its own accord, coincides with them. There is a real difference, I think, between an event that happens after having been told, and the telling of an event that will happen. For an account concerning things that do not [yet] exist contains in itself an element of error, and it is not fair [to have] to wait for a confirmation that comes by accident, nor should one use as compelling proof of having foretold the event with [accurate] knowledge the fact that the event happened after having been foretold; infinity brings everything around. No, the 'good guesser' whom the proverb recommends as the 'best seer' [Eur., frag. 973 Nauck²] is more like a man who looks for clues on the ground and explores the future by means of reasonable forecasts. Prophets of the type of the Sibyl or Bacis have tossed and scattered their predictions at random into the ocean of time—words and phrases referring to experiences and events of all kinds— and although some of them actually come true as a result of chance, what is told now is nevertheless a lie, even if it turns out to be true, should the event happen."

94

The strange appearance of the Pythia and the eerie sound of her voice clearly showed how ancient an institution the oracle was. She did not wear fashionable robes, nor was she perfumed, nor did she sing melodiously like a popular music hall entertainer of the period. In some shrines, aromatic and psychoactive essences were burned. At the oracle of Patras, for example, the priestess prayed and burned incense and then gazed into a mirror in a well. It is likely that the incense in combination with a shiny surface (a form of catoptromancy) helped induce trance. But in Delphi, according to Plutarch, the priestess used only laurel leaves and barley groats, the ingredients also used in magical operations [see no. 6]. This seems doubtful. Plutarch may have preferred not to divulge the type of "entheogen" that was added to the laurel leaves and the barley groats— unless these were of a special kind or treated in a special way. If this is true, the priests at Delphi—like their colleagues at Eleusis—must have guarded the secret very diligently. In any case, prophesying was a harsh, demanding duty for the medium.

Plutarch, On the Oracles of the Pythia 6, pp. 396–97

Sarapion said: "Yes, Boethus, we are sick, as far as our ears and eyes are concerned, for as a result of our soft, luxurious life-style we are accustomed to considering that which is [merely] pleasant as [truly] beautiful and to saying so. Before long we shall criticize the Pythia because she does not chant as melodiously as Glauce, who sings to the kithara, and because she does not wear perfume and purple robes when she descends into the inner shrine, and because she does not burn on the altar cassia or ladanum or frankincense, but only laurel leaves and barley groats. Do you not feel the charm of Sappho's songs," he continued, "—how they soothe and bewitch those who listen to them? But the Sibyl, 'with her ecstatic mouth,' as Heraclitus says, even though her words are unsmiling, unadorned, unperfumed, yet she reaches through the space of a thousand years through the god."

95

Again Plutarch attempts to show, by means of logic rather than empirically, that divination works. This kind of argument often sounds more plausible in Greek than in any translation. Here, as elsewhere, Plutarch operates with the categories of time: past, present, future. He believes in a chain of causes and effects that stretches from the beginnings of time to infinity. What the Pythia sees in one glance, the rational mind—if not the individual, at least the collective mind—ought to discover in due time. Hence the need for statistics as a basis for predictions.

Plutarch, *On the E at Delphi* 6, p. 387 B/C

The god is a prophet, and the art of prophecy concerns the future as it results from the present and the past. There is nothing that comes into being without a cause, nothing that could not reasonably be predicted. Since the present follows the past and the future follows the present very closely, according to a constant process that leads from the beginning to the end, he who understands the natural connections and interrelations of the causes with one another can also declare [Hom., *Il.* 1.70] "the present, the future, and the past." Homer was right to place the present first, then the future, and then the past, for the syllogism based on a hypothetical proposition has as its base that which is; for instance, "if this is, then this [other thing] has preceded it" or "if this is, then this [other thing] will be." The technical and rational part of this, as has been said, is the understanding of the consequence, and the argument derives its premises from sense perception. So, even if it is not much of a statement to make, I shall not hesitate to make it: the tripod of truth is the argument that establishes the relationship between a later and an earlier event and then, taking the existence [of something] as a premise, brings the syllogism to its conclusion.

96

One of Apollonius' famous predictions concerned A.D. 69, the year during which Rome saw three successive emperors (Galba, Otho, and Vitellius), each of whom was in power for only a short time. Apollonius' admiring biographer, Philostratus, tries to defend him from any suspicion of witchcraft. He argues that Apollonius did not claim to be able to change the course of fate by means of magic. Like Apuleius, who also was accused of practicing magic, Apollonius claimed to be a philosopher, a scientist who simply interpreted certain signs that were there for all to see.

Philostratus, *Life of Apollonius of Tyana* 5.12

I have given sufficient proof that Apollonius' foreknowledge of these events was due to supernatural inspiration, and that it would not be reasonable to consider him a magician, but let me add some further arguments. Magicians—and in my opinion they are the most wretched of men—claim to be able to change the course of destiny either by torment-ing daemons or by using weird rites, charms, or plasters. Many of those who have been brought to justice have admitted that this was their kind of expertise. Apollonius, on the other hand, accepted the decrees of destiny and predicted only that they must, by necessity, take their course; but his clairvoyance was divine revelation, not magic. When he saw, in India, the "tripods" and the "wine pourers" and all the other automata I have mentioned, he did not want to know how they worked: he admired them but did not wish to make anything like it.

97

Artemidorus lived in the second century A.D., mostly in Daldis, Lydia, but he traveled widely in order to collect interpretations of dreams and books on dreams. In addition to his treatise *The Art of Judging Dreams,* he wrote works on augury and palmistry.

In the dedication of his book on dreams he tells us that he learned a great deal from talking to professional dream interpreters in many cities. Although they were despised by most respectable citizens, these men had some valuable information to give. We learn, incidentally, that in any ancient city one could expect to find such dream interpreters in the mar-ketplace; perhaps they had their booths there, like the fortune-tellers of our age. They also traveled around to festivals, hoping to find more cus-tomers among the large crowds that these events attracted. Artemidorus does not put himself in the same class as these practitioners, but he re-spects their experience and their knowledge of human nature. He sounds like a man who is passionately interested in his subject but who also wishes to be of help to his fellow man.

At the beginning of his work, Artemidorus establishes a fundamental distinction between "theorematic" and "allegorical" dreams. The former are self-evident, so to speak: they foreshadow an event more or less cor-rectly. The latter need interpretation.

Artemidorus emphasizes how important it is to remember a dream from beginning to end. More often than not, the interpreter will be tempted to analyze an incomplete dream sequence, but when he does that, he only deceives his client and ultimately hurts his own reputation.

Artemidorus then interprets a few dreams, not in any systematic order, it seems, but perhaps to cite examples of those he considers typical. Many of the dreams seem strange to us; many are about incest, sexual perversions, violence. Perhaps only an interpreter who belonged to the same culture could make sense of them.

From the examples that Artemidorus gives (1.2), we see that then, as now, people were "programmed," as it were, by certain experiences, and later—sometimes much later—translated their hopes and fears into dreams by means of these experiences, creating thereby a vocabulary for their own dream language.

The dream about being back in school (1.53) does not have a happy meaning, because most people's school years seem to be unhappy and frustrating.

Dramatic performances had an immediate emotional impact on ancient audiences and a delayed impact in dreams. Since drama was a representation of human experience compressed within a few hours, it served as a symbolic language for emotions that could not be conveyed in any other way.

In 1.78 Artemidorus has something to say about sexual dreams. It seems that people in antiquity often dreamed of sexual intercourse of one kind or another. According to Suetonius' *Life of Julius Caesar* (ch. 7), Caesar dreamed that he slept with his mother, and though he was disturbed by this, the interpreters assured him that he would rule the world, for one's mother is a symbol of the earth.

What Artemidorus writes helps us to understand ancient civilization. Husbands were supposed to have control over their wives and expected obedience from them. To be seen entering or leaving a brothel was slightly embarrassing but not a disgrace. The various interpretations of the brothel as symbol are very curious.

As far as the "Oedipus dream" is concerned (1.79), Artemidorus fully agrees with the interpreters of Caesar's dream almost two centuries earlier.

Crucifixion was widely used in the Greek world as a means of execution, not just in the days of the Roman emperors. To dream of death on the cross is not necessarily bad, Artemidorus points out (2.53), and he advises consideration of the particular person's circumstances.

In the preface to Book 4 he offers some general advice. He is convinced that people who lead healthy, normal, decent lives will not be troubled by strange, disturbing dreams. To that extent we have control over our dreams. Dream interpreters, because of their peculiar profession, tend to have dreams that are quite different from those of the average person.

According to Artemidorus, six criteria ought to be applied to any dream: is it in accordance with nature, with law, with custom, with art, with the person's name, and with time? The distinction between "nature" and "law" seems to correspond roughly to the one between "unwritten" and "written" law, while "custom" somehow belongs to both areas. "Art" means the profession of the dreamer, whose "name" also plays a certain role in the interpretation. "Time" apparently designates the period in the dreamer's life; it is not normal, for instance, for middle-aged men to dream that they are going to school again.

In 4.3 Artemidorus briefly deals with magical practices. He compares magic to blackmail, which, in a sense, it is. To try to blackmail a god into doing us a favor would be as absurd as putting pressure on some influential person. On the other hand, to pray for a dream is not magic, and to thank the gods for a favor is simply good manners.

Once more—in 4.59—Artemidorus emphasizes the need for full information about the dreamer and his dream. He rejects astrology as a supporting science. Essentially, the dream itself tells the story.

Artemidorus, *Oneirocritica*, or *On the Art of Judging Dreams*, excerpts from Books 1–4

Book 1, dedication

There is no book on the interpretation of dreams that I have not acquired, making this my main ambition. The seers of the marketplace are generally despised, and the respectable-looking citizens, raising their eyebrows, call them charlatans, impostors, clowns [or: parasites]. I paid no attention to this slander but associated with them for many years, in the cities of Greece, at the great festivals, in Asia Minor, in Italy, on the major and more densely populated islands, and I was willing to listen to ancient dreams and the events that followed them; for there is no other way to master this discipline.

Book 1, ch. 2

Some dreams are theorematic, some allegorical. Theorematic are those whose fulfillment resembles the vision they offer. A traveler dreamed that he was shipwrecked, and this is what happened. As soon as sleep left him, the ship was sucked down and wrecked, and he, with a few others, saved his life with difficulty. Another man dreamed that he was wounded by a man with whom he had agreed to go hunting the next day. As they left together, he was wounded on the shoulder, just as it had happened in the dream. Someone dreamed that he received money from a friend; the next morning he accepted ten minas from the friend and kept them as a deposit. There are many other examples of this kind.

Allegorical dreams, on the other hand, signify something through something else; in these dreams the soul, according to certain laws of nature, hints at something in the manner of a riddle.

I believe that I must declare, as far as it is possible, the cause that produces and shapes these dreams and give the true explanation of their name.

First, I propose a general definition of the dream that needs no further explanation, unless I am talking to people who love to quarrel. The dream is a motion or production of the soul that has many forms and indicates good or bad things in the future.

Book 1, ch. 12

Let me tell you that dreams that are not remembered completely cannot be interpreted, no matter whether the dreamer has forgotten the middle or the end. For if you want to make sense of a dream [text uncertain] you must explore the point to which the vision leads: only what is remembered from beginning to end can be interpreted.

Just as the seers who offer a sacrifice do not call ambiguous signs untrue—they say only that they do not understand the signs that accompany their sacrifice—thus the interpreter of dreams must not give his opinion or improvise a response concerning things he cannot fully comprehend, for he will lose his prestige, and the dreamer will get hurt.

Book 1, ch. 53

Learning to read and write [in a dream], not having learned it before, predicts something good for the dreamer, but it will be preceded by pain and fear, for students are afraid and suffer pain, even though they learn for their own good. If someone who has already learned to read and write learns it again, this must mean something painful and strange, for one gets elementary education in childhood. Therefore, this indicates incompetence as well as fear and pain. Such a dream promises something good only to him who wants a child, for then not he himself but the child that will be born to him will learn to read and write.

If a Roman learns Greek or a Greek learns Latin, it means that the former will associate with Greeks, the latter with Romans. Having had this kind of dream, many Romans married Greek women or Greeks married Roman women. I know a man who dreamed that he was learning Latin: he was condemned to slavery; it never happens that a slave is taught Greek.

Book 1, ch. 56

To perform in a tragedy or have tragic roles or masks or listen to tragic actors or recite iambic lines: if one remembers the words, the events will be according to the context; if one does not remember them, there will be wretchedness, slavery, battles, violence, dangers, and even things more terrible and cruel than those; for the tragedies are full of them.

To perform in a comedy or listen to comic actors or have comic masks or roles: if they represent Old Comedy, they indicate ribald jokes and verbal fights; if they represent New Comedy, they anticipate the same things as tragedy but promise a satisfactory, happy ending; for such are the plots of comic pieces.

Book 1, ch. 76

To dance in a theater with a made-up face [or: wearing a mask] and the rest of the traditional costume means success and praise; for a poor man it means riches, but they will not last until he is old, for on the stage the actor represents a royal personage and has many servants, but when the play is over, he is left alone.

Book 1, ch. 78

In the chapter on sexual intercourse the best division might be the following: (a) intercourse that is both lawful and natural; (b) unlawful intercourse; (c) unnatural intercourse.

First, concerning lawful intercourse, I have this to say. If you make love with your own wife, and she is willing and agreeable and does not offer any resistance, this is fine for everyone; for one's wife means either one's craft or one's profession—an area from which we derive pleasure, over which we command and have control, as we have over a wife. The dream therefore indicates the profit from such things. People enjoy sex, but they also enjoy profit. If the wife resists and does not surrender her body, it means the opposite. The same interpretation applies to one's mistress.

To have intercourse with prostitutes who are established in brothels indicates a moderate embarrassment and a small expense. For to approach such women means both embarrassment and expense. This dream is favorable to all kinds of enterprises, for these women are called "professionals" by some; they are most accommodating and never say no. It would also seem to be a good sign to enter a brothel and be able to leave it; not being able to get out is bad. I knew someone who dreamed that he went into a brothel and could not leave it; a few days later he was dead. What happened to him corresponded to the dream, for a brothel, like a cemetery, is called a "public place": the cemetery receives the dead, and in the brothel there is a great waste of human sperm. So it makes sense that the brothel would be assimilated to death.

Book 1, ch. 79 (the Oedipus dream)

The chapter on the mother has many different aspects, parts, and sub-divisions unnoticed by many interpreters of dreams so far. It is like this. Sexual intercourse in itself is not sufficient to show the meaning, but the different kinds of embraces and positions of the bodies predict different events. First of all we must talk about the position "body to body," when the mother is still alive, for it does not mean the same thing if she is dead. If someone had intercourse [in a dream] with his mother, "body to body"—in the position which some call "natural"—and she is still alive, and his father is in good health, it means that his father will hate him, because of the jealousy that exists among men in general. If the father is in poor health, he will die [soon], for the son who has the dream will be in charge of his mother both as her son and as [if he were] her husband. It is a propitious dream for any craftsman and artisan, for it is customary to call one's trade one's "mother," and to have intercourse with one's mother could not possibly mean anything else but to work full time and to make a living from one's trade. It is also a good dream for political leaders and politicians, for the mother symbolizes the fatherland. Just as he who has intercourse "according to the rule of Aphrodite" [i.e., in the normal position] has control over the whole body of the woman if she is willing and consents, thus the dreamer will control the politics of his country.

Book 1, ch. 80

To have intercourse with a god or a goddess or to be penetrated by a god means death for one who is ill, for the soul, at this point, when it is about to leave the body in which it dwells, foresees that it will meet and associate with the gods; for the others [i.e., those who are not ill], if they enjoy the experience, it means help from those above; if not, fear and trouble.

Book 2, ch. 53 (dreams about different kinds of death)

To be crucified is good for all seafarers, for the cross is made of beams and nails, just like a ship, and the mast of a ship looks like a cross. It is good for a poor man, for the victim of crucifixion is high up and feeds many birds. It brings hidden things into the open, for the crucified person is plainly visible. It is bad for the rich, for those who are crucified are naked, and their flesh wastes away. . . . To be crucified in a city means [to hold] an office in that city, corresponding to the place of the cross.

Book 2, ch. 55

To descend into Hades and see all the things down there—the things that people believe to be there—means loss of work and loss of income to those who are prosperous and successful, for the inhabitants of Hades are inactive, cold, without motion. For those who are in fear, sorrow, or grief, it means deliverance from cares and worries, for the inhabitants of Hades do not worry and are free from cares. For the others, it means travels—or at any rate it drives them away from the place where they live. Not only did the ancients say of one who went on a long trip that he "went to Hades"—the story itself shows that the inhabitants of Hades are not all in the same place as before.

Book 3, ch. 56

Dreaming of a chef in your house is a good sign if you want to get married; you need a chef for a wedding. It is a good sign for the poor as well, for only people who have plenty of food hire cooks. For those who are ill, it predicts irritations and inflammations and a general imbalance in the body juices, which can lead to acidity, according to the experts in these matters. But it also predicts tears, because of the smoke the chef produces. It also brings hidden things and things that were done in secret into the open, for the creations of the chef are brought out into the open and served to the guests and they appear as what they are [i.e., they are as good as they look].

Book 4, preface

Remember that those who lead a good and useful life never have any ordinary dreams or any absurd fantasies but always dream visions and mostly theorematic ones. For their soul is not, at the surface, troubled by fear or hope, and they are in control of the pleasures of the body. In short, a good person never has an ordinary dream or an absurd fantasy. Do not deceive yourself: the average person and the competent interpreter of dreams do not have the same dreams, for the average person dreams of the same things that he desires or fears [during the day], but those who know, the experts in these matters, signify only the sort of things they want. If someone who is not an expert has a dream, that dream should be interpreted as an ordinary one, not as a dream vision [text uncertain]. Let us assume that someone who is competent in these matters—either because he has consulted books on the interpretation of dreams, or because he has associated with interpreters of dreams, or because he has a natural talent in this direction—is in love with a woman: he will dream not of the beloved one but of a horse or a mirror or a ship or the sea or a female animal or a feminine garment or anything else that signifies a woman. If he is getting ready for a trip, he will not dream of carriages or ships or traveling bags or baggage piled up or any other traveling equipment: he will dream of flying or of an earthquake, of a war, of lightning or any other possible symbols for traveling. If he is afraid of someone or wants to run away from him, he will not see that person [in his dream], but he will flee from a wild animal, break bonds, kill criminals, offer a sacrifice to the gods—in short: he will dream of things that other people do in order to free themselves of fear and trouble. That painter in Corinth who often wanted to kill his master happened to dream that the roof of the house in which he lived collapsed and that he himself was decapitated; nevertheless, his master survived and is still alive today. But since he was able to judge such matters, his soul deluded him in a rather sophisticated way; because to any other person, these dreams would have predicted the death of the master.

To make this less confusing for you, let me tell you that many people— in fact, most people, practically everybody—have only ordinary dreams; there are altogether very few, in fact only the interpreters of dreams, who have the other kind of dreams, the one I just mentioned.

Book 4, ch. 1

It is a general principle that all dreams that are in accordance with nature or law or custom or art or name or time mean something good, and that all dreams contrary to those [six points] are bad and unprofitable. But remember that this theory is not absolute and universal; it only works most of the time. For many dreams have a good outcome, though they go against the reality of everyday life and are not in accordance with nature or those other points. For example, someone dreamed that he was beating his mother. This is certainly a crime, and yet it brought him success, for he happened to be a potter; we call the earth "mother," and the potter works with the earth that he beats. So he worked with great success.

Book 4, ch. 2

The dreams people have when they worry about some business or other, or when they are moved by some irrational urge or desire, you may consider "worrying dreams." We also call them "asked-for dreams," because one asks a god to send a dream concerning some business at hand. But remember: when you ask for a dream, do not burn any incense, and do not say unspeakable names. In short, do not demand anything from the gods that involves magic practices. It would be ridiculous for gods to obey those who demand something with threats, for men of influence refuse the petitions of those who threaten and blackmail them, but grant favors to those who approach them politely. After having had the dream you should sacrifice and give thanks. Those who impose laws on the gods, you should not take seriously; they say, for example: "Should I do this?" or "Will this be granted to me?" or "May I now see the fruit of Demeter? Or, if not, that of Dionysus?" or "If this is good for me and profitable, may I have it? If not, should I give it?" There is a fundamental error in all of this. . . . You must pray to the god about the things that worry you, but the way in which you phrase your request beforehand you must leave to the god or to your soul.

Book 4, ch. 59

You should also first find out about the way of life of the person [who consults you]; I mean, you should inform yourself carefully. And if you cannot get any reliable information from the dreamer, postpone your advice for the moment and ask someone else, lest you make a mistake. . . . Stay away from those who think that dreams must be interpreted according to the horoscope of the dreamer, the good ones as well as the bad ones. They say that the beneficent planets, when they are unable to do something good for you, at least make you feel good in your dreams, and that the maleficent planets, when they are unable to hurt you, at least disturb and frighten you in your dreams. If this were true, no dream would ever be realized; but in fact the good ones and the bad ones are realized, each according to its meaning.

98

As a starting point for his discussion of trance, Iamblichus uses the profound changes that can be observed in the personality of the "medium." The body no longer has the sensations, the reflexes, that it has in a normal state of consciousness. If the body is not subjected to its usual limitations and affections (e.g., feeling pain), then the mind, Iamblichus argues, also must reach a new level. He notes that no trance is exactly like another, and although his explanation is purely speculative, the observation itself may well be valid. Among other things, he mentions levitation and the manifestation of fire. At the same time, he seems to feel that not every "medium" is able to experience the fullness of the vision or share it with others.

Iamblichus, *On the Mysteries of Egypt* 3.4–6

You state that there are many who grasp the future by means of divine possession and divine inspiration and that they are awake as far as their ability to act and their sense perceptions are concerned, but not really conscious or not as conscious as before. I also want to show, in this context, the characteristics of those who are truly possessed by the gods. For if they submit their whole life as a vehicle, as a tool, to the gods who inspire them, they either exchange their human life for a divine life or else they adjust their life to the god and do not act according to their own sense perceptions, nor are they awake like those whose senses are completely awake. They do not perceive the future by themselves, nor do they move like those who act on an impulse. They are not conscious in the way they were before, nor do they concentrate their native intelligence on themselves or manifest any special knowledge.

And here is important proof: many [of those who are in trance] do not get burned, even if they are also close to a fire, for because of the divine inspiration fire does not touch them. When they are actually burned, many do not react, because at this moment they do not live the life of a [normal] creature. Some are pierced by daggers and do not feel [the pain]; others have their backs cut open with hatchets; still others are wounded with knives about their arms and are totally unaware of it. Whatever they do is out of the human sphere. The inaccessible becomes accessible to those who are divinely inspired: they jump into fire and walk through fire; they cross over streams like the priestess in Castaballa. All this goes to show that in their state of divine possession they are no longer in their normal state of consciousness and that they no longer lead the normal life of a person, of a creature, as far as sense perception and volition are concerned. They exchange these for another, more divine kind of life that inspires and possesses them completely.

There are many different kinds of divine trance, and divine inspiration operates in many different ways. It manifests itself through a number of different signs. For one thing, the various gods from whom we receive inspiration produce different kinds of inspiration. For another, the particular kind of divine possession, as it changes, also modifies the nature of the divine inspiration. For either the god takes possession of us, or we become totally part of the god, or else we coordinate our activity with his own. At times we participate in the lowest power of the god, at other times in his intermediate power, and then again in his highest power. Sometimes it is simple participation, sometimes a sharing, sometimes a combination of these types. Either the soul alone enjoys it, or it shares it with the body, or it is the whole person who enjoys it.

As a result, the outward signs of divine possession are manifold as well: movement of the body or of some of its parts, or total lack of any kind of movement; harmonious tunes, dances, melodious voices, or the opposites of these. Bodies have been seen to rise up or grow larger or float in the air, and the opposites of these phenomena also have been observed.

The voice [of the person in trance] seemed to be completely even in volume and in the intervals between sound and silence, and then again there was unevenness. In other instances the sounds swelled and diminished, but occasionally something else happened.

But most importantly, the medium who draws down a divine being sees the spirit descending, sees how great it is, what it is like, and is able to persuade and control it in mysterious ways. The medium sees the shape of the fire before receiving it. Sometimes the fire becomes visible to all who are watching, either as the god descends or as he ascends. Therefore, those who know are able to grasp the real truth, the real power, the real order, that he represents, and they understand in what respect he is qualified to communicate the truth and grant power or maintain it. Those who draw down the spirits without these wonderful experiences are stumbling in the dark, so to speak, and do not know what they are doing, except for certain quite unimportant signs on the body of the person possessed and other trivial manifestations; the full reality of divine inspiration remains hidden to them, and they are without knowledge.

99

Like Plutarch and others before him, Iamblichus attempts to explain how oracles function. He singles out three famous ones: Clarus, near Colophon; Didyma (Branchidae), near Miletus; and Delphi. All of them were oracles of Apollo. A prophetess transmitted the message from the god at Delphi and Didyma, whereas at Clarus a male priest presided. At Clarus, water from a sacred spring underneath the temple played a role, which Iamblichus tries to elucidate. According to him, water only induces a certain disposition in the priest; the real illumination must still come from above. Other rituals have to be observed by the priest-prophet, and they also help to prepare him, but they do not, by themselves, produce the vision.

Similarly, the firelike substance that the Pythia inhales serves only as a preparation. The god is not in that substance; he has to come from somewhere else. The ritual at Didyma is different, but it, too, is a kind of prelude—necessary, it would seem, but not the inspiration itself.

Perhaps all these practices were reproduced elsewhere faithfully, but unsuccessfully, by certain theurgists. Hence Iamblichus comes to the conclusion that oracular prophecy is impossible without the divine presence. In fact, he argues, whatever natural conditions there are have to be created by the god at one time, and the god inspires the ritual that surrounds them. Everything thus comes from the god; he is the ultimate source of prophecy.

Iamblichus, *On the Mysteries of Egypt* 3.11

This phenomenon, therefore, is a kind of possession, and it happens in this way. There is another kind of divination, well known and very impressive. It has many components and is inspired by a god. It is the oracle.

You have this to say concerning it: "There are some who drink water, like the priest of Apollo Clarus at Colophon. Others are sitting near the mouth of a cave, like the priestesses who prophesy at Delphi. Others inhale steam, like the prophetesses of the Branchidae." You mention these three famous oracles, not because they were the only ones (for there were many more that you did not mention), but because they were more important than the others and because you were able to point out the problem with sufficient clarity. I am thinking of the way in which divination is sent by the gods to mankind. For these reasons you were satisfied with those examples. So I, too, shall discuss only these three, omitting the vast majority of oracles.

First, the oracle at Colophon. Everyone agrees that water is used to prophesy. They say that there is a spring in a subterranean structure and that the priest on certain prescribed nights drinks from it after many preliminary ceremonies have been performed. After having drunk he begins to prophesy; but he remains invisible to the visitors present. This shows clearly that the water must be prophetic, but in what way it is prophetic is not, according to the proverb, "for everyone to know." It would appear that a kind of prophetic spirit comes through it, but this is actually not true. For the divine does not spread itself in such a partitioned and disjointed way among its partakers but, offering itself from the outside, it illuminates the spring, filling it with its own prophetic power. And yet not the whole inspiration that the god offers comes from the water; [the water] only produces an aptitude and a purification of the luminous spirit in us through which we become capable of receiving the god.

Another presence of the god precedes this one and shines from on high. This one is not far from anyone who, by his affinity, is in touch with it. It comes all of a sudden and uses the prophet as an instrument. He is no longer himself and has no idea of what he says or where he is. As a result, even after having delivered the prophecy, he recovers with difficulty. Before drinking from the water he has fasted for a whole day and a whole night and, going into trance, has withdrawn all by himself into a part of the sanctuary inaccessible to the crowd. By keeping aloof and distant from human preoccupations, he renders himself pure and ready to receive the god. Therefore, he possesses the inspiration of the god that shines into the pure sanctuary of his soul; the inspiration can take possession without hindrance, and the perfect presence finds no obstacle.

The prophetess at Delphi gives oracles to people through a thin, fire-like spirit that rises from somewhere through a crevice, or she makes predictions sitting in the sanctuary on a bronze tripod or on a four-footed stool that is sacred to the god. In any case she gives herself entirely to a divine spirit, and she shines with a ray from the divine fire. An intense, concentrated fire comes up through the crevice and surrounds her on all sides, filling her with divine radiance. When she takes her place on the seat of the god, she adapts and conforms herself to his firm divinatory power. As a result of both preliminaries she becomes completely the possession of the god. He then appears to her and illuminates her as a separate entity, because he is different from the fire, the spirit, his own seat, and from all the normal and sacred devices that are visible.

The prophetess of the Branchidae also receives the god in herself, whether she is filled with divine radiance as she holds the wand originally handed down by the god, or whether she is seated on an axle, or whether she dips her feet or the border of her garment into water, or whether she breathes in the vapor of the water; by all these [external] things she is prepared to receive the god from the outside and partakes of him.

This is also shown by the large number of sacrifices and by the ritual of the whole ceremony and by all the other acts performed religiously before the delivery of an oracle: the bathing of the prophetess, her fasting for three whole days, her stay in the inner sanctuary, and the fact that she already participates in the light and enjoys it for a long time. All this goes to show that the god is called in prayer to be present and that he comes from outside, and that a marvelous inspiration takes place even before she comes to her accustomed place. It also shows that the god in the spirit rising from the source is separate from the place and more ancient than its present use; that he is in fact the cause of this use and the source of the whole practice of divination.

100

In Porphyry's biography of Plotinus, the "psychic" gifts of the master are briefly mentioned: he identified the slave who had stolen a necklace from a lady who lived in his house; he also predicted the future of some children. When Porphyry lapsed into a state of depression (he called it "melancholy") and contemplated suicide, the master sensed it and counseled him.

It is curious to see that the last great philosopher and theologian of paganism, like the early shamans, was credited with supernatural abilities.

A man like Plotinus, whose life is reasonably well documented and whose writings—at least most of them—have survived, is not a shadowy figure like Orpheus. It would not do to dismiss him as a fraud who impressed his naïve disciples with a few occult tricks. If asked whether this was magic, he might have answered, like Apollonius of Tyana: "No, it is something philosophers know about."

Porphyry, *Life of Plotinus,* par. 61

Plotinus also had an almost supernatural knowledge of human nature. Chione, a highly respectable widow, lived with her children in his house. One day her precious necklace was stolen. The servants were assembled, and Plotinus looked each of them in the eyes. "This is the thief," he said, and pointed at one of them. The man was whipped but denied persistently at first; later he confessed, went to get the stolen object, and brought it back. Plotinus also predicted how each of the children who lived with him would turn out. He described what sort of a person Polemon was and said that he would be amorous and not live long, and this is what actually happened. Once he sensed that I, Porphyry, was planning to commit suicide. I happened to be in his house, and all of a sudden he approached me and said that my intention did not have its roots in my mind but in a certain type of gall disease [literally, "melancholy disease"], and he told me to leave the country. I took his advice and went to Sicily, to a well-known man called Probus; I had heard that he lived in Lilybaeum.

This is how I dropped my intention and why I was prevented from staying with Plotinus until his death.

IOI

Eunapius (fourth–fifth century A.D.) had studied rhetoric, philosophy, and apparently also medicine and earned his living as a "sophist"—a professional lecturer and teacher. He seems to have enjoyed a great reputation, for at one time he exercised a high priestly function, that of "hierophant," at the mystery cult of Eleusis. His *Lives of the Philosophers and Sophists* is full of curious anecdotes like this one concerning Sosipatra, a lady of great prestige who was roughly his contemporary. She represents the curious symbiosis of superior philosophical reasoning and astonishing psychic abilities. In the middle of a serious philosophical discussion she has a telepathic experience involving her lover ("cousin" is a term of endearment), Philometor.

One of her three sons, Antoninus, inherited her gifts and became a famous teacher and visionary himself. Among other things, he predicted

366

the destruction of the great temple of Serapis in Alexandria by the Christians. Antoninus died in A.D. 390, and the temple was destroyed in the following year.

That such a man abstained from theurgy is remarkable, but he may have been afraid, as Eunapius implies, of the strict laws that prohibited the practice of all forms of sorcery. He even refused to discuss theological questions in public.

Eunapius is hostile to the Christians and their cult of martyrs and relics. This, to him, looks suspiciously like witchcraft, for magicians traditionally used parts of corpses and operated with "envoys" from the gods (i.e., daemons). To worship dead bodies in the ancient temple that now served as a church was to desecrate the former pagan sanctuary; to a pagan, death was a pollution, and the presence of a corpse in a temple was unthinkable.

Eunapius, *Lives of the Philosophers and Sophists* 6.9.11–17; 6.10.6–11.1

Once all her friends met in Sosipatra's house. Philometor was not present; he stayed in the country. The problem they discussed was the soul. Several theories were suggested, but then Sosipatra began to speak, and soon her proofs disposed of the arguments that had been proposed. Then she entered into a discussion of the descent of the soul and what part of it is subject to punishment, what part immortal. In the midst of her ecstatic, enthusiastic discourse, she fell silent, as though her voice had been cut off, and after a short while she cried out to the whole group: "What is this? There is cousin Philometor, riding in a carriage! The carriage has just been overturned in a rough spot in the road, and both his legs are in danger! But his servants have dragged him out, and he is all right; his elbows and hands are hurt, but even those wounds are harmless. They are carrying him on a stretcher, moaning!" This is what she said, and it was the truth. Everyone realized that Sosipatra was omnipresent, and whenever anything happened, she was there, which is what the philosophers say about the gods.

She died leaving three sons. The names of two of them do not have to be mentioned, but [the third], Antoninus, was worthy of his parents, for he established himself at the Canobic mouth of the Nile and devoted himself completely to the religious rites as they were practiced there and did his best to live up to his mother's prediction. All the young men who were healthy in mind and thirsted for philosophy studied with him, and the temple was full of candidates for the priesthood. Although he still appeared to be human and spent his time with human beings, he predicted to all his disciples that after his death the sanctuary would no longer exist, that the great, holy temple of Serapis would become a dark, shapeless thing and be transformed into something else, and that a fantastic, hideous gloom would gain control over the most beautiful things on earth. Time confirmed all these prophecies, and the event finally gave him the authority of an oracle.

Antoninus, one of Sosipatra's sons, [as I have said before] went to Alexandria and was impressed by the mouth of the Nile at Canobus and just loved being there; and so he dedicated himself completely to the gods that are worshiped there.

Very soon he reached the affinity with the divine, despised his body, freed himself from the pleasures of the flesh, and applied himself to the wisdom that is unknown to the crowd. Perhaps I ought to say a little more about this. He showed no desire to practice theurgy or anything else that is supernatural, possibly because he was afraid of the imperial policy that was opposed to such practices. But everyone admired his discipline and his strong, inflexible character, and all the students in Alexandria used to see him on the seashore.

For Alexandria, because of the sanctuary of Serapis, was a world of religion all by itself. Those who came there from all parts of the world were equal in number to the local population. After having worshiped the god, they ran to see Antoninus, some—the ones who were in a real hurry—by land, while some were happy to use the river boats that carried them leisurely toward their studies. When they were given an interview, some would propose a scientific problem and would at once be nourished by Plato's philosophy, but those who asked about things divine would "encounter a statue": he would not say a word to any of them, but, fixing his eyes and looking up at the sky, he would sit there without speaking, and he would not give in. No one ever saw him entering easily into a discussion of these things with anyone.

Not so long afterward there was a clear sign that he had some divine element in him. Very soon after he had left the mortal sphere, the cults of Alexandria and the sanctuary of Serapis in particular were completely destroyed—not only the cults, but the buildings as well.

V

ASTROLOGY

Introduction

Astrology, one of the oldest of the occult sciences, is, in a sense, the ancestor of astronomy, but it cannot be entirely separated from it. In fact, the Latin words *astrologia* and *astronomia* both designate what is today called "astrology." Even in English, the term *astronomy* had both meanings until the beginning of the Enlightenment. The Greek word *mathesis* 'learning' can mean specifically "astrology," while *mathematikos* is not so much a "mathematician" as an "astrologer." In the ancient world, as today, astrology was based on mathematics and astronomy. The interest in astronomy and its development as a science in the modern sense can be explained in part by its practical value to the astrologer. And even though astrology may appear to be nonsensical to a modern scientist, it has been called the most "scientific" of all the occult sciences.[1]

Astrology had its beginnings in Mesopotamia, among the Chaldeans, who seem to have been a caste of Babylonian priests, though the name was originally used for the inhabitants of Kaldu in southeastern Babylonia. They probably used their astronomical knowledge to establish calendars and determine the dates of religious festivals. In later antiquity, every astrologer, whether he came from Mesopotamia or not, was called a "Chaldean."[2] Meanwhile, the Assyrians had conquered Babylonia and developed astrological techniques. Their king, Ashurbanipal, compiled an enormous archive in which astrological charts were kept on clay tablets, probably matching predictions with events, but also, it seems, establishing reliable ephemerides—that is, tables showing the computed or observed place of a heavenly body from day to day over many centuries—so that errors could be corrected. Although some lenses made of rock crystal have been found, neither the Babylonians nor the Assyrians may have had precision instruments with which to observe the stars. Perhaps the clear skies of the region made telescopes less necessary than they are today. In any event, the mathematical techniques and the methods of teamwork that were developed during this period were quite advanced.[3]

There are two main types of ancient astrology: (1) "judicial" astrology (first attested in Chaucer), which predicts from celestial or meteorological phenomena the future of the king or the country (whether there will be wars, famines, and floods, or good harvests, peace, and prosperity); and (2) horoscopic astrology, which relates to the character and fortune of an individual. The first type seems to be older than the second; for a long time astrology was apparently a privilege of kings.[4] But both types are based on the belief that the position of the planets in the zodiac determines the future of an individual and, if this individual happens to be a king, that of his country as well.

The horoscope of a child born on April 29, 263 B.C., may be quoted as an example of Babylonian astrology: "At the time [of birth] the Sun was in 13:30° Aries, the Moon in 10° Aquarius, Jupiter at the beginning of Leo, Venus with the Sun, Saturn in Cancer, Mars at the end of Cancer. . . . He will be lacking in wealth. . . . His food will not satisfy his hunger. The wealth that he has in youth will not remain [?]. For thirty-six years he will have wealth. His days will be long." (The rest of the text is obscure.)[5]

In this Babylonian nativity, the Sun is very strong in Aries, the second-best position for it, after its natural place in Leo, and so the prediction mentions longevity and health. But if a planet was in a sign opposed to its natural rulership, only evil could come; thus, in the Babylonian chart, Saturn in Cancer is unfavorable (Cancer is opposite to Capricorn, where Saturn has its home), and so loss of money and possessions, a wasting away of material things, is predicted.

From Babylonia, astrological lore traveled to the other Hellenized parts of the Middle East, especially Egypt, but also to Greece. In the early decades of the third century B.C., a Babylonian priest, Berossus, dedicated a work on Babylonian history (now lost) to King Antiochus I (324–261 B.C.), the second ruler of the Seleucid Empire, an important outpost of Greek civilization in the East. This work, which included astrological doctrine, probably made its way to Egypt, where an ambitious astrological text ascribed to "Nechepso" and "Petosiris" was composed in the second half of the second century B.C. Nechepso and Petosiris claimed to have derived their knowledge from the god Hermes, but it seems reasonable to assume that they were familiar with Babylonian sources.

The new doctrine then spread through the Greek world and was eagerly discussed by the different philosophical schools. Aristotle had already described the stars as beings with supernatural intelligence, incorporeal deities, and ascribed to them a rational sort of influence on life on earth. Most Stoic philosophers accepted astrology because of their belief in fate and their acceptance of the law of cosmic sympathy. Astrology was rejected, however, by skeptics within the later Platonic Academy (e.g., by Carneades) and outside it (e.g., by Sextus Empiricus).

Something ought also to be said about the way astrology was treated in Old Testament times. The people of Israel knew, of course, that it was a prestigious art among their neighbors, the Babylonians and the Assyrians, and there is some evidence that, at times, even in Israel, the powers of the stars were recognized, though these powers were considered subordinate to Yahweh, not independent of him. In one of the oldest surviving pieces of Hebrew literature, the Song of Deborah, written after Barak's victory over Sisera, we read (Judges 5:20): "The stars have fought from heaven above; the stars in their courses have fought against Sisera." But the Song of Deborah is intended as a hymn of thanksgiving to Yahweh.

Isaiah (or rather the "Second Isaiah," a later prophet) scorns the Chaldean astrologers (Isaiah 47:13): "Let your astrologers, your stargazers who predict your future month by month, stand up and save you." He groups these astrologers with the magicians as "advisers" of the king and the people of Babylon: they claim to be able to save their nation, but they are all doomed. This attitude seems to be more typical of the Old Testament.

In the Book of Daniel, which, according to tradition, was composed in the sixth century B.C. at the court of Babylon, Daniel is made chief of the "wise men" of Babylon, that is, the astrologers and magicians (Daniel 2:48), and yet he remains faithful to the laws of his religion (Daniel 1). Hence, it may have been thought permissible for a Jew to practice astrology under certain circumstances. The Book of Daniel is believed by many scholars to have been written in the second century B.C., however, and if that is true, it reflects the ideas of the Hellenistic period.

It was, in fact, in Egypt that astrology found fertile soil, as magic had. Here the precepts formulated by the Chaldeans were organized into a system.[6] Astrologers were now available to ordinary people, and they were consulted on all kinds of matters—business, politics, love. Some astrologers, like the one in Propertius 4.1.7–20, might even claim for themselves the status of a seer or hierophant,[7] thus sharing with the magician a kind of occult knowledge that gave him power and impressed his clients. But there is also genuine "astral mysticism," corresponding to the religious feelings that alchemists sometimes experienced: see Ptolemy's epigram [no. 121] and Vettius Valens' testimony [no. 123] that astrology has freed him from fear and desire.

The earliest Greek horoscopes are preserved on papyri or graffiti from the first century B.C., but the practice itself must be much older. Indeed, the belief in astrology, as well as the belief in daemons and magic, was practically universal for many centuries. The symbol for Taurus, the sign of Venus, whom Julius Caesar claimed as his divine ancestress, was spread by his legions through many countries. Augustus had his horoscope published, and the symbol of Capricorn, his native sign, was stamped on the coins he issued.

Astrological Handbooks

Because astrology was a highly technical subject in antiquity, it was taught from handbooks, some of which have survived. Unfortunately, none of them covers every aspect thoroughly enough for one to learn how to become a practitioner from it. The authors of these handbooks were probably reluctant to divulge their craft as a whole and thus held back certain information for their more advanced students.

Here it is possible to give only a brief survey of the more important texts. Many more are extant in the great libraries of Europe, but only a fraction have been published, even though their contents are roughly known.[8]

One of the earliest texts that is still extant was written under Augustus and Tiberius at the beginning of the first century A.D. It is not a handbook at all, but a didactic poem written in hexameters. About its author, Manilius, almost nothing is known. Since didactic poems are never meant to be exhaustive technical treatises, it is not surprising that no one could learn from this work how to cast a nativity. It offers a certain amount of technical information, but for the most part it deals with the philosophical basis of astrology and the beauty of its concepts. It might be called an invitation to study the subject more thoroughly from other sources, but it does not take the place of such a work.[9]

Ptolemy, whose *Tetrabiblos* was written in the first half of the second century A.D., was one of the greatest scientists of his age as well as a fine mathematician and an able astronomical observer. In this work he attempts to prove "scientifically" the influence of the stars on human life and on life on earth in general. At the beginning he deals with critics and skeptics (anticipating some of the arguments of Sextus Empiricus *Against the Astrologers,* which was written c. A.D. 200). Then he states the basic doctrines of astrology. The planets have their properties through sharing one or more of the four elemental qualities: hot, cold, dry, and moist. Elsewhere he deals with more technical questions, such as the determination of the exact time of birth by means of an astrolabe—no other devices are fully reliable.

Vettius Valens, the author of *Anthologiae* (*Excerpts*), lived at about the same time as Ptolemy. His voluminous work comes closer to a systematic textbook than those just mentioned, even though the title suggests that it is not complete. It seems to have been written for a fairly advanced practicing astrologer who wanted to add to his experience.

Firmicus Maternus (c. A.D. 335) wrote an introduction to astrology entitled *Libri Matheseos*.[10] Like Ptolemy, he deals with such philosophical questions as destiny versus free will and finds a compromise along Neo-platonist lines: the soul, being divine, is not wholly dependent on the powers represented or indicated by the stars. In a slightly different form, this argument would also appeal to a Christian, and it seems that Firmicus did convert to Christianity at one point in his life.[11] He quotes many older authorities—Nechepso, Petosiris, and others—but tries, at the same time, to give the elementary information that they omitted, especially as far as the technique of casting a horoscope is concerned.

From the time of Augustus we have a strange piece of classroom eloquence composed by Arellius Fuscus (*no. 102*), a celebrated professor of rhetoric, for the benefit of his students.[12] It is based on a story about Alexander the Great, who was warned by the Chaldeans (i.e., astrologers) against entering the city of Babylon (Plut., *Alex.* 73, etc.). The story gains its point from the fact that Alexander died in Babylon in 323 B.C. Arellius, however, pretends to be one of Alexander's advisers, urging him to disregard the warnings, and he does it in such a way as to discredit astrology and the techniques of so-called divination altogether.

Pliny the Elder, who preserves so much magical lore, attacks astrology (*Nat. Hist.* 2.6 [= p. 189 of the Loeb Library ed.]). He denies any close alliance or "sympathy" between the stars and mankind; he ridicules the traditional symbolism that connects bright stars with riches, and to him the "celestial mechanism" is just that. At the same time he seems to believe in an influence of the stars that has not yet been discovered (least of all by astrologers): "Their nature is eternal; they weave into the fabric of the world and mingle with its weft." Such a beautiful image! And it was used by a skeptic who would have liked to believe.

Astrology was primarily an occult science or discipline based on mathematics and very complex rules of interpretation, but it coexisted with a more popular brand or version. Not everyone who believed in the influence of the stars could possibly have understood the whole system and cast horoscopes himself. We find the most amazing misunderstandings and oversimplifications of astrological doctrine in the banquet scene (ch. 39) of Petronius' novel *Satyricon,* which was written in the time of Nero. There the author makes fun of a half-educated nouveau riche called Trimalchio, who tries to impress his guests with unusual dishes and fancy table talk. He tells them, among other things, that people born under the sign of Aries will own many sheep and have a lot of wool, but they might also turn out to be quarrelsome pedants. According to the same pseudo-authority, those born under the sign of Libra will become druggists or butchers, because scales will be their indispensable tool. This kind of primitive astrology was probably accepted widely throughout antiquity, but it seems like a parody of the "royal" tradition of the serious astrologers. A good example of practical astrology is the horoscope of Hadrian, who was born in A.D. 76 and died as emperor of Rome in A.D. 138.[13]

The Christian Attitude toward Astrology

For a long time the attitude of the Christian Church toward astrology was ambiguous. We have seen that in the apocryphal Wisdom of Solomon, which was probably written by a Hellenized Jew in Alexandria around the time of Christ's birth, Solomon claims to have received from God all sorts of occult knowledge, including "the changes of the solstices and the vicissitudes of the seasons; the cycles of the years and the positions of the stars."[14] This, no doubt, is a paraphrase of astrology as it was understood in Alexandria at the time. Although the Wisdom of Solomon was and is not universally acknowledged as canonical, it had great influence on early Christian writers; Augustine quotes it almost eight hundred times.

There is no evidence that Jesus and his disciples believed in the power of the stars, but the story of Jesus' birth, as told in the Gospel according to Matthew (2:1–12)—not in the other Gospels—brings the Magi from the East to Bethlehem because they had seen a star that announced to them the birth of the king of the Jews. As pointed out before, these were priest-kings, or Chaldeans, and their knowledge of occult science, including astrology, could easily be defined in terms of chapter 7 of the Wisdom of Solomon; in fact, the Solomon of Wisdom is a combination of the historical Solomon with an oriental priest-king who has occult knowledge, and the book spells out the powers that were commonly ascribed to such "divine men" at the time of the birth of Christ.

Since the Magi recognized in the newborn child a fellow king worthy of their adoration, they must have already seen in him powers that they themselves possessed. Hence, if Jesus had grown up to become a priest-king of this particular type, he would have been the perfect *magus,* the perfect exorcist, the perfect astrologer, but also a great secular ruler. Not all of this was in the stars—or in the Star—and yet the stars did not lie. The story is so much a part of the Christian tradition that it would seem to confirm a general belief in the role of heavenly bodies as messengers of great events rather than as divine powers and agents, which is, in fact, a compromise between Judaism and the astral religion of other Near Eastern civilizations. The only power is with Yahweh, but one should not ignore the signs in the sky.

The "darkness over the whole land" that began while Christ was hanging on the cross and ended shortly before he died is reported by Matthew (27:45), Mark (15:33), and Luke (23:44–45). It may be understood as an eclipse of the sun (at least this seems to be Luke's interpretation, though the text is not certain). If viewed in this way, it would form an antithesis to the bright star that shone at the time of Christ's birth. Thus, Christ's birth and death are seen as cosmic events; the universe could not be indifferent to such happenings.

Curious passages are found in the Book of Revelation: at the beginning (2:28) Jesus promises to the faithful ones the morning star; toward the end (22:16) he himself is compared to the morning star; elsewhere (1:20) stars serve as symbols for angels.[15] This has an interesting parallel. In a magical papyrus (*PGM* I.74–75) a star is called an angel, which could reflect the belief held by contemporary Platonists (Philo of Alexandria, *Plant.* 12, among others) that the stars are living beings endowed with reason.

In his Letter to the Galatians (4:3ff.) Paul chastises the Christian congregations in Galatia for still "worshiping the elements [*ta stoicheia*]" and observing special days, months, seasons, and years. The meaning of *elements* is much disputed, but one plausible explanation is that Paul has in mind the "heavenly bodies," and the special occasions the Galatians still observe are the old pagan festivals connected with the sun, the moon, and other heavenly bodies, for the calendar is based on their motions. Paul warns the Galatians not to make a special celebration to honor the new moon, for instance, because this comes dangerously close to the old astral religion, which is incompatible with the Word of God.

In a well-known passage in his Letter to the Romans (8:38–39), Paul writes: "I am convinced that neither death nor life nor angels nor [supernatural] powers, that neither the present nor the future nor [cosmic] forces above or below, that no other creature can separate us from the love of God which is in Christ Jesus, our Lord." He uses the words *archai* and *dynameis, hypsoma* and *bathos,* which I have translated as "supernatural powers" and "cosmic forces above and below." He probably meant the angelic and daemonic powers who were thought to be organized like an army or a political hierarchy, but he may also have been thinking of the stars and their influence, because *hypsoma* and *bathos* are astrological terms. What Paul tells the Christians in Rome is not to be afraid of daemons or other supernatural powers, some of which may be embodied in stars as astral spirits and thus endowed with a semidivine status.

We have seen that the Scriptures do not offer a clear position on astrology, although Paul certainly regarded it as a threat. His concern shows how deeply rooted these ancient beliefs were.

No wonder we find conflicting views among the early Christian writers. Origen (c. A.D. 185–255), who was perhaps as much a Platonist as a Christian, believed, like Philo, that the stars are rational (or spiritual) beings that take an interest in humans and foretell many things, although they do not cause events to happen. He argued, however, that astrology as a science is beyond human powers. God taught it only to the angels; the astrology practiced on earth is inspired by evil spirits and therefore is not only worthless but dangerous.[16]

Similarly, Tertullian (c. A.D. 160–225) considered astrology to be an art invented by the fallen angels; no Christian should consult one of its practitioners. In his view the Magi had been astrologers, but that did not make the art itself respectable. It had been allowed to exist until the birth of Christ, but anyone who practiced it afterward exposed himself to the wrath of God. In this case Tertullian wholeheartedly agreed with the Roman law that made it a crime for astrologers to enter Rome.[17]

Augustine (A.D. 354–430), in his later years, attacked astrology, although as a young man he had believed in fate as spelled out by the movements of the sun and the moon and the other planets.

Manicheanism was a form of gnosis named after Mani, a religious teacher who was born circa A.D. 216 in Babylonia. The religion he taught was similar to Christianity but it contained many elements that the Church rejected. Mani believed that there was a powerful principle of evil in the world, as opposed to God, the principle of good. He also believed that human lives were ruled by the stars, and since the stars themselves were either daemons or the tools of daemons, man needed a religion that included astrological lore to deal effectively with these powers.[18]

Mani's doctrine appealed to Augustine for a short time, but Augustine eventually turned away from it completely. Some of the most eloquent pages he ever wrote are devoted to a refutation of astrology, as can be seen in the first seven chapters of Book 5 of his *City of God*.

Augustine's main argument concerns babies who are born at almost the same time—particularly twins—but whose lives turn out totally differently: one becomes a senator, the other a slave, for instance. Such cases had been studied by Stoics who believed in astrology—by Posidonius, for example—and they had seemed satisfied by the evidence. Their critics were not. To silence the critics, a Roman Neo-Pythagorean, a contemporary of Cicero's by the name of Publius Nigidius, devised an ingenious experiment. He assembled a group of skeptics around a potter's wheel and, after whirling the wheel with all his strength, tried to strike it as fast as he could at a spot he had already marked.[19] But this proved impossible, for the wheel turned too fast, and the old and new marks did not coincide; in fact, they were at a considerable distance from each other. According to Nigidius, this showed that twins cannot have identical personalities and destinies, because the celestial spheres revolve with such incredible speed that even a few minutes or seconds make all the difference in the world. The experiment must have impressed Nigidius' friends, for they called him "Nigidius Figulus," or "Nigidius the Potter," and that is how he is described in scholarly works to this day.

More than three centuries after Nigidius' death, Augustine was still concerned about the possible merit of the experiment, and he proceeded to refute it, saying that it was more fragile than the pottery made by the rotation of the wheel.

The Stars and the Belief in Fate

Astrology and fatalism[20] go together. Many philosophers and theologians have found this combination appealing; others have objected to astrology on the grounds that it excludes free will. The poet James Kirkup has expressed the dilemma as follows: "I like to believe in astrology; at the same time I feel I shouldn't. But there is something in the fixed order of the stars and in their peculiar aspect at the moment of our birth which is inevitable and fated. I believe in the stars as some rationalists believe in God."[21]

The ancient concept of fate or destiny (*heimarmene*) had its roots in religion,[22] but it was developed by the Stoics, who defined it as the law according to which all things that have happened have happened, all that are happening are happening, and all that will happen will happen. To the Stoics, at least to most of them, the stars were an expression of this concept because they moved according to eternal laws. Hence, almost all Stoics believed in astrology.

Stoic fate is not blind, however. It is rational, and in itself it is a manifestation of the cosmic *logos*, which is divine. This doctrine of fate and necessity was one of the main points of controversy between the Stoa and other philosophical schools, especially the Platonists and the followers of Aristotle, who wished to maintain the autonomy of the human soul and the transcendence and providence of divine powers.[23]

Strangely enough, the astrologer who claimed that he was able to predict someone's fate accurately also believed that he could help that person accept what was foreordained. This acceptance of the inevitable was an important tenet of Stoic ethics. It is reflected in Vettius Valens in a passage that shows that an astrologer could play a role analogous to a modern psychiatrist [*no. 123*]. While announcing a disaster, he might actually soften the blow.

Astrologers who were also practitioners of magic thought they could break or counteract the influence of the stars and offer a way out by recruiting the help of supernatural powers.[24] Christianity and the mystery religions also provided a release from the shackles of determinism through salvation.

Notes on Astrological Technique

The principles and the technique of astrological prediction have not changed a great deal since the late Hellenistic period. We no longer believe in a geocentric universe; three new planets (Uranus, Neptune, and Pluto) have been discovered; and because of the "precession of the equinoxes" the sun is no longer in Aries during the time that it is supposed to be there, from March 21 to April 20; and yet a horoscope today is still, as it was then, "a geocentric map of the solar system at a given moment of time,"[25] and its interpretation follows pretty much the same lines that the ancient astrologers followed.

One of the most important elements of the horoscope is the "ascendant," the degree of the ecliptic that is rising at the moment of birth. Today this is considered to be one of thirty degrees of one of twelve constellations. Originally it may have been a particular star within the constellation, for it was called *horoskopos* 'watcher of the hour'.

The ascendant determines the so-called first house, and this brings us to a curious construction. While the "planets" (which included the sun and the moon) and the twelve signs of the zodiac correspond to heavenly bodies (though the sum of our planets is no longer that of the ancients, and the signs of the zodiac are no longer where they are supposed to be), the division of a chart into twelve houses has no basis in the universe as we know it. This division is based on spherical trigonometry, which in itself must be a mystery to many astrologers. Several systems of establishing the houses are used today, but none of them, it appears, predates the Renaissance. The ancient systems were much simpler.

What is remarkable about the principle of the houses is the fact that it catches in a net, as it were, the main areas or aspects of a person's character and life. The first house, determined by the ascendant, tells the astrologer what he wants to know about the personality, the self, its potential and its realizations. Any planets that happen to be in that section of space at the time of birth will have a special influence on the person's character and destiny.

The second and third houses are easily found by the ancient astrologer after the ascendant has been determined. If Taurus is the ascendant, the second house is in Gemini, the third in Cancer, and so on. The twelfth house will take us back to the sign just preceding the ascendant, in this case Aries.

The second house gives information about the person's property and possessions, his or her financial success. The third house concerns brothers and sisters, but also one's peer group and education. The fourth house has to do with parents, the home, one's roots. The fifth house tells about one's loves, one's children, one's hobbies (a curious but not totally illogical correlation). The sixth house indicates one's health, but also the hard work one has to do. The seventh house is the house of marriage, partnerships, and (ironically) enemies. One is almost tempted to say that in such traditional lore the wisdom of long experience is evident; one has only to think of family relationships in Greek tragedy! The eighth house is the house of death, the subject's, but also that of the people from whom he may inherit. The ninth house was thought to relate to a person's intellectual and spiritual life, his philosophy and religion, but also his travels; there is some logic in this, too, for at least since Herodotus, the chief way to extend one's horizon intellectually was to travel to countries with ancient traditions; there were very few public libraries where one could consult the latest reference works. The tenth house offered clues to one's domicile, profession, social life, status, and conduct of life in general. The eleventh house revealed the nature of one's friendships (as distinguished from the loves revealed by the fifth house), but also, it seems, one's political associations and hence one's political ambitions, for the ancient system of patronage was nominally a "friendship," but it could also be a kind of "mafia." Finally, the twelfth house, graphically close to the first, was the house of troubles and tribulations, illness and betrayal, enemies and disgrace.

Even from this brief survey, it becomes clear that the ancient system of twelve houses preserves a great deal of human experience. At one time there were only eight houses, but as life became more complex, the number apparently had to be increased. Life today is even more complex, and still the ancient system has something to say. It certainly has the capacity to receive many thousands of interpretations. At the very least, it would serve the astrologer as a kind of reminder as he considers the answers to possible questions asked of him. At the same time, it is a great psychological tool, one that was designed long before modern psychology and psychiatry evolved.

The other elements to be considered in interpreting the chart of the zodiac are, as mentioned above, the planets located or placed in the signs.

Each of the planets has its "house" or "houses," which in this case means the sign or signs of the zodiac in which it feels at home: for the sun this is Leo; for the moon it is Cancer; for the others there are two favorite domiciles, one diurnal, one nocturnal. The planets have their greatest and most beneficial influence if they are in the appropriate house at the time of birth—for instance, if Venus is in Libra and the birth takes place during the day, or if Jupiter is in Pisces and the birth takes place at night.

The locations of the planets in the signs of the zodiac and in the twelve trigonometric houses are important, but so, too, are the "aspects": the number of degrees between one planet and another, one planet and the "cusps" (the dividing lines between one house and another). Opposition (180° or thereabouts) and tetragon (ideally 90°) are considered unfavorable, whereas trigon (c. 120°) and sextile (ideally 60°) are considered favorable.

Since it takes the sun about thirty days to pass through one sign of the zodiac, and an enormous number of people with different characters and destinies are born during that time, each sign is subdivided into three decans, or 10° segments roughly corresponding to the ten days the sun seemed to spend there. These decans modify the general character of the sign. One particular planet is in charge of it, but there is also great variety as to the names and functions of the planets.

From our point of view, there is some scientific thinking in all the occult arts of antiquity, at least since the Hellenistic era and afterward, but there is also an element of "pseudoscience" or "superstition" (in the sense of prelogical thought), and the two elements are closely intertwined. The progress made—alchemy developing into chemistry, for instance—rests, up to a certain point, on the separation of reality from fantasy, of exact observation and reasoning from wishful thinking. Let us not forget that, though medicine was not what it is today, there were excellent physicians in Athens or Alexandria or Rome. Some astrologers made valuable astronomical observations and some alchemists stumbled upon great discoveries.

As long as astrology was closely connected with religion, it could not be "scientific" in the true sense of the word. The names of the planets, as they are still used today—Venus or Jupiter—are those of the ancient gods, and they reflect their character, as we know it from the ancient myths. Gradually, the Greek philosophers (who were the first scientists) weakened the authority of the inherited religious conglomerate and laid the foundation for modern science. How could the sun be a god if it was a "mass of incandescent matter," as Anaxagoras declared? Or how could the planetary gods influence our lives if they took no interest in us, as Epicurus, the father of atomism, taught?

Progress was slow, it seems today, because the accumulation of old beliefs and traditions opposed any creative, revolutionary impulse. History offers many examples, from Socrates to Galilei. Some great philosophers, like Plotinus, still believed in certain aspects of magic, and some great scientists, like Ptolemy, were convinced that the stars ruled life on earth.

In a famous passage of his *Annals* (6.22), Tacitus speaks about the astrologer Thrasyllus, a noted scholar and one of Tiberius' closest advisers. To find out whether his predictions were reliable, Tiberius planned to kill him, and Thrasyllus saw from his stars that he was in great danger.

Tacitus' comments are those of an enlightened, highly educated contemporary, and they are well worth quoting. He writes: "When I hear a story like this, I cannot make up my mind whether human lives are ruled by fate and by a necessity that cannot be changed or by coincidence. You will find that even the greatest philosophers of ancient times and those who adopt their doctrines disagree, and that many of them are convinced that the gods do not care about our beginnings, our end, and our existence in general; this is why very often bad things happen to good people and why those who are not so good are fortunate. Others, however, believe that fate controls human lives, although this depends not on the planets, but on the first causes and the natural connexions of causes. At the same time, they admit that we are able to make our choices in our lives; but once we have made a choice, the consequences follow in a certain order."

A little later, Tacitus continues these thoughts: "Besides, most people cannot give up the idea that the moment of birth determines the rest of their life, and whenever something does not happen as predicted it is because those who predicted it misled them by their ignorance. Thus, they say, the art of divination loses its credibility, even though past periods and our own age have witnessed clear proofs [that it can work]."

Evidently, Tacitus himself could not make up his mind. On the one hand, he calls astrology a *superstitio* (*Histories* 2.78.1), and he denounces the astrologers as "disloyal to the powerful and untrustworthy for the hopeful: they will always be banished from our state and kept under control" (*Histories* 1.22.1). When he tells the tragic fate of Libo Drusus who was accused of planning a conspiracy against Tiberius (*Annals* 2.27.2), he mentions that this man had consulted sorcerers, astrologers, and dream interpreters, and he places those in the same category as the necromancers: "The promises of the Chaldaeans, the rituals of the *magi*, the interpreters of dreams . . . [and] those who conjure up the souls of the dead with their incantations." On the other hand, Tacitus shows a certain respect for the more successful practitioners (*Annals* 4.58.2–3).

No doubt most of Tacitus' contemporaries believed that the stars tell the truth. The emperors from time to time banished the astrologers and the sorcerers, sometimes along with the philosophers, probably for political reasons, not because they wished to protect the people from charlatans. It was always possible that a practitioner of the art who knew a little more than the others could predict the time of death of the emperor and hit on the name of his successor.

The idea that we can understand the principle behind the movements of the heavenly bodies and that we can project them into the future on the basis of written records and mathematical calculations may go back to the fourth millennium B.C. The wish to represent the movements of the sun, the moon, and the planets by mathematical tables or by graphic models led to a new kind of higher mathematics, a universal language designed to explore an intellectual process within the mind of a cosmic god who controlled everything on earth and in heaven. If you learned to understand this language, you understood past, present, and future.

The regular movements of the heavenly bodies were a miracle in themselves, and there was a message in the miracle. The various relationships of the planets among themselves could be understood as interactions among divine beings which, collectively, determined all forms of life on earth.

It is very likely that the roots of Greek astrology can be found in the astral religions of Mesopotamia, just as Greek mythology now appears to be an adaptation of older Near Eastern mythologies. Without a firmly established cult of the planetary deities, the whole growth of astrology as a combination of a cosmic religion and scientific astronomy seems unthinkable.

But there may be another component as well. Animal worship is attested in ancient Egypt, and it has left its traces not only in Greek mythology but also in Greek astrology, although the cult itself seems to have disappeared long before Homer. The fact that the Greek and Roman astrologers operated with theriomorphic powers (Aries, Taurus), identified with certain signs of the zodiac, along with anthropomorphic ones (Mars, Mercury), identified with the planets, is often overlooked. Sagittarius, incidentally, may be the Centaur, a combination of man and animal. These powers seem to correspond to ancient animal deities, which were originally the totemic animals of powerful tribes and families. Taurus, for instance, may be none other than the Minotaur, the bull-god worshiped on Minoan Crete.

When we speak of "Greco-Roman astrology" we usually think of the highly sophisticated system that took its shape during the Hellenistic period and included archaic elements as well as a psychological typology borrowed from various philosophical schools. Add to this a symbolism based on religious concepts and give it a mathematical basis. The result is astrology.

Obviously, a system of this kind, having developed in the course of many centuries, had contradictions within itself. How can you reconcile the belief that the astral gods, or any gods whose intentions are revealed by the astral bodies, have absolute power over things on earth with the belief that religion, with its rituals, prayers, and sacrifices, is able to neutralize or modify this power? Whether our future is really determined by the stars in the sky (and this seems to have been the original idea) or by an invisible being whose plans are announced by the stars does not make much difference. If our destiny is predetermined by a god, nothing that we do will change it.

At the same time, torn between fear and hope, people will do almost anything to avoid the worst. Only very few are strong enough to live up to the Stoic ideal of the "wise man" who cheerfully accepts the decrees of fate. In his *Scientific Problems* (*Naturales Quaestiones* 2.35), Seneca writes: "What is the purpose of expiations and [ritual] safeguards, if fate cannot be changed? Allow me to adopt the rigid doctrine of those who abolish such practices and consider them nothing else but placebos for sick minds."

The ancients tended to range their deities in hierarchic structures, mirroring the powerful clans, dynasties, and bureaucracies they had to deal with on earth. In the Homeric epics, the gods are the members of an extended family ruled by Zeus. Every deity has his or her place in the structure. They often fight with each other, as it happens in families, and these feuds may affect mankind. They have their moods, and they are vulnerable in some ways, just like human beings.

From their personal experiences of the caprices of the rich and powerful, the ancients—Babylonians, Persians, Egyptians, and Greeks alike—imagined a heavenly hierarchy similar to the bureaucracies and armies they knew on earth. The supreme god was like a mighty king who had to be respected and pleased at all times.

Astrology, in a sense, is a practical application of the idea of a heavenly hierarchy. The planets and the constellations have their definite places in it, but their powers are not always the same. Although their character is generally known, much depends on their position in the zodiac and in respect to the other planets. All these factors determine whether their influences are strong or weak, good or bad.

If we look at astrology in this way, it seems essentially like a guessing game based on certain rules. Originally, these rules must have been quite simple, but with time they grew more and more complex. By the end of the first millennium B.C., every day of the week, every hour of the day was ruled by a celestial power. For every situation, important or trivial, one could, in principle, consult an astrologer. Should I buy this house? Should I go on this trip? Should I take a bath? Should I get married? Far from being a sort of placebo for sick minds, as Seneca calls it, astrology had now become a source of fears, doubts, and pressures. This is what Paul of Tarsus has in mind when he says: "For our struggle is not against flesh and blood, but against the rulers, against the authorities, against the powers of this dark world and against the spiritual forces of evil in the heavenly realms" (Ephesians 6:12).

NOTES

1. Neugebauer, *The Exact Sciences in Antiquity*, p. 164.
2. Bidez and Cumont, *Les Mages hellénisés.*
3. Saggs, *The Greatness That Was Babylon*, p. 459.
4. Ibid., p. 455.
5. A. Sachs, in *Journal of Cuneiform Studies* 6 (1953): 57.
6. Neugebauer, *The Exact Sciences in Antiquity*, pp. 178ff.; Nilsson, *Geschichte der griechischen Religion*, 1:268.
7. Nock, *Essays on Religion in the Ancient World*, 1:497.
8. The *Catalogus Codicum Astrologicorum Graecorum* surveys the mass of material in astrological handbooks that is preserved in many libraries. The first volumes of the catalogue were compiled under the direction of F. Cumont (Brussels); 12 volumes have been published since 1898.
9. G. P. Goold has produced a fine text and an excellent translation of Manilius (Loeb Classical Library, Cambridge, Mass., 1977).
10. Firmicus' handbook has been translated by J. R. Bram under the title *Ancient Astrology* (Park Ridge, N.J., 1975).
11. The treatise *Why Paganism Is Wrong (De Errore Profanarum Religionum)*, also ascribed to Firmicus, seems to indicate that at one time he was a Christian. It was not impossible to be a Christian and a believer in astrology, though the Church officially condemned astrological doctrine.
12. On Seneca's *Suasoriae* 4.1–3 [*no. 102*], see Cumont, *Astrology and Religion*, pp. 148–49; and L. Bieler, in *Wiener Studien* 52 (1935): 84ff.
13. Neugebauer and Van Hoesen, *Greek Horoscopes*, pp. 90ff.
14. D. Winston, trans., *The Wisdom of Solomon*, Anchor Bible Series, vol. 43 (Garden City, N.Y., 1979), 7:18–19.
15. See F. Boll, *Aus der Offenbarung Johannis* (Leipzig, 1914), pp. 47ff.
16. Thorndike, *A History of Magic and Experimental Science*, 1:436ff.
17. Ibid., pp. 462ff.
18. J. J. O'Meara, *An Augustine Reader* (Garden City, N.Y., 1973), pp. 13ff., 128–29, 319ff.
19. This experiment, briefly reported by Augustine in *City of God* 5.3, has not been properly interpreted, I believe. Nigidius must have smeared some ink on his

finger, set the wheel in motion, and touched it. He then tried to touch that same spot again as the wheel was still spinning.

20. See M. David, *Les Dieux et le destin en Babylonie* (Paris, 1949); Onians, *Origins of European Thought*, pp. 303ff.

21. J. Kirkup, *Sorrows, Passions, and Alarms* (London, 1959), p. 93.

22. Fatalism is the only philosophical principle underlying fairy tales, according to Krappe, *The Science of Folklore*, p. 28. Sometimes the fairies are only agents of fate; certainly there is a linguistic link between the words *fairy* and *fate*.

23. J. Dillon, *The Middle Platonists* (Ithaca, N.Y., 1977), p. 208; G. Luck, in *American Journal of Philology* 101 (1980): 373ff.

24. Arnobius, *Adv. Gent.* 2.13.62.

25. See MacNeice, *Astrology*, p. 244. This excellent work by a student and friend of E. R. Dodds who is chiefly remembered as a fine poet has not received the attention it deserves. The chapter on ancient astrology is especially valuable.

Texts

102

This extract is from a *suasoria,* a type of rhetorical exercise that formed an important part of higher education in the early Roman Empire. Students had to pretend that they were persuading a mythical or historical character to take, or not to take, a certain course of action, after which the teacher would give his own version. Such exercises were considered a good preparation for a career in politics. This piece is taken from a collection of excerpts from model speeches made by famous professors of rhetoric in the Augustan age. In this instance the professor is Arellius Fuscus, one of the teachers who had a certain amount of influence on the poet Ovid, who is said to have excelled in this genre.

What we have is a brief outline of the original speech, some parts of which were more developed than others. It was written down many years later by Seneca the Elder, father of the famous philosopher. It states very clearly the case against astrology—in fact, against all forms of prophecy and prediction. In some parts the Latin text is corrupt, and even where it seems reasonably certain, one cannot always be sure of the meaning.

Arellius first builds up the typical diviner as a kind of superhuman being who surely descends from the gods or the stars (or at least pretends that he does). It is the same kind of irony that we find in Propertius' *Elegies* 4.1, where a Persian or Egyptian astrologer boasts about his divine ancestors. The Latin words *agnoscat suum uatem deus* must therefore mean "let the god [i.e., Apollo] acknowledge the prophet as his own [i.e., his descendant]," not "the god must acknowledge him as a prophet," for the latter could be taken for granted.

The second paragraph begins with the words "If all this were [really] true, why do not men in every generation pursue these studies?" By "these studies" Arellius Fuscus means "all the known techniques of predicting the future" or "all the fraudulent claims that seers make." If astrology were an exact science in which all forecasts came true, everyone would want to be an astrologer. In fact, most people at that time knew a little about astrology—perhaps interpreting it in a garbled, nonsensical way, like the uneducated nouveau riche Trimalchio, in Petronius' *Satyricon* (ch. 35), but usually understanding enough to follow the technical explanations of a professional astrologer.

In the same context Arellius calls the astrologers "those who throw themselves into the battle of the Fates" (reading *proelia* rather than *pignora*, the mechanical repetition of a word that made sense a few lines before but none whatsoever here). This, too, is ironic: the astrologers see themselves as the heroes or protagonists in a sort of cosmic battle, fighting to save their clients from the impact of fate.

Astrologers also like to advertise themselves as psychotherapists, because they can prepare their clients for the blows that fate has in store for them. But their false predictions, Arellius argues, make nervous wrecks of many who are told that they will die soon, but who live on and on in fear and anxiety. Others are given the hope of a long life, but instead meet an early death without being prepared for it; they, too, are fooled by the practitioners of a pseudoscience.

Seneca the Elder, *Suasoriae* 4.1–3 (from a speech by Arellius Fuscus)

[*After having been warned by a seer, Alexander the Great deliberates whether he should enter Babylon.*]

What kind of a man is this who pretends to know the future? Surely the fate of a person who chants prophecies at the order of a god must be very unusual. He cannot be content with the womb from which the rest of us—those who know nothing of the future—are born. No doubt the person who reveals the commands of a god is marked with some divine symbol. Yes, of course: a seer stirs up fear in a king, in the ruler of the universe! That man whose privilege it is to frighten Alexander must be great himself, must stand high above the common lot of mankind. Let him name the stars among his ancestors! Let the god acknowledge the prophet as his own [son or progeny]! He who reveals the future to the nations cannot live his life within the same boundaries [as ordinary men]; his personality must be outside all the necessities of fate.

If all this were true, why do not men in every generation pursue these studies? Why do we not from childhood approach nature and the gods as far as that is possible? After all, the stars are accessible, and we can mix with gods! Why do we sweat away at eloquence? It is useless. Why do we get calloused hands from handling weapons? It is dangerous. Can there be a better investment of talent than knowledge of the future? But those who "throw themselves into the battle of the Fates," as they say, want to know about your birthday, and consider the first hour of your life the indicator of all the years to follow. They observe the motions of the stars, the directions in which they move: whether the Sun stood in threatening opposition or shone kindly on the nativity; whether the baby received the full light [of the Moon], the beginning of her waxing, or whether the Moon was obscured [at the time] and hid her head in darkness; whether Saturn invited the newborn child to become a farmer, Mars a soldier to go to war, Mercury a successful businessman, or Venus graciously promised her favors, or Jupiter would carry the child from humble origins to tremendous heights. So many gods swarming about one head!

So they predict the future? To many they have promised a long life, and yet the day [of death] was suddenly upon them without any warning; to others they have predicted an early death, and yet they lived on, plagued by pointless fears [text uncertain]. To some they have promised a happy life, but Fortune quickly sent them all kinds of harm.

You see, we share an uncertain fate, and these are all fictions concocted by clever astrologers, without any truth in them. Will there be a place on earth, Alexander, that has not witnessed a victory of yours? The Ocean stood open to you, and Babylon should be closed?

103

Agrippa, Augustus' trusted adviser, lectures the ruler on the danger represented by sorcerers and astrologers. They claim to be able to predict the future, and sometimes they seem to be right. In a sense, they are more dangerous when they tell the truth—for instance, when they predict correctly the death of the emperor—than when they are telling lies. Prophecy is necessary and has always been part of Roman rituals, but it has to be done within the proper channels, for example, through the inspection of the entrails of an animal. Astrology is considered a foreign science. But the greatest danger is seen in the formation of secret societies within the state. They can be downright subversive and lead to revolution. We know of several other expulsions of astrologers [mathematici] and sorcerers, sometimes together with philosophers, for instance, in 16 or 17 A.D., under Tiberius, and again in 68 A.D., at the end of Nero's reign.

Dio Cassius 49.43.5; 52.36.1−2

[33 B.C.] Agrippa . . . drove the astrologers and the sorcerers [goetes] out of the city. . . .

[29 B.C., Agrippa addresses Augustus.] You should hate and punish those who introduce foreign elements into our religion, not only for the sake of the gods—for if someone shows disrespect for the gods, he could hardly have respect for anyone else—but also because people of this kind adopt foreign customs, and this may lead to conspiracies and gatherings and secret societies, which is not at all what a monarchy needs. You should not allow people to be atheists or sorcerers. We do need prophecy [*mantike*], and you certainly must appoint predictors and augurs, so people who want to consult them on some matter can approach them. But no *mages* [*mageutai*] whatsoever can be tolerated. For such men often incite the population to revolutions, either by telling the truth or, more often, by telling lies. Quite a few of those who pretend to practice philosophy actually do the same. Just because you have had good experiences with Areius and Athenodorus—fine and decent men—you should not think that all the others who claim to be philosophers are the same. For the men who hide behind such a façade do enormous damage to society as well as to individuals.

104

Manilius, a Stoic, is the author of a didactic poem on astrology. We know very little about him, except that he must have lived under Augustus and Tiberius. His poem, in five books, is by no means a complete introduction to astrology. It deals with certain aspects, leaving others out, and it offers digressions that are often of great interest to us but not strictly necessary from a technical point of view. Manilius may never have intended to cover the whole subject, or he may not have had a chance to finish his work. He, like Lucretius, the Epicurean, offered more than technical or philosophical instruction: he wanted to convert his readers to his own world view. While Lucretius preached Epicureanism as a kind of religion, Manilius preached an astral religion based on Stoic ideas, a religion that promised insight into the nature of the universe.

In the present text Manilius describes astrology as a gift of the god Hermes. If this is not the Greek Hermes but the Egyptian Hermes Trismegistus, it means that Manilius considered astrology to be an Egyptian science, revealed to the priests long ago and kept secret. By studying the divinely revealed principles and applying them to practical matters, these priests established, over the centuries, the science of astrology as Manilius knew it. At the beginning of the long process there was revelation, but afterward a good deal of empirical research was done by men.

According to Manilius, the progress of astrology is just one chapter in the general progress of human civilization. He takes it for granted that magic and the other occult sciences produce concrete results, because they proceed from scientific facts and apply well-tested techniques.

Manilius 1.25–112

It was by a gift of the gods that the earth was permitted a more intimate knowledge of the universe. For if they had wanted to keep it a secret, who would have been clever enough to steal the cosmic mystery that controls everything? Having but a human mind, who could have attempted such a gigantic task, wishing to appear to be a god against the will of the gods and reveal the movements of the heavenly bodies in the zenith and the nadir, underneath the earth, and describe how the stars obey their orbits as they travel through space? You, god of Cyllene [Hermes], are the author and the origin of this great sacred tradition. Thanks to you, we know the farther reaches of the sky, the constellations, the names and movements of the stars, their importance and their influence. You wanted to enlarge the face of the universe; you wanted the power of nature, not only its appearance, to be revered; you wanted mankind to find out in what way god was supreme.

Nature, too, offered her powers and revealed herself. She did not find it beneath her dignity to inspire the minds of kings; she made them touch the summits that are close to heaven. They brought civilization to the savage peoples in the East whose lands are divided by the Euphrates and flooded by the Nile, where the universe returns and soars away, high above the cities of dark nations.

Then the priests who offered worship in temples all their lives and who were chosen to express the prayers of the people obtained by their service the favor of the gods. The very presence of the divine power kindled their pure minds, and god himself brought god into their hearts and revealed himself to his servants.

These were the men who established our noble science. They were the first to see, through their art, how fate depends on the wandering stars. Over the course of many centuries they assigned with persistent care to each period of time the events connected with it: the day on which someone is born, the kind of life he shall lead, the influence of every hour on the laws of destiny, and the enormous differences made by small motions.

They explored every aspect of the sky as the stars returned to their original positions. They assigned to the unchangeable sequences of the fates the specific influence of certain configurations. As a result, experience, applied in different ways, produced an art; examples pointed the way; from long observation it was discovered that the stars control the whole world by mysterious laws, that the world itself moves by an eternal principle, and that we can, by reliable signs, recognize the ups and downs of fate.

Before this, life had been primitive and marked by ignorance. People

had looked at the outward appearance of the creation without any understanding; with amazement they had stared at the strange new light of the
universe. Sometimes they mourned as though they had lost it; then again
they were glad because the stars seemed to be born again [text uncertain].
They could not understand the reasons why the days varied in length and
why the nights did not always fill a standard measure of time; why the
length of shadows was unequal, depending on whether the sun was
withdrawing or returning. Ingenuity had not yet taught mankind crafts
and arts. The earth lay wasted and fallow under ignorant farmers. There
was gold in the hills, but no one went there. The ocean, undisturbed, hid
unknown worlds: men did not dare entrust their lives to the sea and their
prayers to the winds; they thought what little knowledge they had [was]
sufficient.

As time went by, the human mind grew sharper. Hard work made the
poor creatures more ingenious. The heavy lot that each man had to carry
forced him to look out for himself. They began to specialize and compete
intellectually, and whatever [through] intelligence and experience they
discovered by trial, they happily communicated and contributed to the
common good. Their speech—barbarous before—now conformed to
rules of its own. The soil—uncultivated before—was now worked over
for all kinds of crops. The roving sailor traveled across the sea, uncharted
before, and connected by trade routes countries that had not known of
each other before. Gradual progress led to the development of the arts of
war and peace, for experience always generates one skill from the other.
Not to mention the commonplace: men learned to understand the language of birds, to predict the future from entrails, to break snakes by
incantations, to conjure up ghosts and stir the depths of Acheron, to
transform day into night, night into day. Human intelligence, always
eager to learn, overcame everything by trying hard, and human reason
did not set an end or a limit to its efforts until it had climbed up to the sky
and grasped the mysteries of nature by its principles and seen everything
there was to see.

Men understood why clouds are shaken by the impact of tremendous
thunderclaps, why snowflakes in winter are softer than hail in summer,
why flames come out of the ground, why the solid earth quakes, why rain
pours down, what cause produces winds. Reason delivered us from the
awesome feeling that nature inspires: it took Jupiter's lightning and thundering power away and assigned the noise to the winds, the flame to the
clouds. After human reason had connected every phenomenon with its
true cause, it set out to explore the structure of the universe, starting at
the bottom, and attempted to grasp the whole sky; it identified the
shapes, gave the stars their names, observed the cycles in which they

traveled according to eternal laws. It realized that everything moves according to the divine power and the aspects of the universe and that the stars by their manifold configurations change our destinies.

105

Near the beginning of his poem Manilius places a Stoic cosmogony. It is a dramatic account of the creation of the world, comparable with certain passages in Lucretius and with the beginning of Ovid's *Metamorphoses*. These two poets clearly influenced Manilius, but his account is different; he speaks of the elements in rapid motion for a time, until they find their place in the universe: fire soars up to the ethereal zones, earth leaps through water, and so on. The drama of creation is presented in a truly spectacular manner. One idea that emerges is typically Stoic: Nature knows her business quite well and is no "blundering novice"; all the philosopher has to do is study her ways.

The suspension of the earth in space seems to have been a scientific problem much discussed in Manilius' day. He offers a simple explanation. The earth is round, and so is the universe that rotates around it. The sun, the moon, and all the planets are round, and so are the gods. As the universe travels through space (an amazingly modern concept), its rotation produces a kind of centrifugal action. Manilius or the author he is following may have seen a simple physical experiment demonstrating such an action, but one should keep in mind that Manilius' views were not shared by most of his contemporaries.

At the end of the passage, Manilius affirms his belief in a cosmic god whose spirit (*pneuma*) is the breath of the universe. This divine element is immanent in the world and keeps it alive, as it were. The whole cosmos is one huge living and breathing organism, according to this concept, and just as in the human body the condition of one part may affect another part, what happens in one region of the universe may affect what happens in another region. This is a clear statement of the principle of "cosmic sympathy," which is so important in astrology and in the occult sciences in general. Since this principle is often attributed to Posidonius, who firmly believed in all kinds of divination, it is possible that Manilius used him as a source.

Manilius 1.149–254 (154 placed before 159, and 167 placed after 214)

Flying fire soared upward to the ethereal zones, spread along the very top of the starry sky, and made from panels of flames the walls of the world. Next, spirit sank down and turned into light breezes and spread out air through the middle of the empty space of the world. The third element expanded [in the form of] water and floating waves and poured out the ocean born from the whole sea. This happened so that water might breathe out and exhale the light breezes and feed the air, which draws its seeds from it [the water]; also, that the wind might nourish the fire, which is placed directly under the stars. Finally, earth drifted to the bottom, ball-shaped because of its weight: slime, mixed with drifting sand, took shape as the light liquid gradually evaporated. More moisture withdrew and became pure water, and so the oceans were filtered, and land built up, and flat expanses of water came to lie next to hollow valleys. Mountains emerged from the seas. The earth, though still locked on all sides by the ocean, leapt through the waves, and it remained stable because the firmament kept at every point the same distance from it, and by falling from all sides preserved the middle and lowest part from falling. Bodies hit by blows coming from inside remain as they are, and because of the centripetal force, they cannot move very far.

If the earth did not hang in balance, the sun would not, as the stars appear in the sky, drive its chariot from the point of its setting and would not return to its rising; nor would the moon, below the horizon, pursue a course through space; nor would the morning star shine during the early hours of a day after having given its light as evening star at the end of a day. Actually, the earth has not been thrown down to the lowest point. It remains suspended in the center. This is why the whole space [around it] allows passage, so that the firmament may set underneath the earth and rise again. For I cannot believe that the stars that appear at the horizon rise by coincidence, nor that the firmament is created anew again and again, nor that the sun dies every day and is reborn. Over the centuries the shape of the constellations has remained the same. The same sun has risen from the same quarter of the sky. The moon has gone through its phases over the same number of days. Nature keeps to the ways that she herself has made. She is no blundering novice. The days travel around the earth with the light that never fails and show the same hours now to these, and now to other, regions of the earth. If you travel eastward, the East moves constantly farther away, as does the West if you travel westward. What is true for the sun is true for the sky.

Why should one be surprised that the earth is suspended? The firmament itself is suspended, too, and not supported by any base. This is clear from its very movement and from the fact that it travels fast through space. The sun moves without support, as it skillfully directs its chariot now this way and now that, keeping within its turning points in the sky. The moon and the stars travel through cosmic space. Similarly, in accordance with celestial laws, the earth is suspended. Therefore, the earth has been allotted a hollow space in the center of the atmosphere, equidistant at every point from the nadir. It is not flattened out to form a plain, but it has the shape of a sphere, which rises and falls at the same time at every point. This is its natural shape. Thus, the universe itself, because it turns round and round, gives a spherical shape to the stars. We see that the sun and the moon are round, spherical: the moon is looking for light for its extended body, but its globe as a whole does not receive the sun's rays, which hit it at an oblique angle. This is the lasting, abiding form, very much like that of the gods. It has no beginning, no end, in itself, but is like itself on its whole surface, identical with itself throughout. Similarly, the earth stays round, imitating the shape of the universe, and being the lowest of all heavenly bodies, remains in the very center.

For this reason we cannot see all the constellations from every point of the earth. You will never spot the shining light of Canopus until you have crossed the sea and reached the banks of the Nile. Those who live directly under the Bear look for it in vain: they inhabit the slopes of our globe, and the curves of the terrain in between deprive them of the sky and limit their view. The moon proves that the earth is round. When, at night, it is plunged into dark shadows, undergoing an eclipse, it does not frighten all the nations at the same time. First the countries in the East go without your light; then those that are directly under the center of the sky [at the end you roll with tainted wings to those in the West]; later the brass is struck among the nations at the end of the world. If the earth were flat, the moon would rise only once over the whole world, and its eclipse would be bewailed everywhere at the same time. But since the outline of the earth follows a gentle curve, the moon appears now to these lands, now to others, rising and setting at the same time. It moves along a belly-shaped orbit, and it combines an upward with a downward motion. It comes up over some horizons and leaves others behind. Hence we conclude that the earth is round.

On its surface live many different tribes of men and wild beasts and birds of the air. One inhabitable zone stretches toward the North, another is situated in the southern regions: it actually lies beneath our feet, but it imagines itself above us because the terrain hides the gradual slope, and the path ascends and descends at the same time. When the sun has reached the western horizon and looks down on our part of the world, a new day wakes up sleeping cities in that other part and brings back to them with the light of day their round of daily duties. By now, there is night for us, and we invite slumber into our bodies. The ocean divides and at the same time connects the two regions.

This organic structure of the huge universe, its individual parts composed of different elements—air, fire, earth, and the flat sea—is ruled by the divine power of spirit. God breathes through the whole in a mystic

way and governs it by mysterious means. He controls the mutual relationships between all parts through which one [part] transmits its strength
to another and [in turn] receives another's strength. As a result, cosmic
sympathy reigns forever among a variety of phenomena.

106

In his defense of astrology as a part of Stoic doctrine, Manilius naturally
has to attack Epicurus. The Epicureans did not deny that gods existed, but
they rejected any involvement of the gods in human affairs. The Stoics, on
the other hand, believed that there was a permanent force in the history of
the world, and that it excluded the element of chance. The constellations
that Manilius saw in the sky at the beginning of our era were the same
constellations that the Greeks had seen during the Trojan War. To Manilius, this permanence was definitely the expression of a divine will.

But in the course of history the world had seen striking changes. The
descendants of the vanquished Trojans had conquered the descendants of
the victorious Greeks. This, too, had happened in accordance with the
divine will. Thus, for Manilius, nothing is left to chance; everything happens according to a cosmic scheme, and astrology is the science that
explores the hidden intentions of the deity.

Manilius 1.474–531

It is easy to recognize the bright constellations, for they do not show any
deviation in their settings and risings. They all come up at regular times
to display their own light, and appearances and disappearances follow a
certain order. Nothing in that immense structure is more marvelous than
this principle and the fact that everything obeys certain laws. Nowhere
does confusion interfere. Nothing deviates in any direction or moves in a
larger or smaller orb or changes its course. Is there anything else so
overwhelming in appearance, yet so sure in its rhythm?

To me no argument seems as forceful as this, for it shows that the world
moves in accordance with a divine power and is, in itself, god, and has not
been put together at the whim of chance. But this is what Epicurus wants
us to believe: he first built up the walls of the universe from tiny seeds and
dissolved them into these seeds again. He also thought that the seas and
the land and the stars in the sky, as well as the ether, consisted of atoms,
and that in the vast space whole worlds were formed and dissolved again
and new worlds created. He also said that everything would return to the
state of atoms and change its appearance.

But who would believe that such huge conglomerations of matter
could be created from tiny particles without a divine will, and that the

world is the result of casual combination? If chance gave us this universe, let chance govern it! But then why do we see the stars rise in a regular rhythm and accomplish their course as if it had been ordered by a command, never hurrying ahead, never lagging behind? Why do the same stars always grace the summer nights, the same stars always the winter nights? Why does every day impose a certain configuration upon the sky as it comes and a certain configuration as it goes? When the Greeks sacked Troy, the Bear and Orion already moved frontally toward each other; the Bear was content to move in a circle at the top, Orion to ascend toward her from the opposite direction as she turned away, always running over the whole firmament to meet her. Even then men were able to tell the time of dark night by the constellations, and the sky had established a clock of its own. How many realms have tumbled since the sack of Troy? How many nations have been led into captivity? How many times has Fortuna distributed slavery and supremacy throughout the world and reappeared in a different shape? Did it not rekindle the ashes of Troy and give [the Trojans] supreme power without a thought of what had happened? And now it is the turn of Greece to be weighed down by the fate of Asia Minor! Why bother to enumerate the centuries and tell how many times the fiery sun has come back to illuminate the world on its varying courses?

Everything born under the law of mortality must change. The earth does not realize that it is ravaged by the passage of time and that it changes its face over the centuries. But the firmament remains intact: it conserves all its elements; long periods of time do not increase it nor old age diminish it; nor does it swerve from its movement the least bit or lag in its course. It will always be the same because it always was the same. Our forefathers did not see it changed; our descendants will not see it changed. It is god: he will never change. The sun never takes a detour toward the Bears that lie across the sky. It does not change its direction, going from West to East, bringing the dawn to lands that have never seen it. The moon does not grow beyond its normal sphere of light but keeps the rhythm of its waxing and waning. The stars that are attached to the sky do not fall down on the earth but accomplish their orbits in measured periods of time. All this is not the work of chance but the planning of a supreme god.

107

The Milky Way did not play an important role in ancient astrological theory, but as a striking celestial phenomenon it had to be discussed. After reviewing some older theories, Manilius revives one that Cicero's Greek source in the *Republic* 6.16 had proposed: the Milky Way is the place in heaven where the souls of heroes go when they die. These souls are of the same substance as the stars themselves, and so, through their affinity, will be drawn to them. The catalogue of great Roman statesmen and soldiers, following Greek heroes, statesmen, and philosophers, ends with Augustus, who is still alive at the time Manilius' text is written, but who is promised by the poet a preeminent place in heaven after his death. Manilius must remember Cicero's "Dream of Scipio" (*De Republ.*, Book 6) as well as the passage in Virgil's *Aeneid* (6.756ff.) in which Anchises points out to his son in the underworld the series of heroes who will shape Roman history for centuries to come.

From the following text it would seem that the promise of life after death was also a part of astrological doctrine. If one believed in the survival of the individual soul (not all Stoics did), the souls had to be ranked in some way. Thus the Milky Way offered itself as a convenient dwelling place for superior souls. It was prominent and visible—the very opposite of Hades, the great "Invisible One."

Manilius 1.758–804

Could it be that the souls of heroes, the great men who are worthy of heaven, once they are freed from their bodies and released from the earthly sphere, come here to inhabit a heaven of their own, living ethereal years and enjoying the universe? It is here that we honor the descendants of Aeacus, of Atreus, the savage son of Tydeus, and the ruler of Ithaca who conquered nature by his triumphs on land and on sea, as well as the king of Pylus, famous for his triple life-span, the kings of Greece besieging Troy [the camps of the generals and heaven (?) and Troy conquered under Hector (?)] . . . and the black son of Aurora and the Thunderer's offspring, the ruler of Lycia. Nor will I pass you by, virgin daughter of Mars and the other kings that Thrace sent and the nations of Asia Minor and Pella, famous because of the Great [Alexander], nor all the clever men who possessed mental strength and intellectual powers, whose whole status was in themselves: Solon the Just, Lycurgus the Austere, Plato the Heavenly, and he who produced him [i.e., Socrates] and through his condemnation effectively condemned his Athens, and the conqueror of the Persians whose fleets had covered the seas, but also the Roman heroes of whom there is already a large number: the kings, with the exception of Tarquinius; the Horatii, an offspring who was a whole army; Scaevola, who achieved glory by mutilation; Cloelia, a virgin more heroic than men; Cocles, who carried the Roman walls he protected; Corvinus, who acquired his spoils and his name from the raven who was his comrade-in-arms, who carried Phoebus in the bird; Camillus, who, thanks to Jupiter, gained heaven and established Rome (again) by saving it; Brutus, who founded a state he had taken over from a king; Papirius, the avenger in the wars against Pyrrhus; Fabricius and Curius, two equals, and the third victory, Marcellus and Cossus before him, having killed a king [text and meaning uncertain]; the Decii, who competed with their prayers and had similar triumphs; Fabius, who won through delays; Livius, who conquered murderous Hasdrubal with Nero as his colleague in the war; the Scipios as military commanders, sealing together the fate of Carthage; Pompey, conqueror of the world by his three triumphs, after having been leader before his time; Cicero, who gained heaven by his eloquence; moreover, the great sons of Claudius; the prominent members of the family of the Aemilii; the famous Metelli; Cato, who was superior to his fate; and Agrippa, who served under the arms of his own Mars [text uncertain].

The Julii are descended from heaven, taking their origin from Venus, and they will return to a heaven ruled by Augustus, together with Jupiter, among the stars, and there he will see in the assembly of the gods the great Quirinus on an even higher level than the shining circle of the ethereal way. Up there is the seat of the gods; this one, nearby, is for those equal to them, who follow their example through their valor.

108

Manilius speaks once more of the "mutual sympathy" that reigns in the universe and of the "sum total of things," which always remains the same, thus anticipating a law of modern physics, it seems. Manilius believes in a supreme god who has created the universe and keeps it moving, but as he puts it, "movement feeds the creation: it does not change it"—a remarkable phrase.

Manilius 2.60–79

I shall sing of the god who rules mysteriously over nature, the god who permeates the sky, the land, and the sea and who governs the whole immense structure with a unifying bond. I shall sing how the life of the whole universe is based on mutual sympathy and how it moves by the force of reason because a single spirit inhabits all its parts and radiates through the whole world, spreading itself through everything and giving it the shape of a living creature. If the whole mechanism were not built firmly out of sympathetic elements and did not obey a supreme master, and if providence did not rule the tremendous potential of the universe, the earth would not be stable nor would the stars observe their orbits (in fact, the universe would go astray and move aimlessly or else stand still and motionless); nor would the constellations keep their set courses, nor would the night flee the day and then, in turn, chase the day. The rains would not nourish the earth, nor the winds the upper air, nor the sea the clouds, the rivers the sea, the ocean the springs. Nor would the sum total of things remain the same forever through all its parts, having been arranged in a fair manner by the creator to make sure that the waves would not dry up nor the land sink nor the heaven in its motion shrink or extend beyond its normal dimensions. Movement feeds the creation: it does not change it.

109

Manilius now develops the concept of "cosmic sympathy" in an attempt to prove the validity of astrology as a science. Part of his proof is empirical: thus he speaks of sea creatures that change their shapes according to the movement of the moon. Such data had been compiled by Posidonius.

Some of the thoughts expressed in this passage are beautiful and profound and seem to belong to an ancient philosophical tradition that emerges and reemerges throughout antiquity and cannot be traced to a specific school. The rhetorical question "Who could know heaven except by the grace of heaven?" is very similar to Plotinus' axiom that the human eye must have an element of the sun in it in order to see the light of the sun.

But Manilius also operates with a concept dear to the Stoics, the *consensus gentium,* the "agreement of all nations." His argument becomes rather emotional and rhetorical, although in the end he professes not to care whether the majority of mankind listens to him. He must have encountered more than a few skeptics in his lifetime, but he is content to "sing" for the chosen few.

Manilius 2.80–149

Thus everything is organized throughout the whole world and follows a master. This god, and the reason that controls everything, brings down from the heavenly stars the creatures of the earth. Though the stars are very distant and remote, he makes us feel their influence, as they give to the peoples their ways of life and destinies and to every person a character of his own. We do not have to look far for proof: this is why the sky affects the farmland, why it gives and takes away various crops, why it moves the sea by ebb and tide. This constant motion of the sea is sometimes caused by the moon, sometimes provoked by her withdrawal to another part, and sometimes it depends on the yearly course of the sun through the year. This is why certain creatures at the bottom of the sea, imprisoned in a shell, change their shape according to the movement of the moon, imitating your waxing, Delia, and your waning. This is why you, too, turn your face back to your brother's chariot and then turn it away again, reflecting the amount of light he left you or gave you: you are a star at the expense of a star. Finally, take the cattle and the dumb animals on earth: they will never know anything about themselves and the laws of nature, but when nature reminds them, they lift up their souls to the heaven, which is their father; they watch the stars and cleanse their bodies when they see the horns of the waxing moon. They foresee the coming of storms, the return of fair weather. Who can doubt after this that man is connected with heaven . . . [something appears to be missing from the text] . . . man to whom nature gave wonderful gifts: the power of speech, a superior intelligence, and a quick mind? Does not god descend into man alone and dwell in him and seek himself? Not to mention other arts to which is given such an enviable power, a gift beyond our estate . . . [not to mention the fact that nothing is given by a law of equal distribution which shows that the universe is the work of one creator, not of matter; not to mention the fact that fate is predetermined and inescapable, and that it is the characteristic of matter to suffer, of heaven to exert pressure.] . . . who could know heaven except by the grace of heaven? Who could find god unless he were part of god himself? Who could actually see and grasp in his limited mind the enormous structure of this vault that stretches into infinity, the dances of the stars, the never-ending wars of planets and signs . . . [and land and sea under the sky and what is under them] . . . if nature had not blessed our minds with a special vision and had turned a mind related to her toward herself and taught us this marvelous science? How, if not by something that comes from heaven and invites us to heaven and to the sacred fellowship of nature? Who could deny that it would be sacrilege to grasp heaven against its will, to capture it, so to speak, and drag it down into one's soul? But there is no need for long digressions to prove something that is manifest: people do believe in our science, and that must give it authority and weight. Our science never deceives itself nor does it deceive anyone. The method must be followed according to rule, and it is trusted for the right reasons. Things happen as they were foretold. Who would dare to denounce as false what Fortuna confirms? Whose vote would win against such an overwhelming majority?

All this I would like, inspired by the deity, to carry in my song as high as the stars. I do not compose poems in the crowd and for the crowd. Alone, free, I shall drive my chariot, as if racing on an empty course, and no one will come from the opposite direction or drive along with me on the same track. I shall sing a theme for heaven to hear, and the stars will marvel and the world rejoice at the song of its poet. I shall also sing for those to whom the stars generously granted knowledge of their ways and their meaning: a very small group in the whole world. But large is the crowd that loves wealth and gold, power and the insignia of power, a life of leisure full of soft luxury, sweet and entertaining music and pleasant sounds that touch the ears. These things are understood with much less effort than the doctrine of fate. But to learn thoroughly the law of fate is also part of fate.

I I O

Ancient astrology was a science, but it was, at the same time, more and less than its practitioners claimed. Much of it was based on mathematical calculations, but the result of these, the chart, had to be interpreted according to a complex system of rules, and that part was more an art than a science; it could not be learned entirely from textbooks but required a certain amount of experience, and a dose of intuition certainly helped. The astrologer often had a chance to talk to the client and assess him, just as the dream interpreter did. It was different, of course, when a baby was born and the nativity had to be cast then and there.

By Manilius' time the astrologer had become a sort of personal adviser, a psychotherapist. His contact with many different types of clients over the years must have given him an excellent opportunity to study human nature. Manilius may have lived through the last years of the civil war, and this experience may have convinced him that the world is ruled by conflict, by strife. At the same time, friendship and love—the highest values in life, though difficult to attain—are promised by the stars.

We seem to hear the voice of a practitioner of the ancient art of astrology who has lived through difficult times and has shared the secrets of many clients. His experience confirms what his astrological studies tell him: to hate may often seem easier than to love, but it is love that we must recognize as the great cosmic force.

Manilius 2.567–607

The many different relationships between the signs cause enmities and produce hostility in so many ways and in corresponding numbers. For this reason nature has never created out of herself anything that could be more important, more precious than the bonds of friendship. Throughout so many generations of men, so many ages and periods, among so many wars and afflictions, even in times of peace, whenever the situation calls for a friend, it is almost impossible to find one. There was only one Pylades, only one Orestes who offered to die for the friend; in centuries theirs was the only competition for death; it was unique in that one wanted to die and the other refused to yield. And yet two men were able to follow their example: punishment could barely find guilt to punish; the bondsman wished that the accused would not return, and the accused feared that the bondsman would gain him his freedom. But how large is the sum of crimes throughout the centuries! How utterly impossible to absolve earth from its burden of hate! Sons had their fathers murdered for money, and the tombs of mothers . . . [something is missing from the text] Phoebus brought darkness and deserted the earth. Why mention the sack of cities, the profanation of temples, disasters of all kinds in the midst of peace, poisonous mixtures, ambushes in the marketplace, slaughter inside the city walls and a conspiracy that lurks beneath the cloak of friendship? Evil is everywhere among the people, and the whole world is full of insanity. Right and wrong are confused, and injustice makes brutal use of the law itself; crime is more powerful than punishment. No wonder: under many signs men are born for discord; hence peace has disappeared from the world; the bond of trust is rarely found and is given to few; the earth is caught in a conflict with itself, just as heaven is; the human race is ruled by the law of strife.

III

Although Manilius believes in gods or a cosmic god, he also operates with the concept of nature, *physis*. It is difficult to say whether nature is a separate entity or just a convenient term to designate all that is divine and creative and permanent in the universe. Perhaps it is a compromise between traditional polytheism, a more advanced form of Stoicism, and the specific world of the astrologers, who might be bound by Stoic doctrine, but who, in Manilius' time, were more likely to be eclectics. That the universe controls itself is a fundamental idea in this context, and "nature" seems to be just a convenient term for an autonomous, all-embracing organism in which every thought, every dream, every experience, and every action is somehow located and accounted for. Astrology, therefore, can be considered a symbolic language that expresses this truth.

For many ancient thinkers, the nature of the universe was not a scientific fact to be explored by scientific means; it was a mystery, and once fully experienced and understood, it would furnish them with a set of rules to deal with practical problems such as assessing someone's personality and predicting someone's future.

Manilius 3.47–66

Nature, the origin of everything and the guardian of mysteries, built up the enormous structures that form the walls of the world and encircled our globe, which hangs exactly in the center, with a widespread flock of stars. By certain laws she organized heterogeneous parts—air, earth, fire, floating water—into a unity and ordered them to feed one another so that harmony would rule over all these discordant principles and the world might endure, held together by the bonds of a reciprocal covenant. To make sure that nothing was missing from the overall scheme and that everything belonging to the universe was controlled by the universe itself, nature also made the lives and the destinies of mortals dependent upon the stars, so that, in their tireless revolutions they could control the success of human undertakings, the privilege of life, and fame. To those stars [i.e., the signs of the zodiac] which occupy the middle part, the heart of the universe, so to speak, to the stars that outdo the sun, the moon, and the planets but are also outdone by them, nature gave dominion: to each [sign] she consecrated its own role and fixed [there] forever the sum total, so that the idea of fate would be concentrated into a single whole.

112

Manilius here discusses the twelve "houses" into which the astrologers divided the space around the earth. These regions are represented by twelve radii in the standard astrological charts today, with the earth at the center. Unlike the signs of the zodiac, however, they do not correspond to anything in nature: they are a construction. Each house represents an aspect of a person's character and life.

Different methods of predicting someone's life-span were used by the astrologers. This one is based on two rules. First, the astrologer considers the ascendant, that is, the first house. If the first house coincides with Aries (i.e., if the sign of Aries is rising at the moment of birth), this adds 10 ⅔ years to the life of the individual. This is not the whole life-span, for the position of the moon also must be considered. If the moon is in the first house in a favorable position (i.e., in a sign that agrees with her), this grants a life-span of 78 years. It is not clear from the context whether these two figures have to be added: 78 + 10 ⅔ = 88 ⅔. This seems a rather high figure, considering the average life expectancy at that time. If one adds the life-spans granted by all twelve houses and divides by 12, one arrives at an average of just under 55 years. The highest figure is 78, and this would have been considered a ripe old age in Manilius' time. In Cicero's "Dream of Scipio" (*De Republ.* 6.12), which Manilius probably had read, Scipio Africanus the Elder predicts to Scipio Africanus the Younger his death at the age of 56; he gives special significance to this product of 7 × 8, numbers that he calls "perfect." Thus, ancient numerology confirms astrology.

Manilius 3.560–617

I have shown what kind of life, throughout distinct periods of time, comes our way at any given moment. I have also shown to what star each year, each month, each day, each hour, belongs. Now I must explain another principle that applies to the span of a person's life: it tells how many years each sign is supposed to grant. You must consider this theory carefully and keep in mind the figures if you wish to predict the length of a life by the stars. Aries gives 10 ⅔ years, Taurus 12 ⅔, Gemini 14 ⅔, Cancer 16 ⅔, Leo 18 ⅔, Virgo 20 ⅔, and Libra the same number. Scorpio equals the number of years that Leo gives, and those of Sagittarius correspond to those of Cancer. Capricorn gives 14 ⅔, Aquarius 12 ⅔. Aries and Pisces not only share their borderline but also their power: they both give 10 ⅔ years.

In order to understand the calculation in determining the length of life, it is not enough to learn the fixed number of years given by each sign. The "temples" [houses] and "parts" of the sky also have their own gifts to grant, and they add their specific amounts in a well-defined sequence when the whole configuration of stars is right. Now I shall discuss only the decrees of the "temples"; later, when the whole structure of the universe has been clearly understood and the different sections are not scattered here and there in a confusing fashion, the whole combination with its distinct powers will be approached. [Something seems to be missing from the text here.]

If the moon is in a favorable position in the "temple" of the first cardinal point, where the sky returns to the earth, and if it is rising and holds the ascendant, the course of life will be increased to 80 years minus 2. When it is placed in the zenith, it will be the same number (i.e., 80) minus 3. In the region of its setting it is less generous than 80 by 5 (i.e., 75 years). At its very lowest point it is considered to give 60 years plus 12. The trigon of the horoscope [i.e., of the ascendant], which rose first and is on the right side, grants 60 plus 8. The trigon on the left, the one that follows the preceding signs, gives 60 plus 3. The third "temple" from the horoscope, which is also the one next to the zenith, gives 60 years minus 3. The "temple" that appears below, separated by an equal distance, grants as its gift a life of 50 years. The place directly under the rising horoscope allows 40 years to come and go, adds 2 more and leaves you still young. The one that precedes the zone of the rising quarter gives 23 years to those who are born under it and snatches them away when they have just tasted the bloom of youth. The "temple" just above the setting allows 30 years and increases them by 3. The "temple" at the very bottom brings death in childhood: those born at such time will die at the age of 12, their bodies still undeveloped.

113

Manilius is an astrologer and a poet, but he is also a philosopher. In the manner of the philosophers of his age, he offers help and advice to those who are confused, distressed, or worried about the future. Lucretius, over a half century before, had offered the same kind of service, from the Epicurean point of view, in his poem *On Nature,* which Manilius certainly knew. But Manilius is a Stoic; he believes in fate and in divine Providence. Since there is nothing we can do to change the realities of life, and since everything is for the best, even if we do not see it right away, we ought to accept everything that happens to us. This, in fact, is the secret of happiness. Stop worrying about the future, Manilius says: what must be, will be, and there is no way you can influence the course of events.

Although Lucretius and Manilius belong to different schools of thought, they tell us indirectly how unhappy, how neurotic the people were for whom they wrote. We may assume that most of the mental and emotional disorders known to modern psychiatry existed in one form or another in antiquity, even if they were not recognized or described in scientific terms. Most physicians probably did not know how to treat them. In extreme cases exorcists were called in, and for the milder forms of depression or neurosis philosophers were available, but some philosophers, like Apollonius of Tyana, were also exorcists and had the reputation of being sorcerers. Philosophers in general not only lectured; they also listened to their students when they talked about their problems, and offered them advice.

Life had its complexities then as now, and when Manilius says, "We always act as if we are about to live, but we never live," we feel the truth of this today as his contemporaries must have felt it.

Manilius deals particularly with the *paradoxa* of fate. History as he knows it, from the heroic age to Augustan Rome, is full of absurdities. The unexpected, the unpredictable, always happens, yet astrologers claim to be able to foresee even bizarre events. Fate decreed that the ancient power of Troy would survive in one man, Aeneas, and because he landed in Italy, Rome, once a small village, became the center of an empire.

The poet sounds rather smug as he looks down the flight of the centuries and concludes that all this had to happen as it did for the greater glory of Rome. But the lesson he states applies to any person who may feel that some failure or defeat is final and that the future has nothing in store. "Don't despair," the Stoic philosopher says, "and don't try to change what cannot be changed. Put your trust in divine Providence; it will work for you as it did for Rome."

A certain amount of historical lore and personal experience has gone into this diatribe, which is meant to comfort ordinary people in the daily disappointments and frustrations of their lives. After stating his case as forcefully as possible, Manilius adds a caveat: fate cannot be used as an excuse for crime, nor should the good and virtuous lose their rewards, just because it could be said that fate acts through them. This is clearly an attempt to reconcile Stoicism with the legal and moral conventions of the time.

Manilius 4.1–118

Why do we waste the years of our lives worrying? Why do we torture ourselves with fears and vain desires? We grow old before our time with constant anxieties, and we lose the life that we want to prolong. Since there is no limit to our wishes, we can never be happy. We always act as if we are about to live, but we never live. The more someone owns, the poorer he is, because he wants even more: he does not count what he already has but only wishes for what he does not have. Nature needs and demands but little for itself, but we in our prayers build up a high structure from which to fall. With our profits we buy luxuries, and with a life of luxury, extortion. It is the ultimate price of wealth to squander wealth.

Set your minds free, mortal men; let your cares go and deliver your lives from all this pointless fuss. Fate rules the world; everything is bound by certain laws; eternities are sealed by predetermined events. We die the moment we are born, and on the beginning depends the end. Fate is the source of wealth and power and, more often than not, poverty: it gives us at our birth abilities and character, vices and virtues, losses and gains. No one can renounce what is given nor claim what is denied to him. No one can catch Fortune by praying against her will or escape her if she comes close to him. Everyone must bear his appointed lot.

Would the flames have given way before Aeneas? Would Troy, triumphant on the very day of its destruction, have survived in one man if Fate did not make the laws of life and death? Would the she-wolf of Mars have nursed the twins exposed to die? Would Rome have grown out of shacks? Would shepherds have brought the thunder to the Capitoline hill? Would Jupiter have agreed to being locked up in his citadel? Would the world have been conquered by a conquered people? Would Mucius have extinguished the fire with blood from his wounds and returned victorious to Rome? Would Horatius single-handedly have barred the bridge and the city to the attacking enemy? Would a young woman have canceled a treaty? Would three brothers have been killed by the heroism of one? No army won such a victory: Rome relied on a single hero, and it was brought down, even though fate decreed that it should rule the world.

Why mention Cannae and the enemy army close to the walls of Rome? Why mention Varro, who was great because he fled, and Fabius, who was great because he delayed? Did not the fortress of Carthage after the battle of Lake Trasimene admit defeat, although it could have won the war? Did not Hannibal, imagining that he had been caught in our net, pay for the downfall of his race with an inglorious death? Think of the battles in Latium and think of Rome fighting against herself. Think of the civil wars and of the Cimbrian helpless in the presence of Marius, who was helpless in prison himself. This was the man who became an exile after having been consul many times, and he was consul again after having been an exile. His downfall was like that of Libya, where he went into hiding, but then he came out of the ruins of Carthage and conquered Rome. Never would Fortuna have allowed this, had it not been decreed by Fate.

Pompey, you had overthrown Mithridates' empire. You had cleared the sea of pirates. You had been awarded triumphs after wars that had ranged over the whole world. You could now claim the title "the Great." Who would have believed that you were murdered on the shores of Egypt, with only a little wood from a shipwreck to burn your corpse, the remnants of a shattered boat serving as a pyre? Can there be such a complete reversal without the decree of Fate? Julius Caesar was born of heaven and returned to heaven, but after his victory, when he had successfully ended the civil war and held high office in times of peace, he could not escape the violence predicted so many times: holding in his hand information about the conspiracy against him and a list of names, he obliterated with his own blood, before the eyes of the whole Senate, the evidence. Why? Because Fate must prevail.

Should I list cities destroyed, kings overthrown? Need I mention Croesus on the pyre, or Priam's headless corpse on the shore, with not even Troy as his pyre? And Xerxes, whose shipwreck was more terrible than any sea could inflict? Should I bring up the king of Rome whose mother was a slave girl? Fire that was rescued from fire and flames that destroyed a temple but gave way to a man?

How often does sudden death come to the bodies of the strong! How often does death run from itself and roam through the flames! Some have been carried out for burial but returned from the grave: they were given two lives, others barely one. You see how a trivial ailment can kill and a more serious one will get better. Medical science is helpless, logic and experience baffled, therapy harmful, neglect beneficial, and procrastination often stops the disease. Food can be dangerous, poison harmless.

Sons turn out worse than their fathers or rise above their parents: they keep a nature of their own. Success [of a royal house?] comes with one man and goes with another. One who is madly in love can either swim across the sea or ruin Troy. Another's serious manner is well suited to the framing of laws. Sons kill their fathers, parents their children, and brothers meet armed in bloody combat. All this violence is not the work of men: they are forced to commit these atrocities; they are driven to their own punishment and the mutilation of their limbs.

Not every age has brought forth a Decius or a Camillus or a Cato, whose spirits remained unconquered in defeat. The raw material is there in abundance, but it will do nothing against the will of fate. The poor may not necessarily expect to live fewer years, nor can immense wealth buy a long life. Fortuna carries a dead body from a stately home; she commands a pyre and orders a tomb for exalted persons. How great is the power that orders the powerful around!

Is it not true that virtue can be unhappy and vice successful, that rashly conceived actions are rewarded and careful planning fails? Fortuna does not judge the merits of a case and support the deserving; she moves casually and indiscriminately among the crowd.

So there is something else, something greater that forces and controls us and subjects all that is mortal to laws of its own. To the men that are born from it, it assigns the years they will live and the ups and downs of their fortunes. Often it joins the bodies of animals and men, and such a birth will not grow from the seed; for what do we have in common with beasts? When was an adulterer ever punished for his sin by a monstrous birth? It is the stars that introduce new shapes; it is heaven that crossbreeds features. After all, if there were no chain of Fate, why would it be handed down to us? Why, at certain times, are all things that will come to pass prophesied?

And yet this doctrine does not go so far as to defend a crime or to cheat virtue of the rewards that it deserves. No one will hate poisonous plants the less because they do not grow of their own free will but from a particular seed; nor will tasty food be less popular because Nature, not a deliberate choice, gave us these crops. In the same way, men's merits deserve greater glory because they owe their achievements to heaven. On the other hand, we must hate the wicked even more because they are destined for crime and punishment. It does not matter where crime originates; it is still crime. The very fact that I interpret Fate in this way is ordained by Fate.

114

We have a comprehensive astrological handbook in Latin, entitled *Matheseos Libri* (*On Learning*, i.e., *On Astrology*). Its author, Iulius Firmicus Maternus, a senator from Sicily, worked on it between circa 334 and 337 and dedicated it to Mavortius, a high official.

He considers his science as something sacred, something that can only be revealed to those who are worthy and will swear a solemn oath. He compares this commitment to the initiation rites of the mysteries, which also had to be kept secret. He mentions Orpheus, the legendary founder of the Orphic mysteries, but he mentions also Pythagoras and Plato, two philosophers who reserved part of their teaching to a small group of disciples. Firmicus does more or less the same thing: he holds back parts of his science, and it is not possible to become a practicing astrologer just by reading his book. Perhaps he intended to leave the rest to oral instruction.

We look at one horoscope in particular, the only one that concerns a historical person. Firmicus uses it to illustrate the ups and downs of Fortune, and as an example for the importance of the *antiscia,* the shadows thrown by heavenly bodies at each other. This is a rather obscure point of astrological doctrine (it is not the same as the aspects), and it was apparently neglected by some practitioners who, because of that, missed part of the picture.

Firmicus does not give us the name of the native, but he has been identified by ancient historians as Ceionius Rufius Albinus who was consul in 335 and prefect of Rome from 30 December 335 until 10 March 337. This is exactly the period during which Firmicus was busy composing his work. The father of the native whose own life is somehow reflected in the nativity of the son, C. Ceionius Rufius Volusianus, was consul in 311 and again in 314. Firmicus no doubt knew one or the other (or both) personally.

The other treatise that is preserved under his name is of a completely different nature. *De Errore Profanarum Religionum* (*On the Error of the Profane Religions*) is an attack on paganism (especially some mystery cults), which, he says, should be radically suppressed by the state. After having been a great admirer of Plotinus (*Math.* 1.7.14–22), he must have converted to Christianity and abandoned his former loyalties altogether.

Firmicus Maternus, *Mathesis* 2.29, 10–12

From the horoscope that I will furnish below in detail, you may be able to learn how powerful the *antiscia* [i.e., the "shadows" thrown by heavenly bodies at each other] are and how they work in principle.

In this man's nativity the Sun was in Pisces, the Moon in Cancer,

Saturn in Virgo, Jupiter in Pisces, in the same section as the Sun, Mars in Aquarius, Venus in Taurus, Mercury in Aquarius, in the same section as Mars. Scorpio was the ascendant.

The father of this native was sent into exile after having been consul twice. The native himself was exiled for the crime of adultery but suddenly recalled and first appointed administrator of Campania, then governor of Achaea, then governor of Asia Minor, and finally prefect of the city of Rome.

Now someone who knows nothing about the theory of the *antiscia*, seeing the Sun in the same position as Jupiter, in the fifth house from the ascendant, that is, the House of Good Fortune [the following words are corrupt; one would expect a reference to the opposition of Jupiter and Saturn] would have foretold a father who was fortunate, prosperous, powerful, and so on, and made the same prediction for the native himself. But he will be unable to say anything about the exile and the incessant intrigues against him, unless he pays attention to the principle of the *antiscia*. Remember, I said that Pisces sends an *antiscium* to Libra and vice versa. Therefore, the Sun and Jupiter, both positioned in Pisces, are sending an *antiscium* to Libra, the sign in which he [the Sun] is humiliated and brought down; and this happens precisely in the [House of] Bad Fortune. It indicates the notorious exile of the father.

Jupiter, whose power and influence the beam of the *antiscium* transfers from the sign of Pisces to the sign of Libra, placed in the twelfth house, that is, the [House of] Bad Fortune, produced many enemies both for himself and his father, and gave them power.

115

At the beginning of his astrological handbook, Ptolemy attempts to explain in scientific terms why astrology works. To us, this may look like pseudoscience. After all, we know that the sun is not a planet, and new planets have been identified in the solar system, planets whose specific influences remain to be determined. Nevertheless, in Ptolemy's day, this explanation was the best he could come up with, and his authority was such that his theories were widely accepted.

Astrology, Ptolemy argued, was partly empirical, partly intuitive, partly theoretical. Its practitioners seem to have been convinced that, generally speaking, it produced results. Perhaps they forgot their failures and remembered only their successes. But skeptical outsiders demanded some sort of proof, and since statistics of failure and success were hard to evaluate, if they were kept at all, theories like Ptolemy's had to be devised in order to impress the skeptics.

Ptolemy operates with two concepts—that of the "ethereal substance," borrowed from Aristotle, and that of "cosmic sympathy," borrowed from Posidonius—but he also offers some empirical evidence. The influence of the sun and the moon on all sorts of natural processes on earth was recognized and could be substantiated by many observations. Since in astrological terms the sun and the moon were "planets," all planets were thought to influence organic and inorganic conditions on earth.

This particular section of Ptolemy's work is more of a diatribe than a manual. It is aimed at skeptics and critics, and while it uses traditional material (e.g., it points to the farmer's almanac), it also introduces a scientific hypothesis.

Ptolemy, *Tetrabiblus* 1.2.1–8

It is quite clear to everyone and can be explained briefly that a specific force emanates and spreads from the everlasting ethereal substance and that it moves toward the whole region about the earth. This region is constantly subject to change because the main elements of the sublunar [lower] sphere, fire and air, are surrounded and controlled by motions in the [upper] ethereal region. But they themselves surround and control everything else, earth and water and then plants and the creatures that live on earth and in water.

Somehow the sun, together with the atmosphere, always influences everything on earth, not only by the changes that take place during the seasons each year—creatures being born, plants bearing fruit, waters flowing, bodies changing—but also by its daily course around the earth when it gives out heat, moisture, dryness, and fresh air in a logical order and in accordance with its configurations in relation to the zenith.

The moon, being closest to the earth, releases a tremendous discharge on the earth. Most inanimate things and animate creatures live in sympathy with the moon and change along with it: rivers increase and diminish their flow according to the light of the moon; oceans turn their tides in accordance with the rising and setting of the moon; plants and living beings as a whole or in part grow and shrink in rhythm with the moon.

The transitions of fixed stars and plants also produce important conditions in the atmosphere—heat, wind, snow—which in turn influence accordingly what happens on earth. Furthermore, their aspects in relation to each other, as they meet and mix their influences, create many different developments. The power of the sun prevails if one looks at the overall structure of quality [text uncertain], but the other heavenly bodies, to a certain degree, either contribute to this or oppose it. The moon does this more obviously and more continually—for instance, when it is new, at quarter, or full. The other stars do this at greater intervals and less obviously—for example, in their risings and settings and their mutual approaches.

If you look at it this way, it must seem logical to you not only that things already fully formed are by necessity affected by the motions of these heavenly bodies but that the germination of the seed and its maturity are shaped and formed according to the condition of the atmosphere at the time. The more observant farmers and shepherds make guesses about the winds that blow at the time of fertilization and the sowing of the seeds, and they can tell about the quality of the outcome. Important events predicted by obvious aspects of the sun and the moon are registered not by trained scientists but by careful observers in general. For instance, we look at future events, and some of them are caused by a major force and a simpler order, and this is obvious even to untrained minds—well, even to some animals. I am talking of the seasons and the winds as they happen year after year. The sun is generally held responsible for these changes. Things that are less generally known are seen necessarily by trained observers. Sailors, for instance, know the peculiar signs of winds and storms as they come up in certain intervals, caused by the aspects of the moon and the fixed stars with the sun.

116

Like Manilius [no. 104], Ptolemy believes that astrology is a divine art, and that it is revealed to mankind as a special favor of the gods. How, then, can it go wrong, as it admittedly sometimes does? The art itself is not to blame, Ptolemy argues; rather, the fault lies with the imperfect human beings who practice it. To illustrate the problem, he compares astrology with the art of navigation and with medical science. We do not discredit navigation as an art because navigators sometimes make mistakes. What Ptolemy says here about the "beauty" of astrology, he also says in a short poem [no. 121].

We see from this excerpt (as from no. 102) that the art that Ptolemy, Manilius, and others thought divine had its critics in antiquity. Among other things, these critics objected to the habit astrologers had of finding out as much as possible about the native, his family, his background, and so on, instead of limiting themselves to the information they found in the stars. In reply to this, Ptolemy remarks that physicians, too, interest themselves in certain aspects of an illness that are, strictly speaking, outside the realm of medical science. The whole person must be considered, he says. Artemidorus gives the same advice to the interpreter of dreams.

Ptolemy, *Tetrabiblus* 1.2.20

It would be wrong to dismiss this type of [astrological] prediction completely only because it sometimes can be wrong. After all, we do not discredit the art of navigation as such simply because it is often imperfect. When we deal with any art, but especially when we deal with a divine art, we must accept what is possible and be happy with it. It would be wrong to demand—in a typically human, haphazard manner—everything from it and to expect final answers, which it cannot give, instead of quietly appreciating its beauty. We do not blame physicians who talk about the disease in general and about the patient's "idiosyncrasy" when they examine him. Why should we object to astrologers when they include in their diagnosis the native's nationality, country of origin, manner of upbringing, and other given circumstances?

117

According to Ptolemy, medical astrology was first developed in Egypt, and it seems to have been a fairly sophisticated discipline. The physician-astrologer would examine the patient and also cast his nativity, which would give him additional information about the patient's state of health. The stars might tell him about the weak points in the patient's organism, or they might warn him of an impending crisis. If, after having made a prognosis, the physician-astrologer hesitated to choose between two types of treatment, the stars might indicate which one was preferable. Again we see the doctrine of sympathy and antipathy at work.

Ancient medicine obviously was not the science it is today, and so the combination of medicine and astrology should not surprise us. If, in a given society, most people believed that the stars either cause or indicate human illness, along with everything else that happens to human beings, this society would also expect the stars to reveal the cures for the illness, and a physician who ignored astrology altogether might have fewer patients than one who weighed the influences of the stars in his diagnosis.

Ptolemy, *Tetrabiblus* 1.3.17–19

As far as [astrological] predictions are concerned, it seems that even if they are not infallible, their potential at least is most impressive. Similarly, prevention works in some cases, even if it does not take care of everything; and even if these cases are few and insignificant, they should be welcomed and appreciated and considered an unusual benefit.

The Egyptians were aware of this. They developed this technique further than anyone else by thoroughly combining medicine with astrological prognosis. They would never have established certain means of prevention or protection or preservation against conditions that exist or are about to exist in the atmosphere, in general or specifically, if they had been convinced that the future could not be changed or influenced. In fact, they placed the possibility of reacting by a series of natural abilities right after the theory of fate. They combined with the possibility of prediction the useful and beneficial part of the method they called "medical astrology" because they wanted to find out, thanks to astrology, the specific nature of the mixtures in matter and the things that are bound to happen because of the atmosphere and their individual causes. They felt that without this knowledge any remedies must fail, since the same remedies would not be appropriate for all bodies and all affections. On the other hand, their medical knowledge of sympathetic or antipathetic forces in each case and their knowledge of a preventive therapy for an impending illness as well as the cure for an existing disease enabled them as much as possible to prescribe the correct treatment.

118

The ancient astrologers made an effort to determine the moment of their client's birth as closely as possible because they knew that the nature of the universe was changing from second to second. The conventional time-measuring devices used in everyday life were not accurate enough; only an astrolabe would do. The term *astrolabe* originally meant "star-taking," and the instrument used by Ptolemy himself may have been a very simple affair. In the Middle Ages three distinct types of astrolabe emerged: (1) a portable armil, that is, an instrument consisting of a metal ring fixed in the plane of the equator, sometimes crossed by another ring in the plane of the meridian; (2) a planisphere, that is, a polar projection of part of the celestial sphere; (3) a graduated brass ring with a movable index turning upon the center.

The ancients probably knew at least one of these types, but Ptolemy is not very explicit about how to use them. In his time the astrologers still observed the sky, but they also had charts and ephemerids, and they kept records of striking celestial phenomena. They noted the exact time when the moon was full, and so on. Thus the "astral time" of a person's birth could be defined in terms of the lapse in time since the most recent phenomenon was recorded.

Ptolemy, *Tetrabiblus* 1.3.1–3

Often there is a problem about the foremost and principal fact, the fraction of the hour of birth. In general, only observation by a "horoscopic" [i.e., hour-watching] astrolabe at the very moment of birth can, for a trained observer, give the exact time. Almost all other "horoscopic" instruments that most serious astrologers use are in many ways capable of errors: sundials, because of their incorrect position or the incorrect angle of the "gnomon" [i.e., a pin or triangular plate that casts a shadow]; water clocks, because of the stoppage and irregular flow of the water for various reasons, or just by accident. Thus it seems necessary to explain first how to find by a natural, logical method the degree of the zodiac that would be rising, using as a premise the degree of the hour known nearest to [the time of] birth, which is determined by the method of "ascensions." We must then take the syzygy [i.e., conjunction or opposition] of two heavenly bodies immediately preceding the birth—it may be a new moon or a full moon—and when we have determined the exact degree of both luminaries [i.e., sun and moon] if it is a new moon, or, if it is a full moon, the exact degree of the one that is above the earth, we must see what stars control it at the time of birth.

119

Mars and Saturn are generally considered "bad" planets, but their harmful influence can be weakened if they are in "honorable" positions at the time of birth, that is, in a sign where they feel at home—for example, Mars in Aries, Saturn in Aquarius. If both are in hostile signs, they produce the types of people that Ptolemy lists, or perhaps one should say that they create the disposition toward a criminal career. From this catalogue of more or less repulsive types, the astrologer has to pick the one that fits other aspects of the nativity.

Ptolemy, *Tetrabiblus* 3.13.14–15

Saturn associated with Mars in honorable positions produces people who are indifferent [or: steadfast], hard-working, outspoken, obnoxious, boastful cowards, austere in conduct, pitiless, contemptuous, harsh, quarrelsome, rash, chaotic, devious, hijackers, wrathful, inexorable [reading *adeetous* with Camerarius, 2nd. ed., 1553, for *adektous*] demagogues, tyrannical, grasping, haters of their fellow citizens, fond of strife, vengeful, evil through and through daredevils, impatient, pompous, vulgar, pretentious, oppressors, unjust, uncondemned [reading *akatakritous* with Camerarius, 2nd ed., 1553, for *akataphronetous*], haters of their fellow men, inflexible, unchangeable, but at the same time cautious and practical, not to be defeated by their rivals and generally successful. In the opposite positions, he [Saturn, allied with Mars] makes robbers, pirates, forgers, wretches, dirty profiteers, lawbreakers [reading *athesmous* with

Camerarius, 2nd ed., 1553 for *atheous*], cold-hearted, violators, crafty, thieves, perjurers, murderers, eaters of forbidden foods, evildoers, homicides, poisoners, impious, robbers of temples and graves, and totally depraved characters.

120

We know of several astrological handbooks in Greek verse, but most of them are lost. One that is preserved is entitled *Apotelesmatica* (*Influences*) and is attributed to Manetho, an Egyptian high priest of the third century B.C. who compiled a history of Egypt.

The six books, as we have them, seem to have been written by different authors. Books 2, 3, and 6 form a coherent poem whose author has inserted his own horoscope (6.728–50). It is that of a person born in A.D. 80. Book 4 appears to be a complete poem in itself, and Books 1 and 5 are collections of fragments. These portions may date from the second and third centuries A.D.

Our excerpt deals with the nativity of entertainers, such as acrobats and clowns. The author stresses that their work involves hardships and risks, and for him, they definitely belong to a lower social class. It is clearly not very desirable to be born under these stars. At the same time, he conveys a certain degree of compassion with their lives. They travel a lot and they are homeless—like gypsies. The author, whoever he was, has a remarkable gift for description, and he loves unusual words.

Manetho, Apotelesmatica 4.271–85

When the untiring Sun looks at the fiery star of Mars, hitting him with swift rays [i.e., is in the same house] and in quartile aspect to [certain] signs of the zodiac along its heavenly path, namely two-horned Taurus, panting [?] Leo and Aries, the sign of spring for suffering mortals, he [the Sun] creates athletes who are real daredevils, anxious to please their audiences, working long hours, crazy about performing, treading the air with their footsteps, tumblers who jump from [?] the top of the theater [or: circus-tent?], carefully timing their act between heaven and earth, actors, masters of farce and humorous invective, [entertainers] who will grow old in foreign lands, buried by strangers, birds of the earth, creatures who are citizens of no city, dull-witted, needy, ugly, telling obscene jokes, without undergarments, completely baldheaded, whose lives provide as much low-class entertainment as their art.

121

This short poem by Ptolemy sums up what might be called the religious feeling that here and there shines through in his technical handbook [see *no. 116*]. It is not so much an awareness of the power that his craft gives him. It is not a feeling of humility in the face of the universe. It is a religious experience: by interpreting the will of the gods from the movements of the stars, Ptolemy feels that he is directly in touch with the gods.

It has been said that Kepler, the greatest astronomer and astrologer of the seventeenth century, died of malnutrition because he charged such modest fees that he could not pay the grocer's bills. But in his work, too, one encounters a spirit of exaltation that transcends the worries of everyday life.

Ptolemy, *Anthologia Palatina* 9.577

I know that I am mortal, the creature of one day. But when I explore the winding courses of the stars I no longer touch with my feet the earth: I am standing near Zeus himself, drinking my fill of Ambrosia, the food of the gods.

122

This text from the second or third century A.D. was once part of an astrological handbook. It deals with the various constellations of the planets: conjunction (0° distant), opposition (180° distant), and trine (120° distant). The significance of each constellation depends on its own nature (trines are usually favorable), the nature of the planets involved, and the positions of the planets in the signs of the zodiac. The astrologer's art consists in weighing all these factors and in determining their overall meaning.

The symbolism behind this particular reading is fairly obvious: Mercury indicates good opportunities, especially in business deals; Jupiter stands for power, prestige, and authority; Mars suggests aggressiveness. Such symbolism works in different ways on different levels, however, and much depends on the native's position in life.

Tebtunis Papyri, no. 276

. . . If, moreover, Mercury is in conjunction, and Saturn is in an irregular situation, . . . from an unfavorable circumstance. If Mars, at the same time, is in opposition to Saturn, while the constellation [?] mentioned before continues to exist, [this will wipe out?] the profits of transactions.

Saturn in trine with Mars signifies [bad] fortune. Jupiter in trine or in conjunction with Mars makes great kingdoms and empires. Venus in conjunction with Mars brings about fornication and adultery; if, moreover, Mercury is in conjunction with them, they produce scandalous lusts. If Mercury is in conjunction with them, this causes successful business transactions, or [it means that] a man will earn a living by . . . or by his wits [text uncertain]. . . .

If Mars appears in trine with Jupiter or Saturn, this produces great happiness, and he [the native] will acquire great wealth and. . . . If Jupiter and Saturn form this aspect, and Mars comes in conjunction with either . . . he will obtain [wealth] and collect a fortune but spend it and lose everything. If Jupiter, Mercury, and Venus are in conjunction, they bring about glory and empires and great prosperity; if the conjunction takes place at the morning rising [of Venus], that person will have prosperity from youth onward.

123

Vettius Valens, an astrologer of the second century A.D., considers it his duty to tell a client the truth about his future and to help him face that truth. Most people are unable or unwilling to accept their fate; in fact, they like to trick themselves by believing in Chance and cherishing Hope and letting these pseudodivinities control their lives. We are always ready to hope that Fate will not be as harsh as the serious astrologer predicts, and we are more than willing to anticipate a sudden change in Fate due to Chance. Our prayers may foster new hopes, but these hopes are in vain. We must try to be good soldiers of Fate and obey orders as best we can. Or, using another image, we must be like the professional actors, who play their roles and leave the stage when the plot demands their exit. During the performance we must play the role assigned to us by Fate and make the best of it, even if we do not like it very much.

The self-discipline that Vettius Valens demands is the self-discipline of Stoic ethics, and his message is essentially the same as Manilius' [no. 113].

Vettius Valens, Anthologiae 5.6.4–12 (p. 219 Kroll)

Fate has decreed for every human being the unalterable realization of his horoscope, fortifying it with many causes of good and bad things to come. Because of them, two self-begotten goddesses, Hope and Chance, act as the servants of Destiny. They rule our lives and, by compulsion and deception, make us accept what has been decreed. One of them [Chance] manifests herself to all through the outcome of the horoscope, showing herself sometimes as good and kind, but sometimes as dark and cruel. Some she raises up in order to throw them down; others she flings into obscurity to lift them up in greater splendor. The other [Hope] is neither dark nor serene; she always hides herself and goes around in disguise and smiles at everyone like a flatterer and points out to them many attractive prospects that are impossible to attain. By such deceit she rules most people, and they, though tricked by her and dependent on pleasure, let themselves be pulled back to her, and full of hope they believe that their wishes will be fulfilled; and then they experience what they do not expect. Sometimes Hope offers firm expectations, but actually she has abandoned you already and is gone to others. She seems to be close to everyone, and yet she stays with no one.

Those who are not familiar with astrological forecasts and have no wish to study them are driven away and enslaved by the goddesses mentioned above; they undergo every kind of punishment and suffer gladly. Some find part of their expectations fulfilled, so they put up higher stakes and wait for a permanently favorable outcome, without realizing how unstable things are and how easily accidents can happen. Some who have been disappointed in their expectations, not just occasionally but again and again, surrender body and soul to passion and live dishonored and disgraced, or else they exist as the slaves of fickle Chance and treacherous Hope and never are able to achieve anything in life.

But those who make truth and the forecasting of the future their profession acquire a soul that is free and not subject to slavery. They despise Chance, do not persist in hoping, are not afraid of death, and live unperturbed. They have trained their souls to be brave and are not puffed up by prosperity nor depressed by adversity but accept contentedly what comes their way. Since they have renounced all kinds of pleasure and flattery, they have become good soldiers of Fate.

For it is impossible by prayers or sacrifice to overcome the foundation that was laid in the beginning and substitute another more to one's liking. Whatever is in store for us will happen even if we do not pray for it; what is not fated will not happen, despite our prayers. Like actors on the stage who change their masks according to the poet's text and calmly play kings or robbers or farmers or common folk or gods, so, too, we must act the characters that Fate has assigned to us and adapt ourselves to what happens in any given situation, even if we do not agree. For if one refuses, "he will suffer anyway and get no credit" [Cleanth., frag. 527 Arnim].

124

In his textbook Vettius Valens tells us about the joys of astrological research. The following passage reads almost like a prose paraphrase of Ptolemy's short poem [*no. 121*]. To these men, astrology was clearly more than a profession, more than a science: it was a vocation, and it left them no time, nor any desire, for the popular pastimes and amusements of the day, such as horse races, concerts, plays, the ballet. Vettius Valens seems to believe that all so-called pleasant experiences contain in themselves, or are inevitably followed by, an element of pain. This is not true in the case of the investigation of the sky: it conveys an experience of pure joy. This might be said of any kind of research that demands hard work and long hours, progresses slowly, but brings, as a reward, great insights and discoveries. Some alchemists speak of their craft in equally enthusiastic terms.

Vettius Valens, *Anthologiae* 6.1.15–16 (p. 242 Kroll)

I never got carried away by the various kinds of horse races or by the sharp crack of the whip, or by the rhythmic movements of dancers, nor did I enjoy the superficial charm of flutes and poetry and melodious songs or anything else that attracts an audience by a certain art or by jokes. I never took part in any harmful or useful occupations that were divided between pleasure and pain. I had nothing to do with disgraceful and troublesome courtesans [*hetairas,* Usener's conjectural restoration of a missing word]. But once I had experienced the holy, reverent contemplation of celestial phenomena, I wished to cleanse my character of every kind of vice and pollution and leave my soul immortal. I felt that I was communicating with divine beings, and I acquired a sober mind for my research.

125

In his lectures Plotinus, the most eminent Neoplatonist, dealt with magic and occult science in general. He himself appears to have had "psychic" gifts, and he was once told that he possessed a guardian spirit of a higher order than most mortals, and he was also able to protect himself against powerful black magic (Porph., *Plot.*, chs. 53–55, 56–60).

Among the lectures of the master that Porphyry—himself a serious student of occult practices—published in six groups of nine books called the *Enneads,* there is one dealing with astrology (3.1.5). In this context Plotinus does not reject the possibility that the stars may guide our lives; in fact, he accepts the Stoic doctrine of "cosmic sympathy" which underlies much of astrological thought. But for him the stars do not act as causes by themselves; they are only indicators of things to come. They cannot direct our mind, our will, nor can they shape our character. Because the stars are divine beings, they certainly cannot be held responsible for the evil in this world.

If this is the case, Plotinus must assume the existence of a power higher than the stars, a power that rules or influences both the stars and our destinies, and the stars must merely function as a set of cosmic instruments giving important information to those who are able to read them correctly.

For Plotinus all modes of beings are determined by a kind of expansion or "overflow" of a single impersonal and immaterial force that he calls "The One" or "The Good." The problem of evil would require a special discussion: Plotinus considers it essentially a form of nonbeing represented by the world of the senses insofar as it has a material base; thus he eliminates the concept of an evil cosmic soul as an antagonist of "The Good."

In this particular lecture Plotinus wishes to restrict and reduce the exaggerated claims of the astrologers without actually denouncing their craft. As he sees it, there is such a thing as heredity, and beyond heredity and the powers above there is something that we may call "our own," that is, our own individuality. Thus, one's life, one's personality, may be the product of all three influences.

It would follow from this statement that not everything in a person's character and life can be seen in the stars, and that the astrologer who relies only on the stars is bound to give us false or incomplete information about ourselves.

Plotinus seems familiar with the principles and techniques of contemporary astrology. He must have read at least one of the current manuals and noted a number of fallacies in order to discuss them in his lecture. He probably also had contacts with some practitioners through his students. Hence, in spite of his criticism, he may be considered a reliable source, and his treatment of the subject fills a few gaps in our knowledge of ancient astrology.

Plotinus, *Enneads* 3.1.5–6

But perhaps. . . the motion, the course, of the stars controls and guides every single thing, depending on the relative position of the planets, their aspects, their risings, settings, and conjunctions. On this basis people predict everything that will happen in the universe concerning every single person, and especially everyone's destiny and personality. They say that one can see the other living beings and the plants grow and diminish because of their sympathy with the planets, and that they are affected by the planets in other ways as well. Moreover, they claim that the regions of the earth are different from one another in regard to their relationship to the universe, especially to the sun. Living creatures in general, as well as plants, conform to their regions, as do human shapes, sizes, colors, tempers, desires, ways of life, and characters. Hence the motion of the universe controls everything.

In answer to this one must say first of all that [the partisans of astrology] ascribe to . . . [other] principles what is ours—acts of will, passions, weaknesses, impulses—but give us nothing and leave us like rolling stones, not like human beings who have work of their own to do in accordance with their own nature. Surely one must give to us our due; at the same time, some influences from the universe obviously join what is our own and belongs to us. One ought also to distinguish between the things we do ourselves and the things we experience out of necessity, and not attribute everything to these [cosmic forces]. No doubt something reaches us from those regions and from the differences in the atmosphere—for instance, heat and cold in our individual temperature—but something also comes from our parents. We are certainly like our parents in our appearance and also in the irrational impulses of our soul. On the other hand, even if people are similar to their parents in appearance, you may see a great deal of difference in their character, their way of thinking—not corresponding to the regions—so that phenomena of this kind probably come from another principle. Our resistances to our physical temperaments and to our desires might also be mentioned at this point. But the astrologers look at the constellations of the stars and tell us what is happening to every individual, using this as evidence that the events were caused by them, as if the birds, for instance, were the cause of what they [merely] indicate, as would everything the diviners look at when they predict the future. But one can be more precise in looking at this.

Whatever an astrologer predicts, looking at the positions occupied by the stars at the moment of someone's birth, is supposed to happen, not only because the stars suggest it but also because they bring it about. And when they talk about a person's noble birth—meaning that he comes from a distinguished line of fathers and mothers—how is it possible to say this if the parents already had what the astrologers predict from a particular constellation?

They also tell the fate of the parents from the nativity of the children and the character and fate of the children from the nativity of the parents—children that are not yet born!—and they predict the death of a brother from the horoscope of his brother, what will happen to the husband from the horoscope of his wife, and vice versa. Well, how could the position of the stars in relation to an individual cause what has been predicted from the horoscope of the parents? Either the situation as it existed earlier will have to be the cause, or if it is not, the later one cannot be the cause either.

Moreover, the likeness between parents and children shows that good looks and bad looks are inherited and are not caused by the movement of the stars. It is only reasonable to assume that all kinds of living creatures are born at the same time as men, and that all of them ought to have the same fate, since they share the same position of the stars. How are men and other living creatures produced at the same time by certain constellations?

But in truth all individual things come into being in accordance with their own nature: a horse because it comes from a horse; a human being because he or she comes from a human being, and any particular human being because he or she comes from the same type of human being. Admitting that the movement of the universe contributes something—though it must leave the main contribution to the parents—admitting also that the stars act on the physical parts of us in many physical ways, giving us heat and coolness and the physical mixtures resulting from those: how can they influence our character, our way of life, and that which is least dependent on physical mixture, such as becoming a teacher or a geometrician or a gambler or an inventor? And how could a bad character be sent by the stars? They are divine, after all. In general, they are supposed to give all the bad things when they are in bad condition, for instance when they set and pass under the earth—as if something different were happening to them when they set, from our point of view, while, in fact, they always move on the heavenly sphere and keep the same position in relation to the earth. One must not say that a god, looking at another god in one position or another, becomes worse or better, so that they do good things for us when they are feeling good and vice versa.

No, we must say that the stars move for the preservation of the universe. But they also offer another service: those who look at their constellations, as if they were a kind of writing, those who can read this kind of writing, read the future from their patterns, interpreting their meaning by the systematic use of the principle of analogy, just as if someone said: "When the bird flies high, it means outstanding deeds."

126

In this lecture Plotinus continues his discussion of astrological doctrines. During the years of his teaching he often returned to the same themes, approaching them from different angles. Like Socrates, he seems to have formed his thoughts as he moved along, but he preferred the monologue to the dialogue form. Again we see that he was familiar with his subject.

It seems absurd to him to say that the stars are angry at men and punish them by making them unattractive or poor or sickly or wicked. (We should remember that the planets were named after the Greco-Roman gods, who had divine power but not divine love and forgiveness, and who were, in fact, ruled by every human passion and emotion.) Many people in Plotinus' age probably had no difficulty believing that astral gods actually caused all the evils in the world—sickness, crime, war—because they were angry. But this, Plotinus says, is unthinkable.

There is another possibility: the stars are not favorable or unfavorable per se, but they emit a positive or a negative radiation, depending on their position in the universe. Or else some are favorable, others unfavorable, all the time, but their positions modify the intensity of their (positive or negative) radiation.

Plotinus sums up the various doctrines of the astrologers before he delivers his attack on them. First, he considers whether or not the planets have souls. Obviously, if they have souls, they also have a will of their own, and they can intentionally hurt us. But they are divine beings and therefore they do not want to hurt us. They certainly cannot be bribed. If the planets have no will of their own, they might conceivably be forced by their positions and constellations to affect us adversely. Plotinus here seems to refer to that part of astrological doctrine that establishes some kind of pecking order in heaven. A planet may be basically benign but may also be temporarily demoted within the celestial hierarchy and can even be forced to do something bad against its nature.

This whole concept of a celestial empire in which everyone has a certain position but can move up or down, having greater authorities above and lesser authorities below, reflects somehow the hierarchical structure of the great powers of the ancient world: Babylonia, Egypt, Persia, Rome. In such a hierarchy it was possible for a good and enlightened official or commander to hurt the people under him because an order had come from above. It was also possible for a wicked and corrupt governor to do something good, against his will, because he was bound by his instructions. The way huge political and administrative structures had functioned over many centuries must have influenced people's thinking about the greatest structure of all—the universe. They could probably best conceive of it in terms of their own day-to-day experiences in their small world.

In his lecture, Plotinus attacks this kind of model of the universe. He refuses to see the planets as exalted heavenly bureaucrats who are unfair to ordinary people because of pressure from above or because they happen to be in a bad mood at a particular time.

In the first printed edition of the *Enneads,* as well as in Marsilio Ficino's Latin translation, a curious passage (par. 12) appears following paragraph 5. It seems to defend astrology against the kind of criticism that Plotinus levels at it, although it never attacks his main doctrine. Scholars have suggested that this is a short paper delivered by one of Plotinus' students. Ancient philosophers sometimes encouraged their students to contradict them and to try to build a strong case against them, for the sake of argument, as an exercise in dialectics. The teacher was thus forced to find new arguments for his own position or to refute the objections that seemed to weaken it. Paragraph 12 could well be the summary of such a critique, found among the papers of the master and edited along with them. It could also be an excerpt that he himself composed as he read an astrological treatise, planning to use it in class as an *aide-mémoire*. At any rate, it seems to belong here, not after paragraph 11, where most editors place it. The paragraph traditionally numbered 6 does not continue the argument of paragraph 5 but appears to be a rebuttal to paragraph 12.

Plotinus, *Enneads* 2.3.1–5.12.6

1. I have said elsewhere [*Enn.* 3.1.5] that the course of the stars indicates what is going to happen in individual cases, but does not itself, as most people think, cause everything to happen. My argument offered some proofs, but now I must discuss it more accurately and in more detail, for to think of it this way or that makes quite a bit of difference.

People say that the planets in their courses not only cause things in general, such as poverty, wealth, health, and sickness, but also ugliness and beauty, and, what is most important, vices and virtues and also the actions that result from them in every given case, on every given occasion, just as if they were angry at men over matters in which men do not wrong them, since men are the way they are because the planets made them that way.

It is also said that the planets give so-called benefits to people not because they love them but because they [the planets] are either unpleasantly or pleasantly affected according to the place they have reached in their course. It is also said that they are in a different mood when they are in their zenith and when they are descending.

But what is most important? People say that some of the planets are good and others bad and that those which are supposed to be good give bad gifts and the good ones become evil. People also think that the planets, when they look at each other, cause one thing, but when they do not look at each other, something else, as if they were not what they are by themselves but were one way looking at each other, another way not looking at each other.

They also think that a planet is good when he looks at such and such another planet, but if he looks at a different one, he deteriorates, and that it makes a difference whether he looks at him in such and such an aspect or in another one. They also believe that the mixture of all planets is different again, just as a blend of various liquids is different from any of the ingredients. These and others of this kind are the general opinions. We now ought to examine and discuss each point individually; this might be a good starting point.

2. Should we assume that the planets have souls or not? For if they have no souls, they offer nothing but heat or cold. Now, if we assume that some stars are cold, they will influence our destiny only as far as our bodies are concerned, since there is a bodily motion in our direction, one that would not produce a significant change in our bodies, since the effluence from every single star is the same and since they are mixed together into a unity on earth, so that there are only local differences, depending on our distance from the stars. The cold star will have the same kind of influence, but according to its different nature.

How, then, can they make some people wise, some foolish, some schoolteachers, others professors of rhetoric, others kithara players and professionals in other arts, and also some rich, some poor? How can the stars be responsible for the other things that do not have their cause and origin in a blend of bodies? How, for example, can they give a person such and such a brother, a father, a son, a wife, make a person prosper for the time being, or become a general, a king? But if the stars have souls and do all this on purpose, what have we done to them that they would hurt us, especially since they are established in a divine region and are divine themselves? That which makes men evil does not belong to them, nor does anything good or bad happen to them either because of our happiness or our misery.

3. "The planets do not do these things of their own free will but because they are forced by their positions and aspects." But if they are forced, all of them surely ought to do the same things in the same positions and under the same aspects. What difference can it actually make to a planet if it passes now through this portion of the zodiac, now through that? It does not even move along the zodiac itself, but far below it, and wherever it may be, it is in the region of heaven. It would be ridiculous for a planet to become different according to each sign through which it passes and to hand out different gifts and to be different when it is rising, when it is at the center, and when it is declining. For it certainly does not enjoy being at the center, nor is it distressed or inactive when it declines. Another planet does not grow angry when it is rising, nor is it in a good mood when it is declining. One of them is even better when it is declining. For each individual planet is, at any given time, at the center as far as some are concerned, but declining as far as others are concerned, and when it is declining for some, it is at the center for others. Surely it cannot be, at the same time, cheerful and depressed, angry and benevolent. And, of course, it is absurd to say that some of them are cheerful when setting, others when rising. For this

would mean, again, that they can be cheerful and depressed at the same time. And then: why would their grief hurt us? But it is totally inadmissible that they should be cheerful at one time and depressed at another.

They are always in a serene state and enjoy the good they have and the good they see. Each has its own life all by itself, and each has its own good in its action. This has nothing to do with us. Generally speaking, living creatures that have no relationship to us can affect us only incidentally, not through their main activity. Their activity is not aimed at us at all, except that they, like birds, may incidentally act as signs.

4. It is also absurd to say that a planet is happy when it looks at [forms an aspect with] another planet, and that another planet feels differently looking at another one. What enmity could be between them? About what? Why should it make a difference whether two planets form an aspect of 120° or 180° or 90°? And why should one form an aspect of this sort with another and then, when it is in another sign of the zodiac, nearer to it, not form any aspect at all?

Generally speaking, how can they ever do what they are supposed to do? How can each one act by itself? How can all of them together produce an effect that is different from their individual effects? They certainly do not form an agreement between themselves and then act against us, executing their decision and reaching some sort of compromise. None of them forcefully prevents the influence of another, and none of them concedes to another under pressure a field of action. And to say that one planet is glad when he is in the region of another, while the other is affected quite differently when he is in the region of the former—is it not like saying that two people like each other, adding that A likes B while B hates A?

5. Astrologers also claim that one planet is cold, stating in addition that the farther away from us it is, the better for us, as if its evil influence on us were in its being cold; and yet it ought to be good for us when it is in the opposite sign of the zodiac. They also teach that the hot and the cold planet in opposition are both dangerous for us; actually there ought to be a mixture [of temperatures]. They say that one planet enjoys the day and becomes good as it warms up, whereas another one being fiery enjoys the night, as if it were not always day for them, I mean light, and as if the other planet, being high above the earth's shadow, could ever be overtaken by darkness.

Their theory that the full moon in conjunction with such and such a planet is favorable, but unfavorable when she is waning—this theory could be turned upside down, if this sort of thing is admissible at all. For when she is full as far as we are concerned, she would be dark to that planet which moves above her in the other hemisphere, and when she is waning, as far as we are concerned, she would be full from the point of view of that planet; so she ought to do the opposite when she is waning [as far as we are concerned], since she looks at that other planet with her full light. To the moon herself it would make absolutely no difference what phase she is in, since one half of her is always illuminated. It might make a difference if she were getting warm, according to their theory. But the moon could get warm even if she is dark from our point of view; and when she is good to someone, she is full for him; could this not serve as a proof by analogy?

12. The side of the moon which looks toward us is dark in relation to the regions of the earth. It does not hurt the regions above. But since that [which is above] does not help, being far away, this [i.e., the conjunction] is supposed to be less favorable. When the moon is full, it is sufficient for what is below, even if that planet is far away. When the moon shows her dark side to the Fiery Planet (Mars), she is supposed to be good to us, for his power prevails, since it is more fiery than it needs to be for him. The bodies of living creatures that come from there [the higher regions] vary according to their temperature, but none of them is cold. Their position indicates this. The planet called Jupiter has a well-balanced blend of fire, and so does Venus. For this reason, because of their similarity, they are supposed to be harmonious. They are alien in nature to the planet called Mars because of its mixture and to Saturn because of its distance. Mercury, being indifferent, assimilates himself to all, it seems.

All of them contribute their share to the whole, and their relationship with one another is such that it benefits the whole, as does each individual part in one single living creature. They are there for its sake, as, for instance, the gallbladder serves the whole body, but also the organ next to it, for it is its duty to arouse an impulse and also to keep the whole body and the organ next to it from dangerous excess. Similarly, there must be, in the universe, some such organ whose function it is to produce sweetness. There also are eyes. Everything shares a common experience through its irrational part: thus it is one and there is one single harmony.

6. But it is surely total nonsense when astrologers call this planet Mars and this one [reading *Aphroditen tende themenous*] Venus and make them responsible for adultery when they form a certain aspect, as if they satisfied their mutual desire from the wantonness of human beings. Assuming that they look at each other, how could anyone accept that they enjoy the sight but nothing else beyond that? What kind of life is this for the planets, anyway? Innumerable living creatures are born and exist, and to each the planets are supposed to allot such and such a thing: to give them fame, make them wealthy or poor or frivolous, and transfer all their activities to them. How can the planets possibly be responsible for all this?

VI

ALCHEMY

Introduction

The word *alchemy* is derived from the Arabic *alkimya*, which consists of *al* 'the' and a pre-Arabic noun, probably Egyptian *kamt, quemt,* or *chemi,* all of which seem to mean "black" or "black stuff" and could refer to the mud of the Nile, but apparently also to a black powder produced from quicksilver in a metal-manufacturing process developed in Egypt. At one time this particular powder was thought to be the basic substance of all metals.

Alchemy, the forerunner of chemistry, was an occult philosophy or science that sought to bring the macrocosm (the universe) into a close relationship with the microcosm (the human being). It was based on the law of cosmic sympathy and contained elements of astrology, mysticism, religion, and theosophy. A good deal of ancient alchemy is scientific in the modern sense of the word and highly technical in nature. Special apparatuses were constructed and applied under conditions that are reminiscent of modern research. But the ultimate goals of alchemy were not always "scientific" from the present-day point of view. Whatever important discoveries were made seem to have been more or less accidental and were not always fully recognized. Some were even kept secret, then forgotten, and had to be discovered again centuries later.

The main purposes of alchemy were the transmutation of baser metals into silver and gold, the creation of an elixir of life to prolong it, and the creation of a human being (*homunculus*). All these were useful, negotiable achievements that could give enormous power and wealth to the alchemist or to the king who employed him. At the same time, the alchemist seems to have worked on the discovery of his own soul—its purification and perfection.

Let us look at the practical aims in more detail. That precious metals such as gold and silver could be produced from baser ones like copper, iron, lead, and tin was, of course, an illusion, but even fake silver and gold were of great commercial value, as is costume jewelry today. Royalty,

435

nobility, and the rich wore the real thing, but the rest of the people for the most part were quite happy with an imitation. A superficial coloring of the baser metals—perhaps by adding small quantities of real gold or silver—already enabled alchemists to coat objects and thereby approximate the shining quality of silver or gold. The alchemists also came up with alloys that looked enough like precious metals to deceive anyone except a real expert.

In Egypt goldsmiths and metallurgists had considerable experience with various metals. When Hellenistic Egypt attracted Greek scientists, no doubt new progress was made. We have seen that magic in general, as well as astrology and other occult sciences and techniques, developed in Hellenistic Egypt as a result of an exchange of ideas between Egyptian practitioners and Greek scientists. The same might be said about alchemy. Presumably, as in the case of astrology, many ideas and traditions had been generated in Mesopotamia but later drifted toward Egypt, and by that time Greek scientists had arrived in Egypt. This reconstruction is largely speculative. It would seem, however, that any ancient knowledge available at the time of Alexander's conquest could have been developed by disciples of Alexander's own teacher, Aristotle. These disciples were invited by the Ptolemies to come to Egypt and work there.

All ancient civilizations were fascinated by gold—how to find it in the crust of the earth; how to wash it, fuse it, refine it; and, if it did not occur naturally, how to find ways of producing it artificially. Alchemy was no doubt encouraged by the kings of Egypt because it helped create new industries, especially the production of jewelry and cosmetics.

The oldest extant tract on alchemy, the Papyrus Ebers, a sixty-eight-foot roll discovered in the necropolis of Thebes, sometimes called the oldest book in the world, is an important document for *iatrochemistry,* that is, the medical use of chemistry or alchemy. It contains more than eight hundred prescriptions and recipes. One is entitled "a delightful remedy against death" and recommends half an onion mixed with the froth of beer. There is nothing magical about this, for both onions and beer were popular among the Egyptians. Other recipes are clearly based on the laws of sympathy, antipathy, or analogy. To protect one's clothes against mice, one had to rub cat's fat into them; just as living cats kept the mice away, the fat of a dead one worked as a protection. Some of the potions were given symbolic names—for instance, "dragon's blood"—to indicate their power.

Such recipes were kept in the royal archives and in temple libraries for centuries. They were jealously guarded, in the same way that industrial secrets are guarded today, to keep ahead of the competition, but also because they were thought to be based on divine revelation. In later antiquity, Hermes Trismegistus, a combination of the Egyptian god Thoth and the Greek god Hermes, emerged as the god who had discovered alchemy and the other occult sciences and taught them to mankind. By this time alchemy had undergone the influence of Neo-Pythagoreanism, and the belief in numbers as symbols of cosmic forces had begun to play a role.

The Two Aspects of Alchemy

It is important to distinguish between the two aspects of ancient alchemy. On the one hand, it was an applied science, and its aims were practical and commercial. On the other hand, it was almost a religion, a mystic way of life. For us, it may be difficult to reconcile these two aspects, for at any given time or in any given practitioner one of the two aspects may have eclipsed the other. Perhaps we should use the term *alchemy* only when referring to the combination of the two aspects and speak of *ancient chemistry* when the religious element is absent.

The Practical Side

Alchemists were working on drugs that could restore health and prolong life. They also developed dyes and colors. We know that Tyrian purple, for instance, was much in demand in the days of the Roman Empire because of its richness and resistance to the wear of washing. The manufacturing process, which is roughly understood today, was a secret of the Tyrians, and as long as they maintained their monopoly, their profits must have been enormous. To compete, alchemists in other countries tried to develop dyes that were as attractive as Tyrian purple but easier to make and therefore cheaper, and to a certain extent they succeeded, for the indigo-dyed wrappings of some mummies are still amazingly fresh today.

In Hellenistic times and later, Egypt also had an important cosmetics industry. Perfumes, lotions, and different kinds of makeup (rouge for the cheeks, black powder to darken the eyebrows) were exported to other countries.

The ultimate aim of the alchemists—as of chemical researchers today— seems to have been to imitate and accelerate the processes that occur more slowly and less perfectly in nature, to achieve the same results faster and thus less expensively. One could say that they were trying to improve upon nature, to use natural resources in the most rational way.

Chemical processes such as oxidation, reduction, solution, smelting, and alloying were known to the ancient alchemists. Sulfur and mercury showed the most spectacular effects as far as changes in color and substance were concerned; hence, they were among the most popular. The fermentation of barley into beer had been known for thousands of years in the Middle East; the fermentation of grape juice into wine was known to the Greeks of the heroic age; and the distillation of spirits may have been discovered by an Egyptian alchemist toward the end of antiquity, though the technique was apparently forgotten soon afterward and had to be rediscovered in the Middle Ages. The word *alcohol* is Arabic, but it originally designated the fine metallic powder (usually powdered anti-mony) that Near Eastern women put on their eyelids.

Some of the apparatuses used are known. The *alembic* is a simple distilling apparatus invented by Cleopatra (if not the queen herself, some unknown alchemist who worked for her). Its name is derived from an Arabic word that preserves the Greek *ambix* 'cup' or 'beaker', and it consisted of the *cucurbit* 'gourd-shaped vessel', and the *ambix* 'cap', which fed the distilled product into a receiver. According to tradition, the first double boiler also was invented by a woman, Mary the Jewess (it is still called *bain-marie* in French), and consisted of a flat vessel full of hot water in or over which other vessels could be placed so that their contents might be warmed, evaporated, or dried. The *kerotakis* was a closed vessel in which thin leaves of copper and other metals were exposed to the action of various vapors, for instance, the vapor of mercury. This device appears to have been a kind of *alembic*, or *circulatory*, that is, a still or retort that had its neck or necks bent back so as to enter its lower part. The *athanor* ("furnace" in Arabic) was a small domed tower that contained an egg-shaped glass vessel lying in a sandbath over a fire; a constant heat could be maintained using this apparatus.

Egyptian technology, long before the Hellenistic era, had reached a high level. There was, for example, a flourishing industry producing a variety of aromatic oils, perfumes, and blends of incense for domestic use and for export. Carefully blended oils were used for anointing both the living and the dead, but they also served as medications. Kings and priests were anointed with these precious substances, and they were rubbed into the altars and the statues of the gods.

Jars with the residue of perfumes have been found in Egyptian tombs. The ladies—and not only the ladies—wished to be as beautiful and well-groomed in the next world as they had been in this one. But ritual use in the cult of the dead is also possible: incense and aromatic essences could be burned as sacrifices for the deities and the deified dead.

In ancient Egypt, the perfume and incense industry was in the hands of the priests who had their own workshops in the sacred precincts. The making of aromatic oils and certain blends of incense (like the famous *kyphi*) was a sacred art, as we know from Exodus (ch. 30). Both the holy anointing oil and the sacred incense described by Moses were almost certainly psychoactive ("entheogenic") and enabled the priests to "see God" or to hear God's voice. It may be assumed that Moses had learned the composition of these substances from the priests of Egypt.

Under the Ptolemies, thanks to Greek scientists who were now working in Egypt, alchemy must have made rapid advances. We know the names of several successful practitioners, and some works that belong to a later period were based on discoveries made at that time.

A few years ago, the ruins of an enigmatic building were discovered at En Boquet, in the world's lowest point, near the Dead Sea. There is every reason to believe—from the presence of vegetal matter, for instance—that this was an alchemical laboratory that specialized in the production of aromatic essences. The archaeologist who directed the excavations, Mordechai Gichon, called the site "Cleopatra's Workshop." We may never know whether the queen—like the Byzantine empress Zoe much later—personally supervised the production, but her interest in perfumes and poisons is well known.

When Plutarch, in a famous passage (*Life of Antony,* ch. 26) describes Cleopatra on her royal barge, looking like the goddess of love herself, surrounded by servants in theatrical costumes, he does not omit the "wonderful scents from many perfumes," designed no doubt to act on her Roman visitor's senses and, through them, on his brain.

Shakespeare (*Antony and Cleopatra* II 2, vv. 192–98) has developed what he found in Plutarch to conjure up a complex aura of sophisticated seduction by a gorgeous spectacle and a lavish display of powerful scents:

> The barge she sat in, like a burnish'd throne
> sat on the water: the poop was beaten gold,
> purple the sails, and so perfumed that
> the winds were lovesick with them; the oars were silver,
> which to the tune of flutes kept stroke, and made
> the water which they beat to follow faster,
> as amorous of their strokes. . .

Many achievements of ancient technology border on the magical, especially if their secret was well kept. In fact, they could be described as *Magia naturalis.* A good example is Greek Fire, a highly combustible mixture useful in naval warfare because it burned on water. Something like it was already used in Hellenistic times, but its invention is usually attributed to Byzantine alchemists. To a Byzantine theologian with an interest in magic, Michael Psellos, we owe a fascinating description of the secret rituals performed by the empress Zoe (c. 978–1050) in her private laboratory inside the palace; here she experimented with various perfumes, *aromata,* which, as Psellos carefully puts it, she "offered to God" (*Chronographia* 6, chs. 64ff.). In a sense, Zoe continued the tradition of Cleopatra.[1]

Many other simple devices continued in use throughout the Middle Ages. The earliest alchemistic tracts were written in Egyptian, but in the Hellenistic period the most important textbooks seem to have been in Greek. From Greek they were translated into Arabic, and from Arabic into Latin. Thus, a considerable body of information has reached the West, some of it in Greek, some only in translation.

The Spiritual or Mystical Side

The mystical side of alchemy is about as well documented as its practical side. It is marked by a quest for spiritual perfection, just as the search for precious metals involved the perfecting and refinement of raw materials. The process is best illustrated by the aphorism, "Out of other things you will never make the One, until you have first become the One yourself."

Many alchemic operations can be understood as sacrificial offerings, as ceremonies to be accomplished after the alchemist himself has been initiated into some higher mysteries. A long period of spiritual preparation is indispensable. The ultimate goal of this process, as in the mystery religions, is salvation. Thus alchemy appears to be a Hellenistic form of mysticism. Because the soul is divine in origin but tied to matter in this world and isolated from its spiritual home, it must, as far as possible, purify the divine spirit inherent in it from the contamination by matter.[2]

In his search for the *materia prima,* the alchemist discovers hidden powers within his own soul. The symbols he draws and studies help him explore his collective unconscious; the reading and rereading of books derived from divine revelation may create the drowsiness of intoxication; watching the chemical processes in his laboratory for hours on end may produce a kind of trance or an exhaustion that leads to trance.[3]

Thus alchemy can be more than a science; it can be a way of life, like religion or magic. Even when there are no tangible results, the alchemist goes on reading, praying, meditating, and distilling. Perhaps he will make an important discovery, but it will come more or less by accident, as a by-product. Lead never turns into gold, and the philosopher's stone never materializes, but the search for perfection continues.

The alchemist's quest to improve matter, or to ennoble baser substances, appealed to those who had been trained in the great philosophical schools of Greece—to the Platonists, who believed that the creation was basically good, and to the Aristotelians, who believed that nature, though not perfect, strives toward perfection. Indeed, some of the basic philosophical principles of alchemy were no doubt derived from earlier thought. The unity of all things, or rather their unity within diversity, had been postulated by the Eleatic school in the sixth century B.C. For the alchemists this principle was symbolized by the *Ouroboros,* the serpent that "eats its tail" and that carries the legend *hen to pan* 'all is one'. The legend has been explained or paraphrased: "One is all, and by it all, and for it all, and if one does not contain all, all is nothing." This rendering reflects the position of Plotinus, who said: "Everything is everywhere and everything is everything and every single thing is everything" (*Enn.* 5.8.4).

Unifying Concepts

Within the unity of all things there are opposites, such as the four elements—fire and water, air and earth—a doctrine that was known in India and Egypt long before the time of Aristotle. But these opposites are not absolute; one can be transformed into another, and the principle of change, transformation or transmutation, plays an important role in alchemy. Solid water (ice) resembles earth, whereas vaporized water (steam) resembles air, yet water and steam are the same substance. Fire can be thought of as the energy that brings about changes by the heat it produces: fuel is consumed, and the substance that boils in the apparatus changes in character. To the four material elements Aristotle added a fifth, the *quinta essentia,* or ether, a purer form of fire or air, the substance of which the heavenly bodies were thought to be composed, but which is also found in different degrees of admixture in the animal, vegetable, and mineral worlds.

The principle of transformation was clearly all-important to the alchemists. According to Ovid, it was one of the great cosmic laws, and in his *Metamorphoses* he traces the theme from the creation of the world—the transformation of chaos into cosmos—to the transfiguration of Julius Caesar into a star: *In nova fert animus mutatas dicere formas.* There are also hundreds of stories in Greek mythology telling of people being transformed into animals, trees, or stars.

Seeds become flowers and trees, caterpillars become butterflies, and human life from birth to death is a series of transformations or transitions. There is some wonderful magic at work in the universe, some real, some fantastic, like Ovid's fairy tales. If the unity of matter is accepted and the possibility of a powerful transforming agent is admitted, anything can become anything else. In a sense the gods of antiquity were the greatest alchemists; if nothing else worked, a prayer might produce results, and when there were results, the alchemist—like the astrologer or the magician—felt that he himself was a god: this was his reward.

In truth, we have come full circle. Alchemy and magic are closely related; in fact, it is probably impossible to separate them. Many magical texts could be classified as alchemistic recipes. Alchemy and astrology also are related. During alchemistic operations the stars had to be watched, the names of the "planets" were transferred to certain metals, and the astrological symbols of these metals served to designate them: the sun was gold, the moon silver; Mars was iron, Mercury quicksilver; Saturn was lead, Jupiter tin.[4]

NOTES

1. For further discussion of Greek Fire and the empress Zoe, see the epilogue.

2. Festugière, *La Révélation d'Hermès Trismégiste,* 1: 260ff.

3. "Pray, read, read, read, reread, work, and you will find" (*ora, lege, lege, lege, relege, labora, et invenies*) is another aphorism. The mystic aspect of alchemy was described by the American scholar E. A. Hitchcock in *Remarks on Alchemy and the Alchemists* (Boston, 1857). See also T. Burckhardt, *Alchemy: Science of the Cosmos, Science of the Soul,* trans. W. Stoddart (Baltimore, 1967); and Biedermann, *Hand-lexikon der magischen Künste.*

4. Les Belles Lettres (Paris) is planning a new edition of Greek alchemistic texts (the Budé series) in twelve volumes, with introductions, French translations, and notes. The first volume, edited by R. Halleux, with an introduction by H.-D. Saffrey, was published in 1981 under the title *Les Alchimistes grecs.*

Texts

127

The *Ouroboros,* the snake that bites its own tail, is a symbol often used by alchemists. It represents the unity of all forces and processes in the cosmos. To know one single thing by studying it carefully is to know everything. The macrocosm is reflected in the microcosm. The formula that supposedly explains the symbol seems to express the doctrine that the individual reality exists for the sake of universal reality, but also vice versa: the universe is there for the one thing. If the universe were not present, in a mystic sense, in the one thing, there would be no universe.

The mystic language of alchemic texts presents many problems. The written texts are not enough. No doubt the ancient study of alchemy needed a teacher to interpret them and fill in the gaps.

The Ouroboros (1:132–33 Berthelot)

One is all, and by it all, and for it all, and if one does not contain all, all is nothing.

128

The Precepts of Hermes Trismegistus were probably engraved on an emerald tablet at one point to emphasize their value. "Thrice-Greatest Hermes" is a Greek adaptation of the Egyptian god Thoth, and he was thought to have revealed to mankind all the arts and sciences, especially the occult sciences. The text of the *Precepts* is known from two versions: one in Arabic, attributed to Geber (or Jabir) Ibn Hayyan; the other in Latin. The Arabic version may reflect a lost Greek original; the Latin version is believed to depend on the Arabic.

There are thirteen precepts altogether and they are intended as a summary of the science of alchemy. The number *thirteen* may be significant as a "magic" number; but discounting I (a brief preface designed to impress the reader) and XIII (a brief summary), there are only eleven precepts.

II. This precept is an affirmation that the microcosm reflects the macrocosm, and vice versa. The "wonders of the one Thing" expresses in language what the *Ouroboros* symbolizes visually: if you understand one substance perfectly, or if you can actually produce it, you understand the universe. This is a miracle, but then the world is full of miracles.

III. The "One Being" is the supreme god at whose command (the "One Word") the world was created. This god—like the Old Testament Yahweh—can reveal his secrets to mankind, either directly or through an intermediary such as Hermes. Thanks to divine revelation, creating the tiniest substance is, in principle, equivalent to creating the universe. The alchemist is on the same level as his god. But creating one substance is only the beginning of a process that continues ad infinitum. By transformation or adaptation of the "One Thing," other substances are created.

IV. Sun, Moon, Wind, and Earth are essential cosmic forces in any creative process. The Sun and Moon may represent gold and silver in the present context, but they could also be astrological influences that had to be considered in an alchemic operation. The Earth not only brings forth the food that we need but it also contains precious metals. The Wind spreads seeds, but it is also the Spirit, because *pneuma* in Greek covers both meanings.

V. The "One Thing" is *the* most perfect thing in the world (Father of Perfection" seems to be a Semitism, like "Sons of the Kingdom"). If the "One Thing" is done well, the whole world will be in fine condition.

VI. The "power" is the divine power operating through the alchemist. "Earth" represents any solid substance that can be used for a practical purpose. In order to be completely useful to mankind, the spiritual power should be transformed into material things. Alchemy is a domain where spiritual and material forces come into contact with each other and produce something of value.

VII. Earth is the coarse element, Fire the subtle one, but it is possible that the precepts were aimed at processes of refinement or distillation in general. To extract "Fire" from a coarser substance was one of the goals of alchemy.

VIII. The right substance, the right apparatus, the right procedure, was not enough. The alchemist had to acquire and cultivate a certain mental attitude. Nothing could be gained without mystic experience. The ascent and descent of the soul proceed through the planetary spheres (which represent material substances as well as qualities of human character and intellect).

IX. "Virtue" is the conventional translation of the Greek term *arete*, which really means "effectiveness" or "power." To achieve power the alchemist must be a visionary. The creative process in the mind is even more important than the creative process in the test tube. The progress of alchemy as a science depended on new discoveries, new insights, new inventions, and these were thought to be divinely inspired.

X. Here the act of creating a substance in the alchemist's laboratory is compared with the greatest creative act, the creation of the world by the demiurge. The alchemists liked to think of themselves as semidivine figures.

XI. The "wonders that are here established" (or: "performed"?) must refer to the actual alchemistic operations described in a standard textbook or transmitted orally by a master.

XII. Hermes Trismegistus reminds the reader that his precepts are based on divine revelation. The "three parts of cosmic philosophy" are no doubt magic, astrology, and alchemy, for these were the three domains over which the "Great Thoth" of the Egyptians presided. The statement indicates how strongly the author believed that these three occult sciences formed a unity.

The traditional Latin text of the Emerald Tablet is given by H. Kopp, *Beiträge zur Geschichte der Chemie* (Brunswick, 1869), pp. 376–77. The Latin and the Arabic versions are compared by J. Ruska, *Tabula Smaragdina* (Heidelberg, 1926). Among the many attempts to make sense of the text, I mention the following: F. Barrett, *Lives of the Alchymistic Philosophers* (London, 1814), pp. 383–84; E. J. Holmyard, in *Nature* 112 (1923): 525–26; T. L. Davis, in *Journal of Chemical Education* 3 (1926): 863–75; R. Steele and D. W. Singer, in *Proceedings of the Royal Society of Medicine* 21 (1928): 41-57; M. Gaster, in *The Quest* 21 (1930): 165–69; L. Thorndike, in *Isis* 27 (1973): 53–62.

The Precepts of Hermes Trismegistus

I. What I say is not fictitious but reliable and true.

II. What is below is like that which is above, and what is above is like that which is below. They work to accomplish the wonders of the One Thing.

III. As all things were created by the One Word of the One Being, so all things were created by the One Thing by adaptation.

IV. Its father is the Sun and its mother the Moon. The Wind carries it in its belly. Its nurse is the Earth.

V. It is the father of Perfection in the whole world.

VI. The power is strong if it is changed into Earth.

VII. Separate Earth from Fire, the subtle from the coarse, but be prudent and circumspect as you do it.

VIII. Use your mind to its full extent and rise from Earth to Heaven, and then again descend to Earth and combine the powers of what is above and what is below. Thus you will win glory in the whole world, and obscurity will leave you at once.

IX. This has more virtue than Virtue itself, because it controls every subtle thing and penetrates every solid thing.

X. This is the way the world was created.

XI. This is the origin of the wonders that are here established [or, performed?].

XII. This is why I am called "Thrice-Greatest Hermes," for I possess the three parts of cosmic philosophy.

XIII. What I had to say about the operation of the Sun is completed.

129

Zosimus of Panopolis (today Akhmim, on the east bank of the Nile in Egypt) is considered one of the great alchemists of the early Christian era. Scholars believe that he lived in Alexandria at some time during the fourth century A.D. and used its prestigious library. We know that he traveled to Rome at least once, for his own account of the trip survives in a manuscript in Cambridge, England.

The present text is part of his work *On Completion*. It is corrupt in several places, even where the context is clear, and therefore the translation remains tentative.

The work is dedicated to Theosebeia, presumably a wealthy lady who was interested in Zosimus' alchemic researches. He makes it clear to her that the kings of Egypt had traditionally sponsored this kind of research, but under the strictest conditions of secrecy. He obviously has in mind the Ptolemies, who ruled Egypt from 323 until 30 B.C. We do not know whether these Macedonian kings continued an older tradition, but they clearly recognized the value of the natural resources of the country, and they encouraged scientific and technological research. Hellenistic Egypt manufactured metals, jewelry, textiles, perfumes, papyrus, and other goods on a large scale, and its economy depended on the export of these goods throughout the Mediterranean region. Some of these industries were royal monopolies, and the manufacturing processes were carefully guarded secrets. The research chemists who worked for the crown were not allowed to publish the results of their work. Any important discoveries were exploited by the government. In modern terms, the kings owned the patents. Similarly, all mining rights were owned by the government.

All this we learn from Zosimus, who wrote a few centuries later. He

defends the early alchemists who wrote about their work but were prohibited from publishing their most important discoveries. Only the Jews,
he says, were the exception to this rule—they did not respect the prohibi-
tion. There was a large Jewish community in Alexandria. We know of the
Jewish philosopher Philo. And a Jewish alchemist, Mary, is credited with
the invention of the water bath, which is still called *bain-marie* in French
cookbooks. Thus some Jewish scientists of the Ptolemaic period were not
loyal subjects of the crown, according to Zosimus. At the same time, he
credits them with preserving in clandestine fashion valuable knowledge
that would otherwise have been lost completely when Cleopatra's empire
collapsed. No doubt a good deal of Hellenistic technology was lost at that
time because it had been kept secret. The enforced secrecy may explain
why the fairly sophisticated chemistry of the period was classified as
magic tinged with mysticism.

Zosimus, *On Completion,* excerpts (2:239–40 Berthelot)

Here is confirmed the Book of Truth.
Zosimus to Theosebeia greetings!

Madam, the whole kingdom of Egypt depends on these two arts: that
of the appropriate things and that of the minerals. For the so-called
Divine Art, whether in its dogmatic, philosophical part, or in that part
which is mostly guesswork [reading *hypopteuousa* for *hypopiptousa*], has
been given to its guardians for [their] support, and not only itself, but also
those four arts which are called "Liberal Arts" and the "Arts and Crafts."
Their creative application belongs [?] to the kings. Thus, if the king
agrees [?], he who has a share of this knowledge from his ancestors, either
by oral tradition [?] or having deciphered it from the slabs . . . but even he
who had a full knowledge of these things did not practice them, for he
would have been punished. In the same way, the workmen who knew
how to strike the coins of the kingdom were not allowed to do this for
themselves; they would have been punished. Similarly, under the kings of
Egypt those who knew the technique of "cooking" and the secret of the
"procedure" did not practice this for themselves but served the Egyptian
kings, working to fill their treasuries. They had their own inspectors and
supervisors, and there was strict control as far as "cooking" was concerned, not only in itself, but also in respect to the gold mines. For if
anything was found by digging, the law in Egypt demanded that it be
officially registered and delivered.

Some blame Democritus and the ancient authors [in general] that they
did not mention those arts but only the "Liberal Arts." But why blame
them? They could not do otherwise, since they depended [?] on the kings

of Egypt and boasted to be among the "Prophets" of the first order. How could they have revealed, and have made public, knowledge that was reserved for the kings [?], thus giving to others the power that controls wealth? And even if they could have done it [?], they were jealous of their knowledge. Only to the Jews did they secretly explain these techniques and write and hand them down [for them]. This is why we find that Theophilus, son of Theogenes, has recorded the locations of gold mines, and Mary [the Jewess] has described [alchemic] ovens, and other Jews similarly.

130

The Greek text of the *Book of Comarius* reads like a translation from another language, or perhaps it was written by someone whose Greek was inadequate. It is certainly far removed from classical Greek. There are, in addition, textual corruptions introduced by the scribes. Texts that were put to practical use were often tampered with. The successive owners of such handbooks were no doubt practicing alchemists themselves, and they probably annotated their copies. Or if they copied a text, they were likely to leave out material that was of little interest to them. Hence, these treatises have survived in different versions or "recensions," and it is therefore impossible to reconstruct an archetype.

The language is that of a mystic in trance and can, perhaps, only be fully understood by other mystics. Or else it uses words with hidden meanings and is a language that must be learned by those who have been initiated.

An additional problem is created by the apparently deliberate gaps left in such texts by authors who were unwilling to reveal all the secrets of their art and who therefore forced their readers to study with a teacher. Certain things are to be explained later, but the explanations never come, either because the text is incomplete or because the author forgets his promise. (We encounter the same difficulty in astrological literature: none of the treatises we have is a complete textbook enabling the beginner to become a master in a series of steps, following practical examples. This was apparently not the way these subjects were taught.)

The *Book of Comarius* is dedicated to "Cleopatra the Divine," also called "the wise woman," but not necessarily the famous queen. The prayer at the beginning, with its unmistakably Christian character, must be considered a later addition, perhaps by a Byzantine monk who copied (or edited) a pagan treatise. For a long time alchemy was not banned by the Church as a form of magic: on the contrary, as centers of learning, the monasteries were probably among the few places where alchemy could be studied and where texts were available. The prayer at the beginning of this text was perhaps designed to give an edifying character to the work and to place it above suspicion.

Comarius begins with a brief cosmogony and then turns to practical matters such as metals, colors, and apparatuses. A group of philosophers (i.e., scientists) is then introduced, and Cleopatra delivers to them the knowledge she has received from Comarius.

From the more practical precepts, the reader is led to general discourses on the wonders of nature. The symbolism is rich, the language mystic, and the frequent exhortations to the reader to listen to what clearly cannot really be understood increase one's frustration. In the concluding section, alchemy is described as providing a key to the mystery of resurrection, another reason for a Christian to study the subject.

Book of Comarius, Philosopher and High Priest Who Was Teaching Cleopatra the Divine the Sacred Art of the Philosopher's Stone, excerpts (3:289–99 Berthelot)

Lord, God of all powers, Creator of all of nature, creator and maker of all the celestial and supercelestial beings, blessed and eternal ruler! We celebrate you, we bless you, we praise you, we worship the sublimity of your kingdom. For you are the beginning and the end, and every creature visible and invisible obeys you, because you have created them. Since your eternal kingdom has been created as something that is subject to you [?], we implore you, most merciful ruler, in the name of your unspeakable love for mankind, to illuminate our minds and our hearts so that we, too, may glorify you as our only true God and the Father of our Lord Jesus Christ, with your all-holy, good, and life-giving Spirit, now and forever and ever. Amen.

I shall begin this book with the account concerning silver and gold that was given by Comarius, the philosopher, and Cleopatra, the wise woman. The book at hand does not include the demonstrations concerning lights and substances. In this book we have the teaching of Comarius, the philosopher, addressed to Cleopatra, the wise woman.

Comarius, the philosopher, teaches the mystical philosophy to Cleopatra. He is sitting on a throne. He has devoted himself to philosophy, which he ignored before [?]. Even now [?] he has spoken to those who understand mystical insight, and with his hand he has shown that everything is One and consists of four elements.

As an [intellectual] exercise he said: "The earth has been established above the waters, the waters on the tops of mountains. Now, take the earth that is above the waters, Cleopatra, and make a spiritual body from it, the spirit of alum. These things are like the earth and the fire, in respect of their warmth to the fire, in respect of their dryness to the earth. The waters that are on the mountaintops are like the air in respect of their coldness, like the water in respect of their wetness with the air and the fire [?]. Look, from one pearl, Cleopatra, and from another one you have the whole [technique of] dyeing."

Cleopatra took what Comarius had written and began to put into practice the applications of other philosophers, to divide into four parts the beautiful philosophy [?], the one [that teaches that] the matter derived from the natures, as it has been taught and discovered, and an idea of the operations of its difference [?]. Thus [they say?], searching for the beautiful philosophy we have found that it is divided into four parts, and thus we have discovered [?] the general idea of the nature of each of them, the first having blackness, the second whiteness, the third yellowness, the fourth [?] purpleness or refinement. On the other hand, each of these things does not exist from its own general nature [?], but they depend [?] generally on the elements, [and so?] we have a center from which we can proceed systematically. Thus, in between the blackness and the whiteness, the yellowness and the purpleness [?] or refinement, there is the maceration and the washing [out?] of the species. Between the whiteness and the yellowness there is the technique of casting gold, and between the yellowness and the whiteness there is the duality of the composition.

The work is accomplished by the application of the breast-shaped apparatus, the first experiment consisting in separating the liquids from the oxides [?], and this takes a long time.

Next comes the maceration, which consists [?] of the mixture of water and wet oxide [?].

Third, the dissolution of the species, which are burned seven times in an "Askelon vessel." This is how one operates the whitening process and the blackening process of the species by the action of the fire.

Number four is the yellowing process by which one mixes [the substance?] with other yellow liquids and produces wax [?] for the yellowing, in order to achieve the desired goal.

Number five is the fusion, which leads from the yellowing to the gilding.

For the yellowing one must, as mentioned above, divide the composition into two halves. Once it has been halved, one of the parts is mixed with yellow and white liquids, and then you can blend it for any purpose you have in mind.

Again, if the fermentation is a refinement [of the species?], that is to say that refinement and fermentation [constitute the?] perfect transmutation of the composition of the gilding.

This is the way that you, too, must proceed, my friends, when you want to approach this beautiful technique. Look at the nature of plants and their origin. Some descend from the mountains and grow from the earth; some ascend from the valleys; others come from the plains. Look how they develop, for you will [must?] harvest them at special times, on special days; you will pick them from the islands of the sea and from the highest place. Look at the air that is at their service and the nourishment that surrounds them, to make sure that they are not harmed and do not die. Look at the divine water that moistens them and the air that governs them, once they have been incorporated into one essence.

Ostanes and his followers answered Cleopatra: "In you is hidden the whole terrible and strange mystery. Enlighten us in general, but especially about the elements. Tell us how the highest descends toward the lowest, and how the lowest ascends toward the highest and how the one in the middle approaches the highest to unite itself with it and what is the element (that acts) on them. And (tell us) how the blessed waters descend from above in order to see the dead that are lying around, in chains, oppressed in darkness and obscurity inside Hades, and how the remedy of life reaches them and wakes them up from sleep and awakens them to an awakening [reading *eis gregorsin* for *tois ktetorsin* vel sim.], and how the new waters flow toward them, at the beginning of the descent and borne on the couch, descend approaching with the fire, and a cloud carries them, and out of the sea ascends the cloud that carries the waters."

Considering what had been revealed to them, the philosophers rejoiced.

Cleopatra said to them: "When the waters come, they awaken the bodies and the spirits that are enclosed in them and are weak. For again they suffer oppression, and again they will be shut up in Hades, and in a short while they grow and ascend and put on different glorious colors like flowers in spring, and spring itself rejoices and is glad at the beauty they wear.

"For to you who are wise I say this: When you take plants and elements and stones from their places they appear to be mature and [yet they are] not mature; for the fire tests everything. When they are clothed in glory and in shining colors from the fire, then they will appear to you as greater ones through their hidden glory, and [you will see] their exquisite beauty, and fusion [will be] transformed into divinity, for they get nourished in the fire, just as an embryo, nourished in its mother's womb, grows slowly. When the appointed month is near, nothing prevents it from coming out. Such also is the power of this admirable art.

"They suffer in Hades and in the tomb in which they lie from waves and ripples that follow each other, but when the tomb is opened, they will ascend from Hades like the babe from the womb. When the philosophers have contemplated the beauty [of this], just like a loving mother [contemplates] the baby to which she has given birth, they seek to nourish, like a baby, this art, [but] with water instead of milk. For the art imitates [or: is like] the baby and, like the baby, it takes shape, and [there comes a time] when it is perfect in every respect. Here you have the sealed mystery.

"From now on I shall tell you clearly where the elements and plants lie. But first I shall speak in riddles. Climb to the top of the ladder, up the mountain covered with trees, and see: there is a stone on top. Take the arsenic from the stone and use it for whitening divinely. And see: in the middle of the mountain, underneath the arsenic, there is its bride [mercury?, or yellow arsenic, as opposed to the white one?], with whom it unites itself and in whom it finds its pleasure. Nature rejoices in nature, and outside of it there is no union. Descend to the Egyptian Sea and bring back from the sand, from the source, the so-called natron. Unite it with these substances, and they bring out the all-coloring beauty; outside of it there is no union, for the bride is its measure. See, nature corresponds to nature, and when you have assembled everything in an equal proportion, then natures conquer natures and rejoice in one another.

"Look, scientists, and understand! Here you have the fulfillment of the technique of bridegroom and bride having been joined and becoming one. Here you have the plants and their varieties. Look, I have told you the whole truth, and I shall tell it to you again. You must look and understand that from the sea ascend the clouds carrying the blessed waters, and they refresh the earth and make the seeds and the flowers grow. Similarly, our cloud, coming out of our element and carrying the divine waters, refreshes the plants and the elements and does not need anything that is produced by any other soil.

"Here you have the strange mystery, brothers, the completely unknown [mystery]; here you have the truth that has been revealed to you. Look how you sprinkle your soil, how you sprinkle your soil and make your seeds grow in order to harvest when it is ripe.

"Now listen and understand and judge correctly what I say. Take from the four elements the highest arsenic and the lowest arsenic and the white and the red, equal in weight, male and female, so that they are joined to each other. Just as the bird hatches and brings to perfection its eggs in warmth, so you, too, must hatch and polish [or, bring to perfection?] your work by taking it out and watering it in the divine waters and [warming it] in the sun and in burned places, and you must roast it in a gentle flame with the virgin milk and hold it [away] from the smoke. And enclose it in Hades and move it in safety until its structure becomes more solid and does not run away from the fire. Then you take it out of it, and when the soul and spirit have joined each other and become one, then you must throw it on solid silver, and you will have gold [of a quality] that the storehouses of the kings do not have.

"Here you have the mystery of the philosophers. Our fathers made us swear never to reveal it and never to divulge it, since it has divine shape and divine power. For divine is that which is united with the Godhead and accomplishes divine substances, in which the spirit is embodied and the mortal elements are animated; receiving the spirit that comes out of them, they dominate each other and in turn are dominated by each other, just like the dark spirit, which is full of vanity and despondency, the one that has power over the bodies and prevents them from growing white and receiving the beauty and the color in which they were clothed by the Creator (for body, spirit, and soul are weak because of the darkness that stretches over them).

"But once the dark, evil-smelling spirit itself has been disposed of, so that neither the smell nor the color of the darkness appears [any more], then the body is illuminated, and the soul and the spirit rejoice, because [reading *hoti* for *hote*] the darkness has gone away from the body. The soul calls out to the illuminated body: Wake up from Hades! Resurrect from the tomb! Come out alive from the darkness! Enter the process of becoming spiritual, of becoming divine, for the voice of resurrection has sounded, and the remedy of life has come to you. For the spirit rejoices again in the body in which he is, and so does the soul, and it runs fast and full of joy to embrace it, and it does embrace it, and the darkness does not gain power over it because it depends on light, and it cannot be separated from it forever, and it enjoys being in her house, because, hiding it in darkness, she found it filled with light. It was joined with it, since it had become divine according to her [?], and it lives in her. For it put on the light of godliness, and the darkness ran away from them, and all joined in love—the body, the soul, and the spirit—and they have become one in the one that hides the mystery. In the act of their coming together, the mystery was accomplished, the house was sealed, and a statue full of light and godliness was placed there, for the fire brought them together and transformed them, and from the lap of its womb it came forth.

"Similarly, from the womb of the waters and from the air, which ministers to them, it also brought them out from darkness into light, from grief to joy, from sickness to health, from death to life. And it clad them in divine spiritual glory, which they had never worn before, because in them the whole mystery is hidden, and the divine is there unchanged. For it is because of their courage that the bodies enter along with each other and, coming out of the earth, put on light and divine glory, because they grew according to their nature and were changed in their appearance and arose from sleep and came out of Hades. For the womb of the fire gave birth to them, and from it [the womb] they put on the glory. And it brought them to a single unity, and the image was perfected in body and soul and spirit, and they became one. For the fire was subordinated to water, [as was] the earth to the air. Similarly, the air is with the fire, and the earth is with the water, and the fire and the water are with the earth, and the water is with the air, and they are one. For from plants and ashes the One came into being, and it was created divine from nature and by the divine, capturing and controlling all of nature. Look, the natures controlled and conquered the natures, and through this they changed the natures and the bodies and everything from their nature, for he who fled entered into the one who did not flee, and he who controlled entered into the one who did not control, and they were united with each other.

"This mystery that we have learned, brothers, comes from God and from our father, Comarius, the Ancient. Look, brothers, I have told you, the whole hidden truth [handed down] from many wise men and prophets."

The philosophers said to her: "Cleopatra, you have given us ecstasies by telling us what you have. Blessed is the womb that bore you!"

Again, Cleopatra spoke to them: "What I have told you concerns heavenly bodies and divine mysteries. For through their changes and transformations they change the natures and clothe them [?] in an unknown glory, a supreme glory that they did not have before."

The sages said: "Tell us this, too, Cleopatra, Why is it written: 'The mystery of the hurricane. . . . the art is a body, and like a wheel above it; just like the mystery, and the course, and the pole above, and houses and the towers and the most glorious encampments'?"

Cleopatra said: "The philosophers were right to put it [the art] there, where it had been put by the Demiurge and the Lord of all things. And, look, I tell you that the pole will move as a result of the four elements, and that it will never stop. These things have been arranged in our own country, in Ethiopia, and from here the plants, the stones, and the sacred bodies are taken; the one that put them there was a god, not a man. Into everyone the Demiurge placed the seed of power. One greens, the other does not green; one is dry, the other wet; one tends to combine, the other to separate; one dominates, the other is subordinate; and as they meet, some dominate the others, and one rejoices in another body, and one imparts splendor to another. One single nature results that pursues and dominates all natures, and the One itself conquers the nature of fire and earth and transforms its whole nature. And look, I tell you what is beyond it: when it is perfected, it becomes a deadly drug that runs through the body. For just as it enters its own body, it circulates in the [other] bodies. For by decomposition and warmth a drug is obtained that runs unhindered through every kind of body. At this point has the art of philosophy been accomplished."

131

Theophrastus (c. 371–c. 281 B.C.) studied in Athens under Aristotle and became his successor as head of his school, the Peripatus. He lectured and wrote on most of the subjects that his master had investigated, including physics, metaphysics, ethics, politics, physiology, and biology. Of his vast literary output only a fraction has been preserved. Besides his *Characters* (see the portrait of the "Superstitious Person" [*no. 3*]), we have the *Investigation of Plants*, the *Causes of Plants*, and *Concerning Odors*, in which he deals with the production of aromatic essences used as ointments and perfumes or as medications. Olive oil and wine, two of the major products of Attica, were at the base of a large industry that exported cosmetics, spices, and medicines, among other things. In his treatise, Theophrastus already seems to describe the *bain-marie*, an invention usually ascribed to the "Jewess Mary," a famous alchemist in Egypt in a later period.

When he speaks of "tastes" and "odors" he seems to have in mind "things that we taste" and "things that we smell," that is, condiments and perfumes.

What is true of many technical treatises that have come down to us from antiquity, in prose or verse, is true of this text: no one could become a perfumer or a mixer of culinary spices by reading Theophrastus. He only tells us the bare essentials. We must assume that some industrial secrets were involved.

Theophrastus, *Concerning Odors*, 8.14–16, 21–23

Tastes and odors alike are derived from these two things: the methods the makers of spices and perfume-powders apply, that is, mixing dry [solid] substances with dry [solid] substances. The experts who mix ointments or flavor wines, on the other hand, mix liquids with liquids. The third method that is commonly used is that of the perfumer who mixes dry [solid] with liquid substances. This is the way in which all perfumes and ointments are composed. But you should also know which ingredients mix well with which, and what [aromatic] combinations work well together, just as it is in the case of tastes. For those who make mixtures have this very same object in mind: it is as if they were seasoning [a dish]. So much for the ingredients and the methods used by the experts to attain their goal.

The composition and preparation of perfumes have, so to speak, only one object: to make the odors last. This is why olive oil is used as a base, for this substance keeps them for a very long time and is also very convenient to use. Olive oil is by nature not at all well suited to receive an odor, because it is viscous and greasy, and of all the different oils, this is especially true of the greasiest, such as almond oil. But sesame oil and olive oil are most . . . [something seems to be missing in the text].

They [the perfumers] mostly use oil from the Egyptian or Syrian *balanos* [*Balanites aegyptiaca*], for it is the least greasy. The olive oil most in use is that which is pressed from "coarse olives" in the raw state, because it seems to be the least greasy and the thinnest. This is used when it is new, not when it is old. The one that is kept for more than a year is useless, as it has turned thick and greasy. This [the new one] is the most suitable, because it is the least greasy.

Some say that oil from bitter almonds is best for ointments. They are abundant in Cilicia where an ointment is made from them. It is said that this is suitable for the finest perfumes, like the oil from the Egyptian *balanos* by itself; the shells [of the fruits], when thrown into the oil, give it a pleasant smell, for they are [also thrown into the one] made of bitter almonds. It does not really make any sense to seek a base that has very little odor of its own, like the oil that is pressed from "coarse olives" in a raw state, and yet, at the same time, they use these [the oil derived from *balanos* or bitter almonds]. For almond oil is pungent. Perhaps [they do it], because olive oil acquires a bad smell when it is cooked. This needs further investigation.

Almost all spices and aromatic scents except flowers are dry, hot, astringent, and biting. Some also have a certain bitterness, as we said above, for example, iris, myrrh, frankincense, and (perfumed) ointments in general. However, the most common properties are astringency and the warming element; those are actually the effects they produce.

They [spices and perfumes] are all given their astringent quality by exposure to fire, but some of them acquire their special odors even when they are cold and not exposed to fire. It also seems that, just as with flowers [vegetable dyes], some are used in cold and some in warm baths; so it is with odors. But in all cases the cooking—whether to produce the astringent quality or the special odor—is done in vessels standing in water and not in direct contact with the fire, the reason being that the heating must be gentle; if there were direct contact with the flames, there would be considerable waste, and the perfume would smell of burning.

There is less waste when the perfumes acquire their special odors by exposure to fire than when they are left cold, because the perfumes exposed to fire are first steeped in fragrant wine; for then they absorb [*anapinei*] less, while those treated in a cold state, being dry, absorb more, as, for instance, bruised iris root.

The Survival of Pagan Magic

With the advent of Christianity and its rise to power after centuries of persecution, one would expect that, along with the ancient religions, magic in all its forms would disappear. This is not true for all ancient religions, and it is not true for magic. While the gods of Babylonia, Persia, Egypt, Greece, and Rome are gone (though they may live on in various disguises), the faith of the people of the Old Testament is alive today. And as far as pagan magic is concerned, the Church did its best to suppress it but, in a way, had to live with it and even accept or assimilate some of it, as we will see. For centuries, the old and the new coexisted in an uneasy, troublesome, but culturally significant way.

We will first consider the early Church, that is, the first few centuries after the ministry of Jesus. Then we will look at the Byzantine period. Again, one would assume that by that time, around A.D. 1000, the last vestiges of magical concepts and practices had been discarded. But they were still there, under the surface, often in secret, and not only among the lower classes but also among the elite. One could follow this even further, through the later Middle Ages and the Renaissance and show that the Church, while always fighting witchcraft on all fronts, harbored some of the occult lore of past ages. But this would take us too far from our subject.

Spells of the Early Church

How did ancient concepts and rituals that many would call "magical" today survive in early Christianity? Did they really survive? This subject is obviously open to controversy. Much depends on our understanding of magic versus religion. We have seen how difficult it is to draw the line and how much of what seems magic to one culture is religion to another. To put labels on anything that people believe in and are devoted to is awkward, and we can only do it from our own point of view, but we have to try.

Religion and Magic

How could a Christian of the second century distinguish between supernatural phenomena that came from heaven and those that were caused by daemons? How could one know whether something was a true miracle or a trick of magic? What was the essential difference in meaning between the nocturnal visit of a saint and that of an evil spirit, between a pagan amulet and a relic that was carried away from a Christian sanctuary?[1]

The Fight against Magic and Occult Science in General

There are three important sources for our knowledge of the fight against magic in late antiquity:[2]

(a) The historical work of Ammianus Marcellinus (late fourth century), of which only the last books, dealing with the period from 353 to 378 are preserved

(b) The autobiography of Libanius of Antiochia (314–c. 393)

(c) The great collection of imperial decrees known as *Codex Theodosianus,* which became law in 438 and is part of the *Corpus Iuris Civilis*

From two of these sources (the historian and the legal texts), it appears that "magic" was a fairly vague concept. It could include astrology and all techniques of divination but also the possession of amulets and "secret books." The prosecutions we hear about were often arbitrary and not guided by jurisprudence. At the same time, to Ammianus, these interventions of the government are not unjust by themselves; he only objects to excesses of zeal and obvious errors.[3] Libanius, an orator and professor of rhetoric, clearly believes in the powers of magic and feels personally threatened by them.

What seems arbitrary to us in the persecution of magic may have an explanation. The magicians, the astrologers, and sometimes the philosophers along with them were sporadically punished by exile or in other ways because of certain extraordinary events about which we know nothing. In such cases, the population demanded a scapegoat, and it was easy to blame practitioners of the occult. Why "the philosophers" in general, not just the members of one particular school, were sometimes included is not clear—perhaps because they insisted on freedom of thought in an autocratic system.

Between 311 and 361, the government prohibited more than once in concrete terms the practice of magic, along with the traditional method of divination by *haruspicina* (the inspection of the entrails of slaughtered animals) Neoplatonism, and certain Syrian cults. Divination was closely associated with the pagan religions, and many Neoplatonists defended the ancient gods.

The New Testament does not give a precise definition of magic. In Galatians (5:19–21) Paul calls it a sin, along with the cult of idols, impurity, and other transgressions. These are all "works of the flesh," as opposed to "works of the spirit." We can assume that Paul knew magic when he saw it; therefore there was no need for him to describe what it involved.

The magical books that the new converts in Ephesus were persuaded by Paul to burn were worth fifty thousand silver coins, a substantial sum. Anybody who owned such a valuable book must have practiced magic at home, without being a professional *magus*. He (or she) hardly bought such texts for pleasure or edification.[4] If the magical papyri that we have are an analogy, these were practical instructions along the lines of "take this . . . do that . . ." Those who followed the instructions believed in magic. Constantine's laws of 321–24 show that the "knowledge" of magic, not its actual practice, was punishable. This involves the mere possession of forbidden books, amulets, and other paraphernalia. Anyone who had "studied" magic and practiced it as a profession was much more likely to be seen as a criminal.[5] The imperial decrees are in tune with the condemnations of the Church councils and with pastoral instructions.

The Church fathers—Ambrosius, Augustine,[6] Maximus of Turin, and others—attacked magic from a theological point of view. They argued that it is an invention of the fallen angels who taught it to mankind. It is the expression of a mischievous, morbid kind of *curiositas*[7] and one of the resources that daemons use to control the gullible and the feeble-minded. The false miracles performed by magicians are only possible through the help of daemons. If the Church did not deny the reality of daemons, it outlawed the old ways of dealing with supernatural powers. For John Chrysostom, magic, the cult of daemons, idolatry, and devil worship are one and the same thing.

It was strictly forbidden to pray in the ancient temples, to light candles or burn incense near springs and rivers (where Nymphs had been worshiped in the past), to observe the flight of birds, or to wear amulets. Clearly, the once legitimate religious rites of paganism were now treated in the same way as various magic rites, which had always been more or less suspect. The candidates for baptism had to renounce all this in a ritual that has survived in the Church in various forms until the present day.[8]

Forms of Assimilation

How was it possible for the Church to assimilate some forms of pagan magic in spite of its opposition? It was possible mainly because of a human peculiarity called *dipsychia* by Cyril of Alexandria (fourth–fifth century). People with a "double soul"—and they must have been in a majority for a long time—were not completely committed to Christ. Part of their soul was still attached to the ancient customs and rituals. Their "superstitions" had to be eradicated.

Tendencies to blend the old with the new can be seen in marginal or splinter groups. There are old Ethiopian texts, such as the *Instructions in the Secrets* where Christian doctrine and magical concepts form a curious mixture.[9] The Copts seemed to have abandoned their old religion very slowly and, though nominally Christian, still believed in the power of Isis and Horus. There are striking magical elements in the Christianity of the Armenians and Syrians of the first centuries A.D.—enough, at any rate, to provoke the *Letter on Devilish Sorceries and the Godless Conjurations* by John Mandakuni. From other protagonists of orthodoxy we learn, among other things, that the *susurramen magicum,* that is, the humming of secret prayers and incantations, as opposed to loud prayers and praises, was still a problem in Persia in the ninth century.

Magical rituals to guarantee salvation survived in Gnostic communities, mainly in Egypt. During baptism, "barbarous names" (no doubt the old *voces magicae*) were pronounced in order to eliminate the evil influence of heavenly bodies. The dying were comforted with special formulas to support the ascent of their souls. All this was not meant to replace the proper Christian rituals, but it was built into them, so to speak, to add extra power.

The case of Sophronius, bishop of Tella (fifth century), is truly amazing, even though, as a supporter of Nestorius, he may be classified as a heretic.[10] The magical experiments of this dignitary of the Church were described by two presbyters and two deacons before the "Robber Synod" of Ephesus in 449 and denounced by the assembled clergy. Someone had stolen a sum of money from the bishop. He gathered the suspects and first made them swear on the Gospel that they were innocent. Then he forced them to undergo the "cheese-sandwich oracle" (*tyromanteia*). The sandwiches were offered, and the bishop attached a conjuration to a tripod. In principle, the thief would have been unable to eat, but apparently all the suspects ate with a good appetite. So the bishop insisted on another oracle, the *phialomanteia:* he consulted a spirit that was supposed to appear in a dish into which water and oil had been poured. This method finally revealed the thief.

Epilogue

Crimen Magiae

To accuse a person or a group of magical practices was an effective weapon in the arsenal of propaganda and defamation and was used by secular and ecclesiastical authorities time and again. It did not matter whether there was any truth in it or not. The mere suspicion often was enough.

The oldest example—although it still is somewhat controversial—takes us back to the late first century. Acilius Glabrio, a noble Roman, was sentenced to death, along with the consul, Titius Flavius Clemens, by the emperor, Domitian. Clemens' wife, Flavia Domitilla, a granddaughter of a former emperor, Vespasian, was also accused and sent into exile. All three were charged with impiety, participation in Jewish rituals (the early Church being viewed as a Jewish sect by the authorities), and involvement with magic. Acilius Glabrio had previously been forced to fight a lion in the arena and won, which was taken as proof that he was a magician.

But this made it also possible for two seventeenth-century Church historians, Caesar Baronius and Thierry Ruinart, to declare Acilius Glabrio a Christian martyr. When the archaeologist G. B. de Rossi discovered, in 1888, the burial place of the Acilii in the catacomb of Priscilla—a sensation at the time—this was seen as a confirmation of his status, because the name of Acilius' wife was Vera Priscilla. Sainthood was also conferred on Flavia Domitilla, another victim of the persecution. According to scholarly opinion today, the catacombs of Priscilla and Domitilla belong to a later period.[11]

In this case, there were three separate charges, but often Christianity was denounced as a form of magic by pagan polemicists. Celsus (second century), in his attack on the new religion, asserts that Jesus was a man of illegitimate birth who had gone to Egypt to study magic and that the miracles performed by Jesus himself and his disciples were nothing else but magical tricks.[12] For Porphyry, the Neoplatonist, the Apostles were magicians who knew how to exploit the naïveté of the believers.[13]

We have already seen that the Church associates the pagan religions with sorcery and witchcraft. Thus, both sides use essentially the same argument in attacking each other. This is not saying that, for the Christians, all ancient religions were a form of magic. It means that the worshipers of the ancient gods are accused of being involved in illegal activities.[14] Moreover, the Church employs the *crimen magiae* to discredit certain groups and individuals suspected of heresy.[15]

In fourth-century Spain, a Christian of noble birth, Priscillianus of Avila, started an ascetic religious revival that greatly inconvenienced the clergy of northern Spain and southern France. He was accused of witchcraft and condemned by the Council of Bordeaux in 385. Although he appealed directly to the emperor, he was executed, along with six of his supporters. In retrospect, it is almost certain that he had nothing to do with magic, nor could "Priscillianism" be considered a Manichaean sect, that is, a form of heresy.[16] These charges were apparently made up by the establishment to eliminate a charismatic leader.

Simon Magus and Others

The story of Simon Magus is told in Acts 8:9–25. He is described there as a practitioner of magic, but also as the founder of a sect in Samaria (one does not learn in what city) whose members paid homage to him as to "the power of God which is Great." For a long time they were amazed by his "magic," according to Acts, but then they heard the message of the Evangelist Philip, believed him, and allowed themselves to be baptized. Simon follows their example and attaches himself to Philip, astonished by the signs and miracles that happen before his eyes. He obviously realizes that he is witnessing more powerful magic than the one that is familiar to him. The Apostles in Jerusalem hear of the success of their missionary and send Peter and John to Samaria to give the newly baptized, through the laying on of hands, the Holy Spirit as well.

John and Peter do this, but Simon wishes to buy their gift. We are meant to see at once how deeply he is rooted in the ancient world of witchcraft; for magicians expect to be paid and are willing to pay for a new technique. He is sharply rebuked by Peter; after being cursed, he shows his repentance.[17]

At this point one is tempted to ask, How much more could you demand of this man? He welcomes baptism, he receives the Holy Spirit, and he humbly submits to the stern rebuke of the Apostle who has just cursed him. If this is not a truly Christian attitude, what is? But Simon Magus lives on as a shady character, perhaps, because he is sometimes confused, with another Simon, also from Samaria, "Simon of Gitta." This secondary tradition should be separated from the story in Acts, which is the only reliable source for our knowledge of the elder Simon.[18]

Another mysterious figure, Thascius Caecilius Cyprianus, is alleged to have lived in the third century. After having studied magic for ten years with the priests of Memphis, he tried to win Justina, a beautiful Christian woman, by a love charm but changed his mind; he was then converted, became bishop of Antiochia, died as a martyr, and was sainted. All this is more legend than history, for it has all the ingredients of an edifying novel: magic, love, conversion, tragic death, miracles. The story was very popular in late antiquity and in the Middle Ages, and it survives in Greek, Latin, Syrian, Ethiopian, and Arabic. Its influence can be seen in the story of Dr. Faustus. Evidently, it is meant to illustrate the superiority of the new religion.[19]

A more tangible figure is Sextus Julius Africanus who also lived in the third century. He left an encyclopedia entitled *Kestoi* (*Embroidered Girdles*, perhaps in the sense of "charms"). In this colorful compilation, he deals with certain techniques, including the art of producing purple dyes, which had been kept secret for a long time because they were so valuable, like the manufacturing of perfumes in Egypt. We could classify them today as *magia naturalis,* but they are also part of alchemy, which means that the results were not based on research alone but on research plus ritual. Typically, the author is said to have invented a blood-stanching amulet and endowed it with *dynamis* by means of a secret spell.[20] The *Koiranides* or *Kyranides,* an anonymous collection of magical recipes compiled in the third or fourth century, remained in use, though the book was condemned at least once.

Saint Hilarion of Thavatha (291–371) was clearly a historical person, but his *Vita* by Saint Jerome is more legend than biography.[21] There must have been a need for this kind of literature among Christians. A young pagan falls in love with a virgin who is consecrated to God. Of course, he is rejected, whereupon he travels to Memphis, still the metropolis of magic, to learn the occult arts in the temple of Amenhotep-Asclepius. After only one year he returns to Gaza and buries under the threshold of the woman he desires a copper tablet with "monstrous characters" along with other magical objects. The analogies to the Cyprianus story are obvious, but there is a new twist. The ancient love magic works, in a way: the young woman is driven mad, tears the veil off her head, runs out into the street, and calls her lover's name.

Now it is time for a confrontation. In despair, the parents take their daughter to Hilarion, who declares her insane and carries out an exorcism. At once, the daemon that possesses her admits his guilt and leaves. The success of magic was only brief, and the new religion, once more, is triumphant.

In another situation, strangely enough, the saint plays the role of a pagan magician by helping a charioteer (a Christian) to win, to teach the pagans a lesson. He sprinkles the charioteer, his vehicle, and his horses, as well as the barrier at the starting line, with holy water, invoking the name of Jesus. Naturally, his favorite wins, and the pagans are dismayed. The victory in the chariot race is a victory for Jesus.

Thanks to the *Vita* of Saint Severus, written around A.D. 500 by Zacharias Scholasticus of Gaza, we know of a sensational episode that happened in the late fifth century at the law school of Berytus (Beiruth). At this famous school there was not only a Christian student association, organized by Zacharias, but also a fraternity devoted to magic. Its leaders were an Armenian, a Greek from Thessalonica, a Syrian from Heliopolis, and an Egyptian from Thebes. One of the members was in love with a young woman, and his friends decided to sacrifice at midnight a black slave, in order to propitiate the love daemons. One of the professors was also involved. But the conspiracy was discovered, and the authorities ordered an investigation. Magical and astrological books attributed to Zoroaster, Ostanes, and Manetho were confiscated and burned in the presence of the bishop and the whole clergy. The professor as well as the students must have known that they were about to commit a crime, but they were probably hoping to get away with it.

Weather Magic

Religious and magical rituals designed to influence the weather have been performed since the beginning of civilization, because the weather has always been of vital importance for agriculture. How did the Church deal with ancient weather magic? It seems that it had to tolerate it for a while, because, at first, it had nothing to offer in its place. Over a period of time, the Church developed its own procedures, based on the doctrine that God is Lord over the weather and that he can punish his enemies by sending thunderstorms. At the same time, the old concept that bad weather may also be caused by daemons lived on. Hence it was necessary to banish the daemons, and that became the duty of the weather con-jurers. They were called *nephelodioktai* 'cloud chasers' in the East and *tempestarii* 'weather specialists' in the West. At times, weather magic was officially prohibited, but in practice it was allowed, when it was carried out through Christian prayers, rites, and relics: by waving consecrated palm branches, by ringing the bells, but also, strangely enough, by using the *gemma ceraunia* or thunder stone, a magical relic from paganism.

Dynamis

The Church also adopted from paganism the concept that there is a power or life force in the universe, which is available if one knows the right words and rituals. There is a specific Christian *dynamis,* as we will see, but the magical powers of paganism had not completely vanished from the earth. They still resided in the idols of the ancient deities, for instance, and had to be reckoned with. For a long time, the Christians hesitated to destroy the famous sanctuary of Isis Menutho in Alexandria. Then, to neutralize the presumably still active power of the goddess, the bones of two holy martyrs, Cyrus and John, were brought in. Pagan *dynamis* had to be attacked by Christian *dynamis,* the physical destruction preceded by a spiritual offensive. A special exorcism was also required to "Christianize" a pagan temple.

The power is sometimes understood in purely material terms. According to Gregory of Tours (sixth century), the *dynamis* inherent in the tomb of a saint flows into a piece of cloth placed on top of it: "A small piece of cloth lifted from the tomb [of Saint Peter] is so permeated by the divine power that it weighs much more than before."[22] In other words, the presence of *dynamis* can be measured mathematically. What is true of the tomb of a martyr is also true of the relics. It could be argued that the cult of relics is based on this particular concept of power. The Holy Scriptures are loaded with *dynamis*. John Chrysostom only had to touch the Gospel in order to chase away the worries of everyday life. Placed on the head, it drives away headaches. Augustine does not wholly approve of such practices, but he finds them less objectionable than the remedies prescribed by pagan sorcerers. The transfer of *dynamis* is possible through touching or the laying on of hands. For the Church, this physical form of transmitting spiritual power was not magic, because it was sanctified by Jesus and the Apostles.

Daemons as a Fact of Life

Wherever people believe in daemons, magic is being practiced in one form or another, and everything seems to indicate that, during the first few centuries of the Christian era, this belief was as strong as ever, especially among the lower classes, but also among the theologians. It is a very old belief and not limited to one particular country or culture. To feel safe, even a Christian would accept the protection of amulets and other magical devices.

By their very nature, daemons are invisible, but they can assume various shapes. Some of them may look like dogs (perhaps a reminiscence of Anubis or Cerberus), others look like snakes. Their variety is reflected in the famous "Temptation of Saint Anthony," as told in the *Vita* by Athanasius and dramatized by the imagination of painters and poets.[23] They can be found in certain places, for instance near rivers and springs, but also in ruins and near tombs. The "daemons that inhabit the waters" are, of course, the river gods and nymphs of paganism. Generally speaking, the army of daemons is recruited, to a large extent, from the ranks of the ancient gods and demigods that had not lost their power completely. They are joined by the fallen angels and by the Satan of later Judaism after he had become the principle of evil. If possible, daemons like to live in human beings, because there it is warm and dark.

The Church accepted the old popular explanation of illness, especially mental illness and epilepsy in terms of daemoniac possession. Daemons are also the cause of human vices, according to Clement of Alexandria (c. 145–c. 210), who considered the evil spirit of gluttony, *koiliodaimon,* the worst of all the daemons that are active in the human soul. Envy in all its forms (*phthonos, baskania,* the evil eye) is the work of daemons.

Possession is usually considered an abnormal, pathological state, as the treatment of the *energoumenoi* shows. These were people in whom an unclean spirit was thought to be at work, in accordance with Ephesians 2:2, "the prince of the power of the air, the spirit that is now at work in the sons of disobedience." Such people were called "possessed" or "disturbed" or "demonized," all synonyms or euphemisms for "mentally ill." Epileptics were probably placed in the same category. The early Church felt an obligation to deliver these human beings from the spirit that made them different; it separated them from the rest of the congregation and treated them, so to speak, as second-class Christians until they could be successfully exorcised.

The rituals of exorcism (which means literally "conjuration" or "confirmation by oath") were taken over by the Church from Judaism and paganism with certain modifications, but without specific magical accessories. Blowing at a person in order to drive out a daemon was considered effective and became part of the christening ceremony. In certain christening liturgies, for example, in the Greek and the Gallican rites, breath is treated as a real, independent substance, full of *dynamis,* which the priest can address. Some saints were specialists in dealing with daemons, notably Gregory (c. 213–c. 271), the "Worker of Miracles" (Thaumaturgos), also known as "Hunter of Spirits" (Pneumatodiox). He is credited with a spell or an amulet offering protection from a particularly dangerous black daemon with three heads that could emerge from the sea.[24]

It is easy to understand why, between birth and baptism, a ritual of exorcism was considered essential. The child was born with an unclean spirit because of original sin and therefore was especially vulnerable and exposed to the attacks of daemons. The complete ritual included, at one time, not only the water and the breath, but also a pinch of salt placed on the tongue of the child and the anointing oil. The salt is explained as the "salt of wisdom" and a symbol of divine grace. Actually, it serves as a protection, for daemons are afraid of salt. The oil had to be exorcised separately before the child could be anointed, because it might also be inhabited by daemons.

Amulets for Christians?

The attitude of the early Church in this respect is ambiguous. Christian amulets have survived in large numbers, but they were frowned upon by the theologians and condemned from time to time by the Church councils as works of the Devil and a form of idolatry. A distinction is sometimes made between amulets that are only meant to protect the wearer and those that were designed to harm other people (therefore those existed, too!). In general, there was a tendency to avoid pagan mythology and replace it by Christian symbols, but this is not always the case. The old forms, shapes, and decorations are still in use, and people still put their trust in the power of the griffin, the Medusa head, the portrait of Alexander the Great, or the "Abraxas" formula.

At the same time, we see crosses, the fish, names of angels, the "One God" formula, the words "Amen Halleluia," or an invocation of the "Blood of Christ." Passages from the Gospels, sometimes locked in small golden cases, were also considered effective. Healing amulets, called *epidesmata* or *ligaturae* ("objects to be attached") seem to have changed very little in form and function from those popular in pagan times. A typically Christian type of amulet is the *enkolpion* (from *kolpos* 'bosom'), usually a small case in the form of a pectoral cross containing a relic and used as a protection against illness, but also as an aid to religious edification and an object of worship, "a safeguard of our present and a token of our eternal salvation," as Paulinus of Nola (c. 353–431) writes in one of his letters. To protect the inhabitants of a house collectively, phylacteries could be attached to the building. Thus, a Christian inscription over an entrance proclaimed that "Abraham lives here" (the Old Testament patriarch, of course), in analogy to a pagan inscription "Heracles lives here."[25]

Ritual Curses

Bizarre, as it may seem, the early Church did not only develop rituals of blessing and benediction, but also forms of cursing, which can be interpreted as a continuation of pagan black magic. A curse is usually defined as an imprecation, oral or in writing, by a gesture or merely in thought, that harm may come to a person or a thing with the help of supernatural powers. Often, curses are accompanied by threats.

We have seen how Peter cursed Simon Magus, but the victim had at least a chance for repentance and atonement to prevent the worst. Ananias and Sapphira (Acts 5:1–11) paid for the wrath of the Apostle with instant death. Paul cursed the Jews at Corinth, who "opposed and reviled" him, by shaking out his garments and saying to them "Your blood be on your own heads" (Acts 18:1–6).[26] The punishment he demands for the incestuous person in Corinth (1 Corinthians 5:1–5) also aims at the physical death of the offender: "You are to deliver this man to Satan for the destruction of the flesh, that his spirit may be saved in the day of the Lord Jesus." He cursed the Jewish magician Elymas (Acts 13: 10) as a son of the Devil, an enemy of all righteousness, and struck him with temporary blindness.

The Greek terms for "curse" in the New Testament are *anathema, ara,* and *katara*. They are the terms used in pagan contexts, though they may be colored by Hebrew equivalents, and their meanings overlap, except that *ara* can also be "prayer" in general, and *anathema* can also be an "accursed person." Prayers involving curses and threats were incorporated in the ritual of excommunication at an early date. To declare someone *anathema* and to excommunicate that person were practically one and the same thing, especially if the solemn excommunication was imposed according to the ancient curses handed down in the *Pontificale Romanum*. To be excluded from the religious community is essentially a form of death. There can be little doubt that the pagan forms of *damnatio, devotio,* and *exsecratio* lived on in Christian guise.[27] There seems to be a continuity of popular belief, ignorance, common superstition, and—let's face it— just plain human meanness over the centuries, as Christian curse tablets (*tabellae defixionum*) show. At some time between the sixth and eighth centuries they disappear.

Conclusion

It has become clear, I hope, why the Church could not tolerate magic and had to oppose it. Even though it was not identical with any non-Christian religion, it embraced too many relics of former cultures, had absorbed too many elements of pagan religions, and, as a system, had almost a religious character. Above all, its grip on the hopes and the imagination of people was too powerful to be ignored.

On the other hand, it is surprising to see to what extent the early Church absorbed magical practices where they seem to work well and where the new religion had nothing comparable to offer. We should also take into account the continuity of the "magic dream," which transcends all times and all cultures. This is a simple fact of human psychology, and it explains a number of phenomena.

The immense vitality of the new religion manifests itself in the vigorous opposition as well as in the energetic reception. Nothing happens in a vacuum. Everywhere we can find connecting links. Christianity was born and grew strong under the most unfavorable external conditions. After centuries of persecution and suffering, it emerged victorious, but it had also acquired another identity.

Enchantments of Byzantium

Magical concepts and practices survived well into the Byzantine period, even though magic, astrology, divination, and other forms of "pagan superstitions" were condemned by the Church and the emperors.[28] Sorcery and witchcraft, from *magia naturalis* to theurgy,[29] still found adherents, and we know the names of persons who were suspected of being magicians. Even then, many people still believed in daemons, the evil eye, and the protective power of amulets.

Semantics

The old terms are still in use (see the Vocabula Magica), but we also find some new ones, reflecting the changed historical perspective. *Mageia* is still common in the controversy between Christians and non-Christians.[30] Many vestiges of the old religions were branded as witchcraft. The Church declared that all forms of sorcery had come to an end by the fact of the Incarnation. But, in practice, magic still had to be reckoned with.

Some terms are neutral, some loaded with negative meaning, some vague or euphemistic (it could be risky to call certain practices by their real name), while others originally covered only certain aspects of magic and only later, by semantic extension, the whole area. The Latin *sortilegium* is a good example: originally, it meant a technique of divination using lots, *sortes;* then it was applied to other methods of predicting the future, and finally it covered witchcraft in general. By an analogous process, *sortiarius,* the practitioner of *sortilegium,* became "sorcerer."

In Byzantium, *goeteia* retains its negative connotation of "lower form of magic," and *goes* can mean "swindler, charlatan," but *theourgia* is reserved for a higher form of ritual magic that does not deal with ordinary daemons but with the more prominent members of the pantheon. In Christian contexts, it can mean "divine work" in the sense of miracle.

A term covering tricks from the repertoire of *magia naturalis* (but not only those) is *manganeia,* literally "engineering, machinery." From Lucian's satirical biography of Alexander, the *False Prophet,* we know that it was not too difficult to create illusions for naïve congregations. *Pharmakeia* involves mostly the knowledge of drugs (poisons, remedies, hallucinogens), but as this was such an important part of magic, it also designates "witchcraft" in general.

A more general term is *ta hyper anthropon eidenai* 'to know things that are above a human being'. This kind of knowledge could be dangerous and its practical application or the mere possession of magical books and paraphernalia was illegal. Somewhat similar is *periergia,* which originally just meant "curiosity" or "exaggerated curiosity" and then acquired the meaning "magic" (cf. Acts 19:19, *ta perierga*), just like Latin *curiositas*.[31] A related term, *polypragmosyne* 'pursuit of many things', was used to characterize a "busybody" but also the study of magic and the occult arts.

Apomeilixis 'technique of appeasing (gods or daemons)' covers one particular area of magic and is comparable to *thelxis* 'art of soothing'.[32] *Ta arrheta* are things that cannot or should not be expressed in words, things too sacred or too horrible to mention. This term may refer to pagan mysteries but also to "secret abominations." *Katadesmos* is technically a "binding spell," that is, just one particular tool in the magician's kit, but by semantic extension it can also mean other kinds of magical operations, because magic is the "art of binding" par excellence.[33]

In certain contexts, *sophia* or *techne* without an adjective can mean "magic." Thus the great magi of the past can be called "the wise men of old," *hoi archaioi sophoi*, by a Byzantine writer. Similarly, *he hellenike sophia* 'the pagan lore' may refer to magic, while *he hagia sophia* 'the holy wisdom' refers to the doctrine of the Church, just as "evil miracles," meaning illusions produced by magic, are distinguished from "holy miracles."[34] *He pragmateia* 'the business' is sufficiently vague, while *ta hellenika epitedeumata* 'the pagan pursuits' is a little more specific. *Kakotechnia* 'evil art, black magic' is clearly derogatory, like Latin *maleficium* or *nefas.*

Necromancy has its own vocabulary.[35] Since it could involve the desecration of a tomb, it was considered a particularly loathsome crime, but there was also a general feeling that one should not force the shades of the dead to return to life.

A picturesque term for "witch" attested in Byzantine texts is *graus trioditis,* shorthand for "old woman busying herself at the meeting of three ways." These were points outside of cities lined with tombs where Hecate, goddess of the underworld, had been worshiped in pagan times and where all sorts of fortune-tellers, charlatans, and sorcerers used to go about their business. *Trioditis* by itself can mean a "streetwalker." In the Byzantine era, such figures may be partly literary relics, but life being what it is, they were probably still real enough.

Sources and Practitioners

It comes as a surprise that we know of a number of people who practiced magic and worked as astrologers during the Byzantine period, even though the occult arts had been condemned again and again by the Church and the state. An edict of Diocletian who ruled from 284 to 305 had denounced the *maleficia evidentissima* of the astrologers. The same emperor is also remembered for his persecution of the Christians, in 303. In 409 the emperor Honorius decreed that astrologers could avoid deportation only by "burning the books of their error under the eyes of their bishops."[36] It seems that the Christian emperors as well as their pagan predecessors were in fear of all methods of divination because a really skilled practitioner could predict the death of the ruler and the name of his successor.

In spite of the risks, there were scholars and clergymen like Michael Psellus (eleventh century) who took a more than academic interest in the occult. Psellus wrote: "The truth is that my role as a teacher and the variety of interests of those who come to consult me have led me to study every science, and that I can prevent no one from questioning me on that subject."[37]

Magical books, like the *Kestoi* of Sextus Julius Africanus[38] and the anonymous *Koiranides* (see above), were still consulted during the Byzantine era, even though they had been prohibited.[39] Astrologers used a vast compilation by Rhetorius of Egypt (fl. early seventh century), which has been called an "extraordinary collection of excerpts from earlier Greek astrologers, based on what must have been a magnificent library."[40] There obviously was a continuing tradition.

Heliodorus, a Byzantine miracle-worker in the style of Apollonius of Tyana deserves a special mention, because he is the antihero in the *Vita* of Saint Leo of Catania. At one point, Heliodorus makes a pact with the Devil, which places him, like Cyprianus (see above) in the line of the predecessors of Dr. Faustus.[41]

In Byzantine sources, the Roma are sometimes described as expert magicians, snake-charmers and fortune-tellers. They are called Athinganoi, "Untouchables,"[42] a name from which French *tziganes* and German *Zigeuner* are derived. The English name "Gypsy" means "Egyptian" because for a long time it was thought that Egypt, the legendary home of witchcraft, was their country of origin. Today we know that they came from India, and it is probable that they brought with them some ancient lore concerning hallucinogenic plants and ways of influencing the human mind by hypnosis and mass suggestion to Asia Minor, Byzantium, Greece, and finally to western Europe, where their arrival in the later Middle Ages coincided with the height of the witchcraft craze.

Magia Naturalis

One of the Greek words for "magic," *manganeia,* suggests the use of special skills, of machinery or technical devices to produce amazing effects. Among the special skills one should mention ventriloquism, "the art . . . of producing sounds in such a manner that the voice appears to proceed from some person or object other than the speaker, and usually at some distance from him."[43] We hear of performers (known as *engastrimythoi*) who were able to fake trance and deliver oracular responses in the manner of the Pythia in Delphi. Theodore Balsamon said of them, "They proclaim certain things with the evil satanic gaze of the prophetesses of the pagans,"[44] and the second Council of Trullo condemned them. When the great oracles of paganism went into decline in the early imperial period, fake trances might be expected in the sanctuaries, like the one described in Lucan's *Bellum Civile,* but later on, in the Byzantine world, we would rather imagine private séances. Like the famous mediums of the nineteenth century, a skilled performer could give the impression that he or she was really in touch with another world.

Some great inventions were made in late antiquity. We hear of the spectacular machinery of Anthemius of Tralles (sixth century), who created thunder and earthquakes through steam power. These effects worked well in the theater but they could also be used to herald the arrival of a higher spirit to a group of believers. Stage ghosts could be made to appear in a most realistic manner.

Then we have the celebrated Byzantine *automata,* such as the singing birds in a golden tree that could also flutter their wings, the roaring lions made of gold, and the throne of Solomon, which rose high into the air, giving the illusion of supernatural levitation. Such masterpieces of engineering had already been described by Heron of Alexandria (first century), but there was a later genius called Leo the Mathematician (eighth–ninth century) who constructed the pieces of technology adorning the imperial palace in Constantinople. All these devices were truly magical, especially if one did not know how they worked.

One of the greatest achievements usually attributed to Byzantine alchemists is "Greek Fire" ("liquid fire" to the Greeks), a highly combustible mixture that could burn on water and was therefore extremely useful in naval warfare.[45] Actually, a similar composition was already known in the Hellenistic period, but it was further developed in late antiquity. To the original mixture of sulfur, tow, and chips of pinewood, the Byzantine wizards added quicklime and crude mineral oil, probably also resin and pitch. Specially trained technicians sprayed the liquid through a kind of flamethrower (a portable pump with a bronze tube attached to it) at the vessels of the enemy. The effects—both material and psychological—must have been devastating. The composition itself and its proper use in combat were kept secret.

Theurgy

Theourgia, a set of rituals and techniques designed to "work on the deity" and to "make man divine," had several aims, some of them not incompatible with Christianity: to bring divine power into the human soul for the sake of salvation; to achieve mystic union with the deity; to obtain messages from a higher world through a medium in trance; and to animate the statue or icon of the deity.

Behind these aims there seems to be the longing, as Proclus, the Neoplatonist, put it, "to return to our true fathers, the gods,"[46] and the techniques also worked in a Christian context. Today, we would call this a shamanistic concept, because an essential part of shamanism in so-called primitive cultures is the desire to be reunited with the divine spirits of the ancestors. The shaman is the person who can achieve this for himself and, to a lesser extent, for the whole community who participates in his experience.

Psellus' attitude to theurgy is ambiguous. On the one hand, he rejects its pagan form as a concoction of myths concerning oracles and different classes of daemons;[47] on the other hand, he seems to approach it with an open mind. In his search for revelations that would confirm the truth of the Gospel, he was willing to try some unorthodox methods, but in the end the results were not satisfactory.

We owe to him some very curious information about the rituals performed by the empress Zoe (c. 978–1050) in the privacy of her palace.[48] He is very cautious in his account and stresses above all her devotion to Christ, even though her form of worship strongly resembles ancient theurgical practices.

It seems that Zoe owned a miraculous icon representing Jesus, called the Antiphonetes, "He who responds." It was embellished with shiny materials and, as a kind of portable oracle, revealed to her the future by changing its complexion. Zoe would ask the icon specific questions, and when its face turned pale, she became dejected, but when it radiated, she was joyful. In a sense, this was her own personal form of devotion, but there was also some higher form of magic involved, it would appear.

For Psellus also reveals that Zoe, along with her sister, Theodora, and a few trusted servants, used to prepare various perfumes (*aromata*) in her palace. When he says that she "offered *aromata* to God," he probably wants to suggest that she anointed the icon with special substances that she inhaled when she hugged it.[49] It could be the same technique that the pagan theurgists used when they worshiped in front of statues that had been rubbed with aromatic essences. It is not inconceivable that her laboratory was equipped to produce, for her own use, psychoactive or "entheogenic" substances.

There were two main approaches to theurgy. One relied strictly and exclusively on ascetic disciplines—fasting, deprivation of sleep, prayer, meditation, dancing, and so on—to receive messages from a higher world and achieve the desired *unio mystica* with the deity. The other used certain drugs, perfumes, ointments, sounds, light effects, either in combination with ascetic techniques or without them. The most memorable experiences probably came from a combination of both methods.

The type of theurgy propagated by the Neoplatonists was essentially an attempt to bring back the ancient shamanistic techniques disguised as the highest form of theology. These philosophers offered metaphysical explanations of the paranormal occurrences they could observe (smiling statues of the gods, mediums talking in trance), but since such phenomena were unpredictable and varied greatly in quality (some sort of fraud can never be quite excluded), none of their explanations worked. And yet the phenomena themselves had to be genuine, because they proved the reality of the ancient gods.

The devotion of the empress Zoe to her icon is not really different. What Psellus hints at, but with due respect and great caution, is that, under the influence of her *aromata,* she had visions, saw the Jesus icon change color, and probably heard a voice. No one knew better than Psellus that these were pagan practices, outlawed by the Church and the secular authorities. Zoe, of course, was protected by her status.

In another curious passage Psellus describes a séance conducted in 1059 by the Patriarch Michael Caerularius and the monks of Chios.[50] As an expert on such matters he had been asked by the Church authorities to look into these phenomena, and his report led to a formal accusation. We learn that, in order to induce trance, narcotic drugs were ingested, inhaled, or rubbed into the skin. The participants were obviously familiar with various techniques of absorbing psychoactive substances. Inhaling smoke (from frankincense, myrrh, and other gum resins) is, perhaps, the fastest way to the brain, but rubbing a strong ointment into the forehead or the top of the head (the monastic tonsure would have helped) or other parts of the body also worked very well, as we know from the annals of witchcraft in medieval Europe.

No matter how well the monks of Chios mastered the ancient shamanistic techniques, the results, as reported by the investigator, were disappointing. Some of the trance messages believed to come from martyrs, saints, the Virgin Mary, or even from the Holy Trinity were painfully trivial or totally irrelevant. The magic still worked, in a way, but no genuine mystic experiences came from it.

NOTES

The first section of this chapter, "Spells of the Early Church," is based on a paper originally written in German for a Symposium at the University of Jena in 2002. I am grateful to Meinolf Vielberg for his invitation to participate and his permission to use the material in a different form. An English version was published in

MHNH 3 (2003): 29–54. I would like to thank Aurelio Pérez Jiménez, editor of MHNH, for his valuable suggestions and his permission to use the article here, in an abbreviated version. Originally, there were many acknowledgments and references, especially to the *Reallexikon für Antike und Christentum* (*RAC*), most of which have been omitted here. The reader who wishes to do further research should consult the article as published in MHNH.

The second section, "Enchantments of Byzantium," was first published in French in *Critique* (Summer 2003). Here also, I have revised the original text. It is a pleasure to express my gratitude to Jean-Claude Lebenszteijn and Yves Hersant.

1. In general, see David E. Aune, "Magic in Early Christianity," ANRW 2.32.2 (1980), pp. 1507–1757. One should also consult J. Engemann, "Magische Übelabwehr in der Spätantike," *Jahrbücher für Antike und Christentum* 18 (1975): 22–48. For Apuleius as an illustration, see Robert L. Fowler, in *Oxford Readings in Greek Religion,* ed. R. Buxton (Oxford, 2000), 341. On the problem of distinctions, see Henry Maguire, in Maguire, *Byzantine Magic,* p. 2.

2. Richard Gordon, "Imagining Greek and Roman Magic," in Ankarloo and Clark, *Witchcraft,* 2:320–21. Libanius and Ammianus were roughly contemporaries, both natives of Antiochia, both supporters of the Emperor Julian.

3. Ibid., pp. 321–22. For Ammianus, there are two kinds of magic: Persian *mageia,* which combines, as a higher religion, comparable to *theourgia,* Yoga, Zoroastrianism, and Chaldaean astrology; and Western magic, comparable to *goeteia,* which he also calls "secret arts" or "evil arts."

4. *Acts* 19:19; see D. Ogden, in Ankarloo and Clark, *Witchcraft,* pp. 55–56.

5. Constantine's Laws of 321–24 show that the "knowledge of magic" by itself, not only its practice, was punishable. Persons who have "studied magic" and practice it as a profession appear in rhetorical exercises as suspicious characters; see Gordon, in Ankarloo and Clark, *Witchcraft,* pp. 264–65.

6. Augustine, like Ammianus, distinguishes between "lower" and "higher" magic, *goeteia* versus *theourgia;* see Barb, in Momigliano, *The Conflict between Paganism and Christianity,* p. 101.

7. On magic as dangerous *curiositas,* see Luck, *Ancient Pathways and Hidden Pursuits,* pp. 220; 224, n. 1; 226; 231.

8. Cyril of Jerusalem, *Cateches.* 19, 4–20 (= *PG* XXXIII.1078–86).

9. See O. Ranierei, in *EECC,* 1:29.

10. See G. Luck, in Ankarloo and Clark, *Witchcraft,* pp. 155–56.

11. V. Saxer, "Acilius Glabrio," *EECC,* 1:8. H. Marucchi, *Eléments d'archéologie chrétienne,* 2nd ed. (Paris, 1903) seems to glorify Acilius in the manner of romantic fiction by presenting him as a noble Roman who wished to share the lot of the poor and despised and who, perhaps, had talked with the Apostles.

12. On Celsus, see Dickie, *Magic and Magicians in the Greco-Roman Worlds,* pp. 221, 227–29, 233–34, 236–38, 242–43; Dale B. Martin, *Inventing Superstition* (Cambridge, Mass., 2004), pp. 140–59, 160–86.

13. It is not clear whether the Christians were also accused of making poisons; see, for instance, W. Schubart, *Acta Pauli, nach dem Papyrus der Hamburger Staats- und Universitäts-Bibliothek,* 2 vols. (Hamburg, 1936), and A. Barb, "Gift," *RAC* 10 (1978), cols. 1233. *Pharmakeia* and *veneficium* can mean "making poisons" as well as "magic" in general, by semantic extension, as described above. When Paul is

qualified as *maleficus* in *Martyrium Petri* 3 (1, 4), the term probably means "sorcerer." From some *Apocrypha* we know that the Christians were accused of practicing love magic, and apparently some were; see now A. Wypustec, "Un Aspect ignoré des persecutions des chretiens dans l'antiquité," *Jahrbücher für Antike und Christentum* 42 (1999): 50–71. The author (p. 68, n. 97) also comments on the *Vita* of Hilarion.

14. The *Carmen adversus Paganos* is a remarkable testimony for this kind of polemic. It is preserved as an appendix in the *Codex Puteaneus* (sixth century) of the works of Prudentius. The consul Virius Nicomachus Flavianus had threatened to transform the great church of Milan into a stable. In retaliation, the anonymous author accuses the consul's wife of witchcraft. He himself was killed in the Alps, fighting Theodosius. See Ilona Opelt, in *EECC,* 1:144.

15. Irenaeus, bishop of Lyons, the most influential theologian of the second century, condemned Gnosticism in his *Adversus Haereses* by accusing Carpocrates, one of the leading Gnostics, of being a magician; see A. Monaci Castagno, in *EECC,* 1:145.

16. It was alleged by his enemies that Priscillianus had studied magic with an Egyptian, Marcus of Memphis (Sulpicius Severus, *Chronica* 2, 64). See Chadwick, *Priscillianus of Avila.*

17. On Simon Magus, see Valerie Flint, in Ankarloo and Clark, *Witchcraft,* pp. 300ff; Luck, "Witches and Sorcerers," ibid., pp. 125ff.

18. This view took shape during the later nineteenth century and is outlined in the excellent article "Simon Magus" by St. George Stock, in the 11th edition of the *Encyclopaedia Britannica* (1911), 25:126ff. Then it was rejected and simply forgotten for a while. For a recent revival of the idea, see C. Colpe, "Gnosis II," *RAC* 11 (1981), col. 625.

19. The "Confessions" of Cyprian are almost certainly apocryphal. During his period of initiation into the "Mysteries of Memphis" (i.e., magic) he is said to have learned, among many other things, how to produce earthquakes, thus anticipating the illusions staged by Anthemios of Tralles, in the sixth century.

20. See J. R. Vieillefond, *Jules Africain, fragments des Cestes* (Paris, 1932); F. C. R. Thee, *Julius Africanus and the Early Christian View of Magic* (Tübingen, 1984).

21. On Jerome's *Vita Hilarionis,* see Flint, in Ankarloo and Clark, *Witchcraft,* pp. 333, 337, 341–42; Gordon, in Ankarloo and Clark, *Witchcraft,* pp. 202ff.; Wypustec, in *Jahrbücher für Antike und Christentum* 42 (1999).

22. Gregory of Tours, *Gloria Martyr.* 1, 28 (= *PL* 71, 728ff.); see E. Fascher, "Dynamis," *RAC* 4 (1959), col. 451.

23. Athanasius, *Vita Antonii* 9f (= *PG* 26, 85556). It has been suggested that these were genuine visions of the saint, induced partly by ascetic techniques, partly by ergotism (poisoning by ergot which is related to LSD). See R. P. H. Greenfield, in Maguire, *Byzantine Magic,* p. 120, n. 4.

24. See W. Telfer, "The Cultus of St. Gregory Thaumatourgos," *Harvard Theological Review* 29 (1939): 225–344.

25. See Th. Klauser, "Abraham," *RAC* 1 (1950), col. 25; G. Luck, *Die Weisheit der Hunde* (Kröner, 1997), pp. 149, 500. The patriarch is invoked as *deus Abraham* in exorcisms. Generally speaking, the old protective deities of paganism are replaced by the angels of Judaism and the saints in Christian theology.

26. Paul may have assumed that the man was possessed; see W. Speyer, "Gottes-

feind," *RAC* 11 (1981), col. 1034. Perhaps he uttered a lengthy curse of which Luke only retains the essential elements (Speyer, p. 1038). On the symbolic gesture accompanying the curse, see Alan L. Boegehold, *When a Gesture Was Expected* (Princeton, 1999), pp. 73ff.

27. See A. C. Crawley, "Cursing and Blessing," *ERE* 4 (1908), pp. 367–74; W. Doscocil, "Exkommunikation," *RAC* 7 (1969), cols. 1–22. Among the Letters of Synesius (c. 370–c. 414), there is an elaborate Christian curse (no. 58). Synesius was brought up as a pagan, studied with the celebrated Neoplatonist Hypatia and, as far as we know, never formally renounced her doctrines, even as bishop of Ptolemais in Libya. See Ch. Lacombrade, *Synésios de Cyrène* (Paris, 1951), pp. 247–48. Two remarkable cases are discussed by G. Björck, *Der Fluch des Christen Sabinus* (Uppsala, 1938), and P. Moreau, *Une Imprécation funéraire à Néocésarée* (Paris, 1959).

28. An excellent volume on *Byzantine Magic*, edited by Henry Maguire, included essays by Maguire himself, Marie Theres Fögen, Matthew P. Dickie, James Russell, Alexander Kazhdan, John Duffy, Richard P. H. Greenfield, and Robert Mathiesen.

29. This is the way I read Duffy's pages on the empress Zoe (in Maguire, *Byzantine Magic*, pp. 88ff). Peter Struck, "Pagan and Christian Theurgies: Iamblichus, Ps. Dionysius, Religion and Magic in Late Antiquity," *Ancient World* 32.1 (2001): 25–38, does not consider this particular area.

30. See Greenfield, in Maguire, *Byzantine Magic*, pp. 120, n. 5; 125, n. 15; Mathiesen, in ibid., p. 170.

31. See note 7 above.

32. See Hugh Parry, *Thelxis* (Lanham, Md., 1992).

33. See, e.g., M. W. Dickie, "Bonds and Headless Daemons," *Greek, Roman and Byzantine Studies* 40 (1999): 99–140.

34. A. Kazhdan, in Maguire, *Byzantine Magic*, pp. 76–77.

35. Greenfield, in ibid., p. 125, n. 14; Ogden, *Greek and Roman Necromancy*.

36. Fögen, in Maguire, *Byzantine Magic*, pp. 104, 109.

37. Psellus, *Chronogr.* 2, 77–78; see Duffy, in Maguire, *Byzantine Magic*, pp. 88, 94.

38. See note 20 above.

39. Greenfield, in Maguire, *Byzantine Magic*, pp. 129ff.

40. David Pingree, in *Classical Philology* 72 (1977): 203ff.

41. See A. Acconia Longo, in *Rivista di studi bizantini e neoellenici* 26 (1989): 3–98; Kazhdan, in Maguire, *Byzantine Magic*, p. 77.

42. Originally, *Athinganoi* was the name given by the Church to a group of Judaizing heretics in eighth-century Phrygia and Laconia.

43. *Shorter Oxford English Dictionary*, vol. 2 (1973), s. v.

44. F. R. Trombley, in *Oxford Dictionary of Byzantium*, vol. 1 (1991), p. 698.

45. Eric MacGeer, in ibid., s.v. "Greek Fire," seems to consider it a Byzantine invention. He emphasizes how well the secret was kept: even when the enemy captured large amounts of the fuel itself and the necessary equipment, they still had no idea of how to use it.

46. Proclus, *In Platonis Timaeum* I 208 Diehl.

47. Psellus, *Scripta Minora*, ed. by E. Kurtz and F. Drexl (Milan, 1936–41), 1:232ff. See Duffy, in Maguire, *Byzantine Magic*, pp. 86ff.

48. A recipe for the "Perfume of the Empress Zoe" survives in an anonymous tract (eleventh–fourteenth century); see John Scarborough, in *Oxford Dictionary of Byzantium,* vol. 3 (1991), p. 1646. I have not been able to find it. Hallucinogenic mixtures known in Byzantine times included frankincense with ground hemp leaves (hashish). Smoke from this mixture apparently helped a medium to see images in a mirror. This is a form of catoptromancy; see Mathiesen, in Maguire, *Byzantine Magic,* p. 175. We also hear of an incense mixture containing peony root, sweet flag root (*Acorus calamus*), and opium; see Greenfield, in ibid., p. 142, n. 84. Such *aromata* could be placed inside the statues of the ancient gods, to produce, when heated or burned, a mystic communion with the deity; see Duffy, in ibid., pp. 85, n. 5; 89–90. The empress Zoe may have used other, more sophisticated compositions, because she obviously had the resources and the privacy.

49. Duffy, in Maguire, *Byzantine Magic,* pp. 86ff.

50. *Scripta Minora,* 1:232ff.

Psychoactive Substances
in Religion and Magic

The idea that drugs played a role in the great religions of antiquity as they do in tribal societies in Africa and South America is still abhorrent to many scholars today. Perhaps they are willing to admit it for ancient Egypt—but for Greece? For Athens? For the Eleusinian Mysteries? For ancient Israel? And yet the evidence is strong. Psychoactive substances reached the brains of the believers in many different ways: in food and drink, in oil rubbed into the skin, in smoke inhaled. We should not underestimate the expertise of the priests in this area.

Instead of pursuing the idea at this point I would like to say that in magic, drugs were used as well as in religion, probably more regularly and consistently, because so much depended on the moment. This should not come as a surprise. Magic is, in a way, a business transaction between the practitioner and the client. The client wants results, and he wants them here and now. He pays for the service, and he may not be inclined to submit to any spiritual discipline. To a certain extent, ancient religion also has a business-like aspect—the *do ut des* principle. But in magic, this is carried to an extreme.

A quick survey of the *magical papyri* shows how often special incense was burned and aromatic oils were applied. Some of the ingredients are well-known psychoactive substances. Even where no specific recipes are given, we may assume that, more often than not, some kind of smoke was required. Here are a few examples:

1. Manna, styrax, opium, myrrh, frankincense, saffron, bdella, mixed with spurge and fragrant wine (*PGM* IV.1830–40): Manna seems to be a type of *Boswellia* in a powdered form; styrax or storax is *Styrax officinalis,* opium is the juice of *Papaver somniferum,* myrrh is *Commiphora myrrha,* frankincense is (probably) *Boswellia carteri,* saffron is *Crocus sativus,* bdella is *Balsamodendron mukul.* The last ingredient, *ischas,* is not "fig," as it has been translated, but "spurge," that is, *Euphorbia apios.* Incidentally, some of these concoctions could be burned as well as consumed or rubbed into the skin. This is characteristic of many ancient aromatic essences prepared with olive oil or wine.

2. Frankincense, laurel, myrtle, fruit pit, stavesacre, cinnamon leaf, costus. This is pounded and blended with Mendesian wine and honey and made into pills (*PGM* IV.2677–81): Frankincense is, again, a type of *Boswellia,* laurel would be *Laurus nobilis,* myrtle *Myrtus communis.* The "fruit pit" remains

mysterious, while the "wild berry" can be identified as *Delphinion staphisagria*. Cinnamon leaf, also known as malabathrum, is *Cinnamomum tamala,* it seems, and costus is *Saussurea lappa*.

3. Water, myrrh, calf's snout plant, laurel branch. Separately, it seems a fumigation of myrrh, frankincense, and frog's tongue was required (*PGM* V.195–201): "Calf's snout" has been identified as *Antirrhinon orontium*. Frog's tongue is not as fantastic as it sounds, for, like the skin glands of *Bufo marinus,* it may yield a hallucinogenic secretion known as bufotenin. Frogs and toads had their well-documented practical use in medieval witchcraft.

4. Styrax, malabathron (probably *Cinnamomum tamala*), costus (*Saussurea lappa*), frankincense, Indian nard (probably *Nardostachys jatamansi*), cassia (*Cinnamomum cassia*), myrrh (*PGM* XIII.17–20): These essences are thought to please various deities, they are psychoactive, and they can affect the practitioner or the client, or both, establishing the presence of the deity. A similar incense ritual is prescribed for the recitation of the Orphic hymns.

5. Malabathron (see above), styrax, nard (see above), costus, cassia, frankincense, myrrh (*PGM* XIII.350–57): These essences are mixed with wine and burned.

Incense offerings and fumigations were part of many magical rituals, and they were probably carried out even when they are not prescribed specifically. Once we admit the use of holy oils, holy incense, and holy food and drink in ancient religion, we have to admit it for magic as well, because magic is, in so many ways, an imitation of religion on a different level. The *magus* adapted for his own purposes techniques that had worked for the priests for a very long time.

One could even speculate—looking at the curious stories of apprenticeship and initiation—that the typical magus of Hellenistic Egypt had once been attached to one of the great sanctuaries and learned all the rituals and resources. Then he left the temple or was forced to leave and established himself in another profession, which allowed him, nevertheless, to make good use of his experience.

As we consider the psychoactive potential of these mixtures, we should keep in mind the possibility that, in ancient times, people found access to different states of consciousness more easily than we do. They were inclined to believe that higher beings—deities or daemons—could appear and manifest themselves not only to the chosen few, as in the Homeric epics, but to fairly ordinary people, like the characters in Greek novels as well. The point is that the transition from what we call "normal" to a "higher" state of consciousness was smoother and more natural and could be triggered by any number of things. To enhance the transition by manipulations, suggestions, and stimulation of the senses was not difficult for the *magus*. Some "Gipsy tricks" recorded in recent times are probably nothing else than an application of these ancient techniques.

Another factor to consider briefly is the relationship between the *magus* and his client. It is, in a way, a business relationship, as mentioned above, but it is also based on trust. The client comes to the *magus* because he (she) already believes that magic works, just as the person who consults a psychic or an astrologer today believes in psychic gifts or astrological predictions.

Appendix

Magical Smoke

There is evidence beyond the Greek magical papyri that fumigation and incense offerings really worked, perhaps not entirely by themselves, but in combination with other techniques, such as the hypnotic effect of chanting, drumming, and droning and buzzing noises. But "magical smoke" deserves a closer study.

Let us begin with a few comments by William Brashear,[1] to whom we owe among other valuable contributions a bibliography listing the relevant studies from 1914 to 1988. He sees the importance of *epithymata* in magical rituals mainly in creating a *locus magicus* in a profane world full of foul odors (bad smells being associated with evil daemons, just as pleasant odors are associated with benevolent deities). He writes: "The magician . . . burned aromatic substances and anointed his/her body with perfumed salves and ointments. The whole set-up for an epiphany was there: now all that was necessary was for the deity to appear."

So far, so good, but something is missing, I believe, and it is not an entirely new idea. In fact, it has been pointed out long ago (and forgotten again) that the smoke itself was the epiphany. The smoke was inhaled by the magician and his client, and the vision came in trance. The smell of psychoactive substances (and there are many of them, though frankincense and myrrh are prescribed more often than any others) acts on the human brain in a very quick, very predictable way.

No two kinds of frankincense, to use this as an example, have exactly the same effect. There are many varieties, coming from different regions along the ancient incense route, and some of the more potent ones may not be available any more. The blends used in churches today seem to be rather mild, if they can be called psychoactive at all.

To go beyond the evidence of the Greek magical papyri, we will look at an article by Friedrich Pfister published in 1914.[2] It gives the information we need for our purpose, but it also shows that not every smoke offering was designed to induce trance. Aromatic substances were burned in many different contexts, as a bloodless offering to the gods, and the effect on the worshipers was perhaps discovered by accident, long ago. But in some religious ceremonies and in many magical rituals, trance was desired, and the smoke was instrumental, because through it the priest, the medium, the *magus*, the shaman, *and* others could participate in the ultimate experience. To offer a *pharmakon* in a drink was not always practicable (though it was probably done at Eleusis), but smoke has the advantage of reaching a large group, if it is strong enough.

Shamans all over the world use plants in order to travel into another reality, and nature provides them in even more generous profusion than plants for nutrition. The knowledge of the Greeks in this area, even in the earliest times, is astonishing, but they probably took over much of it from other cultures, from the Egyptians, the Scythians, and the Thracians.

Pythagoras, according to Iamblichus (*Life of Pythagoras* 28, 154) prescribed a blend of cedar wood, laurel, cypress, and oak to "honor the gods." Another set of *thymiamata* he recommended (ibid.) includes frankincense, myrrh, millet, "cakes" (*popana*), and honeycombs. Some of these substances are psychoactive. The leaves and branches of *Laurus nobilis*, along with barley flour, were burned in the sanctuary in Delphi to inspire prophetic ecstasy (*Geoponika* 11.2); according to others, equal parts of laurel leaves, seeds of *Hyoscyamus niger,* myrrh, and olibanum were burned. To conjure up Hecate, the hero of the Orphic *Argonautika* (915ff.) burns a mixture of cedar wood, *rhamnos,* and wood of *Populus nigra.*

It seems that exotic types of wood, resin, and spices were imported by the Greeks at an early date, because they were deemed necessary for religious rituals. Over the centuries, they often appear in recipes for incense and ointments. The names of the most commonly used, listed below, all have Semitic roots, even if the plant or the product itself came from the Far East.

    1. Cinnamon, the aromatic bark of *Cinnamomum cassia* or *C. ceylanicum* was brought from Asia (China, Ceylon) to Egypt and Greece probably before Homer.

    2. Frankincense, *Boswellia* spp., came from Somalia and the coastal areas of Arabia. It was known in Egypt during the Eleventh and Twelfth Dynasties already.

    3. The Greeks had at least five different names for the gum resin we call myrrh, *Commiphora* spp. It is mentioned by Herodotus and was brought from East Africa and Arabia.

    4. Ladanum was mainly obtained from *Cistus ladanifer,* a plant found in Greece, but the Greeks apparently learned its use from their eastern neighbors.

    5. Styrax or storax is *Styrax officinalis,* found in Asia Minor, Syria, and Greece.

Among the ceremonial uses of incense, there is a very significant, very curious custom attested only, it seems, in a little-known scholion (on Aeschines' *Speech against Timarchus,* 23–24 Dilts). We are told that, before every assembly (*ekklesia*) of the Athenians, a double sacrifice had to be offered. First, a pig was slaughtered to purify the space and chase away the "unclean daemons that often obstruct the thoughts of people." Then an aromatic blend of essences (*thymiamata*) was offered, in order to attract benevolent spirits, to make sure that, through their presence (*parousia*), the Athenians would reach good decisions. This ritual has all the characteristics of a shamanistic tribal ceremony based on the principle of *similia similibus,* and the term *parousia* is crucial, because through the action of the smoke (a considerable amount of *aromata* would be needed) the presence of benevolent powers was not only imagined but actually felt. But in order to have the experience, the smoke had to be inhaled by the whole assembly, or at least by the priests who performed the ritual and those standing closest to them. Is it conceivable that the mere sight of persons in trance can induce a kind of trance in those who are not directly affected by any psychoactive substance? In some cultures this is almost certainly the case.

    Many other testimonies collected by Pfister show clearly that the incense was *nominally* offered to the deities but *effectively* inhaled and experienced by the priests and some of the people.[3] This, it seems to me, is an exact analogy to the offering of animals: *nominally,* they were supposed to feed the gods and make them strong, kindly disposed, and able to function as gods, but *in fact* the meat was eaten by the priests and some of the people. Naturally, not everybody could get a full meal out of the sacrificial offerings, and to a certain extent the meal was symbolical. The same is true for the incense offering: not everybody could experience personally an epiphany from burning a small or large amount of frankincense. It did work now and then, but often the value of the ritual was purely symbolical, its effects psychological.

If this is true, the well-attested custom of burning frankincense, myrrh, cassia, and so on at funerals (see Apuleius, *Apologia* 32) is not just a sometimes very lavish expression of grief or a display of wealth but a way of staying in touch with the spirit of the deceased and of being assured of their continuing existence in another world. It is well known that Nero did this on a truly extraordinary scale for Poppaea (Pliny, *Nat. Hist.* 12.82–83), perhaps not just to show to the Romans his love for her but to give them an opportunity to feel her presence as a deity, *theos epiphanes*. Ordinary people did this for their dead on a more modest scale, ostensibly to honor them by a sacrifice but also to feel assured of their reality, their continued existence in another sphere, as I think.

A decisive point is made by Pfister, almost casually, in a short paragraph, toward the end of his article.[4] He says: "Occasionally, fumigations also served *to arouse religious hallucinations and ecstatic states of consciousness*" (emphasis added). This is exactly what happened, but not just occasionally, as if by accident, but by design. From the twelve testimonies he cites, I dwell only on two.

The first testimony is from Apuleius, *Apologia* 43: ". . . that the human mind can be put to sleep . . . either through being called away by songs or through the soothing influences of smells, to step outside, so as to forget the present, lose the memory of the body for a while and return to its own nature which is, as we know, immortal and divine." It would be difficult to think of a more precise description of ecstasy under the influence of chants and psychoactive odors. It applies both to religion and magic, depending on set and setting. For Apuleius, the Platonist, this is a perfectly natural occurrence, because it allows the soul to return to its divine origin and affirm its immortality, which transcends all the limitations of this existence on earth, to be free from the encumbrance of the body and share, for a short time, the life of the gods. From his point of view, ecstasy is not a paranormal or pathological state (though it is a privilege), and any means to attain it are legitimate.

After the conversion of Lucius, the hero of Apuleius' *Metamorphoses* (11.4), Isis appears to him, and his vision is clearly that of an animated, speaking statue, with all the attributes of the goddess. The trance that induces the vision is caused, it seems, by the "blessed scents of Arabia" (or: the "scents of Arabia Felix"?). Her feet are called "ambrosian" because they have been rubbed carefully with oils and are closest to the face of the worshiper who kneels before her.

In his classical work on ancient amulets, Campbell Bonner also dealt with the ritual of "animating" *(empsychoun)* an image *(eidolon)*, whether this might be the small figurine of an Eros Paredros (*PGM* XII.14–95) or the large cult statue of a god in a temple. That such a ritual existed in Greece as in Egypt is clear from the testimonies of the Neoplatonist philosophers that Bonner cites and translates,[5] but what it involved is never revealed in so many words. Bonner quotes the older authorities, such as G. Hock, E. Bevan, and Th. Hopfner, and they all seem to agree that we know nothing about a ritual by which, at one point, the deity followed the invitation of the priests to come, take up residence in the statue, and accept the offerings of the worshipers.

Iamblichus, Proclus, and Hermias knew of actions that were believed to animate statues and endow them with power, motion, and expression, but they do not reveal the secret. Iamblichus, in fact, speaks (*On Mysteries* 3.13) scornfully of those who think that they can dispense with the higher theurgic techniques by simply "standing on characters" (probably drawn or painted on the floor). Obviously, this was not enough.

What is it that worked? The secret was kept very well, just as the secret of the entheogens used in the mystery religions was never fully revealed. But an answer is suggested by the passage in *PGM* XII.14ff. mentioned above: the figurine of Eros is to be made of "wax of Etruria, mixed with [every] kind of aromatic plants." The plants are not named specifically, but we can guess what they were: frankincense, myrrh, sweet flag, saffron, and so on. This Eros is a close relative of the Jesus icon of the empress Zoe.

To animate large statues, *aromata* were offered in the form of incense, in massive amounts, if necessary. We are given a hint—but only a hint—in Eunapius' *Lives* (7.2.6–3.3 [see *no. 4*]) when he tells how Maximus the theurgist made a statue of Hecate smile. He offered a grain (!) of incense and sang a kind of hymn.

The second testimony is from Galen, *On Medical Terminology* 187, XIX p. 462 K.[6] "*Enthousiasmos* is a state of ecstasy produced in some people on (?) smoke in the sanctuaries, when they see apparitions, listening to drums or flutes or symbols (?)." The text is corrupt. Rohde corrected "symbols" (*symbolon*) to "cymbals" (*kymbalon*), and Hopfner suggested tentatively *hypo* 'from' for *epi* 'on', which is what one would expect. Now the sense is clear: people in trance experience visions as they inhale the fumes and hear the sound of drums or flutes or cymbals. Galen, the medical authority, is describing religious trance induced by fumigation and music. He does not mention any anointing oils nor does he say what kind of incense was burned. The rhythmic beating of drums or gongs, but also the sound of flutes in a certain mode can have a hypnotic effect, which would reinforce the effect of the inhalation. The key word for such a combination of trance-inducing techniques is *narcohypnosis*. Other techniques include the monotonous, repetitious chanting of words, or gazing intently into mirrors and shining surfaces or at lamps, along with fumigations. The visions (*phasmata*) occur when the worshipers have entered into trance. Needless to say, what worked in religion also worked in magic.

Pythagoras and others were able, it is said, to "prophesy through frankincense," surely not just by observing the movements of the grains and the smoke, but above all by inhaling the smoke. This is the more "advanced" technique of *libanomanteia*.

Hopfner also quotes Herodotus (1.202, 4.74–75) on the rituals of various barbarians such as the Scythians and the Thracians. They inhaled smoke from hemp or (according to Pseudo-Plutarch, *On Rivers* 3.3) from a plant that is said to be "very similar" to *origanon*. Hopfner thinks it is thyme (*Thymus serpyllum*), but it could be another plant of a genus of labiates with aromatic leaves—for instance, wild marjoram (*Origanum vulgare*), sweet marjoram (*O. marjorana*), dittany of Crete (*O. dictamnus*), or pennyroyal (*Mentha pulegium*). It cannot be coincidence, Hopfner says, that several orgiastic cults came to Greece from Thrace and that Orpheus himself was a Thracian.[7] Could this plant be the "entheogen" of the Orphic mysteries?

It is not difficult to explain purifications and apotropaic rituals through foul-smelling substances, such as sulfur, sea onion (*Urginea maritima*), peony root (*Paeonia officinalis*), or bitumen. Once more, the principle of *similia similibus* is at work. Just as the gods are attracted by pleasant smells and manifest themselves in sweet clouds of incense, the evil daemons (they are very sensitive to odors) can be driven away by foul-reeking smoke.

Most of the *epithymata* specified in the Greek magical papyri use frankincense and myrrh, often along with other ingredients. Their predominance in religion would also indicate their value as psychoactive agents. For frankincense, the scientific data presented by D. Martinetz and others are impressive: it probably contains tetrahydrocannabinol, like hashish, and can act in the same way. But this is not true in the same degree of all species of *Boswellia*, and much seems to depend on their place of origin and on the climate of the place where they are burned. The effect also seems to vary according to the mixture with other ingredients. Martinetz and his coauthors are rather cautious in their final statement: "Der bislang medizinisch-hygienisch im Vordergrund stehende Gesichtspunkt, dass das Räuchern bei religiösen Festen . . . die Bildung von Phenolen mit ihrer desinfizierenden, antiseptischen Wirkung nutzte, gibt somit wohl nur einen Teil der Beliebtheit der Räuchermittel im Altertum, dem Mittelalter und der Neuzeit wieder."[8] They say, in effect, that they do not wish to discredit frankincense as a "dangerous drug" in any way. But they add that it is not without interest for the history of religions and the history of civilization in general that resin of olibanum could be understood as a mild narcotic whose effects are appreciated in religious rituals.[9]

Other scientists have been more outspoken, though no one paid much attention to them. Martinetz and his colleagues quote Ludwig Klages (1872–1956), a philosopher and psychologist who also had a degree in chemistry. Klages wrote: "Die seelenkundliche Erforschung der Ekstase bedarf der Ergänzung durch eine Wissenschaft von den Berauschungsmitteln. Opium, Haschisch, Koka, Alkohol, ätherische Öle, Weihrauch, Lorbeer, die Solanaceengifte, selbst Nikotin, Koffein, Thein haben wechselweise dem Entselbstungsdrange der Visionäre gedient, und wir dürfen die grössten Aufschlüsse über das Wesen des Rausches von einer Wissenschaft der Signaturen erwarten, wie sie im Freskostil die Mystik der Renaissance entwarf."[10]

This brilliant visionary concept—almost a manifesto—was formulated a century ago, and since then, much progress has been made by chemists, anthropologists, and ethnopharmacists. We have learned a great deal about ayahuasca and ololiuhqui, not to mention ergot of rye, but somehow frankincense and myrrh have not, until recently, received the attention they deserve.[11]

The evidence concerning myrrh, as presented by Martinetz and his coauthors,[12] is less compelling, at least to a nonscientist. As in the case of frankincense, extensive research has been done, but the results are still not clear. Myrrh, like frankincense, has medical properties. It could be classified as a mild narcotic or as an inebriant, but its status as an "entheogen" remains to be established by science.

Sacred Incense and Holy Anointing Oil in the Old Testament

As I was doing research on psychoactive substances used in religion and magic in antiquity, I happened to come across chapter 30 in the Book of Exodus where Moses prescribes the composition of the sacred incense and the holy anointing oil. It occurred to me, judging from the ingredients, that both substances might act as "entheogens," the incense more powerfully than the oil. I have mentioned this possibility to a number of people, in conversations, talks, and letters, and it has become clear to me how difficult it is to prove such a hypothesis, if proof is possible. Nevertheless, I will try to make a case for it in another publication but at least mention the idea in this book.

Just as frankincense, by itself or, more often, in combination with other substances, could produce visions in the *magus*, it also could create an epiphany for the priest in the service of the Lord. The clues are there, and all of them have been discussed in two scholarly studies,[13] among others, but their authors hesitate to draw the ultimate conclusion—that the inhalation of the sacred incense could create a powerful vision of the deity in the priest. Other factors were probably involved, too: the smell of the holy oil with which the priest, the altar, and other sacred objects within the temple were anointed, the golden surface of the altar that reflected the shine of the lamps, and the prayer discipline.

The idea that Moses himself and the priests who succeeded him relied on "chemical aids" in order to be in touch with the Lord must be disturbing or repugnant to many. It seems to degrade religion—any religion—when one associates it with shamanistic practices.[14] But the question has been asked by Margaret Joyce Field,[15] and she suggests the use of impure nitrous oxide, prepared by dropping crystals of ammonium nitrate on a hot, but not red-hot, metal dish. William James reports his experiments with nitrous oxide, as he tried to alter his normal state of consciousness. The chemical process is not complicated and may have been known to Moses and, before him, to the priests of Egypt.

But the evidence of the Old Testament points in the direction of a blend of frankincense and other substances. The instructions given in the Book of Exodus are precise but can be interpreted in different ways.[16] We gather that the incense blend had to be burned twice daily on a special "golden" altar, that is, a wooden altar with a gold surface, in the sanctuary. The shiny surface, reflecting the light of the sacral lamps nearby, could help induce trance in the priest as he was breathing in the smoke.

Can we prove that the smoke was psychoactive? The fact that the incense mixture contained frankincense and myrrh would support the idea.[17] The other ingredients may have helped, but since there is still some doubt as to their true nature, we do not know enough about their chemistry. What follows is an attempt at reconciling the different opinions resulting from the rabbinical tradition and modern scholarship.

The sacred incense, like the holy anointing oil, has four basic ingredients, but in the case of the incense, seven or more other substances (optional or as substitutes?) could be added and were added over the centuries, it seems. One particularly important formula remained the secret of a priestly family.

These are the four essential parts:

1. "Stacte" and "Balsam" seem to refer to myrrh, *Commiphora myrrha,* or *C. opobalsamum.* "Stacte" means "oozing substance," that is, the gum resin that flows naturally from the plant, not as the direct result of incisions, while "Balsam" is a more generic term, it appears, for it has also been identified as the gum of *Styrax officinalis, Liquidambar orientalis,* or *Liquidambar styraciflua.*

2. Onycha is not a plant, but the covering plate in the shell of the wing shell, *Strombus lentiginosus odoratus,* a mollusk common in the Red Sea, which, when burned, produces a musklike odor. Apparently, it had to be soaked in large amounts of strong white wine or lesser amounts of vetch lye.

3. Galbanum is the gum or resin of *Ferula galbaniflua,* though other identifications, such as *Peucedanum galbaniflorum,* have been proposed.

4. "Pure" frankincense is the gum or resin of *Boswellia carterii* or another species of *Boswellia.*

To these basic ingredients could be added (5) myrrh, most likely another kind of *Commiphora;* (6) cassia, probably from the bark of *Cinnamomum* cassia but possibly *Saussurea lappa;* (7) spikenard, *Nardostachys jatamansi;* (8) saffron, *Crocus sativus;* (9) costus, probably *Aucklandia costus;* (10) cinnamon, *Cinnamomum zeylanicum;* (11) cinnamon bark, probably from the inner bark of *Canella alba.*

Traditionally, four more ingredients were used in addition: (12) "Sodom salt"; (13) a kind of potassium nitrate (*Leptadenia pyrotechnica?*); (14) a different kind of salt; (15) cyclamen.

What we have here looks like a very sophisticated psychoactive incense blend, the results of centuries of research and experiment, one would assume. The formula may have been developed in the temples of Egypt to produce visions of a deity in trance. The words spoken by the Lord to Moses (Exodus 30:6), "where I will meet with you," should be taken in the strictest, literal sense. God will appear to the priest who uses the sacred substance in the proper way. But the sanctions against any frivolous, casual use are formidable, just as they were in ancient Greece and no doubt in Egypt. By its very nature, an "entheogen" is surrounded by taboos, because it gives access to the deity, and the tremendous power it transmits must be controlled.

Among all the detailed instructions preserved in the Book of Exodus, there is not a single reference to an "aroma pleasing to the Lord." The pleasant, aromatic scent is associated with the epiphany of the deity, as in ancient Greece, because the deity appears in the cloud of *aromata* offered by human beings. But the incense burned on the shiny surface of the altar has only one function, the most important of all: to bring down the Lord.

If this interpretation is right, it may give a new understanding of the Gospel account of Jesus' nativity (notably Matthew 2:11). The three Magi offer gold, frankincense, and myrrh to Jesus. The symbolism of these gifts has been understood in many different ways, but there may be a connection with the incense cult of the Old Testament.

The three Magi are kings and high priests in their distant realms. They belong to a mythical time when these offices were not yet separated. But since they are also skilled astrologers, they grasp at once the meaning of the Star of Bethlehem. They recognize in Jesus a future king and high priest who will be able to see and hear

God thanks to their gifts. Frankincense and myrrh, blended and burned, will serve as an entheogen, and from the gold the shiny, reflecting surface of the altar can be made. The idea that the gold has this specific function has been suggested by R. de Langhe.[18]

But here is the point. The Magi themselves require these elements for their own visions, and they cannot think of a more precious gift for Jesus whose future as a religious leader is clear to them. Whether Jesus needed the gifts for this purpose, we cannot know. The Magi simply anticipated his needs from their own.

The holy oil, used to anoint priests, kings, and sacred objects, is also specified in chapter 30 of the Book of Exodus. To judge from the ingredients, it is also psychoactive, but probably to a lesser degree than the incense formula. It consists of:

    1. Pure myrrh, the oleo gum resin from *Commiphora myrrha*

    2. Sweet cinnamon, probably from the dried bark of *Cinnamomum zeylanicum*

    3. Sweet calamus, most likely from *Acorus calamus,* but another name is "fragrant cane," which could be from *Cymbopogon martini*

    4. Cassia, probably from the bark of *Cinnamomum cassia* or *Cassia lignea,* but other plants, such as *Aucklandia costus, Castus speciosus,* and *Saussurea lappa* have also been proposed

Myrrh, as mentioned above, may be considered an inebriant or a mild narcotic, while the psychoactive properties of sweet calamus (asarone) are well established.

The Magical Effect of Panaceas

Looking at some of the universal remedies or cure-alls that were created and touted over the centuries, one cannot help noticing that they often contained one or several psychoactive ingredients. This makes one suspect that they were essentially placebos, but in many cases, people became addicted and damaged their health.

Theriac comes to mind. It was a remedy created by Mithridates VI, king of Pontus (120–63), and modified by Andromachus, the personal physician to the emperor Nero. Originally, it seems to have been a protection against snakebites, but Mithridates took it in order to be immune from all poisons. Gradually, it became a panacea. The ancient formula included opium, frankincense, sea onion, and snake meat, among many other things, and opium apparently remained an ingredient until about 1900. It survived throughout the Middle Ages in one form or another and was prepared ceremoniously in the monasteries and major cities of Europe, to be distributed among the population in case of need. At one time, it contained about sixty ingredients, some of them more psychoactive than others. During the eighteenth century, it came under attack by enlightened physicians, and around 1800 it was simplified but still prescribed. By now, it was generally known that the main effect it had was due to opium. It was last seen, in a very basic form, in a supplement (*Electuarium theriacale*) to the official German Pharmacopoeia in the early nineteenth century.

The complexity of the formula may be explained by one of the guiding principles of ancient medicine, recognized again today: every medication has, besides it therapeutic value, one or several undesirable side effects. It was thought that these could be neutralized by other additives—the more, the better. There is safety in numbers, and a list of sixty ingredients is more impressive than only ten.

A magical drug or elixir of life is recommended in the *Testament of Solomon,* a folktale that contains occult lore, probably composed in Egypt, in the third century A.D. The elixir contained frankincense, myrrh, sea onion, spikenard, and saffron, all ingredients that are proved or reputed to be psychoactive.

The Alamut formula (for want of a better name) was a legendary brew containing hashish. It was prepared at Alamut, a Muslim stronghold near Kasmin in northern Iran, established in the eleventh century by Hasan Ibn Sabbah, the leader of the Assassins, a fanatical sect that had declared a holy war on the Crusaders and on other Muslims. "Assassin" originally meant "consumer of hashish," but through French *assassin* it has come to mean "killer." The members of the sect drank or smoked the substance in order to become immortal, and it made them fearless in battle. Their leader died in 1124 (the "Old Man on the Mountain" was his Syrian counterpart), and the fortress was ransacked in 1256. It is said to have contained a large library, an alchemical laboratory, and a collection of astronomical instruments. In other words: this was a research facility in the ancient Greco-Egyptian style that somehow survived, in an isolated spot, into the Middle Ages.

The idea behind theriac (based on opium) and the Alamut formula (based on hashish) may give us a clue to the concept of the Holy Grail, which came into being during the era of transition between antiquity and the Middle Ages. It was supposed to be a substance, or an object, sometimes associated with the body and blood of Christ, that vouchsafes happiness on earth and bliss in heaven to the chosen few. If you consider the linguistic connections between "holy" and "whole" and "healing," you can understand the Holy Grail both as a mystic (or magical) remedy and a sacrament.

The invention of laudanum is attributed to Paracelsus (1493–1541). He proclaimed it to be the true Elixir of Life and said that it contained gold and pearls, among other things, but the main ingredient seems to have been opium, as in theriac. The name is derived from the Latin *laudandum* 'praiseworthy', or from *ladanum,* that is, *Cistus ladanifer,* which may or may not have been an ingredient. Thomas Sydenham, the "English Hippocrates" (1624–89), produced a similar remedy, also called laudanum, also on the basis of opium, but with alcohol added. It was still popular in the nineteenth century, and writers and artists became addicted to it.

We could mention tobacco, more specifically *Nicotiana rustica,* the "food of the gods." In the New World, tobacco was smoked as part of religious rites. The fumes were offered to the Great Spirit and other deities, just like the frankincense of the Old World. The fumes were also inhaled by the worshipers and led to trance. Since healing rites were performed in trance, tobacco was recommended in America and in Europe for a long time as a cure for almost any physical ill, for toothache, for gout, and as a protection against the plague.

Eau de Cologne is a different matter. Today, we use it as a pleasant, refreshing perfume or toilet water. The popular conception is that only a desperate alcoholic, with nothing else in sight, would reach for a bottle of perfume. But when Eau de Cologne was first produced in Germany, in Cologne, after an Italian formula, it was hailed as *Eau admirable,* and people drank it as a panacea. Under Napoleon I it became mandatory for producers of food and drink in Europe to declare the contents of their articles. The makers of Eau de Cologne would not reveal their formula, it is said, and so their product can only be sold as toilet water since then. However, on Mayotte, a tiny island between Madagascar and the coast of East Africa, Eau de Cologne was until recently, or still is, drunk ritually in order to induce trance.[19]

As a kind of postscript to their book on frankincense and myrrh, Martinetz and his coauthors preserve the recipe to the "Augsburger Lebenselixier." It was created in the eighteenth century and remained popular for more than a century. Among many other things, it contained myrrh, calamus root, gentian root, saffron, and spirits. Once more, we can observe the principle of combining alcohol with a choice of psychoactive plants and pleasant flavors to at least create an illusion of well-being, if not well-being itself.

NOTES

1. W. M. Brashear, *Varia Magica = Papyrologica Bruxellensia* 25 (1991), p. 54.

2. F. Pfister, "Rauchopfer," in *RE* 1.A.1 (1914), cols. 267–85.

3. Ibid., esp. cols. 279–80.

4. Ibid., col. 283.

5. Bonner, *Studies in Magical Amulets Chiefly Graeco-Egyptian,* pp. 15ff.

6. Cited by Th. Hopfner, *Griechisch-ägyptischer Offenbarungszauber,* vol. 2 (Leipzig, 1924; repr., Amsterdam, 1970), pars. 109–10.

7. K. Meuli, "Scythica," *Hermes* 70 (1935): 121–76 = *Gesammelte Schriften,* 2:817–89 (Basel, 1975). This article is still important today. Meuli's discovery of shamanistic elements in Greek religion led the way for Dodds, *The Greeks and the Irrational,* and others.

8. D. Martinetz, K. Loos, and J. Jantzen, *Weihrauch und Myrrhe. Kulturgeschichtliche und wirtschaftliche Bedeutung. Botanik-Chemie-Medizin* (Stuttgart, 1989), pp. 138–39.

9. The publication of the book, followed by a few articles in the press, led to a political debate in Germany. See, for instance, M. Pfeifer, *Der Weihrauch: Geschichte, Bedeutung, Verwendung* (Regensburg, 1997). This book is written from the point of view of the Roman Catholic Church, though it acknowledges the research done by Martinetz et al. Pfeifer (p. 17) reports that the Egyptian word for frankincense is *sntr.* This can be translated as "scent of the deity" or "what qualifies man to communicate with the deity" or "what makes man divine." All three meanings cover different aspects of the mystic experience and show that, for the Egyptians, frankincense was the entheogen par excellence. There are scientists who disagree with Martinetz et al. because their own experiments did not confirm the presence of tetrahydrocannabinol (THC) in frankincense; see, e.g., M. Kessler, *Zur Frage nach psychotropen Stoffen im Rauch von brennendem Gummiharz der Boswellia sacra* (Inaugural-Dissertation Basel, 1991). I am very grateful to Dr. Thomas Schlaepfer, University of Bonn, for pointing out to me this ongoing controversy.

10. Martinetz et al., *Weihrauch und Myrrhe,* pp. 137–38, and L. Klages, *Vom kosmogonischen Eros,* 2nd ed. (Jena, 1926), p. 26. Klages was also the foremost German graphologist of his time. He probably has in mind Marsilio Ficino's note in his translation of Plotinus' *Enneads* 4.4.38 (p. 252 Creuzer). Here, Ficino speaks about the proper way in which the Orphic hymns were recited or sung, with lamps and incense (myrrh for Poseidon, frankincense for Hermes, and so on).

11. Actually, an unknown German professor whose success as a conjurer of spirits came to the attention of Frederick the Great was well aware of the hypnotic properties of frankincense. He told the king his secret (see Th. Fontane, *Wanderungen durch die Mark Brandenburg,* vol. 3 [Berlin, 1960], pp. 292ff.):"Frankincense puts the 'patient' into a doze, a state of drowsiness that is light enough to make him understand everything that I tell him, but also deep enough to prevent him from thinking seriously. Second, it heats his brain to the point that his imagination produces lively pictures of the words he hears." This scientist of the Enlightenment, whoever he was, clearly understood some of the workings of ancient magic. Actually, the effects of frankincense on the brain were already known to Agrippa von Nettesheim (1486–1535), who, in his *De Occulta Philosophia* (1510; repr., 1533), describes a system of mirrors that allows the practitioner to project images of daemons or spirits into a column of smoke from incense. As the smoke changes shape, the spirits appear to move. Smoke ascending in front of a statue seems to animate the image. Adam Lonitzer, a German herbalist, in his *Kreuterbuch* (Frankfurt am Main, 1679), p. 738, also was aware of the psychoactive properties of frankincense. See W. Sellar and M. Matt, *Weihrauch und Myrrhe. Anwendung in Geschichte und Gegenwart* (Munich, 1997); Chr. Rätsch, *Enzyklopädie der psychoaktiven Pflanzen. Botanik, Ethnopharmakologie und Anwendung,* with a foreword by Albert Hofmann (Aarau, 1998), index, s.v. "Boswellia."

12. Martinetz et al., *Weihrauch und Myrrhe,* pp. 169–80.

13. K. Nielsen, *Incense in Ancient Israel,* suppl. to Vetus Testamentum, vol. 38 (Leiden, 1985); P. Heger, *The Development of the Incense Cult in Ancient Israel,* Beihefte zur Zeitschrift für alttestamentliche Wissenschaft, vol. 245 (Berlin, 1997).

14. But see W. La Barre, *Ghost Dance* (New York, 1970), pp. 560ff., 572ff., 598ff.; B. Shanon, *The Antipodes of the Mind* (Oxford, 2002), p. 260, n. 3. Shanon is aware of the hypothesis that many of the world's great religions originated in the use of "entheogens," and he himself has identified two plants in the Sinai Peninsula that are chemically related to Ayahuasca, but he says nothing about the sacred incense. In *The Mystery of Manna* (Rochester, Vt., 2000), D. Merkur argues that the biblical Manna was not just a miraculous kind of food but a psychoactive substance.

15. Margaret Joyce Field, *Search for Security: An Ethno-Psychiatric Study of Rural Ghana* (Evanston, Ill., 1960), pp. 89ff. The author was well qualified to work on such phenomena: she had studied chemistry before becoming a physician specializing in psychiatry, and later she worked as an anthropologist in Africa.

16. See Nielsen and Heger for details. Much valuable information is found in the Internet program "Navigating the Bible" (World ORT). I would like to add that the Copts and the Ethiopians preserved, in their liturgy, some ancient formulas of incense and adapted them to the new faith. There is, for example, a ritual known as the "Confession of Sins over Frankincense" which appears to be a confession in

the sight of God. I have not been able to find the article by E. Hammerschmidt in *Oriens Christianus* 43 (1959): 103–9.

17. See Martinetz et al., *Weihrauch und Myrrhe.*

18. Quoted by G. Ryckmans, *Revue Biblique* 58 (1951): 376, without further comment.

19. See M. Lambeck, *Human Spirits: A Cultural Account of Trance in Mayotte* (Berkeley, 1981).

Vocabula Magica

It will be useful, I think, to list basic words, synonyms, and near synonyms that we find in the sources (Greek and Latin) for magic, its various aspects and specialties, its practitioners. I have tried to make it as comprehensive as possible, although it would be impossible to give a complete vocabulary. I hope that this may serve as a point of departure, and, eventually, the gaps can be filled in by others, once a foundation has been laid. In a way, an unpretentious glossary like this is the best introduction into the complex world of ancient magic, and as far as I know, nothing comparable has been attempted in this format. Even so, the wealth of the language in terms for this particular human activity is impressive, and it shows the enormous importance of the supernatural in daily life. Many terms have several "nontechnical" meanings, but here I shall, as a rule, only give their sense as applied to magic, divination, and so on.

Language (spoken and written) is an evanescent material that preserves facts, human experience, and emotions over a long period of time. It should be studied carefully along with the more tangible material such as the curse tablets and the substances prescribed in magical recipes (which are also transmitted in language).

In an effort to be brief, I have probably oversimplified now and then some of the complexities that are at the very core of religion and magic. This can hardly be avoided in a glossary or abbreviated dictionary of this kind. Often we can only guess the meaning of a word, because it is poorly attested or the context is not clearly understood. We are working in an area where people were often vague on purpose about what they did and what they meant. Some words can have a perfectly normal, harmless meaning, but to those who "knew" they meant something else. I also have not given any of the passages that attest these words, because that would have required a book in itself.

The transliteration of the Greek omits the accents and the distinctions between long and short vowels. But this convention seems to be acceptable today, as long as the reader who wishes to look them up in Liddell-Scott-Jones to find more information keeps in mind the possibility of *epsilon* and *eta, omikron* and *omega.*

493

Greek

abrakadabra. Magical word, probably from Hebrew *ha-bracah-dabrah* 'pronounce the blessing' or a derivation from *abrasax* via *abrasabras* (*sigma* read as Latin *c*).

abrasax or **abraxas.** Magical words, not fully understood, probably referring to a daemon or lower deity.

adynaton 'impossible, miracle, paradox'. Cf. *anomalia, paradoxon, thauma.*

aeromanteia 'divination from phenomena of the lower atmosphere'.

agamos 'unmarried'. Specifically one who died before getting married; one of the "restless dead" useful in magic; cf. *aoros.*

agathodaimon 'good daemon, protecting spirit'. Comparable to guardian angel; cf. *daimon.*

ago 'to lead, bring' (by magic); hence *agoge* 'spell designed to lead a person to the *magus* or his client, spell to attract someone, conjuring ritual' (frequent in love magic). Related: *agogimon* 'love charm'; cf. *epagoge, helko, katago, theagogia.*

agrypnetikon 'spell to produce sleeplessness'. Cf. *oneiropompos.*

agyrtes 'beggar-priest, mendicant sorcerer'. Also *agyrter*. Sometimes associated with *mantis* 'seer, diviner'. The verb *agyrtazo* 'collect by begging' is related to *ageiro* 'gather together' (hence *ageiron* 'one who takes up a collection, mendicant sorcerer', more specifically *en tois kyklois ageiron* 'one who collects money in a circle of spectators'), mostly in a negative sense, 'gather by some form of deceit'. The *metragyrtai* were the "begging priests" of the Great Mother, i.e., the goddess Cybele. The fem. form of *agyrter* is *agyrtria* 'mendicant witch', and *agyrtikos* serves as an adjective, e.g., neuter *agyrtikon* 'way of life of a mendicant sorcerer, jugglery, magical trick'. Cf. *goes.*

Aigyptios 'Egyptian', also 'magician'. Lat. *Aegyptius* (cf. *Babylonius, Chaldaeus*). Cf. *Medos, Thessala.* Verb form *aigyptiazo* 'to practice magic'.

aion 'Eternity'. Power invoked in magic.

alastor 'avenging spirit, evil daemon'. Sometimes the personified curse on a family or a dynasty; probably from *alasthai* 'to roam'. Cf. *Erinys;* Lat. *Furia.*

alazon 'braggart, charlatan, vagrant impostor'. Cf. *apateon, bomolochos.*

alektryomanteia 'divination based on the behavior of a rooster'.

aleuromanteia 'divination based on the observation of wheaten flour'. Cf. *alphito-manteia.*

alexeterion (sc. *pharmakon*) 'remedy, helpful drug or spell'. Cf. *alexipharmakon;* Lat. *(carmen) auxiliare; remedium.*

alexikakos 'averting evil'. Cf. *apostrepsikakos, apotropaios.*

alexipharmakon 'protective drug or spell'. Cf. *alexeterion, pharmakon.*

alimon 'banishing hunger'. A type of magical food (one recipe lists twelve ingredients, including poppy seeds, squill, asphodel, mallows, and honey).

alphitomanteia 'divination through the observation of barley-groats'. Cf. *aleuro-manteia.*

anakaleo 'to summon up [from the dead]'. Cf. *psychagogeo;* Lat. *evoco, invoco.*

analyo 'to undo the effect of a binding spell [*katadesis*]'. Cf. *apolyo.*

ananke 'necessity, compulsion, constraint, fate'. Cf. *heimarmene, katananke.*

anapompe 'digging up [of treasures]'.

anathema. Different, contradictory meanings: 'votive offering', 'dedicated to a deity', i.e. 'consecrated'; or 'accursed'. From *anatithemi* 'to dedicate [to a deity]'; cf. *katathema;* Lat. *sacer. Anathematizo* 'to bind under a curse'.

angelos 'messenger', specifically 'intermediate spirit between gods and men'. Cf. *daimon, pneuma.*

anodos 'way up, emerging [from the underworld]'. Of the appearance of a chthonic deity or a shade. Cf. *katabasis.*

anomalia 'irregularity, abnormality, miracle'. Cf. *adynaton, apithana, paradoxon.*

aoros 'one who died before one's time, one of the untimely [and therefore restless] dead'. Spirit useful in magic. Cf. *agamos, bi(ai)othanatos.*

apateon 'deceiver, rogue', also 'false prophet, shady practitioner'. Associated with *goes* or *planos.* Cf. *alazon, goes.*

apeile 'threat'. Addressed to a god or daemon, as opposed to *epiklesis* or *euche* 'prayer'.

apelastikos 'having the power to drive away'. E.g., a magical herb, a substance, a ritual.

aphanizo 'to make disappear'.

apithana 'unlikely things, incredible happenings, miracles'. Cf. *adynaton, anomalia, paradoxon.*

apokalypsis 'revelation'. E.g., through visions. Cf. *horama;* Lat. *visio.*

apokrypha (ta) 'hidden doctrines, secret wisdom'. Cf. Lat. *arcana, occulta.*

apolysis 'release, deliverance' (from a spell). Cf. *analyo;* Lat. *ligo, solvo.*

apomaktes 'one who rubs, wipes, cleans'. From *apomasso* 'to rub, wipe, clean', esp. in magical rituals. Fem. *apomaktria.* Cf. *kathairo; perimaktria.*

apomanteia 'negative divination'. Opposite to *katamanteia.*

apomeilixis 'appeasement (by magic), soothing ritual'. Cf. Lat. *delenio, -imentum.*

apophthengomai 'to deliver an oracle'. Cf. *chrao.*

apophysao 'to blow away'. E.g., a daemon of sickness, by blowing on the patient.

apopompe 'sending away [by words or rituals]', or 'a kind of curse by which an evil caused by daemons (illness, etc.) is transferred to someone else or sent into the wilderness, the sea, etc.'. The "scapegoat" is *pharmakos.* Cf. *apotrope, epipompe.*

aporrheta 'unspeakable, unmentionable, forbidden things'. Cf. *arrheta;* Lat. *nefas.*

apostrepsikakos 'designed to avert evil'. I.e., a spell, talisman, etc. Cf. *alexikakos, apotropaion,* etc.

apotelesmatika 'influences [of the stars], astrology'.

apotrope 'averting [evil], protective magical or religious rite'. Related words: *apotropaion* 'averting evil', *apotropiasma* 'ritual [sacrifice] to avert evil'. Cf. also *apopompe.*

arai 'curses'. Verb form *araomai* 'to curse'. Cf. Lat. *devotio, dirae.*

arche 'higher power, supernatural agent, authority'. Of angelic or daemonic powers as part of a hierarchy. Cf. *exousia.*

archimagos 'chief *magus*'. Cf. *archiereus* 'chief priest', *archiatros* 'personal physician [of a ruler]', later 'respected physician'.

arete 'superior quality, power, wonder'. Cf. *charis, dynamis;* Lat. *potestas, virtus.*

arrheta 'unspeakable [forbidden] things'. Cf. *aporrheta;* Lat. *nefas. Arrhetopoieo* 'to practice the unmentionable'; cf. *rhadiourgeo.*

asebeia 'impiety', also 'sorcery, witchcraft', as in *graphe asebeias* '[formal] accusation of witchcraft'. Cf. Lat. *impietas.*

Assyrios 'Assyrian'. Type of oriental *magos*. Cf. *Aigyptios, Medos;* Lat. *Chaldaeus,* etc.

astragalomanteia 'kind of divination which uses the knuckle bones of goats or sheep'.

astroboleo 'to bring a star-stroke' (by magic).

astrologos 'astrologer' or 'astronomer' (the borderlines are not clear). Syn. *astrologia, apotelesmatika, genethlialogia* for the former, *astronomos, mathematikos* for the latter.

ataphos 'deprived of burial'. One of the "restless dead," useful in magic. Cf. *agamos, aoros, bi(ai)othanatos.*

autopsia 'direct observation, supernatural vision'. Cf. *horama.*

Bakchos 'worshiper of Dionysus', also 'member or leader of a suspicious cult'. Associated with *mystes, nyktipolos.*

bambakeutria 'witch'. Said to be a Cilician word for *pharmakeutria* (cf. *bambakeia* for *pharmakeia*).

baskania 'jealousy, envy, evil eye'. *Baskanos ophthalmos;* Lat. *malignus oculus. Baskaino* (or *katabaskaino*) 'to hurt [someone] by the evil eye'. Cf. Lat. *fascinatio, fascinum.*

bibliomanteia 'using a book to predict the future'.

bi(ai)othanatos 'one who died by violence [murder, suicide, war, accident]'. Spirit useful in magic. Cf. *agamos, aoros, ataphos.*

bomolochos 'one who hangs out near altars [to steal the meat], buffoon, charlatan'. Cf. *alazon.*

bothros 'pit, trench'. Dug for magical purposes, to establish contact with the powers of the underworld. Cf. Lat. *fossa, scrobis.*

brontomanteia 'prophecy by means of interpreting thunder'.

charakter 'magical symbol'. Cf. *symbolon.*

charis 'grace, spiritual gift, object imbued with spiritual power'. Cf. *arete, dynamis.* Related: *charitesia (ta)* 'magic performed to win favor'.

cheiromanteia 'predictions based on the shape, lines, etc. of the hand'. Related: *cheiroskopos* 'practitioner of *cheiromanteia*'.

chrao 'to give an oracle'. Cf. *apophthengomai.* Related: *chrematismos* 'oracle' (cf. Lat. *oraculum*), *chresterion* 'the sanctuary in which it is offered', *chresmologos* 'soothsayer' (cf. *mantis,* Lat. *sortiarius*). Originally, the diviner picked and interpreted lots (an early form of cartomancy), but later there were books of ready-made predictions (Astrampsychos) from which suitable oracles could be picked. Cf. *kleromanteia.*

chrima, chrisma 'oil, unguent, anointing'.

daimon 'minor [or intermediate] deity, daemon, spirit [good or evil], spirit of a dead person'. Sometimes the higher gods are also called *daimones.* Socrates' *daimonion* is his own personal deity. Related: d*aimonao* or *daimonizomai* 'to be possessed'; *daimon paredros* 'assisting daemon'. Cf. *angelos, pneuma;* Lat. *genius.*

daktylomanteia 'divination by means of a magical ring on a finger'.

daphnemanteia 'laurel-divining'. The wood and the leaves of *Laurus nobilis* were thrown into a fire; a crackling or roaring sound was a good sign.

deisidaimonia '[exaggerated] fear of higher powers'. Hard to distinguish from *theosebeia* '[normal] respect for the gods'. Cf. Lat. *superstitio.*

deo 'to bind (by magic)'. Cf. *katadeo,* etc.

desmeuo 'to bind (by spells)'. Cf. *deo, katadesmeuo,* Lat. *ligo.*

diakopos 'magic to drive asunder, to cause separation'. Opposite to *agoge, agogimon.*

dokimon 'tested charm'.

dromenon 'what is being done, action, ritual, gestures, etc.'. Opposite to *legomenon* 'what is being said' (spoken words, chanted spells) during magical (and religious) operations.

dynamis 'power, specifically magical power'. Almost syn. for *mageia (dynamike techne = efficax scientia).* It roughly corresponds to the anthropological term *mana.* The *magus* has it, but it is also immanent in plants, stones, man-made objects, rituals. Simon Magus was called by his followers "the great power of God." Plural form: *dynameis* 'magical powers'; verb form: *dynamoo* 'to put magical powers into [something]'. *Dynamikos logos* 'powerful spell'. Cf. *charis, arete;* Lat. *potestas, virtus.*

eidolon 'ghostly image, shade'. Cf. *phasma,* Lat. *anima; umbra.* One part left of a person after death, the others being *soma* 'body' (what decays in the tomb) and *psyche* 'soul'.

ekkaleo 'to summon, call forth'. Noun form: *ekklesis.* Cf. Lat. *evoco.*

ekphonesis 'mode of utterance, manner of reciting'.

ekstasis 'displacement, stepping out [of one's normal self], trance'. Related: *theia mania* 'divine madness'; cf. *enthousiasmos,* Lat. *alienatio, externor.*

empeiria 'experience, magical knowledge'. Cf. *oida;* Lat. *ars, experimentum, plusscius, scientia.*

empousa 'female phantom, alluring daemon appearing in various forms'. Cf. *lamia.*

enchytristria 'woman who gathers bones [from a funeral pile] into an urn'. Perhaps 'witch'.

energeia (magike) '[magical] power'. Cf. *arete, dynamis.*

engastrimantis, engastrimythos or *engastrites* 'one who speaks [divines] through the belly; [prophetic] ventriloquist'. Cf. *python, sternomantis.*

engrapho 'to enroll, to deliver [to a higher authority]. Legal term used in religion and magic. Cf. *katagrapho.*

enkilikistria 'woman who purifies around'. Syn. to *periagnistria* but with a reference to the deceitful nature of the Cilicians.

enkoimesis 'sleeping in [a temple], incubation'. Cf. Lat. *incubatio.*

enodioi symboloi 'omens [good or bad] seen in the street'. Cf. Lat. *omen.*

enorkoo 'to adjure' (a daemon). Also *enorkizo;* cf. *exorkismos.*

enthousiasmos 'ecstasy, inspiration, divine possession'. Cf. *ekstasis.*

epagoge 'incantation, spell'. More specifically: ritual to conjure up a ghost in order to harm a person. Related: *epago* 'to bring or send [something] toward [someone]'; *epakton* 'something [a spirit] conjured up against someone'. Cf. *ago, agoge.*

epelysia 'something that comes upon [a person], unexpected spell, act of sorcery'.

epeuchomai 'to curse, imprecate upon'. Cf. *kateuchomai.*

ephesia grammata 'magical formulas or books'.

epichriston '[poisonous] ointment, [healing] salve'. Cf. *katachriston.*

epiklesis 'invocation, invitation, prayer'. Opposite to *apeile* 'threat'. Verb form: *epikaleo* 'to invoke'. Cf. Lat. *advocatio, invocatio.*

epikrateia 'power, superiority'. Cf. *arete, dynamis, exousia.*

epiphaneia 'apparition or arrival of a deity or daemon'. Sometimes accompanied by light (*phos*) and a sweet smell (*euodia*). Cf. *epiphaneia, parousia;* Lat. *adventus; praesentia.*

epipompe 'enchantment'. From *epipempo* 'send against'. Can be a special case of *apopompe* or a curse directing a daemon toward a victim. Cf. *apopompe.*

episteme 'knowledge'. Sometimes has the sense of magical knowledge, e.g., *hieratike episteme* 'sacred knowledge' (i.e., magic, theurgy). Cf. *empeiria, oida, techne;* Lat. *ars, disciplina, scientia.*

epiteleo 'to accomplish, bring to perfection, practice magic'. Cf. *telete.*

epithyma, epithymiama (to) 'fumigation, incense offering' (during religious or magical rituals). Sometimes a combination of pungent (probably psychoactive) and aromatic ingredients, e.g., bird feathers and cypress wood. Frankincense and myrrh etc. are aromatic and may be psychoactive.

epode 'incantation, rhythmic spell chanted over or against someone'. Charms were probably sung or recited in a particular (monotonous, repetitious) way to increase their power by a hypnotic element. They could be soothing and healing but also destructive. The recital was part of an elaborate ritual that included also drugs (*pharmaka*), fumigations, gestures, and movements (*schemata*). He who sings the spell, the enchanter, is called *epodos (epaoidos)*. Cf. Lat. *cantus, carmen, praecantrix.*

eponymia 'meaningful name or epithet'. Used in prayers and invocations. Cf. *onoma;* Lat. *invocatio.* To know the correct name or epithet of a deity was important; hence, the long, cumulative lists.

Erinyes 'female daemons of the underworld, avenging spirits, personified curses'. Cf. *alastor;* Lat. *furia.*

erotikon (sc. *pharmakon*) 'love charm'. Cf. *philtron,* Lat. *amatorium.*

esoterikos 'insider, member of the inner circle, initiate'. Opposite to *exoterikos.*

euche 'prayer'. Cf. *exaitesis,* Lat. *preces.*

eurykles 'ventriloquist'. After a certain E., a master of this art. Cf. *engastrimantis.*

exado, exepaeido 'to draw out by singing' (e.g., daemons of sickness). Cf. *exorkizo;* Lat. *evoco, excanto.*

exagistos 'accursed, abominable'. Cf. *anathema;* Lat. *sacer.*

exaitesis 'petition, prayer'. Cf. *euche.*

exegetes 'interpreter [of dreams, omens, oracles, etc.]'. Cf. Lat. *coniector, interpres.*

exorkismos 'questioning or admonishing under oath', usually 'driving out [of daemons]'. Cf. *enorkoo.*

exoterikos 'outsider'; i.e., not part of the inner circle. Cf. *esoterikos.*

exousia 'power, authority'. Also personified, of divine beings. Cf. *arche, arete, dynamis;* Lat. *potestas.*

gastromanteia 'belly-divining'. From *gastra,* a belly-shaped vessel; it was filled with water, and lighted lamps were placed around it. Cf. *hydromanteia.*

genethlialogia 'astrology'. From *genethlion* (sc. *emar*) 'birthday, horoscope'. Cf. *astrologia, apotelesmatika.*

geomanteia 'earth-divining' (drawing figures in the sand).

glossa 'tongue, speech, language'. As in *en glossais lalein* 'to speak in tongues', i.e., to produce broken, inarticulate speech in trance. Hence the term *glossolalia.*

gnostes 'one who knows [magic, the future, etc.]'. Cf. *oida;* Lat. *plusscius.*

goes 'wizard, sorcerer, juggler, charlatan'. Associated with *agyrtes, alazon* and other negative terms. The word can designate the "wizard" (a low-class type of *magos*) or any quack, humbug, or impostor. The fem. *goeteutria* (in analogy to *pharmakeutria*) is rare. Originally, *goetes* (from *goao* 'to wail') could have been an early Greek shaman whose specialty was a ritual lament over the dead (screams uttered in ecstasy), but it could refer to shrill cries uttered in a normal state of consciousness, during a magical ritual. Related: *goeteia* 'jugglery, witchcraft, deceit'; *goeteuo* 'to bewitch, to charm', (but also 'to play the wizard'); *goeteuma* 'spell, charm'; *goetikos* 'skilled in witchcraft, in juggling'.

graus or **graia** 'old woman', possibly 'witch'. As in *graus trioditis* (late) 'old woman who frequents the crossroads' (lined with tombs, where Hecate could be invoked). Cf. *tymbas;* Lat. *anus, anicula.*

hagnizo 'to cleanse, purify, consecrate' (mostly in religious contexts). Cf. *periagnistria.*

hedonikon 'spell or drug designed to arouse sexual desire'. Cf. *erotikon, philtron.*

heimarmene 'fate, destiny'. Cf. *ananke.*

helko 'to drag' (i.e., force by magic to come). Cf. *ago, agoge, epago, holke.*

hellenikos (late) 'pagan'. As in *hellenike sophia* 'pagan knowledge' (i.e., magic), or *hellenika epitedeumata* 'magical operations'.

henosis 'mystic union with a deity'. Cf. *epiphaneia, systasis.*

heros 'deified mythical ancestor, benefactor, savior figure of an ethnic group or a dynasty, higher being intermediate between gods and men'. Hero worship was common all over Greece but usually localized. A "hero" may be a type of evil daemon and still the object of worship. Cf. *daimon.*

hieratikos 'priestly' (as in *hieratike techne* 'priestly art', but also 'priesthood'). Could be applied to theurgy as a higher form of magic. See *hiereus.*

hiereus 'priest, sacrificer, diviner'; could also be applied to a *magus. Hiereia* 'priestess'; could also be applied, it seems, to the chief witch of a *thiasos* of witches, or it could be a mendicant holy woman. It always depends on who is speaking: the practitioner and his or her followers or the outsiders? Sometimes a term that would seem to imply a certain dignity could also be applied ironically. Cf. *mystagogos.*

hieroskopia 'observation of the organs of a sacrificial victim'. Mainly in religious contexts, but also possible in magical rituals. Cf. Lat. *extispicium, haruspicina.*

hippomanes (to). From *hippos* 'horse' and *mania* 'madness'. Has various meanings: (1) herb (*Datura stramonium?*) or gland that drives horses mad; (2) mucus dripping from the genitals of a mare who is in heat or pregnant; (3) excrescence on the forehead of a newly born foal, eaten at once by the mother; (4) any aphrodisiac. Used in love magic, supposed to arouse mad love in a person. Cf. *epagoge, erotikon.*

holke 'drawing, dragging, pulling' (a person, by means of magic). Cf. *helko.*

horama 'vision [in a dream]'. Cf. *apokalypsis, autopsia.*

horkizo 'to adjure, conjure, exorcise' (originally 'to call upon by an oath'?). Cf. *exorkizo, exorkismos.*

horoskopos 'ascendant [in a horoscope]', also 'astrologer'.

hydromanteia 'divination by means of water'. Related to scrying and crystal gazing. The medium, usually a young boy, was put into trance and observed the reflections in a bowl filled with water. The *magus* asked him what he saw and was thus able to answer questions. Cf. *gastromanteia, lekanomanteia.*

Iao. Stands for YHWH, the Hebrew deity, in the Magical Papyri.

iatromantis 'physician-seer', also 'miracle-worker' (semimythical figures like Abaris, Aristeas, Epimenides, Hermotimus). Another form of shamanism in Greek culture (diagnosis, prescription, and prognosis made in trance).

iatromathematikos 'astrologer who also practices medicine' (by the application of astrology to the human body, its parts and diseases).

indalma 'image, apparition, hallucination'. Cf. *eidolon, phantasma, phasma;* Lat. *umbra.*

iynx (pl. *iynges*) 'magical wheels'. Implement in the form of a wheel, sometimes decorated with gold and threads of wool dyed purple; sometimes a dead bird (wryneck) is attached to it. Perhaps it was set in motion during magical operations, like the *rhombos* 'bull-roarer', to create a noise. "Hecate's wheel" (*Hekatikos strophalos*), a tool used by theurgists, may be a variation of this.

kainotomeo 'to make changes, innovations [in the state, in religion]'. Related to *asebeo* 'to be impious, to commit sacrilege'.

kakodaimon 'evil spirit', also 'person possessed by an evil genius'. Opposite to *agathodaimon.*

kakotechnia '[black] magic'; lit. 'evil art'. Cf. *techne;* Lat. *ars, facinus, maleficium, scientia.*

kapnomanteia 'divination by means of smoke' (e.g., from a sacrifice on an altar). This could be done (1) by observing the movements and shape of the smoke; (2) by breathing in the smoke of certain psychoactive substances (poppy seeds, sesame, frankincense, myrrh). Cf. *libanomanteia.*

katabasis 'descent [into the underworld]', for necromantic purposes. A symbolic ritual took the place of a real descent. Cf. *anodos; bothros.*

katabaskaino 'to hurt [someone] by the evil eye' (intensive form of *baskaino*). Cf. Lat. *effascino* (intensive form of *fascino*).

katachriston '[poisonous or healing] ointment'. Cf. *chrisma, epichriston;* Lat. *nardum.*

katadeo 'to bind [by magic]'. Related: *katadesis* 'act of binding'; *katadesmos* 'binding spell', also 'way of binding down, binding curse, destructive spell'. Cf. *deo, katadesmeuo, philtrokatadesmos;* Lat. *defixio, devotio, ligo.*

katadesmeuo. See *deo*, etc.

katadidomi 'to hand over, consign [a victim to a daemon]'. Cf. *katagrapho, paradidomi.*

kata(ei)do 'to sing a spell to'. Cf. *epode.*

katago. Cf. *ago, agoge.*

katagrapho 'to register, consign, transfer' (someone to the power of the underworld), hence 'to curse'. Originally a legal term. Related: *katagraphe* 'act of registering, etc.'. Cf. *katadidomi, paradidomi;* Lat. *defixio, descriptio, devotio.*

katamanteia. See *apomanteia, manteia.*

katananke 'means of constraint, spell'. Cf. *ananke.*

katapassaleuo 'to nail deep down, to bewitch'. Cf. Lat. *defixio.*

katapharmakeuo 'to dose [or anoint] with drugs, enchant, bewitch'. Cf. *kataphar-masso.*

katapharmasso. See *katapharmakeuo.*

katatatithemi 'to commit, hand over [to a deity]', hence *katathema* 'accursed thing' (object or victim of a curse). Cf. *anathema, katagrapho;* Lat. *sacer.*

katecho 'to inhibit'. Cf. *katadeo; thymokatochon.*

katepa(ei)do 'to subdue by enchantment'. Cf. *epode, kata(ei)do.*

kateuchomai 'to curse'. Cf. *araomai, epeuchomai.*

kathaireo 'to pull down [the moon]'. Cf. *kataspao, kathelko, kataphero;* Lat. *deduco, detraho, devoco.*

kathairo 'to purify (ritually)'; hence *kathartes* 'cleanser, purifier', *katharmos* 'rite of purification', *katharma* 'refuse, outcast, scapegoat'. Cf. *perikathairo* 'to purify all around'.

katoche 'possession [by a god or spirit], trance, ecstasy', i.e., a state conducive to prophetic visions. Cf. *ekstasis, enthousiasmos, theia mania.*

katoptromanteia 'divination by means of mirrors'. Trance could be induced by gazing at polished or shiny surfaces illuminated by lamps, through a kind of self-hypnosis; sometimes trickery seems to have been involved. Cf. *gastromanteia, hydromanteia, lychnomanteia.*

katorytto 'to bury (symbolically)'.

keleo 'to bewitch'. Related: *kelesis* 'enchantment', *kelema* 'spell, charm', *akeletos* 'unbewitched, unbewitchable'. All seem to be derived from an old root.

keromanteia 'wax-divining'. Wax is melted and allowed to drip into water to form various shapes. Similar to "lead-divining," but the term *molybdomanteia* does not seem to be attested.

kestos 'charm, amulet'. Cf. *periapton.*

kledanomanteia 'divination by means of chance utterances'; cf. *palmoskopia*

kleromanteia 'divination by means of casting lots'. Possible materials were wooden sticks, leaves (from olive trees), pebbles, dice. Cf. *astragalomanteia, chrao;* Lat. *sortes, sortilegium.*

klesis 'invocation of powers [in heaven, on earth and in the underworld]'. From *kaleo* 'to call'. Cf. *epiklesis, euche, exaitesis;* Lat. *preces, voco.*

komasia (agalmaton) 'procession of cult images'. Egyptian method of divination, considered a type of *manganeia* by Greeks.

koskinomanteia 'divination by means of a sieve'. A sieve is placed on a pair of tongs which have to be lifted with two fingers only.

kryphia (ta) 'hidden things, secrets'. Cf. Lat. *arcana, occulta.*

kykeon. Sacred potion. Served during the initiation rites at Eleusis, it consisted of barley groats (with ergot, according to Albert Hofmann), grated goat cheese, pennyroyal, honey, and Pramnian wine. Probably hallucinogenic.

kynanthropos 'dog-man', i.e., sorcerer who can transform himself into a dog. Cf. *lykanthropos.*

kyphi. Egyptian mixture of up to thirty-six ingredients, inhaled as incense, rubbed into the skin as an ointment, perhaps also consumed. Probably hallucinogenic, used in the mysteries of Isis as well as in magic.

lamia 'female vampire, ghoul, witch'. Figure of Greek folklore ("devouring one"), which can assume many shapes, that kidnaps small children and eats them. Cf. *empousa.*

laoplanos 'one who deceives the people'. Cf. *agyrtes, planos.*

legomenon (to) 'what is spoken', i.e., words (chants) accompanying the ritual (*to dromenon*).

lekanomanteia 'bowl-divining'. Cf. *hydromanteia.*

lenai 'bacchanals'. Associated by Heraclitus with *bakchoi, magoi, nyktipoloi.*

libanomanteia 'divination through incense' (the smoke from the incense perhaps inducing trance). Cf. *kapnomanteia.*

lithika. Books on the magical properties of stones (esp. precious and semiprecious stones as they were used for healing, for amulets, etc.).

lithomanteia 'divination by way of precious stones or crystal'.

lychnomanteia 'divination by means of a lamp'. Could be combined with *katoptromanteia* or *lekanomanteia* and the burning of *epithymata* to induce trance.

lykanthropos 'werewolf'. Cf. *kynanthropos;* Lat. *versipellis.*

lyo 'to loose, unbind, unfasten'. Opposite to *deo, katadeo.* Cf. *analyo, lysipharmakon* 'to remedy against binding-spells'; Lat. *solvo.*

magos 'Magian'. Member of a Median tribe or caste; then one of the priests and wise men in Persia who carried out the cult of fire by offerings of frankincense and aromatic woods, were advisers to the King, interpreted dreams, practiced astrology, etc.; then enchanter, wizard, and sometimes in a bad sense, impostor, charlatan. *Magos* also serves as an adjective, besides *magikos.* Related: *mageia* 'type of Persian religion' also 'magic' (syn. *mageutike [techne]); mageuma* 'piece of magical art'; *mageuo* 'to be a *magus,* be skilled in Magian lore, bewitch'. *Mageutes* = *magos* is also attested. *Magianos* can be translated by "inscribed with charms" (e.g., an amulet or a bracelet). The root *mag-* apparently has also given *mechane* and survives in Engl. "might," Germ. "Macht." Heraclitus (sixth century B.C.) associates *magoi* with *bakchoi, lenai, mystai, nyktipoloi,* thus creating a complex picture of a kind of exotic charlatan (in his eyes) who operated at night and offered to initiate people into private mysteries, not unlike those of Dionysus. Cf. *goeteia, manganeia, pharmakeia.*

manganeia 'magic by trickery, by technical devices'. From *manganon,* a term covering various pieces of machinery, e.g., "block of a pulley"; hence *manganeuo, manganarios,* etc. Related to *mechane* which is related to *mageia* (see above). The broad range of the term suggests that technical devices were often used to produce miraculous effects. *Magia naturalis* would describe a number of such procedures. Related: *manganarios* 'magician', also 'engineer', and *manganeuterion* 'haunt of impostors', also 'magical workshop'.

manteia 'divination, prophecy'; hence *mantis* 'seer, prophet', *mantike (techne),* *manteuma* 'prophecy, curse that will come true'. Derived from *(theia) mania* '[divine] madness'.

maschalismos 'armpitting'. Specific form of the mutilation of a body to prevent the return of the dead person as a ghost.

mathema '[magical or astrological] knowledge'. Cf. *episteme, mathesis, oida;* Lat. *scientia.*

mechane 'device, machine, trick'. Related: *mechanikos* 'engineer', also 'writer on occult matters'. Cf. *manganeia.*

Medos 'Median, Persian', also 'type of oriental *magus*'. Cf. *Aigyptios,* etc.

megalomysterion 'great mystery'. Cf. *mysterion.*

meliouchos 'he who has the [procreative] member'. Deity invoked in magical rituals.

meniskos 'little moon'. Amulet in the shape of a crescent moon. Cf. Lat. *lunula.*

metragyrtai 'beggar-priests of Cybele, the Mother of the Gods'. They appear in the Greek world in the early fifth century B.C. and attract criticism by their behavior: ecstasy, self-mutilation, promises of salvation through initiation. Cf. *agyrtes.*

miasma 'pollution, defilement', also 'cause of pollution, defilement'. Closely related to our notion of sin.

mimema kerinon 'wax figure, voodoo doll'. Cf. Lat. *imago cerea.*

misethron 'charm for producing hatred', i.e., a spell or drug that makes a person hate another. Opposite to *philtron, stergema.*

moly 'miraculous herb protecting against magic'. Variously identified with a genus of onion or garlic, but also with mandrake, black hellebore, wild rue.

morphoskopos 'observer of forms or figures'. Perhaps same as *physiognomon* 'interpreter of a person's features'.

mystagogos 'priestly guide through the initiation into the Mysteries', but also 'teacher of magic'. Cf. *hiereus, mystes.*

mysteria (ta) 'mystery religions' or 'mystery rites'. Apparently not only applied to the mysteries of Demeter at Eleusis, Dionysus, Orpheus, Isis, etc., but also to "private" religions or esoteric sects propagated by traveling "holy men," perhaps as a sort of "poor man's" imitation or substitute. See *megalomysterion, orpheotelestes.*

mystes 'initiate' (e.g., into "holy magic"). Cf. *mystagogos.*

nekromanteion 'sanctuary where the spirits of the dead were consulted'. Cf. *psychomanteion.* The practice itself is called *nekromanteia* or *nekyomanteia.*

nekydaimon 'divine soul or spirit of a dead person', useful in magic. Cf. *agamoi, aoroi, ataphoi, bi(ai)othanatoi, nekromanteion;* Lat. *larvae, manes, umbrae.*

nekyomanteia 'necromancy, divination by consulting the dead'. This could be the family dead or the spirit of a famous person, a king, as in Aeschylus' *Persians,* where the playwright seems to describe the ritual as a specifically Persian form of *goeteia* or *mageia.*

nepenthes (pharmakon). [Egyptian] drug that soothes grief.

nephelomanteia 'divination based on the shape of clouds'.

niketikon 'winning remedy, victory charm', i.e., spell or amulet promising victory, e.g., in a competition (horse race, etc.).

nyktipolos 'one who wanders by night'. Associated with *bakchos, magos, planos,* etc.

nyktophylax 'night-watchman', also 'friendly daemon who appears by night and cures diseases'.

nympholeptos 'possessed by a Nymph', i.e., frenzied, ecstatic, insane. Cf. Lat. *cerritus, lymphatus.*

ochlagogos 'one who attracts a crowd' (to watch his performance of *thaumata* 'wonders'). Cf. *thaumatopoios;* Lat. *circulator.*

oida 'to know', esp. 'to have supernatural knowledge', as in *ta hyper anthropon eidenai* 'to know more than befits a human being'; the opposite would be *ta kat'anthropon eidenai (prattein).* Cf. *empeiria;* Lat. *ars, plusscius, scientia.*

oikeiosis 'appropriation, affinity, familiarity' (concerning the gods).

oionoskopia 'observation of the flight and sounds of birds' (mainly in a religious context). Related: *oionizesthai* 'to take omens from birds'; *oionistes, oionoskopos* 'interpreter of the movements etc. of birds'.

ololygmos 'howling sounds produced by the practitioner (during magical rituals)'. Cf. Lat. *ululatio.*

oneiromantis 'one who predicts the future on the basis of dreams'. Also called *oneiropolos.* Related: *oneirokrisia*, the art of dream interpretation; *oneiraiteton* 'charm or spell to induce a dream revelation'; *oneiropompe* 'sending of dreams [to a person]'; *oneiropompos* 'daemon who sends dreams'. Cf. also *agrypnetikon.*

onomata (asema) '[meaningless] words or names', *voces magicae.* Cf. *eponymia.*

onychomanteia 'fingernail-divining' (a mixture of soot and oil was smeared on the fingernail of a young boy and inspected in sunlight).

opsis 'vision, apparition' (dream image or phantom). Cf. *autopsia;* Lat. *imago, umbra, visio.*

orgia (ta) 'secret rituals, ecstatic forms of worship, orgiastic celebration'. Cf. *mysteria.*

orpheotelestes 'shady priestlike figure, purifier of the lower classes' (offering salvation through initiation on the basis of books pretending to be by Orpheus).

ousia '[magical] matter, *materia magica*', e.g., hair, fingernails, pieces of clothing of the person one wishes to control. *Mesai ousiai* 'daemons as intermediate beings between gods and men'.

paignia 'amusing tricks' (title of a work by "Democritus," i.e., Bolus of Mendes, mainly dealing with conjuring tricks, it seems), part of *magia naturalis.* Related: *paizein* 'to play magical tricks', *sympaiktes* 'fellow-trickster, accomplice in performing magic'. Cf. *manganeia.*

palmoskopia 'observation of involuntary movements of the body' (e.g., twitching, throbbing). The seer Melampus, a semilegendary figure of the seventh or sixth century B.C. is said to have invented and taught the art of prophesying from these movements (*palmoi*). Cf. *kledanomanteia.*

paradoxon (to) 'unexpected, extraordinary, supernormal, miraculous'. Cf. *anomalia, phoberon, teratodes, thauma;* Lat. *miraculum, portentum.*

parousia 'appearance or arrival of a deity'. Cf. *epiphaneia, theophaneia;* Lat. *adventus, praesentia.*

peisis 'persuasion, persuasiveness', from *peitho* 'to persuade' (with words, by spells or rituals). Cf. *pistis;* Lat. *persuasio.*

periagnizo 'to purify all around'. *Peri-* implies a circular movement characteristic of religious and magical rites. Cf. *enkilikistria, kathairo, perikapnizo, perikathairo, periraino.*

periamma 'amulet' (lit. 'tied around'), also *periapton*, from *periapto* 'to wrap around'. Cf. Lat. *amuletum, remedium.*

periergia 'unhealthy curiosity, interest in and practice of magic'. *Ta perierga* is almost syn. for "magic" and is associated with *mageia* and *pharmakeia. Hierourgiai periergai* must mean 'magical rites'. Cf. *polypragmosyne;* Lat. *curiositas.*

perikapnizo (perithymiao) 'to purify all around by burning incense'. Cf. *periagnizo.*

perikathairo 'to purify all around, purify completely'.

perimasso 'to wipe or knead all around' (to purify). *Perimaktria* 'woman who kneads or wipes all around a person' (e.g., to cleanse that person from the effect of a bad dream).

periousia 'superiority, psychic ability'. Cf. *arete, dynamis, epikrateia.*

Perses 'Persian, type of Near Eastern *magus*'. Cf. *Aigyptios, Medos.*

petalon 'leaf, used in divination or amulet in the shape of a leaf'. *Petaloraptes* 'maker of amulets'.

phantasma 'ghost, apparition'. Cf. *eidolon, indalma, phasma;* Lat. *umbra.*

pharmakon 'poison, remedy'. Hence *pharmatto, pharmakeuo* 'to cast a spell over, practice magic, poison, give a narcotic drug'. *Pharmakeia* is practically syn. to *mageia,* even when no specific drugs are involved, though the distinction is sometimes made. Related: *pharmakeus, pharmakeutes* (fem. *pharmakeutria*) 'poisoner, sorcerer'; *pharmaka deleteria* 'evil drugs', when *pharmakon* 'remedy' is used; *pharmakao* 'to suffer from the effect of drugs or charms'; and *pharmakites* as the object or substance that has been drugged or medicated. There are more formations along these lines. Cf. *alexipharmakon;* Lat. *remedium, veneficium.*

phasma 'vision, apparition, ghost'. Cf. *eidolon, phantasma, pneuma.*

phialomanteia 'divination by means of a *phiale* [i.e., bowl, usually without foot and handle]'. Related to *hydromanteia, lekanomanteia.*

philtron 'love charm', either as a spell or a substance or both in combination. The substance could be slipped into food or drink; it could be rubbed into the skin as a kind of perfume; it could also be applied to objects (the door or the walls of a house, it seems). *Philtrokatadesmos* combines the ideas of "attracting" and "binding." It could be used by women and men to ensure success. Cf. *erotikon;* Lat. *amatorium, poculum.*

phoberon (to) 'fearful, shocking'. Cf. *paradoxon, teratodes, thauma;* Lat. *portentum, prodigium.*

photagogeo 'to draw down the light (the illumination)' by magic (theurgy). Hence *photagogia.* Cf. *theophaneia, theourgia.*

phthonos 'envy' as a motive of witchcraft. Cf. *baskania;* Lat. *invidia.*

phylakterion '[protective] amulet'. It protects by transferring its *dynamis* to the person. Cf. *apotropaion, periamma,* Lat. *amuletum.* (N.B. English "talisman" is usually derived from late Greek *telesma* 'religious rite, consecrated object'.)

physikleidion 'spell designed to open the *physis* [sexual organ] of a woman'.

physis 'proper nature [of a plant, a thing, a substance], appearance, growth'. It is part of the *dynamis* of the plant, the stone, etc. *Physikos* means "natural" but also (in later Greek) "magical." *Physikos* can be a scientist, natural philosopher, but also a *magus.*

pistis 'faith, belief [in magic as well as in religion]'. It is the conviction that a certain *dynamis* works. Cf. *peisis, semeion, tekmerion.*

pittakion 'tablet, label' (with writing, e.g., questions submitted to an oracle).

planos 'wandering, leading astray'; also 'vagabond, impostor, creator of illusions'. Cf. *agyrtes, apateon, goes, laoplanos, thaumatopoios.*

pleonektema 'advantage, superiority, supernatural gift'. Cf. *dynamis, exousia, periousia;* Lat. *plusscius.*

ploutonion 'sanctuary that has a connection with the underworld' (e.g., because of mephitic emanations). Cf. *nekromanteion, psychopompeion.*

pneuma 'wind, breath, spirit, inspiration, divine power'. *Empneustos* 'one who is filled with the spirit, inspired'; cf. *ekstasis, enthousiasmos. Pneuma* can also be the spirit of a dead person. Cf. *phasma.*

polypragmosyne 'morbid curiosity, activities of a busybody, interest in the occult'. Cf. *periergia.*

poppysmos 'special noise [heavy breathing, sucking, smacking or popping]', made by the practitioner during magical and theurgic rituals, typical of shamanism. Cf. *ololygmos, prospneusis, sigmos;* Lat. *stridor, susurrus, ululatio.*

poton (pharmakon) 'drug given in a drink'. Cf. *philtron, poterion, potisma;* Lat. *poculum.*

pragmateia '[magical] operation, ritual'.

praxis '[magical] procedure or ritual, [magical] recipe'.

prognostikos 'soothsayer'. Cf. *chrao.*

proiktes 'beggar, charlatan'. Cf. *bomolochos, goes.*

prophetes 'speaker for a deity, diviner, *magus,* holy man, foreign religious practitioner'. Cf. *chresmologos, mantis.*

prospneusis 'breathing on, manner of breathing'. Cf. *apophysao, poppysmos, sigmos.*

pseudomantis 'false prophet'. Cf. *pseudoprophetes.*

pseudoprophetes 'false prophet, religious charlatan'. Associated with *goes.* Cf. *prophetes, pseudomantis.*

psychagogia 'evocation of souls from the underworld'; also 'entertainment' or 'persuasion' or 'soothing medical treatment'. Related: *psychagogos* 'expert in raising spirits' (to consult them about the future or use them as harmful agents). Cf. *anakaleo;* Lat. *evoco.*

psyche 'life, life force, soul, spirit of a dead person'. Cf. *pneuma, psychagogia,* etc.

psychomanteia 'divination by consulting the spirits of the dead'. *Psychomanteion* 'sanctuary where the dead are conjured up'. Cf. *nekyomanteia, ploutonion.*

psychopompos 'conductor or guide of the souls of the dead'.

python 'prophetic spirit [inside a person], gift of ventriloquism'. Cf. *engastrimythos.*

rhabdos 'wand' (used in magic). *Psychoulkos rhabdos* 'soul-dragging wand'.

rhadiourgia 'frivolity, wickedness', almost same as *goeteia.* Related: *rhadiourgeo* 'to act recklessly', *rhadiourgema* 'roguish trick, crime'.

rhizotomia 'root-cutting, witchcraft', i.e, 'digging up plants [for magical or medical purposes]'. Actually, various parts of the plant could be used, not just the roots. The work was done with bronze sickles (iron tools were considered too "modern" to have the right *dynamis*), with all kinds of precautions (eyes turned away, recitation of protective spells). *Rhizotomoi* 'professional herbalists, sorcerers, healers'. These professionals could be midwives or priests as well. Cf. Lat. *herba, radix.*

rhombos one of three different magical tools: (1) bull-roarer, i.e., flat piece of wood or metal in the shape of a lozenge, attached to a string and producing a whirring sound when rotated during a magical ritual; (2) same as *iynx,* i.e., wheel that can be set whirling clockwise and counterclockwise by two strings which are fed through two wholes; (3) top whipped up with a thong.

rhystike (euche) 'rescue (prayer)'. Religious or magical. Cf. *euche, exaitesis, klesis;* Lat. *preces.*

schema 'ritual vestment' (robe painted with symbols, head dress, mask, makeup, tattoo, gloves, special shoes); also 'ritual gesture' (position, attitude, movement).

semeion 'sign [of a special *dynamis*], miracle, wonder'. Cf. *peisis, tekmerion, thauma;* Lat. *miraculum, portentum, signum.*

sibylla 'ecstatic female seer of a certain type' (localized, attached to sanctuary, but prophesying without answering formal questions).

sigmos: 'hissing sound' (made during rituals). Cf. *poppysmos,* Lat. *susurrus.*

skia 'shadow, shade, ghost'. Cf. *eidolon, phasma;* Lat. *umbra.*

skiomanteia 'divining from shadows'.

sophia 'wisdom, lore, skill, knowledge of magic'. *Sophia thytike* 'sacrificial technique, art of the diviner, supernatural knowledge'. *Archaioi sophoi* 'wise men of old, pagan sorcerers'. *Sophistes* 'skillful practitioner', associated with *goes.*

soteria 'preservation, deliverance, salvation' (through amulets, rituals, initiation into Mysteries, through direct intervention of a deity).

stergema 'love spell'. Cf. *misethron;* Lat. *amor.*

sternomantis 'ventriloquist'. The voice seems to come from the breast, not from the belly. Cf. *engastrimantis.*

symbolon 'token, secret sign' (any object used in magic to which a special function has been assigned). *Symbolodeiktes* 'interpreter of signs, *omina*'; cf. *teratoskopos.* See also *charakter, synthema.*

sympatheia (ton holon) '[cosmic] sympathy'. Principle on which noncausal relationships and "synchronicity" within the universe are based. Latin paraphrase: *amicitiae et odia naturae quibus omnia constant* 'love-and-hate relationships within nature on which everything is based'.

symplegma 'pair of embracing dolls, used in love-magic'. Cf. *mimema kerinon.*

sympratto 'to collaborate'. For instance, the soul of a dead person is thought to "collaborate" with the *magus.*

synthema 'token, symbol, formula'. Cf. *symbolon.*

Syrios 'Syrian, type of Near Eastern *magus*'. Cf. *Aigyptios, Medos, Perses.*

systasis 'encounter with a deity'. Cf. *epiphaneia, henosis, theophaneia.*

techne '[magical] art'. Cf. *episteme, kakotechnia, sophia;* Lat. *ars, scientia.*

tekmerion 'convincing proof' (that magic really works). Cf. *pistis, semeion.*

telete '[religious or magical] ritual act'. Properly "initiation" into one of the Great Mysteries, but could also be applied to private cults propagated by *goetes* and *orpheotelestai* who borrowed the terminology, the rituals, etc., from the mystery religions. *Telesiourgeo* 'to celebrate a rite'. *Telestes* can be same as *goes,* fem. *telestria.* We know of an *Orpheotelestes* named Philippus who was poor but promised his followers prosperity and happiness in the next life if they agreed to be initiated in his "Orphic" mysteries. Cf. *epiteleo.*

teras 'wonder, portent, miracle'. *Teratoskopos* 'interpreter of wonders and prodigies'. *Terateuo* 'to work wonders, to create illusions', *terateia* 'illusion, jugglery', *(to) teratodes* 'strange event, abnormal occurrence'. Cf. *paradoxon, thauma;* Lat. *portentum. Teratourgia, thaumatopoiia* 'creation of wonders'.

thauma 'wonder, miracle, portent'. There are different types of miracles: healing miracles, miracles involving natural phenomena (weather-magic) and paranormal phenomena like telepathy, clairvoyance, precognition, levitation, bilocation, etc. *Thaumatopoiia* 'creation of wonders' includes juggling, acrobatics, marionette performances, etc. *Thaumatopoios, thaumatourgos* 'miracle-worker', also 'magician', 'conjurer' (Lat. *praestigiator*). Cf. *adynaton, anomalia, teras;* Lat. *mirabile, miraculum, portentum.*

theagogia 'evocation of a deity'. Cf. *agoge, theurgia.*

theiasmos 'inspiration, frenzy, ecstasy'. Cf. *ekstasis, enthousiasmos.*

theios aner 'divine man, holy man', i.e., miracle-worker, prophet, healer, shaman. Cf. *thaumatourgos.*

thelxis 'charm, spell'. *Thelkteria* 'offerings to the dead' (cf. *meilikteria*), also 'love philtres'. Cf. Lat. *delenimentum.*

theologos 'one who speaks of the gods, of divine things'. Opposite to *theourgos.*

theophaneia 'appearance, arrival or felt presence of a deity'. Cf. *epiphaneia, henosis, systasis.*

theophoria 'inspiration, frenzy' (bearing the divine spirit within oneself). Cf. *ekstasis, enthousiasmos, theiasmos.*

theourgia 'techniques of influencing the gods' also 'making man divine'. Both approaches have the same goal: to bring about the mystic union with the (pagan) deities through intensive belief, ritual, and meditation. Trance through hypnosis and possibly drugs played a role; trickery cannot be excluded. It is essentially a higher form of *mageia*, as opposed to *goeteia*, in fact a late form of Greek religion that appealed to some Neoplatonists and was partly responsible for Julian's apostasy. It could be seen as an attempt to bring shamanism back in the disguise of theology or philosophy, in order to revive paganism and demonstrate its superiority to the Christian religion. Smiling statues, messages from another world, etc., were supposed to prove that the ancient gods were still alive, powerful, and benevolent.

therepodos 'enchanter of beasts, snake-charmer', also 'healer of animals'.

Thessala 'Thessalian woman, witch'. Cf. *Aigyptios,* etc.

thiasos 'type of close-knit or secret religious society'. Perhaps also coven of witches presided over by a *hiereia* 'priestess'.

thymiama 'perfume, aromatic essence, incense'. Used in religious and magical rituals, could have narcotic or psychedelic effects. Cf. *epithyma.*

thymokatochon 'spell designed to restrain anger'. Cf. *katecho.*

thysia 'burnt offering, sacrifice, ritual'. *Thytes* 'sacrificer' is almost same as *goes, magos, mantis.* Cf. Lat. *sacrificulus.*

tolme also *tolmema* 'recklessness, reckless act'. Can be applied to magic as an immoral, unlawful or irreligious undertaking. Cf. *rhadiourgeo.*

toxikon (to) 'drug, poison'. Cf. *pharmakon.*

tymbas 'witch', i.e., 'one who haunts tombs'. Cf. *graus trioditis;* Lat. *bustuaria.*

tyromanteia 'divination by means of a cheese'. The person suspected of a crime was offered a cheese sandwich. Total lack of appetite was supposed to reveal guilt.

zoidion 'small figure'. Cf. *mimema kerinon;* Lat. *figura cerea.*

Latin

abdita 'hidden things'. Cf. *arcana, clandestina, occulta, secreta.*

abrasax, abraxas. Magical words, not fully understood, probably referring to a daemon or lower deity.

absconditae or *absconsae litterae* 'secret writings, esoteric texts'.

accio, -ire 'to summon', e.g., the spirits of the dead.

Acheron, Acheruns 'underworld', e.g., as a place of punishment or as domicile of avenging spirits. Cf. *Orcus.*

admonitio 'reminder, command, type of significant dream'.

advoco 'to invoke, call upon'. Cf. *invoco, voco;* Gr. *epikaleo.*

Aegyptius 'Egyptian', i.e., Near Eastern type of sage, prophet, or *magus.* Cf. *Babylonius, Chaldaeus.*

alienatio (mentis) 'insanity, trance, ecstasy'. Cf. *arrepticius, externor;* Gr. *ekstasis, mania.*

alligator 'practitioner who [makes and] ties on amulets'. Cf. *ligator, remediator;* Gr.*periamma, periapton.*

amatorium 'love charm, drug that stimulates sexual passion'. Cf. *amor.*

amor 'love potion'. Cf. *amatorium, poculum, potio;* Gr. *erotikon, philtron, stergema.*

anima errans 'wandering soul, spirit of restless dead, *âme en peine*'. Useful for magic in general, whereas *amimula noxia* 'evil spirit' works especially for black magic. Cf. *Manes;* Gr. *ataphos, daimon.*

anus 'old woman, witch'. *Anicula* 'superstitious old woman'. Cf. Gr. *graus.*

apparatus magici 'magical paraphernalia', combined, e.g., with *preces nefariae* and *sacrificia funesta.*

arcana 'hidden things, secrets, mysteries'. *Arcana sacra* 'magical rites', *arcanum nefas* 'black magic'. Cf. *absconditus, clandestinus, occultus.*

argumentum 'story, narrative' (to illustrate the potency of a charm). Cf. *historiola.*

arrepticius (vates) 'ecstatic, in trance, inspired, delirious'. From *arripio* 'to seize, take control'. Cf. *alienatio, externor, lymphatus.*

ars (magica) 'magic'. Also *ars maga, artes magicae, ars illicita (mala, nefanda, polluta, secreta, terribilis).* Cf. *scientia;* Gr. *episteme, kakotechnia, techne.*

augur 'seer'. Mostly in religious context, i.e., an official who interprets the behavior of birds, of lightning, *omina* in general. *Augurium* 'omen, portent, taking of auguries'. Cf. *auspicium.* There were also *auguria privata,* as opposed to *auguria publica,* which could include a variety of methods.

Avernalis 'from lake Avernus' where there was an entrance to the underworld; hence *aqua Avernalis* 'water from lake Avernalis or from the underworld'. Cf. *Acheron.*

Babylonius 'type of Near Eastern *magus,* astrologer, charlatan'. Cf. *Aegyptius, Chaldaeus;* Gr. *Medos.*

Caeretanus 'man from Caere', an ancient Etruscan city. This seems to be the origin of It. *ciarlatano* (via *ceretano*). It is not attested in a negative sense, but the Etruscans were reputed to be experts in religious and magical lore (some Christian writers call them superstitious), and there is the analogy to other groups, such as the Marsi, the Paeligni, etc. Others derive It. *ciarlatano* from *ciarlare* 'to babble'.

caerimoniae (magorum) 'magical rituals'. Cf. *sacra.*

cano, canto 'to sing, chant, recite spells'. Hence a number of words, such as *cantamen, cantio, cantiuncula, canticum, cantus, excanto, decanto, incanto, incantamentum, incantatio, obcanto (occentatio), praecanto,* etc., sometimes qualified by *magicus* or *magnus* (e.g., *cantus magnus* 'mighty song' = *carmina valentia*). While *cantor* seems to be restricted to music, we have *cantatrix anus* 'old witch' or *praecantrix* 'witch, healer'. 'Charm' is derived from late Lat. *carmino*. Cf. Gr. *epode*.

caraius, caraus, caragus, caragius (late) 'type of diviner', associated with *sortilegus*.

carmen 'song, poem, spell'. Sometimes qualified, e.g., *c. magicum* or *c. malum, c. maleficum* (as opposed to *c. auxiliare*), *c. sepulchrale* 'spell evoking the dead from their tombs', *c. veneficum. C. obliquum* seems to be the same thing as *c. malum,* perhaps implying the evil eye.

Cerritus 'possessed by Ceres, frenzied, insane'. Cf. *lunaticus, lymphatus.*

Chaldaeus 'Chaldaean', i.e., *magus,* astrologer, occultist, prophet. Originally 'man from Kaldu' (part of Babylonia). Cf. *Aegyptius, Babylonius;* Gr. *Medos,* etc.

circulator 'itinerant performer [*magus,* juggler] or vendor who gathers crowds around him'. Cf. Gr. *ochlagogos.*

clandestinus 'secret, hidden'. *Supplicia clandestina* 'magical offerings or rituals'. Cf. *arcana, occulta.*

coercitio 'repression, compulsion'. This was a flexible principle within the Roman legal system, which could be applied against magic as well as "new" religions.

Colchicus 'magical', from Colchis, Medea's country of origin. Cf. Gr. *Thessala.*

coniector, -trix 'interpreter of dreams'. Cf. *interpres;* Gr. *exegetes.*

consecratio 'act of isolating a person from society and handing him (her) over to a deity, curse'. Cf. *detestatio, exsecratio, sacer;* Gr. *engrapho.*

Cotytia sacra 'Mysteries of Cotyto, a Thracian goddess', hence 'magical rituals'.

crimen magiae 'indictment of witchcraft'. Cf. Gr. *graphe asebeias.*

curiositas '[unhealthy] curiosity, interest in magic', sometimes qualified as *curiositas nefaria* or *sacrilega.* Cf. Gr. *periergia.*

decanto 'bewitch, conjure up', e.g., *decanto umbras* (in necromantic rituals). Cf. Gr. *kata(ei)do.*

defigo 'to nail down, transfix, bind, bewitch'. The verb is attested in classical Latin, the noun *defixio* 'nailing down, cursing [with a spell]' is only found in glossaries. It is the technical term for curse or curse tablet (*tabella defixionis*). A curse tablet is an inscribed piece of metal (lead), a small thin sheet, buried in graves and near chthonic sanctuaries or thrown into wells and rivers. The victim was thus handed over to the powers of the underworld. Sticking nails into a voodoo doll is also a *defixio.* Cf. *devoveo;* Gr. *(kata)deo, katapassaleuo.*

delenio 'to soothe, charm, apply a magical or medical ointment'. Hence *delenimentum* 'device of enticement, soothing charm, love charm'. Cf. Gr. *apomeilixis, thelgo.*

deligo 'to bind'. Cf. *ligo, obligo, solvo;* Gr. *(kata)deo, lyo.*

dematricula 'female purifier and healer'. Rather obscure figure, may be defined, e.g., as "friendly neighborhood witch."

deprecor 'to invoke, call down [a curse]'. *Deprecatio* 'invocation', is more a religious term, although 'cursing' was also done in religious contexts. It is difficult to distinguish accurately between a number of verbs beginning with *de-* (corresponding to Gr. *kata-*), such as *demando, deprecor, desacrifico, detestor, devoveo,* etc. The prefix usually implies that the prayer, curse, ritual is directed against someone, designed to hurt a person. Cf. *consecratio.*

despuo 'to spit on the ground [or on something] to avert evil'. Cf. *inspuo.*

detestor 'to call down a curse'. Hence *(dira) detestatio.* Cf. *deprecor.*

devoveo 'to curse formally, deliver a person to the powers of the underworld'. Hence *devotio (sepulchralis)* 'formal curse, imprecation, execration'. The language of religion has adopted legal terms, and magic has borrowed from that vocabulary. *Devotio* 'devotional gift [to a deity]'. Cf. *deprecor, voveo;* Gr. *anathema, arai.*

Diana. Goddess of witches, also identified with the moon. Cf. Gr. *Artemis, Hekate.*

dirae 'curses', also as a literary genre. Cf. *detestatio, devotio, exsecratio;* Gr. *arai.*

disciplina 'art, technique', e.g., *magica* or *divina disciplina,* but also *facinerosa* or *malefica disciplina.* Magic could be further described as *disciplina sacrificandi praeterquam more Romano* 'a way of offering sacrifice beyond the Roman ritual'. Cf. *ars, scientia;* Gr. *empeiria, episteme, techne.*

divino 'to practice divination'. Hence the nouns *divinator, divinatio,* e.g., *divinatio artificiosa* 'divination by means of certain tools, substances, techniques', as opposed to precognition by divine inspiration. Cf. *augurium, auspicium, haruspicina;* Gr. *manteia, mantis.*

effascino 'to bewitch, enchant'. Intensive form of *fascino.* Hence *effascinatio* 'sorcery, enchantment'.

elicio 'to summon [spirits, *animas*]' by incantations. Cf. *accio, evoco, excito;* Gr. *nekromanteia, psychagogia.*

evoco 'to summon [spirits]'. Hence *evocatio* 'conjuring, calling up'. Cf. *accio, elicio;* Gr. *epagoge.*

excanto 'to drive out or remove by songs, to make go away by spells', e.g., *fruges excanto* 'to bewitch the field-crops', also 'to chase away [an illness]'. Cf. Gr. *exa(ei)do.*

excito 'to conjure up [the souls of the dead], raise'. Cf. *accio, elicio, evoco.*

exigo 'to drive out'. Cf. Gr. *exorkizo.*

exsecror 'to curse'. Hence *exsecratio* 'imprecation'. Cf. *detestatio, dirae, imprecatio, preces;* Gr. *arai.*

externor 'to move outside, enter trance'. Cf. *alienatio;* Gr. *ekstasis.*

facinus 'black magic, evil sorcery'. Cf. *crimen, nefas;* Gr. *kakotechnia.*

fanaticus 'of or belonging to a sanctuary, inspired by orgiastic rites, frantic'. From *fanum* 'sanctuary, sacred precinct'.

fascino 'to bewitch', e.g., by the evil eye or a spoken curse or a ritual. From *fascinum* 'evil spell'; also 'penis'. Hence *fascinatio,* 'casting of a spell'. Cf. Gr. *baskania.*

fatum 'fate, destiny, death, oracle'. Cf. Gr. *ananke, heimarmene, moira.*

fossa 'pit, ditch' (dug for necromantic rituals). Cf. Gr. *bothros.*

furia 'Fury, avenging goddess, personified curse'. Related to *furor* 'madness, frenzy, ecstasy'. Cf. Gr. *ekstasis Erinys, mania.*

genius 'personified spirit', mostly protective and benign, but *malus genius* (Gr. *kakodaimon*).

gnarus 'one who knows'. Probably vague on purpose, like other terms of this kind. Cf. *peritus, plusscius, sciens;* Gr. *oida.*

Haemonius 'Thessalian' (from the country of witchcraft). *Haemonis* (fem.) and *Haemonia (anus)* are also attested. Cf. Gr. *Thessala.*

hariolus '[ecstatic] seer, prophet, diviner', but usually in a pejorative sense. Associated with *augur, haruspex, vates. Hariola* 'woman who prophesies' (in trance); *hariolor* 'to babble, to talk [inspired] nonsense'.

haruspex 'seer who interprets *omina*'. In Etruscan religion he seems, as a rule, to have looked at all kinds of *omina;* in Roman religion the liver of the sacrificial animal was interpreted, but sometimes all extraordinary events (*portenta, prodigia*). Like *hariolus,* the word may denote a beggar priest or charlatan, as in *haruspex vicanus* 'local soothsayer, freelance diviner' (as opposed to the *harurspices* of the Roman state religion). Also *haruspica* 'woman who interprets the entrails in a way not acceptable to the established religion'. In late antiquity, *haruspex* '*magus* of the pagan type'. *Haruspicina* 'technique of the *haruspex*'.

Hecate. Goddess of the underworld, also identified with the moon, invoked by witches. *Hecateia carmina* 'magical spells'. Cf. *Diana.*

(h)elleborum. Depending on the dose and the combination with other drugs, this plant could be used as a deadly poison, as a hallucinogenic or as a remedy (to treat mental illness). There seem to have been two main varieties: (1) 'black hellebore' = *Helleborus orientalis;* (2) 'white hellebore' = *Veratrum album.*

herba '[magical] plant'. Often combined with *carmen* 'song, spell'. Sometimes qualified as *herba fortis* 'potent herb' or *herba malefica* "evil herb' or *herba mirabilis* 'wonder-working herb'. *Herbaria* is a woman who knows about magical or healing plants. Cf. *radix;* Gr. *rhizotomia.*

historiola (modern term) 'little story'. Mythlike illustration of the power of a charm. Cf. *argumentum.*

illecebrae 'enticement, temptation', e.g., *facinerosae illecebrae* 'wicked enticement', i.e., magic.

imago 'apparition, ghost, phantom, hallucination'. Cf. *anima, umbra;* Gr. *eidolon, indalma, phasma. Imago cerea* 'waxen doll'; cf. Gr. *mimema kerinon, zoidion.*

impietas 'impiety, sorcery'. *Impius* corresponds to Gr. *asebes, atheos.* Cf. *facinus, nefas;* Gr. *asebeia.*

imprecor 'to curse'. Hence *imprecatio* 'calling down curses'. Cf. *deprecor, dirae, exsecratio, preces;* Gr. *arai.*

incanto 'to enchant, charm, bewitch', also 'to endow [an object] with *dynamis*'. Hence *incantamentum, incantatio* 'spell, enchantment', *incantator* 'enchanter, sorcerer'. Cf. *cano, canto;* Gr. *epode.*

incubo 'to sleep in [a temple], waiting for a meaningful dream or a miraculous cure'. Hence *incubatio* (late in this sense). Cf. Gr. *enkoimesis.*

incubus (late) 'evil spirit haunting sleepers', causing nightmares and seeking sexual intercourse with women. Cf. *succubus.*

inspuo. Cf. *despuo.*

internuntius 'intermediary agent', e.g., between gods and men. Cf. Gr. *daimon, mese ousia.*

interpres 'go-between, spokesman of a deity, interpreter of *omina, portenta* or dreams'. Cf. Gr. *exegetes.*

invoco 'to call upon [the gods, the spirits of the dead]'. Hence *invocatio.* Cf. *advoco, invoco;* Gr. *kaleo, anakaleo, epikaleo, katakaleo.*

iunx. Lat. analogy of Gr. *iynx.*

lamella 'thin metal sheet [inscribed with magical characters]'. Also *lamina, lamna.* Cf. *tabella.*

lamia 'female vampire, witch, daemon who eats babies'. Cf. Gr. *empousa.*

Lares 'deified ancestors, related to Manes, worshiped in the house and in the neighborhoods'; also 'protective spirits, kind of daemons attached to the deities of the underworld'. Cf. *lemures.*

larvae 'spirits of the dead, daemons, evil spirits'. Hence *larvatus* 'possessed by evil spirits' (cf. *cerritus, lymphatus*). These spirits could be used for divination, hence *praesagia larvarum.* Cf. *lares, manes;* Gr. *nekydaimon.*

Laverna '[Etruscan] deity of the underworld, patron goddess of thieves'.

lemures 'type of ghosts', originally perhaps 'spirits of dead ancestors'. Partly overlapping with *lares* and *larvae.* According to the ancient explanations (unreliable), all spirits of the dead can be called *lemures*—those who are good are *lares,* those who are bad are *larvae.* Those who are neither are *Manes* (but *Manes* lit. 'the good ones'—perhaps a euphemism, like 'Eumenides').

libri carminum valentium 'collections of magical formulae etc.', probably along the lines of the magical papyri we have. Cf. Gr. *Ephesia grammata.*

ligo 'to bind, compel'. Also 'to tie on [an amulet]'. Cf. *deligo, obligo, solvo;* Gr. *deo, katadeo, lyo. Ligatrix* (late) can be 'sorceress', i.e., one who has expertise in binding spells or making amulets, *ligatura,* lit. 'something that is tied on' also 'amulet'. Cf. *alligator, remedium;* Gr. *periamma, periapton.*

lunatus 'moonstruck, epileptic'.

lunula 'amulet in the shape of a half-moon or a crescent moon'. Cf. Gr. *meniskos.*

lupula 'little she-wolf', also 'prostitute, witch'. Diminutive of *lupa* 'she-wolf, prostitute'. The worlds of magic and prostitution seem to have intersected in ancient societies, but these can also be terms of abuse, like *Harpyia,* etc.

lymphatus 'possessed by a Nymph, insane, frenzied'. Cf. *cerritus, larvatus;* Gr. *nympholeptos.*

magia 'sorcery, magic', also as adj., e.g., *magae artes* as well as *magicae artes.* The sorcerer is called *magus, homo magicus.* Cf. Gr. *mageia, magos.*

maledico 'to slander, abuse', also 'to curse'. *Maledictum* 'insult, curse'.

maleficium 'crime, evil deed, magic'. More specif. *magicum* or *inconcessum maleficium* 'prohibited evil' (parallel with *artes nefandae*). Cf. *maleficus* (sometimes 'sorcerer'), *crimen, facinus, nefas, veneficium;* Gr. *kakotechnia.*

Manes 'the good ones'. Could be euphemism, like Eumenides. Deified ancestral spirits. Cf. *Lares, larvae, lemures.*

manus mala 'hand used in witchcraft', either "laid on" or making a gesture from a distance. Cf. *oculus malignus* 'evil eye'.

Marsus, Marsi, Marsicus. The Marsi, an ethnic group in central Italy were reputed as herbalists, magicians, soothsayers, and snake charmers. *Marsa venena* are the drugs they used, and *nenia Marsa* must have been a lugubrious-sounding spell. Cf. *Sabellus;* Gr. *therepodos.*

materia 'material, substance'. Cf. Gr. *ousia.*

mathematicus (like Gr. *mathematikos*) 'mathematician, scientist, astronomer, astrologer'. Cf. Gr. *mathesis.*

medicamentum 'drug, poison, remedy'. Cf. *remedium;* Gr. *pharmakon.*

minae 'threats, curses, warnings'. Cf. *dirae;* Gr. *apeile.*

miraculum 'marvel, miracle, amazing event, supernatural phenomenon'. Cf. *monstrum, portentum, prodigium;* Gr. *semeion, teras, thauma.*

monstrum 'unnatural, abnormal event, horrible creature'. Cf. *miraculum.*

murmur 'murmur, whisper'. Indistinct way of pronouncing a spell, presumably an evil one, as opposed to the loud, distinct prayers in public. Sometimes specified as *murmur barbarum, dissonum, ferale,* or *infandum,* to stress the exotic, hideous, threatening, and abnormal (illegal) character of the ritual. Cf. *stridor, susurrus magicus;* Gr. *sigmos.*

nardus or *–um* 'nard-oil'. Could serve as a kind of protective cream. Perfumes, like jewelry (amulets) may originally have had a magical, apotropaic character; but they also served as aphrodisiacs.

nefas 'magic as illegal, immoral, or sacrilegious activity'. Cf. *crimen, facinus, impietas, maleficium;* Gr. *arrheta, aporrheta, asebeia. Nefanda* 'wicked, impious actions' can be used in the same sense.

nenia 'spell, incantation' (e.g., with *Marsa*). Originally formalized lament for the dead, accompanied by a flute. What the lament and the spell may have in common is the *ululatio* 'howling'. See *ululatio;* Gr. *ololygmos.*

nocturna (sc. *anus*) 'witch'. Cf. Gr. *nyktipolos.*

obligo 'to bind, compel'. Cf. *ligo, solvo;* Gr. *deo, katadeo, lyo.*

obscaevo 'to represent a good or bad omen'.

occento (orig. *ob-canto*) 'to sing against', i.e., 'to direct a spell against [someone]'. The spell itself is called *malum carmen* or *carmen obliquum.*

occultus 'hidden, secret, esoteric, occult'. Cf. *absconditus, arcanus, clandestinus, secretus;* Gr. *apokrypha.*

oculus malignus 'evil eye', also *oculus obliquus.* Cf. *fascino, manus mala;* Gr. *baskania.*

omen '[good or bad] signs foreshadowing the future'. Hence *ominator* 'one who understands and interprets *omina*'. These signs can occur in a random fashion, by coincidence, or one waits for them; sometimes careful observation of certain phenomena (clouds, lightning, comets) is necessary; there are also many tools and techniques. Cf. *auspicium, divino, haruspex, miraculum, monstrum, ostentum, portentum, prodigium, vates;* Gr. *enodioi symboloi.*

oraculum 'prediction [made in a sanctuary], agent of the prediction, sanctuary where it is made'. Cf. Gr. *chrao, mantis, prophetes.*

Orcus 'underworld as place of punishment or as domicile of evil spirits, god of the underworld, personification of death'. Cf. *Acheron, Acheruns.*

Paeligni. People of central Italy, associated with potent magic; hence *Paeligna anus* 'Samnite witch'. Cf. *Marsi, Sabelli.*

peritus 'expert' (in magic). Cf. *ars, gnarus, plusscius;* Gr. *empeiria, episteme.*

perversitas 'unreasonable, abnormal behavior', e.g., *perversitas magica.* Cf. *crimen, curiositas, facinus, nefas.*

philtra 'charms, drugs, love-potions'. Cf. *poculum.*

phylacterium 'amulet'. Cf. *ligatura, remedium.*

plusscius, –a 'knowing more [than ordinary people]'. Cf. *gnarus, saga;* Gr. *oida.*

poculum 'drinking vessel, drink, drug, poison'. Sometimes qualified as *poculum amoris* or *desiderii,* or *poculum noxium* or *triste.* Cf. *amor, philtra, veneficium;* Gr. *philtron, stergema.*

polleo 'to be strong, powerful, potent, effective' (of magic and medicine, etc.). Forms of *pollens* are sometimes corrupted in the ms. tradition to forms of *pallens* which is supposed to mean "causing paleness," because "pale" obviously does not fit. Conjectural emendation seems necessary. Magic is effective through its *pollentia, potestas.* Cf. *arete, dynamis.*

portentum 'abnormal phenomenon, prodigy, omen, sinister sign'. Cf. *miraculum, omen, prodigium;* Gr. *teras, thauma.*

potentia 'power, ability'. Cf. *pollentia, potestas, virtus;* Gr. *arete, dynamis.*

potestas 'power, control, authority'. Cf. *potentia,* etc.

potio 'drink charged with magic', to arouse love or cause madness, death (not always intended). Since magical potions could be highly toxic in the wrong dose, the word has given "poison" in Engl. and Fr., though *potionatus* already means "poisoned." Cf. *amor, poculum;* Gr. *philtron.*

praecanto 'to chant [a spell] over or for [a person]'. Hence *praecantatio* 'spell, amulet' and *praecantrix* 'purifier, healer, fortune-teller'. Cf. *cano, canto;* Gr. *epode.*

praefiscini or *-fascine* 'so as to avert bad luck'. Cf. *fascinum.*

praesagio 'to forbode, have a foreboding'. Hence *praesagatio, -itio, -ium,* etc. Cf. *sagus, -a.*

praestigia, -ae 'trickery, deceit'. Hence *praestigiator* 'juggler, acrobat, trickster', *praestigiatrix* 'witch, fortune-teller', etc. Cf. *circulator.*

precor 'to pray, wish someone well or ill'. *Preces* 'prayers', also 'curses'; *tacitae preces* '[magical] prayers, uttered silently'; *Thyesteae preces* 'deadly curses'; similarly *funestae* or *infelices* or *nefariae preces.* Related are *imprecor, imprecatio.* Cf. *dirae, exsecratio;* Gr. *arai, euche.*

prodigium 'extraordinary phenomenon' (with good or bad meaning), which explains the relationship between certain signs and certain events; they demand interpretation and remedial action. Cf. *miraculum, monstrum, omen, ostentum, portentum;* Gr. *semeion, teras, thauma.*

propheta 'seer, spokesman for a deity', also 'priestlike figure who performs magic'. Cf. *oraculum;* Gr. *chresmologos, exegetes, mantis, prophetes.*

radix 'root of a plant, used in magic and medicine'. Like *radicula* (dim.), it sometimes implies the whole plant. Cf. Gr. *rhizotomia.*

recanto 'to remove by a spell'. Cf. *cano, canto,* etc.

religio. System of concepts, beliefs, rituals, based on tradition, which regulates the relationship between the gods and the individual, the community.

remedium 'drug, remedy' (magical and medical), specifically 'amulet'. Hence *remediator* 'healer, maker of amulets'. A drug employed in magic is sometimes called *remedium diabolicum, illicitum,* or *sacrilegum.*

revoco 'call back [souls from the underworld]'. Hence *animarum revocator* 'one who conjures up souls'.

ritus (mostly pl.) 'rites, rituals, ceremonies', religious or magical.

Sabellus 'of or belonging to the Sabelli' (Oscan-speaking ethnic group, including the Samnites). *Sabella carmina* 'Samnite spells'. Cf. *Marsae voces,* etc. These peoples, with their distinct culture, were thought to preserve ancient magical lore, like some more exotic nations; cf. *Aegyptius,* etc.

sacer 'belonging to a deity', hence 'sacred, holy' and 'accursed'. Cf. Gr. *anathema, exagistos.* Hence *sacra* 'religious or magical rites', the latter sometimes qualified as *arcana, impia, inaudita, nefaria, nocturna, occulta. Sacerdos* 'priestlike *magus*', *sacri-ficium* 'magical offering' (qualified as *funestum, malum*). Cf. Gr. *hiereus, hiereia, prophetes. Sacro* 'to consecrate' and 'to devote to destruction'; cf. *desecratio. Sacra-mentum* 'oath' (especially the "military oath of allegiance"); later 'mystery, initiation'. Cf. *mysterion. Sacricola* 'worshiper'; can also be a syn. of *saga. Sacrificulus* 'performer of foreign or magical rites', covering a multitude of practices, purification rites and private mysteries. Cf. Gr. *agyrtes, anathema, hiereus, mantis, thytes.*

sagus, -a 'prophetic, psychic, practicing witchcraft'. Related to *sagax* 'keen, sharp, acute' and *sagio* 'sense sharply'. A famous Syrian *saga* is variously described as *sacricola* and *mantis*. This seems to imply that she derived her "superior knowledge" from a special deity or power to whom she offered sacrifices (*sacricola*) and that she gave her advice in the form of prophecies (*mantis*). But *saga (anus)* could be an old woman who practices magic of different kinds (protecting people from harm indicated by bad dreams, making amulets, conjuring up the dead, etc.). Cf. *praesagio.*

scientia efficax 'magic that really works', Gr. *dynamike episteme*. Related terms are *sciens* 'one who knows', *scientissimus, plusscius*. Cf. also *peritus*. One does not want to be too specific about the area of that person's expertise.

scrobis 'pit'. Cf. Gr. *bothros.*

secretum 'secret, mystic rite or symbol, hidden pursuit'. Cf. *abditus, arcanus, occultus.*

sepulc(h)ralis 'connected with tombs', e.g., *sepulchrale carmen* 'spell to conjure up the dead'. Cf. *bustuaria.*

Sibylla 'type of female diviner, ecstatic prophetess', sometimes worshiped as deity. There was a varying number of *Sibyllae* in the ancient world. The *libri Sibyllini,* a collection of predictions, were consulted by a committee of officials in Rome; two collections of *oracula Sibyllina* survive from late antiquity. *Sibyllistes* 'interpreter of the Sibylline oracles, seer'.

signum 'sign, omen'. Cf. *omen, ostentum, prodigium;* Gr. *semeion, thauma.*

solvo 'to free, deliver, release'. Opposite of *ligo*. Cf. Gr. *(apo)lyo.*

sonus (magicus) 'special intonation' used for reciting spells. Cf. *stridor, susurrus;* Gr. *poppysmos, sigmos.*

sors 'lot used for divination [cleromancy]'. *Sortes fatidicae* 'lots that tell one's fate'. *Sortior* 'to predict the future' in general, by lots or—by semantic extension—any other means. *Sortilegus* 'lot picker', i.e., soothsayer, fortune-teller. The lots could be made of different materials—bone, wood, metal, papyrus. The method survives in the Tarot cards. Collections of oracles or literary works could also be used as lots (e.g., pricked with a needle). The Fr. word *sortilège* is derived from Lat. *sortilegium,* while Fr. *sorcier, sorcière* and Engl. "sorcerer" are derived from late Lat. *sortiarius*. By semantic extension the word could be applied to any kind of diviner and then to a practitioner of magic in general.

spargo 'to sprinkle, purify'. Cf. Gr. *perirhaino.*

stridor 'hissing, whistling, whirring sound'. May refer to a specific manner of reciting a spell or the sound of the *rhombus*. Cf. *murmur, susurrus;* Gr. *sigmos.*

strix 'kind of owl, vampire, evil spirit'. There seems to have been a substantial body of myths and folklore concerning this particular kind of creature. Probably related to *striga* 'witch', but difficult to distinguish. The screech-owl was regarded as a bird of ill omen, and witches were able to transform themselves into birds or other animals. Cf. *lamia*.

succubus (late) 'female daemon haunting sleepers, seeking sexual intercourse with men'. Since the prefix *sub-* implies substitution (a daemon taking the place of the wife), one would expect the form *succuba;* the masculine ending was perhaps used in analogy to *incubus*.

sucus (mixtus) 'juice [of a plant]', used for medical or magical purposes.

superstitio 'foreign, false or private form of religion, survival of ancient cults, bizarre folklore'. Originally not negative, but implying exaggerated fear of many different supernatural forces (some of which could be left over from earlier periods or introduced from abroad). *Superstitio exsecranda* or *magica* 'magic', *superstitiosus hariolus* 'ecstatic seer'. Cf. Gr. *deisidaimonia*.

supplicium 'offering or ritual to placate a deity'. *Supplicia clandestina* 'secret offerings', i.e., magical rituals. Cf. *preces nefariae*.

susurrus (magicus) 'whisper, buzzing sound'. Also *susurramen (magicum)*. Cf. *murmur, stridor;* Gr. *sigmos*.

tabella 'flat piece of wood, lead, etc.' (to be inscribed with spells).

tabum 'viscous fluid', sometimes syn. with *venenum*. Cf. *virus*.

Thessala 'Thessalian [woman], witch'.

toxicum 'drug, poison'. Cf. Gr. *pharmakon, toxikon*.

trivium 'meeting place of three roads'. It was lined with tombs, sacred to Hecate, and magic was performed here at night. Cf. Gr. *(graus) trioditis*.

turbo. Magical tool, corresponding to Gr. *rhombos*.

ululatus 'howling, yelling' (in religious or magical context). Cf. Gr. *ololygmos*.

umbra 'shade' (in the underworld), 'ghost' (in the world of the living). Cf. Gr. *eidolon, psyche, skia*.

vanitas 'illusion, pretense', as in *magicae vanitates* 'illusions produced by magic'.

vates 'seer, diviner'. Related to *vaticinor, vaticinium*. Combined with *sacrificulus*. Cf. Gr. *mantis, thytes*.

venenum. Probably from **uenes-nom*, a form of **uenus* in the sense of "propitiatory magic" (cf. Germ. *wünschen*) related to *Venus*, the deity, but also to *veneror* 'to worship'. Originally perhaps "love potion," then any magical or medical drug (herb, potion), then mainly "poison." Many magical drugs were toxic and caused madness or death, if administered in the wrong dose. Like Gr. *pharmakon, pharmakeia*, the Lat. word could include verbal or symbolic actions and supernatural influence as well as material drugs (the original meaning). Hence *veneficium* 'practice of magic, sorcery', also 'potent substance, philtre'; *veneficus, -a,* 'sorcerer, witch, poisoner', sometimes associated with *maleficium, maleficus*. There is also *venenarius* 'dealer in poisons, poisoner'. Cf. *delenimentum, potio, tabum;* Gr. *pharmakon, -eia*.

versipellis 'one who can assume different shapes (e.g., that of a wolf, a dog), werewolf'. Cf. *strix;* Gr. *lykanthropos*.

veteratrix 'experienced [old] woman, witch'. Masc. *veterator* 'old hand (at something)'.

virga 'wand, staff'. Cf. Gr. *rhabdos*.

virtus 'excellence, potency, efficacy'. Cf. *potentia, potestas;* Gr. *arete, dynamis*.

virus 'potent fluid, secretion [from plants or human bodies], poisonous concoction'. Cf. *sucus (mixtus), tabum, venenum.*

vis 'power, potency'. Cf. *virtus,* Gr. *arete, dynamis.*

visio 'vision, appearance'. Cf. Gr. *horama, phantasma.*

voco 'to call' (by a spell). *Vox* 'voice, sound, word', e.g., *voces sacrae* 'magical spells', *voces Marsae* 'Marsian spells'. The words and names used in magic were often unintelligible to outsiders (Gr. *onomata asema*). Cf. *advoco, invoco, murmur, susurrus, ululatus.*

Voveo 'to vow, promise, pray'. Hence *votum* 'vow, prayer'. Cf. *devotio, preces;* Gr. *arai.*

Select Bibliography

Ancient sources are mentioned in the various chapters, in the notes, and in the headnote for each translated text.

Abt, A. *Die Apologie des Apuleius von Madaura und die antike Zauberei.* Giessen, 1908.

Alderink, L. J. *Creation and Salvation in Ancient Orphism.* Chico, Calif., 1981.

Ankarloo, B., and S. Clark, eds. *Witchcraft and Magic in Europe.* Vol. 2: *Ancient Greece and Rome.* London and Philadelphia, 1999. Contains chapters by D. Ogden, G. Luck, R. Gordon, V. Flint.

Armstrong, A. H. "Was Plotinus a Magician?" *Phronesis* 1 (1955): 73ff.

Audollent, A. M. H., ed. *Defixionum Tabellae.* Paris, 1904.

Aune, D. "Magic in Early Christianity." *ANRW* 2.23.2 (1980), pp. 1507–57.

Baccani, D. *Oroscopi greci: Documentazione papirologica.* Messina, 1982.

Barb, A. A. "The Survival of Magic Arts." In *The Conflict between Paganism and Christianity in the Fourth Century,* ed. A. Momigliano, pp. 100–125. Oxford, 1963.

Barnes, J., et al., eds. *Science and Speculation.* Cambridge, 1982.

Barrett, C. K. *The New Testament Background: Selected Documents.* London, 1958.

Barton, T. *Ancient Astrology.* London, 1994.

Beckmann, F. *Zauberei und Recht in Roms Frühzeit. Ein Beitrag zur Geschichte und Interpretation des Zwölftafelrechts.* Münster, 1923.

Bell, H. I. *Cults and Creeds in Graeco-Roman Egypt.* Liverpool, 1952.

Bell, H. I., A. D. Nock, and H. Thompson. "Magical Texts from a Bilingual Papyrus in the British Museum." *Proceedings of the British Academy* 17 (1931): 235ff.

Bernand, A. *Sorciers grecs.* Paris, 1991.

Berthelot, M. P. E. *Collection des anciens alchimistes grecs.* 3 vols. Paris, 1887–88.

Bertholet, A. "Das Wesen der Magie." *Nachrichten der Götting. Gesellsch. der Wissenschaften, Philos.-Histor. Klasse,* 1926–27.

Beth, K. *Religion und Magie: Ein religionsgeschichtlicher Beitrag.* 2nd ed. Leipzig, 1927.

Betz, H. D. "Magic and Mystery in the Greek Magical Papyri." In *Magika Hiera,* ed. C. A. Faraone and D. Obbink, pp. 244–59. Oxford, 1991.

———. *Plutarch's Theological Writings and Early Christian Literature.* Leiden, 1975.

———, ed. *The Greek Magical Papyri in Translation, Including the Demotic Papyri.* Vol. 1. 2nd ed. Chicago, 1992.

Bidez, J. *Vie de Porphyre*. Paris, 1913.

Bidez, J., and F. Cumont. *Les Mages hellénisés*. 2 vols. Paris, 1938.

Biedermann, H. *Handlexikon der magischen Künste*. 2nd ed. Graz, 1973.

Bieler, L. *Theios Aner: Das Bild des göttlichen Menschen in Antike und Frühchristentum*. 2 vols. Vienna, 1935–39.

Biggs, R. D. *SA.ZI.GA: Ancient Mesopotamian Potency Incantations*. Locust Valley, N.Y., 1967.

Blacker C. *The Catalpa Bow*. London, 1975.

Blau, L. *Das altjüdische Zauberwesen*. Strassburg, 1898.

Boll, F., and C. Bezold. *Sternglaube und Sterndeutung: Die Geschichte und das Wesen der Astrologie*. Edited and revised by W. Gundel. Leipzig, 1931.

Bonner, C. *Studies in Magical Amulets Chiefly Graeco-Egyptian*. University of Michigan Studies, Humanist ser. 49. Ann Arbor, Mich., 1950.

———. "Witchcraft in the Lecture Room of Libanius." *Transactions and Proceedings of the American Philological Association* 63 (1932): 34ff.

Borghouts, J. F. *Ancient Egyptian Magical Texts*. Leiden, 1978.

Bouché-Leclercq, A. *L'Astrologie grecque*. Paris, 1899.

———. *Histoire de la divination dans l'Antiquité*. 4 vols. Paris, 1879–82.

Bourguignon, E. *Religion, Altered States of Consciousness and Social Change*. Columbus, Ohio, 1973.

Bowie, E. L. "Apollonius of Tyana: Tradition and Reality." *ANRW* 2.16.21 (1972), pp. 1652–99.

Brashear, W. M. "The Greek Magical Papyri: An Introduction and Survey." *ANRW* 2.18.5 (1995), pp. 3380–3684.

Bremmer, J. N. "Aspects of the Acts of Peter: Women, Magic, Place and Date." In *The Apocryphal Acts of Peter: Magic, Miracles and Gnosticism*, ed. J. B. Bremmer, pp. 1–20. Louvain, 1998.

———. *The Early Greek Concept of the Soul*. Princeton, 1983.

Brenk, F. E. "In the Light of the Moon: Demonology in the Early Imperial Period." *ANRW* 1.16.3 (1984), pp. 2068–2145.

Brown, P. "The Rise and Function of the Holy Man." *Journal of Roman Studies* 61 (1971): 8off.

———. "Sorcery, Demons and the Rise of Christianity from Late Antiquity into the Middle Ages." In *Witchcraft: Confessions and Accusations,* ed. M. Douglas, pp. 7–46. London, 1970.

———, ed. *Religion and Society in the Age of St. Augustine*. London, 1972.

Burkert, W. "GOES. Zum griechischen 'Schamanismus.' " *Rhein. Mus.* 150 (1962): 36–55.

———. *Griechische Religion der archaischen und klassischen Epoche*. Stuttgart, 1977. English translation, Cambridge, Mass., 1985.

———. "Itinerant Diviners and Magicians: A Neglected Element in Cultural Contacts." In *The Greek Renaissance of the Eighth Century BC,* ed. R. Hägg and N. Marinatos, pp. 115–19. Stockholm, 1983.

———. *Lore and Science in Ancient Pythagoreanism*. Translated by E. L. Minar Jr. Cambridge, Mass., 1972.

———. *The Orientalizing Revolution: Near Eastern Influence on Greek Culture in the Early Archaic Age*. Cambridge, Mass., 1992.

Select Bibliography

———. *Structure and History in Greek Mythology and Ritual.* Berkeley, 1979.

Butler, E. M. *Ritual Magic.* Cambridge, 1949.

Cádiz, Depart. de historia antigua de la Univ. *Religión, superstición y magia en el mundo romano.* Cádiz, 1985.

Caro Baroja, J. *The World of the Witches.* Translated by N. Glendinning. London, 1964. Cf. review by G. Luck, *Latomus* 27 (1968): 737.

Caster, M. *Lucien et la pensée religieuse de son temps.* Paris, 1937.

Chadwick, H. *Priscillian of Avila: The Occult and the Charismatic in the Early Church.* Oxford, 1976.

Christidis, A.-Ph., S. I. Dakaris, and I. Votokopoulou. "Magic in the Oracular Tablets from Dodona." In *The World of Ancient Magic,* ed. D. R. Jordan, H. Montgomery, and E. Thomassen, pp. 67–72. Bergen, 1999.

Clerc, J.-B. *Homines magici. Etudes sur la sorcellerie et la magie dans la société romaine impériale.* Bern, 1995.

Coletti Strangi, A. *Gli afrodisiaci nel mondo romano.* Biemme, 1996.

Contenau, G. *La Magie chez les Assyriens et les Babyloniens.* Paris, 1947.

Cramer, F. H. *Astrology in Roman Law and Politics.* Philadelphia, 1954.

Crawley, A. E. "Cursing and Blessing." *Encyclopaedia of Religion and Ethics,* edited by J. Hastings, 4:367–74. New York, 1908–21.

Cumont, F. "Les Anges du paganisme." *Revue de l'histoire des religions* 72 (1915): 159ff.

———. *Astrology and Religion among the Greeks and Romans.* New York, 1912.

———. *L'Egypte des astrologues.* Brussels, 1937.

———. *Les Religions orientales dans le paganisme romain.* 4th ed. Paris, 1929.

Dakaris, S. I. *The Nekyomanteion of the Acheron.* Athens, 1993.

Daniel, R. W., and F. Maltomini. *Supplementum Magicum.* Papyrologica Coloniensia 16.1 and 16.2. Opladen, 1990–92.

Davies, T. W. *Magic, Divination, and Demonology among the Hebrews and Their Neighbours.* London, 1898.

Deissmann, A. *Light from the Ancient East.* Translated by R. M. Strachan. New York, 1927.

Delatte, A. *Anecdota Atheniensia.* Vol. 1. Biblioth. de la Fac. de Philos. et Lettres de l'Univ. de Liege, Fasc. 36. Liege, 1927.

De Martino, E. *Il mondo magico.* Turin, 1948. Reprint, 1975.

des Places, E. "Les Oracles chaldaiques." *ANRW* 2.27.4 (1984), pp. 2299–2335.

Detienne, M. *Les Jardins d'Adonis.* Paris, 1972.

Deubner, L. "Charms and Amulets." *Encyclopaedia of Religion and Ethics,* edited by J. Hastings (1970 ed.), 3:433ff.

———. "Magie und Religion." In *Kleine Schriften zur klassischen Altertumskunde,* ed. O. Deubner, pp. 275–98. Königstein, 1982.

Dickie, M. W. *Magic and Magicians in the Greco-Roman World.* London, 2001.

Dieterich, A. *Abraxas: Studien zur Religionsgeschichte des späteren Altertums.* Leipzig, 1891.

———. *Eine Mithrasliturgie.* 3rd ed. Darmstadt, 1966.

———. "Der Untergang der antiken Religion." In *Kleine Schriften,* ed. R. Wüensch, pp. 275–98. Leipzig, 1911.

Dodds, E. R. *The Ancient Concept of Progress and Other Essays on Greek Literature and Belief.* Oxford, 1973.

——. *The Greeks and the Irrational*. Berkeley, 1951. Cf. review by G. Luck, *Gnomon* 24 (1953): 361ff.

——. *Pagan and Christian in an Age of Anxiety*. Cambridge, 1965.

Douglas, M., ed. *Witchcraft: Confessions and Accusations*. New York, 1970.

Ebner, M., et al. *Lukians Die Lügenfreunde oder: Der Ungläubige*. Darmstadt, 2001.

Edelstein, E. J., and Edelstein, L. *Asclepius: A Collection and Interpretations of the Testimonies*. 2 vols. Baltimore, 1965.

Edelstein, L. "Greek Medicine in Its Relation to Religion and Magic." In *Ancient Medicine: Selected Papers of L. Edelstein*, ed. O. Tempkin and L. Tempkin, pp. 205–46. Baltimore, 1967.

Eitrem, S. "La Magie comme motif littéraire chez les Grecs et les Romains." *Symbolae Osloenses* 21 (1941): 39ff.

——. "The Necromancy in the Persai of Aischylos." *Symbolae Osloenses* 6 (1928): 1ff.

——. "Some Notes on the Daemonology of the New Testament." *Symbolae Osloenses*, Suppl. 20. 2nd ed., Oslo, 1966.

——. "La Théurgie chez les Néoplatoniciens et dans les papyrus magiques." *Symbolae Osloenses* 22 (1942): 49ff.

Eliade, M. *Occultism, Witchcraft and Cultural Fashions*. Chicago, 1976.

——. *Shamanism*. London, 1964.

Ernout, A. "La Magie chez Pline l' Ancien." In *Hommage à J. Bayet*, ed. M. Renard and R. Schilling, pp. 190ff. Collection Latomus LXX. Brussels, 1964.

Evans-Pritchard, E. E. *Theories of Primitive Religion*. Oxford, 1965.

——. *Witchcraft, Oracles and Magic amongst the Azande*. Oxford, 1937.

Faraone, C. A. *Ancient Greek Love Magic*. Cambridge, Mass., 1999.

Faraone, C. A., and D. Obbink. *Magika Hiera*. Oxford, 1991. Contains articles by Faraone, J. H. M. Strubbe, H. S. Versnel, R. Kotansky, J. Scarborough, S. Eitrem, F. Graf, J. J. Winkler, H. D. Betz, and C. R. Phillips III.

Felton, D. *Haunted Greece and Rome: Ghost Stories from Classical Antiquity*. Austin, Tex., 1999.

Ferguson, E. *Demonology of the Early Christian World*. New York, 1984.

Festugière, A.-J. *Hermétisme et mystique païenne*. Paris, 1967.

——. *L'Idéal religieux des Grecs et l'Evangile*. 2nd ed. Paris, 1981.

——. *La Revélation d'Hermès Trismégiste*. 4 vols. Paris, 1944–54.

Festugière, A.-J., and A. D. Nock, eds. and trans. *Corpus Hermeticum*. 4 vols. Paris, 1946–54.

Foerster, W. *Gnosis: A Selection of Texts*. Translated by R. M. Wilson. 2 vols. Oxford, 1972.

Fowden, G. *Egyptian Hermes: A Historical Approach to the Late Pagan Mind*. 2nd ed. Princeton, 1993.

Frazer, J. G. *The Golden Bough: A Study in Magic and Religion*. 12 vols. New York, 1911–15.

Frick, K. "Einführung in die alchemiegeschichtliche Literatur." *Sudhoffs Archiv* 45 (1961): 147ff.

Friedrich, H.-V. *Thessalos van Tralles*. Beiträge zur Klassischen Philologie 28. Meisenheim am Glan, 1968.

Gager, J. G., ed. *Curse Tablets and Binding Spells from the Ancient World*. Oxford, 1992.

Ganschinietz, R. *Hippolytos' Kapitel gegen die Magier*. Texte und Untersuchungen zur Geschichte der altchristlichen Literatur 39.2. Leipzig, 1913.

Giordano, M. *La parola efficace. Maledizioni, giuramenti e benedizioni nella grecia arcaica*. Pisa, 1999.

Gordon, R. "Imagining Greek and Roman Magic." In *Witchcraft and Magic in Europe*, ed. B. Ankarloo and S. Clark, 2:159–375. London, 1999.

Gow, A. S. F. *Theocritus*. Text, translation (vol. 1) and commentary (vol. 2). Cambridge, 1952.

Graf, F. "Excluding the Charming: The Development of the Greek Concept of Magic." In *Ancient Magic and Ritual Power*, ed. M. Meyer and P. Mirecki, pp. 43–62. Leiden, 1995.

———. "How to Cope with a Difficult Life: A View of Ancient Magic." In *Envisioning Magic*, ed. P. Schäfer and H. G. Kippenberg, pp. 93–114. Leiden, 1997.

———. *La Magie dans l'antiquité gréco-romaine*. Paris, 1994. English translation by F. Philip, *Magic in the Ancient World* (Cambridge, Mass., 1997).

———. *Nordionische Kulte. Religionsgeschichtliche und epigraphische Untersuchungen zu den Kulten von Chios, Erythrai, Klazomenai und Phokaia*. Bibliotheca Helvetica Romana 21. Rome, 1985.

———. "Prayer in Magical and Religious Ritual." In *Magika Hiera*, ed. C. A. Faraone and D. Obbink, pp. 188–213. Oxford, 1991.

Grant, F. C. *Hellenistic Religions: The Age of Syncretism*. New York, 1953.

Grant, R. M. *Miracle and Natural Law in Graeco-Roman and Early Christian Thought*. Amsterdam, 1952.

Griffith, F. L., and H. Thompson. *The Demotical Magical Papyrus of Leiden and London*. 3 vols. London, 1904–9.

Gundel, H.-G. *Weltbild und Astrologie in den griechischen Zauberpapyri*. Munich, 1968. Cf. review by J. G. Griffiths, *Classical Review* 19 (1969): 358ff.

Gundel, W., and H.-G. Gundel. *Astrologumena: Die astrologische Literatur in der Antike und ihre Geschichte*. Wiesbaden, 1966.

Gwyn Griffiths, J. "The Great Egyptian Cults of Oecumenical Spiritual Significance." In *Classical Mediterranean Spirituality*, ed. A. H. Armstrong, pp. 39–65. New York, 1986.

Halleux, R., ed. *Les alchimistes grecs*. Paris, 1981. Cf. review by J. Dillon, *Class. Rev.* 36 (1986): 35–38.

Hansen, W. *Phlegon of Tralles, Book of Marvels*. Exeter, 1996.

Hanson, J. S. "Dreams and Visions in the Ancient World and Early Christianity." *ANRW* 2.23.2 (1980), pp. 1395–1427.

Harrison, S. J. *Apuleius: A Latin Sophist*. Oxford, 2000.

Hastings, J., ed. *Encyclopaedia of Religion and Ethics*. 12 vols. New York, 1970.

Hatch, E. *The Influence of Greek Ideas and Usages upon the Christian Church*. Edited and revised by F. C. Grant. New York, 1957.

Heintz, F. *"Simon le Magicien": Actes 8, 5–25 et l'accusation de magie contre les prophètes thaumaturges dans l'antiquité*. Cahiers de la Revue Biblique 39. Paris, 1997.

Hill, D. E. "The Thessalian Trick." *Rhein. Mus.* 116 (1973): 221–38.

Holmyard, E. J. *Alchemy.* Harmondsworth, 1957.

Hopfner, Th. *Griechisch-ägyptischer Offenbarungszauber.* Vols. 1, 2. Leipzig, 1921–24. Reprint, Amsterdam, 1974–90.

———. "Mageia." *RE* 14.1 (1928), cols. 301–93.

———. "Theurgie." *RE* 6.A.1 (1936), cols. 258–70.

Hopkinson, N. *Greek Poetry of the Imperial Period: An Anthology.* Cambridge, 1994.

Horsley, G. H. R., ed. *New Documents Illustrating Early Christianity.* Vols. 1–6. North Ryde, N.S.W., 1981–91.

Hubert, H., and M. Mauss. "Esquisse d'une théorie générale de la magie." *Année sociologique* 7 (1902–3): 1ff.

Hull, J. M. *Hellenistic Magic and the Synoptic Tradition.* Studies in Biblical Theology, 2nd ser., no. 28. Naperville, Ill., 1974.

Humphrey, J. W., J. P. Oleson, and A. N. Sherwood. *Greek and Roman Technology: A Sourcebook.* London, 1998.

Hunink, V. *Apuleius of Madauros, Pro Se De Magia.* 2 vols. Edited with a commentary. Amsterdam, 1997.

Isambert, F. A. *Rite et efficacité symbolique.* Paris, 1979.

Jahn, O. "Über den Aberglauben des bösen Blicks bei den Alten." *Sitzungsberichte der Sächsischen Akademie der Wissenschaften* 8 (1855): 28–110.

Jameson, M., D. R. Jordan, and R. Kotansky. *A Lex Sacra from Selinous.* Greek, Roman and Byzantine Monographs 11. Durham, N.C., 1993.

Janowitz, N. *Magic in the Roman World: Pagans, Jews and Christians.* London, 2001.

Johnston, S. I. *Hekate Soteira: A Study of Hekate's Roles in the Chaldean Oracles and Related Literature.* American Classical Studies. Atlanta, 1990.

———. *Restless Dead: Encounters between the Living and the Dead in Ancient Greece.* Berkeley, 1999.

———, ed. Special issue: "Exploring the Shadows: Ancient Literature and the Supernatural." *Helios* 21.2 (1994).

Jordan, D. R. "*Defixiones* from a Well near the Southwest Corner of the Athenian Agora." *Hesperia* 54 (1985): 205–55.

———. "A Survey of Greek *Defixiones* Not Included in the Special Corpus." *GRBS* 26 (1985): 151–97.

Jordan, D. R., H. Montgomery, and E. Thomassen, eds. *The World of Ancient Magic.* Bergen, 1999.

Karenberg, A., and C. Leitz. *Heilkunde und Hochkultur.* Münster, 2000.

Kieckhefer, R. *Magic in the Middle Ages.* Cambridge, 1990.

Kotansky, R. *The Greek Magical Amulets: The Inscribed Gold, Silver, Copper and Bronze Lamellae.* Papyrologica Coloniensia, vol. 22.1. Opladen, 1994.

Krappe, A. H. *The Science of Folklore.* 1930. Reprint, London, 1974.

Kropp. A. M. *Ausgewählte koptische Zaubertexte.* Vols. 1–3. Brussels, 1930–31.

Lain Entralgo, P. *The Therapy of the Word in Classical Antiquity.* Translated by L. J. Rather and J. M. Sharp. New Haven, 1970.

Lexa, F. *La Magie dans l'Egypte antique.* 3 vols. Paris, 1923–25.

Linden, S. J. *The Alchemy Reader: From Hermes Trismegistus to Isaac Newton.* Cambridge, 2003.

Lindsay, C. W. *A Commentary on Horace's Epodes.* Oxford, 2003.

Lindsay, J. *The Origins of Alchemy in Graeco-Roman Egypt*. London, 1970.

——. *The Origins of Astrology*. London, 1971.

Linforth, I. *The Arts of Orpheus*. Berkeley, 1941.

Lloyd, G. E. R. *Magic, Reason and Experience: Studies in the Development of Greek Science*. Cambridge, 1983.

Lobeck, C. A. *Aglaophamos sive de theologiae mysticae Graecorum causis*. 3 vols. Königsberg, 1829.

Lopez Jimeno, M. del A. *Las tabellae defixionis de la Sicilia griega*. Amsterdam, 1991.

Luck, G. *Ancient Pathways and Hidden Pursuits: Religion, Morals and Magic in the Ancient World*. Ann Arbor, Mich., 2000.

——. *Hexen und Zauberei in der römischen Dichtung*. Zürich, 1962.

——. "Witches and Sorcerers in Classical Literature." In *Witchcraft and Magic in Europe*, ed. B. Ankarloo and S. Clark, 2:91–158. London, 1999.

MacNeice, L. *Astrology*. Garden City, N.Y., 1964.

Maguire, H., ed. *Byzantine Magic*. Cambridge, Mass., 1995.

Majercik, R. *The Chaldaean Oracles: Text, Translation and Commentary*. Studies in Greek and Roman Religion 5. Leiden, 1989.

Mann, J. *Murder, Magic and Medicine*. Oxford, 1994.

Mazal, O. *Wurzeln, Säfte, Samen*. Graz, 1981.

Mead, G. R. S. "Occultism." *Encyclopaedia of Religion and Ethics*, edited by J. Hastings (1970 ed.), 9:444ff.

Merkelbach, R. "Astrologie, Mechanik, Alchemie und Magie im griechisch-römischen Ägypten." *Riggisberger Berichte* 1 (1993): 49–62.

——. *Mithras*. Königstein, 1984.

Merkelbach, R., and M. Totti. *Abrasax: Ausgewählte Papyri religiösen und magischen Inhalts*. Vol. 1. Papyrologica Coloniensia. Opladen, 1990.

Merlan, P. "Plotinus and Magic." *Isis* 44 (1953): 341ff.

Meuli, K. "Scythica." *Hermes* 70 (1935): 121–76. Reprinted in *Gesammelte Schriften*, ed. Th. Gelzer (Basel, 1975), 2:817–89.

Meyer, M., and P. Mirecki, eds. *Ancient Magic and Ritual Power*. Religions in the Graeco-Roman World 129. Leiden, 1995.

Meyer, M., and R. Smith, eds. *Ancient Christian Magic: Coptic Texts of Ritual Power*. San Francisco, 1994.

Michelet, J. *La Sorcière*. 2nd ed. Brussels, 1862.

Momigliano, A., ed. *The Conflict between Paganism and Christianity in the Fourth Century*. Oxford, 1963.

Moreau, A., and J. C. Turpin, eds. *La Magie*. 4 vols. Montpellier, 2000.

Morgan, M. A. *Sepher ha-razim = The Book of Mysteries*. Chico, Calif., 1983.

Moule, C. F. D., ed. *Miracles: Cambridge Studies in Their Philosophy and History*. Cambridge, 1965.

Neugebauer, O. E. *The Exact Sciences in Antiquity*. Princeton, 1951.

Neugebauer, O. E., and H. B. Van Hoesen. *Greek Horoscopes*. Philadelphia, 1959.

Nilsson, M. P. *Geschichte der griechischen Religion*. 2nd ed. 2 vols. Munich, 1955.

——. *Die Religion in den griechischen Zauberpapyri*. Lund, 1949.

Nock, A. D. *Essays on Religion in the Ancient World*. Edited by Z. Stewart. 2 vols. Cambridge, Mass., 1972.

Oesterley, W. O. E. *Immortality and the Unseen World*. London, 1921.

Oesterreich, T. G. *Die Besessenheit*. Langensalza, 1921.

Ogden, D. *Greek and Roman Necromancy*. Princeton, 2001.

———. *Magic, Witchcraft, and Ghosts in the Greek and Roman Worlds: A Sourcebook*. Oxford, 2002.

Onians, R. B. *The Origins of European Thought*. Cambridge, 1951. Cf. review by H. J. Rose, *Journal of Hellenic Studies* 73–74 (1955–56): 175ff.

Parker, R. "Early Orphism." In *The Greek World*, ed. A. Powell, pp. 483–510. London, 1995.

———. *Miasma: Pollution and Purification in Early Greek Religion*. Oxford, 1983.

Perez Jimenez, A., and G. Cruz Andreotti, eds. *Daímon páredros: Magos y prácticas mágicas en el Mundo Mediterráneo*. Madrid and Malaga, 2002.

Petzke, G. *Die Traditionen über Apollonius von Tyana und das Neue Testament*. Studia ad Corpus Hellenisticum Novi Testamenti 1. Leiden, 1970.

Petzoldt, L., ed. *Magie und Religion*. Darmstadt, 1978.

Phillips, C. A., III. "In Search of the Occult: An Annotated Anthology." *Helios* 15 (1988): 151–70.

Préaux, J. "Virgile et le Rameau d'Or." In *Hommage à G. Dumézil*, ed. E. C. Polomé. *Coll. Latomus* 45 (1960): 151ff.

Preisendanz, K. "Fluchtafel (Defixion)." *RAC* 8 (1972), cols. 1–29.

Preisendanz, K., and A. Henrichs. *Papyri Graecae Magicae*. 2nd ed. 2 vols. Stuttgart, 1973–74.

Rea, J. "A New Version of P. Yale Inv. 299." *ZPE* 27 (1977): 15–56.

Read, J. *Prelude to Chemistry*. London, 1936.

———. *Through Alchemy to Chemistry*. London, 1957.

Reitzenstein R. *Die hellenistischen Mysterienreligionen*. 3rd ed. Leipzig, 1927.

———. *Poimandres*. 2nd ed. Leipzig, 1922.

Riddle, J. M. *Dioscorides on Pharmacy and Medicine*. Austin, Tex., 1985.

Ritner, R. K. *The Mechanics of Ancient Egyptian Magical Practice*. Studies in Ancient Oriental Civilizations 54. Chicago, 1993.

Robert, L. "Amulettes grecques." *Journal des savants* 81 (1981): 3–44.

Rutten, M. M. *La Science des Chaldéens*. Paris, 1960.

Ryan, W. F., and C. B. Schmitt, eds. *Ps.-Aristotle, Secret of Secrets*. Warburg Institute Surveys 9. London, 1982.

Saffrey, H.-D. "La Théurgie comme phénomène culturel chez les néoplatoniciens." *Koinonia* 8.2 (1984): 161–71.

Saggs, H. W. F. *The Greatness That Was Babylon*. London, 1962.

Sarton, G. *A History of Science: Hellenistic Science and Culture in the Last Three Centuries B.C.* Cambridge, Mass., 1959.

Schiffman, L. H., and M. D. Swartz. *Hebrew and Aramaic Incantation Texts from the Cairo Genizah*. Sheffield, 1992.

Scott-Moncrieff, P. D. *Paganism and Christianity in Egypt*. Cambridge, 1913.

Semler, J. S. *Commentatio de daemoniacis quorum in Novo Testamento fit mentio*. Halle, 1777.

Simon, B. *Mind and Madness in Ancient Greece*. Ithaca, N.Y., 1978.

Smith, K. F. "Magic (Greek and Roman)." *Encyclopaedia of Religion and Ethics*, edited by J. Hastings (1970 ed.), 1:265ff.

Smith, M. *Jesus the Magician*. New York, 1978.

Speyer, W. "Fluch." *RAC* 7 (1969), cols. 1160–1288.

Sullivan, L. E., ed. *Hidden Truths: Magic, Alchemy and the Occult.* New York, 1987.

Swartz, M. D. *Scholiastic Magic: Ritual and Revelation in Early Jewish Mysticism.* Princeton, 1998.

Tambiah, S. J. *Magic, Science, Religion and the Scope of Rationality.* Cambridge, 1990.

Tambornino, J. *De Antiquorum Daemonismo.* Giessen, 1909.

Tatum, J. *Apuleius and the Golden Ass.* Ithaca, N.Y., 1979.

Tester, S. J. *A History of Western Astrology.* Woodbridge, 1987. Reprint, 1996.

Thee, F. C. R. *Julius Africanus and the Early Christian View of Magic.* Tübingen, 1984.

Thompson, R. C. *The Reports of the Magicians and Astrologers of Nineveh in the British Museum.* 2 vols. London, 1900.

Thorndike, L. *A History of Magic and Experimental Science.* 8 vols. New York, 1923–58.

Thraede, K. "Exorzismus." *RAC* 7 (1969), cols. 44–117.

Tomlin, R. S. O. "The Curse Tablets." In *The Temple of Sulis Minerva at Bath*, ed. B. Cunliffe, pp. 59–277. Oxford, 1988.

Touwaide, A. "Les Poisons dans le monde antique et byzantin." *Revue d'histoire de la pharmacie* 290 (1991): 265–81.

Tupet, A. M. *La Magie dans la poésie latine des origines jusqu'à la fin du règne d'Auguste.* Paris, 1976.

———. "Rites magiques dans l' Antiquité romaine." *ANRW* 2.16.3 (1986), pp. 2591–2675.

Versnel, H. S. "Some Reflexions on the Relationship Magic-Religion." *Numen* 38 (1991): 177–97.

———, ed. *Faith, Hope and Worship: Aspects of Religious Mentality in the Ancient World.* Studies in Greek and Roman Religion 2. Leiden, 1981.

Victor, U. *Lukian von Samosata. Alexandros oder der Lügenprophet.* Leiden, 1997.

Vieillefond, J.-R. *Les "Cestes" de Julius Africanus.* Florence, 1970.

Voutiras, E. "Á propos d'une tablette de malédiction de Pella." *Revue des études grecques* 109 (1996): 678–82.

Wasson, R. G., A. Hofmann, C. A. P. Ruck, and others. *The Road to Eleusis.* Los Angeles, 1998.

Weinreich, O. *Antike Heilungswunder.* Giessen, 1908.

Winkler, J. J. *The Constraints of Desire: The Anthropology of Sex and Gender in Ancient Greece.* New York, 1990.

———. "The Constraints of Eros." In *Magika Hiera,* ed. C. A. Faraone and D. Obbink, pp. 214–43. Oxford, 1991.

Witt, R. E. *Isis in the Graeco-Roman World.* Ithaca, N.Y., 1971.

Wünsch, R. *Antike Fluchtafeln.* 2nd ed. Bonn, 1912.

———. *Antikes Zaubergerät aus Pergamon.* Vol. 6 of *Jahrbuch des deutschen Archäologischen Instituts, Ergänzungsheft.* Berlin, 1905.

———. "Deisidaimoniaka." *Archiv für Religionswissenschaft* 12 (1909): 37–41.

Xella, R., ed. *Magia: Studi di storia delle religioni in memoria di Raffaela Garosi.* Rome, 1976.

Zintzen, C. "Geister (Dämonen)." *RAC* 9 (1976), cols. 640–67.

Index of Ancient Sources

Numbers printed in roman type indicate passages in the ancient source; boldface numbers refer to pages within translations in this volume and italic numbers to other page references herein.

AUTHORS

General Index